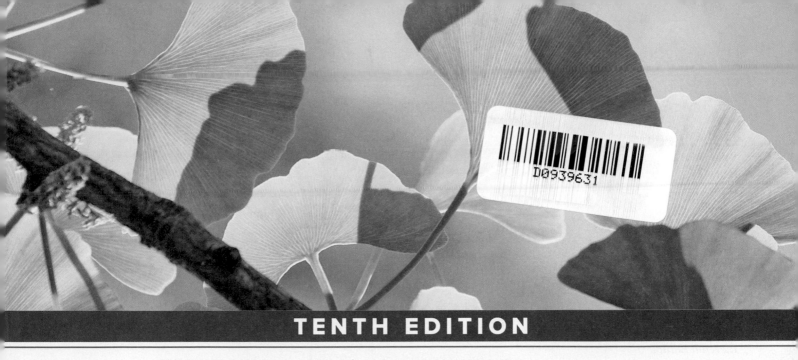

TENTH EDITION

MICROECONOMICS
and Behavior

THE McGRAW HILL SERIES IN ECONOMICS

SURVEY OF ECONOMICS

Brue, McConnell, and Flynn
Essentials of Economics
Fourth Edition

Guell
Issues in Economics Today
Ninth Edition

Mandel
M: Economics—The Basics
Fourth Edition

Schiller
Essentials of Economics
Eleventh Edition

PRINCIPLES OF ECONOMICS

Asarta and Butters
Connect Master: Economics

Colander
Economics, Microeconomics, and
Macroeconomics
Eleventh Edition

**Frank, Bernanke, Antonovics, and
Heffetz**
Principles of Economics,
Principles of Microeconomics,
Principles of Macroeconomics
Seventh Edition

**Frank, Bernanke, Antonovics, and
Heffetz**
Streamlined Editions: Principles of
Economics, Principles of
Microeconomics, Principles of
Macroeconomics
Fourth Edition

Karlan and Morduch
Economics, Microeconomics, and
Macroeconomics
Third Edition

McConnell, Brue, and Flynn
Economics, Microeconomics,
Macroeconomics
Twenty-Second Edition

McConnell, Brue, and Flynn
Brief Editions: Microeconomics
and Macroeconomics
Third Edition

Samuelson and Nordhaus
Economics, Microeconomics, and
Macroeconomics
Nineteenth Edition

Schiller
The Economy Today, The Micro
Economy Today, and The Macro
Economy Today
Fifteenth Edition

Slavin
Economics, Microeconomics, and
Macroeconomics
Twelfth Edition

ECONOMICS OF SOCIAL ISSUES

Guell
Issues in Economics Today
Ninth Edition

Register and Grimes
Economics of Social Issues
Twenty-First Edition

DATA ANALYTICS

Prince
Predictive Analytics for Business
Strategy
First Edition

MANAGERIAL ECONOMICS

Baye and Prince
Managerial Economics and
Business Strategy
Ninth Edition

Brickley, Smith, and Zimmerman
Managerial Economics and
Organizational Architecture
Seventh Edition

Thomas and Maurice
Managerial Economics
Thirteenth Edition

INTERMEDIATE ECONOMICS

Bernheim and Whinston
Microeconomics
Second Edition

Dornbusch, Fischer, and Startz
Macroeconomics
Thirteenth Edition

Frank
Microeconomics and Behavior
Tenth Edition

ADVANCED ECONOMICS

Romer
Advanced Macroeconomics
Fifth Edition

MONEY AND BANKING

Cecchetti and Schoenholtz
Money, Banking, and Financial
Markets
Sixth Edition

URBAN ECONOMICS

O'Sullivan
Urban Economics
Ninth Edition

LABOR ECONOMICS

Borjas
Labor Economics
Eighth Edition

McConnell, Brue, and Macpherson
Contemporary Labor Economics
Twelfth Edition

PUBLIC FINANCE

Rosen and Gayer
Public Finance
Tenth Edition

ENVIRONMENTAL ECONOMICS

Field and Field
Environmental Economics:
An Introduction
Eighth Edition

INTERNATIONAL ECONOMICS

Appleyard and Field
International Economics
Ninth Edition

Pugel
International Economics
Seventeenth Edition

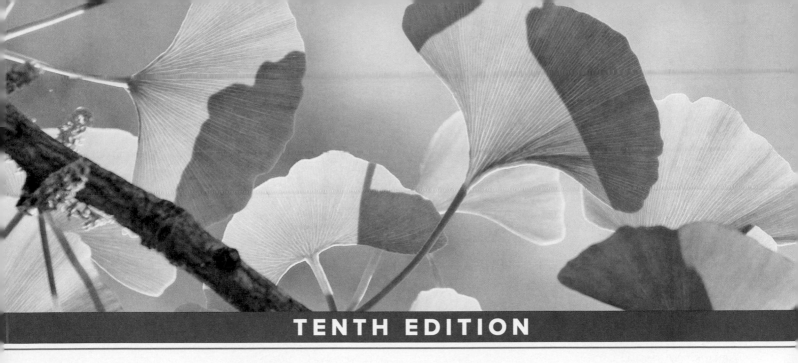

TENTH EDITION

MICROECONOMICS
and Behavior

ROBERT H. FRANK

Cornell University

McGraw Hill

ISBN 978-1-260-57564-4
MHID 1-260-57564-0

Cover Image: ©*Jorge Salcedo/Alamy Stock Photo*

mheducation.com/highered

DEDICATION

FOR ELLEN

ROBERT H. FRANK

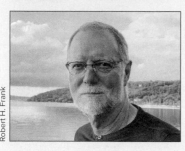

Robert H. Frank

Robert H. Frank is the H. J. Louis Professor of Management and Professor of Economics, emeritus, at Cornell's Johnson School of Management, where he taught from 1972 to 2020. After receiving his B.S. from Georgia Tech in 1966, he taught math and science for two years as a Peace Corps volunteer in rural Nepal. He received his M.A. in statistics in 1971 and his Ph.D. in economics in 1972 from the University of California at Berkeley. He also holds honorary doctorate degrees from the University of St. Gallen and Dalhousie University. During leaves of absence from Cornell, he has served as chief economist for the Civil Aeronautics Board (1978–1980), a Fellow at the Center for Advanced Study in the Behavioral Sciences (1992–1993), Professor of American Civilization at l'École des Hautes Études en Sciences Sociales in Paris (2000–2001), and the Peter and Charlotte Schoenfeld Visiting Faculty Fellow at the NYU Stern School of Business in 2008–2009. His papers have appeared in the *American Economic Review*, *Econometrica*, the *Journal of Political Economy*, and other leading professional journals and for more than two decades, his economics columns appeared regularly in *The New York Times*.

Professor Frank is the co-author of two best-selling principles of economics textbook—*Principles of Economics*, Eighth Edition, and *Principles of Economics: A Streamlined Approach*, Fourth Edition (McGraw Hill, 2021). His research has focused on rivalry and cooperation in economic and social behavior. His books on these themes include *Choosing the Right Pond* (Oxford, 1995), *Passions Within Reason* (W. W. Norton, 1988), *What Price the Moral High Ground?* (Princeton, 2004), *Falling Behind* (University of California Press, 2007), *The Economic Naturalist* (Basic Books, 2007), *The Economic Naturalist's Field Guide* (Basic Books, 2009), *The Darwin Economy* (Princeton, 2011), and *Success and Luck* (Princeton, 2016), and *Under the Influence* (Princeton, 2020), which have been translated into 24 languages. *The Winner-Take-All Society* (The Free Press, 1995), co-authored with Philip Cook, received a Critic's Choice Award, was named a Notable Book of the Year by *The New York Times*, and was included in *BusinessWeek's* list of the 10 best books of 1995. *Luxury Fever* (The Free Press, 1999) was named to the Knight-Ridder Best Books list for 1999.

Professor Frank is a co-recipient of the 2004 Leontief Prize for Advancing the Frontiers of Economic Thought. He was awarded the Johnson School's Stephen Russell Distinguished Teaching Award in 2004, 2010, 2012, and 2018, and the School's Apple Distinguished Teaching Award in 2005.

My goal in writing *Microeconomics and Behavior* was to produce an intellectually challenging text that would also be accessible and engaging to students. The more common approach in this market has been to emphasize one of these dimensions or the other. For example, some texts have done well by sacrificing rigor in the name of user-friendliness. But although such books sometimes keep students happy, they often fail to prepare them for upper-division courses in the major. Others texts have succeeded by sacrificing accessibility in the name of rigor, where rigor all too often means little more than mathematical density. These courses overwhelm many undergraduates, and even those few who become adept at solving well-posed mathematical optimization problems are often baffled by questions drawn from everyday contexts. I have always believed that a text could at once be rigorous *and* user-friendly. And to judge by the breadth of *Microeconomics and Behavior*'s adoption list, many of you apparently agree.

I wrote this book in the conviction that the teaching of intuition and the teaching of technical tools are complements, not substitutes. Students who learn only technical tools rarely seem to develop any real affection for our discipline; and even more rarely do they acquire that distinctive mindset we call "thinking like an economist." By contrast, students who develop economic intuition are stimulated to think more deeply about the technical tools they learn, and to find more interesting ways to apply them. Most important, they usually end up *liking* economics.

Microeconomics and Behavior develops the core analytical tools with patience and attention to detail. At the same time, it embeds these tools in a uniquely diverse collection of examples and applications to illuminate the power and versatility of the economic way of thinking.

ECONOMIC NATURALISM

In more than forty years of teaching, I have found no more effective device for developing intuition than to train students to become "Economic Naturalists." Studying biology enables people to observe and marvel at many details of life that would otherwise have escaped notice. In much the same way, studying microeconomics can enable students to see the mundane details of ordinary existence in a sharp new light. Throughout the text, I try to develop intuition by means of examples and applications drawn from everyday experience. *Microeconomics and Behavior* teaches students to see each feature of the manmade landscape as the reflection of an implicit or explicit cost-benefit calculation.

Year in and year out, the most valuable assignments in my course are the two brief papers in which I ask students to report on their efforts to become economic naturalists. Their specific charge is to use microeconomic principles to answer a question prompted by a personal observation. In recent terms, students have grappled with questions like these: Why do the keypads of drive-up ATM machines have Braille dots? Why do top female models earn more than top male models? Why do brides spend so much money on wedding dresses, while grooms often rent cheap tuxedos (even though grooms could potentially wear their tuxedos on many other occasions and brides will never wear their dresses again)? Why are child safety seats required in cars but not for air travel? Why do airlines charge their highest prices to passengers who buy at the last minute, while the practice is exactly the reverse for Broadway theaters?

The beauty of this assignment is not only that most students enjoy writing these papers, but also that few manage to complete them without becoming life-long economic naturalists. For those who would like to learn more about the assignment, my lecture on it is posted in the Authors@google series here: www.youtube.com/watch?v=QalNVxeIKEE.

A host of Economic Naturalist examples are now available as short, engaging video vignettes available within Connect via the eBook or as assignable homework content. Available videos are denoted in the margin throughout the text.

FOCUS ON PROBLEM-SOLVING

Most economists agree that a critical step in learning price theory is to solve problems. More than any other text currently available in the marketplace, *Microeconomics and Behavior* prepares students for its end-of-chapter problems by taking them through a sequence of carefully crafted examples and self-test questions within each chapter. Because most of these examples and self-tests are drawn from familiar contexts, and because students engage more readily with the concrete than with the abstract, this approach has proven effectiveness. In the absence of such groundwork, many students would reach the end-of-chapter problems with little or no idea how to proceed.

OPTIMAL TOPIC COVERAGE

A guiding principle in the evolution of *Microeconomics and Behavior* has been that topics should be emphasized in proportion both to their importance and to the difficulty that students have in mastering them. Because the basic rational choice model is the building block for much of what comes later in the course, I have devoted considerably more attention to its development than competing texts do. I have also allocated extra space for elasticity and its applications in demand theory, and for the average-marginal distinction in production theory.

As an additional means for discovering which topics are most difficult to master, I have used research in behavioral economics that identifies systematic departures from the prescriptions of the rational choice model. For example, whereas the model says that rational persons will ignore sunk costs, many people are in fact strongly influenced by them. (Someone who receives an expensive, but painfully tight, pair of shoes as a gift is much less likely to wear them than is someone who spent $400 out of his own pocket for those same shoes.) Especially in the chapters on consumer behavior, I call students' attention to situations in which they themselves are likely to make irrational choices. Because student resources are limited, it makes sense to focus on precisely those issues for which knowing price theory is most likely to be helpful.

It may seem natural to wonder whether discussing examples of irrational choices might confuse students who are struggling to master the details of the rational choice model. It's a reasonable question, but my experience has been exactly to the contrary. Such examples actually underscore the normative message of the traditional theory. Students who are exposed to them invariably gain a deeper understanding of the basic theoretical principles at issue. Indeed, they often seem to take an almost conspiratorial pride in being able to see through the errors of judgment that many consumers make. For instructors who want to pursue how cognitive limitations affect consumer behavior in greater detail, there is an entire chapter devoted to this topic. When the first edition of *Microeconomics and Behavior* appeared in 1990, many in the economics profession were skeptical about then emerging field of behavioral economics. But as evidenced by U.C. Berkeley economist Matthew Rabin's receipt of the John Bates Clark Award in 2000 (the honor bestowed every two years by the American Economics Association on the most outstanding American economist under the age of 40) and by the receipt of the Nobel Prize in Economics, first by Daniel Kahneman in 2002 and then by Richard Thaler in 2017, the behavioral approach is now part of the microeconomics mainstream.

A BROADER CONCEPTION OF SELF-INTEREST

Another of my goals has been to incorporate a broader conception of preferences into models of individual choice. Most texts mention at the outset that the rational choice model takes people's tastes as given. They may be altruists, sadists, or masochists; or they may be concerned solely with advancing their narrow material interests. But having said that, most

texts then proceed to ignore all motives other than narrow self-interest. It is easy to see why, because economic research has scored its most impressive gains on the strength of this portrayal of human motivation. It tells us, for example, why Ford discontinued production of its 7,500-pound Excursion SUV in the wake of gasoline price increases; and why thermostats are generally set lower in apartments that have separately metered utilities.

And yet, as students are keenly aware, our *Homo economicus* caricature is patently at odds with much of what we know about human behavior. People vote in presidential elections. They give anonymously to public television stations and private charities. They donate bone marrow to strangers with leukemia. They endure great trouble and expense to see justice done, even when it will not undo the original injury. At great risk to themselves, they pull people from burning buildings, and jump into icy rivers to rescue people who are about to drown. Soldiers throw their bodies atop live grenades to save their comrades. Seen through the lens of the self-interest theory emphasized in most textbooks, such behavior is the human equivalent of planets traveling in square orbits. Indeed, many students are strongly alienated by our self-interest model, which they perceive as narrow and mean-spirited.

Microeconomics and Behavior freely concedes the importance of the self-interest motive in many contexts. But it also highlights the role of unselfish motives in social and economic transactions. Employing elementary game theory, Chapter 12 identifies circumstances in which people who hold such motives have a competitive advantage over pure opportunists. It shows, for example, that people known to have cooperative predispositions can often solve prisoner's dilemmas and other commitment problems in ways that purely self-interested persons cannot.

Our theoretical models of human nature are important, not least because they mold our expectations about how others will behave. Economics is the social science most closely identified with the self-interest model of human behavior. Does this model color our expectations of others, and perhaps even our own behavior? When Cornell psychologists Tom Gilovich, Dennis Regan, and I investigated this question, we found numerous indications that economists are much more likely than others to behave opportunistically in social dilemmas.[1] For example, academic economists were more than twice as likely as the members of any other discipline we surveyed to report that they give

[1]See R. H. Frank, T. D. Gilovich, and D. T. Regan, "Does Studying Economics Inhibit Cooperation?" *Journal of Economics Perspectives,* Spring 1993.

no money at all to any private charity. In an experiment, we also found that economics majors were more than twice as likely as nonmajors to defect when playing one-shot prisoner's dilemmas with strangers.

This difference was not merely a reflection of the fact that people who chose to major in economics were more opportunistic to begin with. We found, for example, that the difference in defection rates grew larger the longer a student had studied economics. Questionnaire responses also indicated that freshmen in their first microeconomics course were more likely at the end of the term to expect opportunistic behavior from others than they were at the beginning.

There are thus at least some grounds for concern that, by stressing only the narrow self-interest motive, economists may have undermined our students' propensities for cooperative behavior. The irony is that the internal logic of the economic model never predicted such narrowly self-interested behavior in the first place.

ADDITIONAL PEDAGOGICAL FEATURES

Unlike most intermediate texts, *Microeconomics and Behavior* contains no boxed applications, which tend to distract students from the thread of argument being developed. Instead, applications and examples are integrated fully into the text. Many of these have the added advantage of being drawn from experiences to which students can personally relate.

The chapter introductions and summaries are another innovative feature of *Microeconomics and Behavior*. Most chapters begin with an anecdote that poses a problem or question that the material developed in the chapter will enable the student to answer. These introductions have proved especially helpful for the many students who find that getting started is often the hardest step. The chapter summaries in most current texts consist of brief annotated lists of the topics covered. The chapter summaries in *Microeconomics and Behavior,* by contrast, are written in a narrative form that carefully synthesizes the material covered in the chapters.

Each chapter concludes with a selection of problems that range in difficulty from routine to highly challenging. These problems have all been class-tested to assure their accuracy and effectiveness in helping students master the most important concepts in the chapters.

Answers to all in-text self-test questions appear at the end of the chapter in which they occur. Variations and extensions of these self-tests are echoed in the end-of-chapter problems, which enable students to approach these

problem sets with greater confidence. Detailed answers to all end-of-chapter problems are included in the solutions manual.

CHANGES IN THE TENTH EDITION

Beyond the usual updating of time-sensitive numerical examples, I have also tried to achieve a **simpler and more unified design** look throughout the text. The design has been refreshed, the Examples and Concept Checks (now named Self-Tests) from the previous edition are emphasized to provide clarity and to facilitate understanding of concepts. Data has been updated accordingly throughout.

A more robust offering of course content in McGraw Hill Connect is now available for this edition. In addition to the test bank, which was available previously in Connect, the end-of-chapter questions have now been added as assignable, automatically graded, content. **Refinements to the SmartBook offer** have also been made. For more information about the assets available to you, refer to the Connect Economics pages that follow.

Economic Naturalism, as described earlier, has long been a central focus of this book. But it is a feature, not a bug, of specific pithy examples involving manual transmissions or Nepalese stone crushers that they reflect a moment in time. In this edition, we have revisited many of Economic Naturalist examples and have found sometimes that new facts lead to different conclusions. New to this edition, a selection of **Economic Naturalist examples have been developed into short video vignettes**, detailing how economics can help you answer a host of interesting questions from everyday experiences. Applicable videos are denoted in the margin throughout the text, as in the margin here. The videos are available within Connect via the eBook, and as assignable homework content with accompanying questions.

▶ Visit your instructor's Connect© course and access your eBook to view this video.

Why do real estate agents often show clients two nearly identical houses, even though one is both cheaper and in better condition than the other?

Connect Economics Asset Alignment with Bloom's Taxonomy

We Take Students Higher

As a learning science company, we create content that supports higher order thinking skills. Within Connect®, we tag assessments accordingly so you can filter your search, assign it, and receive reporting on it. These content asset types can be associated with one or more levels of Bloom's Taxonomy.

The chart below shows a few of the key assignable economics assets with *McGraw Hill Connect* aligned with Bloom's Taxonomy. Take your students higher by assigning a variety of applications, moving them from simple memorization to concept application.

	SmartBook 2.0	Math Preparedness	Videos	Exercises	Interactive Graphs	Application-Based Activities	Econ Everyday Current Events Blog*	Writing Assignment Plus
CREATE								✓
EVALUATE						✓	✓	✓
ANALYZE				✓	✓	✓	✓	✓
APPLY		✓	✓	✓	✓	✓	✓	✓
UNDERSTAND	✓	✓	✓	✓	✓	✓	✓	✓
REMEMBER	✓	✓	✓	✓	✓	✓	✓	✓

Higher Order Thinking Skills ↑

Lower Order Thinking Skills ↓

* Outside of Connect.

SmartBook 2.0

Adaptively aids students to study more efficiently by highlighting where in the chapter to focus, asking review questions and pointing them to passages in the text until they understand. Assignable and assessable.

Math Preparedness

Math preparedness assignments help students refresh important prerequisite topics necessary to be successful in economics. Tutorial videos are included to help illustrate math concepts to students visually.

Videos

Select Economic Naturalist examples have been developed into videos that show how to employ basic economic principles to understand and explain what you observe in the world around you. All videos are closed captioned and are assignable with assessment questions for improved retention.

Why are rotisserie chickens less expensive than fresh chickens?

Exercises

Exercises with algorithmic variations provide ample opportunities for students to practice and hone quantitative skills. Graphing Exercises provide opportunities for students to draw, interact with, manipulate, and analyze graphs.

Interactive Graphs

Interactive Graphs provide visual displays of real data and economic concepts for students to manipulate. All graphs are accompanied by assignable Assessment questions and feedback to guide students through the experience of learning to read and interpret graphs and data.

Application-Based Activities

Immersive real-life scenarios engage students and put them in the role of everyday economists. Students practice their economic thinking and problem-solving skills as they apply course concepts and see the implications of their decisions as they go. Each activity is designed as a 15-minute experience, unless students eagerly replay for a better outcome.

ECON Everyday Current Events Blog

Our Econ Everyday blog saves instructors time bringing current, student-centered content into their course all semester long. Short articles, written for principles-level students, is tagged by topic to bring currency into your course. We also provide discussion questions to help you drive the conversation forward. Visit www.econeveryday.com and subscribe for updates.

Writing Assignment Plus

Writing Assignment Plus delivers a learning experience that helps students improve their written communication skills and conceptual understanding. Faculty can assign, monitor, grade, and provide feedback on writing projects efficiently. Built-in grammar and writing review helps students improve writing quality while an originality check helps students correct central plagiarism before submission. End result? Improved workplace skills of writing in critical thinking.

You're in the driver's seat.

Want to build your own course? No problem. Prefer to use our turnkey, prebuilt course? Easy. Want to make changes throughout the semester? Sure. And you'll save time with Connect's auto-grading too.

65%
Less Time Grading

Laptop: McGraw Hill Education

They'll thank you for it.

Adaptive study resources like SmartBook® 2.0 help your students be better prepared in less time. You can transform your class time from dull definitions to dynamic debates. Find out more about the powerful personalized learning experience available in SmartBook 2.0 at **www.mheducation.com/highered/ connect/smartbook**

Make it simple, make it affordable.

Connect makes it easy with seamless integration using any of the major Learning Management Systems— Blackboard®, Canvas, and D2L, among others—to let you organize your course in one convenient location. Give your students access to digital materials at a discount with our inclusive access program. Ask your McGraw Hill representative for more information.

Padlock: Jobalou/Getty Images

Solutions for your challenges.

A product isn't a solution. Real solutions are affordable, reliable, and come with training and ongoing support when you need it and how you want it. Our Customer Experience Group can also help you troubleshoot tech problems— although Connect's 99% uptime means you might not need to call them. See for yourself at **status. mheducation.com**

Checkmark: Jobalou/Getty Images

Effective, efficient studying.

Connect helps you be more productive with your study time and get better grades using tools like SmartBook 2.0, which highlights key concepts and creates a personalized study plan. Connect sets you up for success, so you walk into class with confidence and walk out with better grades.

Study anytime, anywhere.

Download the free ReadAnywhere app and access your online eBook or SmartBook 2.0 assignments when it's convenient, even if you're offline. And since the app automatically syncs with your eBook and SmartBook 2.0 assignments in Connect, all of your work is available every time you open it. Find out more at **www.mheducation.com/readanywhere**

> *"I really liked this app—it made it easy to study when you don't have your textbook in front of you."*
>
> - Jordan Cunningham,
> Eastern Washington University

No surprises.

The Connect Calendar and Reports tools keep you on track with the work you need to get done and your assignment scores. Life gets busy; Connect tools help you keep learning through it all.

Calendar: owattaphotos/Getty Images

Learning for everyone.

McGraw Hill works directly with Accessibility Services Departments and faculty to meet the learning needs of all students. Please contact your Accessibility Services office and ask them to email accessibility@mheducation.com, or visit **www.mheducation.com/about/accessibility** for more information.

Changes to this edition emphasize updates to content rather than to organization of the text. Significant new material relating to the economics of climate change have been introduced in Chapters 5, 6, 7, and 17. Chapter 10 begins with a mostly new introduction to the theory of perfect competition. Chapter 18 is streamlined and refocused, with the closing "Income Distribution" section updated to reflect the contemporary discussion around basic income and jobs guarantee proposals.

SUPPLEMENTS FOR THE INSTRUCTOR

The following ancillaries are available for quick download and convenient access via the instructor resource site available through McGraw Hill Connect. Instructor resources are password protected for security. The supplements package, which has been revised and improved, consists of the following:

Instructor's Manual: Each chapter contains a Chapter Summary, a Chapter Outline, Teaching Suggestions, a list of Stumbling Blocks for Students, and Additional Problem Suggestions with accompanying solutions.

Solutions Manual: Answers to end-of-chapter Review Questions and Problems have been extracted from the Instructor's Manual and are available here for quick access.

Test Bank: Hundreds of multiple choice and essay questions test students' knowledge of key terms and concepts. All questions have been accuracy checked and are tagged with the corresponding learning objective, level of difficulty, topic, AACSB learning category, and Bloom's taxonomy for easy filtering.

Test Builder in Connect: Available within Connect, Test Builder is a cloud-based tool that enables instructors to format tests that can be printed or administered within an LMS. Test Builder offers a modern, streamlined interface for easy content configuration that matches course needs, without requiring a download.

Test Builder allows you to:

- Access all test bank content from a particular title.
- Easily pinpoint the most relevant content through robust filtering options.
- Manipulate the order of questions or scramble questions and/or answers.
- Pin questions to a specific location within a test.
- Determine your preferred treatment of algorithmic questions.
- Choose the layout and spacing.
- Add instructions and configure default settings.

Test Builder provides a secure interface for better protection of content and allows for just-in-time updates to flow directly into assessments.

PowerPoints: The PowerPoints contain a detailed, chapter-by-chapter review of the important concepts and figures presented in the textbook. You can print, or rearrange the slides to fit the needs of your course.

REMOTE PROCTORING & BROWSER-LOCKING CAPABILITIES

New remote proctoring and browser-locking capabilities, hosted by Proctorio within Connect, provide control of the assessment environment by enabling security options and verifying the identity of the student.

Seamlessly integrated within Connect, these services allow instructors to control students' assessment experience by restricting browser activity, recording students' activity, and verifying students are doing their own work.

Instant and detailed reporting gives instructors an at-a-glance view of potential academic integrity concerns, thereby avoiding personal bias and supporting evidence-based claims.

AACSB STATEMENT

McGraw Hill Global Education is a proud corporate member of AACSB International. Understanding the importance and value of AACSB accreditation, *Microeconomics and Behavior* has sought to recognize the curricula guidelines detailed in the AACSB standards for business accreditation by connecting questions in the text and test bank to the general knowledge and skill guidelines found in the AACSB standards.

The statements contained in *Microeconomics and Behavior* are provided only as a guide for the users of this text. The AACSB leaves content coverage and assessment within the purview of individual schools, the mission of the school, and the faculty. While *Microeconomics and Behavior* and the teaching package make no claim of any specific AACSB qualification or evaluation, we have within *Microeconomics and Behavior* labeled questions according to the general knowledge and skills areas.

MCGRAW HILL CUSTOMER CARE CONTACT INFORMATION

We understand that getting the most from new technology can be challenging. That's why our services don't stop after you purchase our products. You can reach our Product Specialists 24 hours a day to get product-training online. Or you can search our knowledge bank of Frequently Asked

Questions on our support website. For Customer Support, call 800-331-5094, or visit www.mheducation.com/highered/contact.html. One of our Technical Support Analysts will be able to assist you in a timely fashion.

ACKNOWLEDGMENTS

I want to convey my sincere thanks and admiration to my editors at McGraw Hill for their continued willingness to take steps that run counter to market trends. The biggest gambles, of course, were those taken by Scott Stratford, my editor for the first edition. (I hope he is pleased that subsequent developments in the economics profession appear to have ratified the wisdom of those early decisions.) Scott's successors, Anke Weekes, and Christina Kouvelis, have worked attentively on this project. I am extremely grateful for their enthusiastic support.

Tom Barson has made substantial contributions to this revision. I am grateful for his creative insights and suggestions that have made this tenth edition a real step forward. I also want to thank the many reviewers who have been involved in the project, both in this edition and in earlier ones. Their insights and critiques have led to improvements too numerous to list. I hope they are as happy as I am with their influence on the final product.

Charles H. Anderton, *College of the Holy Cross*
Samiran Banerjee, *Emory University*
Charles L. Baum, *Middle Tennessee State University*
Ergin Bayrak, *University of Southern California*
Gary Biglaiser, *University of North Carolina at Chapel Hill*
Inoussa Boubacar, *Clarion University*
James Bradfield, *Hamilton College*
David Brat, *Randolph-Macon College*
Miki Brunyer, *College of Saint Benedict & Saint John's University*
Don Bumpass, *Sam Houston State University*
James Cardon, *Brigham Young University*
Joel Caron, *Salem State University*
Bogachan Celen, *Columbia University*
Anoshua Chaudhuri, *San Francisco State University*
Kwang Soo Cheong, *John Hopkins University*
Dennis Coates, *University of Maryland, Baltimore County*
Tony Cookson, *Montana State University*
Kevin Cotter, *Wayne State University*

Ardeshir J. Dalal, *Missouri State University*
Roger Frantz, *San Diego State University*
Beth Freeborn, *College of William and Mary*
Eric Furstenberg, *University of Virginia*
Keith J. Gamble, *DePaul University*
Amy Glass, *Texas A&M University*
Seth Gershenson, *Michigan State University*
Rae Jean B. Goodman, *U.S. Naval Academy*
Darrin Gulla, *University of Kentucky*
Elif Hafair, *Carnegie Mellon University*
Denise Hare, *Reed College*
Joseph Hughes, *Rutgers University*
Hsiang-Chih Hwang, *Brandeis University & Wellesley College*
Geoffrey A. Jehle, *Vassar College & Columbia University*
Christopher K. Johnson, *University of North Florida*
David R. Kamerschen, *University of Georgia*
Sandra K. Klein, *University of Missouri*
Bill D. Kosteas, *Cleveland State University*
Sang Lee, *Southeastern Louisiana University*
Tom K. Lee, *California State University, Northridge*
Xu Lin, *Wayne State University*
David McAdams, *Massachusetts Institute of Technology*
Robert McComb, *Texas Tech University*
Tamah Morant, *North Carolina State University*
Stephen Morris, *Princeton University*
Anne van den Nouweland, *University of Oregon*
Patrick O'Neill, *University of North Dakota*
Martin Pereyra, *University of Missouri*
C. Barry Pfitzner, *Randolph-Macon College*
Neil Raymon, *University of Missouri at Columbia*
Brian Roberson, *Miami University*
Howard N. Ross, *Baruch College*
John F. Schnell, *University of Alabama at Huntsville*
Nina Sidvena, *University of Washington*
Todd Sorensen, *University of California, Riverside*
Christy Spivey, *University of Texas at Arlington*
Houston H. Stokes, *University of Illinois at Chicago*
John S. Thompson, *Purdue University*
Regina Trevino, *University of California Irvine*
Hui-Kuan Tseng, *University of North Carolina at Charlotte*

As usual, I welcome further comments and suggestions.
Robert H. Frank

BRIEF CONTENTS

CONTENTS

1

Thinking Like an Economist

Much of microeconomics entails the study of how people choose under conditions of scarcity. Many people react to this description by saying that the subject is of little real relevance in developed countries, where material scarcity is largely a thing of the past.

This reaction, however, takes too narrow a view of the Greek shipping magnate scarcity, for there are *always* important resources in short supply. At his death, Aristotle Onassis was worth several billion dollars. He had more money than he could possibly spend and used it for such things as finely crafted whale ivory footrests for the barstools on his yacht. And yet he confronted the problem of scarcity much more than most of us will ever have to. Onassis was the victim of *myasthenia gravis,* a debilitating and progressive neurological disease. For him, the scarcity that mattered was not money but time, energy, and the physical skill needed to carry out ordinary activities.

Time is a scarce resource for everyone, not just the terminally ill. In deciding which movies to see, for example, it is time, not the price of admission, that constrains most of us. With only a few free nights available each month, seeing one movie means not being able to see another, or not being able to have dinner with friends.

Time and money are not the only important scarce resources. Consider the economic choice you confront when a friend invites you to a buffet brunch. You must decide how to fill your plate. Even if you are not rich, money would be no object, since you can eat as much as you want for free. Nor is time an obstacle, since you have all afternoon and would enjoy spending it in the company of your friend. The important scarce resource here is the capacity of your stomach. A smorgasbord of your favorite foods lies before you, and you must decide which to eat and in what quantities. Eating another waffle necessarily means having less room for more scrambled eggs. The fact that no money changes hands here does not make your choice any less an economic one.

Every choice involves important elements of scarcity. Sometimes the most relevant scarcity will involve money, but not always. Coping with scarcity is the essence of the human condition. Indeed, were it not for the problem of scarcity, life would be stripped of much of its intensity. For someone with an infinite lifetime and limitless material resources, hardly a single decision would ever matter. If you made a bad decision today, you could always start with a clean slate tomorrow.

In this chapter we examine some basic principles of microeconomic theory and see how an economist might apply them to a wide variety of choices involving scarcity. Later chapters more formally develop the theory. For now, our only goal is to get an intuitive feel for that distinctive mindset known as "thinking like an economist." And the best way to do that is to work through a series of problems familiar from actual experience.

THE COST-BENEFIT APPROACH TO DECISIONS

If the benefit of an activity exceeds its cost, do it.

Many of the choices economists study can be posed as the following question:

> Should I do activity x?

For the choice confronting a moviegoer, ". . . do activity x?" might be, for example, ". . . see the new *Star Wars* movie tonight?" For the person attending a buffet brunch, it might be ". . . eat another waffle?" Economists answer such questions by comparing the costs and benefits of doing the activity in question. The decision rule we use is disarmingly simple. If $C(x)$ denotes the costs of doing x and $B(x)$ denotes the benefits, it is:

> If $B(x) > C(x)$, do x; otherwise don't.

To apply this rule, we must define and measure costs and benefits. Monetary values are a useful common denominator for this purpose, even when the activity has nothing directly to do with money. We define $B(x)$ as the maximum dollar amount you would be willing to pay to do x. Often $B(x)$ will be a hypothetical magnitude, the amount you would be willing to pay if you had to, even though no money will change hands. $C(x)$, in turn, is the value of all the resources you must give up in order to do x. Here too $C(x)$ need not involve an explicit transfer of money.

For most decisions, at least some of the benefits or costs will not be readily available in monetary terms. To see how we proceed in such cases, consider the following simple decision.

EXAMPLE 1.1   **Comparing Costs and Benefits**

Should I turn down my stereo?

You have settled into your chair and are listening to a vinyl reissue from your favorite punk rock band when you realize that the next two tracks on the record are ones you dislike. If you had a working remote, you could turn down your stereo for the next two songs. But you don't, and so you must decide whether to get up and turn the music down or stay put and wait it out.

The benefit of turning it down is not having the songs you don't like blare away at you. The cost, in turn, is the inconvenience of getting out of your chair. If you are extremely comfortable and the music is only mildly annoying, you will probably stay put. But if you haven't been settled for long or if the music is really bothersome, you are more likely to get up.

Even for simple decisions like this one, it is possible to translate the relevant costs and benefits into a monetary framework. Consider first the cost of getting out of your chair. If someone offered you 1 cent to get up out of a comfortable chair and there were no reason other than the penny to do it, would you take the offer? Most people would not. But if someone offered you $1,000, you would be on your feet in an instant. Somewhere between 1 cent and $1,000 lies your **reservation price,** the minimum amount it would take to get you out of the chair.

To see where the threshold lies, imagine a mental auction with yourself in which you keep boosting the offer by small increments from 1 cent until you reach the

reservation price of activity x the price at which a person would be indifferent between doing x and not doing x.

point at which it is barely worthwhile to get up. Where this point occurs will obviously depend on circumstance. If you are rich, it will tend to be higher than if you are poor, because a given amount of money will seem less important; if you feel energetic, it will be lower than if you feel tired; and so on. For the sake of discussion, suppose your reservation price for getting out of the chair turns out to be $1. You can conduct a similar mental auction to determine the maximum sum you would be willing to pay someone to turn the music down. This reservation price measures the benefits of turning the music down; let's suppose it turns out to be 75 cents.

In terms of our formal decision rule, we then have x = "turn my stereo down," with $B(x) = \$0.75 < C(x) = \$1$, which means that you should remain in your chair. Listening to the next two songs will be unpleasant, but less so than getting up would be. A reversal of these cost and benefit figures would imply a decision to get up and turn the music down. If $B(x)$ and $C(x)$ happened to be equal, you would be indifferent between the two alternatives.

Claudia Veja/Mcment Select/Getty Images

Is it worth the trouble to turn down your stereo?

THE ROLE OF ECONOMIC THEORY

The idea that anyone might actually calculate the costs and benefits of turning down a stereo may sound absurd. Economists have been criticized for making unrealistic assumptions about how people behave, and outsiders are quick to wonder what purpose is served by the image of a person trying to decide how much he would pay to avoid getting up from his chair.

There are two responses to this criticism. The first is that economists don't assume that people make such calculations explicitly. Rather, many economists argue, we can make useful predictions by assuming people act *as if* they made such calculations. This view was forcefully expressed by Nobel laureate Milton Friedman, who illustrated his point by looking at the techniques expert pool players use.[1] He argued that the shots they choose, and the specific ways they attempt to make them, can be predicted extremely well by assuming that players take careful account of all the relevant laws of Newtonian physics. Of course, few expert pool players have had formal training in physics, and hardly any can recite such laws as "the angle of incidence equals the angle of reflection." Nor

[1]Milton Friedman, "The Methodology of Positive Economics," *Essays in Positive Economics,* Chicago: University of Chicago Press, 1953.

People don't always behave as predicted by economic models, but the models provide useful insights about how to achieve important goals.

Taka Wu/Alamy Stock Photo

Professional pool champion Shane Van Boening may not know all the formal laws of Newtonian physics, but the quality of his play suggests that he has a deep understanding of them.

are they likely to know the definitions of "elastic collisions" and "angular momentum." Even so, Friedman argued, they would never have become expert players in the first place *unless* they played as dictated by the laws of physics. Our theory of pool player behavior assumes, unrealistically, that players know the laws of physics. Friedman urged us to judge this theory not by how accurate its central assumption is but by how well it predicts behavior. And on this score, it performs very well indeed.

Like pool players, we must also develop skills for coping with our environments. Many economists, Friedman among them, believe that useful insights into our behavior can be gained by assuming that we act as if governed by the rules of rational decision making. By trial and error we eventually absorb these rules, just as pool players absorb the laws of physics.

A second response to the charge that economists make unrealistic assumptions is to concede that behavior does often differ from the predictions of economic models. Thus, as economist Richard Thaler puts it, we often behave more like novice than expert pool players—ignoring bank shots and having no idea about putting the proper spin on the cue ball to position it for the next shot. Considerable evidence supports this second view.

But even where economic models fail on descriptive grounds, they often provide useful guidance for decisions. That is, even if they don't always predict how we *do* behave, they may often give useful insights into how to achieve our goals more efficiently. If novice pool players have not yet internalized the relevant physical laws, they may nonetheless consult those laws for guidance about how to improve. Economic models often play an analogous role with respect to ordinary consumer and business decisions. Indeed, this role alone provides a compelling reason for learning economics.

COMMON PITFALLS IN DECISION MAKING

Some economists are embarrassed if an outsider points out that much of what they do boils down to an application of the principle that we should perform an action if and only if its benefits exceed its costs. That just doesn't sound like enough to keep a person with a PhD busy all day! There is more to it, however, than meets the eye. People who study economics quickly discover that measuring costs and benefits is as much an art as a science. Some costs seem almost deliberately hidden from view. Others may seem relevant but, on a closer look, turn out not to be.

Economics teaches us how to identify the costs and benefits that really matter. An important goal of this book is to teach you to become a better decision maker. A good starting point is to examine some common pitfalls in decision making. The relevant economic principles are simple and commonsensical, but many people ignore them.

Pitfall 1. Ignoring Implicit Costs

opportunity cost of activity the value of all that must be sacrificed to do the activity.

One pitfall is to overlook costs that are not explicit. If doing activity *x* means not being able to do activity *y,* then the value to you of doing *y* (had you done it) is an **opportunity cost** of doing *x*. Many people make bad decisions because they tend to ignore the value of such forgone opportunities. This insight suggests that it will almost always be instructive to translate questions such as "Should I do *x*?" into ones such as "Should I do *x* or *y*?" In the latter question, *y* is simply the most highly valued alternative to doing *x*. Example 1.2 helps drive this important point home.

| EXAMPLE 1.2 | Implicit Cost |

Should I go skiing today or work as a research assistant?

There is a ski area near your campus. From experience you know that a day on the slopes is worth $60 to you. The charge for the day is $40 (which includes bus fare, lift ticket, and equipment). However, this is not the only cost of going skiing. You must also take into account the value of the most attractive alternative you will forgo by heading for the slopes. Suppose the best alternative is your new job as a professor's research assistant. The job pays $45 per day, and you like it just well enough to be willing to do it for free. The question you face is, "Should I go skiing or work as a research assistant?"

Here the cost of skiing is not just the explicit cost of the ski package ($40) but also the opportunity cost of the lost earnings ($45). The total costs are therefore $85, which exceeds the benefits of $60. Since $C(x) > B(x)$, you should stay on campus and work for your professor. Someone who ignored the opportunity cost of the forgone earnings would decide incorrectly to go skiing.

The fact that you liked the research job just well enough to have been willing to do it for free is another way of saying there were no psychic costs associated with doing it. This is important because it means that by not doing the job you would not have been escaping something unpleasant. Of course, not all jobs fall into this category. Suppose instead that your job is to scrape plates in the dining hall for the same pay, $45/day, and that the job is so unpleasant that you would be unwilling to do it for less than $30/day. Assuming your manager at the dining hall permits you to take a day off whenever you want, let's now reconsider your decision about whether to go skiing.

EXAMPLE 1.3   Costs and Benefits Are Reciprocal

Should I go skiing today or scrape plates?

There are two equivalent ways of looking at this decision. One is to say that one benefit of going skiing is not having to scrape plates. Since you would never be willing to scrape plates for less than $30/day, avoiding that task is worth that amount to you. Going skiing thus carries the indirect benefit of not scraping plates. When we add that indirect benefit to the $60 direct benefit of the skiing, we get $B(x) = \$90$. In this view of the problem, $C(x)$ is the same as before, namely, the $40 ski charge plus the $45 opportunity cost of the lost earnings, or $85. So now $B(x) > C(x)$, which means you should go skiing.

Alternatively, we could have viewed the unpleasantness of the plate-scraping job as an offset against its salary. By this approach, we would subtract $30/day from your $45/day earnings and say that the opportunity cost of not working is only $15/day. Then $C(x) = \$40 + \$15 = \$55 < B(x) = \$60$, and again the conclusion is that you should go skiing.

It makes no difference in which of these two ways you handle the valuation of the unpleasantness of scraping plates. It is critically important, however, that you do it either one way or the other. Don't count it twice!

As Example 1.3 makes clear, costs and benefits are reciprocal. Not incurring a cost is the same as getting a benefit. By the same token, not getting a benefit is the same as incurring a cost.

Obvious as this sounds, it is often overlooked. A case in point was a foreign graduate student who got her degree some years ago and was about to return to her home country. The trade regulations of her nation permitted people returning from abroad to bring back a new automobile without having to pay the normal 50 percent tariff. The student's father-in-law asked her to bring him back a new $20,000 Chevrolet and sent her a check for exactly that amount. This put the student in a quandary. She had been planning to bring back a Chevrolet and sell it in her home country. Because, as noted, new cars normally face a 50 percent import tax, such a car would sell at a dealership there for $30,000. The

EXAMPLE 1.4   Opportunity Cost

Why do most students start college right after finishing high school?

Should I work first or go to college first?

College costs are not limited to tuition, fees, supplies, housing, food—or their equivalent in future loan payments. They also include the opportunity cost of earnings forgone while studying. Earnings increase with experience. Thus the more experience you have, the more income you must forgo to attend college. This opportunity cost is therefore lowest when you are right out of high school.

On the benefit side, one big gain of a college education is sharply higher earnings. The sooner you graduate, the longer you will reap this benefit. Another benefit is the pleasantness of going to college as opposed to working. In general, the kinds of jobs people hold tend to be less unpleasant (or more pleasant) the more education they have. By going to college right away, you thus avoid having to work at the least pleasant jobs. For most people, then, it makes sense to go to college first and work afterward. Certainly it makes more sense to attend college at age 20 than at age 50.

A common exception involves people who are too immature right out of high school to reap the benefits of college work, who often do better by working a year or two before college.

student estimated that she could easily sell it privately for $28,000, which would net her an $8,000 gain. Thus the opportunity cost of giving the car to her father-in-law for $20,000 was going to be $8,000! Not getting this big benefit was a big cost. In the end, it was one the student elected to bear because she valued keeping peace in the family even more. As the cost-benefit principle makes clear, the best decision is not always the one that leaves you with the most money in your pocket.

Example 1.4 is a perfect illustration of Friedman's argument about how to evaluate a theory. High school seniors don't decide when to attend college on the basis of sophisticated calculations involving opportunity costs. On the contrary, most start right out of high school simply because that is what most of their peers do. It is the thing to do.

But this begs the question of how it got to *be* the thing to do. Customs do not originate out of thin air. A host of different societies have had centuries to experiment with this decision. If there were a significantly better way of arranging the learning and working periods of life, some society should have long since discovered it. Our current custom has survived because it is efficient. People may not make explicit calculations about the opportunity cost of forgone earnings, but they often behave *as if* they do.[2]

As simple as the opportunity cost concept is, it is one of the most important in microeconomics. The art in applying the concept correctly lies in being able to recognize the most valuable alternative that is sacrificed by the pursuit of a given activity.

Pitfall 2. Failing to Ignore Sunk Costs

An opportunity cost may not seem to be a relevant cost when in reality it is. On the other hand, sometimes an expenditure may seem relevant when in reality it is not. Such is often the case with *sunk costs,* costs that are beyond recovery at the moment a decision is made.

---

[2]This does not mean that all customs necessarily promote efficiency. For example, circumstances may have changed in such a way that a custom that promoted efficiency in the past no longer does so. In time, such a custom might change. Yet many habits and customs, once firmly entrenched, are very slow to change.

EXAMPLE 1.5   Sunk Cost (Part 1)

Should I drive to Boston or take the bus?

You are planning a 250-mile trip to Boston. Except for the cost, you are completely indifferent between driving and taking the bus. Bus fare is $100. You don't know how much it would cost to drive your car, so you call Budget for an estimate. Budget tells you that for your make of car the costs of a typical 10,000-mile driving year are as follows:

Insurance	$1,000
Interest	2,000
Fuel & Oil	1,000
Maintenance	1,000
Total	$5,000

If a cost has already been incurred and cannot be recovered, it is irrelevant for all decisions about the future.

Suppose you calculate that these costs come to $0.50/mile and use this figure to compute that the 250-mile trip will cost you $125 by car. And since this is more than the $100 bus fare, you decide to take the bus.

If you decide in this fashion, you fall victim to the sunk cost pitfall. Insurance and interest payments do not vary with the number of miles you drive each year. Both are sunk costs and will be the same whether or not you drive to Boston. Of the costs listed, fuel and oil and maintenance are the only ones that vary with miles driven. These come to $2,000 for each 10,000 miles you drive, or $0.20/mile. At $0.20/mile, it costs you only $50 to drive to Boston, and since this is less than the bus fare, you should drive.

Unlike opportunity costs, these costs *should be* ignored. Not ignoring them is a second pitfall in decision making. The principle of ignoring sunk costs emerges clearly in the following example.

In Example 1.5, note the role of the assumption that, costs aside, you are indifferent between the two modes of transport. If you had preferred one mode to the other, we would also have had to weigh that preference. For example, if you were willing to pay $60 to avoid the hassle of driving, the real cost of driving would be $110, not $50, and you should take the bus.

Self-Test questions, such as the one below, are sprinkled throughout the text to help you make sure that you understand important analytical concepts. You will master microeconomics more effectively if you do these exercises as you go along.

SELF-TEST 1.1

How, if at all, would your answer to the question in Example 1.5 be different if the worth of avoiding the hassle of driving is $20 and you average one $28 traffic ticket for every 200 miles you drive?

As a check, the answers to the in-chapter self-test questions are at the end of each chapter. Naturally, the self-tests will be much more useful if you work through them before consulting the answers.

Although our cost-benefit decision rule fails the test of prediction in this experiment, its message for the rational decision maker stands unchallenged. The two groups logically *should* have behaved the same. The only difference between them, after all, is that patrons in the refund group have lifetime incomes that are $5 higher than the others'. Such a

EXAMPLE 1.6   Sunk Cost (Part 2)

The pizza experiment.

A local pizza parlor offers an all-you-can-eat lunch for $5. You pay at the door, then the waiter brings you as many slices of pizza as you like. A former colleague performed this experiment: An assistant served as the waiter for one group of tables.[3] The "waiter" selected half the tables at random and gave everyone at those tables a $5 refund before taking orders. Diners at the remaining tables got no refund. He then kept careful count of the number of slices of pizza each diner ate. What difference, if any, do you predict in the amounts eaten by these two groups?

Eating additional food just to get your money's worth is not a sensible decision strategy.

Diners in each group confront the question "Should I eat another slice of pizza?" Here, the activity x consists of eating one more slice. For both groups, $C(x)$ is exactly zero: Even members of the group that did not get a refund can get as many additional slices as they want at no extra charge. Because the refund group was chosen at random, there is no reason to suppose that its members like pizza any more or less than the others. For everyone, the decision rule says keep eating until there is no longer any extra pleasure in eating another slice. Thus, $B(x)$ should be the same for each group, and people from both groups should keep eating until $B(x)$ falls to zero.

By this reasoning, the two groups should eat the same amount of pizza, on the average. The $5 admission fee is a sunk cost and should have no influence on the amount of pizza one eats. *In fact, however, the group that did not get the refund consumed substantially more pizza.*

---

trivial difference should have no effect on pizza consumption. Members of the no-refund group seemed to want to make sure they "got their money's worth." In all likelihood, however, this motive merely led them to overeat.[4]

What's wrong with being motivated to "get your money's worth"? Absolutely nothing, as long as the force of this motive operates *before* you enter into transactions. Thus it makes perfectly good sense to be led by this motive to choose one restaurant over an otherwise identical competitor that happens to cost more. Once the price of your lunch has been determined, however, the get-your-money's-worth motive should be abandoned. The satisfaction you get from eating another slice of pizza should then depend only on how hungry you are and on how much you like pizza, not on how much you paid. Yet people often seem not to behave in this fashion. The difficulty may be that we are not creatures of complete flexibility. Perhaps motives that make sense in one context are not easily abandoned in another.

SELF-TEST 1.2

Jim wins a ticket from a radio station to see a jazz band perform at an outdoor concert. Mike has paid $18 for a ticket to the same concert. On the evening of the concert there is a tremendous thunderstorm. If Jim and Mike have the same tastes, which of them will be more likely to attend the concert, assuming that each decides on the basis of a standard cost-benefit comparison?

---

[3]See Richard Thaler, "Toward a Positive Theory of Consumer Choice," *Journal of Economic Behavior and Organization* 1, 1980.

[4]An alternative to the "get-your-money's-worth" explanation is that $5 is a significant fraction of the amount of cash many diners have available to spend *in the short run.* Thus members of the refund group might have held back in order to save room for the dessert they could now afford to buy. To test this alternative explanation, the experimenter could give members of the no-refund group a $5 cash gift earlier in the day and then see if the amount of pizza consumed by the two groups still differed.

Pitfall 3. Measuring Costs and Benefits as Proportions Rather Than Absolute Dollar Amounts

When a boy asks his mother "Are we almost there yet?" how will she answer if they are 10 miles from their destination? Without some knowledge of the context of their journey, we cannot say. If they are near the end of a 300-mile journey, her answer will almost surely be yes. But if they have just embarked on a 12-mile journey, she will say no.

Contextual clues are important for a variety of ordinary judgments. Thinking about distance as a percentage of the total amount to be traveled is natural and informative. Many also find it natural to think in percentage terms when comparing costs and benefits. But as the following pair of simple examples illustrates, this tendency often causes trouble.

EXAMPLE 1.7　Comparing Costs and Benefits (Part 1)

Should you drive to Walmart to save $10 on a $40 upgrade to your stereo?

You are about to spend $40 for a Bluetooth adapter for your vintage stereo at the nearby campus store when a friend tells you that the very same adapter is on sale at Walmart for only $20. If Walmart is a 15-minute drive away, where would you buy the adapter? (No matter where you bought it, you must send it to the manufacturer for repairs, if it fails under warranty.)

EXAMPLE 1.8　Comparing Costs and Benefits (Part 2)

Should you drive downtown to save $20 on a $1,000 smart TV?

You are about to buy a new TV with the latest wireless interface at the nearby campus store for $1,020 when a friend tells you that the very same set is on sale at Walmart for only $1,000. If Walmart is a 15-minute drive away, where would you buy the television? (Again, repairs under warranty would entail sending the set to the manufacturer in each case.)

There is no uniquely correct answer to either of these questions, both of which ask whether the benefit of driving to Walmart is worth the cost. Most people say the trip would definitely be worth making for the Bluetooth adapter, but definitely not worth making for the TV. When pressed to explain, they say driving yields a 50 percent savings on the adapter but only a 2-percent savings on the TV.

These percentages, however, are irrelevant. In each case the benefit of driving to Walmart is exactly the $20 savings from the lower purchase price. What's the cost of driving to Walmart? Some might be willing to make the drive for as little as $5, while others might not be willing to do it for less than $50. But whatever the number, it should be the same in both cases. So your answers to the questions just posed should be the same. If you would be willing to make the drive for, say, $8, then you should buy both the adapter and TV at Walmart. But if your reservation price for making the drive is, say, $25, then you should buy both appliances at the nearby campus store.

When comparing costs and benefits, always use absolute dollar amounts, not proportions.

When using the cost-benefit test, you should express costs and benefits in absolute dollar terms. Comparing percentages is not a fruitful way to think about decisions like these.

Pitfall 4. Failure to Understand the Average-Marginal Distinction

So far we've looked at decisions about whether to perform a given action. Often, however, the choice is not whether to perform the action but the extent to which it should be performed. In this more complex case, we can apply the cost-benefit principle by reformulating the question. Instead of asking "Should I do activity x?," we repeatedly pose the question "Should I increase the level by which I am currently engaging in activity x?"

marginal cost the increase in total cost that results from carrying out one additional unit of an activity.

marginal benefit the increase in total benefit that results from carrying out one additional unit of an activity.

To answer this question, we must compare the benefit and cost of an *additional* unit of activity. The cost of an additional unit of activity is called the **marginal cost** of the activity, and the benefit of an additional unit is called its **marginal benefit.**

The cost-benefit rule tells us to keep increasing the level of an activity as long as its marginal benefit exceeds its marginal cost. But as Example 1.9 illustrates, people often fail to apply this rule correctly.

EXAMPLE 1.9	**Marginal Cost and Benefit vs. Average Cost and Benefit**

Should Tom launch another boat?

Tom manages a small fishing fleet of three boats. His current daily cost of operations, including boat rentals and fishermen's wages, is $300, or an average of $100 per boat launched. His daily total revenue, or benefit, from the sale of fish is currently $600, or an average of $200 per boat launched. Tom decides that since his cost per boat is less than his revenue per boat, he should launch another boat. Is this a sound decision?

average cost the average cost of undertaking n units of an activity is the total cost of the activity divided by n.

average benefit the average benefit of undertaking n units of an activity is the total benefit of the activity divided by n.

To answer this question, we must compare the marginal cost of launching a boat with its marginal benefit. The information given, however, tell us only the **average cost** and **average benefit** of launching a boat—which are, respectively, one-third of the total cost of three boats and one-third of the total revenue from three boats. Knowing the average benefit and average cost per boat launched does not enable us to decide whether launching another boat makes economic sense. For although the average benefit of the three boats launched thus far *might* be the same as the marginal benefit of launching another boat, it might also be either higher or lower. The same statement holds true regarding average and marginal costs.

To illustrate, suppose the marginal cost of launching a boat and crew is constant at $100 per boat per day. Then Tom should launch a fourth boat only if doing so will add at least $100 in daily revenue from his total fish catch. The mere fact that the current average revenue is $200 per boat simply doesn't tell us what the marginal benefit of launching the fourth boat will be.

Suppose, for example, that the relationship between the number of boats launched and the daily total revenue is as described in Table 1.1. With three boats per day, the average benefit per boat would then be $200, just as indicated above. If Tom launched a fourth boat, the *average* daily revenue would fall to $160 per boat, which is still more than the assumed marginal cost of $100. Note, however, that in the second column the total revenue from four boats is only $40 per day more than the total revenue from three boats. That means that the marginal revenue from launching the fourth boat is only $40. And since that is less than its marginal cost ($100), launching the fourth boat makes no sense.

TABLE 1.1
How Total Cost Varies with the Number of Boats Launched

Number of boats	Daily total benefit ($)	Daily average benefit ($/boat)
0	0	0
1	300	300
2	480	240
3	600	200
4	640	160

Example 1.10 illustrates how to apply the cost-benefit principle correctly in this case.

EXAMPLE 1.10   Applying the Cost-Benefit Principle

How many boats should Tom launch?

The marginal cost of launching a boat and crew is again constant at $100 per day. If total daily revenue from the catch again varies with the number of boats launched as shown in Table 1.1, how many boats should Tom launch?

     Tom should keep launching boats as long as the marginal benefit of doing so is at least as great as the marginal cost. With marginal cost constant at $100 per launch, Tom should thus keep launching boats as long as the marginal benefit is at least $100.

     Applying the definition of marginal benefit to the total benefit entries in the second column of Table 1.1 yields the marginal benefit values in the third column of Table 1.2. (Because marginal benefit is the change in total benefit that results

---

TABLE 1.2
How Marginal Benefit Varies with the Number of Boats Launched

Number of boats	Daily total benefit ($)	Daily marginal benefit ($/boat)
0	0	
		300
1	300	
		180
2	480	
		120
3	600	
		40
4	640	

when we change the number of boats by one, we place each marginal benefit entry midway between the rows showing the corresponding total benefit entries.) For example, the marginal benefit of increasing the number of boats from one to two is $180, the difference between the $480 total revenue with two boats and the $300 with one.

Comparing the $100 marginal cost per boat with the marginal benefit entries in the third column of Table 1.2, we see that the first three launches satisfy the cost-benefit test, but the fourth does not. Tom should thus launch three boats.

SELF-TEST 1.4

If the marginal cost of launching each boat had not been $100 but $150, how many boats should Tom have launched?

The cost-benefit principle tells us that *marginal* costs and benefits—measures that correspond to the *increment* of an activity under consideration—are the relevant ones for choosing the level at which to pursue the activity. Yet many people compare the *average* cost and benefit of the activity when making such decisions. As Example 1.9 should have made clear, however, increasing the level of an activity may not be justified, even though its average benefit at the current level is significantly greater than its average cost.

USING MARGINAL BENEFIT AND MARGINAL COST GRAPHICALLY

The examples just discussed entail decisions about an activity that could take place only on specific levels—no boats, one boat, two boats, and so on. The levels of many other activities, however, can vary continuously. One can buy gasoline, for example, in any quantity one wishes. For activities that are continuously variable, it is often convenient to display the comparison of marginal benefit and marginal cost graphically.

EXAMPLE 1.11   **Comparing Marginal Benefit and Cost Graphically**

How much should Susan talk to Hal each month?

Susan has a pay-as-you-go phone plan that has a flat-rate charge of 4 cents per minute for calls to her boyfriend Hal. (Fractional minutes are billed at the same rate, so a 30-second call would cost her 2 cents.) The value to Susan, measured in terms of her willingness to pay, of an additional minute of conversation with Hal is shown on curve *MB* in Figure 1.1. How many minutes should she spend on the phone with Hal each month?

The downward slope of curve *MB* reflects the fact that the value of an additional minute declines with the total amount of conversation that has occurred thus far. (As we will see in Chapter 3, it is a common pattern that the more someone has of a good, the less value he assigns to having additional units of it.) Curve *MC* in the diagram measures the cost of each additional minute, assumed to be constant at $0.04. The optimal quantity of conversation is the quantity for which these two curves cross—namely, 400 minutes per month. If Susan speaks with Hal for less than that amount, the marginal benefit from adding another minute would exceed the marginal cost, so she should talk longer. But if they speak for more than 400 minutes per month, the amount she would save by speaking less would exceed the benefit she would sacrifice, which means they should speak less.

Phone call rate
(cents per minute)

MB

Value of an additional
minute

Cost of an
additional
minute

Price = 4 .... MC

Minutes
per month

200   400   600   800

FIGURE 1.1

The Optimal Quantity of Conversation.

The optimal amount of a continuously variable activity is the quantity for which its marginal benefit is just equal to its marginal cost.

SELF-TEST 1.5

If her marginal benefit curve is again as given in Figure 1.1, how many minutes should Susan speak with Hal each month if the flat rate falls to 2 cents per minute?

THE INVISIBLE HAND

One of the most important insights of economic analysis is that the individual pursuit of self-interest is often not only *consistent* with broader social objectives, but actually even *required* by them. Wholly unaware of the effects of their actions, self-interested consumers often act as if driven by what Adam Smith called an *invisible hand* to produce the greatest social good. In perhaps the most widely quoted passage from *The Wealth of Nations*, Smith wrote:

> It is not from the benevolence of the butcher, the brewer, or the baker that we expect our dinner, but from their regard of their own interest. We address ourselves not to their humanity, but to their self-love, and never talk to them of our necessities, but of their advantage.

Smith observed that competition among sellers fostered attempts to develop better products and cheaper ways of producing them. The first to succeed in those attempts enjoyed higher profits than their rivals, but only temporarily. As others copied the new products and methods, their offerings put inevitable downward pressure on prices. Smith's insight, in a nutshell, was that although sellers were seeking only to promote their own advantage, the ultimate beneficiaries were consumers.

Modern economists sometimes lose sight of the fact that Smith did not believe that *only* selfish motives are important.

Adam Smith, L.L.D.

Adam Smith: 1723–1790. Smith's modern disciples often oversimplify his message.

In his earlier treatise, *The Theory of Moral Sentiments,* for example, he wrote movingly about the compassion we feel for others:

> How selfish soever man may be supposed, there are evidently some principles in his nature, which interest him in the fortune of others, and render their happiness necessary to him, though he derives nothing from it, except the pleasure of seeing it. Of this kind is pity or compassion, the emotion which we feel for the misery of others, when we either see it, or are made to conceive it in a very lively manner. That we often derive sorrow from the sorrow of others, is a matter of fact too obvious to require any instances to prove it; for this sentiment, like all the other original passions of human nature, is by no means confined to the virtuous and humane, though they perhaps may feel it with the most exquisite sensibility. The greatest ruffian, the most hardened violator of the laws of society, is not altogether without it.

Smith was well aware, moreover, that the outcome of unbridled pursuit of self-interest is sometimes far from socially benign. As the following example illustrates, the invisible hand mechanism breaks down when important costs or benefits accrue to people other than the decision makers themselves.

EXAMPLE 1.12   **Applying Marginal Benefit and Cost Graphically**

Should I burn my leaves or haul them into the woods?

external cost of an activity
a cost that falls on people who are not directly involved in the activity.

Suppose the cost of hauling the leaves is $20 and the cost to the homeowner of burning them is only $1. If the homeowner cares only about costs that accrue directly to herself, she will burn her leaves. The difficulty is that burning leaves also entails an important **external cost,** which means a cost borne by people who are not directly involved in the decision. This external cost is the damage done by the smoke from the fire. That cost accrues not to the homeowner who makes the decision about burning the leaves but to the people downwind. Suppose the smoke damage amounts to $25. The good of the community then requires that the leaves be hauled, not burned. From the perspective of the self-interested homeowner, however, it seems best to burn them.[5]

External costs and benefits often motivate laws that limit individual discretion. (External costs and benefits will be our focus in Chapter 16.) Most communities, for example, now have laws prohibiting the burning of leaves within city limits. Such laws may be viewed as a way of making the costs and benefits seen by individuals more nearly resemble those experienced by the community as a whole. With a law against burning leaves in effect, the potential leaf burner weighs the penalty of breaking the law against the cost of hauling the leaves. Most people conclude it is cheaper to haul them.

SELF-INTEREST AND *HOMO ECONOMICUS*

Many economists and other behavioral scientists remain skeptical about the importance of duty and other unselfish motives. They feel that the larger material payoffs associated with selfish behavior so strongly dominate other motives that, as a first approximation, we may safely ignore nonegoistic motives.

---

[5]Of course, if the homeowner interacts frequently with the people downwind, self-interest may still dictate hauling the leaves, to preserve goodwill for future interactions. But where the people downwind are anonymous strangers, this motive will operate with less force.

With this view in mind, the stereotypical decision maker in the self-interest model is often given the label *Homo economicus*. *Homo economicus* does not experience the sorts of sentiments that motivate people to vote, or to return lost wallets to their owners with the cash intact. On the contrary, personal material costs and benefits are the only things he cares about. He does not contribute voluntarily to private charities or public television stations, keeps promises only when it pays to do so, and if the pollution laws are not carefully enforced, disconnects the catalytic converter on his car to save on fuel. And so on.

Obviously, many people do not fit the me-first caricature of the self-interest model. They donate bone marrow to strangers with leukemia. They endure great trouble and expense to see justice done, even when it will not undo the original injury. At great risk to themselves, they pull people from burning buildings and jump into icy rivers to rescue people who are about to drown. Soldiers throw their bodies atop live grenades to save their comrades.

To be sure, selfish motives are important. When a detective investigates a murder, for example, her first question is, "Who stood to benefit from the victim's death?" When an economist studies a government regulation, he wants to know whose incomes it enhances. When a senator proposes a new spending project, the political scientist tries to discover which of his constituents will be its primary beneficiaries.

Our goal in much of this text is to understand the kinds of behaviors to which selfish motives give rise in specific situations. But throughout this process, it is critical to remember that the self-interest model is not intended as a prescription for how to conduct your own affairs. On the contrary, we will see in later chapters that *Homo economicus* is woefully ill suited to the demands of social existence as we know it. Each of us probably knows people who more or less fit the *Homo economicus* caricature. And our first priority, most of the time, is to steer clear of them.

The irony here is that being a purely self-interested person entails a degree of social isolation that is not only bad for the soul but also harmful to the pocketbook. To succeed in life, even in purely material terms, people must form alliances and relationships of trust. But what sensible person would be willing to trust *Homo economicus*? Later chapters present specific examples of how unselfish motives confer material rewards on those who hold them. For the present, however, bear in mind that the self-interest model is intended only to capture one part of human behavior, albeit an important one.

Self-interest is one of the most important human motives. But it is not the only important motive.

THE ECONOMIC NATURALIST

Studying biology enables people to observe and marvel at many details of life that would otherwise escape them. For the naturalist, a walk in a quiet woods becomes an adventure. In much the same way, studying microeconomics enables someone to become an "economic naturalist," a person who sees the mundane details of ordinary existence in a sharp new light. Each feature of the manmade landscape is no longer an amorphous mass but the result of an implicit cost-benefit calculation. Following are some examples of economic naturalism.

Many of us respond warmly to the maxim "Anything worth doing is worth doing well." After all, it encourages a certain pride of workmanship that is often sadly lacking. Economic Naturalist 1.1 makes clear, however, that if the maxim is interpreted literally, it does not make any sense. To do something well requires time, effort, and expense. But these are scarce resources. To devote them to one activity makes them unavailable for another. Increasing the quality of one of the things we do thus necessarily means to reduce the quality of others—yet another application of the concept of opportunity cost. Every intelligent decision must be mindful of this trade-off.

▶ Visit your instructor's Connect© course and access your eBook to view this video.

Why does the light come on when you open the refrigerator door but not when you open the freezer?

▶ Visit your instructor's Connect© course and access your eBook to view this video.

Why are child safety seats required in automobiles but not in airplanes?

Economic Naturalist 1.1

Why is airline food so bad?

Everyone complains about airline food. Indeed, if any serious restaurant dared to serve such food, it would quickly go bankrupt. Our complaints seem to take for granted that airline meals should be just as good as the ones we eat in restaurants. But why should they? The cost-benefit perspective says that airlines should increase the quality of their meals if and only if the benefit would outweigh the cost. The benefit of better food is probably well measured by what passengers would be willing to pay for it, in the form of higher ticket prices. If a restaurant-quality meal could be had for, say, a mere $10 increase in fares, most people would probably be delighted to pay it. The difficulty, however, is that it would be much more costly than that to prepare significantly better meals at 39,000 feet in a tiny galley with virtually no time. It could be done, of course. An airline could remove 20 seats from the plane, install a modern, well-equipped kitchen, hire extra staff, spend more on ingredients, and so on. But these extra costs would be more like $100 per passenger than $10. For all our complaints about the low quality of airline food, few of us would be willing to bear this extra burden. In fact, most airlines have eliminated meals from all domestic flights and offer meals only for purchase, to lower operating costs.

Economic Naturalist 1.2

How did automatic transmissions become more efficient than manuals?

For many years, manual transmissions offered better fuel economy than automatics. This was not because manual transmissions were inherently more efficient but because they were less complex than the automatics. That made it cheaper to add fuel-saving fifth or sixth "overdrive" gears to a manual gearbox. Automatic transmissions with additional gears would have offered the same fuel economy benefits, but at a higher price. Since automatic transmissions were mainly sold on convenience, "good enough" three- or four-speed solutions prevailed.

But no more. Today's automatics commonly have 9 or 10 speeds (or use continuously variable technology), and few drivers could make a manual perform nearly as well as an automatic on fuel consumption. What led to this change? We could certainly point to technology, ongoing high gasoline costs, and the imposition of federal fuel efficiency standards. But we must not forget the consumer. By some measures, the percentage of vehicles equipped with manual transmissions sold in the United States has fallen from over 25 percent in 1995 to less than 5 percent in 2018.[6] Automatic transmissions are now competing with each other, not with manuals. It "pays" automakers to react to this change in consumer tastes by investing more heavily in improvements to automatic transmissions.

That said, the end may be in sight for now-dominant automatic transmissions. Automakers are investing even more in vehicle electrification than in transmission technologies. Tomorrow's electric cars will not require traditional multi-speed gearboxes.

---

[6]The sales figures are from www.carmax.com/articles/stick-shift-index. See also National Research Council, *Cost, Effectiveness, and Deployment of Fuel Economy Technologies for Light-Duty Vehicles*, Washington, DC: National Academies Press, 2015, 169, https://doi.org/10.17226/21744.

Everything we see in life is the result of some such compromise. For Roger Federer, playing championship tennis rules out becoming a concert pianist. Yet this obviously does not mean he shouldn't spend any time playing the piano. It just means that he should hold himself to a lower standard there than in the tennis arena.

SHOULD YOU THINK LIKE AN ECONOMIST?

In this chapter, you were given a brief initiation into "thinking like an economist." But should you adopt that perspective? The question goes beyond the strengths and weaknesses of *Homo economicus* that we outlined a few pages back. In recent years, economists and the discipline of economics—often described as mono-lithic entities[7]—have often come under fierce criticism, and if you believe the critics, many of today's social, political, and environmental ills can be traced to "neoliberal" policies "rooted in conventional economic doctrines."[8]

There is no question that economics has much to say about big problems. We would be unlikely to study economics if it did not. But many of the high-level com-plaints may be rooted in a failure to distinguish between **normative** and **positive economics,** which is to say between the politics and values of economic stake-holders (economists included) and actual economic theory.

A specific example helps illustrate the difference. In the pacific Northwest, logging companies are currently cutting down some of the few remaining stands of virgin redwoods to supply contractors with timber to build homes. Many of these trees are more than 2,000 years old—a national, indeed international, treasure we can never hope to replace. To the logging companies, however, they are worth more as lumber than as facilities for carbon capture or monuments to nature's magnificence. Whether the remaining stands of virgin redwoods ought to be protected is, in the end, a **normative question,** one that involves our values every bit as much as the question of whether to forgive student loans or increase tax rates on top incomes.

By itself, economic analysis cannot answer such questions. A society that reveres nature or abhors risks to the environment may well decide the fate of the redwoods differently from one that holds other values, even though members of both societies are in complete agree-ment about all the relevant economic facts and theories. Economic analysis is on firmer ground when it comes to answering **positive questions**—questions about what the conse-quences of specific policies or institutional arrangements will be. If we ban the cutting of redwoods, what will happen to the price of lumber? What substitute building materials are likely to be developed and at what cost? Or will virgin lumber cutting simply move over-seas? How will employment in the logging and housing industries be affected? These aren't all of the relevant questions. Other sciences must be invoked to provide context—say, of the carbon capture impact and time to remediation. But these positive economic questions and their answers are clearly relevant to our thinking about the underlying normative question.

MICROECONOMICS AND MACROECONOMICS

Our focus in this chapter is on issues confronting the individual decision maker. As we pro-ceed, we'll also consider economic models of groups of individuals—for example, the group of all buyers or all sellers in a market. The study of individual choices and the study of group behavior in individual markets both come under the rubric of microeconomics.

The time and effort required to become a championship tennis player rule out the possibility of simultaneously becoming a leading concert pianist.

Leonard Zhukovsky/Shutterstock

normative question a question about what policies or institutional arrangements lead to the best outcomes.

positive question a question about the consequences of specific policies or institutional arrangements.

---

[7]See, for example, Binyamin Appelbaum, *The Economists' Hour: False Prophets, Free Markets, and the Frac-ture of Society*, New York: Little, Brown and Company, 2019. On page 16, Appelbaum presents a justification for speaking of economists "as a homogeneous community."

[8]For a compilation and discussion of frequent current accusations against economics, see Suresh Naidu, Dani Rodrik, and Gabriel Zucman, *Economics for Inclusive Prosperity: An Introduction*, https://econfip.org/wp-content/uploads/2019/02/1.Economics-for-Inclusive-Prosperity-An-Introduction.pdf, which has been reprinted, with a symposium, as "Economics After Neoliberalism," *Boston Review*, Summer 2019, http://bostonreview.net/forum/suresh-naidu-dani-rodrik-gabriel-zucman-economics-after-neoliberalism. Naidu, Rodrik, and Zucman take a very different view of standard economic theory than is taken in this text, but we are aligned on the "economics as an evaluation framework" approach to policy questions.

Macroeconomics, by contrast, is the study of broader aggregations of markets. For example, it tries to explain the national unemployment rate, the overall price level, and the total value of national output.

Economists are much better at predicting and explaining what happens in individual markets than in the economy as a whole. Not only is it difficult to identify unintended consequences of policy changes when working at the economy level, but normative biases (in what is, after all, "policy economics") are particularly difficult to avoid. When prominent economists disagree in the press or on television, the issue is more likely to be from macroeconomics than from microeconomics. But even though economists still have trouble with macroeconomic questions, macroeconomic analysis is undeniably important. After all, recessions and inflation disrupt millions of lives.

Economists increasingly believe that the key to progress in macroeconomics lies in more careful analysis of the individual markets that make up broader aggregates. As a result, the distinction between micro and macro has become less clear in recent years. The graduate training of all economists, micro and macro alike, is increasingly focused on microeconomic analysis.

SUMMARY

- Microeconomics entails the study of choice under scarcity. Scarcity is ever present, even when material resources are abundant. There are always important limitations on time, energy, and the other things we need to pursue our goals.

- Much of the economist's task is to try to answer questions of the form "Should I do activity x?" The approach to answering them is disarmingly simple. It is to do x if and only if its costs are smaller than its benefits. Not incurring a cost is the same as getting a benefit. (LO1)

- The cost-benefit model sometimes fails to predict how people behave when confronted with everyday choices. The art of cost-benefit analysis lies in being able to specify and measure the relevant costs and benefits, a skill many decision makers lack. Some costs, such as sunk costs, often seem relevant but turn out not to be. Others, such as implicit costs, are sometimes ignored, even

though they are important. Benefits too are often difficult to measure. Experience has taught that becoming aware of the most common pitfalls helps most people become better decision makers. (LO2, LO3)

- When the question is not whether to perform an activity but rather at what level to perform it, marginal analysis draws our attention to the importance of marginal benefits and marginal costs. We should increase the level of an activity whenever its marginal benefit exceeds its marginal cost. (LO1)

- The principles of rational choice are by no means limited to formal markets for goods and services. Indeed, some form of implicit or explicit cost-benefit calculation lies behind almost every human action, object, and behavior. Knowledge of the underlying principles casts our world in a sharp new light, not always flattering, but ever a source of stimulating insight. (LO6)

KEY TERMS

average benefit	marginal benefit	opportunity cost of activity
average cost	marginal cost	positive question
external cost of an activity	normative question	reservation price of activity x

REVIEW QUESTIONS

1. What is your opportunity cost of reading a novel this evening? (LO3)

2. Your roommate is thinking of permanently dropping out of school this semester. If his tuition payment for this

semester is non-refundable, should he take it into account when making his decision? (LO3)

3. Give three examples of activities accompanied by external costs or benefits. (LO5)

4. Why is the opportunity cost of attending college higher for a 50 year old than for a 20 year old? *(LO6)*

5. Why should sunk costs be irrelevant for current decisions? *(LO3)*

6. How can the cost-benefit model be useful for studying the behavior of people who do not think explicitly in terms of costs and benefits? *(LO2)*

PROBLEMS

1. Jamal has a flexible summer job. He can work every day but is allowed to take a day off anytime he wants. His friend Don suggests they go to the amusement park on Tuesday. The admission charge for the park is $15 per person, and it will cost them $5 each for gasoline and parking. Jamal loves amusement parks and a day at the park is worth $45 to him. However, Jamal also enjoys his job so much that he would actually be willing to pay $10 per day to do it. *(LO1)*
   a. If Jamal earns $10 if he works, should he go to the amusement park?
   b. If Jamal earns $15 . . . ?
   c. If Jamal earns $20 . . . ?

2. Tom is a mushroom farmer. He invests all his spare cash in additional mushrooms, which grow on otherwise useless land behind his barn. The mushrooms double in size during their first year, after which time they are harvested and sold at a constant price per pound. Tom's friend Dick asks Tom for a loan of $200, which he promises to repay after 1 year. How much interest will Dick have to pay Tom in order for Tom to be no worse off than if he had not made the loan? *(LO3)*

3. The meal plan at University A lets students eat as much as they like for a fixed fee of $500 per semester. The average student there eats 250 lbs. of food per semester. University B charges students $500 for a book of meal tickets that entitles the student to eat 250 lbs. of food per semester. If the student eats more than 250 lbs., he or she pays extra; if the student eats less, he or she gets a refund. If students are rational, at which university will average food consumption be higher? *(LO3)*

4. You are planning a 1,000-mile trip to Florida. Except for cost, you are indifferent between driving and taking the bus. Bus fare is $260. The costs of operating your car during a typical 10,000-mile driving year are as follows: *(LO3)*

Insurance	$1,000
Interest	2,000
Fuel & oil	1,200
Tires	200
License & registration	50
Maintenance	1,100
Total	$5,550

Should you drive or take the bus?

5. Chris and Jane have rented a banquet hall to celebrate their wedding anniversary. Fifty people have already accepted their invitation. The caterers will charge $5 per person for food and $2 per person for drinks. The band will cost $300 for the evening, and the hall costs $200. Now Chris and Jane are considering inviting 10 more people. By how much will these extra guests increase the cost of their party? *(LO3)*

6. You loan a friend $1,000, and at the end of 1 year she writes you a check for $1,000 to pay off this loan. If the annual interest rate on your savings account is 6 percent, what was your opportunity cost of making this loan? *(LO3)*

7. Monica and Rachel live in Ithaca, New York. At 2 PM, Monica goes to the local Ticketmaster and buys a $30 ticket to a basketball game to be played that night in Syracuse (50 miles north). Rachel plans to attend the same game, but doesn't purchase her ticket in advance because she knows from experience that it is always possible to buy just as good a seat at the arena. At 4 PM, a heavy, unexpected snowstorm begins, making the prospect of the drive to Syracuse much less attractive than before. If both Monica and Rachel have the same tastes and are rational, is one of them more likely to attend the game than the other? If so, say who and explain why. If not, explain why not. *(LO3)*

8. Two types of radar weather-detection devices are available for commercial passenger aircraft: the "state-of-the-art" machine and another that is significantly less costly, but also less effective. The Federal Aviation Administration (FAA) has hired you for advice on whether all passenger planes should be required to use the state-of-the-art machine. After careful study, your recommendation is to require the more expensive machine only in passenger aircraft with more than 200 seats. How would you justify such a recommendation to an FAA member who complains that all passengers have a right to the best weather-detecting radar currently available? *(LO1)*

9. A group has chartered a bus to New York City. The driver costs $100, the bus costs $500, and tolls will cost $75. The driver's fee is nonrefundable, but the bus may be canceled a week in advance at a charge of only $50. At $18 per ticket, how many people must buy tickets so that the trip need not be canceled? *(LO1)*

10. Residents of your city are charged a fixed weekly fee of $6 for garbage collection. They may put out as many cans as they wish. The average household puts out three cans per week.

    Now, suppose your city changes to a "tag" system. Each can of garbage must have a tag affixed to it. The tags cost $2 each.

    What effect will the introduction of the tag system have on the total quantity of trash collected? *(LO1)*

11. Suppose that random access memory (RAM) can be added to your computer at a cost of $8 per gigabyte. Suppose also that the value to you, measured in terms of your willingness to pay, of an additional gigabyte of memory is $32 for the first gigabyte, and then falls by one-half for each additional gigabyte. Draw a graph of marginal cost and marginal benefit. How many gigabytes of memory should you purchase? *(LO4)*

12. Suppose in Problem 11 the cost of RAM falls to $4 per gigabyte. How many gigabytes of memory should you purchase now? Suppose additionally that your benefit for an additional gigabyte of memory rises to $144 for the first gigabyte, also falling by one-half for each additional gigabyte. How many gigabytes of memory should you purchase now, with both the lower price and the larger benefit? *(LO4)*

13.* Dana has purchased a $40 ticket to a rock concert. On the day of the concert she is invited to a welcome-home party for a friend returning from abroad. She cannot attend both the concert and the party. If she had known about the party before buying the ticket, she would have chosen the party over the concert. *True or false:* It follows that if she is rational, she will go to the party anyway. Explain. *(LO3)*

14.* Yesterday you were unexpectedly given a free ticket to a Bruno Mars concert scheduled for April 1. The market price of this ticket is $75, but the most you could sell it for is only $50. Today you discover that Taylor Swift will be giving a concert that same evening. Tickets for the Taylor Swift concert are still available at $75. Had you known before receiving your Bruno Mars ticket yesterday that Taylor Swift would be coming, you definitely would have bought a ticket to see her, not Bruno Mars. *True or false:* From what we are told of your preferences, it follows that if you are a rational utility maximizer, you should attend the Taylor Swift concert. Explain. *(LO3)*

15.* Smith recently faced a choice between being (*a*) an economics professor, which pays $60,000/yr, or (*b*) a safari leader, which pays $50,000/yr. After careful deliberation, Smith took the safari job, but it was a close call. "For a dollar more," he said, "I'd have gone the other way."

    Now Smith's brother-in-law approaches him with a business proposition. The terms are as follows:
    - Smith must resign his safari job to work full-time in his brother-in-law's business.
    - Smith must give his brother-in-law an interest-free loan of $100,000, which will be repaid in full if and when Smith leaves the business. (Smith currently has much more than $100,000 in the bank.)
    - The business will pay Smith a salary of $70,000/yr. He will receive no other payment from the business.

    The interest rate is 10 percent per year. Apart from salary considerations, Smith feels that working in the business would be just as enjoyable as being an economics professor. For simplicity, assume there is no uncertainty regarding either Smith's salary in the proposed business or the security of his monetary investment in it. Should Smith join his brother-in-law and, if so, how small would Smith's salary from the business have to be to make it *not* worthwhile for him to join? If not, how large would Smith's salary from the business have to be to make it worthwhile for him to join? *(LO1, LO3)*

16.* You have just purchased a new Chevrolet Equinox for $25,000, but the most you could get for it if you sold it privately is $20,000. Now you learn that Ford is offering its Explorer, which normally sells for $30,000, at a special sale price of $25,000. If you had known before buying the Equinox that you could buy an Explorer at the same price, you would have definitely chosen the Explorer. *True or false:* From what we are told of your preferences, it follows that if you are a rational utility maximizer, you should definitely not sell the Equinox and buy the Explorer. Explain. *(LO1, LO3)*

*Problems marked with an asterisk (*) are more difficult.

ANSWERS TO SELF-TESTS

1.1 Someone who gets a $28 traffic ticket every 200 miles driven will pay $35 in fines, on the average, for every 250 miles driven. Adding that figure to the $20 hassle cost of driving, and then adding the $50 fuel, oil, and maintenance cost, we have $105. This is more than the $100 bus fare, which means taking the bus is best. *(LO1)*

1.2 The $18 Mike paid for his ticket is a sunk cost at the moment he must decide whether to attend the concert. For both Jim and Mike, therefore, the costs and benefits should be the same. If the benefit of seeing the concert outweighs the cost of sitting in the rain, they should go. Otherwise they should stay home. *(LO3)*

1.3 You should use your coupon for the New Delhi trip, because it is more valuable to save $120 than to save $100. *(LO1, LO3)*

1.4 Two boats. Referring to Table 1.2, note that if marginal cost is $150, it now pays to launch the second boat (marginal benefit = $180) but not the third. *(LO1, LO3)*

1.5 At 2 cents per minute, Susan should talk for 600 minutes per month. Refer to the graph as shown. *(LO4)*

Supply and Demand

In April 1979, less than a month after the Carter administration began to ease Nixon-era price controls on domestic crude oil, a major oil supply interruption occurred in the Mideast. Gasoline prices skyrocketed. To head off further increases, the administration implemented a complex system of fuel allocations and gasoline price controls. At the same time, with oil supplies uncertain, it asked U.S. refiners to increase inventories—that is, to send less gasoline to the market. One result was that many urban markets got substantially less gasoline than motorists wanted to buy at the regulated prices. At many service stations, lines of cars stretched many blocks.

Quarrels over position in such queues were common, and many motorists got into fistfights and shouting matches. One was shot and killed for butting into line. Tensions continued until the gasoline lines dwindled with the passing of the summer travel months.

The government's system of price controls and allocations tried to accomplish a task we usually relegate to markets. The gas shortage experience was typical of similar interventions in other times and places. These programs typically produce confusion and conflict. Of course, the unfettered market can itself produce outcomes we don't like. But rarely does it fail to allocate available supplies in a smooth, efficient manner.

You might ask, in light of climate policy options being discussed today, why the Carter administration did not propose a tax on gasoline. It did. It proposed a rebated, "revenue-neutral" gasoline tax as early as 1977, but the proposal failed in Congress.

In Chapter 5, we will look at the objections to the 1977 gas tax proposal and ask whether those objections were supported by economic theory. We begin in this chapter with the basic components of price theory: supply and demand.

CHAPTER PREVIEW

In this chapter we will explore why markets function so smoothly most of the time and why attempts at direct allocation are so often problematic. The "most of the time" in the previous sentence should be noted. There are many kinds of markets, and the theory we develop in this chapter should be used with care when applied to markets where, as in our

---

2

LEARNING OBJECTIVES

After reading this chapter, you should be able to:

LO1 Explain how the demand and supply curves summarize the behavior of buyers and sellers.

LO2 Explain why the equilibrium in a market identifies a price-quantity pair for which buyers and sellers are satisfied.

LO3 Explain how shifts in supply and demand curves cause equilibrium prices and quantities to change.

LO4 Explain why transactions can always be found that make some parties better off without harming others whenever a market is not in equilibrium.

LO5 Explain why attempts to peg prices below or above their equilibrium levels produces negative side-effects and describe both the rationing and allocative functions of prices.

LO6 List some determinants of supply and demand.

LO7 Solve for equilibrium prices and quantities when supply and demand curves are expressed in algebraic form.

Saul Loeb/AFP/Getty Images

Pegging prices below equilibrium levels almost always entails costly side effects.

oil crisis example, a few producers dominate or where an extra-market authority has acted to constrain supply. We will begin to sort out the impacts of these kind of distortions in Chapter 10 and following. That said, the concepts introduced in this chapter provide powerful and intuitive insights into both policy questions and actual market operations. The early part of the chapter will look at basic supply and demand analysis. First, we'll review the usual descriptive features of supply and demand analysis. Next, we'll see that, for given attributes of buyers and sellers, the unregulated competitive market yields the best attainable outcome, in the sense that any other combination of price and quantity would be worse for at least some buyers or sellers.

Despite this attractive feature, market outcomes often do not command society's approval. Concern for the well-being of the poor has motivated the governments of every Western society to intervene in a variety of ways—for instance, by adopting laws that peg prices above or below their equilibrium levels. Such laws, we will see, almost always generate harmful, if unintended, consequences.

A generally more efficient solution to the problems of the poor is to boost their incomes directly. The law of supply and demand cannot be repealed by the legislature. But legislatures can alter the underlying forces that govern the shape and position of supply and demand schedules.

Finally, we will explore supply and demand analysis as a useful device for understanding how taxes affect equilibrium prices and quantities. In particular, it helps dispel the myth that a tax is paid primarily by the party on whom it is directly levied; rather, the burden of a tax falls most heavily on whichever side of the market is least able to avoid it.

SUPPLY AND DEMAND CURVES

Our basic tool for analyzing market outcomes is supply and demand analysis, already familiar to most of you. Let's begin with the following working definition of a market.

Definition: A market consists of the buyers and sellers of a good or service.

Some markets are confined to a single specific time and location. For example, all the participating buyers and sellers (or at least their designated representatives) gather together in the same place for an antiques auction. Other markets span vast geographic territory, and most participants in them never meet or even see one another. The New York Stock Exchange and eBay are examples.

Sometimes the choice of market definition will depend on the bias of the observer. In antitrust cases, for example, current policy prohibits mergers between companies whose combined share of the market would exceed a given threshold. Accordingly, government prosecutors who oppose a merger will often try to define markets as narrowly as possible, thereby making the combined market share as large as possible. The merging companies, by contrast, tend to view their markets in much broader terms, which naturally makes their combined market share smaller. Stouffer's Corporation, when it wanted to merge with Nestlé, told the court that both firms were in the business of selling "frozen dinners." The Justice Department argued to the same court that the two companies were in the business of selling "high-priced ethnic entrees." In general, as in this particular instance, the best market definition will depend on the purpose at hand.

Over the years, economists have increasingly recognized that even subtle product differences matter a great deal to some consumers, and the trend in analysis has been toward ever narrower definitions of goods and markets. Two otherwise identical products are often classified as separate if they differ only with respect to the times or places they are available. An umbrella on a sunny day, for example, is in this sense a very different product from an umbrella during a downpour. And the markets for these two products behave very differently indeed. (My editor tells me that low-quality umbrellas in Manhattan sell for $10 on rainy days, only $5 on sunny days.)

To make our discussion concrete, let's consider the workings of a specific market— say, the one for $1\frac{1}{2}$-pound lobsters in Hyannis, Massachusetts, on July 20, 2019. For this market, our task is to explain both the price of lobsters and the quantity traded. We begin with the basic *demand curve*, a simple mathematical relationship that tells how many lobsters buyers wish to purchase at various possible prices (holding all else constant). The curve *DD* depicted in Figure 2.1, for example, tells us that 4,000 lobsters will be demanded at a price of $8 each, 1,000 at a price of $20, and so on.

If a visitor from Mars were told only that lobsters sell for $8 each, he would have no way of knowing whether they were cheap or expensive. In 1900, an $8 lobster would have been out of reach of all but the wealthiest consumers. In 2019, by contrast, lobsters would have been considered an incredible bargain at that price. Unless otherwise stated, the price on the vertical axis of the demand curve diagram will refer to the **real price** of the good, which means its price relative to the prices of all other goods and services. Thus, the prices on the vertical axis of Figure 2.1 represent lobster prices on July 20, 2019, and the context within which those prices are interpreted by buyers is the set of prices of all other goods on that same date.

The discussion above describes the demand curve as a schedule telling how much of a product consumers wish to purchase at various prices. This is called the *horizontal interpretation* of the demand curve. Under this interpretation, we start with price on the

real price of a product its price relative to the prices of other goods and services.

FIGURE 2.1

The Demand Curve for Lobsters in Hyannis Mass., July 20, 2019

The demand curve tells the quantities buyers will wish to purchase at various prices. Its key property is its downward slope; when price falls, the quantity demanded increases. This property is called the law of demand.

vertical axis and read the corresponding quantity demanded on the horizontal axis. For instance, at a price of $20 per lobster, the demand curve in Figure 2.1 tells us that the quantity demanded will be 1,000 lobsters per day.

A second interpretation of the demand curve is to start with quantity on the horizontal axis and then read the marginal buyer's reservation price on the vertical axis. Thus when the quantity of lobsters sold is 4,000 per day, the demand curve in Figure 2.1 tells us that the marginal buyer's reservation price is $8 per lobster. This second way of reading the demand curve is called the *vertical interpretation.*

law of demand the empirical observation that when the price of a product falls, people demand larger quantities of it.

The demand curve shown in Figure 2.1 happens to be linear, but demand curves in general need not be. The key property assumed of them is that they are downward sloping: the quantity demanded rises as the price of the product falls. This property is often called the **law of demand.** Although we will see in Chapter 4 that it is theoretically possible for a demand curve to be upward sloping, such exceptions are virtually never encountered in practice. To be sure, the negative slope of the demand curve accords in every way with our intuitions about how people respond to rising prices.

As we'll see in more detail in Chapter 4, there are normally two independent reasons for the quantity demanded to fall when price rises. One is that many people switch to a close substitute. Thus, when lobster gets more expensive, some consumers may switch to crab, others to meat or poultry. A second reason is that people are not *able* to buy as much as before. Incomes, after all, go only so far. When price goes up, it is not possible to buy as much as before unless we purchase less of something else.

The demand curve for a good is a summary of the various cost-benefit calculations that buyers make with respect to the good, as we'll see in greater detail in the next chapter. The question each person faces is, "Should I buy the product?" (and usually, "If so, how much of it?"). The cost side of the calculation is simply the price of the product (and implicitly, the other goods or services that could be bought with the same money). The benefit side is the satisfaction provided by the product. The negative slope of the demand schedule tells us that the cost-benefit criterion will be met for fewer and fewer potential buyers as the price of the product rises.

On the seller's side of the market, the corresponding analytical tool is the supply schedule. A hypothetical schedule for our lobster market is shown as line *SS* in Figure 2.2. Again, the linear form of this particular schedule is not a characteristic feature of supply schedules generally. What these schedules do tend to have in common is their upward slope: The quantity supplied rises as the price of a product rises. This property can be called the **law of supply.** For a supplier to be willing to sell a product, its price must cover the marginal cost of producing or acquiring it. As we will see in detail in Chapter 9, the cost of producing additional units often tends to rise as more units are produced, especially in the short run. When this is the case, increased production is profitable only at higher prices.

law of supply the empirical observation that when the price of a product rises, firms offer more of it for sale.

FIGURE 2.2

A Supply Schedule for Lobsters in Hyannis, Mass., July 20, 2019

The upward slope of the supply schedule reflects the fact that costs tend to rise when producers expand production in the short run.

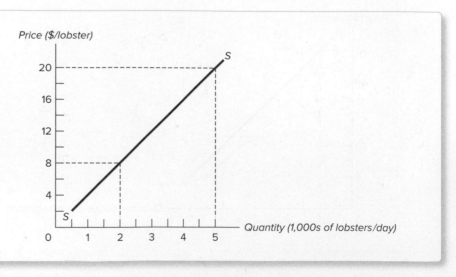

In our lobster market, the reasons for this are clear. Suppliers harvest the lobsters closest to shore first, and then work their way farther offshore as they try to enlarge their catch. The more lobsters they try to harvest, the farther they have to go, and hence the more it costs.

Another factor contributing to the upward slope of the supply curve is substitution on the part of fishermen. As the price of lobsters increases, more producers switch to lobsters, rather than continue to fish for, say, cod or haddock.

Like demand curves, supply curves can be interpreted either horizontally or vertically. Under the horizontal interpretation, we begin with a price, then go over to the supply curve to read the quantity that sellers wish to sell at that price on the horizontal axis. For instance, at a price of $8 per lobster, sellers in Figure 2.2 wish to sell 2,000 lobsters per day.

Under the vertical interpretation, we begin with a quantity, then go up to the supply curve to read the corresponding marginal cost on the vertical axis. For example, if sellers in Figure 2.2 are currently supplying 5,000 lobsters per day, the opportunity cost of the last lobster supplied by the marginal seller would be $20. In other words, the supply curve tells us that the marginal cost of delivering the 5,000th lobster is $20. If someone could deliver a 5,001st lobster for less than $20, she would have had an incentive to do so, in which case the quantity of lobster supplied at a price of $20 would not have been 5,000 per day to begin with. By similar reasoning, when the quantity of lobster supplied is 2,000 per day, the marginal cost of delivering another lobster must be $8.

An alternative way of describing the supply schedule is to call it the set of price-quantity pairs for which suppliers are satisfied. The term "satisfied" has a technical meaning here, which is that any point on the supply schedule represents the quantity that suppliers want to sell, *given the price they face*. They would obviously be happy to get even higher prices for their offerings. But for any given price, suppliers would consider themselves worse off if forced to sell either more or less than the corresponding quantity on the supply schedule. If, for example, the price of lobsters in Figure 2.2 were $8, suppliers would not be satisfied selling either more or fewer than 2,000 lobsters a day.

The demand schedule may be given a parallel description. It is the set of price-quantity pairs for which buyers are satisfied in precisely the same sense. At any given price, they would consider themselves worse off if forced to purchase either more or less than the corresponding quantity on the demand schedule.

▶ Visit your instructor's Connect© course and access your eBook to view this video.

Why are rotisserie chickens less expensive than fresh chickens?

EQUILIBRIUM QUANTITY AND PRICE

With both the supply and demand schedules in hand, we can describe the *equilibrium quantity and price* of lobsters. It is the price-quantity pair at which both buyers and sellers are satisfied. Put another way, it is the price-quantity pair at which the supply and demand schedules intersect. Figure 2.3 depicts the equilibrium in our lobster market, at which a total of 3,000 lobsters is traded at a price of $12 each.

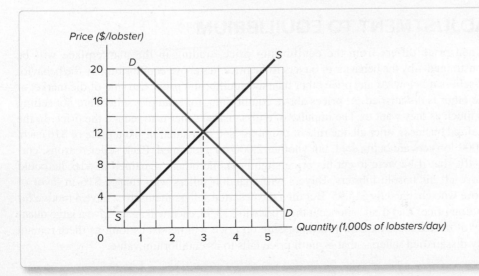

FIGURE 2.3

Equilibrium in the Lobster Market

The intersection of the supply and demand curves represents the price-quantity pair at which all participants in the market are "satisfied": Buyers are buying the amount they want to buy at that price, and sellers are selling the amount they want to sell.

FIGURE 2.4

Excess Supply and Excess Demand

When price exceeds the equilibrium level, there is excess supply, or surplus. When price is below the equilibrium level, there is excess demand, or shortage.

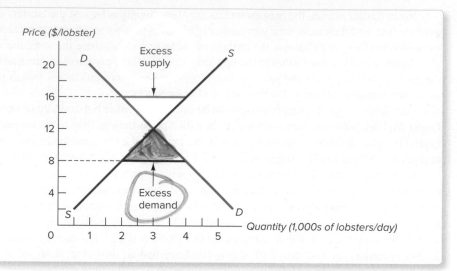

excess supply the amount by which quantity supplied exceeds quantity demanded.

excess demand the amount by which quantity demanded exceeds quantity supplied.

If we were at any price-quantity pair other than the one in Figure 2.3, either buyers or sellers, or both, would be dissatisfied in the sense described above. If the price happened for some reason to lie above the $12 equilibrium level, sellers would tend to be the ones who are frustrated. At a price of $16, for example, buyers would purchase only 2,000 lobsters, whereas sellers would offer 4,000. (See Figure 2.4.) Buyers would be satisfied at a price of $16, but sellers would not. A situation in which price exceeds its equilibrium value is called one of **excess supply,** or *surplus*. At $16, there is an excess supply of 2,000 lobsters.

If, by contrast, the price happened to lie below the equilibrium price of $12, then buyers would be the ones dissatisfied. At a price of $8, for example, they would want to purchase 4,000 lobsters, whereas suppliers would be willing to sell only 2,000. A situation in which price lies below its equilibrium value is referred to as one of **excess demand,** or *shortage*. At a price of $8 in this lobster market, there is an excess demand of 2,000 lobsters. At the market equilibrium price of $12, both excess demand and excess supply are exactly zero.

SELF-TEST 2.1

At a price of $4 in this hypothetical lobster market, how much excess demand for lobsters will there be? How much excess supply will there be at a price of $20?

ADJUSTMENT TO EQUILIBRIUM

When price differs from the equilibrium price, trading in the marketplace will be constrained—by the behavior of buyers if the price lies above equilibrium, by the behavior of sellers if below. At any price other than the equilibrium price, one side of the market or the other is dissatisfied. At prices above equilibrium, for example, sellers are not selling as much as they want to. The impulse of a dissatisfied seller is to reduce the price. In the seafood business, after all, the rule of thumb is "sell it or smell it." At a price of $16 each, 2,000 lobsters are being sold, but another 2,000 go unclaimed. Each seller reasons, correctly, that if he were to cut his price slightly, while others remained at $16, he could move all his unsold lobsters. Buyers will abandon sellers who charge $16 in favor of those who charge only $15.95. But then the deserted sellers themselves have a motive for cutting price. And if all sellers cut their price to $15.95, each will again have a large quantity of unsold lobsters. Downward pressure on price will persist as long as there remain any dissatisfied sellers—that is, until price falls to its equilibrium value.

When price is below $12, buyers are dissatisfied. Under these conditions, sellers will realize that they can increase their prices and still sell as much as they wish to. This upward pressure on price will persist until price reaches its equilibrium value. Put another way, consumers will start bidding against each other in the hope of seeing their demands satisfied.

An extraordinary feature of this equilibrating process is that no one consciously plans or directs it. The actual steps that consumers and producers must take to move toward equilibrium are often indescribably complex. Suppliers looking to expand their operations, for example, must choose from a bewilderingly large menu of equipment options. Buyers, for their part, face literally millions of choices about how to spend their money. And yet the adjustment toward equilibrium results more or less automatically from the natural reactions of self-interested individuals facing either surpluses or shortages.

SOME WELFARE PROPERTIES OF EQUILIBRIUM

Given the attributes—tastes, abilities, knowledge, incomes, and so on—of buyers and sellers, the equilibrium outcome has some attractive properties. Specifically, we can say that no reallocation can improve some people's position without harming the position of at least some others. *If price and quantity take anything other than their equilibrium values, however, it will always be possible to reallocate so as to make at least some people better off without harming others.*

Sticking with the lobster example, suppose price is $8, with suppliers therefore offering only 2,000 lobsters. As indicated in Figure 2.5, the vertical interpretation of the demand curve tells us that when only 2,000 lobsters are available, buyers are willing to pay $16. Similarly, the vertical interpretation of the supply curve tells us that when 2,000 lobsters a day are supplied, the marginal cost of delivering another lobster is only $8. When the value to the buyer of the last lobster caught ($16) is higher than the cost of harvesting it ($8), there's room to cut a deal.

Suppose, for example, a dissatisfied buyer were to offer a supplier $10 for a lobster. The supplier would gladly sell an additional lobster at this price (since, at 2,000 lobsters, an additional lobster costs only $8 to harvest). This transaction would improve the buyer's position by $6 (the difference between the $16 value he attaches to the lobster and the $10 he paid for it). It would also improve the seller's position by $2 (the difference between the $10 she got and the $8 cost of harvesting the extra lobster). No one suffers any harm from this transaction (except the extra lobster!), and the participants reap $8 of additional benefit from it ($6 for the buyer, $2 for the seller). A similar argument can be

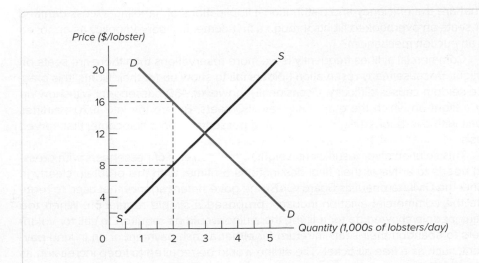

FIGURE 2.5

An Opportunity for Improvement in the Lobster Market

When the quantity traded in the market is below (or above) the equilibrium quantity, it is always possible to reallocate resources in such a way that some people are made better off without harming others. Here, a dissatisfied buyer can pay a seller $10 for an additional lobster, thus making both parties better off.

made concerning any price below the equilibrium value. For any such price, it is always possible to make some people better off without hurting others.

What if the price had been higher than the equilibrium price to begin with? Suppose price is $16 with trading therefore limited by buyers' demands for 2,000 lobsters. (Again, see Figure 2.5.) Now a dissatisfied seller can propose a transaction that will make both the seller and some buyers better off. Suppose, for example, a seller offers an additional lobster for sale for $14. Since buyers value additional lobsters at $16, whoever buys it will be better off by $2. And since lobsters cost only $8 to harvest, the seller will be better off by $6. Again, no one is injured by this transaction, and again the two parties gain a total of $8.

Thus, no matter whether price starts out above or below its equilibrium value, a mutually beneficial transaction will always be possible. We'll examine the welfare properties of the market system in much greater detail in later chapters. But for now, suffice it to say that the equilibrium price and quantity constitute the best outcome attainable, given the initial attributes and endowments of buyers and sellers.

FREE MARKETS AND THE POOR

The fact that market equilibrium is efficient in the sense just described does not mean that it is necessarily desirable in any absolute sense. All markets may be in perfect equilibrium, for example, and yet many people may lack sufficient incomes to purchase even the bare necessities of life. Saying market equilibrium is efficient does not challenge the notion that being poor is difficult, often even painful. Efficiency says merely that, *given the low incomes of the poor,* free exchange enables them to do the best they can. One can hold this view and still believe it desirable to provide public assistance to poor people.

Concern for the well-being of the poor motivates most societies to try to intervene, as in the gasoline price control example mentioned earlier. The difficulty, as in that example, is that these interventions often produce unintended harmful consequences. Indeed, many clearly do more harm than good. As we will see, a more thorough understanding of the workings of the market mechanism would prevent many of the most costly consequences of our current approach.

EXAMPLE 2.1   **Alternate Allocation Mechanisms**

Denied boarding compensation.

What are the efficiency and distributional implications of handling excess demand for seats on overbooked flights through a first-come, first-served policy as opposed to an auction mechanism?

Commercial airlines frequently issue more reservations than there are seats on a flight. Because many reservation holders fail to show up for their flights, this practice seldom causes difficulty. Occasionally, however, 160 passengers will show up for a flight on which there are only, say, 150 seats. Before the late 1970s, airlines dealt with overbooked flights by boarding passengers on a first-come, first-served basis.

This solution gives insufficient weight to the interests of passengers with pressing needs to arrive at their final destinations on time. With this problem clearly in mind, the Civil Aeronautics Board (CAB), the government agency that used to regulate the commercial aviation industry, proposed a simple regulation. When too many people showed up for a flight, the airline would be required to call for volunteers to abandon their seats in return for either a cash payment or an in-kind payment, such as a free air ticket. The airline would be required to keep increasing its offer until it got enough volunteers.

The advantage of the CAB proposal was that it would allow passengers to decide for themselves how pressing their schedules were. People with important meetings could simply refuse to volunteer. Others could agree to wait a few hours, often in return for several hundred dollars or a free trip to Hawaii. By comparison with the first-come, first-served solution, the CAB proposal promised a better outcome for all passengers.

Or at any rate, so it seemed. A consumer-action group immediately objected to the CAB's proposal on the grounds that it was unfair to low-income passengers. The group's complaint was that the auction method of soliciting volunteers would almost always result in the poorest ticket holders being the ones to wait for the next flight.

Now, a poor person will surely be more likely to find a cash payment a compelling reason to volunteer. But by volunteering, a person says that the cash payment is *worth* the wait. The world would indeed be a better place if poor people had higher incomes and were not tempted by their poverty to give up their seats on airplanes. But the consumer group was not proposing to give the poor higher incomes. Rather, it wanted the industry to stick with a system that bumped passengers from overbooked flights irrespective of the value they attached to remaining on board.

Why is an auction a better way to allocate seats on an over-booked flight than first-come, first-served?

It is hard to see how poor people's interests would be served by preventing them from earning extra cash by volunteering to wait for the next flight. And in the end, the CAB adopted its denied-boarding-compensation proposal, to the benefit of air travelers at all income levels.

Many critics of the market system complain that it is unfair to ration goods and services by asking how much people are willing to pay for them. This criterion, they point out, gives short shrift to the interests of the poor. But as Example 2.1 clearly illustrates, serious contradictions plague alternative schemes of allocation. Consider again our hypothetical lobster market. Suppose we are concerned that the equilibrium price of $12 will exclude many deserving poor persons from experiencing the pleasure of a lobster dinner. And suppose that, with this in mind, we adopt a system that periodically gives free lobsters to the poor. Wouldn't such a system represent a clear improvement in the eyes of any person who feels compassion for the poor?

The answer, as in Example 2.1, is that for the same cost we can do even better. When a poor person, or indeed even a rich person, does not buy lobster because the price is too high, she is saying, in effect, that she would prefer to spend her money on other things. If we gave her a lobster, what would she want to do with it? In an ideal world, she would immediately sell it to someone willing to pay the $12 equilibrium price for it. We know there will be such persons because some of the lobsters that would have been bought for $12 were instead given to the poor. The poor person's sale of the lobster to one of these people will bring about a clear improvement for both parties—for the buyer, or else he would not have bought it, and for the seller because the lobster is worth less than $12 to her.

The practical difficulty, as we'll see in detail in later chapters, is that it would take time and effort for our hypothetical poor person to find a buyer for the lobster. In the end, she would probably eat it herself. True enough, she might enjoy her lobster dinner. But by her own reckoning, she would have enjoyed the $12 even more.

The problem is the same with gasoline price controls. The controls were implemented in the sincere belief they were needed to protect the poor from sharply higher gasoline prices. Their effect, however, was to induce a host of behaviors that helped neither rich nor poor.

Despite statements to the contrary by critics of the market system, people are highly responsive to energy prices when they make decisions about how to spend their incomes. If gasoline costs $5.00/gal, for example, many people will form car pools or purchase fuel-efficient cars, even though they would do neither if the price were only $2.50/gal. Whether a long trip is considered worth taking also clearly depends on the price of gasoline.

Regardless of whether fuel is in short supply, it is in everyone's interest—rich or poor—to use it for the activities people value most. But the costs of a policy that does not do this are particularly high when fuel is scarce. Selling gasoline for less than the equilibrium price is just such a policy. It encourages people to use gasoline in wasteful ways.

Rent Controls

For all their differences, displaced manufacturing workers and recent U.S. college graduates have one issue in common: they face the daunting cost of housing in the great job-cluster cities. The costs of relocating to a city like New York or Seattle—or of maintaining oneself there on a low income—make government-imposed solutions such as rent control attractive to many.

Nonetheless, it has been said that the surest way to destroy a city, short of dropping a nuclear bomb on it, is to pass a rent control law. Such laws, like so many others, are motivated by an honest concern for the well-being of low-income citizens as well as wish to keep living in an affordable community. But their economic consequences are no less damaging for being unintended.

Basic supply and demand analysis is again all we need to see clearly the nature of the difficulties. Figure 2.6 depicts the supply and demand schedules for a hypothetical urban apartment market. The equilibrium rent in this market would be $600/month, and at this level there would be 60,000 apartments rented. The city council, however, has passed a law that holds rents at $R_c = \$400$/month, or $200 below the market-clearing value. R_c in this example constitutes a **price ceiling** for rents, a level beyond which rents are not permitted to rise. At $400/month, buyers would like to rent 80,000 apartments, but suppliers are willing to offer only 40,000. There is an excess demand of 40,000 units. And if the rent control level remains fixed at $400/month, excess demand will grow over time as population grows and inflation reduces the value of money.

In an unregulated market, the immediate response would be for rents to rise sharply. But here the law prevents them from rising above R_c. Yet there are other ways the pressures of excess demand can make themselves felt. One is for owners to spend less on maintaining their rental units. If there are two renters knocking at the door of each vacant apartment, clogged drains, peeling paint, broken thermostats, and the like are not apt to receive prompt attention.

Nor are these the most serious difficulties. With an offering of only 40,000 apartments per month, we see in Figure 2.6 that renters would be willing to pay as much as $800/month for an apartment (again, the vertical interpretation of the demand curve). This pressure almost always finds ways, legal or illegal, of expressing itself. In New York City, for example, it is not uncommon to see "finder's fees" or "key deposits" as high as several thousand dollars. Owners who cannot charge a market-clearing rent for an apartment

price ceiling the level above which the price of a good is not permitted by law to rise.

Why are rent-controlled apartments less well maintained than unregulated units?

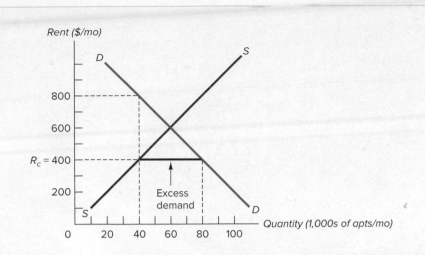

FIGURE 2.6

Rent Controls

With the rent control level set at $400 a month, there is an excess demand of 40,000 apartments a month.

also have the option of converting it to a condominium or co-op, which enables them to sell their asset for a price much closer to its true economic value.

Even when rent-controlled apartment owners do not hike their prices in these various ways, serious misallocations result. A widow steadfastly remains in her seven-room apartment even after her children have left home because it is cheaper than alternative dwellings not covered by rent control. It would be better for all concerned if she relinquished that space to a larger family. But under rent controls, she has no economic incentive to do so.

EXAMPLE 2.2   Excess Demand

Suppose the rent control is lowered (strengthened) to $200/month. What is the excess demand, and how does it compare with the excess demand when rents were limited (more loosely) to $400/month?

At $200/month, buyers would like to rent 100,000 apartments, but suppliers are willing to offer only 20,000. Thus there is an excess demand of 80,000 units. The excess demand is greater than the excess demand of 40,000 units at the $400/month rent control.

SELF-TEST 2.2

In the market for apartments described in Figure 2.6, what would happen if the rent control level were set at $625/mo?

In response to the kinds of problems described above, some rent-control programs have been modified to allow landlords to raise rents when a tenant moves out of an apartment. Such changes reduce, but do not eliminate, misallocations. And they may even create new problems. For example, a landlord who knows that a tenant's departure would permit a rent increase may take any available lawful steps to make the tenant's life unpleasant if he remains.

Of course, the preceding discussion of rent controls does not nearly exhaust the subject of high urban housing costs. For a complete treatment, we would also have to consider, at minimum, how other constraints on supply, such as zoning and density restrictions, serve to drive up home prices and rents. As soon as we did this, we would need to acknowledge that a significant part of household wealth is represented by home

The main problem confronting the poor is that they have too little money. Transferring additional money to the poor does more to help them than attempting to control the prices of things they buy.

Zach Gibson/Getty Images

Legislators can alter many of the forces that determine market outcomes. But they cannot simply repeal the laws of supply and demand.

values. Once you have the goal of protecting home values lined up against the goal of affordable housing, you have a complex normative conflict that goes beyond a basic analysis of supply and demand.

By itself, economics can't strike the balance between the rich or poor. What economic analysis *can* do is point out the existing or likely costs of direct market manipulation or restriction and point to more efficient approaches, such as direct cash transfers or fewer restrictions on housing density. The more "efficient" the approach, the more resources there are to be split between opposing interests. In that sense, efficiency is the normative anchor of positive economics. It will often emerge as the link between the answers provided by economics analysis and the normative questions that motivate our investigations.

If we decide our goal is to help poor people, there are much more effective ways to do it than to give them cheap gasoline, rent-controlled apartments, or free lobsters. One would be to give them additional income and let them decide for themselves how to spend it. Chapter 18 examines some of the practical difficulties involved in transferring additional purchasing power into the hands of the poor. In brief, the most pressing problem is that it is hard to target cash to the genuinely needy without attracting others who could fend for themselves. But as we'll see, economic reasoning also suggests practical ways to overcome this difficulty. There are no simple or easy solutions. But given the enormous losses caused by policies that keep prices below their equilibrium levels, these issues deserve our most serious attention.

Price Supports

price floor a minimum price for a good, established by law, and supported by government's offer to buy the good at that price.

Rent controls are an example of a price ceiling that prevents the price from rising to its equilibrium level. For many agricultural products, the government's policy has been to impose not ceilings but *price supports,* or **price floors,** which keep prices above their equilibrium levels. By contrast to price ceilings, which required merely the announcement of a level beyond which prices could not rise, price supports require the government to become an active buyer in the market.

Figure 2.7, for example, depicts a price support level of P_s in the market for soybeans. Because P_s is above the equilibrium price, there is an excess supply of 200,000 tons/yr. To maintain the price at $P_s = \$400$/ton, the government must purchase 200,000 tons/yr of soybeans. Otherwise farmers would face powerful incentives to cut their prices.

FIGURE 2.7

A Price Support in the Soybean Market

For a price support to have any impact, it must be set above the market-clearing price. Its effect is to create excess supply, which the government then purchases.

An important purpose of farm price supports is to ensure prices high enough to provide adequate incomes for farm families. In practice, however, the supports have proved a costly and inefficient instrument. One problem is the disposition of the surplus bought by the government. To produce this surplus requires valuable labor, capital, fertilizer, and other inputs. Yet often it is simply left to decay in government storage bins. Another difficulty is that much of the surplus is produced by large corporate farms, whose owners have no need for support. For every dollar that price supports put into the hands of a needy family farmer, several more go into the coffers of prosperous agribusinesses. Price supports also raise the food bills of all families, and often raise prices of goods not directly supported. (See Example 2.3 later in this chapter.) If society wants to subsidize small family farms, there are more efficient and direct means than agricultural price supports.[1]

The Rationing and Allocative Functions of Prices

Prices serve two important and distinct functions. First, they ration existing supplies of goods. Scarcity is the universal feature of economic life. People want more of virtually everything than could be supplied at a price of zero. Equilibrium prices curtail these excessive claims by rationing scarce supplies to the users who place the highest value on them. This is the **rationing function of price.** It is a short-run function, in the sense that its focus is the distribution of output that already exists.

The second function of price is that of a signal to direct productive resources among the different sectors of the economy. In industries in which there is excess demand, firms are able to charge more than they need to cover their costs of production. The resulting profits act as a carrot that lures additional resources into these industries. The other side of this coin is that losses act as the stick that drives resources out of those industries in which there is excess supply. This is the so-called **allocative function of price,** the driving force behind Adam Smith's invisible hand. It is a long-run function in the sense that its focus is to induce resources to migrate from industries with excess supply to those with excess demand.

Rent controls subvert both functions of the price mechanism. The rationing function is undercut by the alternative mechanisms that distribute housing with little regard to the value people place on it. The underlying needs of renters are relegated to secondary status. Both luck and the people you happen to know are often decisive. Artificially low rents undercut the allocative function of price by sending a false signal to investors about

rationing function of price the process whereby price directs existing supplies of a product to the users who value it most highly.

allocative function of price the process whereby price acts as a signal that guides resources away from the production of goods whose prices lie below cost toward the production of goods whose prices exceed cost.

[1]For an argument for subsidizing small farms, see Willard W. Cochrane, *The Curse of American Agricultural Abundance*, Lincoln: University of Nebraska Press, 2002, pp. 91–106. Cochrane, a famed agricultural economist, developed in the 1950s the "treadmill" model of farm size expansion (reprinted as pp. 19–44 in the citation), served in the Kennedy administration, published one of the standard histories of U.S. agriculture, and was noted over his long career for opposing broad-based farm "price supports" and advocating for direct transfers to small farmers.

the need for additional housing. Under rent controls, apartment builders earn less than they could by investing their money elsewhere. The cruel irony is that the pressing need in many communities with rent controls is for more low-income housing units, not fewer—which is precisely what the market would produce on its own, assuming there were no additional restrictions, if the poor were given more money.

DETERMINANTS OF SUPPLY AND DEMAND

Supply and demand analysis is useful not only for the normative insight it offers into questions of public policy but also for a rich variety of descriptive purposes. Most important, it predicts how equilibrium prices and quantities will respond to changes in market forces. Because supply and demand curves intersect to determine equilibrium prices and quantities, anything that shifts these curves will alter equilibrium values in a predictable way. In the next several chapters, we investigate in detail the forces that determine the shape and position of market demand curves. For the moment, let's discuss a few whose roles are intuitively clear.

Determinants of Demand

Incomes

For most goods, the quantity demanded at any price rises with income. Goods that have this property are called *normal goods.* So-called *inferior goods* (such as ground beef with high fat content) are the exception. For such goods, the quantity demanded at any price falls when income rises. The idea is that consumers abandon these goods in favor of higher-quality substitutes (such as leaner grades of meat in the ground beef case) as soon as they can afford to.

Tastes

Tastes vary across people and over time. In Western societies, culture instills a taste for sitting on padded furniture, whereas in many Eastern societies, people are conditioned to favor sitting cross-legged on the floor. The demand for armchairs thus tends to be larger in the West than in the East. By the same token, the demand for skirts with hemlines above the knee tends to vary sharply from one decade to another.

Prices of Substitutes and Complements

Bacon and eggs play a complementary role in the diets of some people. For them, a sharp increase in the price of bacon leads not only to a reduction in the quantity of bacon demanded but also to a reduction in the demand for eggs. Such goods are considered *complements:* An increase in the price of one good decreases demand for the other good. In the case of close *substitutes,* such as coffee and tea, an increase in the price of one will tend to increase the demand for the other.

Expectations

Expectations about future income and price levels also affect current purchase decisions. For example, someone who expects higher future income is likely to spend more today than an otherwise identical person who expects lower future income. (After all, with higher expected future income, the need to save diminishes.) Similarly, people will often accelerate their current purchases of goods whose prices are expected to rise in the months to come.

Population

In general, the number of people who buy a product grows as the number of potential buyers grows. Thus, in cities with growing populations, the demand for housing increases from year to year, whereas it tends to fall in cities with declining populations.

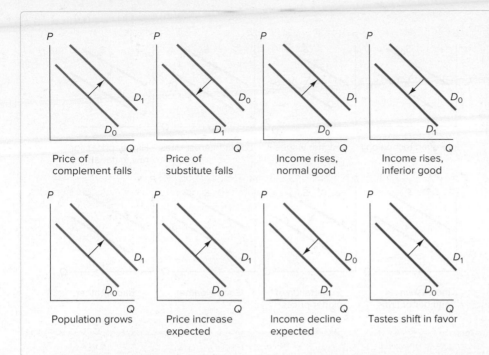

FIGURE 2.8

Factors That Shift Demand Curves

Prices of substitutes and complements, incomes, population, expectation of future price and income changes, and tastes all influence the position of the current demand curve for a product.

Figure 2.8 graphically displays some factors that shift demand curves. We will revisit these factors in more detail in Chapters 4 and 9.

Determinants of Supply

Technology

The amount suppliers are willing to offer at any price depends primarily on their costs of production. These costs, in turn, are closely linked to technology. For instance, the discovery of a more efficient lobster trap will reduce the cost of harvesting lobsters, which results in a rightward shift in the supply schedule.

Factor Prices

A supplier's costs also depend on the payment it must make to its factors of production: labor, capital, and so on. If the price of lobster boats rises, or if the wage paid to lobstermen goes up, the supply schedule for lobsters shifts to the left.

The Number of Suppliers

The more firms that can supply a good, the greater will be the quantity supplied of it at any given price. The supply schedule of personal computers has shifted sharply to the right as more and more companies have begun producing them.

Expectations

Suppliers too take expected changes in prices into account in their current production decisions. For example, if ranchers expect beef prices to rise sharply in the future because of an epidemic affecting young cattle, they are likely to withhold current supplies of mature livestock to take advantage of the higher future prices.[2]

[2]Note that supply is the quantity offered for sale at various prices, not necessarily current production (when suppliers are able to store inventory). Hence, the ranchers reduce sales of cattle in the current period, since they can sell them in a later period when prices are higher.

FIGURE 2.9

Factors That Shift Supply Schedules

Technology, input prices, the number of firms, expectations about future prices, and the weather all affect the position of the supply schedule for a given product.

Weather

For some products, particularly agricultural ones, nature has significant effects on the supply schedule. In years of drought, for example, the supply schedule for many food-stuffs shifts to the left. Figure 2.9 shows the effects of some factors that shift supply schedules. Neither of the preceding lists of supply and demand shifters is meant to be exhaustive. However, having identified weather as a supply shifter, it's worth asking how climate change might map onto the determinants we have identified so far. Climate change is not precisely "weather." The types of weather shocks that affect the supply of food have usually been thought of as random events, albeit within a certain band of expectations based on geography, climate, recent history, etc. A warming climate might increase the frequency of weather shocks, and this change, on top of short-term supply disruptions, might change expectations around what crops were "worth" planting, forcing a long-term adjustment to supply. In parallel, climate change might be experienced as a shock to technology, one that broadly reduced agricultural productivity. This might force farmers to bring marginal, or less productive, acres into production in order to maintain output—a change that would increase greenhouse gas emissions both absolutely and per unit of food produced. Compared to some of the shifters listed earlier, climate change thus brings the threat of systemic (and not just short-term) disruption.

For the sake of simplicity, we develop our theory of prices and of consumer choice mainly using discrete, one-time shifts that result in equally discrete, simple, and predictable responses. Nothing about this approach is intended to diminish the more complex threats posed climate change or other systemic shocks or to deny that such threats may require complex social and political adjustments. By focusing at first on relatively simple markets, we position ourselves to identify the role that markets play in constructive policy responses to complex problems.

Changes in Demand versus Changes in the Quantity Demanded

When economists use the expression *change in demand,* they mean a shift in the entire demand curve. Thus, when the average income level of buyers changes, the demand curve shifts—there is a change in demand. When we say *change in the quantity demanded,* we mean a movement along the demand curve. When the price of a good falls, for example, the result is an increase in the quantity demanded, not an increase in demand.

Analogous interpretations attach to the expressions *change in supply* and *change in the quantity supplied.* These terminological distinctions are important for clear communication both in classroom discussion and on exams. And if the experience of previous generations of students is any guide, it requires effort to keep them straight.

Predicting and Explaining Changes in Price and Quantity

To predict or explain changes in equilibrium prices and quantities, we must predict or account for the shifts in the relevant supply and/or demand schedules. When supply and demand curves have the conventional slopes, the following propositions about equilibrium prices and quantities will hold:

- An increase in demand will lead to an increase in both the equilibrium price and quantity.
- A decrease in demand will lead to a decrease in both the equilibrium price and quantity.
- An increase in supply will lead to a decrease in the equilibrium price and an increase in the equilibrium quantity.
- A decrease in supply will lead to an increase in the equilibrium price and a decrease in the equilibrium quantity.

There is no point in memorizing this list, since each proposition can be easily derived by shifting the relevant curve in a standard supply-demand diagram.

These simple propositions permit us to answer a variety of questions.

Economic Naturalist 2.1

Why do the prices of some goods, such as apples, go down during the months of heaviest consumption while the prices of others, such as beachfront cottages, go up?

The answer is that the seasonal consumption increase is the result of a supply increase in the case of apples, a demand increase in the case of cottages. As shown in Figure 2.10, these shifts produce the observed seasonal relationships between

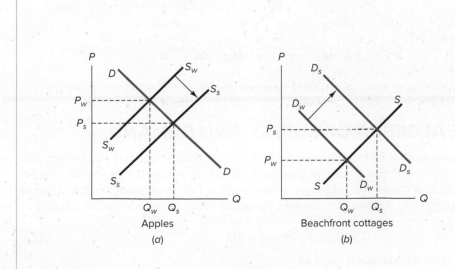

Apples

(a)

Beachfront cottages

(b)

FIGURE 2.10

Two Sources of Seasonal Variation

The quantities consumed of both apples and beachfront cottages are highest in the summer months. (a) Apple prices are at their lowest during the summer because the quantity increase is the result of increased supply. (The subscripts w and s denote winter and summer values, respectively.) (b) Cottage prices are at their highest in summer because the quantity increase is the result of an increase in demand.

equilibrium prices and quantities. (The subscripts *w* and *s* in Figure 2.10 are used to denote winter and summer values, respectively.) When demand increases (as for cottages), the increase in the equilibrium quantity occurs concurrently with an increase in the equilibrium price. When supply increases (as for apples), the increase in the equilibrium quantity occurs concurrently with a decrease in the equilibrium price.

SELF-TEST 2.3

What will happen to the equilibrium price and quantity in the fresh seafood market if each of the following events occurs: (1) a scientific report is issued saying that fish contains mercury, which is toxic to humans, and (2) the price of diesel fuel (used to operate fishing boats) falls significantly?

EXAMPLE 2.3   Increasing Opportunity Cost

If soybeans are one of the ingredients in cattle feed, how does a price support program in the soybean market affect the equilibrium price and quantity of beef?

The price support program raises the price of cattle feed, which causes a leftward shift in the supply schedule for beef. (See Figure 2.11.) This, in turn, results in an increase in the equilibrium price and a reduction in the equilibrium quantity of beef.

FIGURE 2.11

The Effect of Soybean Price Supports on the Equilibrium Price and Quantity of Beef

By raising the price of soybeans, an input used in beef production, the price supports produce a leftward shift in the supply curve of beef. The result is an increase in the equilibrium price and a reduction in the equilibrium quantity.

THE ALGEBRA OF SUPPLY AND DEMAND

The examples thus far have focused on a geometric approach to market equilibrium. This approach is fine for illustrating the basic principles of the theory. But for actually computing numerical values, it usually is more convenient to find equilibrium prices and quantities algebraically. Suppose, for example, the supply schedule for a product is given by

$$P = 2 + 3Q^s, \tag{2.1}$$

and its demand schedule is given by

$$P = 10 - Q^d, \tag{2.2}$$

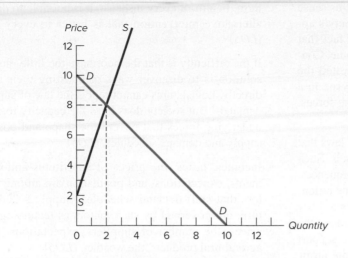

FIGURE 2.12

Graphs of Equations 2.1 and 2.2

The algebraic and geometric approaches lead to exactly the same equilibrium prices and quantities. The advantage of the algebraic approach is that exact numerical solutions can be achieved more easily. The geometric approach is useful because it gives a more intuitively clear description of the supply and demand curves.

where P is the product price and Q^s and Q^d stand for the quantity supplied and the quantity demanded, respectively. In equilibrium, we know that $Q^s = Q^d$. Denoting this common value as Q^*, we may then equate the right-hand sides of Equations 2.1 and 2.2 and solve:

$$2 + 3Q^* = 10 - Q^*, \qquad (2.3)$$

which gives $Q^* = 2$. Substituting $Q^* = 2$ back into either the supply or demand equation gives the equilibrium price, $P^* = 8$.

Needless to say, we could have graphed Equations 2.1 and 2.2 to arrive at precisely the same solution (see Figure 2.12). The advantage of the algebraic approach is that it is much less painstaking than having to produce accurate drawings of the supply and demand schedules.

SELF-TEST 2.4

Find the equilibrium price and quantity in a market whose supply and demand curves are given by $P = 4Q^s$ and $P = 12 - 2Q^d$, respectively.

SUMMARY

- The supply curve is generally an upward-sloping line that tells what quantity sellers will offer at any given price. The demand curve is a downward-sloping line that tells what quantity buyers will demand at any given price. In an unregulated market, the equilibrium price and quantity are determined by the intersection of these two curves. *(LO1, LO2)*

- If price is above its equilibrium, there will be dissatisfied sellers, or excess supply. This condition motivates sellers to cut their prices. By contrast, when prices are below equilibrium, there will be dissatisfied buyers, or excess demand. This condition motivates sellers to charge higher prices. The only stable outcome is the one in which excess demand and excess supply are exactly zero. *(LO2)*

- Given the attributes of buyers and sellers, the equilibrium price and quantity represent the best attainable outcome, in the sense that any other price-quantity pair would be worse for at least some buyers or sellers. *(LO3)*

- Supply and demand analysis is the economist's basic tool for predicting how equilibrium prices and quantities will change in response to changes in market forces. Four simple propositions guide this task: (1) an increase in demand will lead to an increase in both the equilibrium price and quantity; (2) a decrease in demand will lead to a decrease in both the equilibrium price and quantity; (3) an increase in supply will lead to a decrease in the equilibrium price and an increase in the equilibrium quantity; and (4) a decrease in supply will lead to an increase in the equilibrium price and a decrease in the equilibrium quantity. *(LO3)*

- The fact that market outcomes are efficient in this sense does not mean they necessarily command society's approval. On the contrary, we often lament the fact that many buyers enter the market with so little income. Concern for the well-being of the poor has motivated the governments of almost every society to intervene in a variety of ways to alter the outcomes of market forces. *(LO4)*

- Sometimes these interventions take the form of laws that peg prices above or below their equilibrium levels. Such laws often generate harmful, if unintended, consequences. Rent controls, for example, interfere with both the rationing and allocative functions of the price mechanism. They lead to black marketeering and a rapid deterioration of the stock of rental housing. By the same token, price support laws in agriculture tend to enrich large corporate farms while doing little to ease the plight of the small family

farm. In almost every instance, it is possible to design an alternative intervention that is better in every respect. *(LO5)*

- If the difficulty is that the poor have too little money, the solution is to discover ways of boosting their incomes directly. Legislatures cannot repeal the law of supply and demand.[3] But society does have the capacity to alter the underlying forces that govern the shape and position of supply and demand schedules. *(LO5)*

- Incomes, tastes, the prices of substitutes and complements, expectations, and population are among the factors that shift demand schedules. Supply schedules, in turn, are governed by such factors as technology, input prices, the number of suppliers, expectations, and, for agricultural products, the weather. *(LO6)*

KEY TERMS

allocative function of price	law of demand	price floor
excess demand	law of supply	rationing function of price
excess supply	price ceiling	real price of a product

REVIEW QUESTIONS

1. What is the difference between "scarcity" and "shortage"? *(LO1)*

2. What would the supply curve look like for a good that is not scarce? Assuming the good is useful, what would its demand curve look like? Explain why a positive price for a commodity implies that it is scarce. *(LO1)*

3. Give two examples of actions taken by the administration of your college or university whose effect is to prevent specific markets from reaching equilibrium. What evidence of excess supply or excess demand can you cite in these examples? *(LO5)*

4. What is the difference between "a reduction in supply" and "a reduction in the quantity supplied"? *(LO3)*

5. Identify each of the following as (1) a change in demand or (2) a change in the quantity demanded. *(LO3)*
   a. Grape consumption falls because of a consumer boycott.
   b. Grape consumption falls because of a tax on grape producers.

   c. Grape consumption rises because of a good harvest.
   d. Grape consumption rises because of a change in tastes.

6. When there is excess supply, why is any single seller able to sell all she wants to by offering only a small reduction below the current market price? *(LO2)*

7. Give an example of a market in which the allocative function of price is not very important. *(LO5)*

8. Suppose you are a government official and need to collect revenue by taxing a product. For political reasons, you want the burden of the tax to fall mostly on consumers, not firms (who have been substantial contributors to your campaign fund). What should you look for when picking a product to tax? *(LO3)*

9. Which would a rational poor person be more likely to accept and why? *(LO5)*
   a. A $50,000 Mercedes (immediate resale value = $30,000)
   b. $35,000 cash

---

[3]One often hears from critics of economics that, since "markets are a human product," human beings can refashion them at will. This textbook takes a different view. One way to explore the disagreement is to compare what economists Suresh Naidu, Dani Rodrik, and Gabriel Zucman (in the paper we cited in Chapter 1) call "market fundamentalism" with the theories and policy recommendations developed in this text.

PROBLEMS

1. Assume that tea and lemons are complements and that coffee and tea are substitutes. *(LO3)*
   a. How, if at all, will the imposition of an effective ceiling price on tea affect the price of lemons? Explain.
   b. How, if at all, will the imposition of an effective ceiling price on tea affect the price of coffee? Explain.

2. Suppose that the U.S. market for new vinyl LPs in 2018 had supply and demand curves given by $P^s = 15 + 0.65Q^s$ and $P^d = 36 - 0.65Q^d$, where P is in dollars and Q represents millions of LPs sold. *(LO7)*
   a. Use the given curves to estimate the number of LPs and the equilibrium price per LP.
   b. Estimate the total revenue from LP sales in 2018.
   c. Create a supply and demand diagram that represents the 2018 vinyl LP market.

   In 2019, revenues from sales of LPs may exceed revenues from the sale of CDs for the first time since the mid-1990s. Since 2013, revenues from LP sales have more than doubled, while dollar sales of CDs have fallen by two-thirds. Over the same period, while CD prices have held steady, LP retail prices have increased by over 15 percent. *(LO6)*
   d. Which of the determinants of supply and demand discussed in Chapter 2 could explain the weakness of CDs, the comeback of LPs, and the remarkable strength of LP prices?

3. Hardware and software for computers are complements. Discuss the effects on the equilibrium price and quantity *(LO3)*
   a. In the software market, when the price of computer hardware falls.
   b. In the hardware market, when the price of computer software rises.

4. Suppose a newly released study shows that battery-powered toys harm a child's development and recommends that parents adjust their purchasing behavior accordingly. Use diagrams to show the effect on price and quantity in each of the following markets: *(LO3)*
   a. The market for battery-powered toys.
   b. The market for D batteries.
   c. The market for yo-yos (which do not require batteries).

5. Using diagrams, show what changes in price and quantity would be expected in the following markets under the scenarios given: *(LO3)*
   a. *Crude oil:* As petroleum reserves decrease, it becomes more difficult to find and recover crude oil.
   b. *Air travel:* Worries about air safety cause travelers to shy away from air travel.

   c. *Rail travel:* Worries about air safety cause travelers to shy away from air travel.
   d. *Hotel rooms in Hawaii:* Worries about air safety cause travelers to shy away from air travel.
   e. *Milk:* A genetically engineered hormone enables large milk producers to cut production costs.

6. For each scenario in Problem 5, state whether the effect is a change in demand or just a change in quantity demanded. *(LO3)*

7. Suppose demand for seats at football games is $P = 1,900 - (1/50)Q$ and supply is fixed at $Q = 90,000$ seats. *(LO7)*
   a. Find the equilibrium price and quantity of seats for a football game (using algebra and a graph).
   b. Suppose the government prohibits tickets scalping (selling tickets above their face value), and the face value of tickets is $50 (this policy places a price ceiling at $50). How many consumers will be dissatisfied (how large is excess demand)?
   c. Suppose the next game is a major rivalry, and so demand jumps to $P = 2,100 - (1/50)Q$. How many consumers will be dissatisfied for the big game?
   d. How do the distortions of this price ceiling differ from the more typical case of upward-sloping supply?

8. The demand for apartments is $P = 1,200 - Q$ while the supply is $P = Q$ units. The government imposes rent control at $P = \$300$/month. Suppose demand grows in the market to $P = 1,400 - Q$. *(LO7)*
   a. How is excess demand affected by the growth in demand for apartments?
   b. At what price would the government have to set the rent control to keep excess demand at the same level as prior to the growth in demand?

9. Suppose demand is $P = 600 - Q$ and supply is $P = Q$ in the soybean market, where Q is tons of soybeans per year. The government sets a price support at $P = \$500$/ton and purchases any excess supply at this price. In response, as a long-run adjustment, farmers switch their crops from corn to soybeans, expanding supply to $P = (1/2)Q$. *(LO7)*
   a. How does excess supply with the larger supply compare to excess supply prior to the farmers switching crops?
   b. How much more does the government have to spend to buy up the excess supply?

10. Consider two similar cities, Nimbyville and Yimbyville, in different states. In both cities the demand for 1,000-sq ft apartments is $Q^d = 2,000 - 0.75P^s$. This is to say that from a potential market for 2,000 apartment units, the number of apartments demanded goes down 0.75 units for each dollar increase in monthly rent.

In Nimbyville, because of building height restrictions, the supply schedule for 1,000-sq ft apartments is $Q^{sn} = 100 + 2P^{sn}$. In Yimbyville, where there are fewer restrictions, the supply curve begins from a higher base: $Q^{sy} = 400 + 2P^{sy}$. *(LO3)*

a. What are the equilibrium rents paid and 1,000-sq ft apartment units supplied, to the nearest whole dollar or unit, in Nimbyville and Yimbyville?

b. If we changed our assumptions to say that Nimbyville and Yimbyville were adjacent cities, such that one could easily live in one and work in the other, what do you think the effect will be on equilibrium apartment prices in each city?

c. The given supply and demand equations were expressed quantity in terms of price ($Q = a + bP$) instead of price in terms of quantity. Does this make any difference in terms of the equilibrium rents or number of units rented?

11. How would the equilibrium price and quantity change in the market depicted below if the marginal cost of every producer were to increase by $2/lb? (*Hint:* Recall the vertical interpretation of the supply curve discussed in Chapter 1.) *(LO3)*

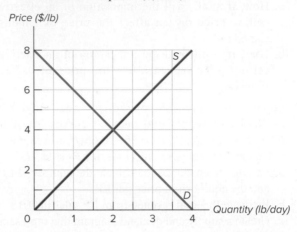

ANSWERS TO SELF-TESTS

2.1 At a price of $4/lobster, the quantity demanded is 5,000 lobsters/day and the quantity supplied is 1,000 lobsters/day, making excess demand equal to 4,000 lobsters/day. At a price of $20/lobster, excess supply is 4,000 lobsters/day. *(LO2)*

2.2 A rent control level set above the equilibrium price has no effect. The rent will settle at its equilibrium value of $600/mo. *(LO2)*

2.3 The fall in the price of diesel fuel shifts the supply curve to the right. The report on mercury shifts the demand curve to the left. As shown in the following diagrams, the equilibrium price will go down (both panels) but the equilibrium quantity may go either up (panel *b*) or down (panel *a*). *(LO3)*

(a)

(b)

2.4 $4Q^* = 12 - 2Q^*$, which yields $Q^* = 2$ and $P^* = 4Q^* = 8$. *(LO7)*

How do Taxes Affect Equilibrium Prices and Quantities?

Supply and demand analysis is also a useful tool for analyzing the effects of various taxes. In this appendix we consider a constant tax per unit of output. How will the equilibrium price and quantity of a product be affected if a tax of $T = 10$ is levied on each unit sold by the producer? There are two equivalent ways to approach this question. The first is to suppose that the tax is levied on the seller. In Figure 2A.1, the line SS denotes the original supply schedule. At a price of $P_0 = 25$, sellers were willing to supply Q_0 units of output. When a tax $T = 10$ is levied on sellers, the market price would have to be $P_0 + 10 = 35$ for them to get the same net payment that they used to receive when the price was $P_0 = 25$. At a price of 35, then, suppliers will offer the same amount of output they used to offer at a price of 25. The resulting after-tax supply schedule is the original supply schedule shifted upward by $T = 10$.

In Figure 2A.2, DD represents the demand curve facing the sellers who have been taxed $T = 10$ per unit of output. The effect of the tax is to cause the equilibrium quantity to fall from Q^* to Q_1^*. The price paid by the buyer rises from P^* to P_1^*; and the price, net of the tax, received by the seller falls to $P_1^* = 10$.

Note in Figure 2A.2 that even though the seller pays a tax of T on each product purchased, the total amount the seller receives per unit lies less than T below the old equilibrium price. Note also that even though the tax is collected from the seller, its effect is to increase the price paid by buyers. The burden of the tax is thus divided between the buyer and the seller.

Price

$35 = P_0 + T$

$T = 10$ S

$25 = P_0$

S'

S

S'

Quantity

Q_0

FIGURE 2A.1

A Tax of $T = 10$ Levied on the Seller Shifts the Supply Schedule Upward by T Units

The original supply schedule tells us what price suppliers must charge in order to cover their costs at any given level of output. From the seller's perspective, a tax of $T = 10$ units is the same as a unit-cost increase of 10 units. The new supply curve thus lies 10 units above the old one.

FIGURE 2A.2

Equilibrium Prices and Quantities When a Tax of $T = 10$ Is Levied on the Seller

The tax causes a reduction in equilibrium quantity from Q^* to Q^*_1. The new price paid by the buyer rises from P^* to P^*_1. The new price received by the seller falls from P^* to $P^*_1 - 10$.

Algebraically, the seller's share of the tax, denoted t_s, is the reduction in the price the seller receives, divided by the tax:

$$t_s = \frac{P^* - (P^*_1 - T)}{T}. \tag{2A.1}$$

Similarly, the buyer's share of the tax, t_b, is the increase in price (including tax) divided by the tax:

$$t_b = \frac{P^*_1 - P^*}{T}. \tag{2A.2}$$

SELF-TEST 2A.1

Verify that $t_s + t_b = 1$.

In general, t_b and t_s depend on the shapes of the supply and demand schedules. If, for example, supply is highly unresponsive to changes in price, t_b will be close to zero, t_s close to 1. Conversely, if demand is highly unresponsive to price, t_b will be close to 1, t_s close to zero. These claims amount to a statement that a tax tends to fall most heavily on the side of the market that can least escape it. If buyers have no substitute products to which they are prepared to turn, the lion's share of the tax will be passed on to them by suppliers. But if suppliers have no alternative other than to go on supplying a product, most of the burden of a tax will fall on them. As long as the supply curve is positively sloped and the demand curve is negatively sloped, however, both t_s and t_b will be positive.

The second way of analyzing the effect of a tax of $T = 10$ per unit of output is to imagine that the tax is collected directly from the buyer. How would that affect the demand curve for the product? In Figure 2A.3, DD is the demand curve before the imposition of the tax. At a price of P_1, buyers would demand a quantity of Q_1. After imposition of the tax, the total amount that buyers have to pay if the product price is P_1 will be $P_1 + 10$. Accordingly, the quantity they demand falls from Q_1 to Q_2. In like fashion, we can reckon the quantity demanded at any other price after imposition of the tax. $D'D'$ is the resulting after-tax demand curve in Figure 2A.3. It is the original demand curve translated downward by 10 units.

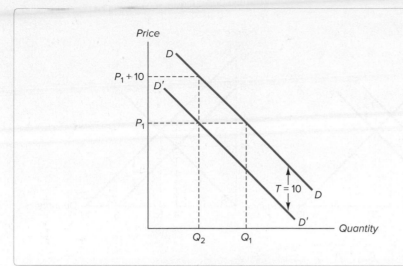

FIGURE 2A.3

The Effect of a Tax of $T = 10$ Levied on the Buyer

Before the tax, buyers would buy Q_1 units at a price of P_1. After the tax, a price of P_1 becomes $P_1 + 10$, which means buyers will buy only Q_2. The effect of the tax is to shift the demand curve downward by 10 units.

If SS in Figure 2A.4 denotes the supply schedule for this market, we can easily trace out the effects of the tax on the equilibrium price and quantity. The equilibrium quantity falls from Q^* to Q_2^*, and the equilibrium pretax price falls from P^* to P_2^*. The total price paid by the buyer after imposition of the tax rises to $P_2^* + 10$.

Is the effect of a tax on the seller any different from the effect of a tax on the buyer? Not at all. To illustrate, suppose the supply and demand curves for a market are given by $P = Q^s$ and $P = 10 - Q^d$, respectively, and consider first the effect of a tax of 2 per unit of output imposed on the seller. Figure 2A.5a shows the original supply and demand curves and the new after-tax supply curve, $S'S'$. The original equilibrium price and quantity are both equal to 5. The new equilibrium price to the buyer (inclusive of tax) and quantity are 6 and 4, respectively. The price received by sellers, net of the tax, is 4.

Now, consider a tax of 2 per unit of output imposed on the buyers. Figure 2A.5b shows the original supply and demand curves and the new after-tax demand curve, $D'D'$. Note that the effects on price and quantity are exactly the same as in the case of the tax levied on sellers shown in panel a.

FIGURE 2A.4

Equilibrium Prices and Quantities after Imposition of a Tax of $T = 10$ Paid by the Buyer

The tax causes a reduction in equilibrium quantity from Q^* to Q_2^*. The new price paid by the buyer rises from P^* to $P_2^* + 10$. The new price received by the seller falls from P^* to P_2^*.

FIGURE 2A.5

A Tax on the Buyer Leads to the Same Outcome as a Tax on the Seller

The price received by sellers (net of the tax), the price paid by buyers (including tax), and the equilibrium quantity will all be the same when the tax is collected from sellers (panel *a*) as when it is collected from buyers (panel *b*).

(a)   (b)

SELF-TEST 2A.2

Consider a market whose supply and demand curves are given by $P = 4Q^s$ and $P = 12 - 2Q^d$, respectively. How will the equilibrium price and quantity in this market be affected if a tax of 6 per unit of output is imposed on sellers? If the same tax is imposed on buyers?

When tax revenues must be raised, many political leaders find it expedient to propose a sales tax on corporations because "they can best afford to pay it." But careful analysis of the effects of a sales tax shows that its burden will be the same whether it is imposed on buyers or sellers. The *legal incidence of the tax* (whether it is imposed on buyers or on sellers) has no effect on the *economic incidence* of the tax (the respective shares of the tax burden borne by buyers and sellers). Economically speaking, the entity from which the tax is actually collected is thus a matter of complete indifference.

A word of caution: When we say that the economic burden of the tax does not depend on the party from whom the tax is directly collected, this does not mean that buyers and sellers always share the burden of taxes equally. Their respective shares may, as noted, be highly unequal. The independence of legal incidence and economic incidence simply means that the burden will be shared in the same way no matter where the tax is placed.

SELF-TEST 2A.3

True or false? The steeper the demand curve for a good relative to the supply curve for that good, the greater the proportion of a tax on that good that will fall on buyers. Explain.

PROBLEMS   Mc Graw Hill connect

1. The government, fearful that a titanium shortage could jeopardize national security, imposes a tax of $2/oz on the retail price of this rare metal. It collects the tax from titanium sellers. The original supply and demand schedules for titanium are as shown in the diagram. Show, in the same diagram, how the short-run equilibrium price and quantity of titanium will be affected by the tax. Label all important points clearly.

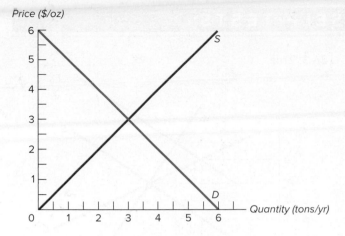

Price ($/oz)

Quantity (tons/yr)

2. In the market for titanium described in Problem 1 (with no tax), suppose that a price floor of $4/oz results in sales of only 2 tons/yr (with no tax). Describe a transaction that will make some buyers and sellers better off without harming others.

3. Suppose the titanium market in Problem 1, with a tax of $2/oz, experiences growth in the demand for titanium because of newfound medical uses. The new demand curve is $P = 8 - Q$. Find the change in government tax revenue due to the heightened demand for titanium.

4. Suppose instead the titanium market in Problem 2, with no tax but a price floor at $4/oz, suffers a reduction in supply because of dwindling titanium reserves. The new supply curve is $P = 2 + Q$. How does excess supply change due to the reduction in supply? Is the price floor still binding (does it cause price to rise from its equilibrium level)?

5. Recall from Chapter 2, Problem 2, the supply and demand curves for new vinyl LPs were given by $P^s = 15 + 0.65Q^s$ and $P^d = 36 - 0.65Q^d$, where P is in dollars and Q represents millions of LPs sold. Suppose that a nationwide tax of $3 is levied on each LP sold, collected from the seller.
   a. What quantity of LPs will be sold in equilibrium?
   b. What price will buyers pay?
   c. Graph the results, showing the old and new equilibrium.
   d. How much will buyers now spend in total?
   e. How much tax will the government collect?

6. For the tax described in Problem 5,
   a. What fraction of the tax does the seller bear?
   b. What fraction of the tax does the buyer bear?
   c. What about the supply and demand curves explains the division of the tax burden?
   d. Does the calculated effect of the tax seem large or small to you? If, in real life, a similar tax turned out to have a larger or smaller effect on sales, what does this suggest about what might have been "wrong" about the supply and demand curves?

7. President Reagan negotiated a "voluntary" import quota on Japanese cars sold in the United States in the early 1980s. Some of his advisers had recommended that he impose a higher import tax (tariff) instead. Assuming the tariff was in the form of a constant tax T per Japanese car sold in the United States and that T was chosen to produce the same quantity reduction as the quota, how will the prices paid for Japanese cars by U.S. consumers compare under the two policies?

8. Many studies on rats and mice have established that charred meat grilled over hot coals causes cancer. Since the government cannot easily regulate home cooking methods, an alternative method has been proposed to discourage the consumption of barbecued meat. The proposal is to place a 100 percent tax at the retail level on charcoal briquets. Suppose the daily demand for charcoal was $P = 120 - 2Q$ and the supply was $P = 30 + Q$, where P is in dollars per bag and Q is the number of 20-lb bags of charcoal sold weekly.
   a. What is the before- and after-tax price of charcoal?
   b. What is the before- and after-tax quantity of charcoal?
   c. How is the tax divided among sellers and buyers?

9. Supply is $P = 4Q$, while demand is $P = 20$, where P is price in dollars per unit and Q is units of output per week.
   a. Find the equilibrium price and quantity (using both algebra and a graph).
   b. If sellers must pay a tax of $T = $4/unit, what happens to the quantity exchanged, the price buyers pay, and the price sellers receive (net of the tax)?
   c. How is the burden of the tax distributed across buyers and sellers and why?

10. Repeat Problem 9, but instead suppose the buyer pays the tax, demand is $P = 28 - Q$, and supply is $P = 20$.

ANSWERS TO APPENDIX SELF-TESTS

2A.1 $t_s + t_b = [(P^* - [P_1^* + T]) + (P_1^* - P^*)]/T = T/T = 1.$

2A.2 The original price and quantity are given by $P^* = 8$ and $Q^* = 2$, respectively. The supply curve with the tax is given by $P = 6 + 4Q^s$. Letting P' and Q' denote the new equilibrium values of price and quantity, we now have $6 + 4Q' = 12 - 2Q'$, which yields $Q' = 1$, $P' = 10$, where P' is the price paid by buyers. $P' - 6 = 4$ is the price received by sellers. Alternatively, the demand curve with a tax of 6 levied on buyers is given by $P = 6 - 2Q^d$, and we have $4Q' = 6' - 2Q'$, which again yields $Q' = 1$. $P'' = 4$, where P'' is the price received by sellers. $P'' + T = P'' + 6 = 10$ is the price paid by buyers.

2A.3 True.

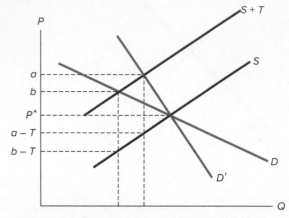

Buyer's share for tax with $D' = (a - P^*)/T$

Buyer's share for tax with $D = (b - P^*)/T$

Rational Consumer Choice

LEARNING OBJECTIVES

After reading this chapter, you should be able to:

LO1 Describe the consumer's budget constraint, the set of all combinations of goods that can be purchased with given income and prices.

LO2 Show how the budget constraint changes when income and prices change.

LO3 Describe the consumer's preference using an indifference map.

LO4 Show how the consumer's budget constraint and indifference map interact to determine the optimal combination of goods to purchase.

You have just cashed your monthly allowance check and are headed to a nearby Starbucks to buy a 4-shot venti soy hazelnut vanilla cinnamon white mocha with caramel, on sale this week for $10. In scenario 1, you lose a $10 bill on your way there. In scenario 2, you buy the drink as planned and then trip and fall as you leave, spilling it on the sidewalk. Try to imagine your frame of mind in each scenario.

a. Would you proceed to buy the drink in scenario 1?

b. Would you re-order the same drink in scenario 2?

Similar questions[1] were recently put to a large class of undergraduates who had never taken an economics course. In response to the first question, 54 percent answered yes, saying they would buy the drink after losing the $10 bill. But only 32 percent answered yes to the second question—68 percent said they would *not* re-order the drink after having spilled the first one. There is, of course, no "correct" answer to either question. The events described will have more of an impact, for example, on a poor consumer than on a rich one. Yet a moment's reflection reveals that your behavior in one scenario logically should be exactly the same as in the other. After all, in both scenarios, the only economically relevant change is that you now have $10 less to spend than before. This might well mean that you will want to give up having the drink; or it could mean saving less or giving up some other good that you would have bought. But your choice should not be affected by the particular way you happened to become $10 poorer. In both scenarios, the cost of the drink is $10, and the benefit you will receive from consuming it is also the same. You should either buy the drink in both scenarios or not buy it in both. And yet, as noted, many people would choose differently in the two scenarios.

[1]These questions are patterned after questions posed by decision theorists Daniel Kahneman and Amos Tversky (see Chapter 7).

Is spilling a $10 drink worse than losing $10 in cash?

CHAPTER PREVIEW

Our task in this chapter is to set forth the economist's basic model for answering questions such as the ones posed above. This model is known as the theory of *rational consumer choice*. It underlies all individual purchase decisions, which in turn add up to the demand curves we worked with in the preceding chapter.

Rational choice theory begins with the assumption that consumers enter the marketplace with well-defined preferences. Taking prices as given, their task is to allocate their incomes to best serve these preferences. Two steps are required to carry out this task. Step 1 is to describe the various combinations of goods the consumer is *able* to buy. These combinations depend on both her income level and the prices of the goods. Step 2 then is to select from among the feasible combinations the particular one that she *prefers* to all others. Analysis of step 2 requires some means of describing her preferences, in particular, a summary of her ranking of the desirability of all feasible combinations. Formal development of these two elements of the theory will occupy our attention throughout this chapter. Because the first element—describing the set of possibilities—is much less abstract than the second, let us begin with it.

THE OPPORTUNITY SET OR BUDGET CONSTRAINT

bundle a particular combination of two or more goods.

For simplicity, we start by considering a world with only two goods,[2] shelter and food. A **bundle** of goods is the term used to describe a particular combination of shelter, measured in square yards per week, and food, measured in pounds per week. Thus, in Figure 3.1, one bundle (bundle *A*) might consist of 5 sq yd/wk of shelter and 7 lb/wk of food, while another (bundle *B*) consists of 3 sq yd/wk of shelter and 8 lb/wk of food. For brevity, we use (5, 7) to denote bundle *A* and (3, 8) to denote bundle *B*. More generally, (S_0, F_0) will denote the bundle with S_0 sq yd/wk of shelter and F_0 lb/wk of food. By convention, the first number of the pair in any bundle represents the good measured along the horizontal axis.

Note that the units on both axes are *flows,* which means amounts per unit of time—pounds per week, square yards per week. Consumption is always measured as a flow. It is important to keep track of the time dimension because without it there would be no way to evaluate whether a given quantity of consumption was large or small. (Suppose all you know is that your food consumption is 4 lb. If that's how much you eat each day, it's a lot. But if that's all you eat in a month, you're not likely to survive for long.)[3]

[2]As economists use the term, a "good" may refer to either a product or a service.
[3]The flow aspect of consumption also helps us alleviate any concern about goods not being divisible. If you consume 1.5 lb/mo, then you consume 18 lb/yr, which is a whole number.

FIGURE 3.1

Two Bundles of Goods

A bundle is a specific combination of goods. Bundle A has 5 units of shelter and 7 units of food. Bundle B has 3 units of shelter and 8 units of food.

Suppose the consumer's income is $M = \$100/\text{wk}$, all of which she spends on some combination of food and shelter. (Note that income is also a flow.) Suppose further that the prices of shelter and food are $P_S = \$5/\text{sq yd}$ and $P_F = \$10/\text{lb}$, respectively. If the consumer spent all her income on shelter, she could buy $M/P_S = (\$100/\text{wk}) \div (\$5/\text{sq yd}) = 20 \text{ sq yd/wk}$. That is, she could buy the bundle consisting of 20 sq yd/wk of shelter and 0 lb/wk of food, denoted (20, 0). Alternatively, suppose the consumer spent all her income on food. She would then get the bundle consisting of $M/P_F = (\$100/\text{wk}) \div (\$10/\text{lb})$, which is 10 lb/wk of food and 0 sq yd/wk of shelter, denoted (0, 10).

Note that the units in which consumption goods are measured are subject to the standard rules of arithmetic. For example, when we simplify the expression on the right-hand side of the equation $M/P_S = (\$100/\text{wk}) \div (\$5/\text{sq yd})$, we are essentially dividing one fraction by another, so we follow the standard rule of inverting the fraction in the denominator and multiplying it by the fraction in the numerator: $(\text{sq yd}/\$5) \times (\$100/\text{wk}) = (\$100 \times \text{sq yd})/(\$5 \times \text{wk})$. After dividing both the numerator and denominator of the fraction on the right-hand side of this last equation by \$5, we have 20 sq yd/wk, which is the maximum amount of shelter the consumer can buy with an income of \$100/wk. Similarly, $M/P_F = (\$100/\text{wk}) \div (\$10/\text{lb})$ simplifies to 10 lb/wk, the maximum amount of food the consumer can purchase with an income of \$100/wk.

In Figure 3.2 these polar cases are labeled K and L, respectively. The consumer is also able to purchase any other bundle that lies along the straight line that joins points K and L. [Verify, for example, that the bundle (12, 4) lies on this same line.] This line is called the **budget constraint** and is labeled B in the diagram.

Recall the maxim from high school algebra that the slope of a straight line is its "rise" over its "run" (the change in its vertical position divided by the corresponding change in its

budget constraint the set of all bundles that exactly exhaust the consumer's income at given prices. Also called the *budget line*.

FIGURE 3.2

The Budget Constraint, or Budget Line

Line B describes the set of all bundles the consumer can purchase for given values of income and prices. Its slope is the negative of the price of shelter divided by the price of food. In absolute value, this slope is the opportunity cost of an additional unit of shelter— the number of units of food that must be sacrificed in order to purchase one additional unit of shelter at market prices.

horizontal position). Here, note that the slope of the budget constraint is its vertical intercept (the rise) divided by its horizontal intercept (the corresponding run): $-(10 \text{ lb/wk})/(20 \text{ sq yd/wk}) = -\frac{1}{2} \text{ lb/sq yd}$. (Note again how the units obey the standard rules of arithmetic.) The minus sign signifies that the budget line falls as it moves to the right—that it has a negative slope. More generally, if M denotes the consumer's weekly income, and P_S and P_F denote the prices of shelter and food, respectively, the horizontal and vertical intercepts will be given by (M/P_S) and (M/P_F), respectively. Thus the general formula for the slope of the budget constraint is given by $-(M/P_F)/(M/P_S) = -P_S/P_F$, which is simply the negative of the price ratio of the two goods. Given their respective prices, it is the rate at which food can be exchanged for shelter. Thus, in Figure 3.2, 1 lb of food can be exchanged for 2 sq yd of shelter. In the language of opportunity cost from Chapter 1, we would say that the opportunity cost of an additional square yard of shelter is $P_S/P_F = \frac{1}{2}$ lb of food.

In addition to being able to buy any of the bundles along her budget constraint, the consumer is also able to purchase any bundle that lies within the *budget triangle* bounded by it and the two axes. D is one such bundle in Figure 3.2. Bundle D costs \$65/wk, which is well below the consumer's income of \$100/wk. The bundles on or within the budget triangle are also referred to as the *feasible set,* or **affordable set.** Bundles like E that lie outside the budget triangle are said to be *infeasible,* or *unaffordable.* At a cost of \$140/wk, E is simply beyond the consumer's reach.

If S and F denote the quantities of shelter and food, respectively, the budget constraint must satisfy the following equation:

$$P_S S + P_F F = M, \tag{3.1}$$

which says simply that the consumer's weekly expenditure on shelter ($P_S S$) plus her weekly expenditure on food ($P_F F$) must add up to her weekly income (M). To express the budget constraint in the manner conventionally used to represent the formula for a straight line, we solve Equation 3.1 for F in terms of S, which yields

$$F = \frac{M}{P_F} - \frac{P_S}{P_F} S. \tag{3.2}$$

Equation 3.2 is another way of seeing that the vertical intercept of the budget constraint is given by M/P_F and its slope by $-(P_S/P_F)$. The equation for the budget constraint in Figure 3.2 is $F = 10 - \frac{1}{2} S$.

BUDGET SHIFTS DUE TO PRICE OR INCOME CHANGES

Price Changes

The slope and position of the budget constraint are fully determined by the consumer's income and the prices of the respective goods. Change any one of these factors and we have a new budget constraint. Figure 3.3 shows the effect of an increase in the price of shelter from $P_{S1} = \$5/\text{sq yd}$ to $P_{S2} = \$10$. Since both weekly income and the price of food are unchanged, the vertical intercept of the consumer's budget constraint stays the same. The rise in the price of shelter rotates the budget constraint inward about this intercept, as shown in the diagram.

Note in Figure 3.3 that even though the price of food has not changed, the new budget constraint, B_2, curtails not only the amount of shelter the consumer can buy but also the amount of food.[4]

affordable set bundles on or below the budget constraint; bundles for which the required expenditure at given prices is less than or equal to the income available.

---

[4]The single exception to this statement involves the vertical intercept (0, 10), which lies on both the original and the new budget constraints.

FIGURE 3.3

The Effect of a Rise in the Price of Shelter
When shelter goes up in price, the vertical intercept of the budget constraint remains the same. The original budget constraint rotates inward about this intercept.

SELF-TEST 3.1

Show the effect on the budget constraint B_1 in Figure 3.3 of a fall in the price of shelter from $5/sq yd to $4/sq yd.

In Self-Test 3.1, you saw that a fall in the price of shelter again leaves the vertical intercept of the budget constraint unchanged. This time the budget constraint rotates outward. Note also in Self-Test 3.1 that although the price of food remains unchanged, the new budget constraint enables the consumer to buy bundles that contain not only more shelter but also more food than she could afford on the original budget constraint.

The following self-test illustrates how changing the price of the good on the vertical axis affects the budget constraint.

SELF-TEST 3.2

Show the effect on the budget constraint B_1 in Figure 3.3 of a rise in the price of food from $10/lb to $20/lb.

When we change the price of only one good, we necessarily change the slope of the budget constraint, $-P_S/P_F$. The same is true if we change both prices by different proportions. But as Self-Test 3.3 will illustrate, changing both prices by exactly the same proportion gives rise to a new budget constraint with the same slope as before.

SELF-TEST 3.3

Show the effect on the budget constraint B_1 in Figure 3.3 of a rise in the price of food from $10/lb to $20/lb and a rise in the price of shelter from $5/sq yd to $10/sq yd.

Note from Self-Test 3.3 that the effect of doubling the prices of both food and shelter is to shift the budget constraint inward and parallel to the original budget constraint. The important lesson of this exercise is that the slope of a budget constraint tells us only about *relative prices,* nothing about prices in absolute terms. When the prices of food and shelter change in the same proportion, the opportunity cost of shelter in terms of food remains the same as before.

Income Changes

The effect of a change in income is much like the effect of an equal proportional change in all prices. Suppose, for example, that our hypothetical consumer's income is cut by half,

FIGURE 3.4

The Effect of Cutting Income by Half

Both horizontal and vertical intercepts fall by half. The new budget constraint has the same slope as the old but is closer to the origin.

from \$100/wk to \$50/wk. The horizontal intercept of the consumer's budget constraint then falls from 20 sq yd/wk to 10 sq yd/wk, and the vertical intercept falls from 10 lb/wk to 5 lb/wk, as shown in Figure 3.4. Thus the new budget, B_2, is parallel to the old, B_1, each with a slope of $-\frac{1}{2}$. In terms of its effect on what the consumer can buy, cutting income by one-half is thus no different from doubling each price. Precisely the same budget constraint results from both changes.

SELF-TEST 3.4

Show the effect on the budget constraint B_1 in Figure 3.4 of an increase in income from \$100/wk to \$120/wk.

Self-Test 3.4 illustrates that an increase in income shifts the budget constraint parallel outward. As in the case of an income reduction, the slope of the budget constraint remains the same.

Budgets Involving More Than Two Goods

In the examples discussed so far, the consumer could buy only two different goods. No consumer faces such narrow options. In its most general form, the consumer budgeting problem can be posed as a choice between not two but N different goods, where N can be an indefinitely large number. With only two goods ($N = 2$), the budget constraint is a straight line, as we just saw. With three goods ($N = 3$), it is a plane. When we have more than three goods, the budget constraint becomes what mathematicians call a *hyperplane,* or *multidimensional plane.* It is difficult to represent this multidimensional case geometrically. We are just not very good at visualizing surfaces that have more than three dimensions.

The nineteenth-century economist Alfred Marshall proposed a disarmingly simple solution to this problem. It is to view the consumer's choice as being one between a particular good—call it X—and an amalgam of other goods, denoted Y. This amalgam is generally called the **composite good.** By convention, the units of the composite good are defined so that its price is \$1 per unit. This convention enables us to think of the composite good as the amount of income the consumer has left over after buying the good X. Equivalently, it is the amount the consumer spends on goods other than X. For the moment, all the examples we consider will be ones in which consumers spend all their incomes. In Chapter 5 we will use the rational choice model to analyze the decision to save. Because savings may be thought of as a form of future consumption, the "intertemporal" model we will develop in Chapter 5 opens the door to giving weight in our choices to a composite good called "the future." We can begin to ask, therefore, what we can or should or are willing to pay today to enjoy a more livable climate down the road.

To illustrate how the composite good concept is used, suppose the consumer has an income of \$$M$/wk, and the price of X is P_X. The consumer's budget constraint may then be

composite good in a choice between a good X and numerous other goods, the amount of money the consumer spends on those other goods.

FIGURE 3.5

The Budget Constraint with the Composite Good

The vertical axis measures the amount of money spent each week on all goods other than X.

represented as a straight line in the X, Y plane, as shown in Figure 3.5. Because the price of a unit of the composite good is $1, a consumer who devotes all his income to it will be able to buy M units. All this means is that he will have M available to spend on other goods if he buys no X. Alternatively, if he spends his entire income on X, he will be able to purchase the bundle $(M/P_X, 0)$. Since the price of Y is assumed to be $1/unit, the slope of the budget constraint is simply $-P_X$.

As before, the budget constraint summarizes the various combinations of bundles that exhaust the consumer's income. Thus, the consumer can have X_1 units of X and Y_1 units of the composite good in Figure 3.5, or X_2 and Y_2, or any other combination that lies on the budget constraint.

Kinked Budget Constraints

The budget constraints we have seen so far have been straight lines. When relative prices are constant, the opportunity cost of one good in terms of any other is the same, no matter what bundle of goods we already have. But sometimes budget constraints are kinked lines. To illustrate, consider the following example of quantity discounts.

EXAMPLE 3.1   Quantity Discounts

Gigawatt Power Company charges $0.10 per kilowatt-hour (kWh) for the first 1,000 kWh of power purchased by a residential customer each month, but only $0.05/kWh for all additional kWh. For a residential customer with a monthly income of $400, graph the budget constraint for electric power and the composite good.

If the consumer buys no electric power, he will have $400/mo to spend on other goods. Thus the vertical intercept of his budget constraint is (0, 400). As shown in Figure 3.6, for each of the first 1,000 kWh he buys, he must give up $0.10, which

FIGURE 3.6

A Quantity Discount Gives Rise to a Nonlinear Budget Constraint

Once electric power consumption reaches 1,000 kWh/mo, the opportunity cost of additional power falls from $0.10/kWh to $0.05/kWh.

means that the slope of his budget constraint starts out at $-\frac{1}{10}$. At 1,000 kWh/mo, the price falls to \$0.05/kWh, which means that the slope of his budget constraint from that point rightward is only $-\frac{1}{20}$.

Note that along the budget constraint shown in Figure 3.6, the opportunity cost of electricity depends on how much the consumer has already purchased. Consider a consumer who now uses 1,020 kWh each month and is trying to decide whether to leave his front porch light on all night, which would result in additional consumption of 20 kWh/mo. Leaving his light on will cost him an extra \$1/mo. Had his usual consumption been only 980 kWh/mo, however, the cost of leaving the front porch light on would have been \$2/mo. On the basis of this difference, we can predict that people who already use a lot of electricity (more than 1,000 kWh/mo) should be more likely than others to leave their porch lights burning at night.

SELF-TEST 3.5

Suppose instead Gigawatt Power Company charged \$0.05/kWh for the first 1,000 kWh of power purchased by a residential consumer each month, but \$0.10/kWh each for all additional kilowatt-hours. For a residential consumer with a monthly income of \$400, graph the budget constraint for electric power and the composite good. What if the rate jumps to \$0.10/kWh for *all* kilowatt-hours if power consumption in a month exceeds 1,000 kWh (where the higher rate applies to all, not just the additional, kilowatt-hours)?

If the Budget Constraint Is the Same, the Decision Should Be the Same

Even without knowing anything about the consumer's preferences, we can use budgetary information to make certain inferences about how a rational consumer will behave. Suppose, for example, that the consumer's tastes do not change over time and that he is confronted with exactly the same budget constraint in each of two different situations. If he is rational, he should make exactly the same choice in both cases. After all, if the budget constraint is the same as before, the consumer has exactly the same menu of possible bundles available as before; and since we have no reason to believe that his ranking of the desirability of these bundles has changed, the most desirable bundle should also be the same. As the following example makes clear, however, it may not always be immediately apparent that the budget constraints are in fact the same.

EXAMPLE 3.2   **Budget Constraints**

On one occasion, Gowdy fills his car's tank with gasoline on the evening before his departure on a fishing trip. He awakens to discover that a thief has siphoned out all but 1 gallon from his 21-gallon tank. On another occasion, he plans to stop for gas on his way out the next morning before he goes fishing. He awakens to discover that he has lost \$80 from his wallet. If gasoline sells for \$4/gal and the round trip will consume 5 gallons, how, if at all, should Gowdy's decision about whether to take the fishing trip differ in the two cases? (Assume that, monetary costs aside, the inconvenience of having to refill his tank is negligible.)

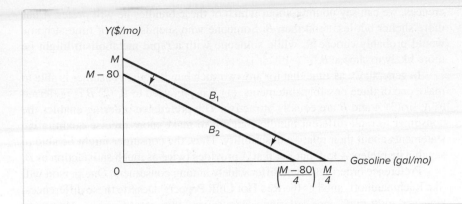

FIGURE 3.7

Budget Constraints Following Theft of Gasoline, Loss of Cash
A theft of $80 worth of gasoline has exactly the same effect on the budget constraint as the loss of $80 in cash. The bundle chosen should therefore be the same, irrespective of the source of the loss.

Suppose Gowdy's income is M/mo. Before his loss, his budget constraint is B_1 in Figure 3.7. In both instances described, his budget constraint at the moment he discovers his loss will shift inward to B_2. If he does not take the trip, he will have $M -$ $80 available to spend on other goods in both cases. And if he does take the trip, he will have to purchase the required gasoline at $4/gal in both cases. No matter what the source of the loss, the remaining opportunities are exactly the same. If Gowdy's budget is tight, he may decide to cancel his trip. Otherwise, he may go despite the loss. But because his budget constraint and tastes are the same in the lost-cash case as in the stolen-gas case, it would not be rational for him to take the trip in one instance but not in the other.

If your preferences are stable and your opportunities are the same in two situations, you should make the same choice in each case.

Note that the situation described in Example 3.2 has the same structure as the one described in the spilled-drink example with which we began this chapter. It too is one in which the decision should be the same in both instances because the budget constraint and preferences are the same in each.

Although the rational choice model makes clear that the decisions *should* be the same if the budget constraints and preferences are the same, people sometimes choose differently. The difficulty is often that the way the different situations are described sometimes causes people to overlook the essential similarities between them. For instance, in Example 3.2, many people erroneously conclude that the cost of taking the trip is higher in the stolen-gas case than in the lost-money case, and so they are less likely to take the trip in the former instance. Similarly, many people were less inclined to repurchase the drink after having spilled the first one than after having lost $10 because they thought, incorrectly, that the drink would cost more under the spilling scenario. As we have seen, however, the amount that will be saved by not buying the LP, or by not taking the trip, is exactly the same under each scenario.

To recapitulate briefly, the budget constraint or budget line summarizes the combinations of bundles that the consumer is able to buy. Its position is determined jointly by income and prices. From the set of feasible bundles, the consumer's task is to pick the particular one she likes best. To identify this bundle, we need some means of summarizing the consumer's preferences over all possible bundles she might consume. We now turn to this task.

CONSUMER PREFERENCES

For simplicity, let us again begin by considering a world with only two goods: shelter and food. A **preference ordering** enables the consumer to rank different bundles of goods in terms of their desirability, or order of preference. Consider two bundles, A and B. For concreteness, suppose that A contains 4 sq yd/wk of shelter and 2 lb/wk of food, while B has 3 sq yd/wk of shelter and 3 lb/wk of food. Knowing nothing about a consumer's pref-

preference ordering a ranking of all possible consumption bundles in order of preference.

Why are brown eggs more expensive than white ones?

erences, we can say nothing about which of these bundles he will prefer. *A* has more shelter but less food than *B*. Someone who spends a lot of time at home would probably choose *A,* while someone with a rapid metabolism might be more likely to choose *B.*

In general, we assume that for any two such bundles, the consumer is able to make one of three possible statements: (1) *A* is preferred to *B,* (2) *B* is preferred to *A,* or (3) *A* and *B* are equally attractive. The preference ordering enables the consumer to rank different bundles but not to make more precise quantitative statements about their relative desirability. Thus, the consumer might be able to say that he prefers *A* to *B* but not that *A* provides twice as much satisfaction as *B.*

Preference orderings often differ widely among consumers. One person will like Rachmaninoff, another the Red Hot Chili Peppers. Despite these differences, however, most preference orderings share several important features. More specifically, economists generally assume four simple properties of preference orderings. These properties allow us to construct the concise analytical representation of preferences we need for the budget allocation problem.

1. Completeness

A preference ordering is *complete* if it enables the consumer to rank all possible combinations of goods and services. Taken literally, the completeness assumption is never satisfied, for there are many goods we know too little about to be able to evaluate. It is nonetheless a useful simplifying assumption for the analysis of choices among bundles of goods with which consumers are familiar. Its real intent is to rule out instances like the one portrayed in the fable of Buridan's ass. The hungry animal was unable to choose between two bales of hay in front of him and starved to death as a result.

2. More-Is-Better

The more-is-better property means simply that, other things equal, more of a good is preferred to less. We can, of course, think of examples of more of something making us worse off rather than better (as with someone who has overeaten). But these examples usually contemplate some sort of practical difficulty, such as having a self-control problem or being unable to store a good for future use. As long as people can freely store or dispose of goods they don't want, having more of something can't make them worse off.

As an example of the application of the more-is-better assumption, consider two bundles: *A,* which has 12 sq yd/wk of shelter and 10 lb/wk of food, and *B,* which has 12 sq yd/wk of shelter and 11 lb/wk of food. The assumption tells us that *B* is preferred to *A,* because it has more food and no less shelter.

3. Transitivity

If you like steak better than hamburger and hamburger better than hot dogs, you are probably someone who likes steak better than hot dogs. To say that a consumer's preference ordering is *transitive* means that, for any three bundles *A, B,* and *C,* if he prefers *A* to *B* and prefers *B* to *C,* then he always prefers *A* to *C.* For example, suppose *A* is (4, 2), *B* is (3, 3), and *C* is (2, 4). If you prefer (4, 2) over (3, 3) and you prefer (3, 3) over (2, 4), then you must prefer (4, 2) over (2, 4). The preference relationship is thus assumed to be like the relationship used to compare heights of people. If Nowitzki is taller than James and James is taller than Bryant, we know that Nowitzki must be taller than Bryant.

Not all comparative relationships are transitive. The relationship "half sibling," for example, is not. I have a half sister who, in turn, has three half sisters of her own. But her half sisters are not my half sisters. A similar nontransitivity is shown by the relationship "defeats in football." Some seasons, Ohio State defeats Michigan, and Michigan defeats Michigan State, but that doesn't tell us that Ohio State will necessarily defeat Michigan State.

Transitivity is a simple consistency property and applies as well to the relation "equally attractive as" and to any combination of it and the "preferred to" relation. For example, if *A* is equally attractive as *B* and *B* is equally attractive as *C*, it follows that *A* is equally attractive as *C*. Similarly, if *A* is preferred to *B* and *B* is equally attractive as *C*, it follows that *A* is preferred to *C*.

The transitivity assumption can be justified as eliminating the potential for a "money pump" problem. To illustrate, suppose you prefer *A* to *B* and *B* to *C*, but you also prefer *C* over *A*, so that your preferences are intransitive. If you start with *C*, you would trade *C* for *B*, trade *B* for *A*, and then trade *A* for *C*. This cycle could continue forever. If in each stage you were charged a tiny fee for the trade, you would eventually transfer all your money to the other trader. Clearly, such preferences are problematic.

As reasonable as the transitivity property sounds, we will see examples in later chapters of behavior that seems inconsistent with it. But it is an accurate description of preferences in most instances. Unless otherwise stated, we will adopt it.

4. Convexity

Mixtures of goods are preferable to extremes. If you are indifferent between two bundles *A* and *B*, your preferences are convex if you prefer a bundle that contains half of *A* and half of *B* (or any other mixture) to either of the original bundles. For example, suppose you are indifferent between $A = (4, 0)$ and $B = (0, 4)$. If your preferences are convex, you will prefer the bundle $(2, 2)$ to each of the more extreme bundles. This property conveys the sense that we like balance in our mix of consumption goods.

Indifference Curves

Let us consider some implications of these assumptions about preference orderings. Most important, they enable us to generate a graphical description of the consumer's preferences. To see how, consider first the bundle *A* in Figure 3.8, which has 12 sq yd/wk of shelter and 10 lb/wk of food. The more-is-better assumption tells us that all bundles to the northeast of *A* are preferred to *A*, and that *A*, in turn, is preferred to all those to the southwest of *A*. Thus, the more-is-better assumption tells us that *Z*, which has 28 sq yd/wk of shelter and 12 lb/wk of food, is preferred to *A* and that *A*, in turn, is preferred to *W*, which has only 6 sq yd/wk of shelter and 4 lb/wk of food.

Now consider the set of bundles that lie along the line joining *W* and *Z*. Because *Z* is preferred to *A* and *A* is preferred to *W*, it follows that as we move from *Z* to *W* we must encounter a bundle that is equally attractive as *A*. (The intuition behind this claim is the same as the intuition that tells us that if we climb on any continuous path on a mountainside from one point at 1,000 feet above sea level to another at 2,000 feet, we must pass through every intermediate altitude along the way.) Let *B* denote the bundle that is equally attractive as *A*, and suppose it contains 17 sq yd/wk of shelter and 8 lb/wk of food.

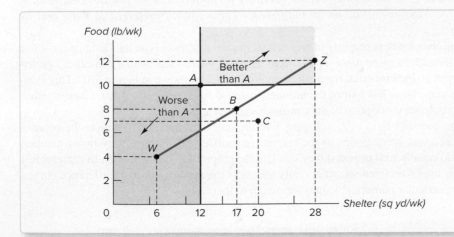

FIGURE 3.8

Generating Equally Preferred Bundles

Z is preferred to *A* because it has more of each good than *A* has. For the same reason, *A* is preferred to *W*. It follows that on the line joining *W* and *Z* there must be a bundle *B* that is equally attractive as *A*. In similar fashion, we can find a bundle *C* that is equally attractive as *B*.

FIGURE 3.9

An Indifference Curve

An indifference curve is a set of bundles that the consumer considers equally attractive. Any bundle, such as *L*, that lies above an indifference curve is preferred to any bundle on the indifference curve. Any bundle on the indifference curve, in turn, is preferred to any bundle, such as *K*, that lies below the indifference curve.

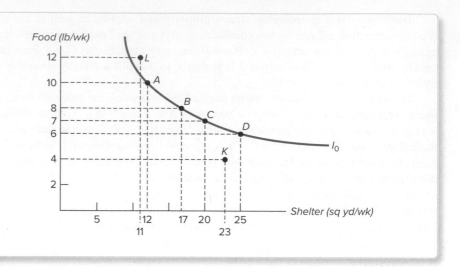

indifference curve a set of bundles among which the consumer is indifferent.

indifference map a representative sample of the set of a consumer's indifference curves, used as a graphical summary of her preference ordering.

(The exact amounts of each good in *B* will of course depend on the specific consumer whose preferences we are talking about.) The more-is-better assumption also tells us that there will be only one such bundle on the straight line between *W* and *Z*. Points on that line to the northeast of *B* are all better than *B;* those to the southwest of *B* are all worse.

In precisely the same fashion, we can find another point—call it *C*—that is equally attractive as *B*. *C* is shown as the bundle (20, 7), where the specific quantities in *C* again depend on the preferences of the consumer under consideration. By the transitivity assumption, we know that *C* is also equally attractive as *A* (since *C* is equally attractive as *B*, which is equally attractive as *A*).

We can repeat this process as often as we like, and the end result will be an **indifference curve,** a set of bundles all of which are equally attractive as the original bundle *A*, and hence also equally attractive as one another. This set is shown as the curve labeled *I* in Figure 3.9. It is called an indifference curve because the consumer is indifferent among all the bundles that lie along it.

An indifference curve also permits us to compare the satisfaction implicit in bundles that lie along it with those that lie either above or below it. It permits us, for example, to compare bundle *C* (20, 7) to bundle *K* (23, 4), which has less food and more shelter than *C* has. We know that *C* is equally attractive as *D* (25, 6) because both bundles lie along the same indifference curve. *D,* in turn, is preferred to *K* because of the more-is-better assumption: It has 2 sq yd/wk more shelter and 2 lb/wk more food than *K* has. Transitivity, finally, tells us that since *C* is equally attractive as *D* and *D* is preferred to *K*, *C* must be preferred to *K*.

By analogous reasoning, we can say that bundle *L* is preferred to *A*. *In general, bundles that lie above an indifference curve are all preferred to the bundles that lie on it. Similarly, bundles that lie on an indifference curve are all preferred to those that lie below it.*

The completeness property of preferences implies that there is an indifference curve that passes through every possible bundle. That being so, we can represent a consumer's preferences with an **indifference map,** an example of which is shown in Figure 3.10. This indifference map shows just four of the infinitely many indifference curves that, taken together, yield a complete description of the consumer's preferences.

The numbers $I_1, \ldots, I_4$ in Figure 3.10 are index values used to denote the order of preference that corresponds to the respective indifference curves. Any index numbers would do equally well provided they satisfied the property $I_1 < I_2 < I_3 < I_4$. In representing the consumer's preferences, what really counts is the *ranking* of the indifference curves, not the particular numerical values we assign to them.[5]

[5]For a more complete discussion of this issue, see pp. 78–86 of the appendix to this chapter.

Food (lb/wk)

Increasing satisfaction

I_4

I_3

I_2

I_1

Shelter (sq yd/wk)

FIGURE 3.10

Part of an Indifference Map

The entire set of a consumer's indifference curves is called the consumer's indifference map. Bundles on any indifference curve are less preferred than bundles on a higher indifference curve and more preferred than bundles on a lower indifference curve.

The four properties of preference orderings imply four important properties of indifference curves and indifference maps:

1. Indifference curves are ubiquitous. Any bundle has an indifference curve passing through it. This property is assured by the completeness property of preferences.

2. Indifference curves are downward-sloping. An upward-sloping indifference curve would violate the more-is-better property by saying a bundle with more of both goods is equivalent to a bundle with less of both.

3. Indifference curves (from the same indifference map) cannot cross. To see why, suppose that two indifference curves did, in fact, cross as in Figure 3.11. The following statements would then have to be true:
   E is equally attractive as D (because they each lie on the same indifference curve).
   D is equally attractive as F (because they each lie on the same indifference curve).
   E is equally attractive as F (by the transitivity assumption).
   But we also know that
   F is preferred to E (because more is better).
   Because it is not possible for the statements E is equally attractive as F and F is preferred to E to be true simultaneously, the assumption that two indifference curves cross thus implies a contradiction. The conclusion is that the original proposition must be true, namely, two indifference curves cannot cross.

4. Indifference curves become less steep as we move downward and to the right along them. As discussed below, this property is implied by the convexity property of preferences.

Food (lb/wk)

D

F

E

Shelter (sq yd/wk)

FIGURE 3.11

Why Two Indifference Curves Do Not Cross

If indifference curves were to cross, they would have to violate at least one of the assumed properties of preference orderings.

Trade-offs between Goods

marginal rate of substitution (MRS) at any point on an indifference curve, the rate at which the consumer is willing to exchange the good measured along the vertical axis for the good measured along the horizontal axis; equal to the absolute value of the slope of the indifference curve.

An important property of a consumer's preferences is the rate at which he is willing to exchange, or "trade off," one good for another. This rate is represented at any point on an indifference curve by the **marginal rate of substitution (MRS),** which is defined as the absolute value of the slope of the indifference curve at that point. In the left panel of Figure 3.12, for example, the marginal rate of substitution at point A is given by the absolute value of the slope of the tangent to the indifference curve at A, which is the ratio $\Delta F_A/\Delta S_A$.[6] (The notation ΔF_A means "small change in food from the amount at point A.") If we take ΔF_A units of food away from the consumer at point A, we have to give him ΔS_A additional units of shelter to make him just as well off as before. The right panel of the figure shows an enlargement of the region surrounding bundle A. If the marginal rate of substitution at A is 2, this means that the consumer must be given 2 lb/wk of food to make up for the loss of 1 sq yd/wk of shelter.

Whereas the slope of the budget constraint tells us the rate at which we can substitute food for shelter without changing total expenditure, the MRS tells us the rate at which we can substitute food for shelter without changing total satisfaction. Put another way, the slope of the budget constraint is the marginal cost of shelter in terms of food, and the MRS is the marginal benefit of shelter in terms of food.

The convexity property of preferences tells us that along any indifference curve, the more a consumer has of one good, the more she must be given of that good before she will be willing to give up a unit of the other good. Stated differently, MRS declines as we move downward to the right along an indifference curve. Indifference curves with diminishing rates of marginal substitution are thus convex—or bowed inward—when viewed from the origin. The indifference curves shown in Figures 3.9, 3.10, and 3.12 have this property, as does the curve shown in Figure 3.13.

In Figure 3.13, note that at bundle A food is relatively plentiful and the consumer would be willing to sacrifice 3 lb/wk of it in order to obtain an additional square yard of shelter. Her MRS at A is 3. At C, the quantities of food and shelter are more balanced, and there she would be willing to give up only 1 lb/wk to obtain an additional square yard of shelter. Her MRS at C is 1. Finally, note that food is relatively scarce at D, and there she would be willing to give up only $\frac{1}{4}$ lb/wk of food to obtain an additional unit of shelter. Her MRS at D is $\frac{1}{4}$.

Intuitively, diminishing MRS means that consumers like variety. We are usually willing to give up goods we already have a lot of to obtain more of those goods we now have only a little of.

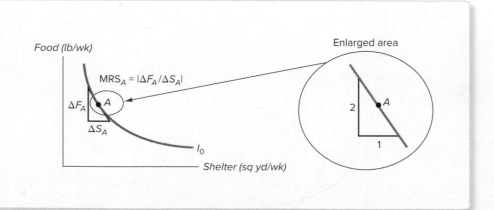

FIGURE 3.12

The Marginal Rate of Substitution

MRS at any point along an indifference curve is defined as the absolute value of the slope of the indifference curve at that point. It is the amount of food the consumer must be given to compensate for the loss of 1 unit of shelter.

[6]More formally, the indifference curve may be expressed as a function $Y = Y(X)$ and the MRS at point A is defined as the absolute value of the derivative of the indifference curve at that point: $MRS = |dY(X)/dX|$.

FIGURE 3.13

Diminishing Marginal Rate of Substitution

The more food the consumer has, the more she is willing to give up to obtain an additional unit of shelter. The marginal rates of substitution at bundles A, C, and D are 3, 1, and 1/4, respectively.

Using Indifference Curves to Describe Preferences

To get a feel for how indifference maps describe a consumer's preferences, let us see how indifference maps can be used to portray differences in preferences between two consumers. Suppose, for example, that both Tex and Mohan like potatoes but that Mohan likes rice much more than Tex does. This difference in their tastes is captured by the differing slopes of their indifference curves in Figure 3.14. Note in Figure 3.14a, which shows Tex's indifference map, that Tex would be willing to exchange 1 lb of potatoes for 1 lb of rice at bundle A. But at the corresponding bundle in Figure 3.14b, which shows Mohan's indifference map, we see that Mohan would trade 2 lb of potatoes for 1 lb of rice. Their difference in preferences shows up clearly in this difference in their marginal rates of substitution of potatoes for rice.

THE BEST FEASIBLE BUNDLE

We now have the tools we need to determine how the consumer should allocate his income between two goods. The indifference map tells us how the various bundles are ranked in order of preference. The budget constraint, in turn, tells us which bundles are affordable. The consumer's task is to put the two together and to choose the most preferred or **best affordable bundle.** (Recall from Chapter 1 that we need not suppose that consumers think explicitly about budget constraints and indifference maps when deciding

best affordable bundle the most preferred bundle of those that are affordable.

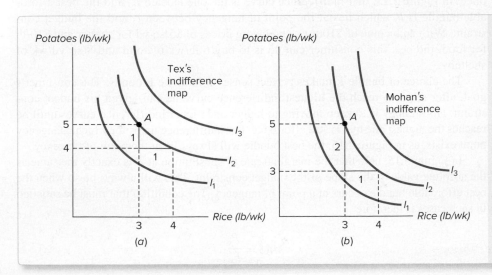

FIGURE 3.14

People with Different Tastes

Relatively speaking, Tex is a potato lover; Mohan, a rice lover. This difference shows up in the fact that at any given bundle Tex's marginal rate of substitution of potatoes for rice is smaller than Mohan's.

FIGURE 3.15

The Best Affordable Bundle
The best the consumer can do
is to choose the bundle on the
budget constraint that lies
on the highest attainable
indifference curve. Here, that
is bundle *F*, which lies at a
tangency between the
indifference curve and the
budget constraint.

what to buy. It is sufficient to assume that people make decisions *as if* they were thinking in these terms, just as expert pool players choose between shots as if they knew all the relevant laws of Newtonian physics.)

Let us again consider the choice between food and shelter that confronts a consumer with an income of $M = \$100/\text{wk}$ facing prices of $P_F = \$10/\text{lb}$ and $P_S = \$5/\text{sq}$ yd. Figure 3.15 shows this consumer's budget constraint and part of his indifference map. Of the five labeled bundles—*A, D, E, F,* and *G*—in the diagram, *G* is the most preferred because it lies on the highest indifference curve. *G,* however, is not affordable, nor is any other bundle that lies beyond the budget constraint. The more-is-better assumption implies that the best affordable bundle must lie *on* the budget constraint, not inside it. (Any bundle inside the budget constraint would be less preferred than one just slightly to the northeast, which would also be affordable.)

Where exactly is the best affordable bundle located along the budget constraint? We know that it cannot be on an indifference curve that lies partly inside the budget constraint. On the indifference curve I_1, for example, the only points that are even candidates for the best affordable bundle are the two that lie on the budget constraint, namely, *A* and *E*. But *A* cannot be the best affordable bundle because it is equally attractive as *D,* which in turn is less desirable than *F* by the more-is-better assumption. So by transitivity, *A* is less desirable than *F*. For the same reason, *E* cannot be the best affordable bundle.

Since the best affordable bundle cannot lie on an indifference curve that lies partly inside the budget constraint, and since it must lie on the budget constraint itself, we know it has to lie on an indifference curve that intersects the budget constraint only once. In Figure 3.15, that indifference curve is the one labeled I_2, and the best affordable bundle is *F,* which lies at the point of tangency between I_2 and the budget constraint. With an income of $100/wk and facing prices of $5/sq yd for shelter and $10/lb for food, the best this consumer can do is to buy 6 lb/wk of food and 8 sq yd/wk of shelter.

The choice of bundle *F* makes perfect sense on intuitive grounds. The consumer's goal, after all, is to reach the highest indifference curve he can, given his budget constraint. His strategy is to keep moving to higher and higher indifference curves until he reaches the highest one that is still affordable. For indifference maps for which a tangency point exists, as in Figure 3.15, the best bundle will always lie at the point of tangency.

In Figure 3.15, note that the marginal rate of substitution at *F* is exactly the same as the absolute value of the slope of the budget constraint. This will always be so when the best affordable bundle occurs at a point of tangency. The condition that must be satisfied in such cases is therefore

$$MRS = \frac{P_S}{P_F}. \tag{3.3}$$

The right-hand side of Equation 3.3 represents the opportunity cost of shelter in terms of food. Thus, with $P_S = \$5/\text{sq yd}$ and $P_F = \$10/\text{lb}$, the opportunity cost of an additional square yard of shelter is $\frac{1}{2}$ lb of food. The left-hand side of Equation 3.3 is $|\Delta F/\Delta S|$, the absolute value of the slope of the indifference curve at the point of tangency. It is the amount of additional food the consumer must be given in order to compensate him fully for the loss of 1 sq yd of shelter. In the language of cost-benefit analysis discussed in Chapter 1, the slope of the budget constraint represents the opportunity cost of shelter in terms of food, while the slope of the indifference curve represents the benefits of consuming shelter as compared with consuming food. Since the slope of the budget constraint is $-\frac{1}{2}$ in this example, the tangency condition tells us that $\frac{1}{2}$ lb of food would be required to compensate for the benefits given up with the loss of 1 sq yd of shelter.

If the consumer were at some bundle on the budget line for which the two slopes are not the same, then it would always be possible for him to purchase a better bundle. To see why, suppose he were at a point where the slope of the indifference curve (in absolute value) is less than the slope of the budget constraint (also in absolute value), as at point E in Figure 3.15. Suppose, for instance, that the MRS at E is only $\frac{1}{4}$. This tells us that the consumer can be compensated for the loss of 1 sq yd of shelter by being given an additional $\frac{1}{4}$ lb of food. But the slope of the budget constraint tells us that by giving up 1 sq yd of shelter, he can purchase an additional $\frac{1}{2}$ lb of food. Since this is $\frac{1}{4}$ lb more than he needs to remain equally satisfied, he will clearly be better off if he purchases more food and less shelter than at point E. The opportunity cost of an additional pound of food is less than the benefit it confers.

SELF-TEST 3.6

Suppose that the marginal rate of substitution at point *A* in Figure 3.15 is 1.0. Show that this means the consumer will be better off if he purchases less food and more shelter than at *A*.

Corner Solutions

The best affordable bundle need not always occur at a point of tangency. In some cases, there may simply *be* no point of tangency—the MRS may be everywhere greater, or less, than the slope of the budget constraint. In this case we get a **corner solution,** like the one shown in Figure 3.16, where M, P_F, and P_S are again given by \$100/wk, \$10/lb and \$5/sq yd, respectively. The best affordable bundle is the one labeled *A,* and it lies at the upper end of the budget constraint. At *A* the MRS is less than the absolute value of the slope of the budget constraint. For the sake of illustration, suppose the MRS at $A = 0.25$, which means that this consumer would be willing to give up 0.25 lb of food to get an additional square yard of shelter. But at market prices the opportunity cost of an additional square yard of shelter is 0.5 lb of food. He increases his satisfaction by continuing to give up

corner solution in a choice between two goods, a case in which the consumer does not consume one of the goods.

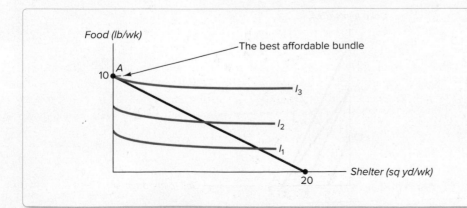

FIGURE 3.16

A Corner Solution

When the MRS of food for shelter is always less than the slope of the budget constraint, the best the consumer can do is to spend all his income on food.

shelter for more food until it is no longer possible to do so. Even though this consumer regards shelter as a desirable commodity, the best he can do is to spend all his income on food. Market prices are such that he would have to give up too much food to make the purchase of even a single unit of shelter worthwhile.

The indifference map in Figure 3.16 satisfies the property of diminishing marginal rate of substitution—moving to the right along any indifference curve, the slope becomes smaller in absolute terms. But because the slopes of the indifference curves start out smaller than the slope of the budget constraint here, the two never reach equality.

Indifference curves that are not strongly convex are characteristic of goods that are easily substituted for one another. Corner solutions are more likely to occur for such goods, and indeed are almost certain to occur when goods are perfect substitutes. (See Example 3.3.) For such goods, the MRS does not diminish at all; rather, it is everywhere the same. With perfect substitutes, indifference curves are straight lines. If they happen to be steeper than the budget constraint, we get a corner solution on the horizontal axis; if less steep, we get a corner solution on the vertical axis.

EXAMPLE 3.3   Corner Solutions

Mattingly is a caffeinated-cola drinker who spends his entire soft drink budget on Coca-Cola and Jolt cola and cares only about total caffeine content. If Jolt has twice the caffeine of Coke, and if Jolt costs \$1/pint and Coke costs \$0.75/pint, how will Mattingly spend his soft drink budget of \$15/wk?

For Mattingly, Jolt and Coke are *perfect substitutes,* which means that his indifference curves will be linear. The top line in Figure 3.17 is the set of all possible Coke-Jolt combinations that provide the same satisfaction as the bundle consisting of 0 pints of Jolt per day and 30 pints of Coke per day. Since each pint of Jolt has twice the caffeine of a pint of Coke, all bundles along this line contain precisely the same amount of caffeine. The first green line down is the indifference curve for bundles equivalent to bundle (0, 20); and the second green line down is the indifference curve corresponding to (0, 10). Along each of these indifference curves, the marginal rate of substitution of Coke for Jolt is always $\frac{2}{1}$ that is, 2 pints of Coke for every pint of Jolt.

In the same diagram, Mattingly's budget constraint is shown as *B*. The slope of his indifference curves is -2; of his budget constraint, $-\frac{4}{3}$. The best affordable bundle is the one labeled *A*, a corner solution in which he spends his entire budget on Jolt. This makes intuitive sense in light of Mattingly's peculiar preferences: he cares only about total caffeine content, and Jolt provides more caffeine per dollar than Coke does. If the Jolt-Coke price ratio, P_J/P_C had been $\frac{3}{1}$ (or any other amount greater than $\frac{2}{1}$), Mattingly would have spent all his income on Coke. That is, we would again have had a corner solution, only this time on the vertical axis. Only if the

---

FIGURE 3.17

Equilibrium with Perfect Substitutes

Here, the MRS of Coke for Jolt is 2 at every point. Whenever the price ratio P_J/P_C is less than 2, a corner solution results in which the consumer buys only Jolt. On the budget constraint *B*, the consumer does best to buy bundle *A*.

price ratio had been exactly $\frac{2}{1}$ might we have seen Mattingly spend part of his income on each good. In that case, any combination of Coke and Jolt on his budget constraint would have served equally well.

Most of the time we will deal with problems that have *interior solutions*—that is, with problems where the best affordable bundle will lie at a point of tangency. An interior solution, again, is one where the MRS is exactly the same as the slope of the budget constraint.

SELF-TEST 3.7

Suppose Bailey always uses exactly two pats of butter on each piece of toast. If toast costs $0.10/slice and butter costs $0.20/pat, find Bailey's best affordable bundle if she has $12/mo to spend on toast and butter. Suppose Bailey starts to watch her cholesterol and therefore alters her preference to using exactly one pat of butter on each piece of toast. How much toast and butter would Bailey then consume each month?

Indifference Curves When There Are More Than Two Goods

In the examples thus far, the consumer cared about only two goods. Where there are more than two, we can construct indifference curves by using the same device we used earlier to represent multigood budget constraints. We simply view the consumer's choice as being one between a particular good X and an amalgam of other goods Y, which is again called the composite good. As before, the composite good is the amount of income the consumer has left over after buying the good X.

In the multigood case, we may thus continue to represent the consumer's preferences with an indifference map in the XY plane. Here, the indifference curve tells the rate at which the consumer will exchange the composite good for X. As in the two-good case, equilibrium occurs when the consumer reaches the highest indifference curve attainable on his budget constraint.

An Application of the Rational Choice Model

As the following example makes clear, the composite good construct enables us to deal with more general questions than we could in the two-good case.

EXAMPLE 3.4　　Rational Choice Model in Action

Is it better to give poor people cash or food stamps?

One objective of SNAP—the program that most people still call "food stamps," although the food redemption coupons have been replaced by EBT cards since 2004—is to alleviate hunger. Under the terms of the program, people whose incomes fall below a certain level are eligible to receive a specified quantity of food stamps. For example, a person with an income of $400/mo might be eligible for $100/mo worth of stamps. These stamps can then be used to buy $100/mo worth of food. Any food he buys in excess of $100/mo he must pay for in cash. Stamps cannot be used to purchase cigarettes, alcohol, and various other items. The government gives food retailers cash for the stamps they accept.

The cost to the government for the consumer in the example given was $100—the amount it had to reimburse the store for the stamps. Would the consumer have been better off had he instead been given $100 directly in cash?

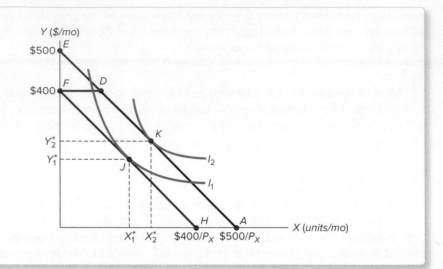

FIGURE 3.18

Food Stamp Program vs. Cash Grant Program

By comparison with the budget constraint under a cash grant (*AE*), the budget constraint under food stamps (*ADF*) limits the amount that can be spent on nonfood goods. But for the consumer whose indifference map is shown, the equilibrium bundles are the same under both programs.

We can try to answer this question by investigating which alternative would get him to a higher indifference curve. Suppose Y denotes the composite good and X denotes food. If the consumer's income is $400/mo and P_X is the price of food, his initial equilibrium is the bundle J in Figure 3.18. The effect of the food stamp program is to increase the total amount of food he can buy each month from $400/P_X$ to $500/P_X$. In terms of the maximum amount of food he can buy, the food stamp program is thus exactly the same as a cash grant of $100.

Where the two alternatives differ is in terms of the maximum amounts of other goods he can buy. With a cash grant of $100, he has a total monthly income of $500, and this is, of course, the maximum amount of nonfood goods (the composite good) he can buy. His budget constraint in this case is thus the line labeled *AE* in Figure 3.18.

With the food stamp program, by contrast, the consumer is not able to buy $500/mo of nonfood goods because his $100 in food stamps can be used only for food. The maximum amount of nonfood goods he can purchase is $400. In Figure 3.18, his budget constraint under the food stamp program is labeled *ADF*. For values of Y less than $400, it is thus exactly the same as his budget constraint under the cash grant program. For values of Y larger than $400, however, his budget constraint under the food stamp program is completely flat.

Note that the consumer whose indifference curves are shown in Figure 3.18 buys exactly the same bundle—namely, bundle K—under both programs. The effect of the food stamp program here is precisely the same as the effect of the cash grant. In general, this will be true whenever the consumer with a cash grant would have spent more on food anyway than the amount of food stamps he would have received under the food stamp program.

Figure 3.19 depicts a consumer for whom this is *not* the case. With a cash grant, he would choose the bundle L, which would put him on a higher indifference curve than he could attain under the food stamp program, which would lead him to buy bundle D. Note that bundle D contains exactly $100 worth of food, the amount of food stamps he received. Bundle L, by contrast, contains less than $100 worth of food. Here, the effect of the food stamp program is to cause the recipient to spend more on food than he would have if he had instead been given cash.

The face value of the food stamps most participants receive is smaller than what they would spend on food. For these people, the food stamp program leads, as noted, to exactly the same behavior as a pure cash grant program.

If you were planning to spend more than $100 on groceries this month anyway, then getting $100 in food stamps is just as good as getting an extra $100 in cash.

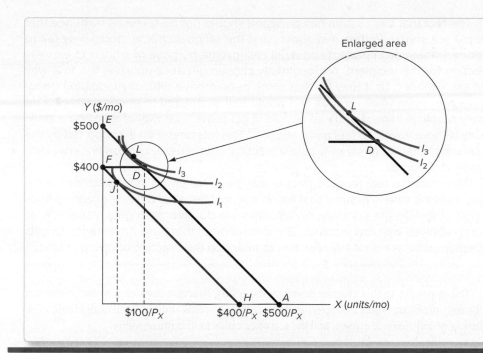

FIGURE 3.19

Where Food Stamps and Cash Grants Yield Different Outcomes

For the consumer whose indifference map is shown, a cash grant would be preferred to food stamps, which force him to devote more to food than he would choose to spend on his own.

The analysis in Example 3.4 raises the question of why Congress did not just give poor people cash grants in the first place. The ostensible reason is that Congress wanted to help poor people buy food, not luxury items or even cigarettes and alcohol. And yet if most participants would have spent at least as much on food as they received in stamps, not being able to use stamps to buy other things is a meaningless restriction. For instance, if someone would have spent $150 on food anyway, getting $100 in food stamps simply lets him take some of the money he would have spent on food and spend it instead on whatever else he chooses.

On purely economic grounds, there is thus a strong case for replacing the food stamp program with a much simpler program of cash grants to the poor. At the very least, this would eliminate the cumbersome step of requiring grocers to redeem their stamps for cash.

As a political matter, however, it is easy to see why Congress might have set things up the way it did. Many taxpayers would be distressed to see their tax dollars used to buy illicit substances. If the food stamp program prevents even a tiny minority of participants from spending more on such goods, it spares many political difficulties.

Example 3.4 calls our attention to a problem that applies not just to the food stamp program but to all other forms of in-kind transfers as well: Although the two forms of transfer are sometimes equivalent, gifts in cash seem clearly superior on those occasions when they differ.

Economic Naturalist 3.1

Why do people often give gifts in kind instead of cash?

Occasionally someone receives a gift that is exactly what he would have purchased for himself had he been given an equivalent amount of money. But we are all far too familiar with gifts that miss the mark. Who has never been given an article of clothing that he was embarrassed to wear? The logic of the rational choice model seems to state unequivocally that we could avoid the problem of useless gifts if we followed the simple expedient of giving cash. And yet virtually every society continues to engage in ritualized gift giving.

The fact that this custom has persisted should not be taken as evidence that people are stupid. Rather, it suggests that the rational choice model may fail to capture something important about gift giving. One purpose of a gift is to express affection for the recipient. A thoughtfully chosen gift accomplishes this in a way that cash cannot. Or it may be that some people have difficulty indulging themselves with even small luxuries and would feel compelled to spend cash gifts on purely practical items. For these people, a gift provides a way of enjoying a small luxury without having to feel guilty about it.[7] This interpretation is supported by the observation that we rarely give purely practical gifts like plain cotton underwear or laundry detergent.

Whatever the real reasons people may have for giving in kind rather than in cash, it seems safe to assume that we do not do it because it never occurred to us to give cash. On the contrary, occasionally we do give cash gifts, especially to young relatives with low incomes. But even though there are advantages to gifts in cash, people seem clearly reluctant to abandon the practice of giving in kind.

The appendix to this chapter develops the utility function approach to the consumer budgeting problem. Topics covered include cardinal versus ordinal utility, algebraic construction of indifference curves, and the use of calculus to maximize utility.

SUMMARY

- Our task in this chapter was to set forth the basic model of rational consumer choice. In all its variants, this model takes consumers' preferences as given and assumes they will try to satisfy them in the most efficient way possible.

- The first step in solving the budgeting problem is to identify the set of bundles of goods the consumer is able to buy. The consumer is assumed to have an income level given in advance and to face fixed prices. Prices and income together define the consumer's budget constraint, which, in the simple two-good case, is a downward-sloping line. Its slope, in absolute value, is the ratio of the two prices. It is the set of all possible bundles that the consumer might purchase if he spends his entire income. *(LO1, LO2)*

- The second step in solving the consumer budgeting problem is to summarize the consumer's preferences. Here, we begin with a preference ordering by which the consumer is able to rank all possible bundles of goods. This ranking scheme is assumed to be complete and transitive and to

exhibit the more-is-better property. Preference orderings that satisfy these restrictions give rise to indifference maps, or collections of indifference curves, each of which represents combinations of bundles among which the consumer is indifferent. Preference orderings are also assumed to exhibit a diminishing marginal rate of substitution, which means that, along any indifference curve, the more of a good a consumer has, the more he must be given to induce him to part with a unit of some other good. The diminishing MRS property accounts for the characteristic convex shape of indifference curves. *(LO3)*

- The budget constraint tells us what combinations of goods the consumer can afford to buy. To summarize the consumer's preferences over various bundles, we use an indifference map. In most cases, the best affordable bundle occurs at a point of tangency between an indifference curve and the budget constraint. At that point, the marginal rate of substitution is exactly equal to the rate at which the goods can be exchanged for one another at market prices. *(LO4)*

KEY TERMS

affordable set	composite good	marginal rate of substitution (MRS)
best affordable bundle	corner solution	preference ordering
budget constraint	indifference curve	
bundle	indifference map	

[7]For a discussion of this interpretation, see R. Thaler, "Mental Accounting and Consumer Choice," *Marketing Science* 4, Summer 1985.

REVIEW QUESTIONS

1. If the prices of all products are rising at 20 percent per year and your employer gives you a 20 percent salary increase, are you better off, worse off, or equally well off in comparison with your situation a year ago? *(LO2)*

2. *True or false:* If you know the slope of the budget constraint (for two goods), you know the prices of the two goods. Explain. *(LO1)*

3. *True or false:* The downward slope of indifference curves is a consequence of the diminishing marginal rate of substitution. *(LO3)*

4. Construct an example of a preference ordering over Coke, Diet Coke, and Diet Pepsi that violates the transitivity assumption. *(LO3)*

5. Explain in your own words how the slope of an indifference curve provides information about how much a consumer likes one good relative to another. *(LO3)*

6. Explain why a consumer will often buy one bundle of goods even though she prefers another. *(LO4)*

7. Why are corner solutions especially likely in the case of perfect substitutes? *(LO4)*

8. *True or false:* If the indifference curve map is concave to the origin, then the optimal commodity basket must occur at a corner equilibrium, except possibly when there are quantity discounts. *(LO4)*

9. If Monique were given $10, she would spend none of it on tuna fish. But when asked, she claims to be indifferent between receiving $10 worth of tuna fish and a $10 bill. How could this be? *(LO4)*

PROBLEMS

Mc Graw Hill connect

1. Acme Seed Company charges $2/lb for the first 10 lb you buy of marigold seeds each week and $1/lb for every pound you buy thereafter. If your income is $100/wk, draw your budget constraint for the composite good and marigold seeds. *(LO1)*

2. Same as Problem 1, except now the price for every pound after 10 lb/wk is $4/lb. *(LO1)*

3. Teagan likes cashews better than almonds and likes almonds better than walnuts. She likes pecans equally well as macadamia nuts and prefers macadamia nuts to almonds. Assuming her preferences are transitive, which does she prefer: *(LO3)*
   a. Pecans or walnuts?
   b. Macadamia nuts or cashews?

4. Originally P_X is $120 and P_Y is $80. *True or false:* If P_X increases by $18 and P_Y increases by $12, the new budget line will be shifted inward and parallel to the old budget line. Explain. *(LO1)*

5. Martha has $150 to spend each week and cannot borrow money. She buys malted milk balls and the composite good. Suppose that malted milk balls cost $2.50 per bag and the composite good costs $1 per unit. *(LO1)*
   a. Sketch Martha's budget constraint.
   b. What is the opportunity cost, in terms of bags of malted milk balls, of an additional unit of the composite good?

6. In Problem 5, suppose that in an inflationary period the price of the composite good increases to $1.50 per unit, but the price of malted milk balls remains the same. *(LO2)*
   a. Sketch the new budget constraint.
   b. What is the opportunity cost of an additional unit of the composite good?

7. In Problem 6, suppose that Martha demands a pay raise to fight the inflation. Her boss raises her salary to $225/wk. *(LO2)*
   a. Sketch the new budget constraint.
   b. What is the opportunity cost of an additional unit of the composite good?

8. Picabo, an aggressive skier, spends her entire income on skis and bindings. She wears out one pair of skis for every pair of bindings she wears out. *(LO3)*
   a. Graph Picabo's indifference curves for skis and bindings.
   b. Now draw her indifference curves on the assumption that she is such an aggressive skier that she wears out two pairs of skis for every pair of bindings she wears out.

9. Suppose Picabo in Problem 8 has $3,600 to spend on skis and bindings each year. Find her best affordable bundle of skis and bindings under both of the preferences described in the previous problem. Skis are $480/pr and bindings are $240/pr. *(LO4)*

10. For Alexi, coffee and tea are perfect substitutes: One cup of coffee is equivalent to one cup of tea. Suppose Alexi has $90/mo to spend on these beverages, and coffee costs $0.90/cup while tea costs $1.20/cup. Find Alexi's best affordable bundle of tea and coffee. How much could the price of a cup of coffee rise without harming her standard of living? *(LO4)*

11. Eve likes apples but doesn't care about pears. If apples and pears are the only two goods available, draw her indifference curves. *(LO3)*

12. Koop likes food but dislikes cigarette smoke. The more food he has, the more he would be willing to give up to achieve a given reduction in cigarette smoke. If food and cigarette smoke are the only two goods, draw Koop's indifference curves. *(LO3)*

13. If you were president of a conservation group, which rate structure would you prefer Gigawatt Power Company to use: the one described in Example 3.1, or one in which all power sold for $0.08/kWh? (Assume that each rate structure would exactly cover the company's costs.) *(LO4)*

14. Paula, a former actress, spends all her income attending plays and movies and likes plays exactly three times as much as she likes movies. *(LO3, LO4)*
    a. Draw her indifference map.
    b. Paula earns $120/wk. If play tickets cost $12 each and movie tickets cost $4 each, show her budget line and highest attainable indifference curve. How many plays will she see?
    c. If play tickets are $12, movie tickets $5, how many plays will she attend?

15. For each of the following, sketch: *(LO3)*
    a. A typical person's indifference curves between garbage and the composite good.
    b. Indifference curves for the same two commodities for Oscar the Grouch on *Sesame Street,* who loves garbage and has no use for the composite good.

16. Boris budgets $9/wk for his morning coffee with milk. He likes it only if it is prepared with 4 parts coffee, 1 part milk. Coffee costs $1/oz, milk $0.50/oz. How much coffee and how much milk will Boris buy per week? How will your answers change if the price of coffee rises to $3.25/oz? Show your answers graphically. *(LO4)*

17. The federal government wants to support education but must not support religion. To this end, it gives the University of Notre Dame $2 million with the stipulation that this money be used for secular purposes only. The accompanying graph shows Notre Dame's pre-federal-gift budget constraint and best attainable indifference curve over secular and nonsecular expenditures. How would the university's welfare differ if the gift came without the secular-use restriction? *(LO4)*

18. Continental Mobile offers an optional call package whereby each month the subscriber gets the first 50 minutes free, the next 100 minutes at $0.25/min, and any additional time at $0.50/min. Draw the budget constraint for cellular minutes and the composite good for a subscriber with an income of $400/mo. *(LO1)*

19. For the Continental Mobile subscriber in Problem 18, what is the opportunity cost of making an additional 20 minutes of calls if he currently makes *(LO1)*
    a. 40 minutes of calls each month?
    b. 140 minutes of calls each month?

20. You have the option of renting a car on a daily basis for $40/day or on a weekly basis for $200/wk. Draw your budget constraint for a budget of $360/trip. *(LO1, LO3, LO4)*
    a. Find your best affordable bundle if your travel preferences are such that you require exactly $140 worth of other goods for each day of rental car consumption.
    b. Alternatively, suppose you view a day of rental car consumption as a perfect substitute for $35 worth of other goods.

21. Tony said that he was exactly indifferent between consuming four slices of pizza and one beer versus consuming three slices of pizza and two beers. He also said that he prefers a bundle consisting of one slice of pizza and three beers to either of the first two bundles. Do Tony's preferences exhibit diminishing marginal rates of substitution? *(LO3)*

22. Your mobile phone company has offered you a choice between the following billing plans: *(LO1)*
    Plan A: Pay $0.05 per call.
    Plan B: Pay an initial $2/wk, which allows you up to 30 calls per week at no charge. Any calls over 30/wk cost $0.05 per call.
    If your income is $12/wk and the composite good costs $1, graph your budget constraints for the composite good and calls under the two plans.

23.* At your school's fund-raising picnic, you pay for soft drinks with tickets purchased in advance—one ticket per bottle of soft drink. Tickets are available in sets of three types:

Small: $3 for 3 tickets
Medium: $4 for 5 tickets
Large: $5 for 8 tickets

If the total amount you have to spend is $12 and fractional sets of tickets cannot be bought, graph your budget constraint for soft drinks and the composite good. *(LO1)*

24.* Consider two Italian restaurants located in identical towns 200 miles apart. The restaurants are identical in every respect but their tipping policies. At one, there is a flat $15 service charge, but no other tips are accepted. At the other, a 15 percent tip is added to the bill. The average food bill at the first restaurant,

exclusive of the service charge, is $100. How, if at all, do you expect the amount of food eaten in the two restaurants to differ? *(LO4)*

25.* Mr. R. Plane, a retired college administrator, consumes only grapes and the composite good $Y(P_Y = \$1)$. His income consists of $10,000/yr from social security, plus the proceeds from whatever he sells of the 2,000 bushels of grapes he harvests annually from his vineyard. Last year, grapes sold for $2/bushel, and Plane consumed all 2,000 bushels of his grapes in addition to 10,000 units of Y. This year the price of grapes is $3/bushel, while P_Y remains $1. If his indifference curves have the conventional shape, will this year's consumption of grapes be greater than, smaller than, or the same as last year's? Will this year's consumption of Y be greater than, smaller than, or the same as last year's? Explain. *(LO4)*

ANSWERS TO SELF-TESTS

3.1 *(LO2)*

3.2 *(LO2)*

3.3 *(LO2)*

3.4 *(LO2)*

3.5 The budget constraint for a residential consumer with Gigawatt Power Company would be kinked outward, as the initial rate for the first 1,000 kWh/mo is lower. For power consumption X up to 1,000 kWh/mo, the budget constraint has a slope of the lower rate $0.05/kWh.

$$Y = 400 - 0.05X \qquad 0 \le X \le 1{,}000 \text{ kWH/mo}$$

For power consumption X above 1,000 kWh/mo, the budget constraint has a slope of the higher rate $0.10/kWh.

$$Y = 450 - 0.10X \qquad X > 1{,}000 \text{ kWH/mo}$$

The kink occurs when $X = 1{,}000$ kWh/mo, where the level of consumption of other goods is $Y = 400 - 0.05X = 400 - 50 = 350$, or equivalently, $Y = 450 - 0.10X = 450 - 100 = 350$. If the rate were instead $0.10/kWh for all kWh that exceeded 1,000 kWh/mo, then the budget constraint for $X > 1{,}000$ kWh/mo would be

$$Y = 400 - 0.10X \qquad X > 1{,}000 \text{ kWh/mo}$$

Problems marked with an asterisk (*) are more difficult.

and would have a discrete jump from $Y = 350$ to $Y = 300$ at $X = 1,000$ kWh/mo. *(LO1, LO2)*

3.6 At bundle A, the consumer is willing to give up 1 lb of food to get an additional square yard of shelter. But at the market prices it is necessary to give up only $\frac{1}{2}$ lb of food to buy an additional square yard of shelter. It follows that the consumer will be better off than at bundle A if he buys 1 lb less of food and 2 sq yd more of shelter. *(LO4)*

3.7 Bailey's budget constraint is $T = 120 - 2B$. Bailey's initial preferences are for two pats of butter for every slice of toast $B = 2T$. Substituting this equation into her budget constraint yields $T = 120 - 4T$, or $5T = 120$, which solves for $T = 24$ slices of toast, and thus $B = 48$ pats of butter each month. Bailey's new preferences are for one pat of butter for every slice of toast $B = T$. Substituting this equation into her budget constraint yields $T = 120 - 2T$, or $3T = 120$, which solves for $T = 40$ slices of toast, and thus $B = 40$ pats of butter each month. Not only has Bailey cut the fat, but she is consuming more fiber too! *(LO3, LO4)*

Jorge Salcedo/Alamy Stock Photo

The Utility Function Approach to the Consumer Budgeting Problem

THE UTILITY FUNCTION APPROACH TO CONSUMER CHOICE

Finding the highest attainable indifference curve on a budget constraint is just one way that economists have analyzed the consumer choice problem. For many applications, a second approach is also useful. In this approach we represent the consumer's preferences not with an indifference map but with a *utility function*.

For each possible bundle of goods, a utility function yields a number that represents the amount of satisfaction provided by that bundle. Suppose, for example, that Tom consumes only food and shelter and that his utility function is given by $U(F, S) = FS$, where F denotes the number of pounds of food, S the number of square yards of shelter he consumes per week, and U his satisfaction, measured in "utils" per week.[1] If $F = 4$ lb/wk and $S = 3$ sq yd/wk, Tom will receive 12 utils/wk of utility, just as he would if he consumed 3 lb/wk of food and 4 sq yd/wk of shelter. By contrast, if he consumed 8 lb/wk of food and 6 sq yd/wk of shelter, he would receive 48 utils/wk.

The utility function is analogous to an indifference map in that both provide a complete description of the consumer's preferences. In the indifference curve framework, we can rank any two bundles by seeing which one lies on a higher indifference curve. In the utility-function framework, we can compare any two bundles by seeing which one yields a greater number of utils. Indeed, as example 3A.1 illustrates, it is straightforward to use the utility function to construct an indifference map.

EXAMPLE 3A.1   Using Utility Function to Construct an Indifference Map

If Tom's utility function is given by $U(F, S) = FS$, graph the indifference curves that correspond to 1, 2, 3, and 4 utils, respectively.

In the language of utility functions, an indifference curve is all combinations of F and S that yield the same level of utility—the same number of utils. Suppose we look at the indifference curve that corresponds to 1 unit of utility—that is, the combinations of bundles for which $FS = 1$. Solving this equation for S, we have

$$S = \frac{1}{F}, \qquad\qquad (3A.1)$$

---

[1]The term "utils" represents an arbitrary unit. As we will see, what is important for consumer choice is not the actual number of utils various bundles provide, but the rankings of the bundles based on their associated utilities.

which is the indifference curve labeled $U = 1$ in Figure 3A.1. The indifference curve that corresponds to 2 units of utility is generated by solving $FS = 2$ to get $S = 2/F$, and it is shown by the curve labeled $U = 2$ in Figure 3A.1. In similar fashion, we generate the indifference curves to $U = 3$ and $U = 4$, which are correspondingly labeled in the diagram. More generally, we get the indifference curve corresponding to a utility level of U_0 by solving $FS = U_0$ to get $S = U_0/F$.

FIGURE 3A.1

Indifference Curves for the Utility Function $U = FS$

To get the indifference curve that corresponds to all bundles that yield a utility level of U_0, set $FS = U_0$ and solve for S to get $S = U_0/F$.

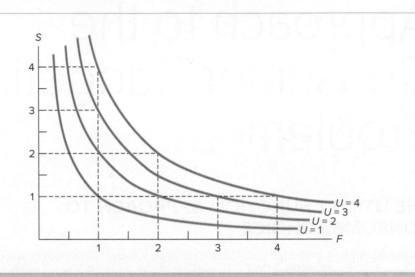

In the indifference curve framework, the best attainable bundle is the bundle on the budget constraint that lies on the highest indifference curve. Analogously, the best attainable bundle in the utility-function framework is the bundle on the budget constraint that provides the highest level of utility. In the indifference curve framework, the best attainable bundle occurs at a point of tangency between an indifference curve and the budget constraint. At the optimal bundle, the slope of the indifference curve, or MRS, equals the slope of the budget constraint. Suppose food and shelter are again our two goods, and P_F and P_S are their respective prices. If $\Delta S/\Delta F$ denotes the slope of the highest attainable indifference curve at the optimal bundle, the tangency condition says that $\Delta S/\Delta F = P_F/P_S$. What is the analogous condition in the utility-function framework?

To answer this question, we must introduce the concept of *marginal utility* (the marginal utility of a good is the rate at which total utility changes with consumption of the good), which is the rate at which total utility changes as the quantities of food and shelter change. More specifically, let MU_F denote the number of additional utils we get for each additional unit of food and MU_S denote the number of additional utils

FIGURE 3A.2

Utility Along an Indifference Curve Remains Constant

In moving from K to L, the loss in utility from having less shelter, $MU_S\Delta S$, is exactly offset by the gain in utility from having more food, $MU_F\Delta F$.

we get for each additional unit of shelter. In Figure 3A.2, note that bundle K has ΔF fewer units of food and ΔS more units of shelter than bundle L. Thus, if we move from bundle K to bundle L, we gain $MU_F \Delta F$ utils from having more food, but we lose $MU_S \Delta S$ utils from having less shelter.

Because K and L both lie on the same indifference curve, we know that both bundles provide the same level of utility. Thus the utility we lose from having less shelter must be exactly offset by the utility we gain from having more food. This tells us that

$$MU_F \Delta F = MU_S \Delta S. \tag{3A.2}$$

Cross-multiplying terms in Equation 3A.2 gives

$$\frac{MU_F}{MU_S} = \frac{\Delta S}{\Delta F}. \tag{3A.3}$$

Suppose that the optimal bundle lies between K and L, which are very close together, so that ΔF and ΔS are both very small. As K and L move closer to the optimal bundle, the ratio $\Delta S / \Delta F$ becomes equal to the slope of the indifference curve at that bundle, which Equation 3A.3 tells us is equal to the ratio of the marginal utilities of the two goods. And since the slope of the indifference curve at the optimal bundle is the same as that of the budget constraint, the following condition must also hold for the optimal bundle:

$$\frac{MU_F}{MU_S} = \frac{P_F}{P_S}. \tag{3A.4}$$

Equation 3A.4 is the condition in the utility-function framework that is analogous to the $MRS = P_F/P_S$ condition in the indifference curve framework.

If we cross-multiply terms in Equation 3A.4, we get an equivalent condition that has a very straightforward intuitive interpretation:

$$\frac{MU_F}{P_F} = \frac{MU_S}{P_S}. \tag{3A.5}$$

In words, Equation 3A.5 tells us that the ratio of marginal utility to price must be the same for all goods at the optimal bundle. The following examples illustrate why this condition must be satisfied if the consumer has allocated his budget optimally.

EXAMPLE 3A.2   Optimal Budget Allocation

Suppose that the marginal utility of the last dollar John spends on food is greater than the marginal utility of the last dollar he spends on shelter. For example, suppose the prices of food and shelter are $1/lb and $2/sq yd, respectively, and that the corresponding marginal utilities are 6 and 4. Show that John cannot possibly be maximizing his utility.

If John bought 1 sq yd/wk less shelter, he would save $2/wk and would lose 4 utils. But this would enable him to buy 2 lb/wk more food, which would add 12 utils, for a net gain of 8 utils.

Abstracting from the special case of corner solutions, a necessary condition for optimal budget allocation is that the last dollar spent on each commodity yield the same increment in utility.

EXAMPLE 3A.3   Optimal Budget Allocation

Mary has a weekly allowance of $10, all of which she spends on newspapers (N) and magazines (M), whose respective prices are $1 and $2. Her utility from these purchases is given by $U(N) + V(M)$. If the values of $u(N)$ and $v(M)$ are as shown in the table, is Mary a utility maximizer if she buys 4 magazines and 2 newspapers each week? If not, how should she reallocate her allowance?

N	$U(N)$	M	$V(M)$
0	0	0	0
1	12	1	20
2	20	2	32
3	26	3	40
4	30	4	44
5	32	5	46

For Mary to be a utility maximizer, extra utility per dollar must be the same for both the last newspaper and the last magazine she purchased. But since the second newspaper provided 8 additional utils per dollar spent, which is four times the 2 utils per dollar she got from the fourth magazine (4 extra utils at a cost of $2), Mary is not a utility maximizer.

N	$U(N)$	$\Delta U(N)$	$\Delta U(N)/P_N$	M	$V(M)$	$\Delta V(M)$	$\Delta V(M)/P_M$
0	0			0	0		
		12	12			20	10
1	12			1	20		
		8	8			12	6
2	20			2	32		
		6	6			8	4
3	26			3	40		
		4	4			4	2
4	30			4	44		
		2	2			2	1
5	32			5	46		

    To see clearly how she should reallocate her purchases, let us rewrite the table to include the relevant information on marginal utilities. From this table, we see that there are several bundles for which $\Delta U(N)/P_N = \Delta V(M)/P_M$—namely, 3 newspapers and 2 magazines; or 4 newspapers and 3 magazines; or 5 newspapers and 4 magazines. The last of these bundles yields the highest total utility but costs $13, and is hence beyond Mary's budget constraint. The first, which costs only $7, is affordable, but so is the second, which costs exactly $10 and yields higher total utility than the first. With 4 newspapers and 3 magazines, Mary gets 4 utils per dollar from her last purchase in each category. Her total utility is 70 utils, which is 6 more than she got from the original bundle.

In Example 3A.3, note that if all Mary's utility values were doubled, or cut by half, she would still do best to buy 4 newspapers and 3 magazines each week. This illustrates the claim that consumer choice depends not on the absolute number of utils associated with different bundles, but instead on the ordinal ranking of the utility levels associated with different bundles. If we double all the utils associated with various bundles, or cut them by half, the ordinal ranking of the bundles will be preserved, and thus the optimal bundle will remain the same. This will also be true if we take the logarithm of the utility function, the square root of it, or add 5 to it, or transform it in any other way that preserves the ordinal ranking of different bundles.

CARDINAL VERSUS ORDINAL UTILITY

In our discussion about how to represent consumer preferences, we assumed that people are able to rank each possible bundle in order of preference. This is called the *ordinal utility* approach to the consumer budgeting problem. It does not require that people be able to make quantitative statements about how much they like various bundles. Thus it assumes that a consumer will always be able to say whether he prefers *A* to *B*, but that he may not be able to make such statements as "*A* is 6.43 times as good as *B*."

In the nineteenth century, economists commonly assumed that people could make such statements. Today we call theirs the *cardinal utility* approach to the consumer choice problem. In the two-good case, it assumes that the satisfaction provided by any bundle can be assigned a numerical, or cardinal, value by a utility function of the form

$$U = U(X, Y), \tag{3A.6}$$

where *X* and *Y* are the two goods.

In three dimensions, the graph of such a utility function will look something like the one shown in Figure 3A.3. It resembles a mountain, but because of the more-is-better assumption, it is a mountain without a summit. The value on the *U* axis measures the height of the mountain, which continues to increase the more we have of *X* or *Y*.

Suppose in Figure 3A.3 we were to fix utility at some constant amount, say, U_0. That is, suppose we cut the utility mountain with a plane parallel to the *XY* plane, U_0 units above it. The line labeled *JK* in Figure 3A.3 represents the intersection of that plane and the surface of the utility mountain. All the bundles of goods that lie on *JK* provide a utility level of U_0. If we then project the line *JK* downward onto the *XY* plane, we have what amounts to the U_0 indifference curve, shown in Figure 3A.4.

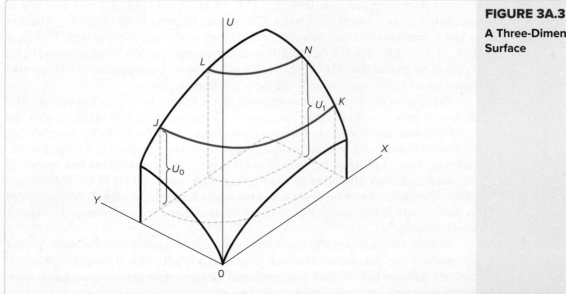

FIGURE 3A.3

A Three-Dimensional Utility Surface

FIGURE 3A.4

Indifference Curves as Projections

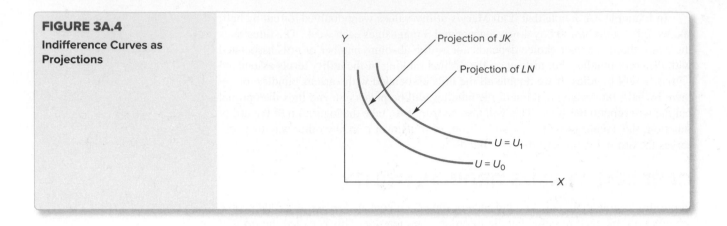

Suppose we then intersect the utility mountain with another plane, this time U_1 units above the XY plane. In Figure 3A.3, this second plane intersects the utility mountain along the line labeled LN. It represents the set of all bundles that confer the utility level U_1. Projecting LN down onto the XY plane, we thus get the indifference curve labeled U_1 in Figure 3A.4. In like fashion, we can generate an entire indifference map corresponding to the cardinal utility function $U(X, Y)$.

Thus we see that it is possible to start with any cardinal utility function and end up with a unique indifference map. *But it is not possible to go in the other direction!* That is, it is not possible to start with an indifference map and work backward to a unique cardinal utility function. The reason is that there will always be infinitely many such utility functions that give rise to precisely the same indifference map.

To see why, just imagine that we took the utility function in Equation 3A.4 and doubled it, so that utility is now given by $V = 2U(X, Y)$. When we graph V as a function of X and Y, the shape of the resulting utility mountain will be much the same as before. The difference will be that the altitude at any X, Y point will be twice what it was before. If we pass a plane $2U_0$ units above the XY plane, it would intersect the new utility mountain in precisely the same manner as the plane U_0 units high did originally. If we then project the resulting intersection down onto the XY plane, it will coincide perfectly with the original U_0 indifference curve.

All we do when we multiply (divide, add to, or subtract from) a cardinal utility function is to relabel the indifference curves to which it gives rise. Indeed, we can make an even more general statement: If $U(X, Y)$ is any cardinal utility function and if V is any increasing function, then $U = U(X, Y)$ and $V = V[U(X, Y)]$ will give rise to precisely the same indifference maps. The special property of an increasing function is that it preserves the rank ordering of the values of the original function. That is, if $U(X_1, Y_1) > U(X_2, Y_2)$, the fact that V is an increasing function assures that $V[U(X_1, Y_1)]$ will be greater than $V[U(X_2, Y_2)]$. And as long as that requirement is met, the two functions will give rise to exactly the same indifference curves.

The concept of the indifference map was first discussed by Francis Edgeworth, who derived it from a cardinal utility function in the manner described above. It took the combined insights of Vilfredo Pareto, Irving Fisher, and John Hicks to establish that Edgeworth's apparatus was not uniquely dependent on a supporting cardinal utility function. As we have seen, the only aspect of a consumer's preferences that matters in the standard budget allocation problem is the shape and location of his indifference curves. Consumer choice turns out to be completely independent of the labels we assign to these indifference curves, provided only that higher curves correspond to higher levels of utility.

Modern economists prefer the ordinal approach because it rests on much weaker assumptions than the cardinal approach. That is, it is much easier to imagine that people can rank different bundles than to suppose that they can make precise quantitative statements about how much satisfaction each provides.

GENERATING INDIFFERENCE CURVES ALGEBRAICALLY

Even if we assume that consumers have only ordinal preference rankings, it will often be convenient to represent those preferences with a cardinal utility index. The advantage is that this procedure provides a compact algebraic way of summarizing all the information that is implicit in the graphical representation of preferences, as we saw in Example 3A.1.

Consider another illustration, this time with a utility function that generates straight-line indifference curves: $U(X, Y) = (\frac{2}{3})X + 2Y$. The bundles of X and Y that yield a utility level of U_0 are again found by solving $U(X, Y) = U_0$ for Y. This time we get $Y = (U_0/2) - (\frac{1}{3})X$. The indifference curves corresponding to $U = 1$, $U = 2$, and $U = 3$ are shown in Figure 3A.5. Note that they are all linear, which tells us that this particular utility function describes a preference ordering in which X and Y are perfect substitutes.

Using Calculus to Maximize Utility

Students who have had calculus are able to solve the consumer's budget allocation problem without direct recourse to the geometry of indifference maps. Let $U(X, Y)$ be the consumer's utility function; and suppose M, P_X, and P_Y denote income, the price of X, and the price of Y, respectively. Formally, the consumer's allocation problem can be stated as follows:

$$\text{Maximize } U(X, Y) \text{ subject to } P_X X + P_Y Y = M. \qquad (3A.7)$$
$$X, Y$$

The appearance of the terms X and Y below the "maximize" expression indicates that these are the variables whose values the consumer must choose. The price and income values in the budget constraint are given in advance.

The Method of Lagrangian Multipliers

As noted earlier, the function $U(X, Y)$ itself has no maximum; it simply keeps on increasing with increases in X or Y. The maximization problem defined in Equation 3A.7 is called a *constrained maximization problem,* which means we want to find the values of X and Y that produce the highest value of U *subject to the constraint that the consumer spend only as much as his income.* We will examine two different approaches to this problem.

One way of making sure that the budget constraint is satisfied is to use the so-called method of *Lagrangian multipliers.* In this method, we begin by transforming the constrained maximization problem in Equation 3A.7 into the following unconstrained maximization problem:

$$\text{Maximize } \pounds = U(X, Y) - \lambda (P_X X + P_Y Y - M). \qquad (3A.8)$$
$$X, Y, \lambda$$

X Y axis graph showing three downward-sloping parallel lines labeled $U = 1$, $U = 2$, and $U = 3$.

FIGURE 3A.5

Indifference Curves for the Utility Function
$U(X, Y) = (\frac{2}{3})X + 2Y$

The indifference curve that corresponds to all bundles yielding a utility level of U_0 is given by $Y = (U_0/2) - (\frac{1}{3})X$.

The term λ is called a Lagrangian multiplier, and its role is to assure that the budget constraint is satisfied. (How it does this will become clear in a moment.) The first-order conditions for a maximum of $\pounds$ are obtained by taking the first partial derivatives of $\pounds$ with respect to X, Y, and λ and setting them equal to zero:

$$\frac{\partial \pounds}{\partial X} = \frac{\partial U}{\partial X} - \lambda P_X = 0, \tag{3A.9}$$

$$\frac{\partial \pounds}{\partial Y} = \frac{\partial U}{\partial Y} - \lambda P_Y = 0, \tag{3A.10}$$

and

$$\frac{\partial \pounds}{\partial \lambda} = M - P_X X - P_Y Y = 0. \tag{3A.11}$$

The next step is to solve Equations 3A.9–3A.11 for X, Y, and λ. The solutions for X and Y are the only ones we really care about here. The role of the equilibrium value of λ is to guarantee that the budget constraint is satisfied. Note in Equation 3A.11 that setting the first partial derivative of $\pounds$ with respect to λ equal to zero guarantees this result.

Specific solutions for the utility-maximizing values of X and Y require a specific functional form for the utility function. We will work through an illustrative example in a moment. But first note that an interesting characteristic of the optimal X and Y values can be obtained by dividing Equation 3A.9 by Equation 3A.10 to get

$$\frac{\partial U/\partial X}{\partial U/\partial Y} = \frac{\lambda P_X}{\lambda P_Y} = \frac{P_X}{P_Y}. \tag{3A.12}$$

Equation 3A.12 is the utility function analog to Equation 3.3 from the text, which says that the optimal values of X and Y must satisfy MRS $= P_X/P_Y$. The terms $\partial U/\partial X$ and $\partial U/\partial Y$ from Equation 3A.12 are called the *marginal utility of X* and the *marginal utility of Y*, respectively. In words, the marginal utility of a good is the extra utility obtained per additional unit of the good consumed. Equation 3A.12 tells us that the ratio of these marginal utilities is simply the marginal rate of substitution of Y for X.

If we rearrange Equation 3A.12 in the form

$$\frac{\partial U/\partial X}{P_X} = \frac{\partial U/\partial Y}{P_Y}, \tag{3A.13}$$

another interesting property of the optimal values of X and Y emerges. In words, the left-hand side of Equation 3A.13 may be interpreted as the extra utility gained from the last dollar spent on X. Equation 3A.13 is thus the calculus derivation of the result shown earlier in Equation 3A.5.

An Example

To illustrate the Lagrangian method, suppose that $U(X, Y) = XY$ and that $M = 40$, $P_X = 4$, and $P_Y = 2$. Our unconstrained maximization problem would then be written as

$$\text{Maximize } \pounds = XY - \lambda(4X + 2Y - 40). \tag{3A.14}$$
$$X, Y, \lambda$$

The first-order conditions for a maximum of $\pounds$ are given by

$$\frac{\partial \pounds}{\partial X} = \frac{\partial(XY)}{\partial X} - 4\lambda = Y - 4\lambda = 0, \tag{3A.15}$$

$$\frac{\partial \pounds}{\partial Y} = \frac{\partial(XY)}{\partial Y} - 2\lambda = X - 2\lambda = 0, \tag{3A.16}$$

and

$$\frac{\partial \pounds}{\partial \lambda} = 40 - 4X - 2Y = 0. \qquad (3A.17)$$

Dividing Equation 3A.15 by Equation 3A.16 and solving for Y, we get $Y = 2X$; substituting this result into Equation 3A.17 and solving for X, we get $X = 5$, which in turn yields $Y = 2X = 10$. Thus (5, 10) is the utility-maximizing bundle.[2]

An Alternative Method

There is an alternative way of making sure that the budget constraint is satisfied, one that involves less cumbersome notation than the Lagrangian approach. In this alternative method, we simply solve the budget constraint for Y in terms of X and substitute the result wherever Y appears in the utility function. Utility then becomes a function of X alone, and we can *maximize* it by taking its first derivative with respect to X and equating that to zero.[3] The value of X that solves that equation is the optimal value of X, which can then be substituted back into the budget constraint to find the optimal value of Y.

To illustrate, again suppose that $U(X, Y) = XY$, with $M = 40$, $P_X = 4$, and $P_Y = 2$. The budget constraint is then $4X + 2Y = 40$, which solves for $Y = 20 - 2X$. Substituting this expression back into the utility function, we have $U(XY) = X(20 - 2X) = 20X - 2X^2$. Taking the first derivative of U with respect to X and equating the result to zero, we have

$$\frac{dU}{dX} = 20 - 4X = 0, \qquad (3A.18)$$

which solves for $X = 5$. Plugging this value of X back into the budget constraint, we discover that the optimal value of Y is 10. So the optimal bundle is again (5, 10), just as we found using the Lagrangian approach. For these optimal values of X and Y, the consumer will obtain $(5)(10) = 50$ units of utility.

Both algebraic approaches to the budget allocation problem yield precisely the same result as the graphical approach described in the text. Note in Figure 3A.6 that the $U = 50$ indifference curve is tangent to the budget constraint at the bundle (5, 10).

A Simplifying Technique

Suppose our constrained maximization problem is of the general form

$$\underset{X,\, Y}{\text{Maximize }} U(X, Y) \text{ subject to } P_X X + P_Y Y = M. \qquad (3A.19)$$

FIGURE 3A.6

The Optimal Bundle when $U = XY$, $P_x = 4$, $P_y = 2$, and $M = 40$

---

[2]The result assumes that the second-order conditions for a local maximum are also met.
[3]Here, the second-order condition for a local maximum is that $d^2U/dX^2 < 0$.

If (X^*, Y^*) is the optimum bundle for this maximization problem, then we know it will also be the optimum bundle for the utility function $V[U(X, Y)]$, where V is any increasing function.[4] This property often enables us to transform a computationally difficult maximization problem into a simple one. By way of illustration, consider the following example:

$$\text{Maximize } X^{1/3}\,Y^{2/3} \text{ subject to } 4X + 2Y = 24. \qquad (3A.20)$$
$$\quad X,\,Y$$

First note what happens when we proceed with the untransformed utility function given in Equation 3A.20. Solving the budget constraint for $Y = 12 - 2X$ and substituting back into the utility function, we have $U = X^{1/3}(12 - 2X)^{2/3}$. Calculating dU/dX *is* a bit tedious in this case, but if we carry out each step carefully, we get the following first-order condition:

$$\frac{dU}{dX} = \left(\tfrac{1}{3}\right)X^{-2/3}(12 - 2X)^{2/3} + X^{1/3}\left(\tfrac{2}{3}\right)(12 - 2X)^{-1/3}(-2) = 0, \qquad (3A.21)$$

which, after a little more tedious rearrangement, solves for $X = 2$. And from the budget constraint we then get $Y = 8$.

Now suppose we transform the utility function by taking its logarithm:

$$V = \ln[U(X, Y)] = \ln(X^{1/3}Y^{2/3}) = \left(\tfrac{1}{3}\right)\ln X + \left(\tfrac{2}{3}\right)\ln Y. \qquad (3A.22)$$

Since the logarithm is an increasing function, when we maximize V subject to the budget constraint, we will get the same answer we got using U. The advantage of the logarithmic transformation here is that the derivative of V is much easier to calculate than the derivative of U. Again, solving the budget constraint for $Y = 12 - 2X$ and substituting the result into V, we have $V = \left(\tfrac{1}{3}\right)\ln X + \left(\tfrac{2}{3}\right)\ln (12 - 2X)$. This time the first-order condition follows almost without effort:

$$\frac{dV}{dX} = \frac{\tfrac{1}{3}}{X} - \frac{2\left(\tfrac{2}{3}\right)}{12 - 2X} = 0, \qquad (3A.23)$$

which solves easily for $X = 2$. Plugging $X = 2$ back into the budget constraint, we again get $Y = 8$.

The best transformation to make will naturally depend on the particular utility function you start with. The logarithmic transformation greatly simplified matters in the example above, but will not necessarily be helpful for other forms of U.

PROBLEMS

1. Mukesh spends all his $100 weekly income on two goods, X and Y. His utility function is given by $U(X, Y) = XY$. If $P_X = 4$ and $P_Y = 10$, how much of each good should he buy?

2. Same as Problem 1, except now Mukesh's utility function is given by $U(X, Y) = X^{1/2}Y^{1/2}$.

3. Note the relationship between your answers in Problems 1 and 2. What accounts for this relationship?

4. Aria consumes only two goods, food and clothing. The marginal utility of the last dollar she spends on food is 12, and the marginal utility of the last dollar she spends on clothing is 9. The price of food is $1.20/unit, and the price of clothing is $0.90/unit. Is Aria maximizing her utility?

5. Miguel has a weekly allowance of $17, all of which he spends on used books (C) and movie rentals (M), whose respective prices are $4 and $3. His utility from these purchases is given by $U(C) + V(M)$. If the values of $U(C)$ and $V(M)$ are as shown in the table, is Miguel a utility maximizer if he buys 2 books and rents 3 movies each week? If not, how should he reallocate his allowance?

C	U(C)	M	V(M)
0	0	0	0
1	12	1	21
2	20	2	33
3	24	3	39
4	28	4	42

[4]Again, an increasing function is one for which $V(X_1) > V(X_2)$ whenever $X_1 > X_2$.

Individual and Market Demand

LEARNING OBJECTIVES

After reading this chapter, you should be able to:

LO1 Show how budget constraints and indifference maps can be used to derive an individual's demand curve.

LO2 Derive an individual's Engel curve and state the difference between normal, inferior, and luxury goods.

LO3 Show how the total effect of a price change can be decomposed into a substitution effect and an income effect.

LO4 Show how to construct the market demand curve for a good as the horizontal sum of the relevant individual demand curves.

LO5 Define the price elasticity of demand for a good and illustrate its use.

LO6 Describe the relationship between price elasticity of demand and how changes in price affect total revenue.

LO7 Describe how the demand for a good may be affected by changes in the distribution of income.

LO8 Define and illustrate income and cross-price elasticities of demand.

A pound of salt costs 30 cents at the grocery store where I shop. My family and I use the same amount of salt at that price as we would if it instead sold for 5 cents/lb or even $10/lb. I also consume about the same amount of salt now as I did as a graduate student, when my income was less than one-tenth as large as it is today.

Salt is an unusual case. The amounts we buy of many other goods are much more sensitive to prices and incomes. For example, when my family and I spent a sabbatical year in New York City, where housing prices are more than four times what they are in Ithaca, we lived in an apartment that was less than half the size of our current house.

CHAPTER PREVIEW

Viewed within the framework of the rational choice model, my behavior with respect to salt and housing purchases is perfectly intelligible. Our focus in this chapter is to use the tools from Chapter 3 to shed additional light on why, exactly, the responses of various purchase decisions to changes in income and price differ so widely. In Chapter 3, we saw how changes in prices and incomes affect the budget constraint. Here we'll see how changes in the budget constraint affect actual purchase decisions. More specifically, we'll use the rational choice model to generate an individual consumer's demand curve for a product and employ our model to construct a relationship that summarizes how individual demands vary with income.

We'll also see how the total effect of a price change can be decomposed into two separate effects: (1) the substitution effect, which denotes the change in the quantity demanded that results because the price change alters the attractiveness of substitute goods, and (2) the income effect, which denotes the change in quantity demanded that results from the change in purchasing power caused by the price change.

Next we'll show how individual demand curves can be added to yield the demand curve for the market as a whole. A central analytical concept we'll developed in this chapter is the price elasticity of demand, a measure of the responsiveness of purchase decisions to small changes in price. We'll also consider the income elasticity of demand, a measure of the responsiveness of purchase decisions to small changes in income. And we'll see that, for some goods, the distribution of income, not just its average value, is an important determinant of market demand.

A final elasticity concept in this chapter is the cross-price elasticity of demand, which is a measure of the responsiveness of the quantity demanded of one good to small changes in the prices of another good. Cross-price elasticity is the criterion by which pairs of goods are classified as being either substitutes or complements.

These analytical constructs provide a deeper understanding of a variety of market behaviors as well as a stronger foundation for intelligent decision and policy analysis.

THE EFFECTS OF CHANGES IN PRICE

The Price-Consumption Curve

Recall from Chapter 2 that a market demand curve tells how much of a good the market as a whole wants to purchase at various prices. Suppose we want to generate a demand schedule for a good—say, shelter—not for the market as a whole but for only a single consumer. Holding income, preferences, and the prices of all other goods constant, how will a change in the price of shelter affect the amount of shelter the consumer buys? To answer this question, we begin with this consumer's indifference map, plotting shelter on the horizontal axis and the composite good Y on the vertical axis. Suppose the consumer's income is $120/wk, and the price of the composite good is again $1 per unit. The vertical intercept of her budget constraint will then be 120. The horizontal intercept will be $120/P_S$, where P_S denotes the price of shelter. Figure 4.1 shows four budget constraints that correspond to four different prices of shelter, namely, $24/sq yd, $12/sq yd, $6/sq yd, and $4/sq yd. The corresponding best afford-able bundles contain 2.5, 7, 15, and 20 sq yd/wk of shelter, respectively. If we were to repeat this procedure for indefinitely many prices, the resulting points of tangency would trace out the line labeled PCC in Figure 4.1. This line is called the **price-consumption curve,** or **PCC.**

price-consumption curve (PCC) holding income and the price of Y constant, the PCC for a good X is the set of optimal bundles traced on an indifference map as the price of X varies.

For the particular consumer whose indifference map is shown in Figure 4.1, note that each time the price of shelter falls, the budget constraint rotates outward, enabling the consumer to purchase not only more shelter but more of the composite good as well. And each time the price of shelter falls, this consumer chooses a bundle that contains more shelter than in the bundle chosen previously. Note, however, that the amount of money spent on the composite good may either rise or fall when the price of shelter falls. Thus, the amount spent on other goods falls when the price of shelter falls from $24/sq yd to

---

FIGURE 4.1

The Price-Consumption Curve
Holding income and the price of Y fixed, we vary the price of shelter. The set of optimal bundles traced out by the various budget lines is called the price-consumption curve, or PCC.

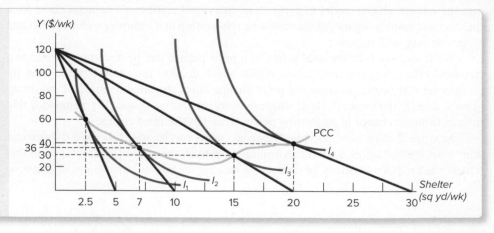

TABLE 4.1
A Demand Schedule

Price of shelter ($/sq yd)	Quantity of shelter demanded (sq yd/wk)
24	2.5
12	7
6	15
4	20

> To derive the individual's demand curve for shelter from the PCC in Figure 4.1, begin by recording the quantities of shelter that correspond to the shelter prices on each budget constraint.

$12/sq yd but rises when the price of shelter falls from $6/sq yd to $4/sq yd. Below, we'll see why this is a relatively common purchase pattern.

The Individual Consumer's Demand Curve

An individual consumer's demand curve is like the market demand curve in that it tells the quantities the consumer will buy at various prices. All the information we need to construct the individual demand curve is contained in the price-consumption curve. The first step in going from the PCC to the individual demand curve is to record the relevant price-quantity combinations from the PCC in Figure 4.1, as in Table 4.1. (Recall from Chapter 3 that the price of shelter along any budget constraint is given by income divided by the horizontal intercept of that budget constraint.)

The next step is to plot the price-quantity pairs from Table 4.1, with the price of shelter on the vertical axis and the quantity of shelter on the horizontal axis. With sufficiently many price-quantity pairs, we generate the individual's demand curve, shown as *DD* in Figure 4.2. Note carefully that in moving from the PCC to the individual demand curve, we are moving from a graph in which both axes measure quantities to one in which price is plotted against quantity.

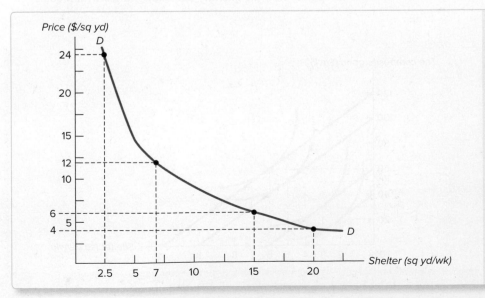

FIGURE 4.2

An Individual Consumer's Demand Curve

Like the market demand curve, the individual demand curve is a relationship that tells how much the consumer wants to purchase at different prices.

THE EFFECTS OF CHANGES IN INCOME

The Income-Consumption Curve

income-consumption curve (ICC) holding the prices of X and Y constant, the ICC for a good X is the set of optimal bundles traced on an indifference map as income varies.

The PCC and the individual demand schedule are two different ways of summarizing how a consumer's purchase decisions respond to variations in prices. Analogous devices exist to summarize responses to variations in income. The income analog to the PCC is the **income-consumption curve, or ICC.** To generate the PCC for shelter, we held preferences, income, and the price of the composite good constant while tracing out the effects of a change in the price of shelter. In the case of the ICC, we hold preferences and relative prices constant and trace out the effects of changes in income.

In Figure 4.3, for example, we hold the price of the composite good constant at $1 per unit and the price of shelter constant at $10/sq yd and examine what happens when income takes the values $40/wk, $60/wk, $100/wk, and $120/wk. Recall from Chapter 3 that a change in income shifts the budget constraint parallel to itself. As before, to each budget there corresponds a best affordable bundle. The set of best affordable bundles is denoted as ICC in Figure 4.3. For the consumer whose indifference map is shown, the ICC happens to be a straight line, but this need not always be the case.

The Engel Curve

Engel curve a curve that plots the relationship between the quantity of X consumed and income.

The analog to the individual demand curve in the income domain is the individual **Engel curve.** It takes the quantities of shelter demanded from the ICC and plots them against the corresponding values of income. Table 4.2 shows the income-shelter pairs for the four budget constraints shown in Figure 4.3. If we were to plot indefinitely many income-consumption pairs for the consumer shown in Figure 4.3, we would trace out the line *EE* shown in Figure 4.4. The Engel curve shown in Figure 4.4 happens to be linear, but Engel curves in general need not be.

Note carefully the distinction between what we measure on the vertical axis of the ICC and what we measure on the vertical axis of the Engel curve. On the vertical axis of the ICC, we measure the amount the consumer spends each week on all goods other than shelter. On the vertical axis of the Engel curve, by contrast, we measure the consumer's total weekly income.

Note also that, as was true with the PCC and individual demand curves, the ICC and Engel curves contain essentially the same information. The advantage of the Engel curve is that it allows us to see at a glance how the quantity demanded varies with income.

FIGURE 4.3

An Income-Consumption Curve

As income increases, the budget constraint moves outward. Holding preferences and relative prices constant, the ICC traces out how these changes in income affect consumption. It is the set of all tangencies as the budget line moves outward.

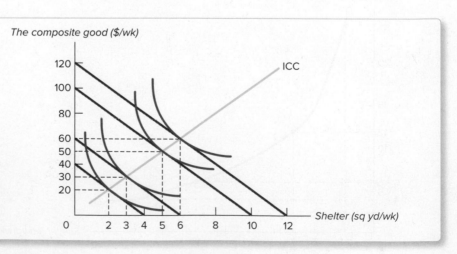

TABLE 4.2
Income and Quantity of Shelter Demanded

Income ($/wk)	Quantity of shelter demanded (sq yd/wk)
40	2
60	3
100	5
120	6

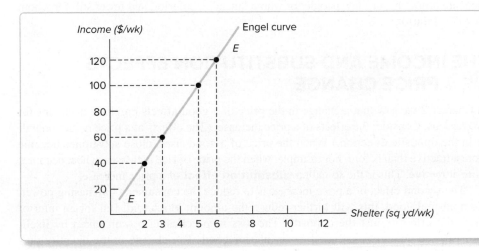

FIGURE 4.4

An Individual Consumer's Engel Curve

Holding preferences and relative prices constant, the Engel curve tells how much shelter the consumer will purchase at various levels of income.

Normal and Inferior Goods

Note that the Engel curve in Figure 4.5a is upward-sloping, implying that the more income a consumer has, the more tenderloin steak he will buy each week. Most things we buy have this property, which is the defining characteristic of a **normal good.** Goods that do not have this property are called **inferior goods.** For such goods, an increase in income leads to a reduction in the quantity demanded. Figure 4.5b is an example of an Engel curve for an inferior good. The more income a person has, the less hamburger he will buy each week.

normal good one whose quantity demanded rises as income rises.

inferior good one whose quantity demanded falls as income rises.

FIGURE 4.5

The Engel Curves for Normal and Inferior Goods

(a) This Engel curve is for a normal good. The quantity demanded increases with income. (b) This Engel curve for hamburger has the negative slope characteristic of inferior goods. As the consumer's income grows, he switches from hamburger to more desirable cuts of meat.

When incomes rise, many consumers switch from low-priced ground beef with high fat content . . .

. . . to leaner, more expensive, cuts of meat.

substitution effect that component of the total effect of a price change that results from the associated change in the relative attractiveness of other goods.

income effect that component of the total effect of a price change that results from the associated change in real purchasing power.

Why would someone buy less of a good following an increase in his income? The prototypical inferior good is one with several strongly preferred, but more expensive, substitutes. Supermarkets, for example, generally carry several different grades of ground beef, ranging from hamburger, which has the highest fat content, to ground sirloin, which has the lowest. A consumer trying to restrict the amount of fat in his diet will switch to a leaner grade of meat as soon as he can afford it. For such a consumer, hamburger is an inferior good.

For any consumer who spends all her income, it is a matter of simple arithmetic that not all goods can be inferior. After all, when income rises, it is mathematically impossible to spend less on all goods at once. It follows that the more broadly a good is defined, the less likely it is to be inferior. Thus, while hamburger is an inferior good for many consumers, there are probably very few people for whom "meat" is inferior, and fewer still for whom "food" is inferior.[1]

THE INCOME AND SUBSTITUTION EFFECTS OF A PRICE CHANGE

In Chapter 2 we saw that a change in the price of a good affects purchase decisions for two reasons. Consider the effects of a price increase. (The effects of a price reduction will be in the opposite direction.) When the price of a good rises, close substitutes become more attractive than before. For example, when the price of rice increases, wheat becomes more attractive. This is the so-called **substitution effect** of a price increase.

The second effect of a price increase is to reduce the consumer's purchasing power. For a normal good, this will further reduce the amount purchased. But for an inferior good, the effect is just the opposite. The loss in purchasing power, taken by itself, increases the quantity purchased of an inferior good. The change in the quantity purchased attributable to the change in purchasing power is called the **income effect** of the price change.

The *total effect* of the price increase is the sum of the substitution and income effects. The substitution effect always causes the quantity purchased to move in the opposite direction from the change in price—when price goes up, the quantity demanded goes down, and vice versa. The direction of the income effect depends on whether the good is normal or inferior. For normal goods, the income effect works in the same direction as the substitution effect—when price goes up [down], the fall [rise] in purchasing power causes the quantity demanded to fall [rise]. For inferior goods, by contrast, the income and substitution effects work against one another.

The substitution, income, and total effects of a price increase can be seen most clearly when displayed graphically. Let us begin by depicting the total effect. In Figure 4.6, the consumer has an initial income of $120/wk and the initial price of shelter is $6/sq yd. This gives rise to the budget constraint labeled B_0, along which the optimal bundle is A, which contains 10 sq yd/wk of shelter. Now let the price of shelter increase from $6/sq yd to $24/sq yd, resulting in the budget labeled B_1. The new optimal bundle is D, which contains 2 sq yd/wk of shelter. The movement from A to D is called the total effect of the price increase. Naturally, the price increase causes the consumer to end up on a lower indifference curve (I_1) than the one he was able to attain on his original budget (I_0).

To decompose the total effect into the income and substitution effects, we begin by asking the following question: How much income would the consumer need to reach his

[1]Another useful way to partition the set of consumer goods is between so-called *necessities* and *luxuries.* A good is defined as a luxury for a person if he spends a larger proportion of his income on it when his income rises. A necessity, by contrast, is one for which he spends a smaller proportion of his income when his income rises. (More on this distinction follows.)

FIGURE 4.6

The Total Effect of a Price Increase

With an income of $120/wk and a price of shelter of $6/sq yd, the consumer chooses bundle A on the budget constraint B_0. When the price of shelter rises to $24/sq yd, with income held constant at $120/wk, the best affordable bundle becomes D. The movement from 10 to 2 sq yd/wk of shelter is called the total effect of the price increase.

original indifference curve (I_0) after the increase in the price of shelter? Note in Figure 4.7 that the answer is $240/wk. If the consumer were given a total income of that amount, it would undo the injury caused by the loss in purchasing power resulting from the increase in the price of shelter. The budget constraint labeled B' is purely hypothetical, a device constructed for the purpose at hand. It has the same slope as the new budget constraint (B_1)—namely, −24—and is just far enough out to be tangent to the original indifference curve, I_0. With the budget constraint B', the optimal bundle is C, which contains 6 sq yd/wk of shelter. The movement from A to C gives rise to the substitution effect of the price change—here a reduction of 4 sq yd/wk of shelter and an increase of 36 units/wk of the composite good.

The hypothetical budget constraint B' tells us that even if the consumer had enough income to reach the same indifference curve as before, the increase in the price of shelter would cause him to reduce his consumption of it in favor of other goods and services. *For consumers whose indifference curves have the conventional convex shape, the substitution*

FIGURE 4.7

The Substitution and Income Effects of a Price Change

To get the substitution effect, slide the new budget B_1 outward parallel to itself until it becomes tangent to the original indifference curve, I_0. The movement from A to C gives rise to the substitution effect, the reduction in shelter due solely to the fact that shelter is now more expensive relative to other goods. The movement from C to D gives rise to the income effect. It is the reduction in shelter that results from the loss in purchasing power implicit in the price increase.

FIGURE 4.8

Income and Substitution Effects for an Inferior Good

In contrast to the case of a normal good, the income effect acts to offset the substitution effect for an inferior good.

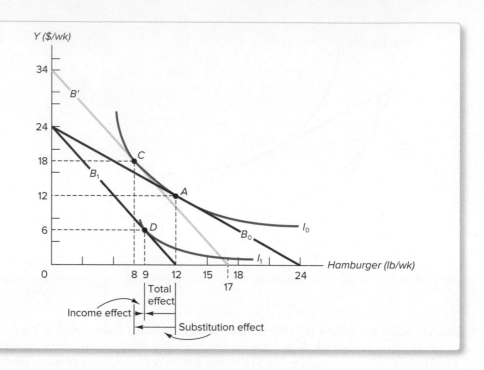

effect of a price increase will always reduce consumption of the good whose price increased.

The income effect stems from the movement from C to D. The particular good shown in Figure 4.7 happens to be a normal good. The hypothetical movement of the consumer's income from \$240/wk to \$120/wk accentuates the reduction of his consumption of shelter, causing it to fall from 6 sq yd/wk to 2 sq yd/wk.

Whereas the income effect reinforces the substitution effect for normal goods, the two effects tend to offset one another for inferior goods. In Figure 4.8, B_0 depicts the budget constraint for a consumer with an income of \$24/wk who faces a price of hamburger of \$1/lb. On B_0 the best affordable bundle is A, which contains 12 lb/wk of hamburger. When the price of hamburger rises to \$2/lb, the resulting budget constraint is B_1 and the best affordable bundle is now D, which contains 9 lb/wk of hamburger. The total effect of the price increase is thus to reduce hamburger consumption by 3 lb/wk. Budget constraint B' once again is the hypothetical budget constraint that enables the consumer to reach the original indifference curve at the new price ratio. Note that the substitution effect (the change in hamburger consumption associated with movement from A to C in Figure 4.8) is to reduce the quantity of hamburger consumed by 4 lb/wk—that is, to reduce it by more than the value of the total effect. The income effect by itself (the change in hamburger consumption associated with the movement from C to D) actually increases hamburger consumption by 1 lb/wk. The income effect thus works in the opposite direction from the substitution effect for an inferior good such as hamburger.

Giffen Goods

Giffen good one for which the quantity demanded rises as its price rises.

A **Giffen good** is one for which the total effect of a price increase is to increase, not reduce, the quantity purchased. Since the substitution effect of a price increase is always to reduce the quantity purchased, the Giffen good must be one whose income effect offsets the substitution effect. That is, the Giffen good must be an inferior good—so strongly inferior, in fact, that the income effect is actually larger than the substitution effect.

Price of potatoes
($/1b)

D

D

Potatoes ($/wk)

FIGURE 4.9

The Demand Curve for a Giffen Good

If a good is so strongly inferior that the income effect of a price increase dominates the substitution effect, the demand curve for that good will be upward sloping. Giffen goods are a theoretical possibility, but are seldom, if ever, observed in practice.

A much-cited example of a Giffen good was the potato during the Irish potato famine of the nineteenth century. The idea was that potatoes were such a large part of poor people's diets to begin with that an increase in their price had a severe adverse effect on the real value of purchasing power. Having less real income, many families responded by cutting back on meat and other more expensive foods, and buying even more potatoes. (See Figure 4.9.) Or so the story goes.

Modern historians dispute whether the potato ever was really a Giffen good. Whatever the resolution of this dispute, the potato story does illustrate the characteristics that a Giffen good would logically have to possess. First, it would not only have to be inferior, but also have to occupy a large share of the consumer's budget. Otherwise, an increase in its price would not create a significant reduction in real purchasing power. (Doubling the price of keyrings, for example, does not make anyone appreciably poorer.) The second characteristic required of a Giffen good is that it have a relatively small substitution effect, one small enough to be overwhelmed by the income effect.

In practice, it is extremely unlikely that a good will satisfy both requirements. Most goods, after all, account for only a tiny share of the consumer's total expenditures. Moreover, as noted, the more broadly a good is defined, the less likely it is to be inferior. Finally, inferior goods by their very nature tend to be ones for which there are close substitutes. The consumer's tendency to substitute ground sirloin for hamburger, for example, is precisely what makes hamburger an inferior good.

The Giffen good is an intriguing anomaly, chiefly useful for testing students' understanding of the subtleties of income and substitution effects. Unless otherwise stated, all demand curves used in the remainder of this text will be assumed to have the conventional downward slope.

EXAMPLE 4.1   Perfect Complements

Suppose skis and bindings are perfect, one-for-one complements and Fatima spends all her equipment budget of $1,200/yr on these two goods. Skis and bindings each cost $200. What will be the income and substitution effects of an increase in the price of bindings to $400 per pair?

Since our goal here is to examine the effect on two specific goods (skis and bindings), we proceed by devoting one axis to each good and dispense with the composite good. On the original budget constraint, B_0, the optimal bundle is denoted A in Figure 4.10. Fatima buys three pairs of skis per year and three pairs of bindings. When the price of bindings rises from $200 per pair to $400 per pair, we get the new budget constraint, B_1, and the resulting optimal bundle D, which contains two pairs of skis per year and two pairs of bindings. An equipment budget of $1,800/yr is what the consumer would need at the new price to attain the same indifference curve she did originally (I_0). (To get this figure, slide B_1 out until it hits I_0, then calculate the cost of buying the bundle at the vertical intercept—here, nine pairs of skis per year at $200 per pair.) Note that because perfect complements have right-angled indifference curves, the budget B' results in an optimal bundle C that is exactly the same as the original bundle A. For perfect complements, the substitution effect is zero. So for this case, the total effect of the price increase is exactly the same as the income effect of the price increase.

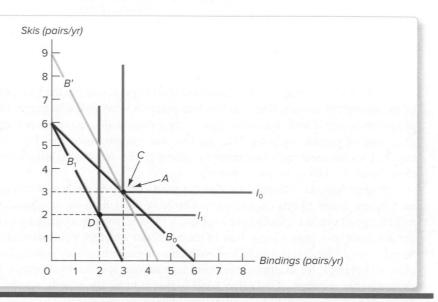

FIGURE 4.10

Income and Substitution Effects for Perfect Complements

For perfect complements, the substitution effect of an increase in the price of bindings (the movement from A to C) is equal to zero. The income effect (the movement from A to D) and the total effect are one and the same.

Example 4.1 tells us that if the price of ski bindings goes up relative to the price of skis, people will not alter the proportion of skis and bindings they purchase. But because the price increase lowers their real purchasing power (i.e., because it limits the quantities of both goods they can buy), they will buy fewer units of ski equipment. The income effect thus causes them to lower their consumption of both skis and bindings by the same proportion.

SELF-TEST 4.1

Repeat Example 4.1 with the assumption that pairs of skis and pairs of bindings are perfect two-for-one complements. (That is, assume that Fatima wears out two pairs of skis for every pair of bindings she wears out.)

EXAMPLE 4.2 | **Perfect Substitutes**

Suppose Elena considers tea and coffee to be perfect one-for-one substitutes and spends $12/wk on these two beverages. Coffee costs $1/cup, while tea costs $1.20/cup. What will be the income and substitution effects of an increase in the price of coffee to $1.50/cup?

Elena will initially demand 12 cups of coffee per week and no cups of tea (point A in Figure 4.11), since each good contributes equally to her utility but tea is more expensive. When the price of coffee rises, Elena switches to consuming only tea, buying 10 cups per week and no coffee (point *D*). Elena would need a budget of $14.40/wk to afford 12 cups of tea (point *C*), which she likes as well as the 12 cups of coffee she originally consumed. The substitution effect is from (12, 0) to (0, 12) and the income effect from (0, 12) to (0, 10), with the total effect from (12, 0) to (0, 10). With perfect substitutes, the substitution effect can be very large: For small price changes (near MRS), consumers may switch from consuming all one good to consuming only the other.

FIGURE 4.11

Income and Substitution Effects for Perfect Substitutes

For perfect substitutes, the substitution effect of an increase in the price of coffee (the movement from *A* to *C*) can be very large.

SELF-TEST 4.2

Starting from the original price in Example 4.2, what will be the income and substitution effects of an increase in the price of tea to $1.50/cup?

Consumer Responsiveness to Changes in Price

We began this chapter with the observation that for certain goods, such as salt, consumption is highly insensitive to changes in price while for others, such as housing, it is much more sensitive. The principal reason for studying income and substitution effects is that they help us understand such differences.

   Consider first the case of salt. When analyzing substitution and income effects, there are two salient features to note about salt. First, for most consumers, it has no close substitutes. If someone were forbidden to shake salt onto his steak, he might respond by shaking a little extra pepper, or even by squeezing some lemon juice onto it. But for most people, these alternatives would fall considerably short of the real thing. Salt's second prominent feature is that it occupies an almost imperceptibly small share of total expenditures. An extremely heavy user of salt might consume a pound every month. If this person's income were $1,200/mo, a doubling of the price of salt—say, from $0.30/lb to $0.60/lb—would increase the share of his budget accounted for by salt from 0.00025 to 0.0005. For all practical purposes, the income effect for salt is negligible.

   In Figure 4.12, the fact that salt has no close substitutes is represented by indifference curves with a nearly right-angled shape. Salt's negligible budget share is captured by the fact that the cusps of these indifference curves occur at extremely small quantities of salt.

   Suppose, as in Figure 4.12, the price of salt is originally $0.30/lb, resulting in the equilibrium bundle *A* in the enlarged region, which contains 1.0002 lb/mo of salt. A price increase to $0.60/lb results in a new equilibrium bundle *D* with 1 lb/mo of salt. The income and substitution effects are measured in terms of the intermediate bundle *C*.

The quantity of salt demanded is highly insensitive to price for two reasons: (1) For many people, there are no attractive substitutes for salt, and (2) salt is so cheap that its price simply isn't worth worrying about.

FIGURE 4.12

Income and Substitution Effects of a Price Increase for Salt

The total effect of a price change will be very small when (1) the original equilibrium bundle lies near the vertical intercept of the budget constraint and (2) the indifference curves have a nearly right-angled shape. The first factor causes the income effect (the reduction in salt consumption associated with the movement from C to D) to be small; the second factor causes the substitution effect (the reduction in salt consumption associated with the movement from A to C) to be small.

▶ Visit your instructor's Connect© course and access your eBook to view this video.

Why do people buy the same amount of (table) salt—even when the price rises substantially?

Geometrically, the income effect is small because the original tangency occurred so near the vertical intercept of the budget constraint. When we are near the pivot point of the budget constraint, even a very large rotation produces only a small movement. The substitution effect, in turn, is small because of the nearly right-angled shape of the indifference curves.

Let us now contrast salt with housing. The two salient facts about housing are that (1) it accounts for a substantial share of total expenditures (more than 30 percent for many people), and (2) most people have considerable latitude to substitute other goods for housing. Many Manhattanites, for example, can afford to live in apartments larger than the ones they now occupy, yet they prefer to spend what they save in rent on restaurant meals, theater performances, and the like. Another substitution possibility is to consume less conveniently located housing. Someone who works in Manhattan can live near her job and pay high rent; alternatively, she can live in New Jersey or Long Island and pay considerably less. Or she can choose an apartment in a less fashionable neighborhood, or one not quite as close to a convenient subway stop. The point is that there are many different options for housing, and the choice among them depends strongly on income and relative prices.

In Figure 4.13, the consumer's income is $120/wk and the initial price of shelter is $0.60/sq yd. The resulting budget constraint is B_0, and the best affordable bundle on it is A, which contains 100 sq yd/wk of shelter. An increase in the price of shelter to $2.40/sq yd causes the quantity demanded to fall to 20 sq yd/wk. The smooth convex shape of the indifference curves represents the high degree of substitution possibilities between housing and other goods and accounts for the relatively large substitution effect (the fall in shelter consumption associated with the movement from A to C). Note also that the original equilibrium bundle, A, was far from the vertical pivot point of the budget constraint. By contrast to the case of salt, here the rotation in the budget constraint caused by the price increase produces a large movement in the location of the relevant segment of the new budget constraint. Accordingly, the income effect for shelter (the fall in shelter consumption associated with the movement from C to D) is much larger than for salt. With both a large substitution and a large income effect working together, the total effect of an increase in the price of shelter (the fall in shelter consumption associated with the movement from A to D) is very large.

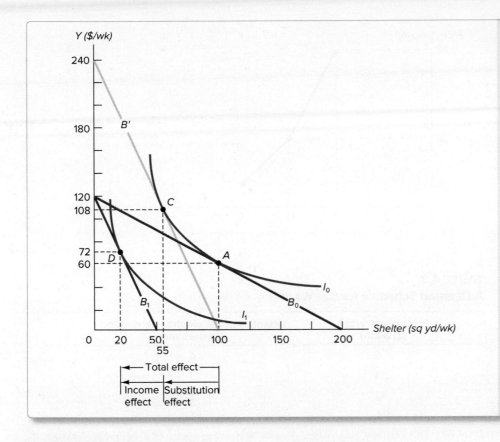

FIGURE 4.13

Income and Substitution Effects for a Price-Sensitive Good

Because shelter occupies a large share of the budget, its income effect tends to be large. And because it is practical to substitute away from shelter, the substitution effect also tends to be large. The quantities demanded of goods with both large substitution and large income effects are highly responsive to changes in price.

EXAMPLE 4.3   Individual Demand Curve for Perfect Complements

James views car washes and gasoline as perfect complements in a 1-to-10 ratio, requiring one car wash for every 10 gallons of gas. Gas costs $3/gal, and James has $144/mo to spend on gas and car washes. (See Figure 4.14.) Construct James's demand curve for car washes by considering his quantity demanded of car washes at various prices (such as $6, $18, and $42; see Figure 4.15).

James's preferences dictate that his optimal bundle must satisfy $G = 10W$, as his indifference curves are L-shaped. James's budget constraint is $3G + P_wW = 144$, or $G = 48 - \frac{Pw}{3}W$. Substituting $G = 10W$, his budget constraint is $30W + P_wW = 144$, which implies $(30 + P_w)W = 144$. At $P_w = 6$, $W = 4$; at $P_w = 18$, $W = 3$; at $P_w = 42$, $W = 2$, as summarized in Table 4.3.

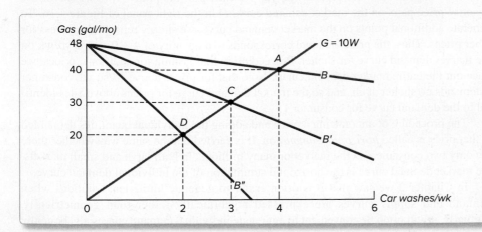

FIGURE 4.14

A Price Increase for Car Washes

With $144/mo, James buys 4 washes/mo when the price is $6/wash (budget constraint B), 3 washes/mo when the price is $18/wash (budget constraint B'), and 2 washes/mo when the price is $42/wash (budget constraint B'').

FIGURE 4.15

James's Demand for Car Washes

The quantity of car washes James demands at various prices forms his demand curve for car washes.

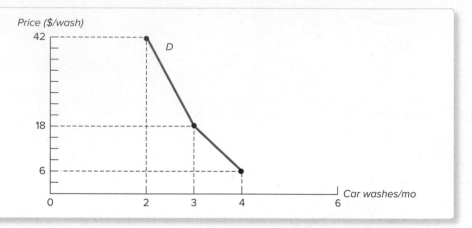

TABLE 4.3

A Demand Schedule for Car Washes

Price of car wash ($/wash)	Quantity of car washes demanded (washes/mo)
6	4
18	3
42	2
114	1

MARKET DEMAND: AGGREGATING INDIVIDUAL DEMAND CURVES

Having seen where individual demand curves come from, we are now in a position to see how individual demand curves may be aggregated to form the market demand curve. Consider a market for a good—for the sake of concreteness, again shelter—with only two potential consumers. Given the demand curves for these consumers, how do we generate the market demand curve? In Figure 4.16, D_1 and D_2 represent the individual demand curves for consumers 1 and 2, respectively. To get the market demand curve, we begin by calling out a price—say, $4/sq yd—and adding the quantities demanded by each consumer at that price. This sum, 6 sq yd/wk + 2 sq yd/wk = 8 sq yd/wk, is the total quantity of shelter demanded at the price $4/sq yd. We then plot the point (4, 8) as one of the quantity-price pairs on the market demand curve D in the right panel of Figure 4.16. To generate additional points on the market demand curve, we simply repeat this process for other prices. Thus, the price $8/sq yd corresponds to a quantity of 4 + 0 = 4 sq yd/wk on the market demand curve for shelter. Proceeding in like fashion for additional prices, we trace out the entire market demand curve. Note that for prices above $8/sq yd, consumer 2 demands no shelter at all, and so the market demand curve for prices above $8 is identical to the demand curve for consumer 1.

The procedure of announcing a price and adding the individual quantities demanded at that price is called *horizontal summation*. It is carried out the same way whether there are only two consumers in the market or many millions. In both large and small markets, the market demand curve is the horizontal summation of the individual demand curves.

In Chapter 2 we saw that it is often easier to generate numerical solutions when demand and supply curves are expressed algebraically rather than geometrically. Similarly, it will often be convenient to aggregate individual demand curves algebraically

FIGURE 4.16

Generating Market Demand from Individual Demands

The market demand curve (D in the right panel) is the horizontal sum of the individual demand curves, D_1 (left panel) and D_2 (center panel).

rather than graphically. When using the algebraic approach, a common error is to add individual demand curves vertically instead of horizontally. A simple example makes this danger clear.

EXAMPLE 4.4   Market Demand

Smith and Jones are the only consumers in the market for beech saplings in a small town in Vermont. Their demand curves are given by $P = 30 - 2Q_J$ and $P = 30 - 3Q_S$ where Q_J and Q_S are the quantities demanded by Jones and Smith, respectively. What is the market demand curve for beech saplings in their town?

When we add demand curves horizontally, we are adding quantities, not prices. Thus it is necessary first to solve the individual demand equations for the respective quantities in terms of price. This yields $Q_J = 15 - (P/2)$ for Jones, and $Q_S = 10 - (P/3)$ for Smith. If the quantity demanded in the market is denoted by Q, we have $Q = Q_J + Q_S = 15 - (P/2) + 10 - (P/3) = 25 - (5P/6)$. Solving back for P, we get the equation for the market demand curve: $P = 30 - (6Q/5)$. We can easily verify that this is the correct market demand curve by adding the individual demand curves graphically, as in Figure 4.17.

FIGURE 4.17

The Market Demand Curve for Beech Saplings

When adding individual demand curves algebraically, be sure to solve for quantity first before adding.

The common pitfall is to add the demand functions as originally stated and then solve for P in terms of Q. Here, this would yield $P = 30 - (5Q/2)$, which is obviously not the market demand curve we are looking for.

SELF-TEST 4.3

Write the individual demand curves for shelter in Figure 4.16 in algebraic form, then add them algebraically to generate the market demand curve for shelter. (*Caution:* Note that the formula for quantity along D_2 is valid only for prices between 0 and 8.)

The horizontal summation of individual consumers' demands into market demand has a simple form when the consumers in the market are all identical. Suppose n consumers each have the demand curve $P = a - bQ_i$. To add up the quantities for the n consumers into market demand, we rearrange the consumer demand curve $P = a - bQ_i$ to express quantity alone on one side $Q_i = a/b - (1/b) P$. Then market demand is the sum of the quantities demanded Q_i by each of the n consumers.

$$Q = nQ_i = n\left(\frac{a}{b} - \frac{1}{b}P\right) = \frac{na}{b} - \frac{n}{b}P.$$

We can then rearrange market demand $Q = na/b - n(P/b)$ to get back in the form of price alone on one side $P = a - (b/n) Q$. The intuition is that each one unit demanded by the market is $1/n$ unit for each consumer. These calculations suggest a general rule for constructing the market demand curve when consumers are identical. If we have n individual consumer demand curves $P = a - bQ_i$, then the market demand curve is $P = a - (b/n)Q$.

EXAMPLE 4.5   Market Demand with Identical Consumers

Suppose a market has 10 consumers, each with demand curve $P = 10 - 5Q_i$, where P is the price in dollars per unit and Q_i is the number of units demanded per week by the ith consumer (Figure 4.18). Find the market demand curve.

FIGURE 4.18

Market Demand with Identical Consumers

When 10 consumers each have demand curve $P = 10 - 5Q_i$, the market demand curve is the horizontal summation $P = 10 - \left(\frac{1}{2}\right)Q$, with the same price intercept and $\frac{1}{10}$ the slope.

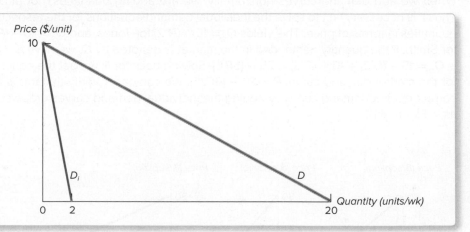

First, we need to rearrange the representative consumer demand curve $P = 10 - 5Q_i$ to have quantity alone on one side:

$$Q_i = 2 - \tfrac{1}{5}P.$$

Then we multiply by the number of consumers, $n = 10$:

$$Q = nQ_i = 10Q_i = 10(2 - \tfrac{1}{5}P) = 20 - 2P.$$

Finally, we rearrange the market demand curve $Q = 20 - 2P$ to have price alone on one side, $P = 10 - \left(\tfrac{1}{2}\right)Q$, to return to the slope-intercept form.

PRICE ELASTICITY OF DEMAND

An analytical tool of central importance is the **price elasticity of demand.** It is a quantitative measure of the responsiveness of purchase decisions to variations in price, and as we'll see in both this and later chapters, it is useful for a variety of practical problems. *Price elasticity of demand is defined as the percentage change in the quantity of a good demanded that results from a 1 percent change in price.* For example, if a 1 percent rise in the price of shelter caused a 2 percent reduction in the quantity of shelter demanded, then the price elasticity of demand for shelter would be −2. The price elasticity of demand will always be negative (or zero) because price changes always move in the opposite direction from changes in quantity demanded.

The demand for a good is said to be *elastic* with respect to price if its price elasticity is less than −1. The good shelter mentioned in the preceding paragraph would thus be one for which demand is elastic with respect to price. The demand for a good is *inelastic* with respect to price if its price elasticity is greater than −1 and *unit elastic* with respect to price if its price elasticity is equal to −1. These definitions are portrayed graphically in Figure 4.19.

When interpreting actual demand data, it is often useful to have a more general definition of price elasticity that can accommodate cases in which the observed change in price does not happen to be 1 percent. Let P be the current price of a good and let Q be the quantity demanded at that price. And let ΔQ be the change in the quantity demanded that occurs in response to a very small change in price, ΔP. The price elasticity of demand at the current price and quantity will then be given by

$$\epsilon = \frac{\Delta Q/Q}{\Delta P/P}. \tag{4.1}$$

The numerator on the right side of Equation 4.1 is the proportional change in quantity. The denominator is the proportional change in price. Equation 4.1 is exactly the same as our earlier definition when ΔP happens to be a 1 percent change in current price. The advantage is that the more general definition also works when ΔP is any other small percentage change in current price.

A Geometric Interpretation of Price Elasticity

Another way to interpret Equation 4.1 is to rewrite it as

$$\epsilon = \frac{\Delta Q}{\Delta P}\frac{P}{Q}. \tag{4.2}$$

price elasticity of demand the percentage change in the quantity of a good demanded that results from a 1 percent change in its price.

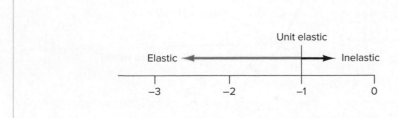

FIGURE 4.19

Three Categories of Price Elasticity

With respect to price, the demand for a good is elastic if its price elasticity is less than −1, inelastic if its price elasticity exceeds −1, and unit elastic if its price elasticity is equal to −1.

Equation 4.2 suggests a simple interpretation in terms of the geometry of the market demand curve. When ΔP is small, the ratio $\Delta P / \Delta Q$ is the slope of the demand curve, which means that the ratio $\Delta Q / \Delta P$ is the reciprocal of that slope. Thus the price elasticity of demand may be interpreted as the product of the ratio of price to quantity and the reciprocal of the slope of the demand curve:[2]

$$\epsilon = \frac{P}{Q} \frac{1}{\text{slope}}. \qquad (4.3)$$

Equation 4.3 is called the *point-slope method* of calculating price elasticity of demand. By way of illustration, consider the demand curve for shelter shown in Figure 4.20. Because this demand curve is linear, its slope is the same at every point, namely, -2. The reciprocal of this slope is $-\frac{1}{2}$. The price elasticity of demand at point A is therefore given by the ratio of price to quantity at A $\left(\frac{12}{2}\right)$ multiplied by the reciprocal of the slope at A $\left(-\frac{1}{2}\right)$, so we have $\epsilon_A = \left(\frac{12}{2}\right)\left(-\frac{1}{2}\right) = -3$.

When the market demand curve is linear, as in Figure 4.20, several properties of price elasticity quickly become apparent from this interpretation. The first is that the price elasticity is different at every point along the demand curve. More specifically, we know that the slope of a linear demand curve is constant throughout, which means that the reciprocal of its slope is also constant. The ratio of price to quantity, by contrast, takes a different value at every point along the demand curve. As we approach the vertical intercept, it approaches infinity. It declines steadily as we move downward along the demand curve, finally reaching a value of zero at the horizontal intercept.

A second property of demand elasticity is that it is never positive. As noted earlier, because the slope of the demand curve is always negative, its reciprocal must also be negative; and because the ratio P/Q is always positive, it follows that the price elasticity of demand—which is the product of these two—must always be a negative number (except at the horizontal intercept of the demand curve, where P/Q, and hence elasticity, is zero). For the sake of convenience, however, economists often ignore the negative sign of price elasticity and refer simply to its absolute value. When a good is said to have a "high" price elasticity of demand, this will always mean that its price elasticity is large in absolute value, indicating that the quantity demanded is highly responsive to changes in price. Similarly, a good whose price elasticity is said to be "low" is one for which the absolute value of elasticity is small, indicating that the quantity demanded is relatively unresponsive to changes in price.

A third property of price elasticity at any point along a straight-line demand curve is that it will be inversely related to the slope of the demand curve. The steeper the demand curve,

FIGURE 4.20

The Point-Slope Method

The price elasticity of demand at any point is the product of the price-quantity ratio at that point and the reciprocal of the slope of the demand curve at that point. The price elasticity at A is thus $\left(\frac{12}{2}\right)\left(-\frac{1}{2}\right) = -3$.

[2]In calculus terms, price elasticity is defined as $\epsilon = (P/Q)[dQ(P)/dP]$.

FIGURE 4.21

Two Important Polar Cases

(a) The price elasticity of the demand curve is equal to $-\infty$ at every point. Such demand curves are said to be perfectly elastic. (b) The price elasticity of the demand curve is equal to 0 at every point. Such demand curves are said to be perfectly inelastic.

the less elastic is demand at any point along it. This follows from the fact that the reciprocal of the slope of the demand curve is one of the factors used to compute price elasticity.

SELF-TEST 4.5

Use the point-slope method (Equation 4.3) to determine the elasticity of the demand curve $P = 32 - Q$ at the point where $P = 24$.

Two polar cases of demand elasticity are shown in Figure 4.21. In Figure 4.21a, the horizontal demand curve, with its slope of zero, has an infinitely high price elasticity at every point. Such demand curves are often called *perfectly elastic* and, as we will see, are especially important in the study of competitive firm behavior. In Figure 4.21b, the vertical demand curve has a price elasticity everywhere equal to zero. Such curves are called *perfectly inelastic.*

As a practical matter, it would be impossible for any demand curve to be perfectly inelastic at all prices. Beyond some sufficiently high price, income effects must curtail consumption, even for seemingly essential goods with no substitutes, such as surgery for malignant tumors. Even so, the demand curve for many such goods and services will be perfectly inelastic over an extremely broad range of prices (recall the salt example discussed earlier in this chapter).

The Unit-Free Property of Elasticity

Another way of measuring responsiveness to changes in price is to use the slope of the demand curve. Other things equal, for example, we know that the quantity demanded of a good with a steep demand curve will be less responsive to changes in price than will one with a less steep demand curve.

Since the slope of a demand curve is much simpler to calculate than its elasticity, it may seem natural to ask, "Why bother with elasticity at all?" One reason is that the slope of the demand curve is sensitive to the units we use to measure price and quantity, while elasticity is not. By way of illustration, notice in Figure 4.22a that when the price of gasoline is measured in $/gal, the slope of the demand curve at point C is −0.02. By contrast, in Figure 4.22b, where price is measured in $/oz, the slope at C is −0.00015625. In both cases, however, note that the price elasticity of demand at C is −3. This will be true no matter how we measure price and quantity. And most people find it much more informative to know that a 1 percent cut in price will lead to a 3 percent increase in the quantity demanded than to know that the slope of the demand curve is −0.00015625.

Some Representative Elasticity Estimates

As the entries in Table 4.4 show, the price elasticities of demand for different products vary substantially, both between and within categories of goods and between different

When weighing costs and benefits, always compare absolute dollar amounts, not proportions. But when describing how quantity demanded responds to changes in price, it's generally best to speak in terms of proportions.

FIGURE 4.22

Elasticity Is Unit-Free

The slope of the demand curve at any point depends on the units in which we measure price and quantity. The slope at point C when we measure the price of gasoline in dollars per gallon (a) is much larger than when we measure the price in dollars per ounce (b). The price elasticity at any point, by contrast, is completely independent of units of measure.

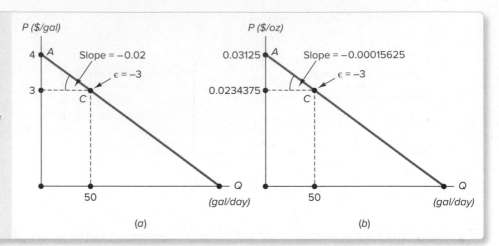

(a) (b)

TABLE 4.4

Price Elasticity of Demand for Selected Products

Good or service*	Price elasticity
Fresh green peas[a]	−2.80
Air travel (vacation)[g]	−1.90
Pork[f]	−1.26
Beer[b]	−1.20
Chicken[f]	−0.81
Air travel (nonvacation)[g]	−0.80
Fruits and vegetables[f]	−0.79
FAFH and alcohol[f]	−0.71
Meat and eggs[f]	−0.31
Cigarettes[c]	−0.25
Cannabis (1972)[e]	−1.00
Cannabis (2017)[d]	−0.42

*Some of these short-run elasticity estimates represent the midpoint of a corresponding range of estimates. Keyed sources are:

[a]Patrick L. Anderson, Richard D. McLellan, Joseph P. Overton, and Gary L. Wolfram, "Price Elasticity of Demand," McKinac Center for Public Policy, 1997, accessed October 13 (1997), 2010. https://scholar.harvard.edu/files/alada/files/price_elasticity_of_demand_handout.pdf.

[b]K. Elzinga, "The Beer Industry," in Walter Adams (Ed.), *The Structure of American Industry*, New York: Macmillan, 1977.

[c]Matthew C. Farrelly and Jeremy W. Bray. "Response to Increases in Cigarette Prices by Race/Ethnicity, Income, and Age Groups—United States, 1976–1993," *Morbidity and Mortality Weekly Report* 47, no. 29, 1998, 605–609.

[d]Dennis Halcoussis, Anton D. Lowenberg, and Zach Roof, "Estimating the Price Elasticity of Demand for Cannabis: A Geographical and Crowdsourced Approach," *Revista de Métodos Cuantitativos para la Economía y la Empresa* 23, 2017, 119–136.

[e]Charles T. Nisbett and Firouz Vakil, "Some Estimates of Price and Expenditure Elasticities of Demand for Marijuana among UCLA Students," *Review of Economics and Statistics*, 1972, 473–475.

[f]Abigail M. Okrent and Julian M. Alston, "The Demand for Disaggregated Food-Away-from-Home and Food-at-Home Products in the United States," ERR-139, U.S. Department of Agriculture, Economic Research Service, August 2012.

[g]Tae H. Oum, W.G. Waters II, and Jong Say Yong, "A Survey of Recent Estimates of Price Elasticities of Demand for Transport," World Bank Infrastructure and Urban Development Department Working Paper, January 1990.

levels within a category. Within the travel category, leisure air travel is more elastic than business travel. Among foods, pork is more elastic than chicken, but because pork and chicken are substitutes, both are more elastic than the parent "meat and eggs" category. We see an extreme example in fresh green peas, which are several levels down in the USDA classification from "fruits and vegetables" and which, at their level, have so many substitutes that they are 3.5 times as elastic as the broad category.

Price elasticities are also sensitive to categorization—is the FAFH ("food way from home") category distorted by the inclusion of alcohol?—and, since elasticities change as social and economic behaviors change, to time. Note that recent estimates for cannabis suggest that it is far more inelastic than when it first hit the radar in the 1960s.

You might ask, given that the price elasticity of demand is different at every point along a linear demand curve, how it is possible to publish "representative" single-value elasticities, as we do in Table 4.4. One explanation is that we calculate representative elasticities using small price changes occurring within a fairly narrow band of "normal" prices. A more technical explanation is that for this work economists use special "constant elasticity" demand curves that allow elasticities to be estimated using statistical techniques. (We will examine constant elasticity demand curves in the appendix to this chapter.)

Demand measurement is a complex area of economics. But, while different studies may produce strikingly different results—depending on the type of categorization, the level of aggregation, method of estimation, and the quality and frequency of data— regularities are observed, especially among broad categories of goods. Transportation, shelter, and "miscellaneous" have the highest elasticities, food and utilities the lowest.[3] Broad categories are less elastic than their components. And, as we shall see, long-run elasticities can be higher than the short-run response would indicate.

ELASTICITY AND TOTAL EXPENDITURE

Suppose you are the administrator in charge of setting tolls for the Golden Gate Bridge, which links San Francisco to Marin County. Suppose that with the toll at $3/trip, 100,000 trips per hour are taken across the bridge. If the price elasticity of demand for trips is −2.0, what will happen to the number of trips taken per hour if you raise the toll by 10 percent? With an elasticity of −2.0, a 10 percent increase in price will produce a 20 percent reduction in quantity. Thus the number of trips will fall to 80,000/hr. Total expenditure at the higher toll will be (80,000 trips/hr)($3.30/trip) = $264,000/hr. Note that this is smaller than the total expenditure of $300,000/hr that occurred under the $3 toll.

Now suppose that the price elasticity had been not −2.0 but −0.5. How would the number of trips and total expenditure then be affected by a 10 percent increase in the toll? This time the number of trips will fall by 5 percent to 95,000/hr, which means that total expenditure will rise to (95,000 trips/hr)($3.30/trip) = $313,500/hr. If your goal as an administrator is to increase the total revenue collected from the bridge toll, you need to know something about the price elasticity of demand before deciding whether to raise the toll or lower it.

This example illustrates the important relationships between price elasticity and total expenditure. The questions we want to be able to answer are of the form, "If the price of a product changes, how will total spending on the product be affected?" and "Will more be spent if we sell more units at a lower price or fewer units at a higher price?" In Figure 4.23, for example, we might want to know how total expenditures for shelter are affected when the price falls from $12/sq yd to $10/sq yd.

The total expenditure, R, at any quantity-price pair (Q, P) is given by the product

$$R = PQ. \tag{4.4}$$

In Figure 4.23, the total expenditure at the original quantity-price pair is thus ($12/sq yd)(4 sq yd/wk) = $48/wk. Geometrically, it is the sum of the two shaded areas E and

[3]Lester D. Taylor and Hendrik S. Houthakker, *Consumer Demand in the United States: Prices, Incomes, and Consumer Behavior*, 3rd ed., New York: Springer, 2010, 138.

FIGURE 4.23

The Effect on Total Expenditure of a Reduction in Price

When price falls, people spend less on existing units (*E*). But they also buy more units (*G*). Here, *G* is larger than *E,* which means that total expenditure rises.

F. Following the price reduction, the new total expenditure is ($10/sq yd)(6 sq yd/wk) = $60/wk, which is the sum of the shaded areas *F* and *G.* These two total expenditures have in common the shaded area *F.* The change in total expenditure is thus the difference in the two shaded areas *E* and *G.* The area *E,* which is ($2/sq yd)(4 sq yd/wk) = $8/wk, may be interpreted as the reduction in expenditure caused by selling the original 4 sq yd/wk at the new, lower price. *G,* in turn, is the increase in expenditure caused by the additional 2 sq yd/wk of sales. This area is given by ($10/sq yd) (2 sq yd/wk) = $20/wk. Whether total expenditure rises or falls thus boils down to whether the gain from additional sales exceeds the loss from lower prices. Here, the gain exceeds the loss by $12, so total expenditure rises by that amount following the price reduction.

If the change in price is small, we can say how total expenditure will move if we know the initial price elasticity of demand. Recall that one way of expressing price elasticity is the percentage change in quantity divided by the corresponding percentage change in price. If the absolute value of that quotient exceeds 1, we know that the percentage change in quantity is larger than the percentage change in price. And when that happens, the increase in expenditure from additional sales will always exceed the reduction from sales of existing units at the lower price. In Figure 4.23, note that the elasticity at the original price of $12 is 3.0, which confirms our earlier observation that the price reduction led to an increase in total expenditure. Suppose, on the contrary, that price elasticity is less than unity. Then the percentage change in quantity will be smaller than the corresponding percentage change in price, and the additional sales will not compensate for the reduction in expenditure from sales at a lower price. Here, a price reduction will lead to a reduction in total expenditure.

SELF-TEST 4.6

For the demand curve in Figure 4.23, what is the price elasticity of demand when *P* = $4/sq yd? What will happen to total expenditure on shelter when price falls from $4/sq yd to $3/sq yd?

The general rule for small price reductions, then, is this: *A price reduction will increase total revenue if and only if the absolute value of the price elasticity of demand is greater than 1.* Parallel reasoning leads to an analogous rule for small price increases: *An increase in price will increase total revenue if and only if the absolute value of the price elasticity is less than 1.* These rules are summarized in the top panel of Figure 4.24, where the point *M* is the midpoint of the demand curve.

FIGURE 4.24

Demand and Total Expenditure

When demand is elastic, total expenditure changes in the opposite direction from a change in price. When demand is inelastic, total expenditure and price both move in the same direction. At the midpoint of the demand curve (*M*), total expenditure is at a maximum.

The relationship between elasticity and total expenditure is spelled out in greater detail in the relationship between the top and bottom panels of Figure 4.24. The top panel shows a straight-line demand curve. For each quantity, the bottom panel shows the corresponding total expenditure. As indicated in the bottom panel, total expenditure starts at zero when Q is zero and increases to its maximum value at the quantity corresponding to the midpoint of the demand curve (point M in the top panel). At that quantity, price elasticity is unity. Beyond that quantity, total expenditure declines with output, reaching zero at the horizontal intercept of the demand curve.

EXAMPLE 4.6   Market Demand for Transit

The market demand curve for bus rides in a small community is given by $P = 100 - (Q/10)$, where P is the fare per ride in cents and Q is the number of rides each day. If the price is 50 cents/ride, how much revenue will the transit system collect each day? What is the price elasticity of demand for rides? If the system needs more revenue, should it raise or lower price? How would your answers have differed if the initial price had been not 50 cents/ride but 75?

Total revenue for the bus system is equal to total expenditure by riders, which is the product PQ. First we solve for Q from the demand curve and get $Q = 1,000 - 10P$. When P is 50 cents/ride, Q will be 500 rides/day and the resulting total revenue will be \$250/day. To compute the price elasticity of demand, we can use the formula $\epsilon = (P/Q)(1/slope)$. Here the slope is $-\frac{1}{10}$, so $1/slope = -10$ (see footnote 4). P/Q takes the value $50/500 = \frac{1}{10}$. Price elasticity is thus the product $\left(-\frac{1}{10}\right)(10) = -1$. With a price elasticity of unity, total revenue attains its maximum value. If the bus company either raises or lowers its price, it will earn less than it does at the current price.

At a price of 50 cents, the company was operating at the midpoint of its demand curve. If the price had instead been 75 cents, it would be operating above the midpoint. More precisely, it would be halfway between the midpoint and the vertical

---

[4]The slope here is from the formula $P = 100 - (Q/10)$.

intercept (point *K* in Figure 4.25). Quantity would be only 250 rides/day, and price elasticity would have been −3 (computed, for example, by multiplying the price-quantity ratio at *K*, $-\frac{3}{10}$, by the reciprocal of the demand curve slope, $-\frac{1}{10}$). Operating at an elastic point on its demand curve, the company could increase total revenue by cutting its price.

FIGURE 4.25

The Demand for Bus Rides

At a price of 50 cents/ride, the bus company is maximizing its total revenues. At a price of 75 cents/ride, demand is elastic with respect to price, and so the company can increase its total revenues by cutting its price.

Determinants of Price Elasticity of Demand

What factors influence the price elasticity of demand for a product? Our earlier discussion of substitution and income effects suggests primary roles for the following factors:

■ **Substitution possibilities.**   The substitution effect of a price change tends to be small for goods with no close substitutes. Consider, for example, the vaccine against rabies. People who have been bitten by rabid animals have no substitute for this vaccine, so demand for it is highly inelastic. We saw that the same was true for a good such as salt. But consider now the demand for a particular brand of salt, say, Morton's. Despite the advertising claims of salt manufacturers, one brand of salt is a more-or-less perfect substitute for any other. Because the substitution effect between specific brands is large, a rise in the price of one brand should sharply curtail the quantity of it demanded. In general, the absolute value of price elasticity will rise with the availability of attractive substitutes.

■ **Budget share.**   The larger the share of total expenditures accounted for by the product, the more important will be the income effect of a price change. Goods such as salt, rubber bands, cellophane wrap, and a host of others account for such small shares of total expenditures that the income effects of a price change are likely to be negligible. For goods like housing and higher education, by contrast, the income effect of a price increase is likely to be large. In general, the smaller the share of total expenditure accounted for by a good, the less elastic demand will be.

■ **Direction of income effect.**   A factor closely related to the budget share is the direction—positive or negative—of its income effect. While the budget share tells us whether the income effect of a price change is likely to be large or small, the direction of the income effect tells us whether it will offset or reinforce the substitution effect. Thus, a normal good will have a higher price elasticity than an inferior good, other things equal, because the income effect reinforces the substitution effect for a normal good but offsets it for an inferior good.

■ **Time.**   Our analysis of individual demand did not focus explicitly on the role of time. But it too has an important effect on responses to changes in prices. Consider the oil price increases of recent years. One possible response is simply to drive less. But many auto trips cannot be abandoned, or even altered, very quickly. A person cannot simply stop going to work, for example. He can cut down on his daily commute by joining a car pool or by purchasing a house closer to where he works. He can also curtail his gasoline consumption by trading in his current car for one that gets better mileage. But all these steps take time, and as a result, the demand for gasoline will be much more elastic in the long run than in the short run.

The short- and long-run effects of a supply shift in the market for gasoline are contrasted in Figure 4.26. The initial equilibrium at A is disturbed by a supply reduction from S to S'. In the short run, the effect is for price to rise to P_{SR} = $6.00/gal and for quantity to fall to Q_{SR} = 5 million gal/day. The long-run demand curve is more elastic than the short-run demand curve. As consumers have more time to adjust, therefore, price effects tend to moderate while quantity effects tend to become more pronounced. Thus the new long-run equilibrium in Figure 4.26 occurs at a price of P_{LR} = $5/gal and a quantity of Q_{LR} = 4 million gal/day.

What is the price elasticity of demand for gasoline? Summarizing then-recent research, Paul Krugman, in 2008, reported internationally averaged short- and long-run figures of –0.30 and –0.70. Levin, Lewis, and Wolak confirmed the short-run figure for the United States in 2017, using high-frequency price data. The confirmation is particularly important, because the U.S. Energy Information Administration published estimates in 2014 that the short-run figure could be as low as –0.02.[5]

Sometimes we see extreme differences between short- and long-run price elasticity values. Hendrik Houthakker and Lester Taylor, in their famous 1970 survey of U.S. consumer price behavior, suggested that for household natural gas, the short-run price elasticity was –0.15, but the long-run was –10.74![6] But the 1930–1965 data used by the authors reflected a period where natural gas was rapidly displacing coal as a household heating option. According to the U.S. Census Bureau, natural gas climbed from heating 11.3 percent of U.S. homes in 1940 to 55.2 percent in 1940.[7] More recent studies, covering periods where natural

The price of elasticity of demand for gasoline is higher in the long run because when the price of gasoline rises, it takes time for people to switch from inefficient vehicles . . .

. . . to more efficient ones.

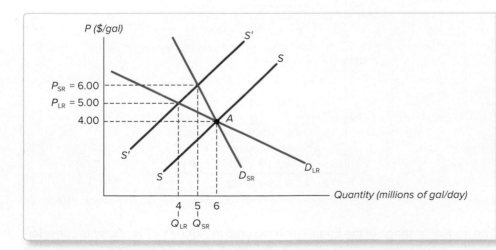

FIGURE 4.26

Price Elasticity Is Greater in the Long Run Than in the Short Run

The more time people have, the more easily they can switch to substitute products. The price effects of supply alterations are therefore always more extreme in the short run than in the long run.

[5]See Paul Krugman, "Gas Price Elasticities," *New York Times*, June 9, 2008, https://economistsview.typepad.com/economistsview/2008/06/gas-price-elast.html. For a survey of gasoline demand studies, see Carol A. Dahl, "What Do We Know about Gasoline Demand Elasticities?" Colorado School of Mines Working Paper, 2006, http://dahl.mines.edu/courses/dahl/dedd/dahl_g06.pdf. A new and innovative study is Laurence Levin, Matthew S. Lewis, and Frank A. Wolak, "High Frequency Evidence on the Demand for Gasoline," *American Economic Journal: Economic Policy* 9, no. 3, 2017, 314–347. For the USEIA report, see Michael Morris, "Gasoline Prices Tend to Have Little Effect on Demand for Car Travel," *Today in Energy*, U.S. Energy Information Administration, December 15, 2104, https://www.eia.gov/todayinenergy/detail.php?id=19191.
[6]H. S. Houthakker and Lester D. Taylor, *Consumer Demand in the United States: Analyses and Projections*, 2nd ed., Cambridge, MA: Harvard University Press, 1970, 86.
[7]www.census.gov/hhes/www/housing/census/historic/fuels.html.

gas use was more stable, have found short-run elasticities in the range of –0.1 to –0.2 and long-run elasticities in the range of –0.3 to –0.4. The figures are very similar to house-hold electricity, –0.9 and –0.27.[8]

THE DEPENDENCE OF MARKET DEMAND ON INCOME

As we have seen, the quantity of a good demanded by any person depends not only on its price but also on the person's income. Since the market demand curve is the horizontal sum of individual demand curves, it too will be influenced by consumer incomes. In some cases, the effect of income on market demand can be accounted for completely if we know only the average income level in the market. This would be the case, for example, if all consumers in the market were alike in terms of preference and all had the same incomes.

In practice, however, a given level of average income in a market will sometimes give rise to different market demands depending on how income is distributed. A simple example helps make this point clear.

EXAMPLE 4.7   The Engel Curve

Two consumers, A and B, are in a market for food. Their tastes are identical, and each has the same initial income level, $120/wk. If their individual Engel curves for food are as given by EE in Figure 4.27, how will the market demand curve for food be affected if A's income goes down by 50 percent while B's goes up by 50 percent?

FIGURE 4.27

The Engel Curve for Food of *A* and *B*

When individual Engel curves take the nonlinear form shown, the increase in food consumption that results from a given increase in income will be smaller than the reduction in food consumption that results from an income reduction of the same amount.

The nonlinear shape of the Engel curve pictured in Figure 4.27 is plausible consider-ing that a consumer can eat only so much food. Beyond some point, increases in income should have no appreciable effect on the amount of food consumed. The implication is that *B*'s new income ($180/wk) will produce an increase in his con-sumption (2 lb/wk) that is smaller than the reduction in *A*'s consumption (4 lb/wk) caused by *A*'s new income ($60/wk).

---

[8]Vipin Arora, "Estimates of the Price Elasticities of Natural Gas Supply and Demand in the United States," 2014, https://mpra.ub.uni-muenchen.de/54232/; and Tatyana Deryugina, Alexander MacKay, and Julian Reif, "The Long-Run Dynamics of Electricity Demand: Evidence from Municipal Aggregation," *Forthcoming in American Economic Journal: Applied Economics.*

What does all this say about the corresponding individual and market demand curves for food? Identical incomes and tastes give rise to identical individual demand curves, denoted D_A and D_B in Figure 4.28. Adding D_A and D_B horizontally, we get the initial market demand curve, denoted D. The nature of the individual Engel curves tells us that B's increase in demand will be smaller than A's reduction in demand following the shift in income distribution. Thus, when we add the new individual demand curves (D_A' and D_B'), we get a new market demand for food (D') that lies to the left of the original demand curve.

FIGURE 4.28

Market Demand Sometimes Depends on the Distribution of Income

A given increase in income produces a small demand increase for B (*b*); an income reduction of the same size produces a larger demand reduction for A (*a*). The redistribution from A to B leaves average income unchanged but reduces market demand (*c*).

The dependence of market demands on the distribution of income is important to bear in mind when the government considers policies to redistribute income. A policy that redistributes income from rich to poor, for example, is likely to increase demand for goods like food and reduce demand for luxury items, such as jewelry and foreign travel.

Demand in many other markets is relatively insensitive to variations in the distribution of income. In particular, the distribution of income is not likely to matter much in markets in which individual demands tend to move roughly in proportion to changes in income.

Engel curves at the market level are schedules that relate the quantity demanded to the average income level in the market. The existence of a stable relationship between average income and quantity demanded is by no means certain for any given product because of the distributional complication just discussed. In particular, note that we cannot construct Engel curves at the market level by simply adding individual Engel curves horizontally. Horizontal summation works as a way of generating market demand curves from individual demand curves because all consumers in the market face the same market price for the product. But when incomes differ widely from one consumer to another, it makes no sense to hold income constant and add quantities across consumers.

As a practical matter, however, reasonably stable relationships between various aggregate income measures and quantities demanded in the market may nonetheless exist. Suppose such a relationship exists for the good X and is as pictured by EE in Figure 4.29, where Y denotes the average income level of consumers in the market for X, and Q denotes the quantity of X. This locus is the market analog of the individual Engel curves discussed earlier.

If a good exhibits a stable Engel curve, we may then define its **income elasticity of demand,** a formal measure of the responsiveness of purchase decisions to variations in the average market income. Denoted η, it is given by a formula analogous to the one for price elasticity:[9]

income elasticity of demand the percentage change in the quantity of a good demanded that results from a 1 percent change in income.

$$\eta = \frac{\Delta Q/Q}{\Delta Y/Y},\qquad(4.5)$$

where Y denotes average market income and ΔY is a small change therein.

[9]In calculus terms, the corresponding formula is $\eta = (Y/Q)\,[dQ(Y)/dY]$.

FIGURE 4.29

An Engel Curve at the Market Level

The market Engel curve tells what quantities will be demanded at various average levels of income.

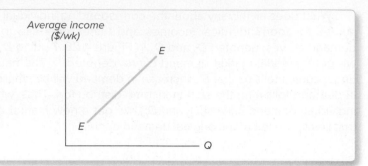

Goods such as food, for which a change in income produces a less than proportional change in the quantity demanded at any price, thus have an income elasticity less than 1. Such goods are called *necessities,* and their income elasticities must lie in the interval $0 < \eta < 1$. Food is a commonly cited example. *Luxuries* are those goods for which $\eta > 1$. Common examples are expensive jewelry and foreign travel. Inferior goods are those for which $\eta < 0$. Goods for which $\eta = 1$ will have Engel curves that are straight lines through the origin, as pictured by the locus EE in Figure 4.30a. The market Engel curves for luxuries, necessities, and inferior goods, where these exist and are stable, are pictured in Figure 4.30b.

The income elasticity formula in Equation 4.5 is easier to interpret geometrically if we rewrite it as

$$\eta = \frac{Y}{Q} \frac{\Delta Q}{\Delta Y}. \tag{4.6}$$

The first factor on the right side of Equation 4.6 is simply the ratio of income to quantity at a point along the Engel curve. It is the slope of the line from the origin (a ray) to that point. The second factor is the reciprocal of the slope of the Engel curve at that point. If the slope of the ray exceeds the slope of the Engel curve, the product of these two factors must be greater than 1 (the luxury case). If the ray is less steep, η will be less than 1 but still positive, provided the slope of the Engel curve is positive (the necessity case). Thus, in distinguishing between the Engel curves for necessities and luxuries, what counts is not the slopes of the Engel curves themselves but how they compare with the slopes of the corresponding rays. Finally, if the slope of the Engel curve is negative, η must be less than zero (the inferior case).

FIGURE 4.30

Engel Curves for Different Types of Goods

(a) The good whose Engel curve is shown has an income elasticity of 1. For such goods, a given proportional change in income will produce the same proportional change in quantity demanded. Thus when average income doubles, from M_0 to $2M_0$, the quantity demanded also doubles, from Q_0 to $2Q_0$. (b) The Engel curves show that consumption increases more than in proportion to income for a luxury and less than in proportion to income for a necessity, and it falls with income for an inferior good.

Economic Naturalist 4.1

Why has the nature of outdoor cooking appliances changed dramatically in recent decades?

A propane grill I bought long ago had been on a downhill slide for several years. First to go was its ignition button, the crude mechanical spark generator that normally fires up the gas. Lighting the grill suddenly became a delicate operation. I would turn on the gas, wait a few seconds, and then throw a match inside. If I threw it in too soon, it would go out before reaching the burner below. But if I waited too long, it would set off a small explosion. Another problem was that the metal baffle that sat atop the burners had rusted through in the middle. This concentrated an enormous amount of heat over a small area near the center of the cooking surface, but very little elsewhere. I was still able to cook reasonably good chicken and small steaks by quickly rotating pieces in and out of the hot zone. But grilling a big fish filet was impossible.

My grill's various deficiencies could surely be repaired, but I had no idea by whom. And even if I did, the cost would almost surely exceed the cost of replacing it. And so, reluctantly, I found myself in the market for a new one.

I was immediately struck by how the menu of available choices had changed in the intervening years. I vaguely remembered earlier models that had built-in storage cabinets and shelf extensions on either side. But even with these options, the most you could have spent was a few hundred dollars. There was nothing—absolutely nothing—like the Viking Professional Grill.

Early Sunbeam Grill, $90

Powered by either natural gas or propane, it comes with an infrared rotisserie that can slowly broil two 20-pound turkeys to perfection as you cook hamburgers for 40 guests on its 828-square-inch grilling surface. It has a built-in smoker system that "utilizes its own 5,000-BTU burner and watertight wood chip drawer to season food with rich woodsy flavor." Next to its grilling surface sit two ancillary range-top burners. Unlike the standard burners on your kitchen stove, which generate 7,500 BTUs, these burners generate 15,000 BTUs, a capability that is useful primarily for the flash-stir-frying of some ethnic cuisines and for bringing large cauldrons of water more quickly to a boil. If you have ever longed to throw together a Szechwan pork dish on your backyard patio, or feared getting off to a late start when you have guests about to arrive and 40 ears of corn left to cook, the Viking has the extra power you may need. The entire unit is constructed of gleaming stainless steel, with enamel and brass accents, and with its fold-out workspaces fully extended, it measures more than seven feet across.

The Frontgate catalog's price of the Viking Professional Grill, not including shipping and handling, is $5,000. Other outdoor cooking appliances are now offered that cost more than ten times that amount.

A well-equipped professional grill (comparable to Viking Professional Grill referenced in text)

What spawned this dramatic boom in the American outdoor luxury grill market? The short answer is that most of the recent growth in income in the United States occurred among the nation's highest earners. For example, although the income of the "middle 60 percent" of households grew by 33 percent (before taxes and transfers) between 1979 and 2016, the corresponding growth for the top 1 percent of earners was 218 percent.[10] Still higher up the income ladder, growth was even more dramatic. Chief executive officers (CEOs) of the largest U.S. corporations, who earned 42 times as much as the average worker in 1980, earned 361 times as much in 2017.[11] Rapid income growth among those with already high incomes spawned increasing demand not only for costly outdoor cooking appliances, but for a broad spectrum of luxury goods.

---

[10]www.cbpp.org/research/poverty-and-inequality/a-guide-to-statistics-on-historical-trends-in-income-inequality. The Center on Budget and Policy Priorities (CBPP) used Congressional Budget Office (CBO) figures for this report.

[11]https://inequality.org/facts/income-inequality/. Figures in the report are from the Institute for Policy Analysis and the AFL/CIO.

Application: Forecasting Economic Trends

If the income elasticity of demand for every good and service were 1, the composition of GNP would be completely stable over time (assuming technology and relative prices remain unchanged). Each year, the proportion of total spending devoted to food, travel, clothing, and indeed to every other consumption category would remain unchanged.

As the entries in Table 4.5 show, however, the income elasticities of different consumption categories differ markedly. And therein lies one of the most important applications of the income elasticity concept, namely, forecasting the composition of future purchase patterns. Ever since the industrial revolution in the West, real purchasing power per capita has grown at roughly 2 percent per year. Our knowledge of income elasticity differences enables us to predict how consumption patterns in the future will differ from the ones we see today.

Thus, a growing share of the consumer's budget will be devoted to goods like restaurant meals and automobiles, whereas ever smaller shares will go to tobacco, fuel, and electricity. And if the elasticity estimates are correct, the absolute amounts spent per person on margarine, pork products, and public transportation will be considerably smaller in the future than they are today.

TABLE 4.5
Income Elasticities of Demand for Selected Products*

Good or service	Income elasticity
Automobiles	2.46
Furniture	1.48
Restaurant meals	1.40
Water	1.02
Tobacco	0.64
Gasoline and oil	0.48
Electricity	0.20
Margarine	−0.20
Pork products	−0.20
Public transportation	−0.36

*These estimates come from H. S. Houthakker and Lester Taylor, *Consumer Demand in the United States: Analyses and Projections,* 2nd ed., Cambridge, MA: Harvard University Press, 1970; L. Taylor and R. Halvorsen, "Energy Substitution in U.S. Manufacturing," *Review of Economics and Statistics,* November 1977; and H. Wold and L. Jureen, *Demand Analysis,* New York: Wiley, 1953.

CROSS-PRICE ELASTICITIES OF DEMAND

cross-price elasticity of demand the percentage change in the quantity of one good demanded that results from a 1 percent change in the price of the other good.

The quantity of a good purchased in the market depends not only on its price and consumer incomes but also on the prices of related goods. **Cross-price elasticity of demand** is the percentage change in the quantity demanded of one good caused by a 1 percent change in the price of the other. More generally, for any two goods, X and Z, the cross-price elasticity of demand may be defined as follows:[12]

$$\epsilon_{XZ} = \frac{\Delta Q_X / Q_X}{\Delta P_Z / P_Z},$$ (4.7)

where ΔQ_X is a small change in Q_X, the quantity of X, and ΔP_Z is a small change in P_Z, the price of Z. ϵ_{XZ} measures how the quantity demanded of X responds to a small change in the price of Z.

[12]In calculus terms, the corresponding expression is given by $\epsilon_{XZ} = (P_Z/Q_X)(dQ_X/dP_Z)$.

TABLE 4.6
Cross-Price Elasticities for Selected Pairs of Products*

Good or service	Good or service with price change	Cross-price elasticity
Butter	Margarine	+0.81
Margarine	Butter	+0.67
Natural gas	Fuel oil	+0.44
Beef	Pork	+0.28
Electricity	Natural gas	+0.20
Entertainment	Food	−0.72
Cereals	Fresh fish	−0.87

*From H. Wold and L. Jureen, *Demand Analysis,* New York: Wiley, 1953; L. Taylor and R. Halvorsen, "Energy Substitution in U.S. Manufacturing," *Review of Economics and Statistics,* November 1977; E. T. Fujii et al., "An Almost Ideal Demand System for Visitor Expenditures," *Journal of Transport Economics and Policy,* 19, May 1985, 161–171; and A. Deaton, "Estimation of Own- and Cross-Price Elasticities from Household Survey Data," *Journal of Econometrics,* 36, 1987, 7–30.

Unlike the elasticity of demand with respect to a good's own price (the *own-price elasticity*), which is never greater than zero, the cross-price elasticity may be either positive or negative. X and Z are defined as *complements* if $\epsilon_{XZ} < 0$. If $\epsilon_{XZ} > 0$, they are *substitutes*. Thus, a rise in the price of ham will reduce not only the quantity of ham demanded, but also, because ham and eggs are complements, the demand for eggs. A rise in the price of coffee, by contrast, will tend to increase the demand for tea. Estimates of the cross-price elasticity of demand for selected pairs of products are shown in Table 4.6.

SELF-TEST 4.7

Would the cross-price elasticity of demand be positive or negative for the following pairs of goods: (*a*) apples and oranges, (*b*) airline tickets and automobile tires, (*c*) computer hardware and software, (*d*) pens and paper, (*e*) pens and pencils?

SUMMARY

- Our focus in this chapter was on how individual and market demands respond to variations in prices and incomes. To generate a demand curve for an individual consumer for a specific good X, we first trace out the price-consumption curve in the standard indifference curve diagram. The PCC is the line of optimal bundles observed when the price of X varies, with both income and preferences held constant. We then take the relevant price-quantity pairs from the PCC and plot them in a separate diagram to get the individual demand curve. *(LO1)*

- The income analog to the PCC is the income-consumption curve, or ICC. It too is constructed using the standard indifference curve diagram. The ICC is the line of optimal bundles traced out when we vary the consumer's income, holding preferences and relative prices constant. The Engel curve is the income analog to the individual demand curve.

We generate it by retrieving the relevant income-quantity pairs from the ICC and plotting them in a separate diagram. *(LO2)*

- Normal goods are those the consumer buys more of when income increases, and inferior goods are those the consumer buys less of as income rises. *(LO2)*

- The total effect of a price change can be decomposed into two separate effects: (1) the substitution effect, which denotes the change in the quantity demanded that results because the price change makes substitute goods seem either more or less attractive, and (2) the income effect, which denotes the change in quantity demanded that results from the change in real purchasing power caused by the price change. The substitution effect always moves in the opposite direction from the movement in price: price increases [reductions] always reduce [increase] the quantity demanded. For normal goods, the income effect also moves in the opposite direction from the price change and thus tends to reinforce the substitution effect. For inferior goods, the income effect moves in the same direction as the price change and thus tends to undercut the substitution effect. *(LO3)*

- The fact that the income and substitution effects move in opposite directions for inferior goods suggests the theoretical possibility of a Giffen good, one for which the total effect of a price increase is to increase the quantity demanded. There have been no documented examples of Giffen goods, and in this text we adopt the convention that all goods, unless otherwise stated, are demanded in smaller quantities at higher prices. *(LO3)*

- Goods for which purchase decisions respond most strongly to price tend to be ones that have large income and substitution effects that work in the same direction. For example, a normal good that occupies a large share of total expenditures and for which there are many direct or indirect substitutes will tend to respond sharply to changes in price. For many consumers, housing is a prime example of such a good. The goods least responsive to price changes will be those that account for very small budget shares and for which substitution possibilities are very limited. For most people, salt has both of these properties. *(LO3)*

- There are two equivalent techniques for generating market demand curves from individual demand curves. The first is to display the individual curves graphically and then add them horizontally. The second is algebraic and proceeds by first solving the individual demand curves for the respective Q values, then adding those values, and finally solving the resulting sum for P. *(LO4)*

- A central analytical concept in demand theory is the price elasticity of demand, a measure of the responsiveness of purchase decisions to small changes in price. It is defined as the percentage change in quantity demanded that is caused by a 1 percent change in price. Goods for which the absolute value of elasticity exceeds 1 are said to be elastic; those for which it is less than 1, inelastic; and those for which it is equal to 1, unit elastic. *(LO5)*

- Another important relationship is the one between price elasticity and the effect of a price change on total expenditure. When demand is elastic, a price reduction will increase total expenditure; when inelastic, total expenditure falls when the price goes down. When demand is unit elastic, total expenditure is at a maximum. *(LO6)*

- The price elasticity of demand depends largely on four factors: substitution possibilities, budget share, direction of income effect, and time. (1) *Substitution possibilities.* The more easily consumers may switch to other goods, the more elastic demand will be. (2) *Budget share.* Goods that account for a large share of total expenditures will tend to have higher price elasticity. (3) *Direction of income effect.* Other factors the same, inferior goods will tend to be less elastic with respect to price than normal goods. (4) *Time.* Habits and existing commitments limit the extent to which consumers can respond to price changes in the short run. Price elasticity of demand will tend to be larger, the more time consumers have to adapt. *(LO6)*

- Changes in the average income level in a market generally shift the market demand curve. The income elasticity of demand is defined analogously to price elasticity. It is the percentage change in quantity that results from a 1 percent change in income. Goods whose income elasticity of demand exceeds zero are called normal goods; those for which it is less than zero are called inferior; those for which it exceeds 1 are called luxuries; and those for which it is less than 1 are called necessities. For normal goods, an increase in income shifts market demand to the right; and for inferior goods, an increase in income shifts demand to the left. For some goods, the distribution of income, not just its average value, is an important determinant of market demand. *(LO7)*

- The cross-price elasticity of demand is a measure of the responsiveness of the quantity demanded of one good to a small change in the price of another. It is defined as the percentage change in the quantity demanded of one good that results from a 1 percent change in the price of the other. If the cross-price elasticity of demand for X with respect to the price of Z is positive, X and Z are substitutes; and if negative, they are complements. In remembering the formulas for the various elasticities—own price, cross-price, and income—many people find it helpful to note that each is the percentage change in an effect divided by the percentage change in the associated causal factor. *(LO8)*

- The appendix to this chapter examines additional topics in demand theory, including the constant elasticity demand curve and the income-compensated demand curve.

KEY TERMS

cross-price elasticity of demand	income elasticity of demand	normal good
Engel curve	income-compensated demand curve	price elasticity of demand
Giffen good	income-consumption curve (ICC)	price-consumption curve (PCC)
income effect	inferior good	substitution effect

REVIEW QUESTIONS

1. Why does the quantity of salt demanded tend to be unresponsive to changes in its price? *(LO3)*

2. Why is the quantity of education demanded in private universities much more responsive than salt is to changes in price? *(LO3)*

3. Draw Engel curves for both a normal good and an inferior good. *(LO2)*

4. Give two examples of what are, for most students, inferior goods. *(LO2)*

5. Can the price-consumption curve for a normal good ever be downward-sloping? *(LO1)*

6. To get the market demand curve for a product, why do we add individual demand curves horizontally rather than vertically? *(LO4)*

7. Summarize the relationship between price elasticity, changes in price, and changes in total expenditure. *(LO6)*

8. Why don't we measure the responsiveness of demand to price changes by the slope of the demand curve instead of using the more complicated expression for elasticity? *(LO5)*

9. For a straight-line demand curve, what is the price elasticity at the revenue maximizing point? *(LO6)*

10. Do you think a college education at a specific school has a high or low price (tuition) elasticity of demand? *(LO5)*

11. How can changes in the distribution of income across consumers affect the market demand for a product? *(LO7)*

12. If you expected a long period of declining GNP, what kinds of companies would you invest in? *(LO8)*

13. *True or false:* For a budget spent entirely on two goods, an increase in the price of one will necessarily decrease the consumption of both, unless at least one of the goods is inferior. Explain. *(LO2)*

14. Mike spends all his income on tennis balls and basketball tickets. His demand curve for tennis balls is elastic. *True or false:* If the price of tennis balls rises, he consumes more tickets. Explain. *(LO6)*

15. *True or false:* If each individual in a market has a straight-line demand curve for a good, then the market demand curve for that good must also be a straight line. Explain. *(LO4)*

16. Suppose your budget is spent entirely on two goods: bread and butter. If bread is an inferior good, can butter be inferior as well? *(LO2)*

PROBLEMS

1. Sam spends $6/wk on orange juice and apple juice. Orange juice costs $2/cup while apple juice costs $1/cup. Sam views 1 cup of orange juice as a perfect substitute for 3 cups of apple juice. Find Sam's optimal consumption bundle of orange juice and apple juice each week. Suppose the price of apple juice rises to $2/cup, while the price of orange juice remains constant. How much additional income would Sam need to afford her original consumption bundle? *(LO2)*

2. Sunil has the same income and faces the same prices as Sam in Problem 1, but he views 1 cup of orange juice as a perfect substitute for 1 cup of apple juice. Find Sunil's optimal consumption bundle. How much additional income would Sunil need to be able to afford his original consumption bundle when the price of apple juice doubles? *(LO2)*

3. Anke has the same income and faces the same prices as Sam and Sunil, but Anke views 1 cup of orange juice and 1 cup of apple juice as perfect complements. Find Anke's optimal consumption bundle. How much additional income would Anke need to afford her original consumption bundle when the price of apple juice doubles? *(LO2)*

4. The market for lemonade has 10 potential consumers, each having an individual demand curve $P = 101 - 10Q_i$, where P is price in dollars per cup and Q_i is the number of cups demanded per week by the ith consumer. Find the market demand curve using algebra. Draw an individual demand curve and the market demand curve. What is the quantity demanded by each consumer and in the market as a whole when lemonade is priced at $P = $1/cup? *(LO4)*

5. a. For the demand curve $P = 60 - 0.5Q$, find the elasticity at $P = 10$. *(LO5)*
   b. If the demand curve shifts parallel to the right, what happens to the elasticity at $P = 10$?

6. Consider the demand curve $Q = 100 - 50P$. *(LO5, LO6)*
   a. Draw the demand curve and indicate which portion of the curve is elastic, which portion is inelastic, and which portion is unit elastic.
   b. Without doing any additional calculation, state at which point of the curve expenditures on the goods are maximized, and then explain the logic behind your answer.

7. Suppose the demand for crossing the Golden Gate Bridge is given by $Q = 10,000 - 1,000P$. *(LO6)*
   a. If the toll (P) is $3, how much revenue is collected?
   b. What is the price elasticity of demand at this point?
   c. Could the bridge authorities increase their revenues by changing their price?
   d. In 2019, the San Francisco Bay area Water Emergency Transportation Authority (WETA) announced it was considering the implementation of hovercraft service as a supplement to existing ferries. Suppose that a fast hovercraft alternative to the Golden Gate Bridge is implemented between Marin County and San Francisco. How would the new service affect the elasticity of demand for trips across the Golden Gate Bridge?

8. Consumer expenditures on safety are thought to have a positive income elasticity. For example, as incomes rise, people tend to buy safer cars (larger cars with side air bags), they are more likely to fly on trips rather than drive, they are more likely to get regular health tests, and they are more likely to get medical care for any health problems the tests reveal. Is safety a luxury or a necessity? *(LO2)*

9. Professors Adams and Brown make up the entire demand side of the market for summer research assistants in the economics department. If Adams's demand curve is $P = 50 - 2Q_A$ and Brown's is $P = 50 - Q_B$, where Q_A and Q_B are the hours demanded by Adams and Brown, respectively, what is the market demand for research hours in the economics department? *(LO4)*

10. Suppose that at a price of $400, 300 tickets are demanded to fly from Ithaca, New York, to Los Angeles, California. Now the price rises to $600, and 280 tickets are demanded. Assuming the demand for tickets is linear, find the price elasticities at the quantity-price pairs (300, 400) and (280, 600). *(LO5)*

11. The monthly market demand curve for calculators among engineering students is given by $P = 100 - Q$, where P is the price per calculator in dollars and Q is the number of calculators purchased per month. If the price is $30, how much revenue will calculator makers get each month? Find the price elasticity of demand for calculators. What should calculator makers do to increase revenue? *(LO6)*

12. What price maximizes total expenditure along the demand curve $P = 27 - Q^2$? *(LO6)*

13. A hot dog vendor faces a daily demand curve of $Q = 1,800 - 15P$, where P is the price of a hot dog in cents

and Q is the number of hot dogs purchased each day. *(LO6)*
   a. If the vendor has been selling 300 hot dogs each day, how much revenue has he been collecting?
   b. What is the price elasticity of demand for hot dogs?
   c. The vendor decides that he wants to generate more revenue. Should he raise or lower the price of his hot dogs?
   d. At what price would he achieve maximum total revenue?

14. Rank the absolute values of the price elasticities of demand at the points A, B, C, D, and E on the following three demand curves. *(LO5)*

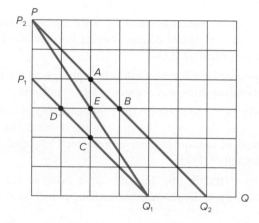

15. Draw the Engel curves for the following goods: food, Hawaiian vacations, cashews, and Target brand sneakers ($4.99/pr). *(LO2)*

16. Is the cross-price elasticity of demand positive or negative for the following pairs of items? *(LO8)*
   a. Tennis rackets and tennis balls
   b. Peanut butter and jelly
   c. Hot dogs and hamburgers

17.* In 2001, X cost $3 and sold 400 units. That same year, a related good Y cost $10 and sold 200 units. In 2002, X still cost $3 but sold only 300 units, while Y rose in price to $12 and sold only 150 units. Other things the same, and assuming that the demand for X is a linear function of the price of Y, what was the cross-price elasticity of demand for X with respect to Y in 2001? *(LO8)*

18.* Luisa cannot tell the difference between rice and wheat and spends all her food budget of $24/wk on these foodstuffs. If rice costs $3/lb, draw Luisa's price-consumption curve for wheat and the corresponding demand curve. *(LO1)*

19.* Repeat the preceding problem on the assumption that rice and wheat are perfect, one-for-one complements. *(LO1)*

---

*Problems marked with an asterisk (*) are more difficult.

20.* Suppose your local espresso bar makes the following offer: People who supply their own half-pint carton of milk get to buy a cup of cappuccino for only $1.50 instead of $2.50. Half-pint cartons of milk can be purchased in the adjacent convenience store for $0.50. In the wake of this offer, the quantity of cappuccino sold goes up by 60 percent and the convenience store's total revenue from sales of milk exactly doubles. *(LO6)*

a. *True or false:* If there is a small, but significant, amount of hassle involved in supplying one's own milk, it follows that absolute value of the price elasticity of demand for cappuccino is 3. Explain.

b. *True or false:* It follows that demand for the convenience store's milk is elastic with respect to price. Explain.

21. According to the Recording Industry Association of America (RIAA), the following table gives the unit sales and average retail price of new vinyl LPs for the years 2013–2018. The price of LPs has increased along with unit sales. Are vinyl LPs a Giffen good? *(LO2)*

Year	Vinyl LP units sold (millions)	Vinyl LP sales (million $)	LP retail price
2013	9.4	$210.7	$22.41
2014	13.2	$314.9	$23.86
2015	16.9	$414.5	$24.53
2016	14.8	$355.4	$24.01
2017	15.6	$388.5	$24.90
2018	16.7	$419.2	$25.10

ANSWERS TO SELF-TESTS

4.1 On Fatima's original budget, B_0, she consumes at bundle A. On the new budget, B_1, she consumes at bundle D. (To say that D has 1.5 pr of bindings per year means that she consumes 3 pr of bindings every 2 yr.) The substitution effect of the price increase (the movement from A to C) is zero. *(LO3)*

Skis (pairs/yr)

Bindings (pairs/yr)

4.2 The income effect, substitution effect, and total effects are all zero because the price change does not alter Elena's optimal consumption bundle. *(LO3)*

Tea (cups/wk)

Coffee (cups/wk)

4.3 The formulas for D_1 and D_2 are $P = 16 - 2Q_1$ and $P = 8 - 2Q_2$, respectively. For the region in which $0 \le P \le 8$, we have $Q_1 = 8 - (P/2)$ and $Q_2 = 4 - (P/2)$. Adding, we get $Q_1 + Q_2 = Q = 12 - P$, for $0 \le P \le 8$. For $8 < P \le 16$, the market demand curve is the same as D_1, namely, $P = 16 - 2Q$. *(LO4)*

4.4 First, we need to rearrange the representative consumer demand curve $P = 120 - 60Q_i$ to have quantity alone on one side: *(LO4)*

$$Q_i = 2 - \tfrac{1}{60}P.$$

Then we multiply by the number of consumers, $n = 30$,

$$Q = nQ_i = 30Q_i = 30(2 - \tfrac{1}{60}P) = 60 - \tfrac{1}{2}P.$$

Price ($/unit)

Quantity (units/wk)

Finally, we rearrange the market demand curve $Q = 60 - \tfrac{1}{2}P$ to have price alone on one side, $P = 120 - 2Q$, to return to the slope-intercept form.

4.5 Since the slope of the demand curve is -1, we have $\epsilon = -P/Q$. At $P = 24$, $Q = 8$, and so $\epsilon = -P/Q = -\frac{24}{8} = -3$. *(LO5)*

4.6 Elasticity when $P = \$4$/sq yd is $\frac{1}{3}$, so a price reduction will reduce total expenditure. At $P = 4$, total expenditure is 48/wk, which is more than the 39/wk of total expenditure at $P = 3$. *(LO6)*

4.7 Substitutes, such as *a, b,* and *e,* have positive cross-price elasticity (an increase in price of one good raises quantity demanded of the other good). Complements, such as *c* and *d,* have negative cross-price elasticity (an increase in price of one good lowers quantity demanded of the other good). *(LO8)*

Jorge Salcedo/Alamy Stock Photo

Additional Topics in Demand Theory

THE CONSTANT ELASTICITY DEMAND CURVE

The demand curves discussed so far have been linear, for which, as noted, price elasticity declines as we move down the demand curve. As we mentioned, not all demand curves have this property; on the contrary, there are others for which price elasticity can remain constant or even rise with movements down the demand curve. The *constant elasticity demand curve* is the name given to a demand curve for which elasticity does not vary with price and quantity. Whereas the linear demand curve has the general form $P = a - bQ$, the constant elasticity demand curve is instead written

$$P = \frac{k}{Q^{1/\epsilon}} \tag{4A.1}$$

where k and ϵ are positive numbers, specific values of which determine the exact shape and position of the curve.[1] The constant k may be thought of as a means of "calibrating" Equation 4A.1—that is, of bringing the values of P and Q into the neighborhood of observed values for good or service of interest. An example with $k = 2$ and $\epsilon = 1$ is pictured in Figure 4A.1.

At times, it will be convenient to use the inverse of Equation 4A.1, which is written

$$Q = \left(\frac{P}{k}\right)^{\epsilon}, \tag{4A.2}$$

where k and ϵ have the same usage. Both equations can be thought of as functions that can be thought of as returning a change in price resulting from a small change in quantity (Figure 4A.1) or as a change in quantity resulting from a small change in price.

Let us examine some points on the curve pictured in Figure 4A.1 and verify that they do indeed have the same price elasticity. Consider first the point $P = 2$, $Q = 1$, and calculate price elasticity as the product of the ratio P/Q and the reciprocal of the slope of the demand curve. To calculate the slope of the demand curve, we need to calculate the ΔQ that occurs in response to a very small ΔP near the point $(1, 2)$. Suppose, for example, we use a price change of $+0.001$. If $P = 2.001$, we can solve from the demand curve (ie., from the equation $P = 2/Q$) to get the corresponding $Q = 2/2.001 = 0.9995$. Thus $\Delta Q = 0.9995 - 1 = -0.0005$, and the slope of the demand curve at $(1, 2)$ may be calculated as $\Delta P/\Delta Q$, or $0.001/(-0.0005) = -2$. The reciprocal of the slope is $-\frac{1}{2}$, and so the price elasticity is $2(-\frac{1}{2}) = -1$.

Consider now the point $(2, 1)$. Again using a ΔP of 0.001, we get a new Q of $2/1.001 = 1.998$, or a ΔQ of -0.002. Thus the slope of the demand curve at $(2, 1)$ is $0.001/(-0.002) = -\frac{1}{2}$, and its reciprocal is -2. The price elasticity at $(2, 1)$ is therefore $(\frac{1}{2})(-2)$, or again -1.

---

[1]Using the formal definition of elasticity, it is easy to show that the elasticity at any price-quantity pair along this demand curve is $-\epsilon$:

$$\frac{P}{Q}\frac{dQ(P)}{dP} = \frac{k/Q^{1/\epsilon}}{Q}\frac{1}{(-1/\epsilon)kQ^{-1/\epsilon-1}} = -\epsilon.$$

FIGURE 4A.1

A Constant Elasticity Demand Curve

Whereas the price elasticity along a linear demand curve declines as quantity increases, it remains the same along a constant elasticity demand curve.

$$P = \frac{2}{Q}$$

SELF-TEST 4A.1

Try several other points along the demand curve in Figure 4A.1 and verify that the price elasticity in every instance is equal to −1. [The answer at the end of the chapter uses the points (0.5, 4) and (4, 0.5).]

It should be obvious from Figure 4A.1 that while the elasticity of demand with respect to price is the same all along the curve, the magnitude of price change is not. Consider a quantity change from .0001 to .0002. This results in a price drop from $20,000 to $10,000—an absurd amount for such a small change in quantity but the "correct" amount for the percentage change in quantity. The example reminds us to use caution when using Equations 4A.1 and 4A.2 for "back of the envelope" calculations on the effect of price changes. It is best to begin by finding a value of k that creates a plausible demand curve for the commodity for the given elasticity and for the range of quantities or prices in question.

As we move downward along any constant elasticity demand curve ($P = k/Q^{1/\epsilon}$), the fall in the ratio P/Q is exactly counterbalanced by the rise in the reciprocal of the slope. A constant elasticity demand curve with $\epsilon > 1$ has the property that a price cut will always increase total expenditures. For one with $\epsilon < 1$, by contrast, a price cut will always reduce total expenditures.

The demand curve given by $P = k/Q$ is a special case of the constant elasticity demand curve called the *constant expenditure demand curve*. At every point along such a demand curve, total expenditure is given by the product $PQ = k$, where k is again a positive constant. Thus, unlike the case of the straight-line demand curve, here people spend exactly the same amount when price is high as they do when price is low. Someone who spends her entire allowance on downloading music files each month, for example, would have a constant expenditure demand curve for downloadable music files. The constant k would be equal to the amount of her allowance.

SELF-TEST 4A.2

What happens to total expenditure when price falls from 4 to 3 along the demand curve given by $P = 4/Q^1/2$?

Segment-Ratio Method

The price elasticity at a given point along a straight-line demand curve may be given one other useful geometric interpretation. Suppose we divide the demand curve into two segments AC and CE, as shown in Figure 4A.2. The price elasticity of demand (in

FIGURE 4A.2

The Segment-Ratio Method

The absolute value of price elasticity at any point is the ratio of the two demand curve segments from that point. At point C, the absolute value of the price elasticity of demand is equal to CE/AC.

absolute value) at point C, denoted $|\epsilon_c|$, will then be equal to the ratio of the two segments.[2]

$$|\epsilon_c| = \frac{CE}{AC}. \tag{4A.2}$$

Equation 4A.2 is called the *segment-ratio* for calculating price elasticity of demand.

Knowing that the price elasticity of demand at any point along a straight-line demand curve is the ratio of two line segments greatly simplifies the task of making quantitative statements about it. Consider the demand curve shown in the top panel of Figure 4A.3. At the midpoint of that demand curve (point M), for example, we can see at a glance that the value of price elasticity is -1. One-fourth of the way down the demand curve (point K in Figure 4A.3), the elasticity is -3; three-fourths of the way down (point L), $-\frac{1}{3}$; and so on. The bottom panel of Figure 4A.3 summarizes the relation between the position on a straight-line demand curve and the price elasticity of demand.

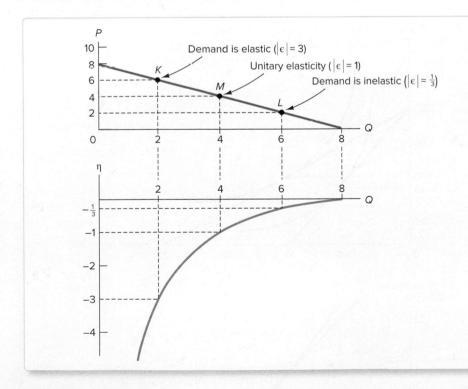

FIGURE 4A.3

Elasticity at Different Positions along a Straight-Line Demand Curve

Using the segment-ratio method, the price elasticities at points K, M, and L (top panel) can be calculated in an instant.

---

[2]To see why this is so, we can make use of some simple high school geometry. First, note that the reciprocal of the slope of the demand curve in Figure 4A.2 is the ratio GE/GC and that the ratio of price to quality at point C is GC/FC. Multiplying these two, we get $|\epsilon_c| = (GE/GC)(GC/FC) = GE/FC$. Now note that the triangles AFC and CGE are similar, which means that the ratios of their corresponding sides must be the same. In particular, it means that the ratio GE/FC, which we just saw is equal to the price elasticity of demand at point C, must also be equal to the ratio CE/AC. And this, of course, is just the result we set out to establish.

THE INCOME-COMPENSATED DEMAND CURVE

The individual demand curves we saw in this chapter take into account both the substitution and income effects of price changes. For many applications, such demand curves will be the relevant tool for predicting people's response to a change in price. Suppose, for example, that gasoline prices rise because of a new OPEC agreement. Such a price increase will have both income and substitution effects, and the individual demand curve described earlier will be the appropriate device for predicting a person's response.

In other situations, however, this demand curve will not be the right tool. During the Carter administration, for example, there was a proposal to tax foreign oil, then cushion the burden of the tax by simultaneously reducing the tax on wage earnings. A tax on oil, taken by itself, would increase the price of oil and produce the corresponding income and substitution effects. But the effect of the simultaneous earnings tax reduction, roughly speaking, would have been to eliminate the income effect of the price increase. The tax comes out of one pocket, but is put right back into the other.

To analyze the effect of such a policy, we must use the **income-compensated demand curve,** which tells the amounts consumers would buy if they were fully compensated for the income effects of changes in price. To generate this curve for an individual, we simply eliminate the income effect from the total effect of price changes. The top panel of Figure 4A.4 shows the income and substitution effects of an increase in the price of shelter from $6/sq yd to $12/sq yd for a consumer whose weekly income is $120. The ordinary demand curve for shelter for the individual pictured here would associate $6 with 10 sq yd/wk and $12 with 6 sq yd/wk. The income-compensated demand curve is always constructed relative to a fixed reference point, the current price. Thus like the ordinary demand curve, it too associates 10 sq yd/wk with the price $6. But with the price $12 it associates not 6 sq yd/wk but 7 sq yd/wk, which is the amount of shelter the

income-compensated demand curve a demand curve that tells how much consumers would buy at each price if they were fully compensated for the income effects of price changes.

FIGURE 4A.4

Ordinary vs. Income-Compensated Demand Curves for a Normal Good

The ordinary demand curve plots the substitution and income effects of a price change. The income-compensated demand curve plots only the substitution effect. For a normal good, the income-compensated demand curve will always be steeper than the ordinary demand curve.

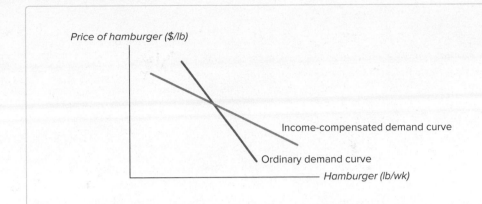

FIGURE 4A.5

Ordinary vs. Income-Compensated Demand Curves for an Inferior Good

The income effect offsets the substitution effect for an inferior good. The income-compensated demand curve, which omits the income effect, is therefore less steep than the ordinary demand curve in the case of an inferior good.

consumer would have bought at $12/sq yd if he had been given enough income to remain on the original indifference curve, I_0.

The individual whose responses are described in Figure 4A.4 happens to regard shelter as a normal good, one for which the quantity demanded increases as income rises. For normal goods, the income-compensated demand curve will necessarily be steeper than the ordinary demand curve. In the case of an inferior good, however, the ordinary demand curve will always be the steeper of the two. The relationship between the two demand curves for an inferior good is as pictured in Figure 4A.5.

In applications, the distinction between ordinary and income-compensated demand curves turns out to be particularly important for questions of tax policy. In the case of Jimmy Carter's gasoline tax proposal, there was an explicit provision for the proceeds of the tax to be returned to the people who paid it. But even without such a provision, the practical impact of a new tax would be roughly the same. After all, when the government raises more revenue from one source it needs to raise less from others. The end result is that the relevant demand curve for studying the effects of a tax on a good is the income-compensated demand curve.

As a practical matter, the distinction between the two types of demand curves is relevant only for goods for which income effects are large in relation to the corresponding substitution effects. In order for the income effect of a price change for a particular good to be large, it is necessary (but not sufficient) that the good account for a significant share of total expenditures. Many of the individual goods and services we buy, however, account for only a tiny fraction of our total expenditures. Accordingly, for such goods the distinction between the two types of demand curve will be unimportant. Even for a good that accounts for a large budget share, the income effect of a price change will sometimes be small. (The good might lie on the border between a normal and an inferior good.) For such goods, too, the distinction between ordinary and income-compensated demand curves will be of little practical significance.

ANSWERS TO APPENDIX SELF-TESTS

4A.1 First consider the point (0.5, 4). If we again let ΔP be 0.001 so that the new P is 4.001, the resulting Q is $2/4.001 = 0.499875$, which means that ΔQ is -0.000125. Price elasticity is therefore equal to $(4/0.5)(-0.000125/0.001) = -1$. Now consider the point (4, 0.5). If we again let ΔP be 0.001, so that the new P is 0.501, the resulting Q is $2/0.501 = 3.992$, which means that ΔQ is -0.008. Price elasticity is therefore equal to $(0.5/4)(-0.008/0.001) = -1$.

4A.2 For $P = 4$, we have $4 = 4\sqrt{Q}$, which yields $Q = 1$, so total expenditure is $4(1) = 4$. For $P = 3$, we have $3 = 4/\sqrt{Q}$, which yields $Q = \frac{16}{9}$, so total expenditure is $(3)(\frac{16}{9}) = (\frac{16}{3})$. So with $\epsilon = 2$ total expenditure rises with a decrease in price.

Applications of Rational Choice and Demand Theories

After reading this chapter, you should be able to:

LO1 Analyze the effect of economic policy proposals by examining how they affect the consumer's budget constraint.

LO2 Use measures of consumer surplus to calculate the benefit from participation in specific markets and design optimal two-part pricing schedules.

LO3 Use the rational choice model to show how changes in prices and incomes affect consumer well-being and identify one source of bias in the consumer price index.

LO4 Use price elasticity of demand to analyze the effects of changes in prices and taxes.

LO5 Employ the intertemporal choice model to examine choices between present and future consumption.

In the 2013–2014 academic year, annual tuition and fees at Cornell University passed the $45,000 level. The university has a special policy whereby children of its faculty who attend Cornell are required to pay only fees, which come to approximately $9,000/yr. Needless to say, this policy provides a strong financial incentive for faculty children to attend Cornell.

The faculty committee on compensation argued for many years that the university should extend the same tuition benefits to faculty children who attend universities other than Cornell. The traditional response of the university was that it could not afford to make such an offer. Under prodding by economists on the committee, however, the administration eventually took a tentative step in this direction by offering to pay 30 percent of tuition and fees at other universities. To its surprise, this new policy not only did not cost the university any money, it actually saved a great deal because the number of faculty children attending Cornell went down significantly once the new policy was in effect. This drop opened up an equivalent number of new positions in the freshman class, and because most of these were filled by tuition-paying students, Cornell actually came out ahead. Faculty families who received the new financial aid also came out ahead, and so did the new students who otherwise would have been unable to attend Cornell. The university had overlooked the opportunity cost of allocating positions to faculty children and had failed to anticipate that so many of them would be vacated because of the new offer.

CHAPTER PREVIEW

Cornell's tuition policy provides yet another lesson that prices affect behavior. In this chapter we consider a variety of applications and examples involving the rational choice and demand theories developed in Chapters 3 and 4. We begin with two examples—a gasoline tax and school vouchers—that illustrate how the rational choice model can shed light on important economic policy questions. Next we consider the concept of consumer surplus, a measure of how much the consumer benefits from being able to buy a given product at a given price. And we'll see how the rational choice model can be used to examine how price and income changes affect welfare.

Next on our agenda are two case studies that illustrate the role of price elasticity in policy analysis. We examine the effect of a fare increase implemented by the Metropolitan Atlanta Rapid Transit Authority and the effect of liquor taxes on alcohol consumption by heavy drinkers.

Finally, we consider how the rational choice model can be adapted to choices that have future consequences.

USING THE RATIONAL CHOICE MODEL TO ANSWER POLICY QUESTIONS

Many government policies affect not only the incomes that people receive but also the prices they pay. Sometimes these effects are the deliberate aim of government policy, but on other occasions they are unintended consequences of policies directed toward other ends. In either case, both common sense and our analysis of the rational choice model tell us that changes in incomes and prices can normally be expected to alter the ways in which consumers spend their money. And as we'll see, the rational choice model can yield crucial insights not always available to policy analysts armed with only common sense.

Application: A Gasoline Tax and Rebate Policy

In 1979, critics used economically flawed arguments to defeat President Carter's proposed tax on gasoline.

A historical case in point—and one that is very relevant to contemporary debates regarding a carbon tax—is a proposal made during the administration of President Jimmy Carter to impose gasoline taxes in order to reduce the gasoline consumption, thereby making the United States less dependent upon foreign sources of oil. While the focus of the Carter proposal was on "conservation," not climate protection, the economics of a gasoline tax proposal are similar to those of a broader carbon tax.

One immediate objection to this proposal was that the resulting rise in gasoline prices would impose economic hardship on the poor. Anticipating this objection, the Carter administration proposed to ease the burden on the poor by using the proceeds of the gasoline tax to reduce the payroll tax (the tax used to finance Social Security). Critics immediately responded that to return the proceeds of the tax in this fashion would defeat its purpose. These critics believed that if consumers got the gas tax back in the form of higher paychecks, they would go on buying just as much gasoline as before. But as we'll see, these critics were woefully in need of instruction in the basic principles of rational choice.

Let's consider an illustrative example. Suppose the price of gasoline is \$1.00/gal, about what it was when President Carter made his proposal; and suppose that a tax of \$0.50/gal is imposed that results in a \$0.50 rise in the price of gasoline.[1] Suppose also that a representative consumer is then given a lump-sum payroll tax rebate that happens to be exactly equal to the amount of gasoline tax he pays. (Here, the term "lump-sum" means that the rebate does not vary with the amount of gasoline he consumes.) True or false: This policy will have no effect on the amount of gasoline this consumer buys. Critics of the Carter proposal would of course answer "true," but once we translate the effects of the proposal into the familiar rational choice framework, we quickly see that the correct response is "false."

To analyze the tax-and-rebate combination, let's consider a consumer whose income is \$150/wk. This consumer's budget constraint before the imposition of the tax is shown

---

[1]Recall from Chapter 2 that the rise in equilibrium price will be exactly the same as the tax when the supply curve for gasoline is perfectly horizontal, an assumption made here for simplicity.

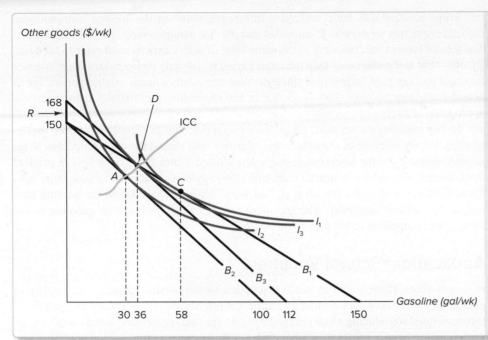

FIGURE 5.1

A Gasoline Tax and Rebate

The tax rotates the original budget constraint from B_1 to B_2. The rebate shifts B_2 out to B_3. The rebate does not alter the fact that the tax makes gasoline 50% more expensive relative to all other goods. The consumer shown in the diagram responds by consuming 22 gal/wk less gasoline.

as B_1 in Figure 5.1.[2] On B_1, he chooses C, which contains 58 gal/wk of gasoline. His budget constraint with a \$1.50/gal price of gasoline would be B_2 if he received no rebate. On B_2, he would consume A, which contains only 30 gal/wk of gasoline. But how do we find the budget constraint that corresponds to a rebate equal to the amount collected from him in gasoline taxes?

The first step is to note that for any given quantity of gasoline consumed, the vertical distance between budget constraints B_1 and B_2 corresponds to the total amount of tax paid on that amount of gasoline. Thus, at 1 gal/wk of gasoline, the vertical distance between B_1 and B_2 would be \$0.50; at 2 gal/wk, it would be \$1.00; and so on.

Our next step is to trace out how the consumer's consumption will vary as a function of the size of the rebate. To do this, note that a rebate is like income from any other source, so what we really want to do is to trace out how the consumer responds to changes in income. As we saw in Chapter 4, the appropriate tool for this task is the income-consumption curve, or ICC. Accordingly, we construct the ICC through bundle A, as shown in Figure 5.1. Recall from Chapter 4 that the ICC in question is the locus of tangency points generated by a series of budget constraints parallel to B_2. ICC shows how consumption of gasoline and other goods increases as the rebate gradually increases. Our goal is to keep increasing the rebate until it is just enough to cover the tax on the gasoline he chooses to buy.

What is the required rebate? Look at bundle D, the point where the ICC through A intersects the original budget constraint B_1. D is the equilibrium bundle on the budget constraint B_3, where the price of gasoline is \$1.50/gal and the consumer has \$(150 + R)/wk = \$168/wk of income. Note that gasoline consumption at D is 36 gal/wk. This means that if we give the consumer a rebate of $R = $18/wk, he will consume bundle D and pay exactly \$18/wk in gasoline taxes. (Note also that \$18 is the vertical distance between B_1 and B_2 when gasoline consumption is 36 gal/wk.)

The critical point is that D lies well to the left of the original bundle C, which means that, despite the rebate, the consumer substantially curtails his gasoline consumption. If gasoline is a normal good, the effect of the rebate is to offset partially the income effect of the price increase. It does nothing to alter the substitution effect.

Why are smaller automobile engines more common in Europe than in the United States?

[2]The equation for B_1 is $Y = 150 - G$, for B_2 it's $Y = 150 - 1.5G$, and for B_3 it's $Y = 168 - 1.5G$, where G is gasoline (gal/wk) and Y is all other goods (\$/wk).

Some readers will have noticed a difference between the income-compensated demand curve that we drew in Figure 4A.4 and the "tax-compensated" curve in Figure 5.1. The former returns the consumer to the same level of utility experienced prior to the price change—but at a greater cost than the latter curve, which only compensates the consumer for the actual tax paid. In practice, since gasoline represents a much smaller percentage of actual consumer budgets than is shown in the diagrams, the difference between the approaches is likely to be small.

In the end, the Carter administration's tax-and-rebate proposal was never implemented, largely because of the objections of critics who lacked the economic knowledge to understand it. In the intervening years, the United States has grown less dependent upon foreign oil, and the concerns motivating "energy conservation" are now more ecological than geopolitical. For all that, "oil wars" have continued, and the Middle East remains an area of instability. The argument for imposing a stiff tax on gasoline seems even more compelling today than it did in 1977.

Application: School Vouchers

In recent years, there has been much discussion of the need to improve the quality of elementary and secondary education in the United States. Many policy analysts have recommended introducing more competition into the market for educational services. To this end there have been proposals that each family be given a voucher that could be used toward the tuition at any school of the family's choosing.

Such proposals contrast with the current system in most school districts, under which all families are required to pay school taxes and are then entitled to "free" tuition at the nearest public school. Under the current system, families who choose to go to private schools do not receive a refund on their school taxes. Critics of the current system complain that because tuition-charging private schools are unable to compete effectively with free public schools, public schools face little pressure to perform.

Setting aside the question of whether a voucher system would lead ultimately to higher educational quality, let's examine the likely effect of vouchers on the overall level of resources devoted to education. We can use the rational choice model to examine the educational choice confronting a representative family.

For simplicity, suppose that the quantity of education measured in terms of classroom-hours per year is fixed, and that when we speak of spending more on education, we mean not buying more hours of education but buying education of higher quality. Suppose the current tax system charges each family P_e of tax for 1 unit of public education, whether or not the family uses it, where "1 unit" is defined as a year's worth of education of the quality currently offered in the public schools. If it does not send its child to public school, the family has the option to purchase 1 or more units of education at a private school, also at the price of P_e per unit. For example, to buy 1.2 units of education at a private school would mean to purchase education of 20 percent higher quality than is currently offered in the public schools. Families are required by law to provide their child with at least 1 unit of education, public or private.

Given these values, we can now derive the current budget constraint for education and other goods for a representative family whose pretax income is Y. If there were no taxes and no public schools, the family's budget constraint would be the line labeled ABD in Figure 5.2. But because each family must pay P_e in school taxes, the vertical intercept of the current budget constraint is not Y but $Y - P_e$. Since 1 unit of public education is "free," the family's budget constraint is horizontal out to 1 unit. If the family then wants to buy more than 1 unit of education under the current system, it must withdraw its child from the public school and enroll her in a private school at an additional cost of P_e per unit. This explains why the current budget constraint drops vertically by P_e at 1 unit of education. Thereafter the budget constraint continues to slope downward at the rate of P_e per unit. Thus the budget constraint for a family considering how much education to purchase is denoted by $A'BCE$ in Figure 5.2.

Many liberals and conservatives agree that school vouchers would expand choice and increase competition in the education sector. But what would be their impact on total education spending?

FIGURE 5.2

Educational Choice under the Current System

The family has a pretax income of Y, out of which it must pay P_e in school taxes. It is entitled to 1 unit of tuition-free public education. In lieu of public education, it may purchase at least 1 unit of private education at the price of P_e per unit. Its budget constraint is thus $A'BCE$, and its optimal bundle is B, which contains 1 unit of public education.

Note in Figure 5.2 that the nonlinear budget constraint makes a tangency solution unlikely for a family with indifference curves like the one shown. For such a family, the optimal bundle is, in effect, a corner solution in which exactly 1 unit of public education is chosen.

Now let's contrast this result with what would happen under a voucher system. Under that system, families again pay P_e in school tax, then get a voucher worth P_e, which may be used toward the purchase of either public or private education. Under the voucher system, the law still requires that families provide at least 1 unit of education for their children. The budget constraint under the voucher system will thus be given by $A'BD$ in Figure 5.3.

Compare Figures 5.2 and 5.3. Note that the principal difference produced by the voucher system is to eliminate the discontinuity at point B of the budget constraint. Parents no longer have to forfeit their school taxes when they switch from public to private schools; they can purchase small increments in education beyond 1 unit without essentially having to "pay double." And indeed, the family in Figure 5.3 responds by choosing bundle G, which contains more than 1 unit of education. The analysis thus suggests that switching to a voucher system will increase the level of spending on education.

In times of budgetary stress, many people will be tempted to conclude that we should avoid any policy that will require additional resources. For these people, several cautionary notes should be stressed. First, our analysis did not take into account the possibility that competition among schools might make schools more efficient in their production of educational services. Thus, while parents might indeed choose to

FIGURE 5.3

Educational Choice under a Voucher System

Unlike the current system, the voucher system allows parents to provide small increases above 1 unit of education at the price of P_e per unit. The budget constraint is now $A'BD$, and the family shown now chooses bundle G, which contains more than 1 unit of education.

purchase more units of education under a voucher scheme, competition might drive the cost per unit down, making the net effect on expenditures hard to determine. Second, much of the additional resources devoted to education as a result of the voucher system would come from parents directly, not from governments. And it is by no means clear that a goal of public policy should be to prevent parents from spending more on education and less on other goods. Finally, a more complete analysis should consider the effect of additional education on economic productivity. After all, any increase in productivity that results from additional education could be used to offset the cost of producing that education. In sum, our analysis in this example focuses on only one part of a much larger picture. But it is an important part, one that policymakers should not neglect.

CONSUMER SURPLUS

consumer surplus a dollar measure of the extent to which a consumer benefits from participating in a transaction.

When exchange takes place voluntarily, economists generally assume it makes all participants better off. Otherwise they would not have engaged in the exchange. It is often useful to have a dollar measure of the extent to which people benefit from a transaction. Such a measure, called **consumer surplus,** is useful for evaluating potential government programs. It is relatively straightforward to measure the costs of, say, building a new road. But an intelligent decision about whether to build the road cannot be made without a reliable estimate of the extent to which consumers will benefit from it.

Using Demand Curves to Measure Consumer Surplus

The easiest way to measure consumer surplus involves the consumer's demand curve for the product. In both panels in Figure 5.4, the line labeled D represents an individual's demand curve for shelter, which sells for a market price of $3/sq yd. In panel (a), note that the most the consumer would have been willing to pay for the first square yard of shelter is $14. Since shelter costs only $3/sq yd, this means that he obtains a surplus of $11 from his purchase of the first square yard of shelter each week. The most he would be willing to pay for the second square yard of shelter is $13, so his surplus from the purchase of that unit will be smaller, only $10. His surplus from the third unit is smaller still, at $9. For shelter or any other perfectly divisible good, the

FIGURE 5.4

The Demand Curve Measure of Consumer Surplus

(a) The height of the demand curve at any quantity measures the most the consumer would be willing to pay for an extra unit of shelter. That amount minus the market price is the surplus he gets from consuming the last unit. (b) The total consumer surplus is the shaded area between the demand curve and the market price.

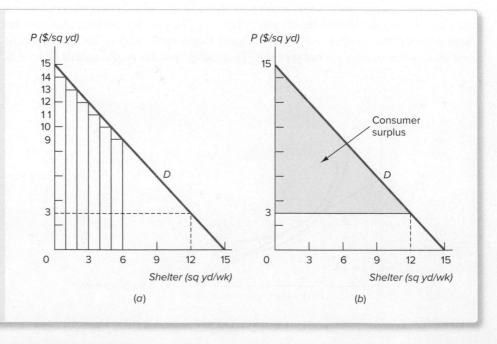

height of the individual's demand curve at any quantity represents the most the consumer would pay for an additional unit of it.[3] In this example, if we subtract the purchase price of $3/sq yd from that value and sum the resulting differences for every quantity out to 12 sq yd/wk, we get roughly the shaded area shown in panel (b). (If we use infinitesimal increments along the horizontal axis, we get exactly the shaded area.) This shaded area represents the individual's consumer surplus from the purchase of 12 sq yd/wk of shelter.

EXAMPLE 5.1   Consumer Surplus

An individual's demand curve for gasoline is given by $P = 10 - Q$, where P is the price of gasoline ($/gal), and Q is the quantity she consumes (gal/wk). If the individual's weekly income is $1,000 and the current price of gasoline is $2/gal, by how much will her consumer surplus decline if an oil import restriction raises the price to $3/gal?

At a price of $2/gal, she consumes only 8 gallons of gasoline per week, which amounts to less than 2 percent of her income. The income effect of the price increase is therefore likely to be insignificant, so we can use the demand curve approximation to measure her consumer surplus before and after the price increase. (See footnote 3.) Figure 5.5 displays her demand curve. Her consumer surplus at

FIGURE 5.5

The Loss in Consumer Surplus from an Oil Price Increase

At a price of $2/gal, consumer surplus is given by the area of triangle *AFF*. At a price of $3/gal, consumer surplus shrinks to the area of triangle *ACD*. The loss in consumer surplus is the difference between these two areas, which is the area of the shaded region.

the price of $2/gal is given by the area of the triangle *AEF* in Figure 5.5, $CS = \frac{1}{2}(10 - 2)8 = $32/wk$. Following the price increase, her consumption falls from 8 to 7 gal/wk, and her surplus shrinks to the area of the triangle *ACD*, $CS' = \frac{1}{2}(10 - 3)7 = $24.50/wk$. Her loss in consumer surplus is the difference between these two areas, which is the area of the trapezoid *DCEF*, the shaded region in Figure 5.5. This area is equal to $CS - CS' = 32 - 24.5 = $7.50/wk$.

[3]These statements about willingness-to-pay are literally true only if the demand curve we are talking about is an income-compensated demand curve like the one discussed in the appendix to Chapter 4 (see page 123). If the demand curve shown were an ordinary demand curve of the sort we have been using, it would tell us that the consumer would be willing to buy 1 unit at a price of $14, 2 units at a price of $13, and so on. From this it would not be strictly correct to conclude that, having already paid $14 for the first unit, the consumer would then be willing to spend an *additional* $13 for the second unit. If the income effect of the demand for the good is positive, the fact that the consumer is now $14 poorer than before means that he would be willing to pay somewhat less than $13 for the second unit. But since income effects for most goods are small, it will generally be an acceptable approximation to measure consumer surplus using the ordinary demand curve. In a widely cited article, Robert Willig has argued that the demand curve method will almost always yield an acceptable approximation of the true value of consumer benefits. See R. Willig, "Consumer Surplus without Apology," *American Economic Review,* 66, 1976, 589–597.

Application: Two-Part Pricing

Economic reasoning suggests that a voluntary exchange will take place between a buyer and a seller if and only if that exchange makes both parties better off. On the buyer's side, we may say that willingness to exchange depends on the buyer's expectation of receiving consumer surplus from the transaction.

Economic theory does not tell us much about how the gains from exchange will be divided between the buyer and the seller. Sometimes the buyer will be in an advantageous bargaining position, enabling her to capture most of the benefits. Other times the buyer's options will be more limited, and in these cases, her consumer surplus is likely to be smaller. Indeed, as Economic Naturalist 5.1 illustrates, the seller can sometimes design a pricing strategy that captures *all* the consumer surplus.

Economic Naturalist 5.1

Why do some tennis clubs have an annual membership charge in addition to their hourly court fees?

Why do many tennis clubs have both annual membership fees and court rental fees?

A suburban tennis club rents its courts for $25 per person per hour. John's demand curve for court time, $P = 50 - \frac{1}{4}Q$, where Q is measured in hours per year, is given in Figure 5.6. Assuming there were no other tennis clubs in town, what is the maximum annual membership fee John would be willing to pay for the right to buy court time for $25/hr?

The answer to this question is the consumer surplus John receives from being able to buy as much court time as he wants at the $25/hr price. This is equal to the area of triangle *ABC* in Figure 5.6, which is $CS = \frac{1}{2}(50 - 25)100 = \$1,250/\text{yr}$. If the club charged a fee higher than that, John would be better off not renting any court time at all.

FIGURE 5.6

An Individual Demand Curve for Tennis Court Time

At a price of $25/hr, John receives $1,250/yr (the shaded area) of consumer surplus from renting court time. The maximum annual membership fee the club can charge is $1,250.

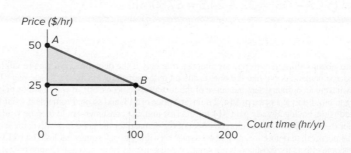

SELF-TEST 5.2

In Economic Naturalist 5.1 how much would the maximum annual membership fee be if the club charged only $20/hr for court time?

Economic Naturalist 5.1 sheds light on many of the pricing practices we observe throughout the economy. Many amusement parks, for example, charge a fixed admission fee in addition to a charge for each ride. Some shopping clubs charge a fixed membership fee for the right to buy from their stores, with Amazon Prime famously giving this practice a new online twist. Pricing schemes like these are often called **two-part pricing.** Their effect is to transfer some of the consumer surplus from the buyer to the seller.

two-part pricing a pricing scheme that consists of a fixed fee and a marginal charge for each unit purchased (also called two-part tariffs).

Companies obviously like two-part price structures but can't always sustain them. Mobile phone companies used to charge a fixed monthly fee in addition to charges based on actual calls made or received. As calls became commoditized by service innovations and competition, the unit price component was moved to text messages and then to data. With "unlimited data" beginning to dominate plan pricing, mobile phone companies are facing new choices. Should they focus on providing a high-bandwidth network? Or should they become content providers, like current cable and satellite

Economic Naturalist 5.2

Why do some amusement parks charge only a fixed admission fee, with no additional charge even for rides with long lines?

The price of a one-day pass at Disney's Magic Kingdom is around $100 for children under 10. This pass includes unlimited access to all rides and attractions in the theme park, the only catch being that on certain rides—such as the popular Space Mountain roller coaster—waiting lines can be more than an hour long. Given persistent excess demands for some rides at a price of zero, why doesn't Disney charge an additional fee for each use of its most popular rides?

Economic theory predicts that the price of any good or service will rise in the face of excess demand. Long waiting lines like the ones described above thus pose a challenge for economists. In this case, a possible explanation may be that the people who have to pay for the rides (parents) are different from the ones who demand them (their children). Since their parents are paying, children want to ride the most thrilling rides whether the price is $0 or $5 per ride. At a price high enough to eliminate waiting lines, it would be possible to go on the most popular rides dozens of

Why doesn't Disney charge extra for its most popular rides?

times a day, and many children would want to do exactly that. Parents could always ration access by saying no, of course. But not many parents look forward to a vacation in which they must spend the entire day saying no to their children. For these parents, Disney's current pricing policy is perhaps an ideal solution. It enables them to say to their children, "Go on whichever rides you want, as many times as you want," and then allow waiting lines to perform the essential rationing function.

operators? If they take the second path, they will collide with content-streaming services, which have puzzled consultants and business scholars by not even attempting to establish two-part pricing.[4]

OVERALL WELFARE COMPARISONS

The concept of consumer surplus helps us identify the benefits (or costs) of changes that occur in particular markets. Often we will want to assess whether consumers are better or worse off as a result of changes not just in one market but in many. Here too our model of rational choice lets us draw a variety of useful inferences. Consider the following example.

EXAMPLE 5.2   Budget Constraints

Jin spends all his income on two goods: X and Y. The prices he paid and the quantities he consumed last year are as follows: $P_X = 10$, $X = 50$, $P_Y = 20$, and $Y = 25$. This year P_X and P_Y are both 10, and Jin's income is $750. Assuming his tastes do not change, in which year was Jin better off, last year or this?

To answer this question, begin by comparing Jin's budget constraints for the 2 years. Note first that his income last year was equal to what he spent, namely, $P_X X + P_Y Y = 1,000$. For the prices given, we thus have the budget constraints shown in Figure 5.7a.

FIGURE 5.7

Budget Constraints for 2 Years

(a) If the consumer's budget constraint for this year contains the same bundle he bought last year (bundle A), he will be at least as well off this year as last. (b) If, in addition, relative prices are different in the two years, he will necessarily be able to buy a better bundle this year (bundle D).

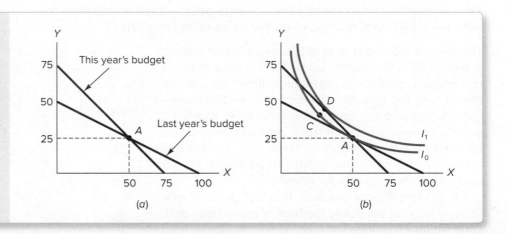

(a)   (b)

In Figure 5.7a, we see that Jin's budget constraint for this year contains the very same bundle he bought last year. Since his tastes have not changed, this tells us he cannot be worse off this year than last. After all, he can still afford to buy the same bundle as before. But our standard assumptions about preference orderings enable us to draw an even stronger inference. If his indifference curves have the usual convex shape, we know that an indifference curve—call it I_0—was tangent to last year's budget constraint at the point A in Figure 5.7b. We also know that this year's budget constraint is steeper than last year's, which tells us that part of I_0 must lie inside this year's budget triangle. On I_0, bundle A is equally preferred to bundle C. And because more is better, we know that D is preferred to C. It thus follows that D is preferred to A, and so we know that Jones was able to purchase a bundle of goods this year that he likes better than the one he bought last year. It follows that Jin was better off this year than last.

---

[4]Rafi Mohammed, "Why Is Every Streaming Service Using the Same Pricing Model?" *Harvard Business Review*, November 12, 2019, https://hbr.org/2019/11/why-is-every-streaming-service-using-the-same-pricing-model.

SELF-TEST 5.3

Jin spends all his income on two goods: X and Y. The prices he paid and the quantities he consumed last year are as follows: $P_X = 15$, $X = 20$, $P_Y = 25$, and $Y = 30$. This year the prices have changed ($P_X = 15$ and $P_Y = 20$), and Jin's income is now $900. Assuming his tastes have not changed, in which year was Jin better off, last year or this?

Application: The Welfare Effects of Changes in Housing Prices

Consider the following two scenarios:

1. You have just purchased a house for $200,000. The very next day, the prices of all houses, including the one you just bought, double.

2. You have just purchased a house for $200,000. The very next day, the prices of all houses, including the one you just bought, fall by half.

In each case, how does the price change affect your welfare? (Are you better off before the price change or after?)

I recently asked a class of first-year graduate students in economics these questions. The overwhelming majority responded that you are better off as a result of the price increase in scenario 1, but worse off as a result of the price drop in scenario 2. Although most students seemed confident about these two responses, only one turns out to be correct.

To see why, first consider the case in which all housing prices double. Suppose your total wealth just before purchasing your house was $400,000. Let the size of your current house correspond to 1 unit of housing and let the price of other goods (the composite good) be 1. Your original budget constraint under scenario 1 will then correspond to the line labeled B_1 in Figure 5.8. Its vertical intercept, $400,000, is the maximum amount you could have spent on other goods. Its horizontal intercept, 2 units of housing, corresponds to the maximum quantity of housing you could have bought (that is, a house twice as large as your current house). On B_1, the equilibrium at A represents your original purchase. At A, you have 1 unit of housing and $200,000 left for other goods.

After the price of your house doubles, your budget constraint becomes the line labeled B_2 in Figure 5.8. To calculate the vertical intercept of B_2, note that your current house can now be sold for $400,000, which, when added to the $200,000 you had left over after buying your house, yields a maximum of $600,000 available for other goods. The horizontal intercept of B_2 tells us that when the price of housing doubles to $400,000/unit,

FIGURE 5.8

Rising Housing Prices and the Welfare of Homeowners

When the price of housing doubles, your budget constraint becomes B_2, which also contains your original bundle A. Because C, the optimal bundle on B_2, lies on a higher indifference curve than A, the effect of the housing price increase is to make you better off.

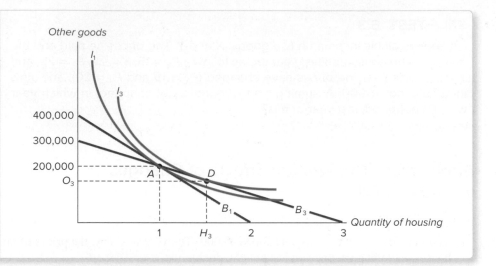

FIGURE 5.9

Falling Housing Prices and the Welfare of Homeowners

When the price of housing falls by half, your budget constraint becomes B_3, which also contains your original bundle A. Because D, the optimal bundle on B_3, lies on a higher indifference curve than A, the effect of the housing price drop is to make you better off.

your \$600,000 will buy a maximum of only 1.5 units of housing. Note finally that on B_2 your optimal bundle is C, which contains $H_2 < 1$ units of housing and $O_2 > \$200,000$ worth of other goods. And since bundle C lies on a higher indifference curve than bundle A, you are better off than before the price increase.

Not surprisingly, when the price of housing goes up, your best response is to buy fewer units of housing and more units of other goods. Note that you are insulated from the harm of the income effect of the price increase because the price increase makes the house you own more valuable.

So far, so good. Now consider what for many students was the more troubling case—namely, scenario 2, in which housing prices fall by half. Again adopting the units of measure used in scenario 1, your budget constraint following the fall in housing prices is the line labeled B_3 in Figure 5.9. To get its vertical intercept, note that sale of your current house will now yield only \$100,000, which, when added to the \$200,000 you already have, makes a maximum of \$300,000 available for the purchase of other goods. To calculate the horizontal intercept of B_3, note that when the price of housing falls to \$100,000, your \$300,000 will now buy a maximum of 3 units of housing. Given the budget constraint B_3, the best affordable bundle is the one labeled D, which contains $H_3 > 1$ units of housing and $O_3 < 200,000$ units of other goods. As in scenario 1, the effect of the relative price change is again to move you to a higher indifference curve. This time, however, your direction of substitution is the opposite of the one in scenario 1: Because housing is now cheaper than before, you respond by purchasing more units of housing and fewer units of other goods.

In each scenario, note that your new budget constraint contains your original bundle, which means that you have to be at least as well off after the price change as before. Note also that in each case the change in relative prices means your new budget constraint contains bundles beyond your original indifference curve, making it possible to achieve a better outcome in each scenario.

Application: A Bias in the Consumer Price Index

The consumer price index (CPI) measures changes in the "cost of living," the amount a consumer must spend to maintain a given standard of living. Published each month by the Bureau of Labor Statistics, the CPI is calculated by first computing the cost of a representative bundle of goods and services during a reference period and then dividing that cost into the current cost of the same bundle. Thus, if it cost \$100 to buy the representative bundle in the reference period and \$150 to buy the same bundle today, the CPI would be 1.5. Announcing this figure, government spokespersons would explain that it meant the cost of living had increased by 50 percent compared with the reference period.

What the CPI fails to take into account, however, is that when prices of different goods rise by different proportions, consumers do not generally buy the same bundle of goods as before. Typically, they substitute away from those goods whose prices have risen most. By reallocating their budgets, consumers are able to escape at least part of the harmful effects of price increases. Because the CPI fails to take substitution into account, it overstates increases in the cost of living.

A simple example using the rational choice model makes this point unmistakably clear. Suppose the only goods in the economy were rice and wheat and that the representative consumer consumed 20 lb/mo of each in the reference period. If rice and wheat each cost $1/lb in the reference period, what will be the CPI in the current period if rice now costs $2/lb and wheat costs $3/lb? The cost of the reference period bundle at reference period prices was $40, while at current prices the same bundle now costs $100. The CPI thus takes the value of $100/$40 = 2.5. But is it really correct to say that the cost of living is now 2.5 times what it was?

To consider an extreme case, suppose our representative consumer regarded rice and wheat as perfect one-for-one substitutes, meaning that her indifference curves are negatively sloped 45° lines. In Figure 5.10, her original bundle is A and her original indifference curve (which coincides exactly with her original budget constraint) is I_0. How much income would she need in the current period to achieve the same level of satisfaction she achieved in the reference period? At the new prices, the slope of her budget constraint is no longer -1, but $-3/2$. With a budget constraint with this new slope, she could reach her original indifference curve most cheaply by buying bundle C in Figure 5.10. And since the cost of C at current prices is only $80, we can say that the cost of maintaining the original level of satisfaction has gone up by a factor of only 2.0, not 2.5.

In general, we can say that the extent to which the CPI overstates the cost of living will go up as substitution possibilities increase. The bias will also be larger when there are greater differences in the rates of increase of different prices.

FIGURE 5.10

The Bias Inherent in the Consumer Price Index

For this consumer, rice and wheat are perfect substitutes. When the price of each was $1/lb, she bought 20 lb/mo of each in the reference period, for a total expenditure of $40/mo. If the current prices of rice and wheat are $2/lb and $3/lb, respectively, the expenditure required to buy the original bundle is $100/mo. The CPI is the ratio of these two expenditures, $100/$40 = 2.5. But the consumer can attain her original indifference curve, I_0, by buying bundle C, which costs only $80 at current prices. The cost of maintaining the original level of satisfaction has thus risen by a factor of only 2.0.

Quality Change: Another Bias in the CPI?

Gathering data on the prices of goods and services might seem like a straightforward task. In practice, however, it is complicated by the existence of discounts, rebates, and other promotional offers in which the actual transaction price may be substantially different from the official list price.

Yet important as they are, accurate price data are not sufficient for estimating changes in the cost of living. We must also account for changes in quality. And this, unfortunately, turns out to be a far more complicated task than measuring changes in prices.

A brief historical look at the automobile industry illustrates the difficulty. The U.S. Department of Commerce reported that the average price for a new vehicle in 1994 was $19,675, a 5.1 percent increase over 1993 and a 72.8 percent increase over 1984.[5] During that same 10-year span, the CPI rose only 42.6 percent. Does this mean that the prices of cars rose much more rapidly during that period than those of other goods and services? Not necessarily. After all, cars produced in 1994 came with many features not found on earlier models. For example, whereas approximately 90 percent of cars sold in the United States in 1994 came equipped with air bags and about 40 percent with antilock brakes, virtually none had these features in 1984. The number of cars with convenience equipment such as rear window defrosters and power windows once confined to luxury models rose more than 50 percent during the same decade.

The Department of Commerce now calculates a special automotive CPI, which deducts the cost of such additional features in an effort to measure changes in the prices of comparably equipped cars. This index rose only 32.2 percent between 1984 and 1994—or about 10 percent *less* than the overall CPI.

Although these adjustments obviously help, they capture only a small part of the automobile quality changes that have been occurring in recent years. For example, the automotive CPI made no allowance for the fact that 1994 cars had achieved a 40 percent reduction in hydrocarbon emissions and a 60 percent reduction in oxides of nitrogen relative to 1984 cars. Nor did the index allow for the fact that 1994 cars were much more reliable, crashworthy, and corrosion resistant than cars from a decade earlier.

The pace of auto quality improvement is vividly illustrated by a comparison of the 1995 Honda Civic DX sedan—one of the company's smallest and cheapest cars during that model year—with Honda's top-of-the-line Accord sedan from 1982. Besides having a bevy of safety features not found on the older Accord, the '95 Civic had a larger interior; a quieter, cleaner-burning, yet more powerful engine (102 horsepower versus 75); better tires and brakes; and a much more sophisticated suspension. The '95 Civic accelerated from 0 to 60 mph in 9.1 seconds, compared with 12.2 seconds for the '82 Accord; the '95 Civic got 40 miles per gallon on the highway, while the '82 Accord got only 32. Whereas the '95 Civic's finish will survive six northern winters in near-showroom condition, similar exposure left the '82 Accord riddled with rust. The '82 Accord had a sticker price of $8,995, but since it was in short supply, many dealers sold it for about $10,000. The '95 Civic had a sticker price of $12,360, and most dealers sold it at a substantial discount. So even with the passage of 13 years, the nominal dollar transaction price was not much higher for the Civic than for the older Accord. The '95 Civic's sticker price, adjusted for changes in the overall CPI, translates into $8,995 in 1982 dollars—in effect, a much better car for less money.

If the Civic–Accord comparison is representative, it seems that the government's attempts to adjust for automobile quality improvements have fallen short. With the growth of global competition, quality has been improving rapidly not just in automobiles but in other goods and services as well. And we may be sure that, as in the auto industry, many of the relevant changes will have escaped the Department of Commerce's notice.

---

[5]The data in this section are drawn from Csaba Csere, "Do Cars Cost Too Much, or Do We Just Like Costly Cars?" *Car and Driver,* June 1995, 9.

Failure to account fully for quality of improvements has the same effect as failure to account for substitution. Both cause the official cost-of-living index to overstate the true increase in prices.

The CPI has extremely important implications for the federal budget deficit, for this is the index used to determine the cost-of-living adjustments received by Social Security recipients and beneficiaries of a host of other government programs. Even a slight upward bias in the CPI can swell the budget deficit by many billions of dollars.

USING PRICE ELASTICITY OF DEMAND

In the sphere of applied economic analysis, few tools are more important than the concept of price elasticity of demand. In this section we examine historical applications of this concept in two very different settings.

Application: The MARTA Fare Increase

To cover a rising budget deficit in 1987, the Metropolitan Atlanta Rapid Transit Authority (MARTA) raised its basic fare from 60 to 75 cents/ride. In the 2 months following the fare increase, total system revenues rose 18.3 percent in comparison with the same period a year earlier.[6] Assuming a linear demand curve and that the observed changes in ridership are the result of the fare increase, what do these figures tell us about the original price elasticity of demand for rides on the MARTA system? If Q_1 denotes the original quantity of riders and ΔQ the change in riders due to the fare increase, and if ΔP and P_1 denote the price change and original price, respectively, we want to use the information given to calculate the expression $\epsilon = (\Delta Q/Q_1)/(\Delta P/P_1)$. Suppose the demand curve for rides on MARTA is as shown by the curve labeled D in Figure 5.11. The fact that total revenues went up by 18.3 percent may be expressed as follows:

$$\frac{75(Q_1 + \Delta Q) - 60Q_1}{60Q_1} = 0.183, \qquad (5.1)$$

where $\Delta Q < 0$ is the fall in ridership. Equation 5.1 reduces to

$$\frac{15Q_1 + 75\Delta Q}{60Q_1} = 0.183, \qquad (5.2)$$

FIGURE 5.11

The MARTA Fare Increase

Knowing the percentage change in total expenditure and the percentage change in price enables us to calculate the price elasticity of demand.

P (cents/ride)

75
60

D

Q (rides/day)

Q_1
$Q_1 + \Delta Q$

---

[6]See Bert Roughton, Jr., "MARTA Sees Ridership Dip with Fare Hike," *Atlanta Constitution*, October 8, 1987, 7.

which, in turn, solves for

$$\frac{\Delta Q}{Q_1} = -0.0536. \tag{5.3}$$

Since we know that $\Delta P/P_1 = \frac{15}{60} = 0.25$, this tells us that $\epsilon = -0.0536/0.25 = -0.2144$. The demand for MARTA rides thus turns out to be highly inelastic with respect to price, which is consistent with the fact that the fare increase led to a substantial increase in total expenditure.

SELF-TEST 5.4

In the example just discussed, suppose that MARTA had raised its fare from $1.00 to $1.10 and that, in response, system revenue rose by 2 percent. What would that tell us about the elasticity of demand for MARTA tickets at the original price of $1.00? (Again assume that the demand curve for tickets is linear.)

Application: The Price Elasticity of Demand for Alcohol

How does the consumption of alcoholic beverages respond to changes in their price? For many decades, the conventional wisdom on this subject responded, "not much." Unfortunately, however, estimates of the price elasticity of demand for alcohol tend to be unreliable. The problem is that liquor prices usually don't vary sufficiently to permit accurate estimates.

In a careful study,[7] Philip Cook made use of some previously unexploited data on significant changes in alcohol prices. He suggested that the price elasticity of demand for alcohol may be much higher than we thought.

Cook's method was to examine changes in alcohol consumption that occur in response to changes in state liquor taxes. Of the 48 contiguous states, 30 license and tax the private sale of liquor. Periodically, most of these states increase their nominal liquor taxes to compensate for the effects of inflation. The pattern is for the real value of a state's liquor tax to be highest right after one of these tax increases, then to erode steadily as the cost of living rises. The fact that taxes are not adjusted continuously to keep their real value constant provides the real price variability we need to estimate the responsiveness of alcohol purchases to price changes.

There were 39 liquor tax increases in Cook's 30-state sample during the period 1960–1975. In 30 of these 39 cases, he found that liquor consumption declined relative to the national trend in the year following the tax increase. His estimate of the price elasticity of demand was −1.8, a substantially higher value than had been found in previous studies.

Cook's interpretation of his findings provides an interesting case study in the factors that govern price elasticity. One salient fact about the alcohol market, he noted, is that heavy drinkers, though a small fraction of the total population, account for a large fraction of the total alcohol consumed. This fact had led many people to expect that alcohol consumption would be unresponsive to variations in price. The common view of heavy drinkers, after all, is that they drink primarily out of habit, not because of rational deliberations about price. Stated another way, analysts always expected the substitution effect to be small for these people. But even if the substitution effect were zero for heavy drinkers, there would remain the income effect. The budget share devoted to alcohol tends to be large among heavy drinkers for two reasons. The obvious one is that heavy drinkers

---

[7]Philip J. Cook, "The Effect of Liquor Taxes on Drinking, Cirrhosis, and Auto Accidents," in *Alcohol and Public Policy,* Mark Moore and Dean Gerstein (eds.), Washington, DC: National Academy Press, 1982.

buy a lot of liquor. Less obvious, perhaps, is that their incomes tend to be significantly smaller than average. Many heavy drinkers have difficulty holding steady jobs and often cannot work productively in the jobs they do hold. The result is that the income effect of a substantial increase in the price of liquor forces many heavy drinkers to consume less. In support of this interpretation, Cook observed that mortality from cirrhosis of the liver declines sharply in the years following significant liquor tax increases. This is a disease that for the most part afflicts only people with protracted histories of alcohol abuse, and clinical experience reveals that curtailed drinking can delay or prevent its onset in long-term heavy drinkers.

THE INTERTEMPORAL CHOICE MODEL

The choices we have considered thus far have involved trade-offs between alternatives in the present—the choice between food now and clothing now, between travel now and stereo equipment now, and so on. There was no hint that the alternative chosen today might affect the menu of alternatives available in the future.

Yet such effects are a prominent feature of many important decisions. Our task in this section is to enlarge the basic consumer choice model in Chapter 3 to accommodate them.

We will begin with a simple model that compares abstract present and future "consumption" bundles. We do this for simplicity. There is no requirement that present and future bundles be the same. Within a category, for example, one can balance the size of an apartment rented today with the opportunity to buy one's own home tomorrow. Even more broadly, the intertemporal choice model can be extended to weigh our standard of living today against the *livability* of our planet tomorrow. How much should we pay today to assure ourselves of a future, climate-stable world? Acknowledged or not, intertemporal choice is part of every discussion of our response to climate change.

Intertemporal Consumption Bundles

People may either consume all their income now or save part for the future. How would rational consumers distribute their consumption over time? To keep the analysis manageable, suppose there are only two time periods, *current* and *future*. In the standard, or *atemporal*, choice model in Chapter 3, the alternatives were different goods that could be consumed in the current period—apples now versus oranges now, etc. In our simple *intertemporal choice model*, the alternatives instead will be *current consumption* (C_1) versus *future consumption* (C_2). As we indicated, each of these is an amalgam—the functional equivalent of the composite good. We set aside the questions of bundle composition or of how to apportion current and future consumption among specific consumption goods.

In the atemporal choice model, any bundle of goods can be represented as a point in a simple two-dimensional diagram. We use an analogous procedure in the intertemporal choice model. In Figure 5.12, for example, current consumption of $6,000 combined with

C_2 *(future consumption)*

9,000 ---- D

6,000 ---------- E

3,000   6,000

C_1 *(current consumption)*

FIGURE 5.12

Intertemporal Consumption Bundles

Alternative combinations of current and future consumption are represented as points in the C_1, C_2 plane. By convention, the horizontal axis measures current consumption; the vertical axis, future consumption.

future consumption of $6,000 is represented by the bundle E. Bundle D represents current consumption of $3,000 and future consumption of $9,000.

The Intertemporal Budget Constraint

Suppose you receive $50,000 income now and $60,000 in the future. Suppose also that if you deposit some of your current income in a bank, you can receive your principal plus 20 percent in the future period. Similarly, if you wish to borrow against your future income, you may receive $1 now for every $1.20 you must repay in the future. (See Figure 5.13.) To construct your intertemporal budget constraint, first note that you can always merely consume your income in each period, so $C_1 = \$50,000$ and $C_2 = \$60,000$ must be a point on your intertemporal budget constraint. Another option is to deposit all $50,000 (maximum lending) and thus receive $1.2(50,000) = \$60,000$ in addition to your $60,000 future income for $C_2 = \$120,000$ future consumption with no current consumption ($C_1 = 0$). Yet another option is to borrow $\$60,000/1.2 = \$50,000$ (maximum borrowing) in addition to your $50,000 current income for $C_1 = \$100,000$ current consumption with no future consumption ($C_2 = 0$). The equation for your intertemporal budget constraint is $C_2 = \$120,000 - 1.2C_1$, or, equivalently, $1.2C_1 + C_2 = \$120,000$.

In general, suppose you receive M_1 of your income in the first period and M_2 in the second, and can either borrow or lend at the interest rate r. What is the most you can consume in the future period? Maximum future consumption occurs when you set all your current income aside for future use. Setting aside M_1 in the current period at the interest rate r means your deposit will grow to $M_1(1 + r)$ by the future period. So the most you can possibly consume in the future is that amount plus your future income, or $M_1(1 + r) + M_2$.

What is the most you could consume in the current period? The answer is your current income plus the maximum amount you can borrow against your future income. The most you can borrow against a future income of M_2 is called the **present value** of M_2, denoted $\mathrm{PV}(M_2)$. It is the amount that, if deposited today at the interest rate r, would be worth exactly M_2 in the future period. Accordingly, we can find the present value of M_2 by solving $\mathrm{PV}(M_2)(1 + r) = M_2$ for $\mathrm{PV}(M_2)$:

present value the present value of a payment of X dollars T years from now is $X/(1 + r)^T$, where r is the annual rate of interest.

$$\mathrm{PV}(M_2) = \frac{M_2}{1 + r}. \tag{5.4}$$

For example, if M_2 were $110,000 and the interest rate were 10 percent (that is, $r = 0.10$), the present value of M_2 would be $\$110,000/1.1 = \$100,000$. Present value is a simple equivalence relationship between sums of money that are payable at different points in time. If $r = 0.10$, then $100,000 today will be worth $110,000 in the future. By the same token, $110,000 in the future is worth $100,000 today when the interest rate is 10 percent.

FIGURE 5.13

The Intertemporal Budget Constraint

For every dollar by which current consumption is reduced, it is possible to increase future consumption by $1.2.

FIGURE 5.14

Intertemporal Budget Constraint with Income in Both Periods, and Borrowing or Lending at the Rate *r*

The opportunity cost of $1 of present consumption is $(1 + r)$ dollars of future consumption. The horizontal intercept of the intertemporal budget constraint is the present value of lifetime income, $M_1 + M_2/(1 + r)$.

It is not necessary, of course, to borrow or save the maximum amounts possible. The consumer who wishes to shift some of her future income into the current period can borrow any amount up to the maximum at the rate of $1/(1 + r)$ dollars today for every dollar given up in the future. Or, she can save any amount of her current income and get back $(1 + r)$ dollars in the future for every dollar not consumed today. The intertemporal budget constraint, shown as B in Figure 5.14, is thus again the straight line that joins the maximum current consumption and maximum future consumption points. And its slope will again be $-(1 + r)$. As in the atemporal model, here too the slope of the budget constraint may be interpreted as a relative price ratio. This time it is the ratio of the prices of current and future consumption. Current consumption has a higher price than future consumption because of the opportunity cost of the interest forgone when money is spent rather than saved. It is conventional to refer to the horizontal intercept of the intertemporal budget constraint as the *present value of lifetime income*.

SELF-TEST 5.5

You have $50,000 of current income and $42,000 of future income. If the interest rate between the current and future period is 5 percent, what is the present value of your lifetime income? What is the maximum amount you could consume in the future? What is the equation describing your intertemporal budget constraint?

As in the atemporal case considered in Chapter 3, the intertemporal budget constraint is a convenient way of summarizing the consumption bundles that someone is *able* to buy. And again as before, it tells us nothing about which particular combination a person will *choose* to buy.

Intertemporal Indifference Curves

To discover which bundle the consumer will select from those that are feasible, we need some convenient way of representing the consumer's preferences over current and future consumption. Here again the analytical device is completely analogous to one we used in the atemporal case. Just as a consumer's preferences over two current consumption goods may be captured by an indifference map, so too may his preferences over current and future goods be represented in this fashion. In Figure 5.15, the consumer is indifferent between the bundles on I_1, which are less desirable than those on I_2, and so on.

FIGURE 5.15

An Intertemporal Indifference Map

As in the atemporal model, movements to the northeast represent increasing satisfaction. The absolute value of the slope of an indifference curve at a point is called the marginal rate of time preference (MRTP) at that point. The MRTP at A is $|\Delta C_2/\Delta C_1|$

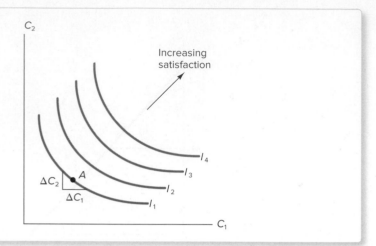

marginal rate of time preference (MRTP) the number of units of consumption in the future a consumer would exchange for 1 unit of consumption in the present.

The absolute value of the slope of the intertemporal indifference curve at any point is the marginal rate of substitution between future and current consumption. At point A in Figure 5.15, it is given by $|\Delta C_2/\Delta C_1|$, and this ratio is also referred to as the **marginal rate of time preference (MRTP)** at A.[8] If $|\Delta C_2/\Delta C_1| > 1$ at A, the consumer is said to exhibit *positive time preference* at that point. This means that he requires more than 1 unit of future consumption to compensate him for the loss of a unit of current consumption. If $|\Delta C_2/\Delta C_1| < 1$ at a point, he is said to exhibit *negative time preference* at that point. Such a person is willing to forgo 1 unit of current consumption in return for less than 1 unit of future consumption. Finally, if $|\Delta C_2/\Delta C_1| = 1$ at a point, the consumer is said to have *neutral time preference* at that point. With neutral time preference, present and future consumption trade off against one another at the rate of 1 to 1.

As in the atemporal case, it appears justified to assume that the marginal rate of time preference declines as one moves downward along an indifference curve. The more current consumption a person already has, the more she will be willing to give up in order to obtain an additional unit of future consumption. For most of us, then, the question of whether time preference is positive, negative, or neutral will be a matter of where we happen to be on our indifference maps. The scion of a wealthy family who is unable to borrow against the \$5 billion he is due to inherit in 2 years very likely has strongly positive time preference. By contrast, the primitive farmer whose food stocks are perishable is likely to have negative time preference in the wake of having harvested a bumper crop.

The optimal allocation between current and future consumption is determined exactly as in the atemporal model. The consumer selects the point along his budget constraint that corresponds to the highest attainable indifference curve. If the intertemporal indifference curves have the conventional convex shape, we ordinarily get a tangency solution like the one shown in Figure 5.16. If the MRTP is everywhere larger than (or everywhere smaller than) the slope of the budget constraint, corner solutions result, just as in the atemporal case.

Note in Figure 5.16 that the marginal rate of time preference at the optimal bundle (C_1, C_2) is positive, because the absolute value of the slope of the budget constraint is $1 + r > 1$. In the example pictured in the diagram, the consumer has the same income in each time period, but consumes slightly more in period 2.

The optimal allocation will of course be different for different consumers. The optimum shown in Figure 5.17*a*, for example, is for a consumer whose preferences are much more heavily tilted in favor of future consumption. The one shown in Figure 5.17*b*, by contrast, is for a consumer who cares much more about present consumption. But in

---

[8]In calculus terms, the marginal rate of time preference is given by $|dC_2/dC_1|$.

FIGURE 5.16

The Optimal Intertemporal Allocation

As in the atemporal model, the optimal intertemporal consumption bundle (bundle *A*) lies on the highest attainable indifference curve. Here, that occurs at a point of tangency.

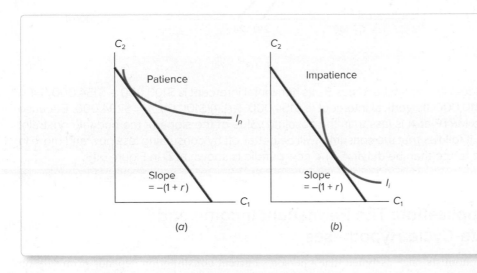

FIGURE 5.17

Patience and Impatience

(*a*) The patient consumer postpones the bulk of consumption until the future period. (*b*) The impatient consumer consumes much more heavily in the current period. But in equilibrium, the marginal rate of time preference $(1 + r)$ is the same for both types of consumers.

each case, note that the slope of the indifference curve at the optimal point is the same. As long as consumers can borrow and lend at the interest rate r, the marginal rate of time preference at the optimal bundle will be $(1 + r)$ (except, of course, in the case of corner solutions). For interior solutions, positive time preference is the rule, regardless of the consumer's preferences.

It is conventional to assume that both current and future consumption are normal goods. Thus an increase in the present value of lifetime income, all other factors constant, will cause both current and future consumption to rise.

EXAMPLE 5.3   Marginal Rate of Time Preference

You have current income of $100,000 and future income of $154,000, and can borrow and lend at the rate $r = 0.1$. Under these conditions, you consume exactly your income in each period. True or false: an increase in r to $r = 0.4$ will cause you to save some of your current income.

Line *B* in Figure 5.18 is the original budget constraint. Its horizontal intercept is the present value of lifetime income when $r = 0.1$: $100,000 + $154,000/1.1 = $240,000. Its vertical intercept is future income plus $(1 + r)$ times current income: $154,000 + (1.1)($100,000) = $264,000. The optimal bundle occurs at *A*, by assumption, which implies that the MRTP at *A* is 1.1. When the interest rate rises to 0.4, the intertemporal

FIGURE 5.18

The Effect of a Rise in the Interest Rate

When the interest rate goes up, the intertemporal budget constraint rotates about the current endowment point. If the current endowment point (A) was optimal at the lower interest rate, the new optimal bundle (D) will have less current consumption and more future consumption.

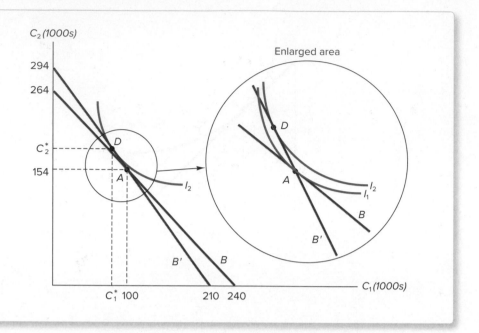

budget constraint becomes B'. Its horizontal intercept is \$100,000 + \$154,000/1.4 = \$210,000. Its vertical intercept is \$154,000 + (1.4)(\$100,000) = \$294,000. Because the MRTP at A is less than the absolute value of the slope of the budget constraint B', it follows that the consumer will be better off by consuming less now and more in the future than he did at A. The new bundle is shown at D in Figure 5.18.

Application: The Permanent Income and Life-Cycle Hypotheses

Economists once assumed that a person's current consumption depends primarily on her current income. Thus if a consumer received a windfall roughly equal to her current income, the prediction was that her consumption would roughly double.

In the 1950s, however, Milton Friedman, Franco Modigliani, Richard Brumberg, and others argued that the intertemporal choice model suggests otherwise.[9] To illustrate, consider a consumer with current and future incomes both equal to 120, who can borrow and lend at the rate $r = 0.2$. Line B in Figure 5.19 is the consumer's intertemporal budget constraint, and the optimal bundle along it is A. Note that the horizontal intercept of B is the present value of lifetime income, namely, 120 + (120/1.2) = 220.

Notice what happens when this consumer's current income rises from 120 to 240. His budget constraint is now B', and the optimal bundle is D. The effect of increasing current income is thus to increase not only current consumption (from 80 to 150) but future consumption as well (from 168 to 228). Because intertemporal indifference curves exhibit diminishing marginal rates of time preference,[10] the consumer generally does best not to concentrate too much of his consumption in any one period. By spreading his windfall over both periods, he is able to achieve a better outcome.

Friedman's *permanent income hypothesis* says that the primary determinant of current consumption is not current income but what he called **permanent income.** In terms of our simple intertemporal choice model, permanent income is simply the present

permanent income the present value of lifetime income.

[9]See Franco Modigliani and R. Brumberg, "Utility Analysis and the Consumption Function: An Interpretation of Cross-Section Data," in K. Kurihara (ed.), *Post Keynesian Economics,* London: Allen & Unwin, 1955; and Milton Friedman, *A Theory of the Consumption Function,* Princeton, NJ: Princeton University Press, 1957.
[10]Diminishing marginal rate of time preference is the intertemporal analog of diminishing marginal rate of substitution in the atemporal model.

FIGURE 5.19

Permanent Income, Not Current Income, Is the Primary Determinant of Current Consumption

The effect of a rise in current income (from 120 to 240) will be felt as an increase not only in current consumption (from 80 to 150), but also in future consumption (from 168 to 228).

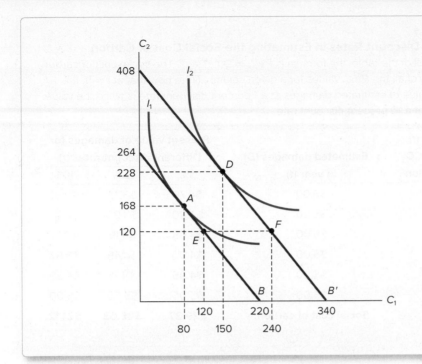

value of lifetime income. (Following the increase in current income in Figure 5.19, permanent income is $240 + 120/1.2 = 340$.) When we consider that in reality the future consists of not just one but many additional periods, it becomes clear that current income constitutes only a small fraction of permanent income. (If there were 10 future periods we were concerned about, for example, then a 10 percent increase in current income would cause permanent income to increase by just over 2 percent.)[11] Accordingly, Friedman argued, a given proportional change in current income should give rise to a much smaller proportional change in current consumption, just as we saw in Figure 5.19. (The *life-cycle hypothesis* of Modigliani and Brumberg tells essentially the same story.)

Application: The Social Cost of Carbon

One of the most important and controversial applications of intertemporal choice theory concerns establishing and framing policy choices around the social cost of carbon (SCC). According to William Nordhaus, co-winner of the Nobel Prize in economics in 2018, the SCC "designates the economic cost caused by an additional tom of carbon dioxide emissions or its equivalent."[12] Another way of putting it, and one that aligns with the language we used in setting up the intertemporal budget constraint, is to say that the SCC is the *present value* of all the future costs of emitting a ton of carbon dioxide today. In the 2016 version of his DICE "integrated assessment model,"[13] Nordhaus estimated the SCC for 2015 to be $31 per ton of CO_2. The estimate is hugely controversial, with climate change skeptics saying it is far too high and climate activists saying it is far too low.[14]

---

[11] Again, we assume an interest rate of $r = 0.2$.

[12] William D. Nordhaus, "Social Cost of Carbon in DICE Model," Proceedings of the National Academy of Sciences, 114 (7), February 2017, 1518–1523; DOI: 10.1073/pnas.1609244114. Nordhaus' definition is echoed by the Environmental Defense Fund: "The social cost of carbon is a measure of the economic harm from [such impacts as extreme weather events, rising health care costs, destruction of property, increased food prices, and more], expressed as the dollar value of the total damages from emitting one ton of carbon dioxide into the atmosphere." https://www.edf.org/true-cost-carbon-pollution.

[13] https://sites.google.com/site/williamdnordhaus/dice-rice.

[14] For example, see the reactions to Nordhaus's Nobel award on the WUWT blog: David Middleton, "'Nobel Prize for Climate Catastrophe'… Seriously?" WUWT, December 21, 2019, https://wattsupwiththat.com/2018/12/21/the-nobel-prize-for-climate-catastrophe-seriously/; Mark Chapman, "Is Nordhaus' Discount Rate Really Too Low?" WUWT, January 4, 2019, https://wattsupwiththat.com/2019/01/04/is-nordhaus-discount-rate-really-too-low/.

TABLE 5.1

Effect of Discount Rates in Estimating the Social Cost of Carbon

In each cell of the table, the formula is $PV_{D(t)} = D(t)/(1 + r)^t$. The social cost of carbon is the sum of all the $PV_{D(t)}$ values for a given column. Note how that at $t = 5$, the present value of estimated damages at a 1 percent discount rate is twice the value obtained at a 10 percent discount rate.

Year (t) since CO_2 emission	Estimated damages (D) in year (t)	Present value of damages for Different discount rates (r)		
		1%	5%	10%
5	$5.00	$4.76	$3.73	$2.31
4	$5.00	$4.80	$3.95	$2.70
3	$5.00	$4.85	$4.19	$3.15
2	$5.00	$4.90	$4.45	$3.67
1	$5.00	$4.95	$4.71	$4.29
0	$5.00	$5.00	$5.00	$5.00
Social cost of carbon:		**$29.27**	**$26.03**	**$21.12**

Much of the controversy in estimating the SCC comes from selecting what Nordhaus calls the "goods discount rate," which is essentially identical to the r component from our Equation 5.4. (Recall that the slope of the budget line in Figure 5.13 is $1 + r$.) In order to understand how the discount rate affects the SCC, let's consider a restricted case (Table 5.1) in which the estimated damages from CO_2 emissions extend just 5 years into the future. Even for this short period, it can be readily seen that the choice of the discount rate has a large effect on the SCC.

Nordhaus takes what he calls a "descriptive" approach to setting the discount rate. His r of 4.25 percent is intended to reflect observed savings rates and returns on capital investment in the actual U.S. economy. But Nordhaus's activist critics take a more "prescriptive" approach. As Mark Chapman puts it, rather than take the discount rate from observable markets, activists "believe that it is the government's ethical duty to work out, from first principles, how discounting should be undertaken across generations rather than inferring this indirectly from the limited number of participants who influence market yields."[15] Prescriptively (or normatively) reducing the discount rate would have a large effect on the SCC estimation. By Nordhaus's calculations, lowering the discount rate to 2.5 percent would raise the SCC from $31 to $128.50 per ton.[16]

Despite disagreements over the SCC estimate, we should keep in mind that the main point of establishing a social cost of carbon is to allow us to make informed, if still imperfect, cost-benefit decisions around the threats to our environment. If we can prevent $1.00 of damage for less than $1.00, we should do it. Actual estimation of the social cost of carbon requires more sophisticated mathematical tools than are examined in this text. But the *choice* forced upon us by climate change can be illustrated very well by extending simple intertemporal model we have already developed.

Consider Figure 5.20. The budget constraint B1 represents the same two-period trade-off of $100,000 of current income (C_1) versus $120,000 of future income (C_2), at interest rate $r = .2$, that was presented in Figure 5.13. We have added an indifference curve to show that the consumer's preference is to spend $50,000 in C_1 and $60,000 in C_2, a choice that corresponds to the consumer's cash income in each period.

But let us add the assumption that the consumer who operates within this budget does so in a way that releases 50,000 units of CO_2 per period. Each unit of CO_2 emitted

---

[15]See Chapman, "Is Nordhaus' Discount Rate Really Too Low?"
[16]See Table 1 in Nordhaus, "Social Cost of Carbon in DICE Model," 1520.

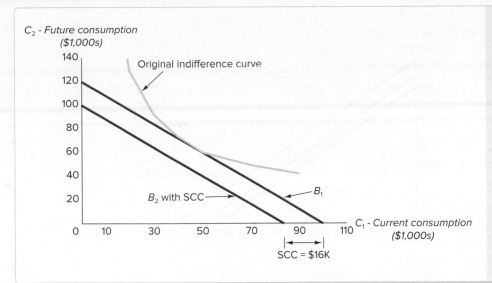

FIGURE 5.20

Impact of Future Environmental Damages on Consumer Intertemporal Budget Constraints

The social cost of carbon (the present value of a future period remediation tax of $20,000) causes the consumer's intertemporal budget constraint to contract by $16,000 on the x-axis.

causes 40 cents of damage in the next period *only*. Under this extremely simple assumption, and using the same discount rate for environmental damage that we used for the budget constraint, the social cost of carbon in period 1 would be $20,000/(1 + .2) = $16,000.

Of course, our consumer does not actually experience in period 1 the damage he is causing in period 2. In technical terms, the harm caused by the consumer—even if in this case he is harming his future self—is called an "externality." We will study externalities in Chapter 16, and this will enable us to develop a more complete treatment of concepts like the social cost of carbon and environmental damage in general. But for now, let's "internalize" the social cost of carbon and say that in period 2, an arbitrary authority is going to impose a dollar-for-dollar tax on the consumer to clean up the damages caused by his carbon emissions in period 1. This $20,000 "tax," again discounted by $1 + r$, has the effect of creating a new budget line B2, parallel to B1, that is reduced by $16,000 on the x-axis and $20,000 on the y-axis of Figure 5.20. The result is that if the consumer persists in spending $50,000 in period 2, he will only receive $40,000 of income in period 2. Obviously, a social cost of carbon higher than $0.40/unit, if it were offset by a dollar-for-dollar "tax," would create an even worse outcome in the future period.

What can the consumer do? Let us make a second (again extremely simplifying) assumption—that the $0.40/unit of period 2 damage can be entirely and permanently eliminated by paying a carbon tax of $0.20/unit in the current period, as shown in Figure 5.21. Let's even assume (magically) that this tax forces a complete conversion to a zero-emissions regime so that it does not have to paid again in period 2. On his new budget line B_3, our consumer would still see a reduction in income, relative to B_1, but would enjoy an improved financial position relative to B_2 and, of course, much less risk of carbon-related climate catastrophe. Under the rational choice model we have developed, the benefits exceed the cost, so the choice is clear.

But not, perhaps, for everyone. Up to now we have treated environmental harm and remediation as the trade-off faced by a single consumer. But the choice to adopt a carbon tax is not individual, it's social—and at the social level, our simple representative consumer model can easily break down. Suppose that, in the economy inhabited by our consumer, it requires $50,000 a year just to get by (see the vertical dotted line in Figure 5.21). On budget line B_3, by consuming $50,000 in the first period, our consumer would still receive only $48,000 in the second period—too little to live on. Wealthier consumers— say, those making many times or perhaps only a few times as much—may readily agree to the carbon tax, even if their carbon consumption is higher than our model consumer's, because they will still end up with adequate income (net of tax) in both present and future

FIGURE 5.21

A Carbon Tax under Intertemporal Choice

A carbon tax of $10,000 ($B_3$) improves the consumer's position over B_2, but still leaves future consumption below the "Just get by" level.

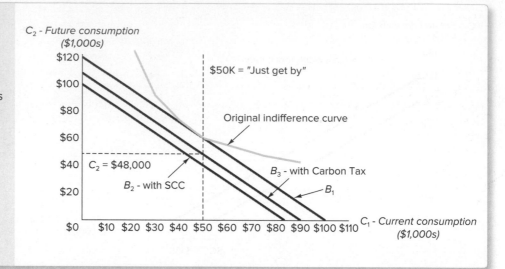

periods. But our illustrated consumer will likely resist the tax: Why accept a certain and visible hardship over uncertain, invisible risk? As with the Carter administration gasoline tax proposal that we examined earlier, an income-compensating scheme may be needed for a carbon tax to win broad public support.

With this political constraint in mind, many climate advocates have called for the imposition of a revenue-neutral carbon tax—one for which all revenue collected is returned to consumers in amounts independent of their own carbon emissions. A simple version of this proposal would redistribute the total revenue collected in equal lump-sum amounts to all taxpayers. Alternatively, a carbon tax could be made progressive—as, for example, by limiting eligibility for rebates to low- and middle-income families.

Note also that high-income families consume substantially more energy than others. They live in bigger houses, drive bigger cars, and take many more plane trips to distant destinations, for instance. These families would therefore contribute a disproportionate share of the revenue from a carbon tax. In short, distributional objections to a carbon tax would be easy to address. A revenue-neutral carbon tax could be structured so that a substantial majority of the population received monthly rebate checks that were larger than the amounts they had paid in in carbon taxes.

Factors Accounting for Differences in Time Preference

Even with a "revenue neutral" feature, carbon taxation may remain a hard sell until a majority of stakeholders can see that the consequences of inaction are palpable and certain. Uncertainty regarding the future is one reason to prefer current to future consumption. In countries at war, for example, people often live as though there were no tomorrow, as indeed for many of them there will not be. By contrast, a peaceful international climate, secure employment, stable social networks, good health, and a variety of similar factors tend to reduce uncertainty about the future, in the process justifying greater weight on future consumption.

Intertemporal indifference maps, like the atemporal variety, also vary according to the disposition of the individual. My first son, for example, has strongly positive time preferences in most situations. (His indifference curves are very steep with respect to the current consumption axis.) Ever since he was a small boy, he always ate his favorite part of his meal first, then worked his way through to his least favored items. Only with pressure would he eat his vegetables at all, and even then he always ate them last. My second son is the polar opposite case. He always starts with the foods he likes least, carefully husbanding his favorite items for the end of his meal. This contrast in their behavior at the dinner table pervades virtually every other aspect of their lives.

Time preference depends also on the circumstances at hand. Experimental studies have isolated certain situations in which most people have strongly positive time preference, others in which they show strongly negative time preference. Carnegie-Mellon University economist George Loewenstein, for example, told experimental subjects to imagine they had won a kiss from their favorite movie star and then asked them when they would most like to receive it. Even though getting it right away was one of the options, most subjects elected to wait an average of several days. These choices imply negative time preference, and Loewenstein explained that most subjects simply wanted a little while to savor the anticipation of the kiss.[17]

Loewenstein also told a group of subjects to imagine that they were going to receive a painful electric shock and then asked them when they would like to receive it. This time most subjects chose to get it right away. They apparently wanted to spend as little time as possible dreading the shock. But since an electric shock is a "bad" rather than a "good," these choices too imply negative time preference.

While negative time preferences are occasionally observed in individual cases and can be invoked among many people by suitably chosen experiments, a preference for present over future consumption is more common. For example, if we put a can of honey-roasted cashews in front of Loewenstein's experimental subjects, not many of them would want to wait a few days to anticipate the pleasure of eating them. On the contrary, the nuts would probably disappear in short order, even if that meant spoiling dinner an hour away.

Nineteenth-century economist Eugen von Böhm-Bawerk suggested that one reason for such behavior is that current consumption opportunities confront our senses directly, whereas future ones can only be imagined. The pleasure of eating the roasted nuts, for example, is both intense and immediate. Even those people who would strongly prefer the meal to the nuts often lack the self-control to wait. Böhm-Bawerk believed that our "faulty telescopic faculty" was no good reason to assign greater weight to current than to future pleasures. Uncertainty aside, he felt that people would reap greater satisfaction from their lives if they weighed the present and the future equally.

SUMMARY

- In this chapter our primary focus was on applications of the rational choice and demand theories developed in Chapters 3 and 4. We also considered the concept of consumer surplus, which measures the amount by which a consumer benefits by being able to buy a given product at a given price. We saw that consumer surplus is well approximated by the area bounded above by the individual demand curve and below by the market price. Two-part pricing structures are a device by which a portion of consumer surplus is transferred from the buyer to the seller. (LO1, LO2)

- The rational choice model is also useful for evaluating the welfare effects of price and income changes. It suggests why the consumer price index, the government's measure of changes in the cost of living, may often overstate the true cost of achieving a given level of satisfaction. (LO3)

- The intertemporal choice model is analogous to the atemporal choice model in Chapter 3. In the two-dimensional case, it begins with a commodity graph that depicts current and future consumption levels of a composite good.

The consumer's initial endowment is the point, (M_1, M_2), that corresponds to current and future income. If the consumer can borrow and lend at the rate r, his intertemporal budget constraint is then the line passing through the endowment point with a slope of $-(1 + r)$. The opportunity cost of a unit of current consumption is $1 + r$ units of future consumption. The horizontal intercept of the intertemporal budget constraint is the present value of all current and future income, which is also called the present value of lifetime wealth. (LO5)

- The consumer's intertemporal preferences are represented with an indifference map with the same properties as in the atemporal case. A consumer is said to exhibit positive, neutral, or negative time preference at a point if his marginal rate of time preference (the absolute value of the slope of his indifference curve) at that point is greater than 1, equal to 1, or less than 1, respectively. In the case of interior solutions, equilibrium occurs at a tangency between the intertemporal budget constraint and an indifference curve. Because

[17]See George Loewenstein, "Anticipation and the Valuation of Delayed Consumption," *Economic Journal*, 97, September 1987, 666–684.

the slope of the intertemporal budget constraint exceeds 1 when $r > 0$, consumers exhibit positive time preference in equilibrium, irrespective of the shape of their indifference curves. *(LO5)*

- An important application of the intertemporal choice model is to the study of decisions about how much to save. The permanent income and life-cycle hypotheses employ the model to demonstrate that it is the present value of lifetime wealth, not current income alone, that

governs current consumption (and hence current savings). *(LO5)*

- The intertemporal choice model can describe social as well personal trade-offs between present and future periods. An important example is the social cost of carbon (SCC), which uses intertemporal discounting to estimate the total future costs of a ton of current period carbon emissions. *(LO5)*

KEY TERMS

consumer surplus	permanent income	two-part pricing
marginal rate of time preference (MRTP)	present value	

REVIEW QUESTIONS

1. Explain in your own words why a gasoline tax whose proceeds are refunded to the consumer in a lump-sum amount will nonetheless reduce the consumption of gasoline. *(LO4)*

2. Explain in your own words what a two-part pricing scheme is and why sellers might use one. *(LO2)*

3. Do you think a college education has a high- or low-price (tuition) elasticity of demand? *(LO3)*

4. Explain in your own words why even long-term heavy drinkers might be highly responsive to increases in the price of alcohol. *(LO3)*

5. Explain why 1 plus the interest rate in the intertemporal choice model is analogous to the relative price ratio in the consumer choice model discussed in Chapter 3. *(LO5)*

6. Bus services are generally more energy efficient than cars yet the trend over the past 30 years has been a decline in the proportion of commuters taking buses despite an increase in real energy prices. Why? *(LO3)*

7. Jennifer, who earns an annual salary of $20,000, wins $25,000 in the lottery. Explain why she most likely will not spend all her winnings during the next year. *(LO5)*

PROBLEMS

1. Using a diagram like Figure 5.2, explain why, under our current method of educational finance, a rich family is much more likely than a poor family to send its children to a private school. *(LO1)*

2. When the price of gasoline is $1/gal, you consume 1,000 gal/yr. Then two things happen: (1) The price of gasoline rises to $2/gal and (2) a distant uncle dies, with the instruction to his executor to send you a check for $1,000/yr. If no other changes in prices or income occur, do these two changes leave you better off than before? *(LO3)*

3. Desmond demands strawberries according to the schedule $P = 4 - (Q/2)$, where P is the price of strawberries ($/pint) and Q is the quantity (pint/wk). Assuming that the income effect is negligible, how much will he be hurt if the price of strawberries goes from $1/pint to $2/pint? *(LO2)*

4. You can rent a movie download from your cable provider for $4 per movie per day. If your demand curve for movie rentals is given by $P = 20 - 2Q$, where P is the rental price ($/day) and Q is the quantity demanded (movies per year), what is the maximum annual amount you be willing to pay for movie downloads? *(LO2)*

5. Jane spent all her income on hot dogs and caviar. Her demand curve for caviar was inelastic at all prices for caviar. Unfortunately, an accident at a nuclear power plant caused the supply of caviar to fall and the price to rise. What happened to Jane's consumption of hot dogs? Explain. *(Note:* You should assume that the accident had no effect on the price of hot dogs or Jane's preference for caviar.) *(LO4)*

6. Jordan spends all her income on two goods, X and Y. The prices she paid and the quantities she consumed last year are as follows: $P_X = 15$, $X = 20$, $P_Y = 25$, and $Y = 30$. If the prices next year are $P_X = 6$ and $P_Y = 30$,

and Jordan's income is 1,020, will she be better or worse off than she was in the previous year? (Assume that her tastes do not change.) *(LO3)*

7. Yanni lives in a world with two time periods. His income in each period, which he receives at the beginning of each period, is $210. If the interest rate, expressed as a fraction, is 0.05 per time period, what is the present value of his lifetime income? Draw his intertemporal budget constraint. On the same axes, draw Yanni's intertemporal budget constraint when $r = 0.20$. *(LO5)*

8. Suppose Yanni from Problem 7 views current and future consumption as perfect, one-for-one substitutes for one another. Find his optimal consumption bundle. *(LO5)*

9. Suppose Yanni from Problem 7 views current and future consumption as one-to-one complements. Find his optimal consumption bundle. *(LO5)*

10. Karen earns $75,000 in the current period and will earn $75,000 in the future period. *(LO5)*
    a. Assuming that these are the only two periods, and that banks in her country borrow and lend at an interest rate $r = 0$, draw her intertemporal budget constraint.
    b. Now suppose banks offer 10 percent interest on funds deposited during the current period, and offer loans at this same rate. Draw her new intertemporal budget constraint.

11. Find the present value of $50,000 to be received after 1 year if the annual rate of interest is *(LO5)*
    a. 8 percent
    b. 10 percent
    c. 12 percent

12. Crusoe will live this period and the next period as the lone inhabitant of his island. His only income is a crop of 100 coconuts that he harvests at the beginning of each period. Coconuts not consumed in the current period spoil at the rate of 10 percent per period. *(LO5)*
    a. Draw Crusoe's intertemporal budget constraint. What will be his consumption in each period if he regards future consumption as a perfect, one-for-one substitute for current consumption?
    b. What will he consume each period if he regards 0.8 unit of future consumption as being worth 1 unit of current consumption?

13. Sureka earns $55,000 in the current period and will earn $60,000 in the future period. What is the maximum interest rate that would allow her to spend $105,000 in the current period? What is the minimum interest rate that would allow her to spend $120,500 in the future period? *(LO5)*

14. Mia receives $100 of income this period and $100 next period. At an interest rate of 10 percent, she consumes all her current income in each period. She has a diminishing marginal rate of time preference between consumption next period and consumption this period. *True or false:* If the interest rate rises to 20 percent, Mia will save some of her income this period. Explain. *(LO5)*

15. At current prices, housing costs $50 per unit and the composite good has a price of 1 per unit. A wealthy benefactor has given Chris, a penniless person, 1 unit of housing and 50 units of the composite good. Now the price of housing falls by half. *True or false:* Chris is better off as a result of the price change. Explain. *(LO3)*

16.* Antonio and Isabella are economists. In an attempt to limit their son Hector's use of the family car, they charge him a user fee of 20 cents/mile. At that price he still uses the car more than they would like, but they are reluctant to antagonize him by simply raising the price further. So Antonio and Isabella ask him the following question: What is the minimum increase in your weekly allowance you would accept in return for having the fee raised to 40 cents/mile? Hector, who is a known truth-teller and has conventional preferences, answers $10/wk. *(LO1)*
    a. If Antonio and Isabella increase Hector's allowance by $10/wk and charge him 40 cents/mile, will he drive less than before? Explain.
    b. Will the revenue from the additional mileage charges be more than, less than, or equal to $10/wk? Explain.

17.* All book buyers have the same preferences, and under current arrangements, those who buy used books at $22 receive the same utility as those who buy new books at $50. The annual interest rate is 10 percent, and there are no transaction costs involved in the buying and selling of used books. Each new textbook costs $m to produce and lasts for exactly 2 years. *(LO5)*
    a. What is the most a buyer would pay for the use of a new book for 1 yr?
    b. How low would m have to be before a publisher would find it worthwhile to print books with disappearing ink—ink that vanishes 1 yr from the point of sale of a new book, thus eliminating the used-book market? (Assume that eliminating the used-book market will exactly double the publisher's sales.)

18.* Christina wants to work exactly 12 hr/wk to supplement her graduate fellowship. She can either work as a clerk in the library at $6/hr or tutor first-year graduate students in economics. Pay differences aside, she is indifferent between these two jobs. Each of three first-year students has a demand curve for tutoring given by $P = 10 - Q$, where P is the price in dollars per hour, and Q is the number of hours per week. If Christina has the option of setting a two-part tariff for her tutoring services, how many hours per week should she tutor and how many hours should she work in the library? If she does any tutoring, what should her rate structure be? *(LO2)*

*Problems marked with an asterisk (*) are more difficult.

19.† Eastern University is committed to its current policy of allowing the children of its faculty to attend the university without paying tuition. Suppose the demand curve of Eastern faculty children (CFCs) for slots in other universities is given by $P = 30 - 5Q_0$, where P is the tuition price charged by other universities (in thousands of dollars) and Q_0 is the number of CFCs who attend those universities. Eastern is now considering a proposal to subsidize some proportion k of the tuition charged to CFCs who attend other universities. Suppose Eastern knows that it can fill all its available slots with non-CFCs who pay tuition at the rate of $45,000/yr. Assuming that all CFCs who do not attend other universities will go to Eastern, what value of k will maximize Eastern's tuition revenues, net of outside subsidies, if the tuition price at all other universities is $24,000/yr? *(LO1)*

20.† How will your answer to the preceding problem differ if the tuition charged by outside universities is $12,000/yr? What is the economic interpretation of a value of k greater than 1? *(LO1)*

21.* Michaela runs a small movie theater, whose customers all have identical tastes. Each customer's reservation price for the movie is $5, and each customer's demand curve for popcorn at her concession stand is given by $P_c = 4 - Q_c$, where P_c is the price of popcorn in dollars and Q_c is the amount of popcorn in quarts. If the marginal cost of allowing another patron to watch the movie is zero, and the marginal cost of popcorn is $1, at what price should Michaela sell tickets and popcorn if her goal is to maximize her profits? (Assume that Michaela is able to costlessly advertise her price structure to potential patrons.) *(LO2)*

ANSWERS TO SELF-TESTS

5.1 Initial consumer surplus at $P = \$3$ (and $Q = 7$ gal/wk) is $CS = \frac{1}{2}(10 - 3)7 = \$24.50$/wk. Consumer surplus at the higher price $P' = \$4$ (and $Q' = 6$ gal/wk) is $CS' = \frac{1}{2}(10 - 4)6 = \$18$/wk. The loss in consumer surplus is given by the area of $DCEF$, which equals $24.5 - 18 = \$6.50$/wk. *(LO2)*

5.3 The two budget lines and last year's optimal bundle are shown in the following diagram. A closer look at the tangency point (enlarged area) shows that this year Jin can now afford to purchase a bundle he prefers to the one he bought last year. *(LO3)*

5.2 The maximum membership fee is now given by the area of triangle $AB'C'$, which is $CS = \frac{1}{2}(50 - 20)120 = \$1800$/yr. *(LO2)*

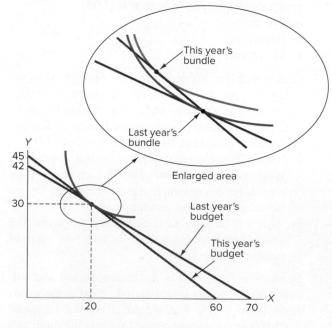

*Problems marked with an asterisk (*) are more difficult.
†Problems marked with a dagger (†) are most easily solved using calculus.

5.4 Again let P_1 and Q_1 denote the original price and quantity, and ΔP and ΔQ denote the respective changes, with $\Delta Q < 0$. The fact that the new total revenue is 2 percent higher than before tells us that

$$[1.10(Q_1 + \Delta Q) - 1.00(Q_1)] = 0.02[1.00(Q_1)].$$

Rearranging terms, we have

$$0.08Q_1 = -1.10\Delta Q,$$

which solves for

$$\Delta Q / Q_1 = -0.08/1.10.$$

And since we know that $\Delta P / P_1 = 0.10$, we have

$$\epsilon = (\Delta Q / Q_1)/(\Delta P / P_1) = (-0.08/1.10)/0.10 = -0.727. \ (LO4)$$

5.5 $PV = \$50,000 + \$42,000/1.05 = \$90,000$. Maximum future consumption $= 50,000(1.05) + \$42,000 = \$94,500$. The equation for your intertemporal budget constraint is $C_2 = \$94,500 - 1.05C_1$. (LO5)

The Economics of Information and Choice under Uncertainty

6

LEARNING OBJECTIVES

After reading this chapter, you should be able to:

LO1 State and apply the costly-to-fake principle.

LO2 State and apply the full-disclosure principle.

LO3 Apply the concept of probability to calculate the expected values of uncertain events and use the Von Neumann—Morgenstern expected utility model to analyze and predict behavior under uncertainty.

LO4 Explain how the law of large numbers facilitates risk management and apply the concepts of adverse selection and moral hazard.

LO5 Explain how statistical discrimination affects outcomes in labor markets and insurance markets.

When a toad and his rival vie for the same mate, each faces an important strategic decision. Should he fight for her or set off in search of another? To fight is to risk injury, but to continue searching entails costs as well. At the very least, it will consume time. And there is no guarantee that the next potential mate will not herself be the object of some other toad's affections.

Each toad's assessment of the other's fighting capabilities plays an important role in this decision. If one's rival is considerably larger, the likelihood of prevailing will be low and the likelihood of injury high, so it will be prudent to continue searching. Otherwise, it may pay to fight.

Many of these decisions must be made at night, when it is hard to see, so toads have found it expedient to rely on various nonvisual clues. The most reliable is the pitch of the rival's croak. In general, larger toads have longer and thicker vocal cords, and hence a deeper croak. Hearing a deep croak in the night, a toad may reasonably infer that a big toad made it. Indeed, experiments have shown that the common toad is much more likely to be intimidated by a deep croak than a high-pitched one.[1]

CHAPTER PREVIEW

Information is an important input for decision making, not only for toads, but for consumers and firms as well. Our models in previous chapters assumed perfect information. In practice, however, we are often woefully ill informed. Our concern in the first part of

[1]See John Krebs and Richard Dawkins, "Animal Signals: Mind Reading and Manipulation," in J. Krebs and N. Davies (eds.), *Behavioral Ecology: An Evolutionary Approach,* 2d ed., Sunderland, MA: Sinauer Associates, 1984.

this chapter is with the question of how we gather and evaluate relevant information. Because many of the issues that will concern us arise in simple form in the context of the toad's problem, it provides a convenient starting point for our discussion. We'll see that the principles that govern communication between toads help us understand such diverse issues as product warranties, hiring practices, and even how people choose partners in personal relationships. We'll also examine statistical discrimination, the process by which people use group characteristics to help estimate the characteristics of specific individuals.

Although the quality of decisions can often be improved by the intelligent gathering of information, it is almost impossible to acquire all potentially relevant information. Our task in the second part of this chapter is to expand the consumer choice model of Chapter 3 to accommodate decisions made under uncertainty.

THE ECONOMICS OF INFORMATION

Communication between Potential Adversaries

The problems of communication between parties whose goals are potentially in conflict are fundamentally different from those involving parties with common goals. Toads searching for mates obviously fall into the former category, as in general will any two parties to an economic exchange. The seller, for example, sometimes has an incentive to overstate the quality of his product. The buyer, likewise, often has an incentive to understate the amount she is willing to pay for it. And the potential employee may be tempted to misrepresent his qualifications for the job.

Bridge partners, by contrast, clearly have common goals. When a bridge player uses standard bidding conventions to tell his partner something, his partner takes the message at face value. Neither player has anything to gain by deceiving the other. Communication here is a pure problem of information transfer. A message need only be decipherable. Error aside, its credibility is not in question.

A very different logic applies, however, when the interests of would-be communicators are in conflict, or even potentially so. Suppose, for example, the bridge player whispers to the opponent on her left, "I always bid conservatively." What is the opponent to make of such a remark? It is perfectly intelligible. Yet if all parties are believed to be rational, the relationship between them is such that the statement can convey no real information. If being known as a conservative bidder would be an advantage, that would be reason enough for a player to call herself one, true or not. The statement is neither credible nor incredible; it simply contains no information.

The streetwise shopper knows to be wary of inflated claims about product quality. But how exactly does she distinguish a good product from a bad one? How, similarly, does a producer persuade a potential rival that he will cut his price sharply if the rival enters his market? Statements like "I will cut my price" are problematic in the same sense discussed for opposing bridge players. Since the producer has an incentive to utter such statements whether true or not, they should convey no information.

We do know, however, that adversaries can communicate information that has strategic value. Toads, after all, are able to broadcast information of this sort. But they do not do it merely by saying "I am a big toad." The big toad's implicit claim is credible only because of the physical barriers that prevent the small toad from uttering a deep croak. The toad's croak is an example of a signal: a means of conveying information.

signaling communication that conveys information.

The toad example illustrates two important properties of **signaling** between potential adversaries: (1) signals must be costly to fake; and (2) if some individuals use signals that convey favorable information about themselves, others will be forced to reveal information even when it is considerably less favorable. Each principle is important for understanding how economic agents gather and interpret information. Let's begin by stating each principle in terms of its application in the toad example and then examining its application in a variety of economic contexts.

THE COSTLY-TO-FAKE PRINCIPLE

For a signal between adversaries to be credible, it must be costly (or, more generally, difficult) to fake. If small toads could costlessly imitate the deep croak that is characteristic of big toads, a deep croak would no longer *be* characteristic of big toads. But they cannot. Big toads have a natural advantage, and it is that fact alone that enables deepness of croak to emerge as a reliable signal.

This **costly-to-fake principle** has clear application to signals between people. It is at work, for example, in the following episode from Joe McGinnis's *Fatal Vision*. Captain Jeffrey MacDonald, an Army Green Beret physician, has been told he is suspected of having killed his wife and daughters. The Army has assigned him a military defense attorney. Meanwhile, however, MacDonald's mother recruits Bernard Segal, a renowned private attorney from Philadelphia, to defend her son. When Segal calls MacDonald in Fort Bragg, North Carolina, to introduce himself, his first question is about MacDonald's Army attorney:

> "Are his shoes shined?"
>
> "What?!" MacDonald sounded incredulous. Here he was, all but accused of having murdered his own wife and children, and in his very first conversation with the Philadelphia lawyer who presumably had been hired to set things right, the first question the lawyer asks is about the condition of the other lawyer's shoes.
>
> Segal repeated the question. "And this time," he said later, "I could almost hear Jeff smiling over the phone. That was when I first knew I had a client who was not only intelligent but who caught on very quickly. He said, no, as a matter of fact, the lawyer's shoes were kind of scruffy. I said, 'Okay in that case, trust him. Cooperate with him until I can get down there myself.' The point being, you see, that if an Army lawyer keeps his shoes shined, it means he's trying to impress the system. And if he was trying to impress the system in that situation—the system being one which had already declared a vested interest, just by public announcement of suspicion, in seeing his client convicted—then he wasn't going to do Jeff any good. The unshined shoes meant maybe he cared more about being a lawyer."

The condition of the attorney's shoes was obviously not a perfect indication of his priorities in life. Yet they did provide at least *some* reason to suspect that he was not just an Army lackey. Any attorney who wore scruffy shoes merely to convey the impression that he was not looking to get ahead in the Army actually *wouldn't* get ahead. So the only people who can *safely* send such a signal are those who really do care more about their roles as attorneys.

Some economic applications of the costly-to-fake principle follow:

Product Quality Assurance

Many products are so complex that consumers cannot inspect their quality directly. In such cases, firms that offer high quality need some means of communicating this fact to potential buyers. Otherwise, they will not be able to charge high enough prices to cover their added costs.

One way to solve this problem is for the firm to develop a reputation for delivering high quality.[2] But conditions will not always allow a firm to do this. Consider the case of sidewalk vendors who sell wristwatches on the streets of any large city. If such a "firm" decides to go out of business, it can do so with virtually no losses. It has no headquarters,

costly-to-fake principle for a signal to an adversary to be credible, it must be costly to fake.

---

[2]This illustration is based on Benjamin Klein and Keith Leffler, "The Role of Market Forces in Assuring Contractual Performance," *Journal of Political Economy,* August 1981.

no costly capital equipment, no loyal customers to worry about—indeed, no sunk costs of any kind. Even if a vendor had supplied quality products on the same street corner for years, that would provide no assurance that he would still be in business tomorrow. And if he *were* planning to go out of business, his incentive would be to sell the lowest-quality merchandise he could pass off. In short, a firm with no obvious stake in the future has an inherently difficult time persuading potential customers it will make good on its promises.

The incentives are different for a firm with extensive sunk costs. If such a firm goes out of business, it loses the value of substantial investments that cannot be liquidated. Accordingly, the material interests of these firms favor doing everything they can to remain in business. And if buyers know that, they can place much greater trust in the promise of a high-quality product. If such a firm charged a price commensurate with high quality and then delivered shoddy merchandise, it would get too little repeat business to survive, and would thus have incurred its sunk costs in vain.

These observations suggest a reason for believing that heavily advertised products will in fact turn out to have higher quality, just as their slogans proclaim. An extensive national advertising campaign is a sunk cost, its value lost forever if the firm goes out of business. Having made such an investment, the firm then has every incentive to deliver. That firms believe many consumers have spotted this pattern is evidenced by the fact that they often say ". . . as seen on national TV . . ." in their magazine ads.

Choosing a Trustworthy Employee

In many situations employees have an opportunity to cheat their employers. Many productive activities would have to be abandoned if firms were unable to hire employees who would not cheat in these situations. The firm needs a signal that identifies a prospective employee as trustworthy. One basis for such a signal might be the relationship between a person's character and the costs or benefits of membership in specific groups. For example, perhaps trustworthy people generally enjoy working in volunteer charitable organizations, which untrustworthy people instead tend to consider highly burdensome. In such cases, the groups people decide to join will convey statistically reliable information about their character.

This notion seems borne out in the procedure by which many professional couples in New York City recruit governesses for their children. The care of children is one of those tasks in which trustworthiness is of obvious importance since it is difficult to monitor the caretaker's performance directly. The very reason for needing someone else to look after them, after all, is that you are not there to do so yourself. Bitter experience has apparently persuaded many New Yorkers that the local labor market is not a good place to recruit people who perform reliably without supervision.

The solution many of these couples have adopted is to advertise for governesses in Salt Lake City newspapers. The couples have discovered that persons raised in the Mormon tradition are trustworthy to a degree that the average New Yorker is not. The signal works because someone who merely wanted to *appear* trustworthy would find it unpalatable, if not impossible, to have remained in the Mormon tradition. The tradition involves continuing, intensive moral indoctrination, an experience most purely opportunistic persons would find too taxing to endure. Like the deepness of a toad's croak as a signal of its size, membership in the Mormon tradition is a good signal of trustworthiness because it would be so costly for an opportunistic person to simulate.[3]

[3]While it may pay, based on group characteristics, to trust Mormons, the same characteristics may make Mormons (and other close-knit groups) overly trusting of each other. Utah, by some accounts, has long been a hotspot for fraudulent investment schemes. The FBI's term for this phenomenon is "affinity fraud." www.fbi.gov/news/stories/beware-of-affinity-fraud.

Choosing a Hard-Working, Smart Employee

As a final illustration of the costly-to-fake principle, consider a degree with honors from an elite university. Employers are looking for people who are smart and willing to work hard. There are obviously a great many people in the world who have both these traits yet do not have an elite degree. Even so, employers are reasonably safe in assuming that a person who has such a degree is both smart and hard-working, for it is not obvious how anyone without that combination of traits could go about getting an elite degree with honors.

No one really questions the fact that the graduates of elite institutions generally turn out to be productive employees. But there is a lively debate indeed about the extent to which attendance at these institutions actually *causes* high productivity. People who think it does point to the fact that the graduates of elite institutions earn significantly higher salaries. Skeptics caution, however, that the entire differential cannot be attributed to the quality of their education. The problem is that the students at the best institutions were undoubtedly more productive to begin with. These institutions, after all, screen their applicants carefully and accept only those with the strongest records of achievement.

Choosing a Relationship

Most people want mates who are kind, caring, healthy, intelligent, physically attractive, and so on. Information about physical attractiveness may be gathered at a glance. But many of the other traits people seek in a mate are difficult to observe, and people often rely on behavioral signals that reveal them. To be effective, such signals must be costly to fake. Someone who is looking for, say, a highly disciplined partner might thus do well to take special interest in people who run marathons in less than $2\frac{1}{2}$ hours. And even the degree of interest a person shows in a prospective partner will sometimes reveal a lot.

Economic Naturalist 6.1

Why is coyness often an attractive attribute?

Groucho Marx once said he wouldn't join any club that would have him as a member. To follow a similar strategy in the search for a relationship would obviously result in frustration. And yet Groucho was clearly on to something. There may be good reasons for avoiding a seemingly attractive searcher who is too eager. If this person is as attractive as he or she seems, why such eagerness? Such a posture will often suggest unfavorable values for traits that are difficult to observe. The properties of effective signals thus make it clear why coyness, within limits, is so adaptive. It is difficult, apparently, for eager persons to disguise their eagerness.

The same properties also have implications for the institutional arrangements under which people search for partners. An often decried difficulty of modern urban life is that heavy work schedules make it hard for people to meet one another. In response, commercial dating services offer to match people with ostensibly similar interests and tastes. Participants in these services are thus spared the time and expense of getting to know people with whom they have few interests in common. They also avoid uncertainty about whether their prospective partner is interested in meeting someone. And yet while marriages often result from commercial dating services, many people have found them a bad investment. The apparent reason is that, without meaning to, they act as a screening device that identifies people who have trouble initiating their own relationships. To be sure, sometimes a participant's trouble is merely that he or she is too busy. But often it is the result of personality problems or other, more worrisome difficulties. People who participate in dating services are indeed easier to meet, just as the advertisements say. But signaling theory says that, on the average, they may be less worth meeting.

Conspicuous Consumption as Ability Signaling

Suppose you have been unjustly accused of a serious crime and are looking for an attorney to represent you. And suppose your choice is between two lawyers who, so far as you know, are identical in all respects, except for their standard of consumption. One wears a threadbare polyester suit off the rack and arrives at the courthouse in a 15-year-old, rust-eaten Chevy sedan. The other wears an impeccably tailored sharkskin suit and drives a new BMW 745i. Which one would you hire?

Our simple signaling principles suggest that the latter attorney is probably a better bet. The reason is that a lawyer's ability level in a competitive market is likely to be mirrored closely by his income, which in turn will be positively correlated with his consumption. There is obviously no guarantee that the lawyer who spends more on consumption will have higher ability. But as in other situations involving risk, here too people must be guided by the laws of probability. And these laws say unequivocally to choose the better-dressed lawyer.

For important decisions involving people we do not know well, even weak signals of ability are often decisive. Close employment decisions are an obvious example. First impressions count for a lot during job interviews, and as apparel manufacturers are fond of reminding us, we never get a second chance to make a first impression. Placement counselors have always stressed the importance of quality attire and a good address in the job search process. Even when the employer *knows* how good an applicant is, she may still care a great deal about how that person will come across to others. This will be especially true in jobs that involve extensive contact with outsiders who do *not* know how good the employee is.

Judging from their spending behavior, many single people seem to believe that their marriage prospects hinge critically on what clothes they wear and what cars they drive. At first glance, this seems curious because by the time most people marry, they presumably know one another well enough for such things not to count for much. Even so, many potential mates have been rejected at the outset for seeming "unsuitable." The trappings of success do not guarantee that a person will marry well, but they do strengthen the chances of drawing a second glance.

The importance of consumption goods as signals of ability will be different for different occupations. Earnings and the abilities that count most among research professors are not strongly correlated, and most professors think nothing of continuing to drive a 15-year-old automobile if it still serves them reliably. But it might be a big mistake for an aspiring investment banker to drive such a car in the presence of his potential clients.

Economic Naturalist 6.2

Why do residents of small towns spend less on their professional wardrobes than their counterparts in big cities?

As in the case of an investment banker hoping to attract new clients, it's clear that a person's incentive to spend additional money on conspicuous consumption goods will be inversely related to the amount and reliability of independent information that other people have about his abilities. The more people know about someone, the less he can influence their assessments of him by rearranging his consumption in favor of observable goods. This may help explain why consumption patterns in small towns, which have highly stable social networks, are so different from those in big cities. The wardrobe a professional person "needs" in Iowa City, for example, costs less than half as much as the one that same person would need in Manhattan or Los Angeles. Similarly, because the reliability of information about a person increases with age, the share of income devoted to conspicuous consumption should decline over time. The more mature spending patterns of older people may say as much about the declining payoffs to ability signaling as about the increasing wisdom of age.

Note that conspicuous consumption as an ability signal confronts us with a dilemma. The concept of a tasteful wardrobe, like the notion of a fast car, is inescapably relative. To make a good first impression, it is not sufficient to wear clothes that are clean and mended. We must wear something that looks better than what most others wear. This creates an incentive for everyone to save less and spend more on clothing. But when *everyone* spends more on clothing, relative appearance remains unchanged. Conspicuous consumption is thus essentially a *positional good,* one whose attractiveness depends on how it compares with goods in the same category consumed by others. In the familiar stadium metaphor, all spectators leap to their feet to get a better view of an exciting play, only to find the view no better than if all had remained seated. Here, too, the aggregate outcome of individually rational behavior is markedly different from what people hoped.

Why do lawyers in small towns buy cheaper suits than lawyers in big cities?

As a group, it might pay to spend much less on conspicuous consumption and to save much more for retirement. But if conspicuous consumption strongly influences estimates of ability, it may not pay any individual, acting alone, to take this step.

THE FULL-DISCLOSURE PRINCIPLE

A second important principle illustrated by the toad example can be called the **full-disclosure principle,** which says that if some individuals stand to benefit by revealing a favorable value of a trait, others will be forced to disclose their less favorable values. This principle helps answer the initially puzzling question of why the smaller toads bother to croak at all.[4] By croaking, they tell other toads how small they are. Why not just remain silent and let them wonder?

Suppose all toads with croaks pitched higher than some threshold did, in fact, remain silent. Imagine an index from 0 to 10 that measures the pitch of a toad's croak, with 10 being the highest and 0 the lowest; and suppose, arbitrarily, that toads with an index value above 6 kept quiet (see Figure 6.1).

It's easy to see why any such pattern would be inherently unstable. Consider a toad with an index of 6.1, just above the cutoff. If he remains silent, what will other toads think? From experience, they will know that *because* he is silent, his croak must be pitched higher than 6. But how much higher?

Lacking information about this particular toad, they cannot say exactly. But they can make an educated statistical guess. Suppose toads were uniformly scattered along the pitch scale. This means that if we picked a toad at random from the entire population

full-disclosure principle
individuals must disclose even unfavorable qualities about themselves, lest their silence be taken to mean that they have something even worse to hide.

Initial croaking threshold

Croak ⟵——————⟶ Don't croak

0 1 2 3 4 5 6 7 8 9 10
Lowest pitch   Highest pitch

FIGURE 6.1

The Information Implicit in Silence

If only those toads with a pitch below 6.0 bother to croak, toads who remain silent reveal that their pitch is, on the average, significantly higher than 6.0.

[4]See Krebs and Dawkins, "Animal Signals."

Why does the small toad croak at all, thereby telling rivals they need not fear him?

of toads, the pitch of its croak would be equally likely to take any value along the pitch scale. With the croaking threshold at 6, however, a toad who remained silent would be systematically different from a randomly selected toad. In particular, experience would tell that the average index for toads who remain silent is 8 (halfway between 6 and 10). Any toad with an index less than 8 would, by the fact of his silence, create the impression that he is smaller than he really is. Our toad with an index of 6.1 would therefore do far better to croak than not.

Thus, if the threshold for remaining silent were 6, it would pay all toads with an index less than 8 to croak. If they do, of course, the threshold will shift from 6 to 8. But a threshold of 8 will not be stable either. With the cutoff at that level, it will pay all toads with an index less than 9 to croak. *Any* threshold less than 10 is for similar reasons destined to unravel. This process happens not because the small toads want to call attention to their smallness by croaking. Rather, they are forced to do so in order to keep from appearing smaller than they really are.

The full-disclosure principle derives from the fact that potential adversaries do not all have access to the same information. In the toad case, the asymmetry is that the silent toad knows exactly how big he is, while his rival can make only an informed guess. As the following illustrations demonstrate, similar asymmetries give rise to important signals between economic agents.

Product Warranties

Information asymmetries help explain, for example, why the producer of a low-quality product might disclose that fact by offering only very limited warranty coverage. The asymmetry here is that producers know much more than consumers about how good their products are. The firm that knows it has the best product has a strong incentive to disclose that information. A credible means of doing so is a liberal guarantee. (This device is credible because of the costly-to-fake principle—a low-quality product would break down frequently, making it too costly to offer a liberal guarantee.)

Once this product appears with its liberal guarantee, consumers immediately know more than before, not only about *its* quality, but about the quality of all remaining products as well. In particular, they know that the ones without guarantees cannot be of the highest quality. Lacking any other information about an unguaranteed product, a prudent consumer would estimate its quality as the average level for such products. But this means consumers will underestimate the quality of those products that are just slightly inferior to the best product.

Consider the situation confronting the producer of the second-best product. If it continues to offer no guarantee, consumers will think its product is worse than it really is. Accordingly, this producer will do better to offer a guarantee of its own. But because of its product's slightly lower quality, the terms of its guarantee cannot be quite so liberal as those for the best product.

With the second-best product now guaranteed, the class of remaining unguaranteed products is of still lower average quality than before. The unraveling process is set in motion, and in the end, all producers must either offer guarantees or live with the knowledge that consumers rank their products lowest in quality. The terms of the guarantees will in general be less liberal the lower a product's quality. Producers clearly do not want to announce their low quality levels by offering stingy warranty coverage. Their problem is that failure to do so would make consumers peg their quality levels even lower than they really are.

Regulating the Employment Interviewer

Another illuminating application of the full-disclosure principle is the difficulty it predicts for government policies that try to restrict the amount of information corporations can demand of job applicants. Consider, for example, the legislation that prohibits employers from asking about marital status and plans for having children.

Before the enactment of this legislation, employers routinely solicited such information, particularly from female job candidates. The information helps predict the likelihood of withdrawal from the labor force, and the employer's motive in asking for it was to avoid investing in the hiring and training of workers who would not stay long. Since the demographic information is costly to fake (few people would refrain from marrying in order to appear less likely to drop out of the labor force), it can be a signal between parties whose interests might be in conflict. The purpose of the legislation was to prevent employers from favoring job candidates on the basis of demographic status.

To achieve this, however, it is not sufficient merely to prohibit employers from asking about demographic categories. For if a woman realizes that her own particular categories place her in the most favored hiring category, she has an incentive to *volunteer* information about them. This sets up the familiar unraveling process whereby all but the least favorable information will eventually be volunteered by job candidates. The candidate who fails to volunteer information, however unfavorable, is simply assumed to be in the least favorable category. If the legislation were to achieve its desired intent, it would somehow have to prohibit job candidates from volunteering the information at issue.

People and things belong to categories, some of which are, by consensus, better than others. To be trustworthy is better than to be untrustworthy, hard-working better than lazy, and so on. The general message of the full-disclosure principle is that lack of evidence that something resides in a favored category will often suggest that it belongs to a less favored one. Stated in this form, the principle seems transparently simple. And yet its implications are sometimes far from obvious.

The Lemons Principle

For example, as the following Economic Naturalist illustrates, the full-disclosure principle helps resolve the long-standing paradox of why new cars usually lose a large fraction of their market value the moment they are driven from the showroom.

Economic Naturalist 6.3

Why do "almost new" used cars sell for so much less than brand new ones?

A new car purchased on Monday for $30,000 might sell for only $22,000 as a used car the following Friday. The explanation for this large price reduction clearly cannot be that the car has suffered physical depreciation of more than 25 percent in less than a week.

► Visit your instructor's Connect© course and access your eBook to view this video.

Economists struggled for years to make sense out of this curious pattern of events. In an uncomfortable departure from their characteristic professional posture, some even speculated that consumers held irrational prejudices against used cars. Berkeley economist George Akerlof, however, suggested that mysterious superstitions might not be necessary. In his "The Market for 'Lemons,'" one of the most widely cited economics papers in the past several decades, he offered an ingenious alternative explanation (which became the first clear statement of the full-disclosure principle).[5]

Why do "almost new" used cars sell for so much less than brand-new ones?

Akerlof began with the assumption that new cars are, roughly speaking, of two basic types: good ones and "lemons." The two types look alike. But the owner of each car knows from experience which type hers is. Since prospective buyers cannot tell which type is which, good cars and lemons must

[5]George Akerlof, "The Market for 'Lemons,'" *Quarterly Journal of Economics,* 1970.

sell for the same price. We are tempted to think the common price will be a weighted average of the respective values of the two types, with the weights being the proportions accounted for by each type. In the new-car market, in fact, this intuition proves roughly correct.

In the used-car market, however, things work out differently. Since good cars are worth more to their owners than lemons are to theirs, a much larger fraction of the lemons find their way quickly into the used-car market. As used-car buyers notice the pattern, the price of used cars begins to fall. This fall in price then reinforces the original tendency of owners of good cars not to sell. In extreme cases, the *only* used cars for sale will be lemons.

Akerlof's insight was to realize that the mere fact that a car was for sale constituted important information about its quality. This is not to say that having a lemon is the only reason that prompts people to sell their cars. Even if it were just a minor reason, however, it would still keep the owner of a good car from getting full value for it in the secondhand market. And that may be all that is needed to initiate the by now familiar unraveling process. Indeed, trouble-free cars rarely find their way into the used-car market except as a result of heavy pressure from external circumstances. ("Going overseas, must sell my Volvo station wagon" or "Injured hand, must sell my stick shift BMW.")

Akerlof's explanation thus vindicates our intuition that physical depreciation is an insufficient reason for the sharp price differential between new and used cars. The gap is much more plausibly understood as a reflection of the fact that cars offered for sale, taken as a group, are simply of lower average quality than cars not offered for sale.

The Stigma of the Newcomer

The full-disclosure principle also suggests why it might once have been more difficult than it is now to escape the effects of a bad reputation by moving. In the current environment, where mobility is high, a dishonest person would be attracted to the strategy of moving to a new location each time he got caught cheating. But in less mobile times, this strategy would have been much less effective, for when societies were more stable, trustworthy people had much more to gain by staying put and reaping the harvest of the good reputation they worked to develop. In the same sense that it is not in the interests of the owner of a good car to sell, it was not in the interests of an honest person to move. In generally stable environments, movers, like used cars, were suspect. Nowadays, however, there are so many *external* pressures to move that the mere fact of being a newcomer carries almost no such presumption.

CHOICE UNDER UNCERTAINTY

No matter how much time and energy we spend gathering information, we must make most choices without complete knowledge about the relevant alternatives. The choice between, say, taking a ski trip or buying a new smartphone can be made more intelligently if we consult sources such as the National Weather Service and *Consumer Reports*. And yet, in the end, we simply cannot rule out possibilities of bad weather or defective phones. Such risks are a prominent feature of many of our most important decisions. Our task in the remainder of this chapter is to enlarge the basic consumer choice model in Chapter 3 to accommodate them.

Probability and Expected Value

When choosing a university to attend, a person to marry, an occupation to pursue, or even a movie to see, there are likely to be important characteristics you are uncertain about at the moment of choice. Sometimes your choice is between two alternatives that are equally risky (the choice, for example, between two blind dates); other times it will be between a little-known alternative and a relatively familiar one (for instance, the decision whether to transfer to another university or to stay where you are).

Economic decisions made under uncertainty are essentially gambles. We have a variety of intuitions about what makes for an attractive gamble, and many of these intuitions carry over into the realm of economic choices. To illustrate, consider the following series of gambles involving the toss of a fair coin.

Gamble 1.   If the coin comes up heads, you win $100; if tails, you lose $0.50.

This is a gamble you are unlikely ever to be offered in a profit-making casino. The winning outcome is 200 times larger than the losing outcome and the two outcomes are equally likely. Only people whose religious faith proscribes gambling would consider turning this gamble down, and even for them, the choice might be difficult. (They might, for example, think it best to take the gamble and donate their winnings to charity.)

Gamble 2.   If heads, you win $200; if tails, you lose $100.

With a winning outcome only twice as large as the losing outcome, this bet is obviously less attractive than the first, but it too would be accepted by many people.

Finally, consider a third gamble. It is the same as the second except the payoffs are multiplied by 100.

Gamble 3.   If heads, you win $20,000; if tails, you lose $10,000; losers are allowed to pay off their loss in small monthly payments spread out over 30 years.

If put to the test, most people would refuse this bet, even though its payoffs are in exactly the same proportion as those in gamble 2. It is the task of a theory of choice under uncertainty to explain this pattern of behavior.

One important property of a gamble is its **expected value,** a weighted average of all its possible outcomes, where the weights are the respective probabilities. The probability that a fair coin comes up heads when tossed is 1/2. One way of interpreting this statement is to say that it means that if a fair coin were tossed a very large number of times, it would come up heads half the time, tails the other half of the time. Thus, the three bets described above have expected values of:

expected value the sum of all possible outcomes, weighted by its respective probability of occurrence.

$$EV_1 = (1/2)\$100 + (1/2)(-\$0.50) = \$49.75; \qquad (6.1)$$

$$EV_2 = (1/2)\$200 + (1/2)(-\$100) = \$50; \qquad (6.2)$$

and

$$EV_3 = (1/2)\$20,000 + (1/2)(-\$10,000) = \$5,000, \qquad (6.3)$$

where the notation EV_i denotes the expected value of gamble $i,$ where $i = 1, 2, 3.$

A gamble is clearly more attractive if it has a positive expected value rather than a negative one. But from the way most people respond to these three hypothetical gambles, it is clear that having a positive expected value is by no means sufficient to make a gamble attractive. On the contrary, gamble 3 has the highest expected value of the three, yet is the one least likely to be accepted. By contrast, gamble 1, which has the lowest expected value, is the one most likely to be chosen.

Now, the lesson is obviously not that having a higher expected value is a bad thing in itself. Rather, it is that in addition to the expected value of a gamble, most people also consider how they feel about each of its possible outcomes. The feature that makes gamble 3 so unattractive to most people is that there is a 50-50 chance of the extremely unpleasant outcome of losing $10,000. Gamble 2 also contains an unpleasant possibility, namely, a 50-50 chance of losing $100. But this is an outcome many people feel they could live with. Gamble 1 is by far the easiest choice for most people because its positive outcome is large enough to make a difference, while its negative outcome is too small to really matter.

The Von Neumann–Morgenstern Expected Utility Model

The formal economic theory of choice between uncertain alternatives was advanced by John von Neumann, a distinguished mathematician at the Institute for Advanced Study, and Oskar Morgenstern, a Princeton economist. Its central premise is that people choose the alternative that has the highest **expected utility.** Their theory of expected utility maximization assumes a utility function U that assigns a numerical measure to the satisfaction associated with different outcomes. *The expected utility of a gamble is the expected value of utility over all possible outcomes.*

expected utility the expected utility of a gamble is the expected value of utility over all possible outcomes.

For the sake of simplicity, we will consider the outcome of a gamble to be defined uniquely by the amount of total wealth to which it corresponds. For example, if a consumer with an initial wealth level of 1,000 accepted gamble 1 above and won, the outcome would be a total wealth of $1,000 + 100 = 1,100$, and the consumer's utility would be $U(1,100)$. If he lost, his wealth would be $1,000 - 0.50 = 999.50$, his utility $U(999.50)$. More generally, if M_0 is the consumer's initial wealth level, the expected utility of accepting the first gamble would be:

$$EU_1 = (1/2)U(M_0 + 100) + (1/2)U(M_0 - 0.50). \tag{6.4}$$

If you refuse gamble 1, your expected utility will simply be the utility of the wealth level M_0, namely, $U(M_0)$. Faced with this choice, the von Neumann–Morgenstern expected utility criterion tells you to accept the gamble if and only if EU_1 is larger than $U(M_0)$.

EXAMPLE 6.1 **Expected Utility**

Suppose Mohammed's utility function is given by $U(M) = \sqrt{M}$. If Mohammed has an initial wealth of 10,000, which of the above gambles has the highest expected utility?

The three expected utilities are given by:

$$EU_1 = (1/2)\sqrt{10{,}100} + (1/2)\sqrt{9{,}999.50} = 100.248,$$

$$EU_2 = (1/2)\sqrt{10{,}200} + (1/2)\sqrt{9{,}900} = 100.247,$$

and

$$EU_3 = (1/2)\sqrt{30{,}000} + (1/2)\sqrt{0} = 86.603,$$

so gamble 1 is the most attractive of the three for Mohammed.

The key insight of the theory is that the expected values of the outcomes of a set of alternatives need not have the same ranking as the expected utilities of the alternatives. Differences in these orderings arise because utility is often a nonlinear function of final wealth. In the empirically most common case, utility is assumed to be a *concave* function of total wealth, which means that the utility function has the characteristic profile shown in Figure 6.2. More formally, a function $U(M)$ is said to be concave if for any pair of values M_1 and M_2, the function lies above the chord joining the points $[M_1, U(M_1)]$ and $[M_2, U(M_2)]$. The utility function $U = \sqrt{M}$ is a concave function of M. A utility function that is concave in M is also said to exhibit **diminishing marginal utility** of wealth. Marginal utility is simply the slope of the utility function,[6] and a utility function with diminishing marginal utility is one whose slope declines as M increases.

diminishing marginal utility for a utility function defined on wealth, one in which the marginal utility declines as wealth rises.

[6]See the appendix to Chapter 3 for a more extended discussion of marginal utility.

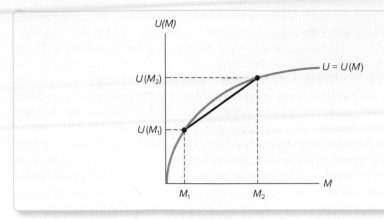

FIGURE 6.2

A Concave Utility Function

Any arc of a concave utility function lies above the corresponding chord.

Intuitively, the meaning of diminishing marginal utility of wealth is that the more wealth a consumer has, the smaller will be the increase in his utility caused by a 1-unit increase in wealth.

Persons whose utility functions are concave in total wealth are said to be **risk averse,** which means that they would always refuse a gamble whose expected value is zero. Gambles with an expected value of zero are called **fair gambles.**

Consider, for example, a gamble G in which you win $30 if the coin comes up heads, but lose $30 if tails. The expected value of this gamble is $(1/2)30 + (1/2)(-30) = 0$, so it is a fair gamble. For a person with an initial wealth level of 40 and utility function given by $U = U(M)$, the expected utility of this gamble is

$$EU_G = 0.5U(40 - 30) + 0.5U(40 + 30) = 0.5U(10) + 0.5U(70). \qquad (6.5)$$

For any fair gamble, the expected value of your wealth if you accept the gamble is the same as the certain value of your wealth if you refuse the gamble. Here, the expected value of wealth when you take the gamble is equal to 40. If you refuse the gamble, you will have a certain wealth level of 40, which yields utility equal to $U(40)$. Expected utility theory says that if $EU_G > U(40)$, you should accept the gamble; otherwise you should refuse it.

The expected utility of a gamble has a straightforward geometric interpretation. We first construct the chord that joins the points on the utility function that correspond to losing and winning the gamble, respectively (that is, the points A and C in Figure 6.3). For the utility function shown in Figure 6.3, the expected utility of the gamble is equal to

risk averse preferences described by a utility function with diminishing marginal utility of wealth.

fair gamble a gamble whose expected value is zero.

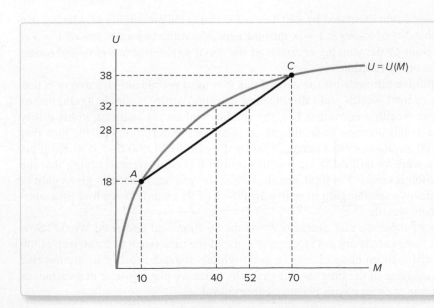

FIGURE 6.3

A Risk-Averse Person Will Always Refuse a Fair Gamble

The expected utility of a gamble lies on the chord joining points A and C. If the probability of winning is 1/2, the expected utility lies halfway between A and C. Since a point on the arc of a concave function always lies above the corresponding point on the chord, the expected utility of a fair gamble will always be less than the utility of refusing the gamble.

$0.5(18) + 0.5(38) = 28$. Note that this value corresponds to the point on the chord between A and C that lies directly above the expected value of wealth under the gamble (40). Note that the expected utility of refusing the gamble is simply $U(40) = 32$, which is clearly larger than the expected utility of the gamble itself.

Indeed, it is clear from Figure 6.3 that a risk-averse person will refuse not only fair gambles but even some that have positive expected value. For the particular utility function shown, all gambles that result in an expected value of final wealth less than 52 yield a lower expected utility than that of standing pat with the initial wealth level 40.

The gambles we have considered so far have been ones decided by the toss of a coin. With probability 1/2, a good outcome occurred; with probability 1/2, a bad outcome. In general, however, the probability of winning a gamble can be any number between 0 and 1. But as the following example and exercise illustrate, the expected utility of a gamble may still be interpreted as a point on the chord joining the winning and losing endpoints, even when the probability of winning is something other than 1/2.

EXAMPLE 6.2   **Expected Value of Wealth**

Your utility function is $U = \sqrt{M}$ and your initial wealth is 36. Will you accept a gamble in which you win 13 with probability 2/3 and lose 11 with probability 1/3?

The expected utility of the gamble is given by

$$EU_G = (2/3)\sqrt{36 + 13} + (1/3)\sqrt{36 - 11} = 14/3 + 5/3 = 19/3.$$

If you refuse the gamble, your utility will be $\sqrt{36} = 6$, which is smaller than 19/3, so you should accept the gamble.

SELF-TEST 6.1

Graph the utility function in Example 6.2 for $0 < M < 50$. Locate the points on the utility function that correspond to the winning and losing outcomes of the gamble in Example 6.2. Draw the chord between these two points, labeling the winning endpoint C, the losing endpoint A. What fraction of AC must you move from C before reaching the expected utility of the gamble?

The general rule illustrated by Self-Test 6.1 is that if the probability of winning is p and the probability of losing is $1 - p$, then the expected utility lies a fraction of $1 - p$ to the left of point C, the winning endpoint of the chord joining the winning and losing points on the utility function.

One intuitive rationale for the assumption that most people are risk averse is that increments to total wealth yield diminishing marginal utility—which, again, means that the more wealth a consumer has, the smaller will be the increase in his utility caused by a 1-unit increase in wealth. Most of us are comfortable with the idea that an extra $100 means more to a person if his total wealth is $4,000 than it would if his total wealth were $1 million. Note that this intuition is equivalent to saying that the utility function is concave in total wealth—which in turn implies that a given gain in wealth produces a smaller gain in utility than the loss that would be caused by a comparable loss in wealth.

Whether people are risk averse is of course an empirical question. We do know that at least some people are not risk averse some of the time (such as those who climb sheer rock cliffs, or go hang-gliding in gusty winds). Indeed, most of us are not risk averse at least some of the time (as, for example, when we play roulette in a casino, or any other game of chance with negative expected value).

FIGURE 6.4

The Utility Function of a Risk-Seeking Person Is Convex in Total Wealth

Any arc of a convex function lies below the corresponding chord. For a risk seeker, the expected utility of a fair gamble, EU_G, will always exceed the utility of refusing the gamble, $U(M_0)$.

Consider a person with an initial wealth of M_0 who is confronted with a gamble that pays B with probability $1/2$ and $-B$ with probability of $1/2$. If this person is a **risk seeker,** her utility function will look like the one pictured in Figure 6.4. It is *convex* in total wealth, which implies that the expected utility of accepting a fair gamble, EU_G, will be larger than the utility of refusing it, $U(M_0)$. Geometrically, a convex utility function is one whose slope increases with total wealth.

risk seeking preferences described by a utility function with increasing marginal utility of wealth.

SELF-TEST 6.2

Consider a person with an initial wealth level of 100 who faces a chance to win 20 with probability 1/2 and to lose 20 with probability 1/2. If this person's utility function is given by $U(M) = M^2$, will she accept this gamble?

A person is said to be **risk neutral,** finally, if he is generally indifferent between accepting or refusing a fair gamble. The utility function of a risk-neutral person will be linear, like the one shown in Figure 6.5.

risk neutral preferences described by a utility function with constant marginal utility of wealth.

SELF-TEST 6.3

Consider a person with an initial wealth level of 100 who faces a chance to win 20 with probability 1/2 and to lose 20 with probability 1/2. If this person's utility function is given by $U(M) = M$, will she accept this gamble?

FIGURE 6.5

Risk Neutrality

A risk-neutral consumer is indifferent between accepting or refusing a fair gamble, because the expected utility of accepting, EU_G, is the same as the certain utility of refusing, $U(M_0)$.

EXAMPLE 6.3   **Risk Neutral**

Suppose it is known that some fraction z of all personal computers are defective. The defective ones, however, cannot be identified except by those who own them. Consumers are risk neutral and value nondefective computers at $2,000 each. Computers do not depreciate physically with use. New computers sell for $1,000, used ones for $500. What is z?

Because of the lemons principle, we know that all used computers that are for sale must be defective. (The owners of nondefective computers could not sell them for what they are worth in the used market, so they hold on to them.) Accordingly, the price of a used computer is the same as the value of a new defective one. (Recall that being used, by itself, doesn't cause the machines to depreciate.) Because consumers are risk neutral, the price of a new computer—$1,000—is simply a weighted average of the values of nondefective and defective computers, where the weights are the respective probabilities. Thus, we have

$$\$1,000 = \$500z + \$2,000\,(1 - z), \tag{6.6}$$

which solves for $z = 2/3$.

SELF-TEST 6.4

Suppose one in every four new personal computers is defective. The defective ones, however, cannot be identified except by those who own them. Consumers are risk neutral and value nondefective computers at $2,000 each. Computers do not depreciate physically with use. If used computers sell for $600, how much do new ones sell for?

The gambles we have considered thus far have had only two outcomes. In general, however, a gamble can have any number of possible outcomes. The expected value of a gamble with more than two outcomes is, as before, a weighted sum of the possible outcomes, where the weights are again the respective probabilities. For example, a gamble with three possible outcomes, B_1, B_2, and B_3, which occur with probabilities p_1, p_2, and p_3, respectively, has an expected value of $p_1 B_1 + p_2 B_2 + p_3 B_3$. Because the probabilities must add up to 1, we know that $p_3 = (1 - p_1 - p_2)$. The expected utility of this gamble is therefore $p_1 U(B_1) + p_2 U(B_2) + (1 - p_1 - p_2)U(B_3)$.

To gain added facility with the concepts of the expected utility model, it is helpful to work through some simple numerical examples. In the next example we use a payoff tree to illustrate the outcomes and probabilities for a decision under uncertainty.

EXAMPLE 6.4   **Expected Utility**

Sarah has a von Neumann–Morgenstern utility function given by $U = 1 - 1/M$, where M is the present value of her lifetime income. If Sarah becomes a teacher, she will make $M = 5$ with probability 1. If she becomes an actress, she will make $M = 400$ if she becomes a star, but only $M = 2$ if she fails to become a star. The probability of her becoming a star is 0.01. Ellis is an infallible judge of acting talent. After a brief interview, she can state with certainty whether Sarah will become a star if she chooses to pursue a career in acting. What is the most she would be willing to pay for this information?

To answer this question, we must first calculate Sarah's expected utility if she lacks access to Ellis's information. If she were to become a teacher, she would have a lifetime income of 5 with probability 1, so her expected utility would be simply

$$U_T = 1 - 1/5 = 0.8.$$

If instead she pursued an acting career, her expected utility would be

$$EU_A = 0.01(1 - 1/400) + 0.99(1 - 1/2) = 0.505.$$

Because her expected utility is higher by becoming a teacher rather than an actress, she will become a teacher and have an expected utility of 0.8.

Now suppose she has access to an interview with Ellis that will reveal with certainty whether she would become a star if she pursued an acting career. And suppose the charge for this interview is P, where P is measured in the same units as M (see Figure 6.6).

The clear advantage of having the information Ellis provided is that if she says she would succeed as an actress, she can then avail herself of that lucrative, but otherwise too risky, career path. If Ellis says she would not succeed, however, she can choose teaching with no regrets. Her expected utility if she pays P for the interview is given by

$$EU_I = 0.01[1 - 1/(400 - P)] + 0.99[1 - 1/(5 - P)]. \tag{6.7}$$

To find the maximum amount that Ellis can charge for an interview, we set EU_I equal to Sarah's expected utility if she lacks information and solve for P (recall that if she lacks information, she becomes a teacher and gets $U_T = 0.8$):

$$EU_I = 0.01[1 - 1/(400 - P)] + 0.99[1 - 1/(5 - P)] = U_T = 0.8. \tag{6.8}$$

As an exercise, you can verify that a value of P of approximately 0.0494 solves this equation. For any price less than that, Sarah should pay Ellis for her evaluation. But if Ellis charges more than 0.0494, Sarah should skip the interview and become a teacher.

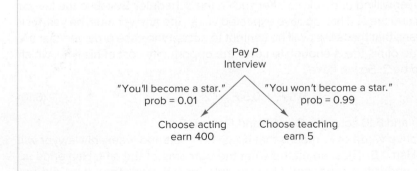

Pay P
Interview

"You'll become a star."   "You won't become a star."
prob = 0.01   prob = 0.99

Choose acting   Choose teaching
earn 400   earn 5

FIGURE 6.6

The Value of Reducing Uncertainty

Under the assumed payoffs, the expected utility of becoming an actress is less than the expected utility of becoming a teacher. But because a successful actress earns so much more than a teacher, information about whether an acting career would be successful has obvious economic value.

As the preceding example clearly illustrates, information that helps reduce uncertainty has economic value. And this is reflected in the fact that we employ vocational testing services, guidance counselors, and a variety of other professionals to generate just this type of information.

EXAMPLE 6.5   Expected Benefit

Han, who was injured by a defective product, is weighing the decision whether to sue the manufacturer. His utility function is given by $U(M) = 1 - (1/M)$, where M is his total wealth. His total wealth if he does not sue is $M_0 = 7$. If he sues, he would win with probability 0.5, in which case he would receive a damage award of 5. If he loses, he will receive nothing in damages. Suppose the opportunity cost of the time required for a lawyer to file a suit on Han's behalf is 2. Will Han file a suit if he has to pay the lawyer a fee of 2? Can a risk-neutral lawyer offer Han a fee schedule whose expected value is sufficient to cover the lawyer's opportunity cost (that is, whose expected value is at least 2) and that simultaneously will induce Han to sue? If so, describe such a fee schedule.

From the perspective of Han and his lawyer, the economic cost of filing a suit is 2, the opportunity cost of the lawyer's time. The expected benefit of filing the suit is the probability of winning (0.5) times the damage award if he wins (5), or 2.5. Thus the expected value of filing the lawsuit is $2.5 - 0.5 = 0.5 > 0$. But the question for Han is not whether filing the suit has positive expected value but rather whether it will increase his expected utility. If Han sues and pays his lawyer 2, his total wealth (net of the lawyer's fee) will be $7 + 5 - 2 = 10$ if he wins and $7 - 2 = 5$ if he loses. His expected utility if he files suit will thus be $0.5[1 - (1/10)] + 0.5[1 - (1/5)] = 0.85$. If he does not sue, his wealth will be 7 for sure, which means his utility will be $1 - (1/7) = 0.86 > 0.85$. Thus if he has to pay his lawyer a fee of 2, he will not sue.

Han's aversion to risk prevents him from filing a suit that has positive expected value. Luckily for him, his lawyer happens to be risk neutral. That means the lawyer can design a fee schedule under which the lawyer assumes all the risk of an unsuccessful filing. What would such a fee schedule look like?

Let F_1 be the lawyer's fee if Han sues and wins and F_2 be the fee if Han sues and loses. Because Han is risk averse, the best possible fee structure from his perspective would be one in which his income is the same irrespective of the suit's outcome:

$$7 + 5 - F_1 = 7 - F_2. \tag{6.9}$$

Is his lawyer willing and able to offer such a fee schedule? Because the lawyer is risk neutral and the suit has positive expected value, the answer must be yes. Risk neutrality means that the lawyer will be content to accept the case provided that the expected value of his fee is enough to cover the opportunity cost of his time, which is assumed to be 2. So we have

$$0.5\,F_1 + 0.5\,F_2 = 2. \tag{6.10}$$

Equations 6.9 and 6.10 solve for $F_1 = 4.5$ and $F_2 = -0.5$.

The negative value of F_2 means that if Han files suit and loses, his lawyer will actually pay Han 0.5. Thus, no matter what the outcome of the suit, Han ends up with $M = 7.5$ under the proposed fee schedule, or 0.5 more than if he did not sue. (Note that 0.5 is exactly the expected value of the lawsuit.) Thus if Han's lawyer offers him the proposed fee schedule, he will sue because his expected utility if he does so—$U = (1 - 1/7.5) = 0.87$—will be higher than if he does not sue (0.86).

The example illustrates the principle that in transactions involving risk, a risk-neutral seller can make the transaction more attractive to a risk-averse buyer by acting, in effect, as an insurance company.

SELF-TEST 6.5

In Example 6.5, find the values of F_1 and F_2 that would have made Han indifferent between filing a suit and not filing it.

The answer to the question asked in Self-Test 6.5 is called the **certainty equivalent value** of the gamble associated with filing the lawsuit. The certainty equivalent value of a gamble is the sum of money for which an individual would be indifferent between receiving that sum and taking the gamble.

Exposure to risk is an undesirable thing for risk-averse consumers, enough so that they are often willing to sacrifice substantial resources in order to reduce it. Thus, the certainty equivalent value of a gamble is less than the expected value of a gamble for risk-averse consumers. As you showed in Self-Test 6.5, the consumer in Example 6.5 would have been willing to accept an expected value lower by 0.5 rather than run the risk of having to absorb the full cost of an unsuccessful lawsuit.

certainty equivalent value the certainty equivalent value of a gamble is the sum of money for which an individual would be indifferent between receiving that sum and taking the gamble.

Are Entrepreneurs Risk-Seeking?

Suppose that, in place of the usual $5 lottery ticket, your local convenience store offered a ticket with a 75 percent chance of paying nothing, a near 25 percent chance of a small-to-substantial payoff, and a two-in-a-thousand chance of paying a billion dollars or more. Given that the odds just described are considerably better than those offered by current multi-state lotteries, you might be tempted to reach for your wallet. But then you realize that the price of the ticket is not $5. And the winning number will not be announced this coming Saturday. With this ticket, you may not find out for 10 years or more whether you have won anything, and until you do find out, the price of the ticket is half your paycheck.

According to economists Robert Hall and Susan Woodward, more than 22,000 startup entrepreneurs (or small teams of entrepreneurs) accepted similar terms from venture capitalists between 1987 and 2008. Because virtually all individuals capable of winning venture capital funding face large opportunity costs—as employees of established companies, they would be highly compensated—Hall and Woodward concluded that entrepreneurs emerge from a group whose distinguishing attributes include lower-than-average risk aversion and higher-than-average assets.[7]

Of course, these two attributes may be related. Risk aversion may decrease with wealth since the ability to absorb a loss of any fixed size would be higher for wealthier persons. Nonetheless, as authors of a recent survey have cautioned, it would be a mistake to conclude that entrepreneurship is "a luxury good that is consumed more by wealthier individuals."[8] For as Hall and Woodward recognized, even among those who can afford to take the risk, entrepreneurs are likely set apart by their "strong preferences for that role over employment" and by displaying such confidence they often "exaggerate the likely payoffs of their own products."[9] Subsequent research has gone on to ask not only whether entrepreneurs are "overconfident," but also whether their overcommitment to a specific vision may be one reason the failure rate of startups is so high.[10] In sum, entrepreneurs

---

[7]Robert E. Hall and Susan E. Woodward, "The Burden of the Nondiversifiable Risk of Entrepreneurship," *American Economic Review*, 100(3), 2010, 1163–1194. A broader study, unrelated to venture capital financing, had already concluded that "the propensity to own a business is a non-linear function of wealth." See Erik Hurst and Annamaria Lusardi, "Liquidity Constraints, Household Wealth, and Entrepreneurship," *Journal of Political Economy*, 12(2), 2004, 319–347.

[8]Thomas Åstebro, Holger Herz, Ramana Nanda, and Roberto A. Weber, "Seeking the Roots of Entrepreneurship: Insights from Behavioral Economics," *Journal of Economic Perspectives*, 28(3), 2014, 49–70.

[9]Hall and Woodward, "The Burden of the Nondiversifiable Risk of Entrepreneurship," 1164.

[10]Åstebro et al., "Seeking the Roots of Entrepreneurship: Insights from Behavioral Economics," reviews a broad range of entrepreneur characteristics and motivations.

may indeed be less risk-averse than others, but there is no clear evidence that lottery-like payoffs are their primary motivation.

INSURING AGAINST BAD OUTCOMES

When the risks that different consumers confront are *independent* of one another (that is, when the likelihood of a bad outcome happening to one consumer is independent of the likelihood of one happening to another), it will often be possible for consumers to act collectively to achieve a result they all prefer.

Risk Pooling

Recall gamble 3 considered earlier in this chapter, in which you could flip a coin and win $20,000 if it came up heads but lose $10,000 if it came up tails. Although this is obviously a much better than fair gamble (its expected value is $5,000), most people would be reluctant to accept it because it would be so difficult to deal with a loss of $10,000. But suppose you could join 9,999 other people in an agreement under which you each accept the gamble, then pool the resulting gains and losses and share them equally. Would you enter that agreement?

You'd be almost crazy not to, because with 10,000 independent flips of a fair coin, the number of heads will lie between 4,900 and 5,100 more than 95 percent of the time. The upshot is that if you join the agreement, not only is the expected value of your share of the winnings $5,000 (the same as if you gambled alone), more important, your share of the winnings is extremely likely to be close to $5,000. The only way you could lose money under this agreement would be if 10,000 flips of a fair coin came up tails more than two-thirds of the time. The odds of that happening are so remote that you really don't need to worry about it.

Risk sharing, or *risk pooling,* works because of a statistical property called the **law of large numbers.** This law says that if an event happens independently with probability p for each of a large number of individuals, then the *proportion* to whom it happens in a given year will rarely deviate significantly from p. Suppose the event is that of a fire destroying a private home, and that it happens with probability 0.001 for each home in a given year. For a small collection of individual homes, the proportion destroyed by fire can vary sharply from year to year. But in a sample of, say, 1,000,000 homes, we can be reasonably sure that the number destroyed by fire in a given year will be very close to 1,000 (so that the proportion destroyed—1,000/1,000,000—would be 0.001).

For individuals, or even small groups of individuals, accidental losses pose a problem of inherent uncertainty. But for a large group of individuals, the proportion of people who will have accidents is extremely stable and predictable. And this property of the law of large numbers makes it possible for people to reduce their risk exposure through pooling arrangements.

Another method of risk sharing is the practice of joint ownership of business enterprises. When a new business starts, two things can happen. The business can succeed, in which case its owners earn a lot of money. Alternatively—and much more likely—it can fail, in which case they lose all or part of their initial investments. Starting a business is thus a gamble, much like any other. Consider a business venture that requires an initial investment of $10,000. Suppose that with probability 1/2 you lose this initial investment, and with probability 1/2 you not only get it back but also earn a dividend of $20,000. This venture is thus essentially the same as gamble 3 considered earlier. It is clear that while the expected value of this enterprise is positive (namely, $5,000), many people would find it unacceptably risky. But if 100 people pooled their resources and shared the investment, the venture would suddenly look exactly like gamble 2—each person would stand to lose $100 with probability 1/2 or gain $200 with probability 1/2. Without changing the business venture itself at all, it has suddenly become attractive to a great many more people.

law of large numbers a statistical law that says that if an event happens independently with probability p in each of N instances, the proportion of cases in which the event occurs approaches p as N grows larger.

Partnerships, joint stock companies, racehorse syndicates, and a host of other similar institutional arrangements enable people to translate unacceptably large risks into much more palatable small ones. Someone with a lot of wealth to invest can keep her risk to a minimum by investing it in numerous independent projects. There is a good chance that *some* of these projects will fail, but very little chance that a substantial portion of them will.

Another example of collective action to reduce uncertainty is the operation of insurance markets. Consider the case of automobile liability insurance. An accident that causes death or serious injury can easily result in a court judgment of several million dollars against the driver. The likelihood of such a bad outcome is remote, but the consequences are so dire that few families could bear them. Private insurance companies offer a means for consumers to share this risk. By contributing an annual premium of several hundred dollars each, the policyholders create a pool of revenues that is large enough to settle the small handful of judgments awarded each year. Because of the law of large numbers, insurance companies can predict very accurately how much revenue they will need to cover their benefit claims. In effect, each party accepts a sure small loss (its insurance premium) in return for a guarantee of not having to bear a much larger one.

For the average consumer, insurance for sale in a private marketplace will always be an unfair gamble, in the specific sense defined earlier. To see why, note first that if an insurance company paid out exactly the same amount in benefits as it collected in premiums, then buying insurance would be a fair gamble—the amount a policyholder got back in benefits would be equal, on the average, to the amount she paid in premiums. But a private insurance company must collect more in premiums than it pays out in benefits, because it must also cover its administrative costs. Sales agents, bookkeepers, claims investigators, and the rent on the company's offices must all be paid for out of premiums. So, on the average, consumers get back less in benefits than they pay in premiums. That most people prefer a small unfair gamble (buying insurance) to a much larger fair one (taking their chances without insurance) is often cited as evidence that most people are risk averse.

The Reservation Price for Insurance

What is the most a consumer would pay for insurance against a loss? Suppose a risk-averse consumer with an initial wealth of 700 has the utility function $U(M)$, as shown in Figure 6.7. If he faces the prospect of a loss of 600 with probability 1/3, his expected

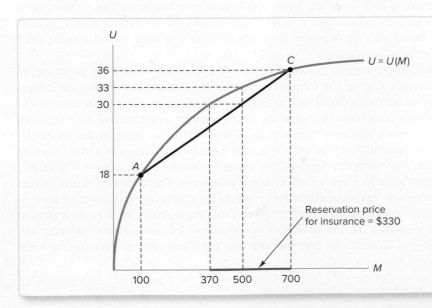

FIGURE 6.7

The Reservation Price for Insurance

The consumer's initial wealth is 700, and he faces a loss of 600 with probability 1/3. His expected utility is 30. Because he gets the same expected utility from a certain wealth level of 370, he would be willing to pay as much as 700 − 370 = 330 for insurance against the loss.

utility is $(1/3)U(100) + (2/3)U(700) = (1/3)(18) = (2/3)(36) = 30$. (See Figure 6.7, and note that his expected utility lies on the chord joining A and C at the point directly above $M = 500$, his expected wealth without insurance.) Now suppose this consumer could buy an insurance policy that completely covered the loss. What is the most he would be willing to pay for such a policy? From Figure 6.7, we see that if he paid 330 for it, his utility would be $U(700 - 330) = U(370) = 30$, whether or not a loss occurred. Since this is exactly the same as his expected utility if he did not buy the policy, he would be indifferent between buying and not buying it. His *reservation price* for the policy, the most he would be willing to pay for it, is thus 330. Note that $700 - 330 = 370$ is the *certainty equivalent value* of the gamble of getting $700 - 600$ with probability $1/3$ and 700 with probability $2/3$. If I is the actual price of the insurance, and is less than 330, then the consumer will buy the policy and get consumer surplus from it of $330 - I$.

Adverse Selection

When a trading opportunity is presented to a heterogeneous group of potential traders, those who accept it will be different—and often worse—on the average, than those who do not. For example, the used cars that are for sale are of lower quality than the used cars that are not for sale; and the participants in dating services are generally less worth meeting than nonparticipants. Both illustrate the lemons principle, and are also sometimes referred to as examples of **adverse selection.** Adverse selection is the process by which "undesirable" members of a population of buyers or sellers are more likely to participate in a voluntary exchange.

adverse selection the process by which the less desirable potential trading partners volunteer to exchange.

Adverse selection is especially relevant to insurance markets, where it often eliminates exchange possibilities that would be beneficial to both consumers and insurance companies alike. To remain in business, an insurance company must have revenues from premiums that cover the claims it pays out plus its administrative expenses. Its premiums therefore must closely reflect the likelihood of claims being filed. Not all potential consumers, however, are equally likely to file claims. In the automobile collision insurance case, for example, some drivers are several times more likely to have accidents than others.

If insurance companies could identify the most risky drivers, they could adjust their premiums accordingly. To some extent, of course, they attempt to do precisely that, charging higher rates for drivers with a history of accidents or serious traffic violations or even for those having no prior insurance history. (More below on how they also set different rates for people with identical records who belong to different groups.) But these adjustments are at best imperfect. Some people who have had neither an accident nor a traffic ticket are nonetheless much more at risk than many drivers with blemished records. Within any broad category of policy, there will inevitably be wide variation in the riskiness of potential policyholders.

Competitive pressure in the insurance market will in general force premiums to reflect the average level of risk for policies in a given category. This means that drivers who know they are much riskier than average face an attractive price on insurance. The other side of this coin, however, is that the same premium is unattractive to drivers who know they are much less risky than average. The result is that many of the least risky drivers will be induced to self-insure—that is, to forgo buying insurance and simply take their chances. And when that happens, the average riskiness of the drivers who do buy insurance goes up, which necessitates a rise in premiums. This increase, in turn, makes the insurance even less attractive to less risky drivers, inducing still more of them to self-insure. In the end, all but the worst drivers may be excluded from participation in the insurance market. This is an unfortunate outcome for many careful drivers, who would gladly pay an insurance premium that was anywhere close to the expected value of their losses.

Economic Naturalist 6.4

Why was American health reform legislation so complicated?

The runup to the 2020 presidential election was replete with hotly debated proposals for "Medicare for All" (M4A), prominent on the platforms of some candidates for the Democratic nomination.

Some of the M4A impetus comes from dissatisfaction with the complexity of the 2010 Affordable Care Act (ACA), or "Obamacare." Indeed, at passage, the ACA ran to over 2,400 pages. The law's drafters could have proposed a simpler and more efficient system—something more like the single-payer systems that have been adopted by most other industrial countries. Why didn't they?

Adopting a simpler approach would have meant abandoning the nation's current system of employer-provided health plans. These plans are a deeply flawed model for providing health care, but a majority of American still have them, and current single-payer M4A proposals must contend with the fact that employer-provided coverage remains popular with those who have it. That popularity pushed single-payer options off the table in 2009–2010 and may again do so well beyond the 2020 election. Any lesser proposal to eliminate complexity from the ACA will still have to reckon that each of Obamacare's major features was critical for extending the then-current system to provide near-universal coverage.

Nearly every economic analysis of the health care industry rests on the observation that individually purchased private insurance is not a viable business model for providing medical services. Such insurance is broadly affordable only if most policyholders are healthy most of the time.

The fundamental problem is that insurers can often identify specific people—like those with serious pre-existing conditions—who are likely to need expensive care. Any company that issued policies to such people at affordable rates would be driven into bankruptcy, its most profitable customers lured away by competitors offering lower rates made possible by selling only to healthy people.

This is an example of the adverse selection problem just discussed. Because of it, unregulated private markets for individual insurance cannot accommodate the least healthy—those who most desperately need health insurance.

Many countries solve this problem by having the government provide health insurance for all. In some, like Britain, the government employs the care providers. Others, like France, reimburse private practitioners—as does the Medicare program for older Americans.

The United States probably would have adopted one of those models had it not been for historical accidents that led to widespread adoption of employer-provided plans in the 1940s. To control costs of World War II mobilization, regulators capped growth of private-sector wages, making it hard for employers to hire desperately needed workers.

But because many fringe benefits weren't capped, employers spied a loophole: They could sweeten their employment packages by offering additional benefits, like health insurance. Its cost was deductible as a business expense, and in 1943 the Internal Revenue Service ruled that its value was not taxable as employee income. By 1953, employer health plans covered 63 percent of workers, up from only 9 percent in 1940.

Eligibility for favorable tax treatment hinged on the plans being available to all employees, a feature that helped to mitigate the adverse selection problem. Although hiring workers with pre-existing conditions meant paying higher premiums, tight labor markets made many employers willing to bear that cost, because insurance was an effective recruiting tool.

Employer plans are thus a significant improvement over individual private insurance, but they are still deeply flawed. If you lose your job, you can lose your coverage. This problem was cast into sharp relief by persistent high unemployment in the wake of the 2008 financial crisis. In no other industrial country do we see communities organizing bake sales to help defray the cost of an uninsured neighbor's cancer treatments.

The decline in the number of workers covered by employer plans began long before the recent crisis. According to census data, 65 percent of workers had employer-backed plans in 2000, but only 55 percent were covered by 2010. This decline has been driven in part by rapid increases in health care costs.

Economists agree that no matter how those costs are apportioned on paper, any money spent on employer-sponsored plans ultimately comes at the expense of wages. Real wages have risen little in receipt decades, and the prospect that they will keep stagnating portends further erosions in coverage. So quite apart from the inherent failings of the employer model, it simply wouldn't be able to deliver broad health coverage over the long term.

The Affordable Care Act was actually modeled after proposals advanced by the Heritage Foundations, the American Enterprise Institute, and other conservative research organizations in the 1990s. The main provisions were intended to eliminate the most salient problems associated with the then-current system.

One provision establishes insurance exchanges, where participating companies must offer coverage to all customers, irrespective of pre-existing conditions. Another imposes a financial penalty on those who fail to obtain coverage—the so-called individual mandate. And a third prescribes subsidies to make insurance more affordable for low-income families. (The Massachusetts plan engineered by Mitt Romney as governor in 2006 took an almost identical approach.)

Without each of its three main provisions, the law wouldn't work. The individual mandate was the most controversial. Critics denounced it as a violation of people's liberty. Paradoxically, the slim majority on the Supreme Court that affirmed the mandate's constitutionality seemed to embrace that view, likening the mandate to requiring citizens to eat broccoli for their own good. The court defended the constitutionality of the mandate by calling it a tax rather than a penalty.

But that interpretation struck many economists as a misreading of the mandate's purpose. It wasn't that people should buy health insurance because it would be good for them. Rather, it was that failure to do so would cause significant harm to others. Society will always step in to provide care—though in much more costly and often delayed and ineffective forms—to the uninsured who fall ill. To claim the right not to buy health insurance is thus to assert a right to impose enormous costs on others. Many legal scholars argued that the Constitution guarantees no such right.

No one can be sure how the push for M4A or the ongoing legal and political challenges to ACA will play out. But if an employer-based system remains the starting point, as is certainly possible, no one should assume that it will be easier to draft superior legislation.

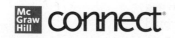

▶ Visit your instructor's Connect© course and access your eBook to view this video.

Why might a patient be more likely to receive an expensive magnetic resonance imaging (MRI) exam for a sore knee if covered under a conventional health insurance plan rather than a Health Maintenance Organization (HMO) plan?

Moral Hazard

moral hazard incentives that lead people to file fraudulent claims or to be negligent in their care of goods insured against theft or damage.

Another phenomenon with important implications for insurance markets is **moral hazard,** which occurs when insurance creates incentives for people to behave in inefficient or even fraudulent ways. Consider the case of "Nub City," the small Florida town given that nickname by insurance investigators who were skeptical about its curious pattern of accident claims:

> Over 50 people in the town have suffered "accidents" involving the loss of various organs and appendages, and claims of up to $300,000 have been paid out by insurers. Their investigators are positive the maimings are self-inflicted; many witnesses to the "accidents" are prior claimants or relatives

of the victims, and one investigator notes that "somehow they always shoot off parts they seem to need least."[11]

Because the amount an insurance company charges in premiums must be sufficient to cover the amount it pays out in claims, fraudulent insurance claims cause premiums to be higher than they otherwise would be. But moral hazard also causes insurance premiums to rise for reasons unrelated to fraud. Many people whose cars are insured, for example, are less likely to take simple steps to reduce the likelihood of their being damaged or stolen. Similarly, someone whose house is insured against fire damage is less likely for that reason to install a sprinkler system that would limit fire damage. Taking precautions is costly, and people who know their losses are fully covered by insurance are less likely to take them.

Both adverse selection and moral hazard play a role in the entrepreneurship example discussed earlier. Why are venture capital terms so strict? Hall and Woodward explain:

> Venture capitalists face a daunting problem in evaluating proposals for startups. One of the reasons that entrepreneurs receive submarket salaries during the startup phase is to induce self-selection among applicants for venture funding. Only entrepreneurs with confidence in the commercial value of their ideas will seek funding if the entrepreneur's payoff from an unsuccessful startup is negative.[12]

STATISTICAL DISCRIMINATION

As noted above, automobile insurance companies often try to tailor their rates to the driving records of individual policyholders. In addition, most companies charge different rates to people with identical driving records if they happen to belong to groups with significantly different average risk. Perhaps the most conspicuous example is the extremely high rate for single male drivers under 25 years of age. The average accident rate for drivers in this group is much higher than for any other demographic category. Even so, plenty of males under 25 are exceptionally good drivers. There are surely several such persons in your class. The difficulty is that insurance companies cannot identify them at a reasonable cost.

In California, many auto insurance companies charge different rates depending on what part of a city you live in. Their rationale is that traffic congestion, theft, vandalism, uninsured drivers, and other factors that influence claims differ greatly from neighborhood to neighborhood.[13] The awkward result, however, is that people who live just 50 yards from one another in adjacent zip codes sometimes end up paying substantially different insurance rates.

Many have complained that such rate differentials are inherently unfair. But before judging the insurance companies, it is important to understand what would happen to one that abandoned these differentials. Suppose, for example, that a company decided to sell insurance at the same price to all drivers with clean records. If it retained its current list of policyholders, this would mean lowering its current rates for people in unsafe neighborhoods, teenage males, and other high-risk groups, and raising them for everyone else. But why should older drivers from safe neighborhoods then remain with the company? They could save by switching to a company that had stuck with the old rate structure, and many of them would surely do so. By the same token, members of high-risk groups who now hold policies with other companies would have a strong incentive to switch to the one with the new rate structure. In the end, the company would be left with only policyholders from high-risk groups. The company could stick with its new program of charging the same rate for everyone, but that rate would have to be high enough to cover the claims generated by the highest-risk group of all.

Recognizing this problem, some states are considering laws that would prohibit group insurance rating. The argument is that if *all* companies are forced to offer a single rate, members of low-risk groups cannot escape rate increases by switching to other companies. The difficulty with this approach, however, is that the government cannot force private insurance

---

[11]*Wall Street Journal,* December 23, 1974.
[12]Hall and Woodward, "The Burden of the Nondiversifiable Risk of Entrepreneurship," 1166.
[13]See Eric Smith and Randall Wright, "Why Is Automobile Insurance in Philadelphia So Damned Expensive?" *American Economic Review,* 82, 1992, 756–772.

companies to provide insurance against their will. As a result, many companies will pull out of those areas that are costliest to serve, leaving their former customers to fend for themselves.

Application: Always Self-Insure against Small Losses

As noted earlier, insurance provided in private markets will have negative expected value because of the resources used by the company to administer its policies. The phenomenon of adverse selection provides another reason to self-insure when the size of the potential loss is manageable. It says that insurance premiums must be large enough to cover the cost of serving the typical policyholder, who will have a greater risk of losses than the average person. Still another reason that insurance premiums exceed the expected value of the average person's losses is the problem of moral hazard.

Despite the fact that insurance premiums must cover administrative expenses, adverse selection, and the costs of moral hazard, most of us still find it prudent to insure against major losses, like damage to our homes by fire. But many people also insure against a host of much smaller losses.

> Because insurance companies must cover their costs, their average premium must exceed their average claim payment. So for the average customer, buying insurance is a gamble with negative expected value. In the long run, you'll come out ahead if you don't buy insurance against small losses.

Buying insurance against minor losses violates the principle that you should always pick the alternative with the highest expected outcome when only small outcomes are at stake. Automobile collision insurance policies typically offer a choice of the amount of each claim to leave uncovered—the "deductible provision," as it is called. If you choose the $200 deductible provision, for example, your insurance policy will cover all but the first $200 of any damage claim. Policies with this provision are cheaper than those without, because the company not only does not have to pay the first $200 in damages, but also avoids the trouble and expense of processing numerous small damage claims. Because of this additional cost reduction, the amount you expect to save in premiums is larger than the extra amount you expect to spend on repairs. And the higher deductible provision you choose, the greater the expected savings will be. Rather than insure fully against collision damage, it thus makes much more sense to choose a large deductible provision and deposit the savings in an interest-bearing account.

How large a deductible provision? The larger the better, subject to the proviso that you have enough resources on hand to take care of the uncovered portion of any damage claim. Indeed, for many middle- and upper-income consumers, and for those with older cars that are not worth very much, the most sensible strategy is not to buy automobile collision insurance at all.

But what if you follow this strategy and then someone smashes your new $20,000 automobile beyond repair? Naturally, you will feel bad. But be careful not to fall victim to the bad-outcome-implies-bad-decision fallacy. After all, the odds of such an accident were very low to begin with, and even having had one, your premium savings over the course of a lifetime will be more than enough to cover the damages. Relative to the alternative of buying collision insurance, going without collision insurance is a better-than-fair gamble, and if you are wealthy enough to withstand the worst outcome, you should take it.

Caution: Always Consider Insuring against Major Losses

Lest there be any misunderstanding, the advice of the last section does not apply to major losses. If a major loss is defined as one that will deprive you of a significant fraction of your lifetime wealth, you should probably insure against such losses. You should carry major medical insurance, with deep coverage against both catastrophic illness and loss of income from disability; you should carry an umbrella liability insurance policy against the possibility of a ruinous court judgment; if you live on a flood plain, you should carry flood insurance; and so on.

Ironically, however, many people leave these life-shattering risks uncovered, while at the same time insuring themselves fully against the possible theft of their television sets. The savvy expected utility maximizer will know to avoid this ill-advised pattern of behavior.

The appendix to this chapter discusses search theory and the winner's curse.

Can We Insure against Climate Catastrophe?

As we saw in Chapter 5, William Nordhaus, in his DICE model, treats CO_2 emission reduction as an "investment," at least in the sense that the costs and benefits of mitigation strategies are evaluated against a normal rate of return embedded in a "discount rate"—the "r" in our intertemporal choice setup. The DICE model, like other integrated assessment models, asks what stream of investment, such as a carbon tax, needs to begin today in order to reduce carbon emissions to a certain level at a certain point in the future.

Other economists, most notably the late Martin Weitzman of Harvard, have asked whether climate change is more an insurance problem than an investment problem. What if averting climate catastrophe is less about stopping the *flow* of CO_2 emissions and more about mitigating the damage that is evolving from the *stock* of CO_2 that has already been released? Weitzman pointed to a range of climate science studies that suggested a "disastrous collapse of planetary welfare," based on CO_2 levels already observed, was a "tiny" but "non-negligible" possibility. Since the possibility of catastrophe could neither be eliminated nor precisely estimated, he called his finding the "Dismal Theorem."

How should we deal with "high-impact, low-probability catastrophes"? In the face of such deep uncertainty, Weitzman insisted, standard future discounting, standard damage reckoning, and standard cost-benefit analysis all break down. Provocatively, he suggested that short-term greenhouse gas emissions reduction might *not* be the priority in such a situation. Instead, emphasis should be given to "buying insurance," in the sense of developing carbon sequestration or "geoengineering" technologies that could be brought to play in a worst-case scenario.

The argument between the Nordhaus approach and the Weitzman approach remains very much alive. Because the disagreement is *about* uncertainty, it can't be resolved *with* certainty. Weitzman therefore argued for a balanced approach that avoids overcommitment:

> [A] tricky balance is required between being overawed by the Dismal Theorem into abandoning cost-benefit analysis altogether and being underawed by the Dismal Theorem into believing that [climate catastrophe] is just another empirical issue to be sorted out by nosiness-as-usual CBA.[14]

There is little doubt that it will be difficult to reach agreement on the balance that Weitzman describes. Climate scientists who foresee catastrophe will likely find discount-based approaches too "business-as-usual." Planners whose goal is to define and implement specific policies will complain the Dismal Theorem approach is too alarmist to be useful. Perhaps most economists will be in the former camp and will continue to focus primarily on the quantifiable trade-offs embodied in measures to reduce CO_2 emissions. Their intuition ("When you're in a hole, stop digging.") is powerful one. The contribution of Martin Weitzman is the reminder that, once the hole is past a certain depth, some thought must be given to making it livable.

---

[14]The extacted quotation and other in-text quotes are from Martin L. Weitzman, "On Modeling and Interpreting the Economics of Catastrophic Climate Change," *The Review of Economics and Statistics* 91(1), 2009, 1–19. A less technical discussion, one that develops the "insurance" theme more explicitly, is Martin L. Weitzman, "A Review of the Stern Review on the Economics of Climate Change," *Journal of Economic Literature* 45(3), 2007, 703–724. An updated treatment in a more balanced context is Gernot Wagner and Martin L. Weitzman, *Climate Shock: The Economic Consequences of a Hotter Planet*, Princeton, NJ: Princeton University Press, 2015. A response to Weitzman's 2009 article is William D Nordhaus, "An Analysis of the Dismal Theorem," Cowles Foundation, 2009, http://cowles.yale.edu/sites/default/files/files/pub/d16/d1686.pdf. But see also the symposium, with contributions by Weitzman, Nordhaus, and Robert Pindyck, in the *Review of Environmental Economics and Policy* 5(2), 2011, https://academic.oup.com/reep/issue/5/2. Weitzman based his 2009 article concerns on a panel of studies referenced in the "Physical Science Basis" module of Fourth Assessment Report (2007) of the Intergovernmental Panel on Climate Change, Table 9.3, p. 721f, www.ipcc.ch/report/ar4/wg1/. More recent versions of the IPCC climate assessment report are available at www.ipcc.ch.

SUMMARY

- Potential parties to an economic exchange often have many common goals, but in an important respect they must be viewed as adversaries. In both product and labor markets, both buyers and sellers face powerful incentives to misrepresent their offerings. *(LO1)*

- For messages between potential adversaries to be credible, they must be costly to fake. A firm with extensive sunk costs, for example, can communicate credibly that it offers a reliable product because if it fails to satisfy its customers, it stands to lose a lot of money. By contrast, a street vendor, for whom the costs of going out of business are very low, has a more difficult time persuading buyers he offers high quality. *(LO1)*

- Messages between potential adversaries must also satisfy the full-disclosure principle, which means that if one party is able to disclose favorable information about itself, others will feel pressure to disclose parallel information, even if considerably less favorable. The producer of a low-quality product does not *want* to signal his product's inferior status by offering only limited warranty coverage. But unless he does so, many buyers will make an even less favorable assessment. *(LO2)*

- When a trading opportunity confronts a mixed group of potential traders, the ones who accept it will be different—and in some way worse—on the average than those who reject it. Cars that are offered for sale in the secondhand market are of lower quality than those that are not for sale; participants in dating services are often less worth meeting than others; and so on. These are illustrations of the lemons principle. *(LO4)*

- The analytical tool for dealing with choice under uncertainty is the von Neumann–Morgenstern expected utility model. This model begins with a utility function that assigns a numerical measure of satisfaction to each outcome, where outcomes are defined in terms of the final wealth to which they correspond. The model says that a rational consumer will choose between uncertain alternatives so as to maximize his expected utility, a weighted sum of the utilities of the outcomes, where the weights are their respective probabilities of occurrence. *(LO3)*

- The central insight of the expected utility model is that the ordering of the expected values of a collection of gambles is often different from the ordering of the expected utilities of those gambles. The differences arise because of nonlinearities in the utility function, which in turn summarize the consumer's attitude toward risk. The concave utility function, any arc of which always lies above the corresponding chord, leads to risk-averse behavior. Someone with such a utility function will always refuse a fair gamble, which is defined as one with an expected value of zero. A person with a convex utility function, any arc of which lies below the corresponding chord, is said to be a risk seeker. Such a person will always accept a fair gamble. A person with a linear utility function is said to be risk neutral, and is always indifferent between accepting and refusing a fair gamble. *(LO3)*

- Because of adverse selection, firms are under heavy competitive pressure to find out everything they possibly can about potential buyers and employees. This pressure often results in statistical discrimination. In insurance markets, people from groups with different accident rates often pay different premiums, even though their individual driving records are identical. This pricing pattern creates an understandable sense of injustice on the part of individuals adversely affected by it. In competitive markets, however, any firm that abandoned this policy could not expect to survive for long. *(LO4, LO5)*

- Insurance purchased in private markets is generally an unfair gamble, not only because of the administrative costs included in insurance premiums, but also because of adverse selection and moral hazard. The fact that most people nonetheless buy substantial amounts of insurance is taken as evidence of risk aversion. This observation is further supported by the pervasiveness of risk-sharing arrangements such as joint stock ownership. *(LO4)*

- Climate change mitigation has investment and insurance components that can point in different policy directions. Because reducing future CO_2 emissions involves discounting, it is an investment-like activity that is best encouraged by a carbon tax. Mitigating the impact of previous emissions is more like an insurance activity. Directed research into technologies such as carbon sequestration or geoengineering may be the best way to "buy insurance" against unlikely-but-possible adverse climate events. *(LO4)*

KEY TERMS

adverse selection	expected value	risk averse
certainty equivalent value	fair gamble	risk neutral
costly-to-fake principle	full-disclosure principle	risk seeking
diminishing marginal utility	law of large numbers	signaling
expected utility	moral hazard	

REVIEW QUESTIONS

1. Why must a signal between potential adversaries be costly to fake? *(LO1)*

2. Explain why, despite the potential adversarial relationship between sellers and buyers, commercial advertising nonetheless transmits information about product quality. *(LO1)*

3. What practical difficulty confronts laws that try to regulate what questions can be asked of job applicants during employment interviews? *(LO2)*

4. How does statistical discrimination affect the distribution of insurance premiums within a group? *(LO5)*

5. How does statistical discrimination affect the average insurance premium paid by members of different groups? *(LO5)*

6. Why is it intuitively plausible to assume that most people are risk averse? *(LO3)*

7. Give some examples of behavior that seem inconsistent with the assumption of risk aversion. *(LO3)*

8. Explain, in your own words, why it makes sense to self-insure against minor losses. *(LO4)*

9. Give some examples in which people do not self-insure against minor losses. *(LO4)*

PROBLEMS

McGraw Hill connect

1. Suppose the messiness of apartments is measured on a scale from 0 to 100, with 0 the cleanest and 100 the messiest. Suppose also that the distribution of apartments by messiness is as shown in the diagram. That is, suppose 10 percent of the apartments lie between 0 and 20, 20 percent between 20 and 40, and so on.

Suppose, finally, that all parents tried to teach their children never to let anyone in to see their apartments if they were over 80 on the messiness scale. If such a rule of thumb were widely observed, what would be your best estimate of the messiness index of someone who said, "You can't come in now, my place is a pit"? In a world in which everyone makes use of all available information, would you expect this rule of thumb to be stable? What do you conclude from the fact that people really do sometimes refuse admission on the grounds that their apartments are too messy? *(LO2)*

2. Explain in detail what will happen to an insurance company that charges teenage males the same rates for automobile insurance as it charges its other customers. *(LO5)*

3. It is known that some fraction *d* of all new cars is defective. Defective cars cannot be identified as such except by the people who own them. Each consumer is risk neutral and values a nondefective car at $6,000. New

cars sell for $4,000 each, used ones for $1,000. If cars do not depreciate physically with use, what is *d*? *(LO4)*

4. A new motorcycle sells for $9,000, while a used motorcycle sells for $1,000. If there is no depreciation and risk-neutral consumers know that 20 percent of all new motorcycles are defective, how much do consumers value a nondefective motorcycle? *(LO4)*

5. The exhaust system on your 2010 Honda Accord needs to be replaced, and you suspect that the price of a new exhaust system is the same as what you would get if you tried to sell the car. If you know that the car is otherwise okay, what relevance does Akerlof's model of lemons have to your decision about whether to purchase a new exhaust system? *(LO4)*

6. What grounds are there for assuming that a randomly chosen social worker is less likely to cheat you in cards than a randomly chosen person? *(LO5)*

7. At the turn of this century, most banks required tellers to have a high school diploma. Even though the tasks currently performed by tellers in most banks can still be performed by persons who have mastered the high school curriculum, many banks now require that their tellers have college diplomas. Assuming that the real costs of college education are lower now than at the turn of the century and that these costs are lower for persons of higher ability, construct an explanation for why banks might have raised their hiring standards. *(LO1)*

8. What is the expected value of a random toss of a die? (Fair and six-sided.) *(LO3)*

9. A fair coin is flipped twice and the following payoffs are assigned to each of the four possible outcomes:

H-H: win 20; H-T: win 9; T-H: lose 7; T-T: lose 16.

What is the expected value of this gamble? *(LO3)*

10. Suppose your utility function is given by $U = \sqrt{M}$, where M is your total wealth. If M has an initial value of 16, will you accept the gamble in the preceding problem? *(LO3)*

11. Suppose you have \$10,000 to invest. A broker phones you with some information you requested on certain junk bonds. If the company issuing the bonds posts a profit this year, it will pay you a 40 percent interest rate on the bond. If the company files for bankruptcy, you will lose all you invested. If the company breaks even, you will earn a 10 percent interest rate. Your broker tells you there is a 50 percent chance that they will break even and a 20 percent chance that the company will file for bankruptcy. Your other option is to invest in a risk-free government bond that will guarantee 8 percent interest for 1 year. *(LO3)*
    a. What is the expected interest rate for the junk bond investment?
    b. Which investment will you choose if your utility function is given by $U = M^2$?
    c. Which investment will you choose if your utility function is given by $U = \sqrt{M}$?

12. Suppose your current wealth, M, is 100 and your utility function is $U = M^2$. You have a lottery ticket that pays \$10 with a probability of 0.25 and \$0 with a probability of 0.75. What is the minimum amount for which you would be willing to sell this ticket? *(LO3)*

13. Your utility function is $\sqrt{M}$. Your current wealth is \$400,000. There is a 0.00001 probability that your legal liability in an automobile accident will reduce your wealth to \$0. What is the most you would pay for insurance to cover this risk? *(LO3)*

14. A farmer's hens lay 1,000 eggs/day, which he sells for 10 cents each, his sole source of income. His utility function is $U = \sqrt{M}$, where M is his daily income. Each time a farmer carries eggs in from the hen house, there is a 50 percent chance he will fall and break all the eggs. Assuming he assigns no value to his time, is he better off by carrying all the eggs in one trip or by carrying 500 in each of two trips? *(Hint:* There are three possibilities when he takes two trips: 1,000 broken eggs, 500 broken eggs, and no broken eggs. What is the probability of each of these outcomes?) *(LO3)*

15. Your current wealth level is $M = 49$ and you are forced to make the following wager: If a fair coin comes up heads, you get 15; you lose 13 if it comes up tails. Your utility function is $U = \sqrt{M}$. *(LO3)*
    a. What is the expected value of this gamble?
    b. What is its expected utility?
    c. How would your answers change if the payoff for tails fell to a loss of 15?
    d. What is the most you would pay to get out of the gamble described in part (c)?

16. Jane has an investment opportunity that pays 33 with probability 1/2 and loses 30 with probability 1/2. *(LO3)*
    a. If her current wealth is $M = 111$, and her utility function is $U = \sqrt{M}$, will she make this investment?
    b. Will she make it if she has two equal partners? (Be sure to calculate the relevant expected utilities to at least two decimal places.)

17. Amanda has a von Neumann–Morgenstern utility function given by $U = \sqrt{M}$, where M is her income. If she becomes an economics professor, she will make $M = 81$/yr with probability 1. If she becomes an attorney, she will make $M = 900$/yr if she becomes a partner in a Wall Street firm, but only $M = 25$/yr if she fails to make partner. The probability of her becoming a partner is 0.2. Ellis is an infallible judge of legal talent. After a brief interview, he can state with certainty whether Amanda will become a partner. What is the most Amanda would be willing to pay for this information? (Set up the relevant equation. You don't need to solve it.) *(LO3)*

18.* In the preceding problem, assuming that the interview is costless for Ellis to conduct, is he getting the highest possible expected income for himself by charging Amanda the same fee regardless of the outcome of the interview? *(LO3)*

19.* There are two groups of equal size, each with a utility function given by $U(M) = \sqrt{M}$, where $M = 100$ is the initial wealth level for every individual. Each member of group 1 faces a loss of 36 with probability 0.5. Each member of group 2 faces the same loss with probability 0.1. *(LO4)*
    a. What is the most a member of each group would be willing to pay to insure against this loss?
    b. In part (a), if it is impossible for outsiders to discover which individuals belong to which group, will it be practical for members of group 2 to insure against this loss in a competitive insurance market? (For simplicity, you may assume that insurance companies charge only enough in premiums to cover their expected benefit payments.) Explain.
    c. Now suppose that the insurance companies in part (b) have an imperfect test for identifying which individuals belong to which group. If the test says that a person belongs to a particular group, the probability that he really does belong to that group is $x < 1.0$. How large must x be in order to alter your answer to part (b)?

20.* There are two groups, each with a utility function given by $U(M) = \sqrt{M}$, where $M = 144$ is the initial wealth level for every individual. Each member of group 1 faces a loss of 44 with probability 0.5. Each member of group 2 faces the same loss with probability 0.1. *(LO4)*

*Problems marked with an asterisk (*) are more difficult.

a. What is the most a member of each group would be willing to pay to insure against this loss?

b. If it is impossible for outsiders to discover which individuals belong to which group, how large a share of the potential client pool can the members of group 1 be before it becomes impossible for a private company with a zero-profit constraint to provide insurance for the members of group 2? (For simplicity, you may assume that insurance companies charge only enough in premiums to cover their expected benefit payments and that people will always buy insurance when its price is equal to or below their reservation price.) Explain.

21* Given a choice between A (a sure win of 100) and B (an 80 percent chance to win 150 and a 20 percent chance to win 0), Sejal picks A. But when she is given a choice between C (a 50 percent chance to win 100 and a 50 percent chance to win 0) and D (a 40 percent chance to win 150 and a 60 percent chance to win 0), she picks D. Show that Sejal's choices are inconsistent with expected utility maximization. *(LO3)*

ANSWERS TO SELF-TESTS

6.1 The expected utility of the gamble corresponds to point *D,* which lies one-third of the way from *C* to *A.* *(LO3)*

6.2 If she accepts the gamble, her expected utility is given by $EU_G = (1/2)(120^2) + (1/2)(80^2) = 10,400$. Her utility if she refuses the gamble is only $100^2 = 10,000$, and so she should accept the gamble. *(LO3)*

6.3 If she accepts the gamble, her expected utility is given by $EU_G = (1/2)(120) + (1/2)(80) = 100$. Her utility if she refuses the gamble is also 100, and so she is indifferent between accepting and refusing the gamble. *(LO3)*

6.4 As in Example 6.3, the key step here is to see that the only used computers for sale will be defective. Because of the lemons principle, the owner of a good computer could not sell it for what it is worth to him in the secondhand market. So if the value of a defective computer is $600, then the value of a new computer to a risk-neutral buyer must be $(1/4)(\$600) + (3/4)(\$2,000) = \$1,650$. *(LO4)*

6.5 Han would be indifferent between filing the suit and not filing it under a fee schedule for which his income, including damage awards and net of lawyer's fees, would be exactly 7 no matter how the suit was decided. That happens when $F_1 = 5$ and $F_2 = 0$. In this case, the expected value of smith's lawyer's fee would be $0.5(5) + 0.5(0) = 2.5$, or 0.5 more than the opportunity cost of the lawyer's time. Under this fee structure, the lawyer would capture the entire expected value of the lawsuit. *(LO3)*

*Problems marked with an asterisk (*) are more difficult.

Jorge Salcedo/Alamy Stock Photo

Search Theory and the Winner's Curse

THE SEARCH FOR HIGH WAGES AND LOW PRICES

If all jobs paid the same and were in all other respects equally desirable, there would be no reason to continue searching once you received your first job offer. But jobs are, of course, not all the same. In particular, some make much fuller use of your particular mix of talents, training, and skills than others. The better the requirements of a given job match your inventory of personal characteristics, the more productive you will be, and the more your employer will be able to pay you. If you are a slick-fielding shortstop who can hit 30 home runs and steal 30 bases each year, for example, you are worth a lot more to the Boston Red Sox than to a local Burger King.

Whatever your mix of skills, your problem is to find the right job for you. The first thing to note is that your search cannot—indeed, should not—be exhaustive. After all, there are more job openings in the United States at any moment than a single person could possibly hope to investigate. Even if it were somehow possible to investigate them all, such a strategy would be so costly—in terms of both money and time—that it would surely not be sensible.

For simplicity, suppose we abstract from all dimensions of job variation other than wage earnings. That is, let us assume that there is a distribution of possible job vacancies to examine, each of which carries with it a different wage. Also for simplicity, suppose that you are risk neutral, plan to work for one period of time, and that the per period wage payments for the population of job vacancies are uniformly distributed between $100 and $200, as shown in Figure 6A.1. What this means is that if you examine a job vacancy at random, its wage payment is equally likely to take any of the values between $100 and $200. Suppose, finally, that it costs $5 to examine a job vacancy.

You have begun your search, and the first job you examine pays $150. Should you accept it, or pay $5 and look at another? (If you do examine another job and it turns out to be worse than your current offer, you can still accept the current offer.) To decide intelligently here, you must compare the cost of examining another offer with the expected benefits. If there are to be any benefits at all, the new offer must be greater than $150.

Wage ($/period)

100   200

FIGURE 6A.1

A Hypothetical Uniform Wage Distribution

The wage paid by a randomly selected new job offer is equally likely to take any of the values between $100 and $200 per time period. On the average, a new job offer will pay $150.

FIGURE 6A.2

The Expected Value of an Offer That Is Greater Than $150

The probability that the next job offer will exceed $150 is 0.5. An offer that is known to exceed $150 is equally likely to lie anywhere between $150 and $200. Its expected value will be $175.

The probability of that happening is 0.5 (in Figure 6A.2, the ratio of the area of the shaded rectangle to the area of the total rectangle).

Suppose the new offer does, in fact, exceed $150. What is its expected value? In Figure 6A.2, note that since an offer greater than $150 is equally likely to fall anywhere in the interval from $150 to $200, its average value will be $175, which is a gain of $25 over your current offer. Hence the expected gain from sampling another offer when you have $150 offer in hand—call it EG(150)—is the product of these two factors: (1) the probability that the new offer exceeds the old one, and (2) the expected gain if it does. Thus we have

$$EG(150) = (1/2)(\$25) = \$12.50. \tag{6A.1}$$

Since the expected gain of sampling another offer exceeds the $5 cost and you are risk neutral, you should continue searching.

How large should an offer be before you should accept it? The answer to this question is called the *acceptance wage,* denoted w^*. If you are risk neutral, it is the wage for which the expected monetary benefits of sampling another offer are exactly equal to the costs. More generally, it would be the wage for which the expected utility gain from sampling another offer is exactly offset by the loss in utility from the cost of search. The risk-neutral case is much simpler to analyze and still illuminates all the important issues.

If the current offer is w^*, note in Figure 6A.3 that the probability of getting a better one is $(200 - w^*)/100$ (which is again the ratio of the area of the shaded rectangle to the area of the total rectangle). Assuming the new offer does land between w^* and 200, its expected value will be halfway between the two, or $(200 + w^*)/2$. This expected value is $(200 - w^*)/2$ units bigger than w^*.

FIGURE 6A.3

The Acceptance Wage

The acceptance wage, w^*, is the wage level for which the cost of an additional search is exactly equal to its expected benefit. The expected benefit is the product of the probability that a new offer will pay more than w^* $[(200 - w^*)/100]$ and the average gain when it does so $[(200 - w^*)/2]$. To find w^*, set this product equal to the cost of search (here $5) and solve for w^*.

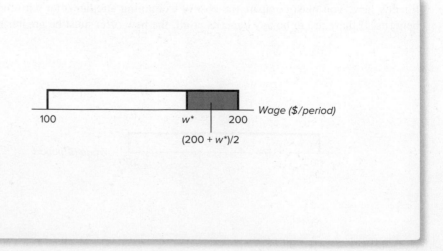

The expected gain of sampling another offer is again the probability that the new offer exceeds w^* times the expected wage increase if it does. Thus we have

$$EG(w^*) = \left(\frac{200 - w^*}{100}\right)\left(\frac{200 - w^*}{2}\right) = \frac{(200 - w^*)^2}{200}. \qquad (6A.2)$$

By the definition of the acceptance wage for a risk-neutral searcher, this expected gain is equal to the cost of sampling another offer:

$$EG(w^*) = \frac{(200 - w^*)^2}{200} = 5, \qquad (6A.3)$$

which reduces to

$$w^* = 200 - \sqrt{1{,}000} = 168.38. \qquad (6A.4)$$

In this example, then, the optimal decision rule will be to continue searching until you find an offer at least as high as 168.38. When wages are uniformly distributed, as here, you should end up, on the average, with a wage that is midway between 200 and w^*. Note, however, that following this rule does not necessarily mean you will always do better than if you accept a current offer that is less than w^*. If you are extremely unlucky, for example, you might start off with an offer of $160 and then search 20 times before finding an offer greater than w^*. Your total earnings net of search costs could then be at most $100, which is obviously worse than $160.

SELF-TEST 6A.1

If the cost of search is $1, and wage offers are uniformly distributed between 10 and 60, what is the smallest wage you should accept?

Analogous reasoning leads to a similar optimal decision rule for someone who is searching for a low-priced product. As we will see in Chapter 11, most firms employ a variety of discount pricing methods, with the result that there will generally exist a relatively broad distribution of prices in the markets for most products. Again for simplicity, assume a price distribution that is uniform on the interval $(0, P)$, as shown in Figure 6A.4.

The acceptance price, P^*, is determined in much the same way as the acceptance wage from the job search case. If the price of the product you have just sampled is P^*, the probability of getting a lower price on your next try is P^*/P (as before, the ratio of the area of the shaded rectangle to the area of the total rectangle). If you do find a lower

FIGURE 6A.4

A Hypothetical Price Distribution

The price of a product selected randomly from this distribution is equally likely to be any number between 0 and P. The probability of finding a price below P^* is P^*/P, which is simply the fraction of all prices that lie below P^*. A price that is known to be below P^* has an average value of $P^*/2$.

FIGURE 6A.5

The Acceptance Price as a Function of the Cost of Search

As search becomes more costly (as *C* rises), it pays to settle for higher-priced products.

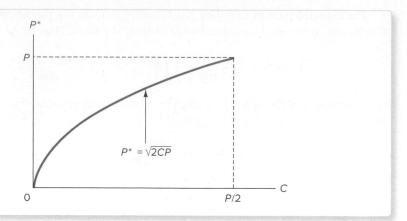

price, your savings, on the average, will be $P^*/2$. Your expected gain from another search at P^* is therefore

$$\text{EG}(P^*) = \left(\frac{P^*}{2}\right)\left(\frac{P^*}{P}\right) = \frac{P^{*2}}{2P}. \tag{6A.5}$$

If the cost of another search is *C,* the expression for the acceptance price will be

$$P^* = \sqrt{2PC}. \tag{6A.6}$$

In both the wage- and price-search cases, the acceptance levels depend on the cost of search: when the cost of examining an additional option rises, your acceptance wage falls, and your acceptance price rises. In the price-search case, the relationship between P^* and C (as given in Equation 6A.6) is shown in Figure 6A.5.

EXAMPLE 6A.1   Acceptance Price

Suppose you are searching for a low price on a price distribution that is uniform on the interval (1, 2). How will your acceptance price change if the cost of search rises from 0.05 to 0.10?

The expression for the acceptance price given in Equation 6A.6 is for a price distribution that is uniform on the interval (0, *P*). Note that the minimum value of the price distribution here is not 0 but 1. The acceptance price for this price distribution will be exactly 1 unit higher than the acceptance price for a uniform price distribution on the interval (0, 1). With a cost of search of 0.05, we see from Equation 6A.6 that the latter acceptance price will be $\sqrt{0.10} = 0.316$, which means that the acceptance price for the uniform price distribution on (1, 2) will be 1.316. With a search cost of 0.10, the acceptance price for the uniform distribution on (0, 1) rises to $\sqrt{0.20} = 0.447$, so the new acceptance price for the uniform distribution on (1, 2) will be 1.447.

Note the essential similarity between the wage- and price-search problems and the toad's decision considered at the beginning of Chapter 6. Like the rational wage- or price-searcher, a rational toad would weigh the costs of an additional search against the expected benefits. He would arrive at an "acceptance pitch," such that if his rival's croak were pitched any higher he would stay and fight.

THE WINNER'S CURSE

When Northwestern University psychologist Max Bazerman was teaching at Boston University some years back, he and his colleague William Samuelson performed the following experiment in their microeconomics classes.[1] First they placed $8 worth of coins in a clear glass jar. After giving their students a chance to examine the jar carefully, they then auctioned it off—coins and all—to the highest bidder. They also asked each student to submit a written estimate of the value of the coins in the jar.

On the average, students behaved conservatively, both with respect to their bids and to the estimates they submitted. Indeed, the average estimate was only $5.13, about one-third less than the actual value of the coins. Similarly, most students dropped out of the bidding well before the auction price reached $8.

Yet the size of the winning bid in any auction depends not on the behavior of the *average* bidder, but on the behavior of the *highest* bidder. In 48 repetitions of this experiment, the top bid averaged $10.01, more than 20 percent more than the coins were worth. Bazerman and Samuelson thus made almost $100 profit at the collective expense of their winning bidders.

At that price, the winners may consider it an important lesson learned cheaply. The stakes were higher when oil company executives were taught the same lesson in the early 1970s. For the first time, the federal government conducted an auction of potentially valuable oil leases in the Gulf of Mexico. Companies had no experience bidding on such leases, but they did have access to standard geological methods for estimating their value. In hindsight, we can now see that the oil leases fetched prices that were too high. The winning bidders—who paid prices in the millions for their leases—would have earned a much higher return on their investments had they deposited the same money in a savings account.

The general principle that the winning bid for an item often exceeds its true value is known as the *winner's curse*. The startling thing about the winner's curse is that it does not require anyone to use a biased estimate of the value of the prize. The problem is that all estimates involve at least some element of randomness. An estimate is said to be *unbiased* if, on the average, it is equal to the true value. Temperature forecasts, for instance, are unbiased; they are too high some days, too low on others, but their long-run average values track actual temperatures almost perfectly. By the same token, even if each bidder's estimate is unbiased, it will on some occasions be too high, on others too low. And the winner of the auction will of course be the bidder whose estimate happens to be too high by the greatest margin.

A fully rational bidder will take into account the fact that the winning bid tends to be too high. Referring again to the coin auction, suppose that someone's best estimate of the value of the coins in the jar is $9. Knowing that the winning bid will tend to be too high, he can then protect himself by adjusting his bid downward. If other bidders are fully rational, they too will adjust their bids, and the identity of the winning bidder should be the same as before.

How big should the downward adjustment be? A moment's reflection makes it clear that the more bidders there are, the larger the adjustment should be. Suppose the true value of the good being auctioned is $1,000. To illustrate what is meant by an unbiased estimate, imagine that each potential bidder draws a ball from an urn containing 201 balls consecutively numbered from 900 to 1,100. (Once its number is inspected, each ball is returned to the urn.) The expected value of the number on any given ball is 1,000, no matter how many bidders there are. But the expected value of the *highest* number drawn will increase with the number of bidders. (If a million people drew balls from such urns, it is almost certain that someone would get 1,100, the maximum possible value; but if only five people drew, the highest number would be much smaller, on the average.) Accordingly, the more bidders there are, the more you should adjust your estimate downward.

To illustrate the mechanics of the adjustment process, consider an auction in which the true value of the item for sale is 0.5, and in which each bidder uses an estimate that

[1]For a more detailed account of this experiment, see David Warsh, "The Winner's Curse," *Boston Globe*, April 17, 1988.

FIGURE 6A.6

An Unbiased Estimate with a Uniform Distribution

Each potential bidder has an estimate of the value of the resource that is equally likely to take any value between 0 and 1. The true value of the resource is the average value of these estimates, which is 0.5.

is uniformly distributed between 0 and 1. This estimate is equally likely to take any value between 0 and 1, so it has an expected value of 0.5, which means it is unbiased (see Figure 6A.6).

If there were only one bidder at this auction, the expected value of the highest estimate would be 0.5, and so there would be no need for him to make an adjustment. If there were N bidders, however, what would be the expected value of the highest estimate? Suppose we put the N estimates in ascending order and call them $X_1, X_2, \ldots, X_N$, so that X_N denotes the highest of the N estimates. Since the estimates all come from a uniform distribution, the expected values of $X_1, X_2, \ldots, X_N$ will be evenly spaced along the interval. As noted, when $N = 1$ we have only X_1, and its expected value, 0.5, lies right in the middle of the interval.

What about when $N = 2$? Now our two estimates are X_1 and X_2, and their expected values are as shown in the second panel of Figure 6A.7. This time the highest estimate has an expected value of $2/3$. In the third panel note that the highest of 3 estimates has an expected value of $3/4$. In the bottom panel, finally, the highest of 4 estimates has an expected value of $4/5$. In general, the highest of N estimates will have an expected value of $N/(N + 1)$. (See footnote 2.)

If the estimates were all drawn from a uniform distribution on $(0, C)$, not on $(0, 1)$, the expected value of the highest estimate would be $CN/(N + 1)$.

FIGURE 6A.7

The Expected Value of the Highest Estimate N = 1, 2, 3, and 4

When more people make estimates of the value of a resource, the expected value of the highest estimate increases. When the estimates are uniformly distributed on the interval (0, 1), the largest of N estimates (X_N) has an average value of $N/(N + 1)$.

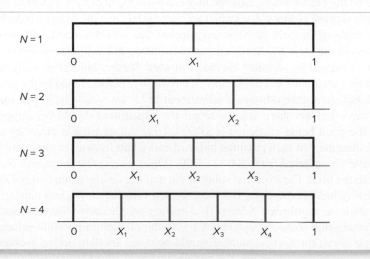

[2]The random variables $X_1 \ldots, X_N$ are known as the "order statistics" of a sample of size N. To find the expected value of X_N, note first that X_N is less than any value z if and only if each of the N sampled values is less than z. For the uniform distribution on (0, 1), the probability of that event is simply Z^N. This is the cumulative distribution function of X_N. The probability density function of X_N is therefore $d(z^N)/dz$, or Nz^{N-1}. The expected value of X_N is thus given by

$$\int_0^1 zNz^{N-1}dz = \frac{N}{N+1}.$$

EXAMPLE 6A.2   Winner's Curse

Suppose 50 people are bidding for an antique clock, and each has an unbiased estimate of the true value of the clock that is drawn from a uniform distribution on the interval (0, *C*), where *C* is unknown. Your own estimate of the value of the clock is $400. How much should you bid?

Your problem is to adjust your estimate so that if it happens to be the highest of the 50, you will not bid more, on the average, than the true value of the clock, which is $C/2$. The expected value of the highest of 50 estimates is $(50/51)C$, so if your estimate of 400 happens to be the highest, we have, on the average,

$$(50/51)C = 400, \tag{6A.7}$$

which solves for $C = 408$. This is your adjusted estimate of the value of C on the assumption that yours was the highest of the 50 unadjusted estimates. Since the true value of the clock is $C/2$, you should therefore bid only $204.

SELF-TEST 6A. 2

If there had been only four bidders in Example 6A.2, how much should you have bid?

As a practical matter, do bidders really adjust their behavior to eliminate the winner's curse? An evolutionary argument can be made to the effect that there will be an automatic tendency for this to happen. The idea is that bidders who fail to adjust their estimates downward will end up losing money each time they win an auction and will eventually go bankrupt. Those who survive may not understand the winner's curse at all. They may simply be people who happen for other reasons to bid cautiously.

When extremely large sums of money are at stake and bankruptcy is a real possibility, the evolutionary argument has obvious force. But Michael Manove, a Boston University economist, suggests that it will not apply in all circumstances. He notes that even when a person pays too much for something at auction, it is often possible to recoup the loss by putting forth additional effort. In such cases, the person will regret having paid too much, but his economic survival will not be at stake—only his leisure time and peace of mind. In Manove's scheme, it is the careless optimists who ignore the winner's curse and win all the auctions. They are then sent scrambling to stay on their feet, and in the end, many of them manage to do so. Their utility is lower than if they had not won the auctions. The irony is that they may nonetheless drive out the more realistic bidders from many markets.

To illustrate his point, Manove cites his own decision about whether to accept the vice chairmanship of his department. Someone weighing this decision knows that being vice chairman carries with it a known financial stipend and involves an unknown amount of work. Manove accepted, saying that the stipend seemed worth it in view of his estimate of the amount of work involved. The position proved much more time-consuming than he predicted, however, and in the end Manove came out slightly richer, but much less happy, than if he had turned it down. His account illustrates the by now familiar caution that the rational choice model sometimes falls short on purely descriptive grounds. But here again, the model offers useful guidance by calling attention to the specific situations in which you are most likely to err.

I have known about the winner's curse for years, and yet I still bid whatever I think something is worth whenever I go to an antique auction. Am I being irrational? The answer depends on what I intend to do with the things I end up buying. Many of the participants at the auctions I attend are dealers, and I would indeed be irrational if I were a dealer and failed to adjust my estimates. But I am not a dealer. I keep whatever I buy for my own use. Since each item is unique, there is no issue of whether I could purchase it more cheaply elsewhere. For me the only test my bid has to pass is whether the item is worth that amount to me.

EXAMPLE 6A.3   Expected Profit

Suppose you are the economic advisor for a firm that is trying to decide whether to acquire the Bumbler Oil Company, whose only asset is an oil field that has a net value X under its current management. The owners of Bumbler know the exact value of X, but your company knows only that X is a random number that is uniformly distributed between 0 and 100. Because of your company's superior management, Bumbler's oil field would be worth $1.5X$ in its hands. What is the highest value of P that you can bid and still not expect to take a loss if your company acquires Bumbler Oil?

If your company bids P and if X is greater than P, then Bumbler will refuse the offer and the deal is off. Your company earns zero profit in that case. If Bumbler accepts your company's offer, then we know that $X < P$. Since X is uniformly distributed between 0 and 100, the expected value of X, given that $X < P$, is $P/2$. This means that the expected value of Bumbler's oil field to your company is 1.5 times that, or $0.75P$. If your company bids P and Bumbler accepts, then the expected profit of your company will be $0.75P - P = -0.25P$. So for any positive P, your company expects to lose $0.25P$ if Bumbler accepts its offer. Your company's best strategy is therefore not to bid at all.

Some Pitfalls for the Expected Utility Maximizer

The expected utility model offers intelligent guidance about how to choose rationally in the face of uncertainty. The normative usefulness of the model is underscored by the fact that people often appear sorely in need of its guidance. One well-known example, based on the work of the French economist M. Allais, suggests that most people behave inconsistently with respect to certain kinds of choices. To illustrate, first consider the following pair of alternatives:

>   *A:* A sure win of $30
>   versus
>   *A':* An 80 percent chance to win $45.

Confronted with these alternatives, most people choose *A,* the sure win.[3] If a person is risk averse, there is nothing surprising about this choice, even though the expected value of alternative *A'* is $36.

   Now consider the following pair of alternatives:

>   *B:* A 25 percent chance to win $30
>   versus
>   *B':* A 20 percent chance to win $45.

This time most people choose the less certain alternative, namely, *B'*. Taken in isolation, this choice is also unsurprising, for the expected value of *B* ($7.50) is significantly lower than that of *B'* ($9), and both alternatives involve some risk. The problem is that the most popular pair of choices (*A* and *B'*), taken together, contradict the assumption of expected utility maximization. To see why, suppose the chooser is a utility maximizer with a utility function $U(M)$ and an initial wealth level of M_0. His choice of *A* over *A'* then implies that

$$U(M_0 + 30) > 0.8U(M_0 + 45) + 0.2U(M_0). \tag{6A.8}$$

---

[3]See Amos Tversky and Daniel Kahneman, "The Framing of Decisions and the Psychology of Choice," *Science,* 211, 1981, 453–458.

In turn, his choice of B' over B implies that

$$0.2U(M_0 + 45) + 0.8U(M_0) > 0.25U(M_0 + 30) + 0.75U(M_0). \qquad (6A.9)$$

Rearranging the terms of inequality 6A.9, we have

$$0.25U(M_0 + 30) < 0.2U(M_0 + 45) + 0.05U(M_0). \qquad (6A.10)$$

Dividing both sides of inequality A6.10 by 0.25, finally, we have

$$U(M_0 + 30) < 0.8U(M_0 + 45) + 0.2U(M_0), \qquad (6A.11)$$

which is precisely the reverse order of inequality 6A.8, the one implied by the choice of A over A'. And hence the contradiction.

Psychologists Daniel Kahneman and Amos Tversky have labeled this kind of inconsistency the "certainty effect." As a purely descriptive matter, they argue that "a reduction in the probability of an outcome by a constant factor has a larger impact when the outcome was initially certain than when it was merely probable."[4] Thus, in the first pair of alternatives, the movement from A to A' represented a 20 percent reduction in the chances of winning (from 100 to 80 percent), the same as the reduction when moving from B to B' (25 to 20 percent). But because the first reduction was from an initially certain outcome, it was much more aversive.

Note that Kahneman and Tversky are not saying that there is anything irrational about liking a sure thing. Their point is simply that our choices in situations where both alternatives are risky seem to imply a lesser degree of risk aversion than does our behavior in situations where one of the alternatives is risk-free.

Part of the attraction of the sure alternative is the regret many people expect to feel when they take a gamble and lose. The expected utility maximizer will want to be careful, however, to avoid the "bad-outcome-implies-bad-decision" fallacy. To illustrate this fallacy, suppose someone offers you the following gamble: You are to draw a single ball from an urn containing 999 white balls and one red ball. If you draw a white ball, as you most probably will, you win $1,000. If you draw the lone red ball, however, you lose $1. Suppose you accept the gamble and then draw the red ball. You lose $1. Do you now say you made a bad decision? If so, you commit the fallacy. The decision, when you made it, was obviously a good one. Almost every rational person would have decided in the same way. The fact that you lost is too bad, but it tells you nothing about the quality of your decision. By the same token, if you choose an 80 percent chance to win $45 rather than a sure win of $30, there is no reason to regret the quality of your decision if you happen to lose.

As a general rule, human nature obviously prefers certainty to risk. At the same time, however, risk is an inescapable part of the environment. People naturally want the largest possible gain *and* the smallest possible risk, but most of the time we are forced to trade risk and gain off against one another. When choosing between two risky alternatives, we are forced to recognize this trade-off explicitly. In such cases, we cannot escape the cognitive effort required to reach a sensible decision. But when one of the alternatives is riskless, it is often easier simply to choose it and not waste too much effort on the decision. What this pattern of behavior fails to recognize, however, is that choosing a sure win of $30 over an 80 percent chance to win $45 does precious little to reduce any of the uncertainty that really matters in life.

On the contrary, *when only small sums of money are at stake, a compelling case can be made that the only sensible strategy is to choose the alternative with the highest expected value.* The argument for this strategy, like the argument for buying insurance, rests on the law of large numbers. Here, the law tells us that if we take a large number of independent gambles and pool them, we can be very confident of getting almost exactly the sum of their expected values. As a decision maker, the trick is to remind yourself that each small risky choice is simply part of a much larger collection. After all, it takes the sting out of an occasional small loss to know that following any other strategy would have led to a virtually certain large loss.

[4]Ibid., p. 456.

To illustrate, consider again the choice between the sure gain of $30 and the 80 percent chance to win $45, and suppose you were confronted with the equivalent of one such choice each week. Recall that the gamble has an expected value of $36, $6 more than the sure thing. By always choosing the "risky" alternative, your expected gain—over and beyond the gain from the sure alternative—will be $312 each year. Students who have had an introductory course in probability can easily show that the probability you would have come out better by choosing the sure alternative in any year is less than 1 percent. *The long-run opportunity cost of following a risk-averse strategy for decisions involving small outcomes is an almost sure* loss *of considerable magnitude.* By thinking of your problem as that of choosing a *policy* for dealing with a large number of choices of the same type, a seemingly risky strategy is transformed into an obviously very safe one.

PROBLEMS

1. You are searching for a high wage from a wage distribution that is uniform on the interval (5, 8). The cost of each search is 0.06. What is the smallest wage you should accept?

2. A class of 100 students is participating in an auction to see who gets a large jar of quarters. Each student has an unbiased estimate of the total value of the coins. If these estimates are drawn from the interval (0, *C*), where *C* is not known, and your own estimate is $50, how much should you bid?

3. Suppose you are the economic advisor for a firm that is trying to decide whether to acquire Bumbler Oil Company, whose only asset is an oil field that has a net value X under its current management. The owners of Bumbler know the exact value of X but your company knows only that X is a random number that is uniformly distributed between 0 and 100. Because of your company's superior management, Bumbler's oil field would be worth $X + 40$ in its hands.
   a. What is the most your company can bid and not expect to take a loss?
   b. Assuming your company is the only bidder, what bid maximizes your company's expected profits?

4. If the wages you are offered are uniformly distributed between $75 and $150, and if the cost of looking for another job is $2, what is the minimum wage you should accept?

5. Earthly Bliss dating service charges $100 per date that it arranges. All of its dates will accept an offer of marriage. In your estimation the quality of the potential spouses offered by the dating service can be measured by an index that runs from 0 to 100. The potential spouses are uniformly distributed over this range. Suppose you value a spouse at $50 per index point. If your dates were drawn at random from the Earthly Bliss pool, at what value of the index would you stop searching?

6. You are a buyer for a used-car dealer. You attend car auctions and bid on cars that will be sold at the dealer. The cars are sold "as is" and there is seldom an opportunity to make a thorough inspection. Under these conditions, the lower bound for the value of a car can be zero. A 1981 Dodge Aries has been offered at the auction. You are one of 20 bidders. Your estimate of the value of the car is $200. If all the bidders have unbiased estimates drawn from a uniform distribution with an unknown upper bound, what is the most you can bid for the car and not have your client expect to lose money?

ANSWERS TO APPENDIX SELF-TESTS

6A.1 Let w^* again denote the acceptance wage. The probability of finding a higher wage is $(60 - w^*)/50$. The average gain, given that you do find a higher wage, is $(60 - w^*)/2$. So the expected gain is the product of these, $(60 - w^*)^2/100$. Equating this to the cost of search, 1, and solving for w^*, we have $w^* = 50$.

6A.2 With 4 bidders, the expected value of the largest estimate is $(4/5)C$. Equating this to 400, and solving, we get $C = 500$, and so you should bid 250.

7

Departures from Standard Rational Choice Models (With and Without Regret)

Behavioral economics has been my profession's runaway growth area of recent decades. Scholars in this area work largely at the intersection of economics and psychology, although some also make use of theories and evidence from biology, sociology, and other disciplines. Much of the field's attention has focused on systematic biases in people's judgments and decisions. As the late Amos Tversky, a Stanford University psychologist and a founding father of behavioral economics, liked to say, "My colleagues, they study artificial intelligence. Me? I study natural stupidity."

In the early 1980s, I taught one of the first undergraduate courses in behavioral economics. Because few students had heard of this nascent field, my first challenge was to come up with a course title that might lure some to enroll. In the end, I decided to call it "Departures from Rational Choice." Naturally, there was no standard syllabus then. After much thought, I decided to cover material under two broad headings: "Departures from Rational Choice Without Regret," and "Departures from Rational Choice With Regret." For this chapter's title, I've chosen a slightly modified version of that early course title, for reasons that will become clear presently.

Under the first heading, I listed studies that describe departures from the predictions of standard rational choice models that people do not seem to regret. A case in point is the way people typically react to one-sided offers in the so-called ultimatum game. In this game, the experimenter gives one subject some money—say, $100—and then tells him to propose a division of that sum between himself and a second subject. If the second accepts, each walks away with the amount proposed. For instance, if the first proposes "$60 for me and $40 for you" and the second accepts, the first gets $60 and the second gets $40. But here's the twist: If the second subject rejects the proposal, the $100 reverts to the experimenter, and each subject receives nothing.

Standard rational choice models predict that the first subject will make a one-sided proposal—such as $99 for himself and $1 for the second subject—since he knows that it would be in the second subject's interest to accept rather than get nothing. But such offers are rarely proposed, and when they are, they are almost invariably rejected. Subjects who reject one-sided offers seldom voice regret about having done so.

Does that mean they're irrational? There is actually far from universal agreement on just what rationality means.

Under the ". . . with regret" heading of that course's syllabus, I included studies that document the many systematic cognitive errors to which people are prone. For example, although standard rational choice models say that people will ignore sunk costs, such costs often influence choices in conspicuous ways, as we saw in Chapter 1.

Suppose, for example, that you're about to depart for a sporting event or concert at an arena 50 miles away when an unexpected heavy snowstorm begins. If your ticket is nonrefundable, your decision of whether to drive to the event should not be influenced by the amount you paid for it. Yet a fan who paid $100 for his ticket is significantly more likely to make the dangerous drive than an equally avid fan who happened to receive his ticket for free. The first fan is probably guilty of a cognitive error. People typically seem to regret the decisions they make on the basis of such errors once they become aware of them.

In short, standard rational choice models, which presume that people are self-interested in the narrow sense and draw inferences without error from all information available to them, don't always predict accurately what real people will do in actual environments.

CHAPTER PREVIEW

We begin this chapter with an example of how unselfish motivations can be incorporated into the rational choice model—in this case, a straightforward application of the present-aim standard. But our real challenge will be to explore how such motivations might have come to be held in the first place. We are all comfortable with the notion that someone who deliberately strives to be more spontaneous is doomed to fail. So, too, we'll see that people whose only goal is to promote their own interests face a difficulty of a similar sort. There are important problems that selfish people simply aren't able to solve very well. We'll see that it's possible to do a much better job of predicting people's behavior when we take certain unselfish sources of motivation into account.

We'll also see that better predictions of behavior are possible when we take explicit account of not just the sunk-cost fallacy but also a variety of other systematic cognitive errors to which people appear prone. We'll examine several behavioral models of choice that often do a much better job of predicting actual decisions than the rational choice model. It will be important to remember, however, that these behavioral models claim no normative significance. They tell us, for instance, that we often *do* tend to ignore sunk costs, not that we *should* ignore them.

The rational choice model says we can make better decisions by ignoring sunk costs, and most people, on reflection, strongly agree. The value of behavioral models is that they call our attention to situations in which we are likely to make mistakes. Such models are an important tool for helping us avoid common pitfalls in decision making.

PRESENT AIM AND SELF-INTEREST STANDARDS OF RATIONALITY

Two important definitions of rationality are the so-called *present-aim* and *self-interest* standards.[1] A person is rational under the present-aim standard if she is efficient in the pursuit of whatever aims she happens to hold at the moment of action. No attempt is

[1]See Derek Parfit, *Reasons and Persons,* Oxford: Clarendon, 1984.

made, under this standard, to assess whether her aims themselves make any sense. If someone has a preference for self-destructive behavior, for example, the only requirement for rationality under the present-aim standard is that she pursue that behavior in the most efficient available way. Under the self-interest standard, by contrast, it is assumed at the outset that people's motives are congruent with their narrow material interests. Motives such as altruism, fidelity to principle, a desire for justice, and the like are simply not considered under the self-interest standard.

In textbook accounts of rational choice, economists often embrace the present-aim standard. Tastes are given exogenously, we say, and there is no logical basis for questioning them. In the words of the nineteenth-century economist Jeremy Bentham, a taste for pushpins is no less valid than a taste for poetry.

The difficulty with the present-aim standard is what we might call the "crankcase oil" problem. If we see a person drink the used crankcase oil from his car, and he then writhes in agony and dies, we can assert that he must have *really* liked crankcase oil. (Why else would he have drunk it?) Virtually any behavior, no matter how bizarre, can be "explained" after the fact by simply assuming a taste for it. Thus the chief attraction of the present-aim model turns out also to be its biggest liability. Because it allows us to explain everything, we end up explaining nothing.

With this difficulty in mind, most economists assume some version of the self-interest standard of rationality in their actual research. This is the approach we took in previous chapters, and as we have seen, it generates many powerful insights into human behavior. It helps explain, for example, why car pools form in the wake of increases in gasoline prices; why the members of "service" organizations, such as the Rotary and Kiwanis clubs, are more likely to be real estate salespersons, dentists, insurance agents, and others with something to sell than to be postal employees or airline pilots; and so on. Without question, self-interest is an important human motive.

Yet narrow self-interest is surely not the only human motive. Travelers on interstate highways leave tips for waitresses they will never see again. Participants in bloody family feuds seek revenge even at ruinous cost to themselves. People walk away from profitable transactions whose terms they believe to be "unfair." The British spent vast sums to defend the desolate Falklands from Argentina, even though they had little empire left to deter future aggression against. (The Argentine writer Jorge Luis Borges likened the war to two bald men fighting over a comb.) In these and countless other ways, people do not seem to be pursuing their own narrow interests. I no longer feel comfortable calling such behavior irrational because, as we'll see, rational persons have reason to be grateful that they're not always driven by narrowly selfish motives. But what is clear, in any event, is that the behavior of such people is not well predicted by the self-interest version of rational choice theory. And that's why this chapter's title differs slightly from the title of my earlier course.

An Application of the Present-Aim Standard: Altruistic Preferences

Because we know from experience that not everyone has the narrowly selfish preferences assumed by the self-interest model, it is tempting to broaden the analysis by simply adding additional tastes—by assuming, for example, that people derive satisfaction from a variety of behaviors that conflict with narrowly defined self-interest, such as donating money to charity, voting, disposing of litter properly, and so on. Let us explore how the notion that some people have altruistic preferences can be incorporated formally into our model of rational choice.

Consider, for example, the case of Franny, who cares not only about her own income level but also about Zooey's. Such preferences can be represented in the form of an indifference map defined over their respective income levels, and might look something like the one shown in Figure 7.1. Note that Franny's indifference curves are negatively sloped, which means that she is willing to tolerate a reduction in her own income in return for a sufficiently large increase in Zooey's. Note also that her indifference curves exhibit diminishing marginal rate of substitution (MRS) which means that the more income Franny has, the more she is willing to give up in order to see Zooey have more.

The question that Franny confronts is whether she would be better off if she gave some of her income to Zooey. In order to answer this question, we first need to display the relevant budget constraint confronting Franny. Suppose her initial income level is $50,000/yr and that Zooey's is $10,000, as denoted by the point labeled A in Figure 7.2. What are Franny's options? She can retain all her income, in which case she stays at A. Or she can give some of it to Zooey, in which case she will have $1 less than $50,000 for every $1 she gives him. Her budget constraint here is thus the locus labeled B in Figure 7.2, which has a slope of −1.

If Franny keeps all her income, she ends up on the indifference curve labeled I_1 in Figure 7.2. But because her MRS exceeds the slope of her budget constraint at A, it is clear that she can do better. The fact that MRS > 1 at A tells us that she is willing to give up more than a dollar of her own income to see Zooey have an extra dollar. But the slope of her budget constraint tells us that it costs her only a dollar to give Zooey an extra dollar. She is therefore better off if she gives some of her income to Zooey. The optimal transfer is represented by the tangency point labeled C in Figure 7.2. The best she can do is to give $19,000 of her income to Zooey.

Note, however, that the conclusion would have been much different if Franny had started not at A but at D in Figure 7.2. Then her budget constraint would have been only that portion of the locus B that lies below D. (She does not have the option of making negative gifts to Zooey!) And since her MRS at D is less than 1, she will do best to give no money to Zooey at all. (Recall from Chapter 3 that such outcomes are called corner solutions.)

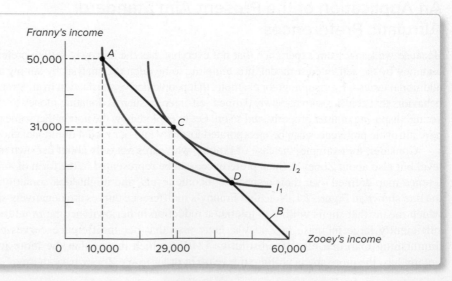

EXAMPLE 7.1   Altruistic Preferences

Sienna's utility function is given by $U_S = M_S M_J$, where M_S is Sienna's wealth level and M_J is Jayden's. Initially, Sienna has 90 units of wealth and Jayden has 10. If Sienna is a utility maximizer, should she transfer some of her wealth to Jayden, and if so, how much? Draw Sienna's initial indifference curve and the indifference curve when each has 50 units of wealth. Also draw Sienna's budget constraint in the $M_S M_J$ plane.

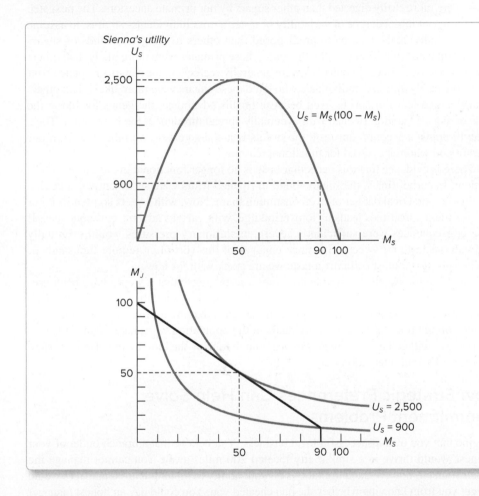

FIGURE 7.3

A Utility-Maximizing Altruist

The top panel shows that Sienna's utility is maximized by keeping only 50 units of wealth for herself. The red line in the bottom panel is Sienna's budget constraint in the $M_S M_J$ plane. Note that the $U_S = 2,500$ indifference curve is tangent to that budget constraint at $M_S = 50$.

Together, Sienna and Jayden have a total of 100 units of wealth. This means that if Sienna's wealth is M_S, then Jayden's is $100 - M_S$. Sienna's utility function may thus be written as $U_S = M_S(100 - M_S)$, which is plotted in the top panel of Figure 7.3. Note that Sienna's utility attains a maximum of 2,500 when $M_S = 50$. At the initial allocation of wealth, Sienna's utility is only 900. So if Sienna is a utility maximizer, she should transfer 40 units of her wealth to Jayden. The heavy line in the bottom panel is Sienna's budget constraint in the $M_S M_J$ plane. Note that the $U_S = 2,500$ indifference curve is tangent to this budget constraint when $M_S = M_J = 50$.

THE STRATEGIC ROLE OF PREFERENCES

The attractive feature of the present-aim standard of rationality is that it lets us broaden our analysis to embrace nonegoistic motives whose existence is well documented. Yet as noted, the lingering methodological difficulty is that unless we impose some constraints on ourselves, the present-aim standard allows us to explain virtually any bizarre behavior

A primate with a strong preference for ripened fruit was more likely to survive and reproduce because the sugars in ripened fruit are easier to digest.

by simply positing a taste for it. Our dilemma is how to expand our view of human motives without at the same time becoming vulnerable to the crankcase oil objection.

Biologists have discovered a way out of this dilemma, one that rests on an analysis that is quintessentially microeconomic in character. In biology, an organism's tastes are not arbitrarily given, as they are in economic models. Rather, biologists assume that tastes are forged by the pressures of natural selection to help organisms solve important problems in their environments. Consider the example of the common human taste for sweets. How would biologists explain such a taste? Their argument is straightforward. It begins with the observation that certain kinds of sugars—in particular, those commonly found in ripened fruit—were more easily digested than other sugars by our primate ancestors. The next step is to assume an initial degree of variability of tastes across individuals—that is, to assume that some individuals were more predisposed than others to "like" the kinds of sugars found in ripened fruit. Motivated by this taste, these primates were more likely than others to eat ripened fruit. Because nutrients were generally scarce and the sugars in ripened fruit were more easily digested, individuals who liked these sugars were more likely than others to survive and leave offspring. And because of this advantage, the genes for liking the kinds of sugars found in ripened fruit eventually spread throughout the population. Thus, in the biologist's account, our taste for sweets is a characteristic we inherited from our ancestors, in whom it evolved for functional reasons.

There is evidence that this particular taste is no longer functional in our current environment. In earlier times, the sugars found in ripened fruits were sufficiently scarce that there was no practical danger of overconsuming them. Now, with sweets so plentiful, our taste for them sometimes leads us to overindulge, with various adverse consequences. If these consequences were sufficiently severe, evolutionary pressures would eventually diminish our taste for sweets. But since changes of this sort often require thousands of generations, it is almost certainly a taste we are stuck with for now.

The taste for sweets is a simple preference, in the sense that it would have been useful to an individual irrespective of whether others in the population shared that taste. Other tastes, however, are more complex, in the sense that the usefulness of having them depends on the fraction of other individuals in the population who share them. This second type we will call a *strategic preference,* one that helps the individual solve important problems of social interaction.

How Strategic Preferences Can Help Solve Commitment Problems

Imagine that you own a successful local business. You believe that a branch outlet of your business would thrive in a similar city located 200 miles away. You cannot manage the branch yourself, however, and limitations on your ability to monitor a hired manager would prevent you from knowing whether she had cheated you. You could pay an honest manager $100,000 (twice the going rate) and still expect a net gain of $100,000 by opening the outlet. But you know that anyone you hire will face powerful incentives to cheat. Suppose that by managing dishonestly, she could augment her own return by $200,000, but that you would then lose $100,000 on the venture. In that event, you would have no recourse, since there would be no way to know, much less prove, that your manager had cheated you. Would you open the branch outlet?

Rational choice theory predicts you'll do so only if your expected gain is positive. You must therefore predict how a hired manager would evaluate the choices confronting her if you open the branch outlet. If you believe that everyone is self-interested in the narrow sense, you'd predict that any manager you hired would cheat you, which means that you'd lose $100,000 if you opened the outlet. So you wouldn't open it.

This decision constitutes what the late Harvard and Maryland economist Tom Schelling called a commitment problem.[2] Failure to open the outlet leads to a worse

[2]Thomas C. Schelling, *The Strategy of Conflict,* Cambridge, MA: Harvard University Press, 1960.

outcome for both you and the manager than if you had opened the outlet and the manager had run it honestly. If an applicant could somehow commit herself to manage honestly, she would want to. But simply claiming to be honest won't do the trick, since even a dishonest manager would have every incentive to make that claim.

Note that the mere existence of an honest manager is not sufficient to solve the commitment problem just described. The business owner must also be able to identify someone he has good reason to believe will manage honestly. Are there signals that might lead a skeptical owner to predict someone would manage honestly?

Since the publication of Charles Darwin's 1872 book, *The Expression of Emotion in Man and Animals,* much has been learned about the observable manifestations of inner motivational states. Psychologists, for example, have confirmed Darwin's claim that certain facial expressions are characteristic of specific emotions that guide people's choices. These expressions, which are the result of complex combinations of facial muscle movements, are extremely difficult to produce on demand, yet appear spontaneously when the corresponding emotion is experienced.

Consider, for instance, the schematic expression in Figure 7.4. The distinct configuration of the eyebrows—elevated in the center of the brow, sloping downward toward the sides—is produced by a specific combination of the pyramidal muscles (located near the bridge of the nose) and the corrugator muscles (located near the center of the brow). Only 15 percent of experimental subjects are able to produce this expression on demand. By contrast, virtually all subjects exhibit it spontaneously when they experience grief, sadness, or concern.

Psychologists have also found that posture and other elements of body language, the pitch and timbre of the voice, the rate of respiration, and even the cadence of speech are systematically linked to underlying motivational states. Because the relevant linkages are beyond conscious control in most people, it is difficult to conceal from others the experience of certain emotions, and equally difficult to feign the characteristic expressions of these emotions on occasions when they are not actually experienced. For this reason, we are able to use such clues to form estimates of the emotional makeup of others, which in turn help us to form judgments about their preferences.[3] In addition to facial expressions and other physical symptoms of emotion, we rely on reputation and a variety of other clues to predict the behavior of potential partners.[4]

FIGURE 7.4

The Expression of Grief, Sadness, or Concern

Specific emotions summon characteristic facial expressions. Because these expressions are extremely difficult to display through conscious manipulation of the relevant facial muscles, the expressions serve as reliable indicators of the underlying motivational states.

---

[3]The term "preferences" may not fully capture the essence of what we are trying to assess in potential partners. "Character" or "moral sentiments" may come closer.
[4]For a discussion of the role of reputation and other factors, see Chapter 4 of my *Passions Within Reason.*

A Simple Thought Experiment

Perhaps the following simple thought experiment will help you decide whether you think you are able to make reliable character judgments about other people.

Imagine you have just gotten home from a crowded concert and discover you have lost $1,000 in cash. The cash had been in your coat pocket in a plain envelope with your name written on it. Do you know anyone, not related to you by blood or marriage, who you feel certain would return it to you if he or she found it?

For the sake of discussion, I will assume that you are not in the unenviable position of having to answer no. Think for a moment about the person you are sure would return your cash; call her "Virtue." Try to explain *why* you feel so confident about her. Note that the situation was one where, if she had kept the cash, you could not have known it. On the basis of your other experiences with her, the most you could possibly know is that she did not cheat you in *every* such instance in the past. Even if, for example, she returned some lost money of yours in the past, that would not prove she didn't cheat you on some other occasion. (After all, if she *had* cheated you in a similar situation, you wouldn't know it.) In any event, you almost certainly have no logical basis in experience for inferring that Virtue would not cheat you now. If you are like most participants in this thought experiment, you simply believe you can fathom her inner motives: You are sure she would return your cash because you are sure she would feel terrible if she did not.

If your assessment of Virtue is correct, then hiring her to manage the branch outlet of your business would be a win-win move. She would earn $100,000 more than the going rate for managers (even though not as much as she could have by cheating you). And because she doesn't cheat you, your return is also $100,000 more than if you hadn't opened the branch outlet.

For preferences to serve as commitment devices, it is not necessary to be able to predict other people's preferences with certainty. Just as a weather forecast of a 20 percent chance of rain can be invaluable to someone who must plan outdoor activities, so can probabilistic assessments of character traits be of use to people who must choose someone to trust. It would obviously be nice to be accurate in every instance. But it will often suffice to be right only a fraction of the time. And most people firmly believe they can make reasonably accurate character judgments about people they know well. If you share this belief, you are in a position to see clearly why the unbridled pursuit of self-interest will often be self-defeating.

Here are two more examples of commitment problems and how nonegoistic preferences can help solve them:

- **The deterrence problem.** Suppose Liko has a $500 leather suitcase that Chynna covets. If Chynna steals it, Liko must decide whether to press charges. If he does, he will have to go to court. He will get his suitcase back and Chynna will spend 60 days in jail, but the day in court will cost him $600 in lost earnings. Since this is more than the suitcase is worth, it would clearly not be in his material interest to press charges. (To eliminate an obvious complication, suppose Liko is about to move to a distant city, so there is no point in his adopting a tough stance in order to deter future theft.) Thus, if Chynna knows Liko is a purely rational, self-interested person, she is free to steal the briefcase with impunity. Liko may threaten to press charges, but his threat would be empty.

  But now suppose that Liko is *not* a pure egoist—that if Chynna steals his suitcase, Liko will become outraged and think nothing of losing a day's earnings, or even a week's, in order to see justice done. If Chynna knows this, she will not steal the suitcase. If people expect us to respond nonegoistically to the theft of our property, we will seldom need to because it will not be in their interests to steal it. Being predisposed to respond nonegoistically serves much better here than being guided only by material self-interest.

- **The bargaining problem.** In this example, Chynna and Liko face the opportunity of a profitable joint venture. There is some task that they alone can do, which will net them $1,000 total. Suppose Liko has no pressing need for extra money, but Chynna has important bills to pay. It is a fundamental principle of bargaining theory that the party who needs the transaction least is in the strongest position. The difference in their circumstances thus gives Liko the advantage. Needing the gain less, he can threaten, credibly, to walk away from the transaction unless he gets the lion's share of the take, say, $900. Rather than see the transaction fall through, it will then be in Chynna's interest to capitulate.

But suppose Liko knows that Chynna cares not only about how much money she receives in absolute terms but also about how the total is divided between them. More specifically, suppose Liko knows that Chynna is committed to a norm of fairness that calls for the total to be divided evenly. If Chynna's commitment to this norm is sufficiently strong, she will refuse Liko's one-sided offer, even though she would do better, in purely material terms, by accepting it. The irony is that if Liko knows this, he will not confront Chynna with a one-sided offer in the first place.

TASTES NOT ONLY *CAN* DIFFER, THEY *MUST* DIFFER

Imagine a mutation that caused honest people to be born with an identifying mark, such as an "H" on the forehead. Dishonest people lack this mark. Honest types would receive the premium wages. If the two types could be distinguished without effort, the honest types, who are more valuable to employers, would prevail in the Darwinian struggle for survival. The only equilibrium would be a population consisting entirely of honest people.[5]

In general, though, there aren't any perfectly reliable and costlessly observable character traits. It's usually difficult to figure out who's who, and in an environment in which everyone was trustworthy, it wouldn't pay to be vigilant in the choice of trading partners—just as it wouldn't pay to buy an expensive security system for your apartment if you lived in a neighborhood in which there had never been a burglary. Thus, a population consisting exclusively of honest types could not be a stable equilibrium, because reduced levels of vigilance would enable dishonest types to invade any such population. So if character traits are costly to observe, the only sustainable equilibrium is one where there is a mixed population consisting of both honest and dishonest individuals. In short, the examples we've discussed suggest that character traits such as honesty not only *can* differ across individuals, they *must* differ.

This message stands in stark contrast to the message of a celebrated article by University of Chicago economists George Stigler and Gary Becker, who at the time were strongly critical of explanations of behavior based on the assumption of differing tastes.[6] To say that people behave differently merely because they have different tastes, they argued, is an intellectual cop-out, an abandonment of the scholar's quest to get to the bottom of things. The best explanation of behavioral differences, in their view, is one that assumes people have the same tastes but have different incomes and face different prices.

Note that Stigler and Becker were stating the classical criticism of the present-aim version of rational choice theory—namely, that it serves up an instant explanation of any and all behavior. We may agree wholeheartedly with this criticism, yet this should not blind us to the fact that differences in tastes do exist—indeed must exist—and often imply important differences in behavior. The advantage of the commitment model is that its view of tastes as means rather than ends helps constrain the open-ended nature of the present-aim standard. The commitment model's functional view of preferences suggests that the repertoire of tastes be expanded beyond the simple egoistic tastes assumed in the self-interest model, but only upon showing that the holding of a specific taste is advantageous (or at least not fatally disadvantageous) in a material sense.

---

[5]For the details of the argument supporting this claim, see chapter 3 of my 1988 book, *Passions Within Reason.*
[6]George Stigler and Gary Becker, "De Gustibus Non Est Disputandum," *American Economic Review,* 67, September 1977. In fairness, I should add that Gary Becker later embraced a much richer view about the admissible range of preferences.

Economic Naturalist 7.1

Why do people vote in presidential elections?

The self-interest version of the rational choice model predicts that people will not vote in presidential elections. The reason, in a nutshell, is that while there are almost always costs involved in voting, there is virtually no chance that a single vote will tip the balance of the election—not even in excruciatingly close contests like the one in 2000, when a small number of ballots in Florida decided the national election.

Since presidential elections are never decided by a single vote, why do people incur the cost of going to the polls?

But consider a person who has been taught that it is a citizen's duty to vote in presidential elections. If this message has sunk in at a deep level, its effect is to alter the person's preferences. For such a person, voting now becomes an end in itself, something that provides satisfaction.[7]

Application: Predicting Variations in Voter Turnout

If we assume that a person regards voting as a duty, her decision as to whether to vote can be analyzed in much the same way as we analyze other economic choices. To illustrate, consider a consumer whose utility is given by the following function:

$$U = 2M + 100V, \tag{7.1}$$

where M is the dollar value of her annual consumption of the composite good, and V takes the value 1 if she votes and 0 if she does not. Suppose further that this consumer finances her consumption by working at a job that pays \$50/hr for as many hours as she chooses to work. And suppose, finally, that in order to vote she must spend a total of 30 minutes traveling to and from the polling place, where she also must stand in line before casting her ballot. If she regards her transit time and waiting time as neither more nor less unpleasant than working an equivalent amount of time at her job, how long must the line at the polls be before she will decide not to vote?

Suppose we let t represent the length of the line at the polls, measured in hours. Then the total time required to vote, including travel time, is equal to $(t + 0.5)$ hr. Given that she can earn \$50/hr at her job, the opportunity cost of her voting is thus \$$(50t + 25)$. And since she gets 2 units of utility from each dollar of consumption of the composite good

---

[7]Here too, it might seem more descriptive to say that a person votes not because it gives her pleasure but because she thinks it is the right thing to do. Analytically, however, both descriptions may be represented by saying that the act of voting augments utility.

(see Equation 7.1), the opportunity cost of voting in utility terms is equal to $100t + 50$. On the benefit side, she stands to gain 100 units of utility by voting. The maximum acceptable length of the polling line is the value of t that equates the costs and benefits of voting in utility terms. This value of t is found by solving the equation

$$100t + 50 = 100, \tag{7.2}$$

which yields $t = \frac{1}{2}$, or 30 minutes. So the model predicts that if the line at the polling place is shorter than 30 minutes, she will vote; if longer, she will not vote; and if equal to 30 minutes, she will be indifferent between voting and not voting. The same model also shows how a storm that increases transit time to the polls will tend to reduce voter turnout.

Application: Concerns about Fairness

As an additional illustration of how predictions change when we take nonegoistic motives into account, consider the following example set forth by the German economist Werner Guth. Guth and his colleagues investigated how people behave in a simple game designed to test for the presence of concerns about fairness.

The game is called the *ultimatum bargaining game* and involves two players, an *allocator* and a *receiver*. It begins by giving the allocator a fixed sum of money, say, $20. The allocator must then make a proposal about how the money should be divided between himself and the receiver—for example, he might propose $10 for himself and $10 for the receiver. The receiver's task is then either to accept or to reject the proposal. If he accepts it, then they each receive the amounts proposed. If he rejects it, however, each player receives nothing. The $20 simply reverts to the experimenters. The players in the game are strangers to one another and will play the game only once.

What does the self-interest model predict will happen here? To answer this question, we begin by assuming that each player cares only about his final wealth level, not about how much the other player gets. Now suppose the allocator proposes to keep $P_A = \$15$ for himself and to give the remaining $\$20 - P_A = \$5$ to the receiver, and that the receiver accepts this proposal. If M_A and M_R were their respective wealth levels before the experiment, their final wealth levels will then be $M_A + \$15$ and $M_R + \$5$.

If, on the other hand, the receiver rejects the allocator's proposal, then their final wealth levels will be M_A and M_R. Knowing this, the allocator can conclude that the receiver will get a higher wealth level by accepting the proposal than by rejecting it, provided only that P_A is less than $20. If the money cannot be divided into intervals any smaller than 1 cent, the self-interest model thus predicts unequivocally that the allocator will propose to keep $19.99 for himself and to give the remaining 1 cent to the receiver. The receiver may not be pleased about this one-sided offer, but the self-interest model says he will accept it nonetheless, because $M_R + \$0.01 > M_R$. By the logic of the self-interest model, the receiver reasons that, although a gain of 1 cent is not much, it is better than nothing, which is what he would get if he refused the offer. Because the game is played only once, there is no point in refusing in the hope of encouraging a more favorable offer next time.

What prediction would we reach if we acknowledge that the receiver cares not just about his final wealth level but also about fairness? It is perhaps natural to say that the fairest split of the surplus in an ultimatum bargaining game is 50-50. Let S denote the total sum of money to be divided, and let $P/S = (20 - P_A)/S$ be the share of this surplus the receiver would get if he accepted the proposal. A convenient way to express the receiver's concern about fairness is by saying that his satisfaction declines as the ratio P/S deviates—in either direction—from the value 0.5. Thus, the receiver's indifference map defined over M_R and P/S might look roughly as shown in Figure 7.5. The indifference curves shown embody the additional assumption that a one-sided division is more objectionable if it favors the other person—which is another way of saying that the MRS rises more sharply when we move to the left from $P/S = 0.5$ than when we move to the right.[8]

---

[8]The point made in this example would be essentially the same if the receiver's indifference curves in Figure 7.5 were downward sloping throughout.

FIGURE 7.5

The Trade-Off between Absolute Wealth and Relative Gain

In many situations, the fairest division of a surplus is when each party receives an equal share. When people value fairness for its own sake, the indifference curves between final wealth and own share of the surplus are U-shaped, which means that people need to be compensated for accepting divisions that deviate from equality.

Let us now evaluate the one-sided proposal predicted by the standard self-interest model, where $P_A = \$19.99$ and $P = \$0.01$. If the receiver accepts this proposal, he will end up at the point $(0.01/20, M_R + 0.01)$, labeled C in Figure 7.6. If, on the other hand, he rejects the proposal, he will have virtually the same wealth level, M_R. If rejecting may be considered to result in a P/S value of 0.5 (since neither party gains ground at the other's expense), the receiver will thus end up at point D in Figure 7.6. And because D lies on a higher indifference curve than C, he does best to reject the proposal. (If he accepted it, the trivial increase in his wealth would be insufficient to compensate for the disutility of the one-sided transaction.) More important, if the allocator knows that the receiver has such preferences, he will never make a one-sided offer in the first place.

In the forgoing example, it cost the receiver only a penny to punish the allocator for making a one-sided offer. Are people willing to turn down one-sided offers when substantially larger losses are involved? Werner Guth and his colleagues conducted these experiments with amounts as large as $50. They found that, even at this level, it is common to see the receiver reject if the allocator offers less than 20 percent of the total.

At some point, of course, concerns about fairness are likely to give way to concerns about the absolute gain itself. It would be surprising indeed if the receiver rejected a proposal that he get 10 percent of, say, $1 million. Here, most people would surely find the pair $(0.1, M_R + \$100,000)$ more attractive than $(0.5, M_R)$.

FIGURE 7.6

The Gain from Rejecting a One-Sided Offer

Accepting a one-sided offer places the receiver at point C. By refusing the offer, he ends up at D, where, even though his final wealth is slightly lower, he is on a higher indifference curve.

EXAMPLE 7.2   **A Symmetric Problem**

Hatfield's utility function is given by $U_H = M_H / \sqrt{M_M}$, where M_H is Hatfield's wealth level and M_M is McCoy's. McCoy's utility function takes a similar form: $U_M = M_M / \sqrt{M_H}$. Suppose $M_H = M_M = 4$ initially, and suppose there is a task, neither pleasant nor unpleasant, that Hatfield and McCoy can perform together and that will generate an additional 2 units of wealth for the two men to divide. Neither man can perform the task alone or with anyone else. What is the smallest payment Hatfield would accept in return for this task? (McCoy is paid the difference between 2 and the amount paid to Hatfield.) Is this task feasible?

The utility functions in this example are ones in which each person feels better when his own wealth increases but feels worse when the other person's wealth increases. The effect of the task is to increase the wealth of both people. The question is thus whether the positive effect of having more income from performing the task outweighs the negative effect of the other person also having more income. Hatfield's initial utility level is $4/\sqrt{4} = 2$. Suppose he does the task with McCoy and receives a payment of P, leaving $2 - P$ for McCoy. Hatfield's utility level would then be $U_H = (4 + P)/\sqrt{(4 + 2 - P)} = (4 + P)/\sqrt{(6 - P)}$. The lowest acceptable utility payment for Hatfield is the one that keeps his utility at the same level as if he did not participate: $(4 + P)/\sqrt{(6 - P)} = 2$. Rearranging terms, we have $P^2 + 12P - 8 = 0$, which solves for $P = 0.63$.[9] Since the problem is symmetric, this is also the minimum payment that would be acceptable to McCoy. And since the total gain from doing the project (2) is more than enough for each person to get 0.63, they will do it. For example, if each takes a payment of 1, each will have a utility level of $(4 + 1)/\sqrt{(4 + 1)} = \sqrt{5}$, which is greater than the initial utility level of 2.

The Importance of Tastes

The self-interest model assumes certain tastes and constraints and then calculates what actions will best serve those tastes. This model is widely used by economists and other social scientists, game theorists, military strategists, philosophers, and others. Its results influence decisions that affect us all. In its standard form, it assumes purely egoistic tastes—namely, for present and future consumption goods of various sorts, leisure, and so on. Envy, guilt, rage, honor, sympathy, love, and the like typically play no role.

The examples in this chapter, by contrast, emphasize the role of these emotions in behavior. The rationalists speak of tastes, not emotions, but for analytical purposes, the two play exactly parallel roles. Thus, a person who is motivated to avoid the emotion of guilt may be equivalently described as someone with a "taste" for honest behavior.

Tastes have important consequences for action. The inclusion of tastes that help solve commitment problems substantially alters the predictions of self-interest models. We saw that it may pay people to feel concerned about fairness for its own sake, because feeling that way makes them better bargainers. Without taking into account concerns about fairness, we cannot hope to predict what prices stores will charge, what wages workers will demand, how long business executives will resist a strike, what taxes governments will levy, how fast military budgets will grow, or whether a union leader will be reelected.

[9]Recall that the solution to an equation of the form $ax^2 + bx + c = 0$ is given by

$$x = \frac{-b \pm \sqrt{b^2 - 4ac}}{2a}.$$

The presence of conscience also alters the predictions of self-interest models. These models predict clearly that when interactions between people are not repeated, people will cheat if they know they can get away with it. Yet evidence consistently shows that many people do not cheat under these circumstances. Self-interest models also suggest that the owner of a small business will not contribute to the lobbying efforts of trade associations. Like one man's vote, her own contribution will seem too small a part of the total to make any difference. Yet many small businesses do pay dues to trade associations, and many people do vote. Charitable institutions also exist on a far grander scale than would ever be predicted by self-interest models.

There is nothing mystical about the emotions that drive these behaviors. On the contrary, they are an obvious part of most people's psychological makeup. What we have seen is why it might be advantageous, even in purely material terms, to have concerns that motivate unselfish behavior.

Is Material Gain an "Appropriate" Motive for Morality?

Some may object that the prospect of material gain is somehow an improper motive for adopting moral values. But this objection misconstrues the fundamental message of this section, which is that nonegoistic motives confer material advantage only if the satisfaction people take from doing the right thing is *intrinsic* to the behavior itself. Otherwise, the person will lack the necessary motivation to make self-sacrificing choices when no one is looking, and once other people sense that aspect of his character, material advantages will not, in fact, follow. By the very nature of the commitment problem, moral sentiments cannot lead to material advantage unless they are heartfelt.

Departures from Traditional Rational Choice Models (With Regret)

Cornell University has two sets of faculty tennis courts, one outdoor, one indoor. Membership in the outdoor facility is available for a fixed fee per season, with no additional charge based on actual court use. The indoor facility, by contrast, has not only a seasonal fee but also a $25 per hour charge for court time. The higher charges of the indoor facility reflect the additional costs of heat, electricity, and building maintenance. The indoor facility opens in early October, when the Ithaca weather can be anything from bright sunshine and mild temperatures to blowing sleet and snow. The outdoor courts remain open, weather permitting, until early November.

Demand on the indoor facility is intense, and people who want to play regularly must commit themselves to reserve a specific hour each week. Having done so, they must pay for the hour whether or not they use it. During good weather, almost everyone prefers to play on the outdoor courts, which are nestled in one of Ithaca's scenic gorges.

Here is the problem: You are committed to pay for an indoor court at 3 PM on Saturday, October 20, the only hour you are free to play that day. It is a warm, sunny autumn afternoon. Where should you play, indoors or out?

Surprisingly, many of my noneconomist partners balk when I say that playing on the outdoor courts is the only sensible thing to do. "But we've already paid for the indoor court," they invariably complain. I ask, "If both courts cost the same, which would you choose?" They immediately respond, "Outdoors." I then explain that both courts *do* cost the same—because our fee for the hour is going to be $25 no matter which place we play—indeed, no matter whether we play at all. The $25 is a sunk cost and should have no effect on our decision. Yet, even at this point, many people seem to feel uncomfortable about wasting the indoor court we have paid for. The alternative, however, is to waste an opportunity to play outdoors, which we all agree is something even more valuable! True enough, it is bad to be wasteful, but *something* is going to be wasted, no matter which place we play.

Eventually, most people come around to the notion that it is more sensible to abandon the indoor court, even though paid for, and play outdoors on sunny fall days. The rational choice model says unequivocally that this is what we should do. But it does not seem to be the natural inclination of most people. On the contrary, in the absence of a prodding economist, most people who have paid for an indoor court end up using it, even on the most pleasant days.

BOUNDED RATIONALITY

The late Nobel laureate Herbert Simon was among the first to impress upon economists that human beings are incapable of behaving like the rational beings portrayed in standard rational choice models. Simon was a pioneer in the field of artificial intelligence and stumbled upon this realization in the process of trying to instruct a computer to "reason" about a problem. He discovered that when we ourselves confront a puzzle, we rarely reach a solution in a neat, linear fashion. Rather, we search in a haphazard way for potentially relevant facts and information, and usually quit once our understanding reaches a certain threshold. Our conclusions are often inconsistent, even flatly incorrect. But much of the time, we come up with serviceable solutions. In Simon's terms, we are "satisficers," not maximizers.

Subsequent economists have taken Simon's lead and developed a sophisticated literature on decision making under incomplete information. We now realize that when information is costly to gather, and cognitive processing ability is limited, it is not even rational to make fully informed choices of the sort portrayed in simple models. Paradoxically, it is irrational to be completely well informed! The literature on decision making under incomplete information, far from being a challenge to the rational choice model, has actually bolstered our confidence in it.

But there is another offshoot of Simon's work, one that is less friendly to the rational choice model. This research, strongly influenced by cognitive psychologists Daniel Kahneman and Amos Tversky, demonstrates that even with transparently simple problems, people often violate the most fundamental axioms of rational choice. Choosing whether to play tennis indoors or out is a case in point. The relevant facts in this problem could hardly be any simpler, and yet, as noted, people consistently choose irrationally. Such examples, Kahneman and Tversky showed, are by no means isolated. On the strength of this work, Kahneman was awarded the Nobel Prize in economics in 2002, an honor that Tversky undoubtedly would have shared had it not been for his untimely death in 1996.

Losing a $10 ticket on your way to a concert is no worse than losing a $10 bill.

One of the most cherished tenets of the rational choice model is that wealth is fungible. Fungibility implies, among other things, that our total wealth, not the amount we have in any particular account, determines what we buy. Kahneman and Tversky, however, provided a vivid experimental demonstration to the contrary.[10] They tell one group of people to imagine that, having earlier purchased tickets for $10, they arrive at the theater to discover they have lost them. Members of a second group are told to picture themselves arriving just before the performance to buy their tickets when they find each of them has lost $10 on the way to the theater. People in both groups are then asked whether they will continue with their plans to attend the performance. In the rational choice model, the forces governing this decision are the same for both groups. Losing a $10 ticket should have precisely the same effect as losing a $10 bill. (Recall from Chapter 3 the rule that if tastes and budget constraints are the same, decisions should also be the same.) And yet, in repeated trials, most people in the lost-ticket group say they would not attend the performance, while an overwhelming majority—88 percent—in the lost-bill group say they would.

Kahneman and Tversky explained that people apparently organize their spending into separate "mental accounts" for food, housing, entertainment, general expenses, and so on. People who lose their tickets act as if they debit $10 from their mental entertainment accounts, while those who lose $10 debit their general expense accounts. For people in the former group, the loss makes the apparent cost of seeing the show rise from $10 to $20, whereas for those in the second it remains $10.

[10]See Amos Tversky and Daniel Kahneman, "The Framing of Decisions and the Psychology of Choice," *Science*, 211, 1981, 453–458.

FIGURE 7.7

Utility of a Pair of Events That Increases Total Wealth

Under the rational choice model, any combination of events that increases total wealth will also increase total utility.

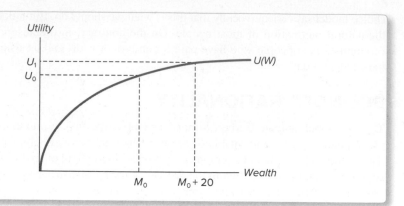

The rational choice model makes clear that the second group's assessment is the correct one. And on reflection, most people do, in fact, agree that losing a ticket is no better reason not to see the performance than losing a $10 bill.

The Asymmetric Value Function

The rational choice model says that people should evaluate events, or collections of events, in terms of their overall effect on total wealth. Suppose A is the event that you get an unexpected gift of $100 and B is the event that you return from vacation to find an $80 invoice from the city for the repair of a broken water line on your property. According to the rational choice model, you should regard the occurrence of these two events as a good thing, because their net effect is a $20 increase in your total wealth.

Kahneman and Tversky found, however, that people seem to weigh each event separately, and attach considerably less importance to the gain than to the loss—so much less that many people actually refuse to accept pairs of events that would increase their overall wealth!

In the rational choice model, this of course can never happen. Confronted with the two events A and B described above, a person with an initial wealth of M_0 knows exactly how to react. The combined effect of A (a $100 gain) and B (an $80 loss) is to increase his wealth to $M_0 + 20$. And since utility is an increasing function of total wealth, the two events taken together cause utility to increase from U_0 to U_1, as shown in Figure 7.7.

Kahneman and Tversky proposed that people evaluate alternatives not with the conventional utility function, but instead with a *value function* that is defined over *changes* in wealth. One important property of this value function is that it is much steeper in losses than in gains. In Figure 7.8, for example, note how it assigns a much larger value, in absolute terms, to a loss of $80 than to a gain of $100. Note also that the value function is concave in gains and convex in losses. This property is the analog of diminishing marginal

FIGURE 7.8

The Kahneman-Tversky Value Function

Unlike the traditional utility function, the value function is defined over *changes* in total wealth. It is steeper in losses than in gains, concave in gains, and convex in losses.

utility in the traditional model. It says that the impact of incremental gains or losses diminishes as the gains or losses become larger.

Kahneman and Tversky emphasized that their value function is a purely descriptive device. They are trying to summarize regularities in the ways people actually seem to make choices. They make no claim that people *should* choose in the ways predicted by their value function.

According to Kahneman and Tversky, people typically evaluate each item of a collection of events separately and then make decisions on the basis of the sum of the separate values. In this example, $V(100)$ is much smaller, in absolute terms, than $V(-80)$. Because the algebraic sum of the two is less than zero, anyone who employs this decision mechanism will refuse the pair of opportunities A and B, even though their net effect is to increase total wealth by $20.

There are really two important features of the Kahneman and Tversky value function. One is that people treat gains and losses asymmetrically, giving the latter much heavier weight in their decisions than the former. The second is that people evaluate events first and then add the separate values together. The first of these features does not necessarily imply irrational behavior. There is nothing inconsistent, after all, about feeling that a loss causes more pain than the happiness caused by a gain of the same magnitude. What *does* often appear irrational is the second step—treating each event separately, rather than considering their combined effect.

This is essentially a question about how to frame events. If someone pointed out to a person that the net effect of two events A and B was to increase her wealth by $20, she would probably agree to allow the events to happen. Framed as an entity, they are obviously an improvement over the status quo. The problem is that, in actual decisions, it may seem more natural to frame the events separately.

Another example helps illustrate this point. Recently, a corporation made available to its employees a new medical insurance plan. The old plan paid 100 percent of all covered medical expenses, and the premium was approximately $500/yr per family. The new plan has a $200 deductible feature—people must pay the first $200 in medical expenses each year, but once that threshold is reached, the insurance again pays 100 percent. The premium for the new plan is $250/yr, half that of the old plan. Employees have the option of staying with the old plan or switching to the new.

Seen through the lens of the rational choice model, the new plan dominates the old. The $250 savings in premiums is more than enough to compensate for the $200 deductible feature. Families that incur less than $200/yr in medical expenses do even better under the new plan. Nonetheless, many employees are adamant in their wish to remain on the old plan. If some people code the $250 premium savings and the $200 extra in medical bills as separate events, the asymmetric value function predicts just such behavior. As indicated in Figure 7.9, the $200 loss weighs in more heavily than the $250 gain.

FIGURE 7.9

Rejection of a Dominant Insurance Plan

Because the savings in premiums ($250) is larger than the largest possible increase in uncovered expenses ($200), the new plan is necessarily better than the old. But if people code gains and losses separately, they may nonetheless refuse to switch to the new policy.

Sunk Costs

Another basic tenet of the rational choice model is that sunk costs should be ignored in decisions. In the tennis example, we saw that it is this principle, not sunk cost, that is sometimes ignored. Economist Richard Thaler argues that such examples are not isolated, that people in fact show a general tendency not to ignore sunk costs. Thaler is the author of the all-you-can-eat pizza experiment discussed in Chapter 1. Recall that in the experiment diners whose admission charges were refunded ate substantially fewer slices of pizza than others. Thaler offered several other vivid illustrations of the pattern.

One is a thought experiment in which you are asked first to imagine that you have bought a pair of fashionable shoes for $600, only to discover that they are painfully tight. They improve slightly after being broken in, but still cause considerable discomfort. Do you continue wearing these shoes or give them away? Would your response be any different if you had not bought the shoes but instead had received them as a gift?

Under the rational choice model, it should not matter whether you bought the shoes or were given them. Either way, you own them now, and the only question is whether the discomfort they cause is serious enough to discontinue wearing them. People in both categories should be equally likely to discontinue wearing the shoes. Contrary to this prediction, however, people are much more likely to say they would abandon the shoes if they received them as a gift. Having shelled out $600 apparently makes many people determined to endure them.

Out-of-Pocket Costs Versus Implicit Costs

Thaler suggested that our tendency not to ignore sunk costs may be given a simple interpretation in terms of the Kahneman and Tversky value function. In terms of the tennis example, failure to play on the outdoor courts on a nice day is coded mentally as a forgone gain, whereas not playing on the $25 indoor court you have already paid for is coded as a loss. Even though the gain is larger than the loss here, the greater steepness of the value function in the loss domain creates a bias in favor of the indoor court.

Much the same interpretation is supported by a number of other plausible examples.[11] Consider a person who in 1992 bought a case of wine for $5/bottle. Today the same wine sells for $100/bottle. Her wine merchant offers her $60/bottle for it and she refuses, even though the most she would pay for the same wine today is $35/bottle. The rational choice model rules out such behavior. But if out-of-pocket expenses (for example, for the purchase of additional wine) are coded as losses, while implicit costs (for example, of not selling the wine to the merchant) are coded as forgone gains, then the asymmetric value function allows for just such a response.

An even more common example is the case of tickets to premium entertainment events. Tickets for the best seats to the 2019 Super Bowl sold for $2,500 through official channels, but in the open market went for prices as high as $25,000. Thousands of fans used their $2,500 tickets to attend the game, thus passing up the opportunity to sell them for $25,000. Very few of these fans, however, would have spent $25,000 to buy a ticket for the game.

Thaler offered the parallel example of the man who would refuse to mow his neighbor's lawn for $40 yet mows his own identical lawn, even though his neighbor's son would be willing to mow it for him for only $20. This behavior, as well as the behavior of the Super Bowl fans, is also consistent with the notion that out-of-pocket expenses are coded as losses, implicit costs as forgone gains.

---

[11]See R. Thaler, "Toward a Positive Theory of Consumer Choice," *Journal of Economic Behavior and Organization*, 1980.

AFFECTIVE FORECASTING ERRORS

Choosing intelligently between a pair of alternatives often requires only an accurate prediction of how each will affect us right away. For example, in choosing between rice and potatoes as a starch for dinner, we need only predict which one will be more satisfying that evening. Most people are reasonably good at this.

In many other cases, intelligent choice requires that we predict not only which alternative will be more satisfying at the moment but also how the experience of each would evolve over time if chosen. Yet adaptation typically receives little attention when people confront purchase decisions.[12] For the most part, we estimate the attractiveness of a good or activity by trying it and seeing how it affects us. When considering whether to pay extra for a house with a view, for instance, we sit in its living room and stare out for a while; when considering a new car, we take it for a test drive; and so on. And on the basis of these initial impressions, we then make our purchase decisions.

Does ignoring adaptation make some choices misleadingly attractive relative to others? The answer clearly depends on whether we adapt differently over time to experiences in different categories. If we do not, failure to account for adaptation will introduce no bias. For example, if the initial impression of every activity overstated its eventual attractiveness by a factor of, say, three, all activities might prove disappointing, but our choices among them would not be distorted.

Distortions surely will result, however, if we adapt more quickly or completely in some areas than in others. Thus if we choose among potential experiences in accordance with how strongly we react to them initially, the logical implication is that we will invest too heavily in experiences whose attractiveness declines steeply over time and too little in those whose attractiveness declines less steeply, or even grows, over time. A central, if often implicit, theme in the psychological literature on the determinants of life satisfaction is that adaptation is, in fact, highly variable across categories.

The psychologists Leaf Van Boven and Thomas Gilovich have found, for example, that people tend to adapt much more quickly to the consumption of goods than to the consumption of experiences.[13] Thus, although most people experience a rush of satisfaction when they first acquire television sets with bigger screens or refrigerators with greater capacity, these feelings almost invariably tend to decay rapidly. Once we become accustomed to the bigger TV or the more spacious refrigerator, its favorable features fade into the background. We are no longer conscious of them.

In contrast, the time profiles of our reactions to increases in many other forms of consumption have essentially the opposite configuration. For example, our subjective experience of vigorous exercise or of trying to play a musical instrument may even be mildly unpleasant at first, but for most people these experiences become more pleasurable as additional time passes. To the extent that we ignore our tendencies to adapt differently in different spheres, we will spend too much on some goods, too little on others.

Consider, for example, a woman trying to decide whether to trade in her Toyota Corolla for a new Porsche Boxster. She could meet the payments on the new car by working an additional Saturday each month, which in her case would mean not spending that Saturday with friends. The rational choice model suggests that she will work the extra Saturday if the satisfaction afforded by the Porsche outweighs the satisfaction provided by the company of her friends. But never having owned a Porsche, she cannot be sure how that experience would affect her. Nor can she know how things would evolve if she continued to spend the extra Saturday with friends. In both cases, she must make rough guesses about the future.

Introspection may provide reasonably good estimates of how these experiences will affect her satisfaction in the short run. But in the problem at hand, the relevant short- and

Psychologists find that people report greater long-run satisfaction when they purchase experiences (top) than when they purchase material goods.

[12]For a discussion, see George Loewenstein and David Schkade, "Wouldn't It Be Nice? Predicting Future Feelings," in D. Kahneman, E. Diener, and N. Schwartz (eds.), *Well-Being: The Foundations of Hedonic Psychology,* New York: Russell Sage Foundation, 1999.

[13]See Leaf Van Boven and Thomas Gilovich, "To Do or to Have? That Is the Question," *Journal of Personality and Social Psychology,* 85, December 2003, 1193–1202.

long-run effects are likely to be different. Because the Porsche is much faster and handles much better than her Toyota, her test drive will provide an initial thrill. Over time, however, she will grow accustomed to the new car's capabilities, and its capacity to stimulate will decay. The contribution to subjective well-being of additional time spent with friends will have a markedly different time profile. As relationships continue over time, the satisfaction they provide tends to increase rather than diminish.

In the long run, then, extra time spent with friends might well prove to be the better choice. Yet the short-run increment in satisfaction might easily be higher with the new car. And because these short-run effects are the most vivid and readily available sources of information at the moment of decision, they may bias choice in favor of the car.

Failure to take adaptation into account has similar implications for the decision about how much to save. Here the problem stems from how the amount we consume at one point in time affects our ability to derive pleasure from a given consumption level later on. By way of illustration, consider the following hypothetical choice between two different consumption profiles that could be financed from the same stream of lifetime earnings. In each case, suppose that you and all others in your age cohort will earn a salary of $50,000 each and every year from age 21 until retirement at age 65. In one instance, suppose you and the others spend exactly your salaries of $50,000 each year, as shown by the level consumption profile labeled *A* in Figure 7.10. Alternatively, suppose you and the others start out by saving $10,000 a year (or, to put it another way, suppose you start out by consuming only $40,000 a year), then gradually diminish your rate of saving until, by middle age, you begin drawing down your savings in ever larger amounts to finance additional consumption. If we ignore for simplicity the fact that your savings will generate interest, this pattern yields the rising consumption profile labeled *B* in Figure 7.10. Note that although profile *B* starts out $10,000 lower than profile *A* and ends up $10,000 higher, total lifetime consumption is the same on each profile. Which one would you choose (assuming that in either case you will receive the same generous pension during retirement)?

When I put an essentially similar question to a sample of more than 100 Cornell seniors a few years ago, almost 80 percent chose *B*, the rising consumption profile. Evidence suggests that this profile will in fact be the more satisfying of the two.[14] Here again, the idea is that our evaluations of almost everything—including material living standards—depend on our frames of reference. One frame of reference for evaluating our material standard of living involves comparing what we currently have to what others have. The choice to save $10,000 out of a $50,000 salary becomes very different if

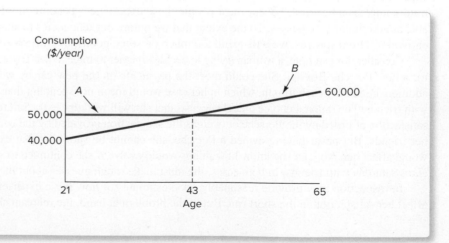

FIGURE 7.10

Static and Rising Consumption Profiles

Which consumption profile would you choose: *A*, in which everyone consumes $50,000 every year, or *B*, in which everyone starts out consuming $40,000 a year and ends up consuming $60,000? When asked this question, a large sample of undergraduates voiced a strong preference for *B*.

[14]See D. C. Shin, "Does Rapid Economic Growth Improve the Human Lot?" *Social Indicators Research,* 8, 1980, 199–221; and Robert Frank and Robert Hutchens, "Wages, Seniority, and the Demand for Rising Consumption Profiles," *Journal of Economic Behavior and Organization,* 21, 1993, 251–276.

friends, neighbors, or colleagues who make the same salary are spending all $50,000. But since everyone is assumed to follow the same consumption profile in this example, this comparison adds nothing of interest. A second frame of reference involves comparing what we currently have to what we ourselves had in the recent past, and it is this frame of reference that proves decisive for the problem at hand. For example, someone who consumes $50,000 this year is more likely to be satisfied with her standard of living if she consumed $45,000 last year than if she had consumed $55,000. People who consume too much too soon thus establish a more demanding frame of reference within which their later consumption must be evaluated.

The more we save during the early course of the life cycle, the steeper, and hence more satisfying, our consumption profiles will be. As obvious as this might seem, however, many of us never consciously consider the extent to which our current spending habits affect our evaluations of future living standards. To the extent that we ignore this relationship, we will tend to save too little. Here again, our failure to take adaptation into account may lead to costly—and avoidable—errors.

Perhaps the most vivid example of failure to account for future adaptation is the drug abuser's failure to anticipate increasing tolerance to his drug of choice. Thus a cocaine abuser typically gets launched on his downward spiral in the expectation that repeated ingestion of the drug will yield the same rush of euphoria he experienced on his first trial. He quickly discovers, however, that larger and larger doses are required to produce this effect. And before long, it becomes necessary to ingest prodigious quantities of the drug merely to avoid feelings of profound dysphoria. We may be sure that fewer people would take the first steps along this miserable trajectory if their patterns of future adaptation were clear to them at the outset.

JUDGMENTAL HEURISTICS AND BIASES

As the examples considered so far make it clear, people often make irrational decisions even when they have the relevant facts at their fingertips. Yet another difficulty confronting the rational choice model is that we often draw erroneous inferences about what the relevant facts are. More important, many of the errors we make are systematic, not random. Kahneman and Tversky identified three particularly simple heuristics, or rules of thumb, that people use to make judgments and inferences about the environment.[15] These heuristics are efficient in the sense that they help us economize on cognitive effort and give roughly correct answers much of the time. But they also give rise to large, predictable errors in many cases. Let us consider each of the three heuristics in turn.

Availability

We often estimate the frequency of an event, or class of events, by the ease with which we can summon examples from memory. Much of the time, there is a close positive correlation between the ease with which we can do so and the true frequency of occurrence. It is easier, after all, to recall examples of things that happen often.

But frequency of occurrence is not the only factor that determines ease of recall. If people are asked, for example, whether there are more murders than suicides in New York State each year, almost everyone confidently answers yes. And yet there are always more suicides! Kahneman and Tversky explained that we think there are more murders because murders are more "available" in memory. Memory research demonstrates that it is much easier to recall an event the more vivid or sensational it is. Even if we had heard about equally many suicides as murders, it is on this account likely that we will be able to remember a much larger proportion of the murders.

Other elements in the mechanics of memory can also affect the availability of different events. Ask yourself, for example, whether there are more words in the English language that start with the letter r than words that have r as their third letter. Most people answer confidently that many more words start with *r*, but in fact many more words have *r* as their third letter. We store words in memory much as they are stored in a dictionary—alphabetically, beginning with the first letter. We know plenty of words with *r* as their third letter, but it is no easier to remember them than it is to find them in a dictionary.

Events also tend to be more available in memory if they have happened more recently. A large body of research indicates that people tend to assign too much weight to recent information when making assessments about relative performance. In baseball, for example, a player's lifetime batting average against a certain pitcher is the best available predictor of how he will do against that pitcher in his next time at bat. It is apparently not uncommon, however, for a manager to bench a hitter against a pitcher he has performed poorly against the last couple of times out, even though he hit that same pitcher very well during a span of many years. The problem is that the manager estimates the player's performance by examples of it that spring easily to mind. And the most recent examples are the easiest ones to think of.

Economically, the availability bias is important because we often have to estimate the relative performance of alternative economic options. Managers of companies, for example, must weigh the merits of different employees for promotion. The most effective managers will be those who guard against the natural tendency to put too much weight on recent performance.

Representativeness

Kahneman and Tversky also discovered an interesting bias in the way we attempt to answer questions of the form, "What is the likelihood that object *A* belongs to class *B*?" For example, suppose Steve is a shy person and we want to estimate the likelihood that he is a librarian rather than a salesperson. Most people are eager to respond that Steve is much more likely to be a librarian, because shyness is thought to be a representative trait for librarians but rather an unusual one for salespersons. Such responses are often biased, however, because the likelihood of belonging to the category in question is influenced by many other important factors besides representativeness. Here, it is heavily influenced by the relative frequencies of salespersons and librarians in the overall population.

A simple example conveys the essence of the problem. Suppose that 80 percent of all librarians are shy, but only 20 percent of all salespeople. Suppose further that there are nine salespeople in the population for every librarian. Under these reasonable assumptions, if we know that Steve is shy and that he is either a librarian or a salesman, what is the probability that he is a librarian? The relevant numbers for answering this question are displayed in Figure 7.11. There, we see that even though a much larger proportion of librarians are shy, there are more than twice as many shy salespersons as there are shy librarians. The reason, of course, is that there are so many more salespeople than librarians. Out of every 100 people here, 26 of them are shy—18 salespersons and 8 librarians. This means that the odds of a shy person being a librarian are only 8/26, or just under

FIGURE 7.11

Distribution by Type of Librarians and Salespersons

Even though shyness is more representative of librarians than of salespersons, a shy person is much more likely to be a salesperson than a librarian. The reason is that there are many more salespersons than librarians.

Shy librarians 8

Shy salespersons 18

Non-shy librarians 2

Non-shy salespersons 72

one-third. Yet most people who confront this example are reluctant to say that Steve is a salesperson, because shyness is so unrepresentative of salespersons.

SELF-TEST 7.1

Suppose 90 percent of all librarians are shy but only 20 percent of all salespersons are, and that there are 4 times as many salespersons as librarians. What is the likelihood that a randomly chosen shy person is a librarian, given that he or she is either a salesperson or a librarian?

Another example of the representativeness bias is the statistical phenomenon known as the *regression effect,* or *regression to the mean.* Suppose a standard IQ test is administered to 100 people and that the 20 who score highest have an average score of 122, or 22 points above the average for the population. If these same 20 people are then tested a second time, their average score will almost always be substantially smaller than 122. The reason is that there is a certain amount of randomness in performance on IQ tests, and the people who did best on the first test are likely to include disproportionately many whose performances happened to be better than usual on that particular test.

We have substantial firsthand experience with regression effects in our daily lives (for example, the sons of unusually tall fathers tend to be shorter than their fathers). Kahneman and Tversky noted, however, that we often fail to make adequate allowance for it in our judgments because, they conjectured, we feel intuitively that an output (for example, an offspring) should be representative of the input (for example, the parent) that produced it.

Economic Naturalist 7.2

Why does the rookie of the year in baseball often have a mediocre second season?

Toronto third baseman Erik Hinske hit .279 with 24 home runs and 84 runs batted in when he won the American League's Rookie of the Year Award in 2002. During his second year with the Blue Jays, however, his average dropped to .243 with only 12 home runs and 63 runs batted in. Hinske's performance decline in 2003 fits a pattern observed in baseball and other professional sports in which the rookie of the year typically performs at a much lower level in the next season. Why this pattern?

The phenomenon in question is called the "sophomore jinx." A related phenomenon is the "*Sports Illustrated* jinx," which holds that an athlete whose picture appears on the cover of *Sports Illustrated* one week is destined to do poorly the next. Shirley Babashoff, an Olympic swimming medalist, was once said to have refused to have her picture on the cover of *SI* for fear of the jinx.[16] Both these supposed jinxes, however, are easily explained as the result of regression to the mean. Someone gets to be

What accounts for the "sophomore jinx"?

rookie of the year only after having had an extraordinarily good season. Similarly, athletes appear on the cover of *SI* only after an unusually strong performance. Their subsequent performance, even if still well above average, will almost inevitably fall below the standard that earned them their accolades.

---

[16]See Thomas Gilovich, *How We Know What Isn't So,* New York: The Free Press, 1991.

An especially pernicious consequence of our failure to take into account regression to the mean is the effect it has on our estimates of the relative efficacy of praise and blame. Psychologists have long demonstrated that praise and other forms of positive reinforcement are much more effective than punishment or blame for teaching desired skills. But people would be unlikely to draw this inference from experience if they were unmindful of the importance of regression to the mean.

The reason is that, quite independently of whether a person is praised or blamed, a good performance is likely to be followed by a lesser one and a bad performance by a better one. Someone who praises good performances is therefore likely to conclude, erroneously, that praise perversely *causes* worse performance. Conversely, someone who denigrates poor performance is likely to spuriously take credit for the improvement that in fact results from regression effects. The co-movements of praise, blame, and performance would convince all but the most sophisticated analyst that blame works and praise doesn't. Managers who are trying to elicit the most effective performances from their employees can ill afford to make this mistake.

Anchoring and Adjustment

In one common strategy of estimation, known as "anchoring and adjustment," people first choose a preliminary estimate—an anchor—and then adjust it in accordance with whatever additional information they have that appears relevant. Kahneman and Tversky have discovered that this procedure often leads to biased estimates, for two reasons. First, the initial anchor may be completely unrelated to the value to be estimated. And second, even when it is related, people tend to adjust too little from it.

To demonstrate the anchoring and adjustment bias, Kahneman and Tversky asked a sample of students to estimate the percentage of African countries that are members of the United Nations. Each person was first asked to spin a wheel that generated a number between 1 and 100. The student was then asked whether his estimate was higher or lower than that number. And finally, the student was asked for his numerical estimate of the percentage. The results were nothing short of astonishing. Students who got a 10 or below on the spin of the wheel had a median estimate of 25 percent, whereas the corresponding figure for those who got a 65 or above was 45 percent.

Each student surely *knew* that the initial random number had no possible relevance for estimating the percentage of African nations that belong to the U.N. Nonetheless, the numbers had a dramatic effect on the estimates they reported. In similar problems, any number close at hand seems to provide a convenient starting point. Kahneman and Tversky reported that giving the students monetary payoffs for accuracy did not alter the size of the bias.

In another illustration, two groups of high school students were asked to estimate the product of 8 numbers within 5 seconds. The first group was given this expression:

$$8 \times 7 \times 6 \times 5 \times 4 \times 3 \times 2 \times 1,$$

while the second group was given exactly the same numbers in reverse order:

$$1 \times 2 \times 3 \times 4 \times 5 \times 6 \times 7 \times 8.$$

The time limit prevents most students from performing the entire calculation (which would lead to the correct answer of 40,320). What many of them apparently do is to perform the first few multiplications (their anchor), and then project an estimate of the final result. For both groups of students, these anchors turn out not to be very appropriate and the projections turn out to be grossly insufficient. The resulting bias displays exactly the predicted pattern: The median estimate for the first group was 2,250; for the second group, only 512.

An important economic application of the anchoring and adjustment bias is in estimating the failure rates of complex projects. Consider, for example, starting a new business. To succeed, it is necessary that each of a large number of events happen. Satisfactory financing must be obtained, a workable location found, a low-cost production process designed, sufficiently skilled labor hired, an effective marketing campaign implemented, and so on. The enterprise will fail if any one of these steps fails. When many steps are involved, the failure rate is invariably high, even when each step has a high probability of success. For example, a program involving 10 steps, each with a success rate of 90 percent, will fail 65 percent of the time. When estimating failure rates for such processes, people tend to anchor on the low failure rate for the typical step, from which they make grossly insufficient adjustments. The anchoring and adjustment bias may thus help explain why the overwhelming majority of new businesses fail.

The anchoring bias can also show up at the leadership level. Recent studies of entrepreneurship have asked whether the high failure rate of startups might be related to their founders' "overprecise" commitment to the original vision—to the degree that necessary adjustments in strategy, when made, are too small and come too late.[17]

THE PSYCHOPHYSICS OF PERCEPTION

Yet another pattern in the way we perceive and process information has importance in economic applications. It derives from the so-called **Weber-Fechner law** of psychophysics. Weber and Fechner set out to discover how large the change in a stimulus had to be before we could perceive the difference in intensity. Most people, for example, are unable to distinguish a 100-watt light bulb from a 100.5-watt light bulb. But how large does the difference in brightness have to be before people can reliably identify it? Weber and Fechner found that the minimally perceptible difference is roughly proportional to the original intensity of the stimulus. Thus the more intense the stimulus is, the larger the difference has to be, in absolute terms, before we can tell the difference.

Thaler suggested that the Weber-Fechner law seems to be at work when people decide whether price differences are worth worrying about. Suppose, for example, you are about to buy a USB hub in a store for $25 when a friend informs you that the same hub is selling for only $20 in another store only 10 minutes away. Do you go to the other store? Would your answer have been different if you had been about to buy a television for $1,050 and your friend told you the same set was available at the other store for only $1,045? Thaler found that most people answer yes to the first question and no to the second.

In the rational choice model, it is inconsistent to answer differently for the two cases. A rational person will travel to the other store if and only if the benefits of doing so exceed the costs. The benefit is $5 in both cases. The cost is also the same for each trip, whether it is to buy a USB hub or a television. If it makes sense to go in one case, it also makes sense in the other.

Weber-Fechner law the property of perception whereby the just noticeable difference in a stimulus tends to be proportioned to the value of the stimulus.

The Difficulty of Actually Deciding

In the rational choice model, there should be no difficult decisions. If the choice between two alternatives is a close call—that is, if the two alternatives are predicted to yield approximately the same utility—then it should not make much difference which is chosen. But if one of the options clearly has a higher expected utility, the choice should again be easy. Either way, the chooser has no obvious reasons to experience anxiety and indecision.

In reality, of course, we all know that difficult decisions are more the rule than the exception. There are many pairs of alternatives over which our utility functions just don't seem to assign clear, unambiguous preference rankings. The difficulty is most pronounced when the alternatives differ along dimensions that are hard to compare. If the three things we care about in a car are, say, comfort, fuel economy, and safety, it will be easy to decide between two cars if one is safer and more comfortable and has better gas mileage than the other. But what if one is much more comfortable and has much worse gas mileage? In principle, we are supposed to have indifference curves that tell us the rate at which we would be willing to trade one characteristic for the other. In practice, however, we often seem to find it difficult to summon the information implicit in these curves.

[17]Thomas Åstebro, Holger Herz, Ramana Nanda, and Roberto A. Weber, "Seeking the Roots of Entrepreneurship: Insights from Behavioral Economics," *Journal of Economic Perspectives*, 28(3), 2014, 49–70.

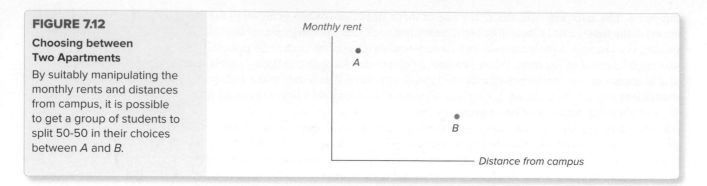

FIGURE 7.12

Choosing between Two Apartments

By suitably manipulating the monthly rents and distances from campus, it is possible to get a group of students to split 50-50 in their choices between *A* and *B*.

And the very act of trying to do so often seems to provoke disquiet. For instance, it is not uncommon for people to dwell on the possibility that they will regret whichever choice they make. ("If I pick the more comfortable car, what will happen if I then get transferred to a job that requires a long daily commute?")

Such difficulties appear to cast doubt on a fundamental axiom of rational choice theory, namely, that choices should be independent of irrelevant alternatives. This axiom is often illustrated by a story like the following. A man comes into a delicatessen and asks what kind of sandwiches there are. The attendant answers that they have roast beef and chicken. The patron deliberates for a few moments and finally asks for a roast beef sandwich. The counterman says, "Oh, I forgot to mention, we also have tuna." To this the patron responds, "Well, in that case I guess I'll have chicken." According to the rational choice model, the availability of tuna should matter only if it is the alternative the patron most prefers. There is no intelligible basis for its availability to cause a switch from roast beef to chicken.

In collaboration with Itamar Simonson, Tversky performed some intriguing experiments that suggest choice may not, in fact, always be independent of irrelevant alternatives.[18] One of their examples is the choice between apartments that differ along two dimensions, monthly rent and distance from campus. From a student's·point of view, an apartment is more attractive the closer it is to campus and the lower its monthly rent. A group of students was asked to choose between two apartments like the pair shown in Figure 7.12. Notice in the figure that neither apartment dominates the other. *A* is more expensive, but *B* is farther from campus. We expect that students who are relatively more concerned about rent will choose apartment *B*, while those who care primarily about commuting time will pick *A*. By manipulating the distance and rent, it is easy to get a group of students to divide roughly 50-50 between the two apartments.

So far, no surprises. But now the researchers add a third apartment, *C*, to the list of choices, giving us the set depicted in Figure 7.13. Notice that *C* is *dominated* by *B*—that is, it is both farther from campus *and* more expensive than *B*. In terms of the rational choice model, it is a classic example of an irrelevant alternative. Faced with the choice *A*, *B*, and *C*, no rational consumer would ever choose *C*. And indeed, in actual experiments, hardly anyone ever does.

FIGURE 7.13

Adding an Irrelevant Alternative

Because *C* is dominated by *B*, no one should ever choose it. But while no one does choose *C*, its availability makes people much more likely to choose *B*.

[18]See Itamar Simonson and Amos Tversky, "Choice in Context: Tradeoff Contrast and Extremeness Aversion," *Journal of Marketing Research*, 29, August 1992, 281–295.

The surprise is that options like *C* turn out to affect people's choices between the remaining options. Tversky and Simonson discovered that when an apartment like *C* is added to the pair *A* and *B,* the effect is to shift people's choices substantially in favor of *B.* Before *C* was available, students divided 50-50 between *A* and *B.* Once *C* was added, however, more than 70 percent of the students chose *B,* the option that dominates *C.*

Many people apparently find the original choice between *A* and *B* a difficult one to make. The appearance of *C* gives them a comparison they can make comfortably, namely, the one between *B* and *C.* The researchers hypothesized that this creates a "halo effect" for *B,* which makes it much more likely to be chosen over *A.* Perhaps a similar effect might cause the availability of tuna to cause someone to switch his decision from roast beef to chicken. Whatever the reason for such behavior, it clearly violates the axiom that choice is independent of irrelevant alternatives.

Economic Naturalist 7.3

Why do real estate agents often show clients two houses that are nearly identical, even though one is both cheaper and in better condition than the other?

As in the examples just discussed, the fact that one house dominates another may endow the first house with a halo that makes it more attractive relative to houses that are better than it on at least some dimensions. For example, an agent might have a client who is having difficulty making up her mind between a Greek revival house and a Queen Anne Victorian. By showing the client a similar Queen Anne Victorian that is priced higher and is less well maintained than the first, she might clinch the sale in favor of the dominant Queen Anne Victorian. Again, people seem to dislike choosing between alternatives that are difficult to compare. Experienced real estate agents often avoid this problem by giving their clients an opportunity to focus on an easy choice.

▶ Visit your instructor's Connect© course and access your eBook to view this video.

Why do real estate agents often show clients two nearly identical houses, even though one is both cheaper and in better condition than the other?

THE SELF-CONTROL PITFALL

Another reason that behavior doesn't always track the predictions of simple rational choice models is that people often have difficulty carrying out plans they believe to be in their own interests. Thomas Schelling observed, for example, that most cigarette smokers say they want to quit.[19] Many of them, with great effort, have done so. (Both Schelling and I are members of this group and can testify to the difficulty.) Many more, however, have tried to quit and failed.

One way of solving the self-control problem is captured by the example of Homer's Ulysses, who was faced with having to sail past dangerous reefs where the sirens lay. Ulysses realized that once he was within earshot of the sirens' cries, he would be drawn irresistibly toward them and sail to his doom on the reefs. Able to foresee this temporary change in his preferences, he came up with an effective commitment device: He instructed his crewmen to strap him tightly to the mast and not to release him, even though he might beg them to, until they had sailed safely past.

Similar sorts of commitment devices are familiar in modern life. Fearing they will be tempted to spend their savings, people join "Christmas clubs," special accounts that prohibit withdrawals until late autumn; they buy whole-life insurance policies, which impose

[19]See Thomas Schelling, *Choice and Consequence,* Cambridge, MA: Harvard University Press, 1984.

substantial penalties on withdrawals before retirement. Fearing they will spoil their dinners, they put the salted nuts out of easy reach. Fearing they will gamble too much, they limit the amount of cash they take to Atlantic City. Fearing they will stay up too late watching TV, they move the television out of the bedroom.

The moral of the burgeoning self-control literature is that *devising* a rational intertemporal consumption plan is only part of the problem. There is also the task of *implementing* it. But here too, rational deliberation can help us avoid some of the most important pitfalls. The consumer who has just given up smoking, for example, can predict that he will desperately want a cigarette if he goes out drinking with his friends on Friday nights. And he can also insulate himself from that temptation by committing himself to alternative weekend activities for the next month or so. By the same token, the person who wants to shield herself from the temptation to spend too much may have part of her pay diverted automatically into a savings account, and this is precisely what millions of people do.

These issues once again highlight the distinction between the positive and normative roles of the rational choice model discussed in Chapter 1. Thus, because the rational choice model takes no account of self-control problems and the like, it will sometimes fail to predict how people actually behave. But note carefully that this does not mean that the model, even in its narrowest form, is wrong or useless. For here, as in other instances, it can play the important normative role of guiding people toward better decisions, ones that accord more fully with their real objectives.

COGNITIVE ILLUSIONS AND PUBLIC POLICY

Many of the examples we have used to illustrate cognitive bias and other departures from rationality have been simple thought experiments or even simpler staged experiments: returning a wallet, allocating a payoff, estimating the product of a long list of figures. But behavioral economics also supports the evaluation of the great policy questions of our time.

Perhaps the greatest question we face concerns our response to the climate crisis. In October 2018, the United Nations' Intergovernmental Panel on Climate Change (IPCC) reported that in the absence of decisive measures to curtail greenhouse gas emissions, we are now on track to experience catastrophic increases in average global temperatures by 2040.[20] Of course, forecasts of climate models are notoriously imprecise. Temperatures might well rise by less, or considerably more, than predicted. But the current rise of only 1°C (1.8°F) has already produced floods, droughts, and fires on a scale unseen in human history. America received a foretaste of the potential impact of climate change in November 2018, when the Camp Fire killed 85 people and essentially destroyed the community of Paradise, California. As this chapter goes to press, it is Australia's turn. Wildfires there have killed dozens of people and consumed an area the size of West Virginia. The wildfires are of such intensity that in some areas, according to the International Red Cross, they have "created their own weather systems, generating pyrocumulonimbus clouds, trapping heat and generating strong wind and lightning strikes, in turn sparking further fires."[21] These events seem almost designed to underscore the first sentence of David Wallace-Wells's recent *The Uninhabitable Earth*: "It's worse, much worse, than you think."[22]

It is clear that if temperature increases come anything close to the IPCC's worst projections, many millions of people will die, and much of the earth's wealth will be destroyed. Under severe-case scenarios, the social cost of carbon we investigated in Chapter 5 would eventually become astronomical—and the actions required would overwhelm the discounting mechanisms embodied in the integrated assessment models of William Nordhaus and others. Actions to reduce or reverse global warming will require time to work, and so the time to act is now.

Reactions to this challenge vary greatly from country to country. In the United States, supporters of a set of policy proposals called the "Green New Deal" have introduced an expansive legislative agenda that attacks climate change and economic inequality

[20]Intergovernmental Panel on Climate Change, *Special Report: Global Warming of 1.5°*, October 2018, www.ipcc.ch/sr15.
[21]www.ifrc.org/docs/Appeals/20/IBAUbf080120.pdf.
[22]David Wallace-Wells, *The Uninhabitable Earth: Life after Warming*, New York: Tim Duggan Books, 2019.

simultaneously. Some critics have focused on the seeming unaffordability of these proposals. Others have objected that tackling both problems at once will simply make failure
in both domains more likely. Green New Deal proponents counter that unless we include
policies to mitigate rising inequality's impact, it will be impossible to assemble a sufficiently broad political coalition to overcome our current gridlock around climate change.

Without specifically endorsing any version of the Green New Deal or any of its components, we can still state that the insights developed in this chapter suggest that funding
the Green New Deal would be less impractical than many critics think. A phrase used
more than once in my most recent book[23] is *the mother of all cognitive illusions*. I use this
phrase to describe the belief, held by many wealthy voters, that higher top tax rates will
require them to make painful sacrifices. It is easy to understand this belief. We learned in
this chapter that it is very likely indeed that increased taxes get "coded as a loss" on individual taxpayer's Kahneman-Tversky asymmetric value function. Still, that belief is
demonstrably false. It is not just that, as the wealthy themselves would be quick to concede, they already have far more than anyone might reasonably be said to need. It's that
higher taxes will not compromise their ability of the wealthy to buy the special extras they
want. Those extras—think of New York City penthouse condominiums—are invariably in
short supply. Getting them requires bidding against others who also want them, and the
ability to bid successfully depends only on *relative* disposable income which would be
completely unaffected by a wealth tax or an increase in high-bracket income taxes.

Of course, the rich think higher taxes would hurt them because they know higher
taxes would reduce their disposable incomes in absolute terms. But almost every income
decline they have actually experienced was one in which their own income fell while the
incomes of peers remained unchanged—as happens, for example, when someone experiences a business reverse, home fire, health crisis, or a divorce. In the wake of such events,
it really is harder to bid successfully for what you want. But things are totally different
when the rich all pay higher taxes. The same full-floor apartments with commanding
360° views end up in the same hands as before.

Proper understanding of behavioral economics won't remove all disagreements over
what policies are desirable or effective, but it should challenge many of our first-take
prejudices around what level of response to climate crisis is possible.

SUMMARY

- The self-interest model, which assumes that everyone behaves opportunistically, makes many predictions that are at odds with observed behavior. People who violate those predictions often express no regret about having done so. *(LO1)*

- Commitment problems often arise when people are unable to make credible promises or threats that would require them to act against their own narrow interests in the future. Failure to make credible threats and promises can be costly. Being known not to have strictly self-interested preferences can be extremely useful for solving commitment problems. *(LO2)*

- In order for such preferences to be advantageous, others must be able to discover that one has them. If preferences could be observed without cost or uncertainty, there would be only cooperative people in the world. But because costs and uncertainty are an inherent part of the process, there will always be at least some of the opportunistic people assumed in conventional self-interest models. *(LO3)*

- People who are concerned about the interests of others need not suffer on that account, even in purely material terms. Because others can recognize the kind of people they are, opportunities will be open to them that would not be open to opportunists. *(LO3)*

- Many other predictions of the standard rational choice model are at odds with observed behavior because people fail to discover efficient ways to achieve their goals. People often fail to ignore sunk costs. They play tennis indoors when, by their own account, they would prefer to play outside. They behave differently when they lose a ticket than when they lose an equivalent amount of cash. In such cases, people often regret their departures from rational choice. *(LO4)*

[23]Robert H. Frank, *Under the Influence: Putting Peer Pressure to Work*, Princeton, NJ: Princeton University Press, 2020. The concluding section to this chapter draws heavily from chapters 11 and 12 of this book.

- People often use mental accounting systems that reduce the complexity of their decisions, sometimes at the expense of consistency with the axioms of rational choice. *(LO4)*

- An important class of departures from rational choice appears to result from the asymmetric value function described by Kahneman and Tversky. In contrast to the rational choice model, which uses a utility function defined on total wealth, Kahneman and Tversky's descriptive theory uses a value function defined over changes in wealth. Unlike the traditional model, it gives losses much heavier decision weight than gains. This feature makes decisions extremely sensitive to how alternatives are framed. For example, if a loss is combined with a slightly larger gain, the net effect typically receives a positive evaluation, as it would under the rational choice model. But Kahneman and Tversky suggest that when gains and losses occur as discrete events, people tend to evaluate their effects separately, in which case the impact of the loss tends to outweigh that of the larger gain. A loss combined with a slightly larger gain produces a positive effect, whereas taken separately their net effect is negative. *(LO4)*

- Another source of suboptimal decisions is failure to anticipate how we will adapt to different consumption experiences over time. In choosing between two goods, people tend to favor the alternative that provides greater satisfaction at the moment of decision. Evidence suggests, however, that the satisfaction provided by some goods and activities tends to decay quickly over time, whereas for others it decays less quickly or even increases. The upshot is a tendency to spend too much on goods and activities in the former category, and too little on those in the latter. *(LO5)*

- Another important departure from rational choice occurs in the heuristics, or rules of thumb, people use to make estimates of important decision factors. The availability heuristic says that one way people estimate the frequency of a given class of events is by the ease with which they can recall relevant examples. This leads to predictable biases because actual frequency is not the only factor that governs ease of recall. People tend to overestimate the frequency of vivid or salient events, and of other events that are especially easy to retrieve from memory. *(LO6)*

- Another important heuristic is representativeness. People estimate the likelihood that an item belongs to a given class by how representative it is of that class. This thinking often leads to substantial bias because representativeness is only one of many factors that govern this likelihood. For example, shyness may indeed be a trait representative of librarians, but because there are so many more salespeople than librarians, it is much more likely that a randomly chosen shy person is a salesperson than a librarian. *(LO6)*

- Anchoring and adjustment is a third heuristic that often leads to biased estimates of important decision factors. This heuristic says that people often make numerical estimates by first picking a convenient (but sometimes irrelevant) anchor and then adjusting from it (usually insufficiently) on the basis of other potentially relevant information. *(LO6)*

- Another departure from rational choice traces to the psychophysics of perception. Psychologists have discovered that the barely perceptible change in any stimulus is proportional to its initial level. This seems to hold true as well when the stimulus in question is the price of a good or service. People think nothing of driving across town to save $5 on a $25 radio, but would never dream of doing so to save $5 on a $1,000 TV set. *(LO7)*

- Departures from rational choice may also occur because people simply have difficulty choosing between alternatives that are hard to compare. The rational choice model assumes that we have complete preference orderings, but in practice, it often seems to require a great deal of effort for us to decide how we feel about even very simple alternatives. *(LO7)*

- Finally, departures from rational choice may occur because people lack sufficient willpower to carry out plans they believe to be in their own interests. In such instances, people may try to place tempting, but inferior, alternatives out of reach. *(LO8)*

- Behavioral models of choice often do a much better job of predicting actual decisions than the rational choice model. It is important to remember, however, that the behavioral models claim no normative significance. That is, the mere fact that they predict, for example, that people often *do* ignore sunk costs should not be taken to mean that people *should* ignore them. The rational choice model says we can make better decisions by ignoring sunk costs, and most people, on reflection, strongly agree. In this respect, behavioral models of choice are an important tool for helping us avoid common pitfalls in decision making. *(LO8)*

- In evaluating public policy proposals, we must consider their impact on people's wealth or income relative to their peers, and not just their absolute gain or loss in dollar terms. *(LO9)*

KEY TERM

Weber-Fechner law

REVIEW QUESTIONS

1. Summarize in your own words the major difficulties of the present-aim and self-interest standards of rationality. *(LO1)*

2. Explain the role of rational analysis in the psychologist's model of human motivation. *(LO1)*

3. Describe two commitment problems you personally encountered during the last year. *(LO2)*

4. What role in solving commitment problems is played by the observability of preferences? *(LO2)*

5. Suppose you were the owner of a small business and were asked the maximum you would be willing to pay in order to attend a course in the traditional theory of rational choice. In which case would your answer be larger: (1) if it were known that people always behave in strict accordance with the predictions of rational

choice theory; or (2) if it were known that people's behavior, yours included, often departs systematically from the predictions of rational choice theory? *(LO4)*

6. Why is it rational to make decisions with less than complete information? *(LO4)*

7. Is there anything irrational about weighing gains less heavily than losses? *(LO4)*

8. The policy of one school was to punish students for being late, while the corresponding policy in an otherwise identical school was to reward students for being on time. If effectiveness is measured by behavior on the day following punishment or reward, which policy would seem to be more effective? Is this standard of effectiveness a good one? *(LO6)*

PROBLEMS

1. Alphonse's utility function is given by

$$U_A = M_A M_G,$$

where M_A and M_G are the wealth levels of Alphonse and Gaston, respectively. If Alphonse's initial wealth level is 100 while Gaston's is only 20, how much of his wealth will Alphonse give to Gaston? *(LO1)*

2. Abdul's utility function is given by

$$U_A = M_A^2/M_B,$$

where M_A is Abdul's wealth level and M_B is Bindi's wealth level. Bindi's utility function is given by *(LO1)*

$$U_B = M_B^2/M_A.$$

Suppose $M_A = M_B = 10$ initially, and suppose there is a joint project that Abdul and Bindi can undertake that will generate an additional 10 units of wealth to divide between them. The project is neither pleasant nor unpleasant. What is the minimum payment Abdul must be given to secure his agreement to perform the project? What is the minimum payment Bindi must be given? Will they perform the project? *(LO1)*

3. Now, suppose Bindi's utility function is given by $U_B = M_B^2$ in Problem 2. And suppose Abdul signs a contract saying that he will donate 20 to a cause he opposes in the event that he receives less than 90 percent of any money he earns jointly with Bindi. Will Bindi accept a take-it-or-leave-it offer of 1 unit from Abdul? *(LO1)*

4. Describe the advantages and disadvantages of electing a political leader who is known to favor harsh

military reprisals against foreign aggression, even when such reprisals are highly injurious to our own national interests. *(LO2)*

5. Olivia's utility is given by $U = 3M + 60V$, where M is the dollar value of her annual consumption of the composite good and V takes the value 1 if she votes and 0 if she does not. Olivia finances her consumption by working at a job that pays \$30/hr for as many hours as she chooses to work. In order to vote she must spend a total of 20 minutes traveling to and from the polling place, where she must stand in line before casting her ballot. If she regards her transit time and waiting time as neither more nor less unpleasant than working an equivalent amount of time at her job, how long must the line at the polls be before Olivia will decide not to vote? *(LO1)*

6. Suppose your happiness is given by a Kahneman-Tversky value function like the one shown in the diagram. *(LO4)*

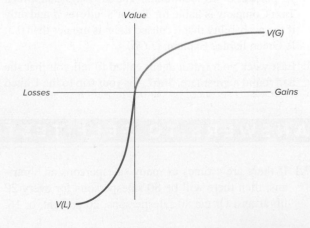

You have decided to put the most favorable spin on the various combinations of events that occur in your life. For each of the following pairs of events, will you be happier if you consider their effects separately or if you first combine them and consider only their net effect?

a. A gain of $500 and a loss of $50.

b. A gain of $50 and a loss of $500.

c. A gain of $500 and a gain of $600.

d. A loss of $500 and a loss of $600.

7. Honda has hired you as a consultant to give it marketing advice about how to sell its new all-terrain vehicle. On the basis of the material covered in this chapter, suggest two specific marketing strategies for Honda to consider. *(LO6, LO7)*

8. Give two examples of how the framing of alternatives tends to produce systematic effects on people's choices. *(LO4)*

9. Studies have shown that in the New York City subway crime rates fall in the years following increased police patrols. Does this pattern suggest that the increased patrols are the *cause* of the crime reductions? *(LO6)*

10. Claiborne is a gourmet. She makes it a point never to visit a restaurant a second time unless she has been served a superb meal on her first visit. She is puzzled at how seldom the quality of her second meal is as high as the first. Should she be? *(LO6)*

11. Dalgliesh the detective fancies himself a shrewd judge of human nature. In careful tests it has been discovered that he is right 80 percent of the time when he says that a randomly chosen suspect is lying. Dalgliesh says that Jones is lying. The polygraph expert, who is right 100 percent of the time, says that 40 percent of the subjects interviewed by Dalgliesh are telling the truth. What is the probability that Jones is lying? *(LO6)*

12. A witness testifies that the taxicab that struck and injured Taylor in a dark alley was green. On investigation, the attorney for Green Taxi Company discovers that the witness identifies the correct color of a taxi in a dark alley 80 percent of the time. There are two taxi companies in town, Green and Blue. Green operates 15 percent of all local taxis. The law says that Green Taxi Company is liable for Taylor's injuries if and only if the probability that it caused them is greater than 0.5. Is Green liable? Explain. *(LO6)*

13. Last week your travel agent called to tell you that she had found a great fare, $667, for your trip to the United Kingdom later this month. This fare was almost $400 below the APEX (advance purchase excursion) fare. You told her to book it immediately and went around the department telling everyone about your great bargain. An hour later she called you back and told you that the reservation agent at British Airways had made a mistake and that the quoted fare did not exist. Your agent said she would hunt around and do the best she could for you. A few days later she found a ticket consolidator that could book you on the same British Airways flight for $708, a figure still well below what you originally had expected to pay. This time you didn't go around the department bragging about your bargain. How might the material in this chapter be used to shed light on your behavior? *(LO4)*

14. In planning your next vacation, you have narrowed your choices down to two packages offered by your travel agent, a week in Hawaii for $1,200 or a week in Cancun for $900. You are indifferent between these choices. You see an online ad for a week in Hawaii, with accommodations identical to those offered by your agent, for $1,300. According to the theory of rational choice, should the information in the online ad influence your vacation plans? Explain. *(LO6)*

15. Eun will drive across town to take advantage of a 40 percent off sale on a $40 blouse but will not do so to take advantage of a 10 percent off sale on a $1,000 computer. Assuming that her alternative is to pay list price for both products at the department store next to her home, is her behavior rational? *(LO7)*

16. Harper is having difficulty choosing between two tennis rackets, *A* and *B*. *B* has substantially more power than *A*, but substantially less control. According to the rational choice model, how will the availability of a third alternative—racket *C*, which has slightly less power than B and also slightly less control—influence Harper's final decision? If Harper behaves like most ordinary decision makers in this situation, how will the addition of racket *C* matter? *(LO6)*

17. In the fall, Wilson puts 50 coconuts from his harvest into a cave just before a family of bears goes in to hibernate. As a result, he is unable to get the coconuts out before the bears emerge the following spring. Coconuts spoil at the same rate no matter where he stores them, and yet he continues this practice each year. Why might he do this? *(LO8)*

ANSWERS TO SELF-TESTS

7.1 If there are 4 times as many salespersons as librarians, then there will be 80 salespersons for every 20 librarians. Of the 80 salespersons, 20 percent, or 16, will be shy. Of the 20 librarians, 90 percent, or 18, will be shy. Thus, the likelihood that a shy person is a librarian is $18/(18 + 16) = 0.53$. *(LO6)*

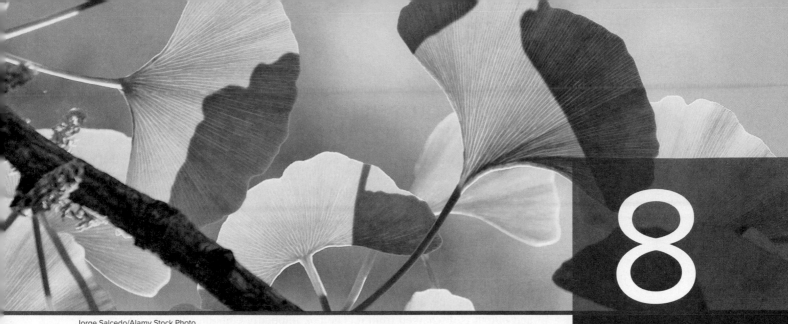

Production

Many people think of production as a highly structured, often mechanical process whereby raw materials are transformed into finished goods. And without doubt, a great deal of production—like a mason's laying bricks for the walls of a house—is of roughly this sort. Economists emphasize, however, that production is also a much more general concept, encompassing many activities not ordinarily thought of as such. We define it as *any activity that creates present or future utility.*

A process can be unconventional and still constitute production. On *Saturday Night Live*, Tina Fey has quipped that "The show doesn't go on because it is ready; it goes on because it's 11:30." But whether her lines are memorized or improvised, Fey is as much a production worker as the artisan whose chisel and lathe mold an ashwood log into a Louisville Slugger bat. The person who delivers a singing telegram is also engaged in production; so is the doctor who gives my child a tetanus shot; the lawyer who draws up my will; the people who collect my garbage on Wednesday mornings; the postal worker who delivers my tax return to the IRS; and even the economists who write about production.

CHAPTER PREVIEW

In our discussions of consumer choice during the preceding chapters, an existing menu of goods and services was taken for granted. But where do these goods and services come from? In this chapter we'll see that their production involves a decision process very similar to the one we examined in earlier chapters. Whereas our focus in earlier chapters was on the economic decisions that underlie the demand side of the market relationship, our focus in the next eight chapters is on the economic decisions that underlie the supply side.

In this chapter we describe the production possibilities available to us for a given state of technology and resource endowments. We want to know how output varies with the application of productive inputs in both the short run and the long run. Answers to these questions will set the stage for our efforts in the next chapter to describe how firms choose among technically feasible alternative methods of producing a given level of output.

235

A Production Worker

entrepreneurship creating, maintaining, and assuming responsibility for a business enterprise.

production function the relationship that describes how inputs like capital and labor are transformed into output.

THE INPUT-OUTPUT RELATIONSHIP, OR PRODUCTION FUNCTION

There are several ways to define production. One definition, mentioned above, is that it is any activity that creates present or future utility. Production may be equivalently described as a process that transforms inputs (factors of production) into outputs. (The two descriptions are equivalent because output is something that creates present or future utility.) Among the inputs into production, economists have traditionally included land, labor, capital, and the more elusive category called **entrepreneurship**.[1] To this list, it has become increasingly common to add such factors as knowledge or technology, organization, and energy.

A **production function** is the relationship by which inputs are combined to produce output. Schematically, it may be represented as the box in Figure 8.1. Inputs are fed into it, and output is discharged from it. The box implicitly embodies the existing state of technology, which has been improving steadily over time. Thus, a given combination of productive inputs will yield a larger number of cars with today's technology than with the technology of 1970.

A production function may also be thought of as a cooking recipe. It lists the ingredients and tells you, say, how many pancakes you will get if you manipulate the ingredients in a certain way.[2]

Yet another way of describing the production function is to cast it in the form of a mathematical equation. Consider a production process that employs two inputs, capital (K) and labor (L), to produce meals (Q). The relationship between K, L, and Q may be expressed as

$$Q = F(K, L), \tag{8.1}$$

where F is a mathematical function that summarizes the process depicted in Figure 8.1. It is no more than a simple rule that tells how much Q we get when we employ specific quantities of K and L. By way of illustration, suppose the production function for meals is given by $F(K, L) = 2KL$, where K is measured in equipment-hours per

FIGURE 8.1

The Production Function

The production function transforms inputs like land, labor, capital, and entrepreneurship into output. The box in the diagram embodies the existing state of technological knowledge. Because knowledge has been accumulating over time, we get more output from a given combination of inputs today than we would have gotten in the past.

Inputs
(land, labor, capital, and so forth)

Production function

Outputs
(cars, polio vaccine, home-cooked meals, FM radio broadcasts, and so forth)

[1]An entrepreneur is thus, by definition, a risk-taker.
[2]In some recipes, the ingredients must be mixed in fixed proportions. Other recipes allow substitution between ingredients, as in a pancake recipe that allows milk and oil to be substituted for eggs. Production functions can be of either of these two types.

TABLE 8.1
The Production Function $Q = 2KL$

		Labor (person-hours/wk)				
		1	**2**	**3**	**4**	**5**
	1	2	4	6	8	10
Capital	**2**	4	8	12	16	20
(equipment-hours/wk)	**3**	6	12	18	24	30
	4	8	16	24	32	40
	5	10	20	30	40	50

The entries in the table represent output, measured in meals per week, and are calculated using the formula $Q = 2KL$

week,[3] L is measured in person-hours per week, and output is measured in meals per week. For example, 2 equipment-hr/wk combined with 3 person-hr/wk would yield $2(2)(3) = 12$ meals/wk with this particular production function. The relationship between K, L, and weekly output of meals for the production function $Q = 2KL$ is summarized in Table 8.1.

Intermediate Products

Capital (as embodied, for example, in the form of stoves and frying pans) and labor (as embodied in the services of a chef) are clearly by themselves insufficient to produce meals. Raw foodstuffs are also necessary. The production process described by Equation 8.1 is one that transforms raw foodstuffs into the finished product we call meals. In this process, foodstuffs are *intermediate products,* which many economists treat as inputs like any others. For the sake of simplicity, we will ignore intermediate products in the examples we discuss in this chapter. But this feature could be built into all these examples without changing any of our essential conclusions.

Fixed and Variable Inputs

The production function tells us how output will vary if some or all of the inputs are varied. In practice, there are many production processes in which the quantities of at least some inputs cannot be altered quickly. The FM radio broadcast of classical music is one such process. To carry it out, complex electronic equipment is needed, and also a music library and a large transmission tower. Records and compact discs can be purchased in a matter of hours. But it may take weeks to acquire the needed equipment to launch a new station, and months or even years to purchase a suitable location and construct a new transmission tower.

The **long run** for a particular production process is defined as the shortest period of time required to alter the amounts of *every* input. The **short run,** by contrast, is defined as that period during which one or more inputs cannot be varied. An input whose quantity can be altered in the short run is called a **variable input.** One whose quantity cannot be altered—except perhaps at prohibitive cost—within a given time period is called a **fixed input.** In the long run, all inputs are variable inputs, by definition. In the classical music broadcast example, compact discs are variable inputs in the short run, but the broadcast tower is a fixed input. If sufficient time elapses, however, even it becomes a variable input. In some production activities, like those of a street-corner hot dog stand, even the long run does not involve an extended period of time. We begin in the next section by

long run the shortest period of time required to alter the amounts of all inputs used in a production process.

short run the longest period of time during which at least one of the inputs used in a production process cannot be varied.

variable input an input that can be varied in the short run.

fixed input an input that cannot vary in the short run.

[3]Here, 1 frying pan-hr/wk is 1 frying pan used for 1 hour during the course of a week. Thus, a frying pan that is in use for 8 hr/day for each day of a 5-day workweek would constitute 40 frying pan-hr/wk of capital input.

considering short-run production and then we move on to long-run production in the following section.

PRODUCTION IN THE SHORT RUN

Consider again the production process described by $Q = F(K, L) = 2KL$, the simple two-input production function described in Table 8.1. And suppose we are concerned with production in the short run—here, a period of time in which the labor input is variable but the capital input is fixed, say, at the value $K = K_0 = 1$. With capital held constant, output becomes, in effect, a function of only the variable input, labor: $F(K, L) = 2K_0L = 2L$. This means we can plot the production function in a two-dimensional diagram, as in Figure 8.2a. For this particular $F(K, L)$, the short-run production function is a straight line through the origin whose slope is 2 times the fixed value of K: Thus, $\Delta Q/\Delta L = 2K_0$. In Figure 8.2b, note that the short-run production rotates upward to $F(K_1, L) = 6L$ when K rises to $K_1 = 3$.

SELF-TEST 8.1

Graph the short-run production function for $F(K, L) = \sqrt{K}\sqrt{L}$ when K is fixed at $K_0 = 4$.

As you saw in Self-Test 8.1, the graphs of short-run production functions will not always be straight lines. The short-run production function shown in Figure 8.3 has several properties that are commonly found in production functions observed in practice. First, it passes through the origin, which is to say that we get no output if we use no variable input. Second, initially the addition of variable inputs augments output at an increasing rate: moving from 1 to 2 units of labor yields 10 extra units of output, while moving from 2 to 3 units of labor gives 13 additional units. Finally, the function shown in Figure 8.3 has the property that beyond some point ($L = 4$ in the diagram), additional units of the variable input give rise to smaller and smaller increments in output. Thus, the move from 5 to 6 units of labor yields 14 extra units of output, while the move from 6 to 7 units of labor yields only 9. For some production functions, the level of output may actually decline with additional units of the variable input beyond some point, as happens here for $L > 8$. With a limited amount of capital to work with, additional workers may eventually begin to get in one another's way.

The property that output initially grows at an increasing rate may stem from the benefits of division of tasks and specialization of labor. With one employee, all tasks must be done by the same person, while with two or more employees, tasks may be divided and employees may better perform their dedicated tasks. (Similar logic applies to specializing in one task within any period of time.)

FIGURE 8.2

A Specific Short-Run Production Function

Panel *a* shows the production function, $Q = 2KL$, with K fixed at $K_0 = 1$. Panel *b* shows how the short-run production function shifts when K is increased to $K_1 = 3$.

(a)

(b)

FIGURE 8.3

Another Short-Run Production Function

The curvilinear shape shown here is common to many short-run production functions. Output initially grows at an increasing rate as labor increases. Beyond $L = 4$, output grows at a diminishing rate with increases in labor.

The final property noted about the short-run production function in Figure 8.3—that beyond some point, output grows at a diminishing rate with increases in the variable input—is known as the **law of diminishing returns.** And although it too is not a universal property of short-run production functions, it is extremely common. The law of diminishing returns is a short-run phenomenon. Formally, it may be stated as follows:

> As equal amounts of a variable input are sequentially added while all other inputs are held fixed, the resulting increments to output will eventually diminish.

Employing the logic of Economic Naturalist 8.1, the British economist Thomas Malthus argued in 1798 that the law of diminishing returns implied eventual misery

law of diminishing returns if other inputs are fixed, the increase in output from an increase in the variable input must eventually decline.

Economic Naturalist 8.1

Why can't all the world's people be fed from the amount of grain grown in a single flowerpot?

The law of diminishing returns suggests that no matter how much labor, fertilizer, water, seed, capital equipment, and other inputs were used, only a limited amount of grain could be grown in a single flowerpot. With the land input fixed at such a low level, increases in other inputs would quickly cease to have any effect on total output.

Thomas Malthus failed to anticipate the capacity of productivity growth to keep pace with population growth. But his basic insight—that a planet with fixed resources can support only so many people—remains valid.

for the human race. The difficulty is that agricultural land is fixed and, beyond some point, the application of additional labor will yield ever smaller increases in food production. The inevitable result, as Malthus saw it, is that population growth will drive average food consumption down to the starvation level.

Whether Malthus's prediction will be borne out in the future remains to be seen. But he would never have imagined that food production per capita would grow more than twenty-fold during the ensuing two centuries. Note carefully, however, that the experience of the last 200 years does not contradict the law of diminishing returns. What Malthus did not foresee was the explosive growth in agricultural technology that has far outstripped the effect of a fixed supply of land. Still, the ruthless logic of Malthus's observation remains. No matter how advanced our technology, if population continues to grow, it is just a matter of time before limits on arable land spell persistent food shortages.

The world's population has grown rapidly during the years since Malthus wrote, more than doubling during the last 50 years alone. Are we in fact doomed to eventual starvation? Perhaps not. As the late economist Herbert Stein once famously remarked, "If something can't go on forever, it will stop." And indeed, population specialists now predict that the earth's population will peak late in this century and then begin to decline.[4] If we don't blow (or burn) ourselves up in the meantime, there is thus a good chance that we will escape the dire fate that Malthus predicted.

Technological improvements in production are represented graphically by an upward shift in the production function. In Figure 8.4, for example, the curves labeled F_1 and F_2 are used to denote the agricultural production functions in 1808 and 2008, respectively. The law of diminishing returns applies to each of these curves, and yet the growth in food production has kept pace with the increase in labor input during the period shown.

FIGURE 8.4

The Effect of Technological Progress in Food Production

F_1 represents the production function for food in the year 1808. F_2 represents the corresponding function for 2008. The effect of technological progress in food production is to cause F_2 to lie above F_1. Even though the law of diminishing returns applies to both F_1 and F_2, the growth in food production between 1808 and 2008 has more than kept pace with the growth in labor inputs over the same period.

[4]See Wolfgang Lutz, Warren Sanderson and Sergei Sherbov, "The Uncertain Timing of Reaching 8 Billion, Peak World Population, and Other Demographic Milestones," *Population & Development Review*, 37 (3), September 2011, 571–578.

TOTAL, MARGINAL, AND AVERAGE PRODUCTS

Short-run production functions like the ones shown in Figures 8.3 and 8.4 are often referred to as **total product curves.** They relate the total amount of output to the quantity of the variable input. Also of interest in many applications is the *marginal product* of a variable input. It is defined as *the change in the total product that occurs in response to a unit change in the variable input (all other inputs held fixed).* A business manager trying to decide whether to hire or fire another worker has an obvious interest in knowing what the **marginal product** of labor is.

More formally, if ΔL denotes a small change in the variable input, and ΔQ denotes the resulting change in output, then the marginal product of L, denoted MP_L, is defined as

$$MP_L = \frac{\Delta Q}{\Delta L}. \tag{8.2}$$

Geometrically, the marginal product at any point is simply the slope of the total product curve at that point, as shown in the top panel of Figure 8.5.[5] For example, the marginal product of labor when $L = 2$ is $MP_{L=2} = 12$. Likewise, $MP_{L=4} = 16$ and $MP_{L=7} = 6$ for the total product curve shown in Figure 8.5. Note, finally, that MP_L is negative for values of L greater than 8.

The marginal product curve itself is plotted in the bottom panel in Figure 8.5. Note that it rises at first, reaches a maximum at $L = 4$, and then declines, finally becoming negative for values of L greater than 8. Note also that the maximum point on the marginal product curve corresponds to the inflection point on the total product curve, the point where its curvature switches from convex (increasing at an increasing rate) to concave (increasing at a decreasing rate). Note also that the marginal product curve reaches zero at the value of L at which the total product curve reaches a maximum.

total product curve a curve showing the amount of output as a function of the amount of variable input.

marginal product change in total product due to a 1-unit change in the variable input.

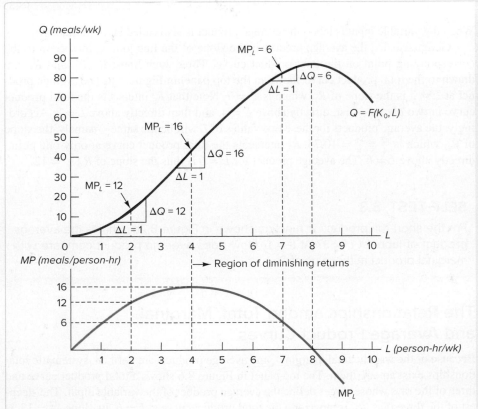

FIGURE 8.5

The Marginal Product of a Variable Input

At any point, the marginal product of labor, MP_L, is the slope of the total product curve at that point (top panel). For the production function shown in the top panel, the marginal product curve (bottom panel) initially increases as labor increases. Beyond $L = 4$, however, the marginal product of labor decreases as labor increases. For $L > 8$ the total product curve declines with L, which means that the marginal product of labor is negative in that region.

[5]The formal definition of the marginal product of a variable input is given by $MP(L) = \partial F(K, L)/\partial L$.

As we will see in greater detail in later chapters, the importance of the marginal product concept lies in the fact that decisions about running an enterprise most naturally arise in the form of decisions about *changes*. Should we hire another engineer or accountant? Should we reduce the size of the maintenance staff? Should we install another copier? Should we lease another delivery truck?

To answer such questions intelligently, we must compare the benefit of the change in question with its cost. And as we will see, the marginal product concept plays a pivotal role in the calculation of the benefits when we alter the level of a productive input. Looking at Figure 8.5, we may identify a range of values of the variable input that a rational manager would never employ. In particular, as long as labor commands a positive wage, such a manager would never want to employ the variable input in the region where its marginal product is negative ($L > 8$ in Figure 8.5). Equivalently, he would never employ a variable input past the point where the total product curve reaches its maximum value (where $MP_L = 0$).

SELF-TEST 8.2

What is the marginal product of labor when $L = 3$ in the short-run production function shown in Figure 8.2a? When $L = 1$? Does this short-run production function exhibit diminishing returns to labor?

---

average product total output divided by the quantity of the variable input.

The **average product** of a variable input is defined as the total product divided by the quantity of that input. Denoted AP_L, it is thus given by

$$AP_L = \frac{Q}{L}. \tag{8.3}$$

When the variable input is labor, the average product is also called labor productivity.

Geometrically, the average product is the slope of the line joining the origin to the corresponding point on the total product curve. Three such lines, R_1, R_2, and R_3, are drawn to the total product curve shown in the top panel in Figure 8.6. The average product at $L = 2$ is the slope of R_1, which is $\frac{14}{2} = 7$. Note that R_2 intersects the total product curve in two places—first, directly above $L = 4$, and then directly above $L = 8$. Accordingly, the average products for these two values of L will be the same—namely, the slope of R_2, which is $\frac{43}{4} = \frac{86}{8} = 10.75$. R_3 intersects the total product curve at only one point, directly above $L = 6$. The average product for $L = 6$ is thus the slope of R_3, $\frac{72}{6} = 12$.

SELF-TEST 8.3

For the short-run production function shown in Figure 8.2a, what is the average product of labor at $L = 3$? At $L = 1$? How does average product compare with marginal product at these points?

The Relationships among Total, Marginal, and Average Product Curves

Because of the way the total, marginal, and average products are defined, systematic relationships exist among them. The top panel in Figure 8.6 shows a total product curve and three of the rays whose slopes define the average product of the variable input. The steepest of the three rays, R_3, is tangent to the total product curve at $L = 6$. Its slope, $\frac{72}{6} = 12$, is the average product of labor at $L = 6$. The marginal product of labor at $L = 6$ is defined as the slope of the total product curve at $L = 6$, which happens to be exactly the slope of R_3, since R_3 is tangent to the total product curve. Thus $AP_{L=6} = MP_{L=6}$, as shown in the bottom panel by the fact that the AP_L curve intersects the MP_L curve for $L = 6$.

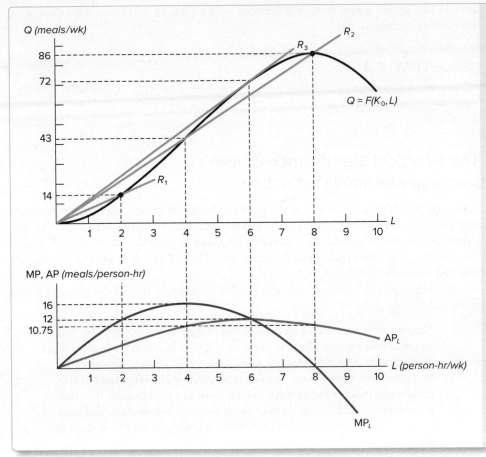

FIGURE 8.6

Total, Marginal, and Average Product Curves

The average product at any point on the total product curve is the slope of the ray to that point. For the total product curve shown in the top panel, AP_L rises with $L = 6$, then declines. At $L = 6$, $MP_L = AP_L$. For any $L < 6$, $MP_L > AP_L$, and for any $L > 6$, $MP_L < AP_L$.

For values of L less than 6, note in the top panel in Figure 8.6 that the slope of the total product curve is larger than the slope of the ray to the corresponding point. Thus, for $L < 6$, $MP_L > AP_L$, as reflected in the bottom panel. Note also in the top panel that for values of L greater than 6, the slope of the total product curve is smaller than the slope of the ray to the corresponding point. This means that for $L > 6$, we have $AP_L > MP_L$, as shown in the bottom panel in Figure 8.6.

Note finally in Figure 8.6 that for extremely small values of L, the slope of the ray to the total product curve becomes indistinguishable from the slope of the total product curve itself. This tells us that for $L = 0$, average and marginal products are the same, which is reflected in the bottom panel in Figure 8.6 by the fact that both curves emanate from the same point.[6]

The relationship between the marginal and average product curves may be summarized as follows: *When the marginal product curve lies above the average product curve, the average product curve must be rising; and when the marginal product curve lies below the average product curve, the average product curve must be falling. The two curves intersect at the maximum value of the average product curve.* A moment's reflection on the definitions of the two curves makes the intuitive basis for this relationship clear. If the contribution to output of an additional unit of the variable input exceeds the average contribution of the variable inputs used thus far, the average contribution must rise. This effect is analogous to what happens when a student with a 3.8 grade point average joins a fraternity whose other members have an average GPA of 2.2: The new member's presence causes the group's GPA to rise. Conversely, adding a variable input whose marginal product is less than the average product of existing

Whenever the last unit of an activity exceeds the average level of the activity, the average must be rising. Conversely, when the last unit is smaller than the average, the average must be falling.

---

[6]For the production function shown, that point happens to be the origin, but in general it need not be.

units is like adding a new fraternity member with a GPA of 1.7. Here, the effect is for the existing average to fall.[7]

> **SELF-TEST 8.4**
>
> Consider a short-run production process for which $AP_{L=10} = 7$ and $MP_{L=10} = 12$. Will $AP_{L=10.1}$ be larger or smaller than $AP_{L=10}$ for this process?

The Practical Significance of the Average-Marginal Distinction

The distinction between average and marginal products is of central importance to anyone who must allocate a scarce resource between two or more productive activities. The specific question is, How should the resource be allocated in order to maximize total output? The following examples make clear the issues posed by this problem and the general rule required to solve it.

Read through the following scenario carefully and try to answer the question posed at the end:

> Suppose you own a fishing fleet consisting of a given number of boats, and can send your boats in whatever numbers you wish to either of two ends of an extremely wide lake, east or west. Under your current allocation of boats, the ones fishing at the east end return daily with 100 pounds of fish each, while those in the west return daily with 120 pounds each. The fish populations at each end of the lake are completely independent, and your current yields can be sustained indefinitely. Should you alter your current allocation of boats?

Most people, especially those who have not had a good course in microeconomics, answer confidently that the current allocation should be altered. Specifically, they say that the fishing fleet owner should send more boats to the west side of the lake. Yet, as the following example illustrates, even a rudimentary understanding of the distinction between the average and marginal products of a productive resource makes clear that this response is not justified.

EXAMPLE 8.1   Interior Solution

In the fishing fleet scenario just described, suppose the relationship between the number of boats sent to each end and the number of pounds caught per boat is as summarized in Table 8.2. Suppose further that you have four boats in your fleet, and that two currently fish the east end while the other two fish the west end. (Note that all of these suppositions are completely consistent with the facts outlined in the scenario.) Should you move one of your boats from the east end to the west end?

From the entries in Table 8.2, it follows that your total output under the current allocation is 440 pounds of fish per day (100 pounds from each of the two boats

---

[7]Mathematically, the result that MP intersects AP at the maximum value of AP can be shown by noting that the necessary condition for a maximum of AP is that its first partial derivative with respect to L be zero:

$$\partial(Q/L)/\partial L = [L(\partial Q/\partial L) - Q]/L^2 = 0,$$

from which it follows that $\partial Q/\partial L = Q/L$.

TABLE 8.2
Average Product, Total Product, and Marginal Product (lb/day) for Two Fishing Areas

Number of boats	East end			West end		
	AP	TP	MP	AP	TP	MP
0	0	0		0	0	
			100			130
1	100	100		130	130	
			100			110
2	100	200		120	240	
			100			90
3	100	300		110	330	
			100			70
4	100	400		100	400	

The average catch per boat is constant at 100 pounds per boat for boats sent to the east end of the lake. The average catch per boat is a declining function of the number of boats sent to the west end.

at the east end, 120 from each of the two at the west end). Now suppose you transfer one boat from the east end to the west end, which means you now have three boats in the west and only one in the east. From the figures in Table 8.2, we see that your total output will now be only 430 pounds per day, or 10 pounds per day less than under the current allocation. So, no, you should not move an extra boat to the west end. Neither, for that matter, should you send one of the west end boats to the east end. Loss of a boat from the west end would reduce the total daily catch at that end by 110 pounds (the difference between the 240 pounds caught by two boats and the 130 that would be caught by one), which is more than the extra 100 pounds you would get by having an extra boat at the east end. The current allocation of two boats to each end is optimal.

Example 8.1 is an instance of an important class of problems in which managers must decide how to allocate an input across several alternative processes used for producing a given product. *The general rule for allocating an input efficiently in such cases is to allocate the next unit of the input to the production activity where its marginal product is highest.* This form of the rule applies to resources, such as boats, that are not perfectly divisible, and also to cases in which the marginal product of a resource is always higher in one activity than in another.[8] For a resource that is perfectly divisible, and for activities for which the marginal product of the resource is not always higher in one than in the others, the rule is to *allocate the resource so that its marginal product is the same in every activity.*

Many people, however, "solve" these kinds of problems by allocating resources to the activity with the highest *average* product, or by trying to equalize *average* products across activities. The reason that this particular wrong answer often has appeal is that people often focus on only part of the relevant production process. By sending only two boats to the west end, the average catch at that end is 20 pounds per day greater than the average catch per boat at the east end. But note that if you send a third boat to the west end, that boat's contribution to the total amount of fish caught at the west end will be only 90 pounds per day (the difference between the 330 pounds caught by three boats and 240 pounds caught by two). What people often tend to overlook is that the third boat at the west end catches some of the fish that would otherwise have been caught by the first two.

As the figures in Table 8.2 illustrate, the opportunity cost of sending a third boat to the west end is the 100 pounds of fish that will no longer be caught at the east end. But since that

[8]See Example 8.2.

third boat will add only 90 pounds to the daily catch at the west end, the best that can be done is to keep sending two boats to each end of the lake. The fact that either of the two boats currently fishing at the east end could catch 10 pounds per day more by moving to the west end is no cause for concern to a fishing fleet owner who understands the distinction between average and marginal products.

SELF-TEST 8.5

Explain why we cannot necessarily conclude that you should throw more fastballs in the following scenario: You are a baseball pitcher who throws two different kinds of pitches: fastball and curve. Your team statistician tells you that at the current rate at which you employ these pitches, batters hit .275 against your curve, but only .200 against your fastball. Should you alter your current mix of pitches?

Example 8.1 produced what economists call an *interior solution*—one in which each of the production activities is actually employed. But not all problems of this sort have interior solutions. As the next example will make clear, one activity sometimes dominates the other.

EXAMPLE 8.2   Production Decision

Same as the fishing fleet Example 8.1, except now the marginal product of each boat sent to the west end of the lake is equal to 120 lb/day.

The difference between this example and Example 8.1 is that this time there is no drop-off in the rate at which fish are caught as more boats are sent to the west end of the lake. So this time the average product of any boat sent to the west end is identical to its marginal product. And since the marginal product is always higher for boats sent to the west end, the optimal allocation is to send all four boats to that end.

Cases such as the one illustrated in Example 8.2 are by no means unusual. But by far the more common, and more interesting, production decisions are the ones that involve interior solutions such as the one we saw in Example 8.1, where some positive quantity of the productive input must be allocated to each activity.

EXAMPLE 8.3   Efficient Allocation

Suppose that from the last seconds you devoted to Problem 1 on your first economics exam you earned 4 extra points, while from the last seconds devoted to Problem 2 you earned 6 extra points. The total number of points you earned on these two questions were 20 and 12, respectively, and the total time you spent on each was the same. The total number of points possible on each problem was 40. How—if at all—should you have reallocated your time between problems?

The rule for efficient allocation of time spent on exams is the same as the rule for efficient allocation of any resource: the marginal product of the resource should be the same in each activity. From the information given, the marginal product of your time spent on Problem 2 was higher than the marginal product of your time spent on Problem 1. Even though the average product of your time spent on Problem 1 was higher than on Problem 2, you would have scored more points if you had spent a few seconds less on Problem 1 and a few seconds more on Problem 2.

PRODUCTION IN THE LONG RUN

The examples discussed thus far have involved production in the short run, where at least one productive input cannot be varied. In the long run, by contrast, all factors of production are by definition variable. In the short run, with K held fixed in the production function $Q = F(K, L)$, we were able to describe the production function in a simple two-dimensional diagram. With both K and L variable, however, we now require three dimensions instead of two. And when there are more than two variable inputs, we require even more dimensions.

This creates a problem similar to the one we encountered in Chapter 3 when the consumer was faced with a choice between multiple products: We are not very adept at graphical representations involving three or more dimensions. For production with two variable inputs, the solution to this problem is similar to the one adopted in Chapter 3.

To illustrate, consider again the production function discussed earlier in this chapter:

$$Q = F(K, L) = 2KL, \tag{8.4}$$

and suppose we want to describe all possible combinations of K and L that give rise to a particular level of output—say, $Q = 16$. To do this, we solve $Q = 2KL = 16$ for K in terms of L, which yields

$$K = \frac{8}{L}. \tag{8.5}$$

The (L, K) pairs that satisfy Equation 8.5 are shown by the curve labeled $Q = 16$ in Figure 8.7. The (L, K) pairs that yield 32 and 64 units of output are shown in Figure 8.7 as the curves labeled $Q = 32$ and $Q = 64$, respectively. Such curves are called **isoquants,** and are defined formally as *all combinations of variable inputs that yield a given level of output.*[9]

Note the clear analogy between the isoquant and the indifference curve of consumer theory. Just as an indifference map provides a concise representation of a consumer's preferences, an *isoquant map* provides a concise representation of a production process.

isoquant the set of all input combinations that yield a given level of output.

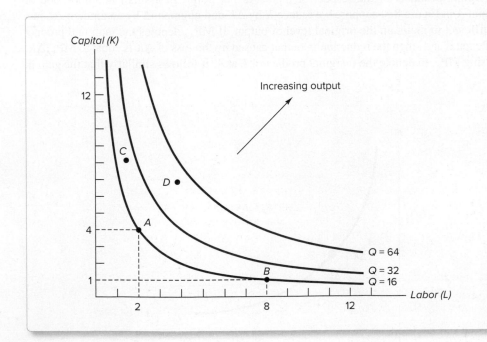

Capital (K)

Increasing output

Labor (L)

FIGURE 8.7

Part of an Isoquant Map for the Production Function $Q = 2KL$

An isoquant is the set of all (L, K) pairs that yield a given level of output. For example, each (L, K) pair on the curve labeled $Q = 32$ yields 32 units of output. The isoquant map describes the properties of a production process in much the same way as an indifference map describes a consumer's preferences.

[9]"Iso" comes from the Greek word for "same," which also appears, for example, in the meteorological term "isobars," meaning lines of equal barometric pressure.

On an indifference map, movements to the northeast correspond to increasing levels of satisfaction. Similar movements on an isoquant map correspond to increasing levels of output. A point on an indifference curve is preferred to any point that lies below that indifference curve, and less preferred than any point that lies above it. Likewise, any input bundle on an isoquant yields more output than any input bundle that lies below that isoquant, and less output than any input bundle that lies above it. Thus, bundle C in Figure 8.7 yields more output than bundle A, but less output than bundle D.

The only substantive respect in which the analogy between isoquant maps and indifference maps is incomplete is the significance of the labels attached to the two types of curves. From Chapter 3 recall that the actual numbers assigned to each indifference curve were used to indicate only the relative rankings of the bundles on different indifference curves. The number we assign to an isoquant, by contrast, corresponds to the actual level of output we get from an input bundle along that isoquant. With indifference maps, we are free to relabel the indifference curves in any way that preserves the original ranking of bundles. But with isoquant maps, the labels are determined uniquely by the production function.

The Marginal Rate of Technical Substitution

marginal rate of technical substitution (MRTS) the rate at which one input can be exchanged for another without altering the total level of output.

Recall from our discussion of consumer theory in Chapter 3 that the marginal rate of substitution is the rate at which the consumer is willing to exchange one good for another along an indifference curve. The analogous concept in production theory is called the **marginal rate of technical substitution,** or **MRTS.** It is the rate at which one input can be exchanged for another without altering output. In Figure 8.8, for example, the MRTS at A is defined as the absolute value of the slope of the isoquant at A, $|\Delta K/\Delta L|$.

In consumer theory, we assumed that the marginal rate of substitution diminishes with downward movements along an indifference curve. For most production functions, the MRTS displays a similar property. Holding output constant, the less we have of one input, the more we must add of the other input to compensate for a one-unit reduction in the first input.

A simple but important relationship exists between the MRTS at any point and the marginal products of the respective inputs at that point. In a small neighborhood of point A in Figure 8.8, suppose we reduce K by ΔK and augment L by an amount ΔL just sufficient to maintain the original level of output. If MP_{KA} denotes the marginal product of capital at A, then the reduction in output caused by the loss of ΔK is equal to $MP_{KA}\Delta K$. Using MP_{LA} to denote the marginal product of L at A, it follows similarly that the gain in

FIGURE 8.8

The Marginal Rate of Technical Substitution

The MRTS is the rate at which one input can be exchanged for another without altering total output. The MRTS at any point is the absolute value of the slope of the isoquant that passes through that point. If ΔK units of capital are removed at point A, and ΔL units of L are added, output will remain the same at Q_0 units.

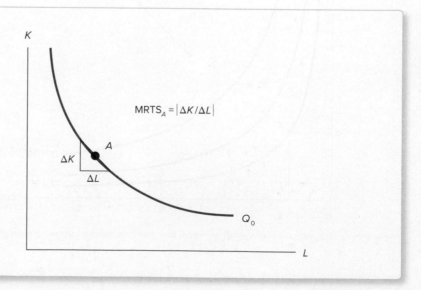

output resulting from the extra ΔL is equal to $MP_{LA}\Delta L$. Finally, since the reduction in output from having less K is exactly offset by the gain in output from having more L, it follows that

$$MP_{KA}\Delta K = MP_{LA}\Delta L. \qquad (8.6)$$

Cross-multiplying, we get

$$\frac{MP_{LA}}{MP_{KA}} = \frac{\Delta K}{\Delta L}, \qquad (8.7)$$

which says that the MRTS at A is simply the ratio of the marginal product of L to the marginal product of K. This relationship will have an important application in the next chapter, where we will take up the question of how to produce a given level of output at the lowest possible cost.

SELF-TEST 8.6

Given a firm's current level of capital and labor inputs, the marginal product of labor for its production process is equal to 3 units of output. If the marginal rate of technical substitution between K and L is 9, what is the marginal product of capital?

In consumer theory, the shape of the indifference curve tells us how the consumer is willing to substitute one good for another. In production theory, an essentially similar story is told by the shape of the isoquant. Figure 8.9 illustrates the extreme cases of inputs that are perfect substitutes (a) and perfect complements (b). Figure 8.9a describes a production process in which cars and gasoline are combined to produce trips. The input of gasoline comes in two brands, Mobil and Shell, which are perfect substitutes for one another. We can substitute 1 gallon of Shell for 1 gallon of Mobil and still produce the same number of trips as before. The MRTS between Mobil and Shell remains constant at 1 as we move downward along any isoquant.

Figure 8.9b describes a production process for typing letters using the two inputs of coders and computers. In this process, the two inputs are perfect complements. Here, inputs are most effectively combined in fixed proportions. Having more than one computer per coder doesn't augment production, nor does having more than one coder per computer.

FIGURE 8.9

Isoquant Maps for Perfect Substitutes and Perfect Complements

In panel a, we get the same number of trips from a given total quantity of gasoline, no matter how we mix the two brands. Mobil and Shell are perfect substitutes in the production of automobile trips. In panel b, computers and coders are perfect complements in the process of typing letters.

RETURNS TO SCALE

A question of central importance for the organization of industry is whether production takes place most efficiently at large scale rather than small scale (where "large" and "small" are defined relative to the scale of the relevant market). This question is important because the answer dictates whether an industry will end up being served by many small firms or only a few large ones.

The technical property of the production function used to describe the relationship between scale and efficiency is called *returns to scale*. The term tells us what happens to output when all inputs are increased by exactly the same proportion. Because returns to scale refer to a situation in which all inputs are variable, *the concept of returns to scale is an inherently long-run concept.*

A production function for which any given proportional change in all inputs leads to a more than proportional change in output is said to exhibit **increasing returns to scale.** For example, if we double all inputs in a production function with increasing returns to scale, we get more than twice as much output as before. As we will see in Chapters 11 and 12, such production functions generally give rise to conditions in which a small number of firms supply most of the relevant market.

Increasing returns to scale often result from the greater possibilities for specialization in large organizations. Adam Smith illustrated this point by describing the division of labor in a pin factory.[10]

> One man draws out the wire, another straightens it, a third cuts it, a fourth points it, a fifth grinds it at the top for receiving the head; to make the head requires two or three distinct operations. . . . I have seen a small manufactory . . . of this kind where only ten men were employed . . . [who] could, when they exerted themselves, make among them about twelve pounds of pins in a day. There are in a pound upwards of four thousand pins of middling size. Those ten persons, therefore, could make among them upwards of forty-eight thousand pins in a day. Each person, therefore, making a tenth part of forty-eight thousand pins might be considered as making four thousand eight hundred pins in a day. But if they had all wrought separately and independently . . . they could not each of them have made twenty, perhaps not one pin in a day. . . .

The airline industry is often cited as one with increasing returns to scale. Industry professionals have long stressed that having a large number of flights helps an airline fill each flight by feeding passengers from its incoming flights to its outgoing flights. Local airport activities also exhibit increasing returns to scale. Because of the law of large numbers,[11] moreover, it follows that maintenance operations, flight crew scheduling, and other inventory-related activities are all accomplished more efficiently on a large scale than on a small scale. Similarly, ticket-counter space, ticket agents, reservations equipment, baggage-handling equipment, ground crews, and passenger-boarding facilities are all resources that are utilized more efficiently at high activity levels. Increasing returns to scale constitute the underlying explanation for why the industry has been moving toward ever larger airlines in the last decade.

A production function for which a proportional change in all inputs causes output to change by the same proportion is said to exhibit **constant returns to scale.** In such cases, doubling all inputs results in a doubling of output. In industries in which production takes place under constant returns to scale, large size is neither an advantage nor a disadvantage.

Finally, a production function for which a proportional change in all inputs causes a less than proportional change in output is said to exhibit **decreasing returns to scale.** Here large size is a handicap, and we do not expect to see large firms in an industry in which production takes place with decreasing returns to scale. As we will see in

increasing returns to scale the property of a production process whereby a proportional increase in every input yields a more than proportional increase in output.

constant returns to scale the property of a production process whereby a proportional increase in every input yields an equal proportional increase in output.

decreasing returns to scale the property of a production process whereby a proportional increase in every input yields a less than proportional increase in output.

---

[10]Adam Smith, *The Wealth of Nations,* New York: Everyman's Library, 1910 (1776), Book 1, p. 5.
[11]See Chapter 6.

Chapter 10, the constant and decreasing returns cases often enable many sellers to coexist within the same narrowly defined markets.

A production function need not exhibit the same degree of returns to scale over the entire range of output. On the contrary, there may be increasing returns to scale at low levels of output, followed by constant returns to scale at intermediate levels of output, followed finally by decreasing returns to scale at high levels of output.

Economic Naturalist 8.2

Why do builders use prefabricated frames for roofs but not for walls?

When construction crews build a wood-frame house, they usually construct framing for the walls at the construction site. By contrast, they often buy prefabricated framing for the roof. Why this difference?

There are two key differences between wall framing and roof framing: (1) cutting the lumber for roof framing involves many complicated angle cuts, whereas the right-angle cuts required for wall framing are much simpler; and (2) sections of roof framing of a given size are all alike, whereas wall sections differ according to the placement of window and door openings. Both properties of roof framing lead to substantial economies of scale in production. First, the angle cuts they require

Why do builders build custom frames for walls but use prefabricated frames for roofs?

can be made much more rapidly if a frame or "jig" can be built that guides the lumber past the saw-blade at just the proper angle. It is economical to set up such jigs in a factory where thousands of cuts are made each day, but it usually does not pay to use this method for the limited number of cuts required at any one construction site. Likewise, automated methods are easy to employ for roof framing by virtue of its uniformity. The idiosyncratic nature of wall framing, by contrast, militates against the use of automated methods.

So the fact that there are much greater economies of scale in the construction of roof framing than wall framing helps account for why wall framing is usually built at the construction site while roof framing is more often prefabricated.

This is not to say that economies of scale in wall framing cannot be achieved. If we move from the example of custom individual houses to that of an suburban condo development where perhaps 20 buildings, each with identical interior layouts, are being erected at the same time, we have entered the situation where you may very well see a crane lifting prefabricated wall units into place and workers simply nailing these units to the floor.

Showing Returns to Scale on the Isoquant Map

A simple relationship exists between a production function's returns to scale and the spacing of its isoquants.[12] Consider the isoquant map in Figure 8.10. As we move outward into the isoquant map along the ray labeled *R,* each input grows by exactly the same proportion. The particular production function whose isoquant map is shown in the diagram exhibits increasing returns to scale in the region from *A* to *C*. Note, for example, that when we move from *A* to *B*, both inputs double while output goes up by a factor of 3; likewise, when we move from *B* to *C*, both inputs grow by 50 percent while output grows by 100 percent. In the region from *C* to *F,* this same production function exhibits constant

[12]The discussion in this section applies to *homothetic* production functions, an important class of production functions defined by the property that the slopes of all isoquants are constant at points along any ray.

FIGURE 8.10

Returns to Scale Shown on the Isoquant Map

In the region from *A* to *C*, this production function has increasing returns to scale. Proportional increases in input yield more than proportional increases in output. In the region from *C* to *F*, there are constant returns to scale. Inputs and output grow by the same proportion in this region. In the region northeast of *F*, there are decreasing returns to scale. Proportional increases in both inputs yield less than proportional increases in output.

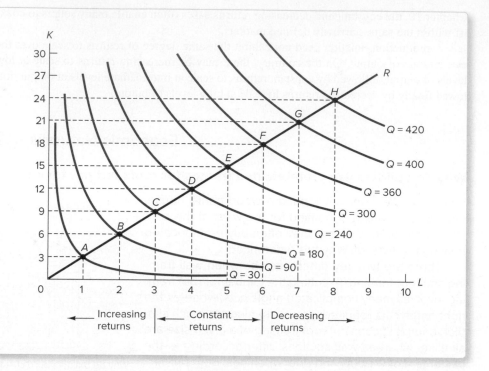

returns to scale. Note, for example, that when we move from *D* to *E*, both inputs grow by 25 percent and output also grows by 25 percent. Finally, the production function whose isoquant map is shown in Figure 8.10 exhibits decreasing returns to scale in the region to the northeast of *F*. Thus, when we move from *F* to *G*, both inputs increase by 16.7 percent while output grows by only 11.1 percent.

The Distinction between Diminishing Returns and Decreasing Returns to Scale

It is important to bear in mind that decreasing returns to scale have nothing whatsoever to do with the law of diminishing returns. Decreasing returns to scale refer to what happens when all inputs are varied by a given proportion. The law of diminishing returns, by contrast, refers to the case in which one input varies while all others are held fixed. As an empirical generalization, it applies with equal force to production functions having increasing, constant, or decreasing returns to scale.

The Logical Puzzle of Decreasing Returns to Scale

If the production function $Q = F(K, L)$ is a complete description of the corresponding production process, it is difficult to see how any production function could ever exhibit decreasing returns to scale in practice. The difficulty is that we ought to be able to duplicate the process used to produce any given level of output, and thereby achieve constant returns to scale. To illustrate, suppose first that $Q_0 = F(K_0, L_0)$. If we now want to produce $2Q_0$ units of output, we can always do so by again doing what we did the first time—namely, by again combining K_0 and L_0 to get Q_0 and adding that to the Q_0 we already have. Similarly, we can get $3Q_0$ by carrying out $F(K_0, L_0)$ three times in succession. Simply by carrying out the process again and again, we can get output to grow in the same proportion as inputs, which means constant returns to scale. And for reasons similar to the ones discussed above for the airline industry, it will often be possible to do even better than that.

In cases in which it is not possible to at least double our output by doubling both *K* and *L*, we seem forced to conclude that there must be some important input besides *K* and *L* that we are failing to increase at the same time. This input is variously referred to as "organization" or "communication," the idea being that when a firm gets past a certain size, it somehow starts to get out of control. Others claim that it is the shortage of managerial or entrepreneurial resources that creates bottlenecks in production. If there is indeed some unmeasured input that is being held fixed as we expand K and L, then we are still in the short run by definition. And there is no reason to expect to be able to double our output by doubling only *some* of our inputs.

The appendix to this chapter considers several mathematical extensions of production theory. Topics covered include applications of the average-marginal distinction, specific mathematical forms of the production function, and a mathematical treatment of returns to scale in production.

SUMMARY

- Production is any activity that creates current or future utility. A production function summarizes the relationship between inputs and outputs. The short run is defined as that period during which at least some inputs are fixed. In the two-input case, it is the period during which one input is fixed, the other variable. *(LO1)*

- The marginal product of a variable input is defined as the change in output brought forth by an additional unit of the variable input, all other inputs held fixed. The law of diminishing returns says that beyond some point the marginal product declines with additional units of the variable input. *(LO2, LO4)*

- The average product of a variable input is the ratio of total output to the quantity of the variable input. Whenever marginal product lies above average product, the average product will increase with increases in the variable input. Conversely, when marginal product lies below average product, average product will decline with increases in the variable input. *(LO4)*

- An important practical problem is that of how to allocate an input across two productive activities to generate the maximum possible output. In general, two types of solutions are possible. A corner solution occurs when the marginal product of the input is always higher in one activity than in the other. In that case, the best thing to do is to concentrate all the input in the activity where it is more productive. *(LO4)*

- An interior solution occurs whenever the marginal product of the variable input, when all of it is placed in one activity, is lower than the marginal product of the first unit of the input in the other activity. In this case, the output-maximizing rule is to distribute the input across the two activities in such a way that its marginal product is the same in both. Even experienced decision makers often violate this simple rule. The pitfall to be on guard against is the tendency to equate not marginal but average products in the two activities. *(LO4)*

- The long run is defined as the period required for all inputs to be variable. The actual length of time that corresponds to the short and long runs will differ markedly in different cases. In the two-input case, all of the relevant information about production in the long run can be summarized graphically by the isoquant map. The marginal rate of technical substitution is defined as the rate at which one input can be substituted for another without altering the level of output. The MRTS at any point is simply the absolute value of the slope of the isoquant at that point. For most production functions, the MRTS will diminish as we move downward to the right along an isoquant. *(LO5, LO6)*

- A production function is said to exhibit constant returns to scale if a given proportional increase in all inputs produces the same proportional increase in output, decreasing returns to scale if a given proportional increase in all inputs results in a smaller proportional increase in output, and increasing returns to scale if a given proportional increase in all inputs causes a greater proportional increase in output. Production functions with increasing returns to scale are also said to exhibit economies of scale. Returns to scale constitute a critically important factor in determining the structure of industrial organization. *(LO7)*

KEY TERMS

average product	isoquant	production function
constant returns to scale	law of diminishing returns	short run
decreasing returns to scale	long run	total product curve
entrepreneurship	marginal product	variable input
fixed input	marginal rate of technical	
increasing returns to scale	substitution (MRTS)	

REVIEW QUESTIONS

1. List three examples of production that a noneconomist might not ordinarily think of as production. *(LO1)*

2. Give an example of production in which the short run lasts at least 1 year. *(LO5)*

3. Why should a person in charge of hiring productive inputs care more about marginal products than about average products? *(LO4)*

4. A news article stated that when a certain government official moved from New York to California, the average IQ level in both states went up. Interpret this remark in the context of the average-marginal relationships discussed in the chapter. *(LO4)*

5. How is an isoquant map like an indifference map? In what important respect do the two constructs differ? *(LO6)*

6. Distinguish between diminishing returns to a variable input and decreasing returns to scale. *(LO2, LO7)*

7. *True or false:* If the marginal product is decreasing, then the average product must also be decreasing. Explain. *(LO4)*

8. A factory adds a worker and subsequently discovers that the average product of its workers has risen. *True or false:* The marginal product of the new worker is less than the average product of the plant's workers before the new employee's arrival. *(LO4)*

9. Currently, 2 units of labor and 1 unit of capital produce 1 unit of output. If you double both the inputs (4 units of labor and 2 units of capital), what can you conclude about the output produced under constant returns to scale? Decreasing returns to scale? Increasing returns to scale? *(LO7)*

PROBLEMS

1. Graph the short-run total product curves for each of the following production functions if K is fixed at $K_0 = 4$. *(LO1)*
   a. $Q = F(K, L) = 2K + 3L$.
   b. $Q = F(K, L) = K^2L^2$.

2. Do the two production functions in Problem 1 obey the law of diminishing returns? *(LO2)*

3. Suppose the marginal product of labor is currently equal to its average product. If you were one of ten new workers the firm was about to hire, would you prefer to be paid the value of your average product or the value of your marginal product? Would it be in the interests of an employer to pay you the value of your average product? *(LO4)*

4. The following table provides partial information on total product, average product, and marginal product for a production function. Using the relationships between these properties, fill in the missing cells. *(LO4)*

Labor	Total product	Average product	Marginal product
0		0	
1	180		
2			140
3	420		
4		120	

5. As an IT manager, you must decide how to allocate programmers between "support"—that is, doing bug fixes and responding to production issues—and the development of new features and systems. Both tasks are measured in completed "tickets," and for each activity, the weekly average product, total product, and marginal product are given in the accompanying table. Ticket completions of both types are equally valued by your company. Your programmers work in teams of 10. Currently you allocate two teams (20 programmers) to support and three teams (30 programmers) to development. How should you reallocate your teams, if at all, to achieve the maximum number of competed tickets per week? *(LO4)*

Number of teams	Support AP	Support TP	Support MP	Development AP	Development TP	Development MP
0	0	0		0	0	
1	40	40	40	45	45	45
2	40	80	40	40	80	35
3	40	120	40	35	105	25
4	40	160	40	30	120	15
5	40	200	40	25	125	5

6. As the IT manager described in Problem 5, you do a work study and discover that the marginal product for a

support team is actually a flat 50 tickets a week. What then becomes the best allocation of teams? *(LO4)*

7. A firm's short-run production function is given by

$$Q = \frac{1}{2}L^2 \qquad \text{for } 0 \le L \le 2$$

and

$$Q = 3L - \frac{1}{4}L^2 \qquad \text{for } 2 < L \le 7.$$

   a. Sketch the production function.
   b. Find the maximum attainable production. How much labor is used at that level?
   c. Identify the ranges of L utilization over which the marginal product of labor is increasing and decreasing.
   d. Identify the range over which the marginal product of labor is negative. *(LO1, LO4)*

8. Each problem on an exam is worth 20 points. Suppose that from the last seconds you devoted to Problem 10 on the exam you earned 2 extra points, while from the last seconds devoted to Problem 8 you earned 4 extra points. The total number of points you earned on these two problems were 8 and 6, respectively, and the total time you spent on each was the same. How—if at all—should you have reallocated your time between them? *(LO4)*

9. Suppose capital is fixed at 4 units in the production function $Q = KL$. Draw the total, marginal, and average product curves for the labor input. *(LO1)*

10. Identify the regions of increasing, constant, and decreasing returns to scale on the isoquant map shown. *(LO7)*

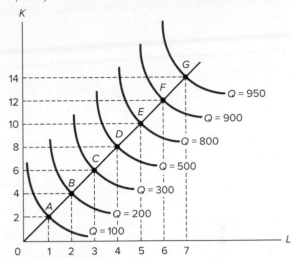

11. When Paul Samuelson switched from physics to economics, Robert Solow is said to have remarked that the average IQ in both disciplines went up. A bystander responded that Solow's claim must be wrong because it implies that the average IQ for academia as a whole (which is a weighted average of the average IQ levels for each discipline) must also have gone up as a result of the switch, which is clearly impossible. Was the bystander right? Explain. *(LO4)*

ANSWERS TO SELF-TESTS

8.1 For $K = 4$, $Q = \sqrt{4}\,\sqrt{L} = 2\,\sqrt{L}$. *(LO1)*

8.2 The slope of the total product curve in Figure 8.3*a* is 2 for all values of L. So $MP_{L=3} = 2$. *(LO4)*

8.3 The slope of the ray to any point on the total product curve is 2, and so $AP_{L=3} = 2$. When the total product curve is a ray, as here, $AP_L = MP_L$ is constant for all values of L. *(LO4)*

8.4 Because $AP_{L=10} < MP_{L=10}$, AP will rise when L increases, and so $AP_{L=10.1} > AP_{L=10}$. *(LO4)*

8.5 We cannot say that the pitcher should throw more fastballs without first knowing how a change in the proportion of pitches thrown would alter the effectiveness of both types of pitches. In particular, throwing more fastballs is likely to decrease the effectiveness not only of the additional fastballs thrown, but of all other fastballs as well. And if this loss exceeds the gain from switching from curves to fastballs, more fastballs should not be thrown. *(LO4)*

8.6 From the relationship $MP_L/MP_K = MRTS$, we have

$$3/MP_K = 9, \text{ which yields } MP_K = \frac{1}{3}. \text{ (LO4)}$$

Mathematical Extensions of Production Theory

APPLICATION: THE AVERAGE-MARGINAL DISTINCTION

Suppose that when your tennis opponent comes to the net, your best response is either to lob (hit the ball over his head) or to pass (hit the ball out of reach on either side). Each type of shot is more effective if it catches your opponent by surprise. Suppose someone who lobs all the time will win a given point only 10 percent of the time with a lob, but that someone who virtually never lobs wins the point on 90 percent of the rare occasions when he does lob. Similarly, suppose someone who tries passing shots all the time wins any given point only 30 percent of the time with a passing shot, but someone who virtually never tries to pass wins 40 percent of the time when he does try. Suppose, finally, that the rate at which each type of shot becomes less effective with use declines linearly with the proportion of times a player uses it. What is the best proportion of lobs and passing shots to use when your opponent comes to the net?[1]

The payoffs from the two types of shots are summarized graphically in Figure 8A.1. Here, the "production" problem is to produce the greatest possible percentage of winning shots when your opponent comes to the net. $F(L)$ tells you the percentage of points you will win with a lob as a function of the proportion of times you lob (L). $F(L)$ is thus, in effect, the average product of L. $G(L)$ tells you the percentage of points you will win with a passing shot, again as a function of the proportion of times you lob. The negative slope of $F(L)$ reflects the fact that lobs become less effective the more you use them. Similarly, the positive slope of $G(L)$ says that passing shots become more effective the more you lob. Your problem is to choose L^*, the best proportion of times to lob.

To find the optimal value of L, we must first discover how the percentage of total points won, denoted P, varies with L. For any value of L, P is simply a weighted average of the percentages won with each type of shot. The weight used for each type of shot is simply the proportion of times it is used. Noting that $(1 - L)$ is the proportion of passing shots when L is the proportion of lobs, we have

$$P = LF(L) + (1 - L)G(L). \qquad (8A.1)$$

The expression $LF(L)$ is the percentage of total points won on lobs. $(1 - L)G(L)$, similarly, is the percentage of total points won on passing shots. From Figure 8A.1, we see

[1]This example was suggested by Harvard psychologists Richard Herrnstein and James Mazur, in "Making Up Our Minds: A New Model of Economic Behavior," *The Sciences*, November/December 1987, 40–47.

FIGURE 8A.1

Effectiveness vs. Use: Lobs and Passing Shots

that the algebraic formulas for $F(L)$ and $G(L)$ are given by $F(L) = 90 - 80L$ and $G(L) = 30 + 10L$. Substituting these relationships into Equation 8A.1 gives

$$P = 30 + 70L - 90L^2, \tag{8A.2}$$

which is plotted in Figure 8A.2. The value of L that maximizes P turns out to be $L^* = 0.389$, and the corresponding value of P is 43.61 percent.[2]

Note in Figure 8A.3 that at the optimal value of L, the likelihood of winning with a lob is almost twice as high (58.9 percent) as that of winning with a passing shot (33.9 percent). Many people seem to find this state of affairs extremely uncomfortable—so

FIGURE 8A.2

The Optimal Proportion of Lobs

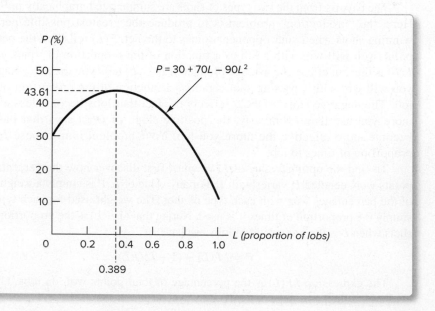

[2]The calculus-trained student can find L^* without having to plot P as a function of L simply by solving

$$\partial P / \partial L = 70 - 180L = 0,$$

which yields $L^* = \frac{7}{18} = 0.389$, which, upon substitution into Equation 8A.2, yields $P = 43.61$.

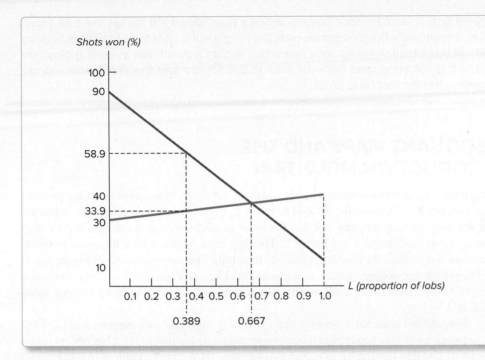

FIGURE 8A.3

At the Optimizing Point, the Likelihood of Winning with a Lob is Much Greater Than of Winning with a Passing Shot

much so that they refuse to have anything to do with it. In extensive experimental studies, Harvard psychologists Richard Herrnstein and James Mazur found that people tend to divide their shots not to maximize their overall chances of winning, but to equate the *average product* of each type. Note in Figure 8A.3 that this occurs when $L = 2/3$, at which point the percentage of points won with either shot is 36.7. At this value of L, however, the *marginal product* of a passing shot will be much higher than for a lob, because it will strongly increase the effectiveness of all your *other* lobs. (Of course, an extra passing shot will also reduce the effectiveness of your other passing shots, but by a much smaller margin.)

The situation here is analogous to the allocation example involving the fishing boats mentioned in Chapter 8. There is no more reason to want the average return to each tennis shot to be the same than there is to want the average product on each end of the lake to be the same. And yet the tendency to equate average rather than marginal products is a very common pitfall, one that even experienced maximizers have to be on guard against. Let us consider one final example.

EXAMPLE 8A.1

True or false? The best football coach is the one who always chooses the play that will gain the most yardage.

If you answered "true," you have not been paying attention. The best coach is the one who selects the best mix of plays, just as the best tennis player is the one who selects the best mix of shots. In the National Football League, passing plays gain almost twice as much yardage, on the average, as running plays. Why don't coaches call more passes? Because the passing game loses effectiveness if it is used too frequently. From the big difference in average gains for the two types of plays, it is apparent that most coaches are aware that the run is necessary to set up the pass. But many ostensibly expert commentators seem completely oblivious to this point. Trailing by 4 points with 20 seconds to go with fourth and goal at the

4-yard line, a team is more likely to score a touchdown if it throws the ball. However, a team will win more games over the long run if it nonetheless uses a running play in this situation every once in a while. But let a coach call a running play and fail in this situation, and both the fans in the stands and the announcers in the booth will insist that he is an idiot.

ISOQUANT MAPS AND THE PRODUCTION MOUNTAIN

Previously, we derived isoquants algebraically by holding output constant in the production function and then solving for K in terms of L. But there is also a geometric technique for deriving the isoquant map, one that is similar to the derivation of the indifference map discussed in the appendix to Chapter 3. This approach begins with a three-dimensional graph of the production function, perhaps something like the one shown in Figure 8A.4. It resembles the sloping surface of a mountain. The value on the Q axis measures the height of the mountain, or total output, which continues to increase as we employ more of K or L.

Suppose in Figure 8A.4 we were to fix output at some constant amount, say, Q_0. That is, suppose we cut the production mountain with a plane parallel to the KL plane, Q_0 units above it. The line labeled AB in Figure 8A.4 represents the intersection of that plane and the surface of the production mountain. All the input bundles that lie on AB yield an output level of Q_0. If we then project line AB downward onto the KL plane, we get the Q_0 isoquant shown in Figure 8A.5. As defined in Chapter 8, an isoquant is a locus of K, L pairs that produce the same level of output.

Suppose we then intersect the production mountain with another plane, this time Q_1 units above the KL plane. In Figure 8A.4, the second plane intersects the production mountain along the line labeled CD. It represents all input bundles that yield Q_1. Projecting CD down onto the KL plane, we thus get the isoquant labeled Q_1 in Figure 8A.5. In like fashion, we can generate an entire isoquant map corresponding to the production function $Q = F(K, L)$.

FIGURE 8A.4

The Production Mountain

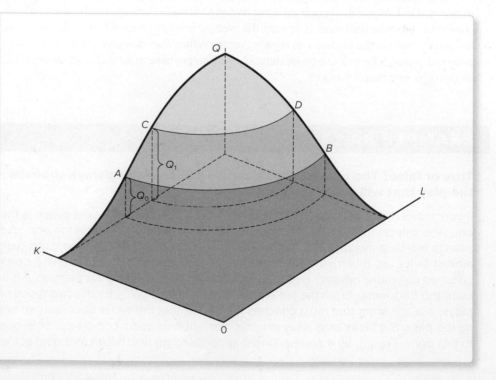

FIGURE 8A.5

**The Isoquant Map Derived
from the Production Mountain**

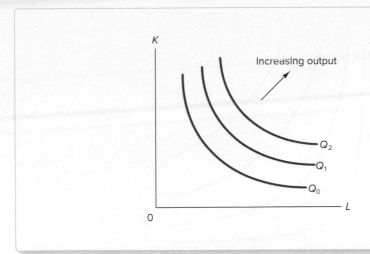

SOME EXAMPLES OF PRODUCTION FUNCTIONS

In this section we will examine two of the many different production functions that are commonly used in economic analysis.

The Cobb-Douglas Production Function

Perhaps the most widely used production function of all is the Cobb-Douglas, which in the two-input case takes the form

$$Q = mK^\alpha L^\beta, \tag{8A.3}$$

where α and β are numbers between zero and 1, and m can be any positive number.

To generate an equation for the Q_0 isoquant, we fix Q at Q_0 and then solve for K in terms of L. In the Cobb-Douglas case, this yields

$$K = \left(\frac{m}{Q_0}\right)^{-1/\alpha} (L)^{\beta/\alpha}. \tag{8A.4}$$

For the particular Cobb-Douglas function $Q = K^{1/2}L^{1/2}$, the Q_0 isoquant will be

$$K = \frac{Q_0^2}{L}. \tag{8A.5}$$

A portion of the isoquant map for this particular Cobb-Douglas production function is shown in Figure 8A.6.

The number assigned to each particular isoquant in Figure 8A.6 is exactly the level of output to which it corresponds. For example, when we have 2 units of K and 2 units of L, we get $Q = \sqrt{2}\sqrt{2} = 2$ units of output. Recall from Chapter 3 that the numbers we used to label the indifference curves on an indifference map conveyed information only about *relative* levels of satisfaction. All that was required of our indexing scheme in that context was that the *order* of the numbers we assigned to the indifference curves reflect the proper ranking of the corresponding satisfaction levels. With isoquants, the situation is altogether different. We have, in effect, no choice about what labels to assign to them.

Calculus-trained students can easily verify the following expressions for the marginal products of labor and capital in the Cobb-Douglas case:

$$MP_K = \frac{\partial Q}{\partial K} = \alpha mK^{\alpha-1}L^\beta \tag{8A.6}$$

FIGURE 8A.6

Isoquant Map for the Cobb-Douglas Production Function $Q = K^{1/2}L^{1/2}$

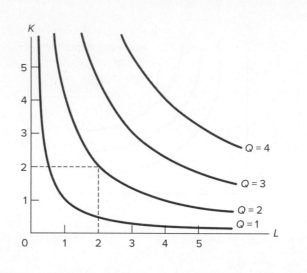

and

$$\text{MP}_L = \frac{\partial Q}{\partial L} = \beta m K^\alpha L^{\beta-1}. \tag{8A.7}$$

The Leontief, or Fixed-Proportions, Production Function

The simplest among all production functions that are widely used is the *Leontief,* named for the Nobel laureate Wassily Leontief, who devised it. For the two-input case, it is given by

$$Q = \min(aK, bL). \tag{8A.8}$$

If you are unfamiliar with this curious functional form, its interpretation is simply that Q is equal to either aK or bL, whichever is smaller. Suppose, for example, that $a = 2$, $b = 3$, $K = 4$, and $L = 3$. Then, $Q = \min(2 \times 4, 3 \times 3) = \min(8, 9) = 8$. The isoquant map for $Q = \min(2K, 3L)$ is shown in Figure 8A.7.

FIGURE 8A.7

Isoquant Map for the Leontief Production Function $Q = \min(2K, 3L)$

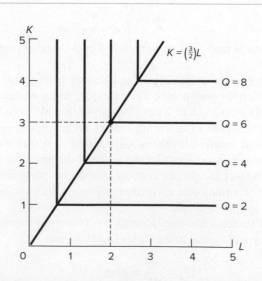

To see why the Leontief is also called the fixed-proportions production function, note first in Figure 8A.7 that if we start with 3 units of K and 2 units of L, we get 6 units of output. If we then add more L—so that we have, say, 3 units of L instead of 2—we still get only $Q = \min(2 \times 3, 3 \times 3) = \min(6, 9) = 6$ units of output. By the same token, adding more K when we are at $K = 3$ and $L = 2$ will not lead to any additional output. In the Leontief case, K and L are used most effectively when $aK = bL$—in the example at hand, when $2K = 3L$. In Figure 8A.7, the locus of points for which $2K = 3L$ is shown as the ray $K = \left(\frac{3}{2}\right)L$. It is along this ray that the cusps of all the right-angled isoquants of this Leontief production function will lie.

Recall from Chapter 3 that in the case of perfect complements, the indifference curves had the same right-angled shape as the isoquants for the Leontief production function. This meant that the MRS was infinite on the vertical arm of the indifference curve, zero on the horizontal arm, and undefined at the cusp. For exactly parallel reasons, the MRTS in the Leontief case will be infinite on the vertical arm of the isoquant, zero on the horizontal, and undefined at the cusp.

A MATHEMATICAL DEFINITION OF RETURNS TO SCALE

Mathematically, to increase all inputs in the same proportion means simply to multiply all inputs by the same number $c > 1$. By way of illustration, consider the production function we discussed in Chapter 8, $Q = F(K, L) = 2KL$. For this particular function, when we multiply each input by c we get

$$F(cK, cL) = 2(cK)(cL) = c^2 2KL = c^2 F(K, L). \tag{8A.9}$$

The result of multiplying each input by c in this production function is thus to multiply the original output level by c^2. Output thus grows more than in proportion to input growth in this case [with proportional growth, we would have had output equal to $cF(K, L)$], so this production function has increasing returns to scale. Thus, for example, if $c = 2$ (a doubling of each input), we get $F(2K, 2L) = 2(2K)(2L) = 4(2KL)$, a quadrupling of output.

Drawing on these observations, the definitions of our three cases may be summarized as follows:

$$\text{Increasing returns: } F(cK, cL) > cF(K, L); \tag{8A.10}$$

$$\text{Constant returns: } F(cK, cL) = cF(K, L); \tag{8A.11}$$

and

$$\text{Decreasing returns: } F(cK, cL) < cF(K, L). \tag{8A.12}$$

The following two exercises will help cement your ability to apply these definitions to specific examples.

SELF-TEST 8A.1

Does the production function $Q = \sqrt{K}\sqrt{L}$ have increasing, constant, or decreasing returns to scale?

SELF-TEST 8A.2

Does the production function $Q = K^{1/3}L^{1/3}$ have increasing, constant, or decreasing returns to scale?

In the case of the Cobb-Douglas production function, $Q = mK^\alpha L^\beta$, Equations 8A.10 through 8A.12 imply a simple relationship between the parameters α and β and the degree of returns to scale. Specifically, if $\alpha + \beta > 1$, there are increasing returns to scale; $\alpha + \beta = 1$ means constant returns to scale; and $\alpha + \beta < 1$ means decreasing returns to scale. To illustrate for the constant returns case, suppose $Q = F(K, L) = mK^{\alpha}L^{\beta}$, with $\alpha + \beta = 1$. Then we have

$$F(cK, cL) = m(cK)^{\alpha} (cL)^{\beta}, \tag{8A.13}$$

which reduces to

$$c^{(\alpha + \beta)}mK^{\alpha}L^{\beta} = cmK^{\alpha}L^{\beta} = cF(K, L), \tag{8A.14}$$

which, by Equation 8A.11, is the defining characteristic of constant returns to scale.

PROBLEMS

1.* Do the following production functions have increasing, decreasing, or constant returns to scale? Which ones fail to satisfy the law of diminishing returns?
   a. $Q = 4K^{1/2}L^{1/2}$
   b. $Q = aK^2 + bL^2$
   c. $Q = \min(aK, bL)$
   d. $Q = 4K + 2L$
   e. $Q = K^{0.5}L^{0.6}$
   f. $Q = K_1^{0.3}K_2^{0.3}L^{0.3}$

2.* What is the marginal product of labor in the production function $Q = 2K^{1/3}L^{1/3}$ if K is fixed at 27?

3. Can the Cobb-Douglas production function be used to portray a production process in which returns to scale are increasing at low output levels and are constant or decreasing at high output levels?

4. Suppose that a firm with the production function

   $$Q = \min(2K, 3L)$$

   is currently using 6 units of capital and 5 units of labor. What are the marginal products of K and L in this case?

5. The average number of yards gained by a college football team on a passing play is $8 + 12r$, where r is the fraction of their total plays that are running plays. Their average gain per running play is $10 - 8r$. What is their optimal fraction of running plays? At this value of r, what is the average gain per pass? The average gain per run? (This problem and the next one are similar to the tennis example considered earlier.)

6. Suppose you are a baseball pitcher with two pitches, fastball and curve. Your opponents' batting averages against these two pitches are as shown in the diagram below. If your goal is to minimize your opponents' overall batting average, what is the optimal proportion of fastballs? At this proportion, what are opponents' batting averages against your two pitches?

ANSWERS TO APPENDIX SELF-TESTS

8A.1 $F(K, L) = \sqrt{K} \sqrt{L}$, so $F(cK, cL) = \sqrt{cK} \sqrt{cL} = \sqrt{c^2} \sqrt{K} \sqrt{L} = cF(K, L)$, and so it has constant returns to scale.

8A.2 $F(K, L) = K^{1/3}L^{1/3}$, so $F(cK, cL) = (cK)^{1/3}(cL)^{1/3} = c^{2/3}K^{1/3}L^{1/3} = c^{2/3}F(K, L) < cF(K, L)$, and so it has decreasing returns to scale.

*This problem is most easily solved using the calculus definition of marginal product.

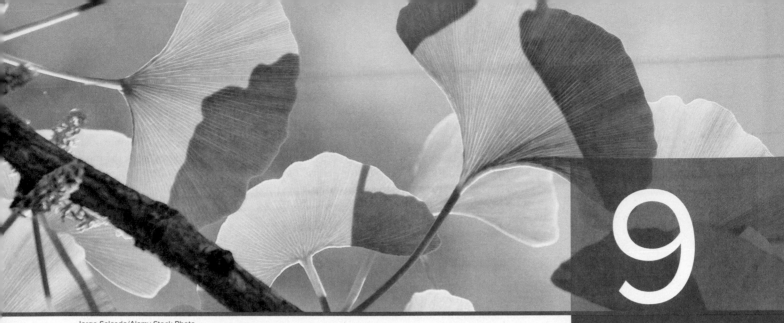

9

Costs

LEARNING OBJECTIVES

After reading this chapter, you should be able to:

LO1 Decompose short-run total costs of production into fixed costs and variable costs.

LO2 Explain how the shape of the short-run total cost curve relates to the shape of the short-run production function.

LO3 Explain the relationship between average variable cost, average total cost, and marginal cost.

LO4 Explain why the optimal allocation of production across multiple facilities requires that marginal cost be the same in each.

LO5 Explain how the relationship between the average and marginal product of a variable input is reflected in the relationship between the average and marginal cost curves.

LO6 Characterize the optimal input combination for producing a given level of output in the long run and explain why an input's marginal product divided by its price must take the same value for every input.

LO7 Explain how the degree of returns to scale in production is related to long-run production costs.

In the late 1960s, just after finishing college, I was a high school math and science teacher in Sanischare, a small village in eastern Nepal. During my two years there, one of the country's few roads was in the process of being built through Sanischare. Once the right-of-way was cleared and the culverts and bridges laid in, the next step was to spread gravel over the roadbed. As at almost every other stage of the process, the methods employed at this step were a page torn from another century. The Nepalese workmen squatted by the side of the road in the blazing sun, tapping away at large rocks with their hammers. In a 12-hour day, each worker would produce a small mound of gravel, not enough to cover even one running foot of roadbed. But there were a lot of people working, and eventually the job was done.

In the United States, of course, we don't hire people to hammer rocks into gravel by hand. Instead, we have huge machines that pulverize several tons of rock each minute. The reason for this difference seemed obvious to me at the time: Nepal, being a very poor country, simply couldn't afford the expensive equipment used in industrialized nations. But this explanation, I now realize, is wrong. As we will see, it still would have made sense for Nepal to make gravel with manual labor even if it had had vast surplus revenues in its national treasury, because labor is very cheap relative to capital equipment there.

CHAPTER PREVIEW

In this chapter our goal is to translate the theory of production developed in Chapter 8 into a coherent theory of costs. In Chapter 8 we established the relationship between the quantities of inputs employed and the corresponding level of output. Here, we will forge the link between the quantity of output produced and the cost of producing it.

Our first step will be to tackle the question of how costs vary with output in the short run. This question turns out to be more involved than it sounds, for there are seven different types of costs to keep track of—total cost, variable cost, fixed cost, marginal cost, average total cost, average variable cost, and average fixed cost. This array sounds bewildering at first, but the links between the different cost concepts are actually clear and simple. And each turns out to be important for the study of firm behavior, our principal concern in the chapters to follow.

Of even greater importance for the structure and conduct of industry is the question of how costs vary with output in the long run. Here, we will begin with the question of how to produce a given level of output—say, a mile of road—at the lowest possible cost. A given quantity can be produced many ways: We need to find the cheapest way, the most appropriate method for existing factor prices. The answer to this question enables us to explore how costs are related to returns to scale in production.

COSTS IN THE SHORT RUN

To see how costs vary with output in the short run, it is convenient to begin with a simple production example of the sort we discussed in Chapter 8. Suppose Zara's Cleaners washes bags of laundry using labor (L) and capital (K). Labor is purchased in the open market at a wage rate w = \$10/person-hr.[1] Capital is fixed in the short run. The relationship between the variable input and the total number of bags washed per hour is summarized in Table 9.1. Note that output initially grows at an increasing rate with additional units of the variable input (as L grows from 0 to 4 units), then grows at a diminishing rate (as L grows from 4 to 8 units).

The total cost of producing the various levels of output is simply the cost of all the factors of production employed. If Zara owns her own capital, its implicit rental value is an opportunity cost, the money Zara could have earned if she had sold her capital and invested the proceeds in, say, a government bond (see Chapter 1). Suppose Zara's capital is fixed at 120 machine-hr/hr, the rental value of each of which is r = \$0.25/machine-hr,[2] for a total capital rental of \$30/hr. This cost is **fixed cost (FC)**, which means that it does not vary in the short run as the level of output varies. More generally, if K_0 denotes the amount of capital and r is its rental price per unit, we have

fixed cost (FC) cost that does not vary with the level of output in the short run (the cost of all fixed factors of production).

$$FC = rK_0. \tag{9.1}$$

Other examples of fixed cost might include property taxes, insurance payments, interest on loans, and other payments to which the firm is committed in the short run and which do not vary as the level of output varies. Business managers often refer to fixed costs as *overhead costs*.

variable cost (VC) cost that varies with the level of output in the short run (the cost of all variable factors of production).

Variable cost (VC) is defined as the total cost of the variable factor of production at each level of output.[3] To calculate VC for any given level of output in this example, we simply multiply the amount of labor needed to produce that level of output by the hourly wage

TABLE 9.1
The Short-Run Production Function for Zara's Cleaners

Quantity of labor (person-hr/hr)	Quantity of output (bags/hr)
0	0
1	4
2	14
3	27
4	43
5	58
6	72
7	81
8	86

The entries in each row of the right column tell the quantity of output produced by the quantity of variable input in the corresponding row of the left column. This production function initially exhibits increasing, then diminishing, returns to the variable input.

[1] A person-hour is one person working for 1 hour. In Chapter 14 we will consider how input prices are determined. For the present, we simply take them as given.
[2] A machine-hour is one machine working for 1 hour. To say that Zara's capital is fixed at 120 machine-hr/hr means that she has 120 machines that can operate simultaneously.
[3] In production processes with more than one variable input, variable cost refers to the cost of *all* such inputs.

TABLE 9.2
Outputs and Costs

Q	FC	VC	TC
0	30	0	30
4	30	10	40
14	30	20	50
27	30	30	60
43	30	40	70
58	30	50	80
72	30	60	90
81	30	70	100
86	30	80	110

The fixed cost of capital is $30/hr, and the cost per unit of the variable factor (L) is $10/hr. Total cost is calculated as the sum of fixed cost and variable cost.

rate. Thus, the variable cost of 27 bags/hr is ($10/person-hr) (3 person-hr/hr) = $30/hr. More generally, if L_1 is the quantity of labor required to produce an output level of Q_1 and w is the hourly wage rate, we have

$$VC_{Q1} = wL_1. \qquad (9.2)$$

Note the explicit dependence of VC on output in the notation on the left-hand side of Equation 9.2, which is lacking in Equation 9.1. This is to emphasize that variable cost depends on the output level produced, whereas fixed cost does not.

Total cost (TC) is the sum of FC and VC. If Zara wishes to wash 43 bags/hr, the total cost of doing so will be $30/hr + ($10/person-hr) (4 person-hr/hr) = $70/hr. More generally, the expression for total cost of producing an output level of Q_1 is written

total cost (TC) all costs of production: the sum of variable cost and fixed cost.

$$TC_{Q1} = FC + VC_{Q1} = rK_0 + wL_1. \qquad (9.3)$$

Table 9.2 shows fixed, variable, and total cost for corresponding output levels for the production function given in Table 9.1. The relationships among the various cost categories are most clearly seen by displaying the information graphically, not in tabular form. The short-run production function from Table 9.1 is plotted in Figure 9.1. Recall from Chapter 8 that the initial region of upward curvature ($0 \leq L \leq 4$) of the production function corresponds to increasing returns to the variable input. Beyond the point $L = 4$, the production function exhibits diminishing returns to the variable input.

FIGURE 9.1

Output as a Function of One Variable Input

This production process shows increasing returns to the variable input up to $L = 4$, and diminishing returns thereafter.

GRAPHING THE TOTAL, VARIABLE, AND FIXED COST CURVES

Not surprisingly, the shape of the variable cost curve is systematically related to the shape of the short-run production function. The connection arises because the production function tells us how much labor we need to produce a given level of output, and this quantity of labor, when multiplied by the wage rate, gives us variable cost. Suppose, for example, we want to plot the variable cost of producing 58 units of output. (See Figures 9.1, 9.2.) We first note from the production function shown in Figure 9.1 that 58 units of output require 5 units of labor, which, at a wage rate of $10/person-hr, gives rise to a variable cost of (5)(10) = $50/hr. So in Figure 9.2, the output level of 58 is plotted against a variable cost of $50/hr. Similarly, note from the production function that 43 units of output require 4 units of labor, which, at the $10 wage rate, gives rise in Figure 9.2 to a variable cost of $40/hr. In like fashion, we can generate as many additional points on the variable cost curve as we choose.

Of particular interest is the relationship between the curvature of the production function and that of the variable cost curve. Note in Figure 9.1 that $L = 4$ is the point at which diminishing returns to the variable factor of production set in. For values of L less than 4, there are increasing returns to L, which means that increments in L produce successively larger increments in Q in that region. Put another way, in this region a given increase in output, Q, requires successively smaller increments in the variable input, L. As a result, variable cost grows at a diminishing rate for output levels less than 43. This is reflected in Figure 9.2 by the concave shape of the variable cost curve for output levels between 0 and 43.

Once L exceeds 4 in Figure 9.1, we enter the region of diminishing returns. Here, successively larger increments in L are required to produce a given increment in Q. In consequence, variable cost grows at an increasing rate in this region. This is reflected in the convex shape of the variable cost curve in Figure 9.2 for output levels in excess of 43.

Because fixed costs do not vary with the level of output, their graph is simply a horizontal line. Figure 9.2 shows the fixed, variable, and total cost curves (FC, VC, and TC) for the production function shown in Figure 9.1. Note in the figure that the variable cost curve passes through the origin, which means simply that variable cost is zero when we produce no output. The total cost of producing zero output is equal to fixed costs, FC. Note also in the figure that the vertical distance between the VC and TC curves is everywhere equal to FC. This means that the total cost curve is parallel to the variable cost curve and lies FC units above it.

FIGURE 9.2

The Total, Variable, and Fixed Cost Curves

These curves are for the production function for Zara's Cleaners, shown in Figure 9.1. The variable cost curve passes through the origin, which means that the variable cost of producing zero units of output is equal to zero. The TC curve, which is the sum of the FC and VC curves, is parallel to the VC curve and lies FC = 30 units above it.

EXAMPLE 9.1   Graphing the Cost Functions

Suppose the production function is given by $Q = 3KL$, where K denotes capital and L denotes labor. The price of capital is \$2/machine-hr, the price of labor is \$24/person-hr, and capital is fixed at 4 machine-hr/hr in the short run. Graph the TC, VC, and FC curves for this production process.

Unlike the production process shown in Figure 9.1, the process in this example is one in which there are everywhere constant returns to the variable factor of production. As shown in Figure 9.3, output here is strictly proportional to the variable input.

FIGURE 9.3

The Production Function $Q = 3KL$, with $K = 4$

This short-run production function exhibits constant returns to L over the entire range of L. There is neither a region of increasing returns nor a region of diminishing returns to L.

To derive the total cost function from this production function, we must first discover how much capital and labor are required to produce a given level of output in the short run. Since K is fixed at 4 machine-hr/hr, the required amount of labor input is found by solving $Q = 3KL = 3(4)L$ for $L = Q/12$. The total cost of producing Q units of output per hour is therefore given by

$$TC(Q) = (\$2/\text{machine-hr})(4 \text{ machine-hr/hr})$$

$$+ (\$24/\text{person-hr})\left(\frac{Q}{12}\text{ person-hr/hr}\right) = \$8/\text{hr} + \$2Q/\text{hr}. \tag{9.4}$$

The \$8/hr expenditure on capital constitutes fixed cost. Variable cost is total cost less fixed cost, or

$$VC_Q = 2Q. \tag{9.5}$$

The total, variable, and fixed cost curves are plotted in Figure 9.4.

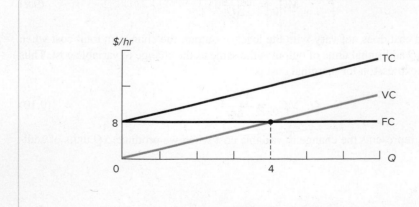

FIGURE 9.4

The Total, Variable, and Fixed Cost Curves for the Production Function $Q = 3KL$

With K fixed at 4 machine-hr/hr in the short run and a price of K of $r = \$2$/machine-hr, fixed costs are \$8/hr. To produce Q units of output per hour requires $Q/12$ person-hr/hr of labor. With a price of labor of \$24/person-hr, variable cost is \$2Q/hr. Total cost is \$8/hr + \$2Q/hr.

OTHER SHORT-RUN COSTS

average fixed cost (AFC) fixed cost divided by the quantity of output.

Average fixed cost (AFC) is fixed cost divided by the quantity of output. For the production function shown in Table 9.1, for example, the average fixed cost of washing 58 bags/hr is ($30/hr) ÷ (58 bags/hr) = \$0.517/bag. More generally, the average fixed cost of producing an output level of Q_1 is written

$$\text{AFC}_{Q_1} = \frac{\text{FC}}{Q_1} = \frac{rK_0}{Q_1}. \tag{9.6}$$

Note in Equation 9.6 that, unlike FC, AFC depends on the level of output produced.

average variable cost (AVC) variable cost divided by the quantity of output.

Average variable cost (AVC) is variable cost divided by the quantity of output. If Kelly washes 72 bags/hr, his AVC will be ($10/person-hr) (6 person-hr/hr) ÷ 72 bags/hr = \$0.833/bag. The average variable cost of producing an output level Q_1 may be written as

$$\text{AVC}_{Q_1} = \frac{\text{VC}_{Q_1}}{Q_1} = \frac{wL_1}{Q_1}. \tag{9.7}$$

average total cost (ATC) total cost divided by the quantity of output.

Average total cost (ATC) is total cost divided by the quantity of output. And since total cost is the sum of total fixed cost and total variable cost, it follows that ATC is the sum of AFC and AVC. For example, the ATC of washing 58 bags/hr is ($30/hr) ÷ (58 bags/hr) + ($10/person-hr) (5 person-hr/hr) ÷ (58 bags/hr) = \$0.517/bag + \$0.862/bag = \$1.379/bag. The average total cost of producing Q_1 units of output is given by

$$\text{ATC}_{Q_1} = \text{AFC}_{Q_1} + \text{AVC}_{Q_1} = \frac{rK_0 + wL_1}{Q_1}. \tag{9.8}$$

marginal cost (MC) change in total cost that results from a 1-unit change in output.

Marginal cost (MC), finally, is the change in total cost that results from producing an additional unit of output.[4] In going from 58 to 72 bags/hr, for example, total costs go up by \$10/hr, which is the cost of hiring the extra worker needed to achieve that increase in output. Since the extra worker washes an extra 14 bags/hr, the marginal cost of the additional output in per-bag terms is ($10/hr) ÷ (14 bags/hr) = \$0.714/bag. More generally, if ΔQ denotes the change in output from an initial level of Q_1, and ΔTC_{Q_1} denotes the corresponding change in total cost, marginal cost at Q_1 is given by

$$\text{MC}_{Q_1} = \frac{\Delta\text{TC}_{Q_1}}{\Delta Q}. \tag{9.9}$$

Because fixed cost does not vary with the level of output, the change in total cost when we produce ΔQ additional units of output is the same as the change in variable cost. Thus an equivalent expression for marginal cost is

$$\text{MC}_{Q_1} = \frac{\Delta\text{VC}_{Q_1}}{\Delta Q}, \tag{9.10}$$

where ΔVC_{Q_1} represents the change in variable cost when we produce ΔQ units of additional output.

---

[4]In calculus terms, the definition of marginal cost is simply $\text{MC}_Q = d\text{TC}_Q/dQ$.

Graphing the Short-Run Average and Marginal Cost Curves

Since FC does not vary with output, average fixed cost declines steadily as output increases. Suppose McGraw-Hill's fixed costs in producing this text were approximately $200,000. If only 1,000 copies were produced, its average fixed cost would be $200/book. But if the publisher produces 20,000 copies, AFC will fall to $10/book. McGraw-Hill's best-selling economics principles text, by Campbell McConnell, Stanley Brue, and Sean Flynn is considerably longer than this book, and yet its average fixed cost comes to little more than $1/book. The process whereby AFC falls with output is often referred to as "spreading overhead costs."

For the fixed cost curve FC shown in the top panel in Figure 9.5, the corresponding average fixed cost curve is shown in the bottom panel as the curve labeled AFC. Like all other AFC curves, it takes the form of a rectangular hyperbola. As output shrinks toward zero, AFC grows without bounds, and it falls ever closer to zero as output increases. Note that the units on the vertical axis of the AFC curve are dollars per unit ($/unit) of output, and that the vertical axis of the FC curve, by contrast, is measured in dollars per hour($/hr).

Geometrically, average variable cost at any level of output Q, which is equal to VC/Q, may be interpreted as the slope of a ray to the variable cost curve at Q. Notice in

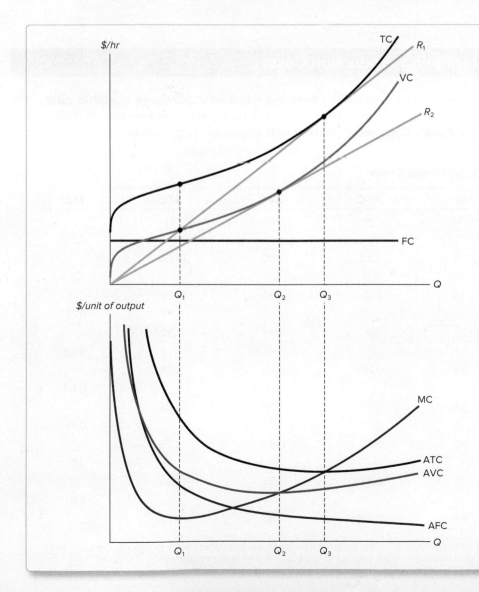

FIGURE 9.5

The Marginal, Average Total, Average Variable, and Average Fixed Cost Curves

The MC curve intersects the ATC and AVC curves at their respective minimum points.

the top panel in Figure 9.5 that the slope of a ray to the VC curve declines with output up to the output level Q_2; thereafter it begins to increase. The corresponding average variable cost curve, shown in the bottom panel in Figure 9.5, therefore reaches its minimum value at Q_2, the output level at which the ray R_2 is tangent to the variable cost curve. Beyond that point, the AVC curve increases with output.

The graph of the ATC curve is generated in an analogous fashion. For any level of output, ATC is the slope of the ray to the total cost curve at that output level. For the total cost curve in the top panel in Figure 9.5, the corresponding ATC curve is plotted in the bottom panel of the diagram. Note that the minimum point on ATC in the bottom panel occurs at Q_3, the output level for which the ray R_1 is tangent to the TC curve in the top panel.

Recall that because TC = FC + VC, it follows that ATC = AFC + AVC (simply divide both sides of the former equation by output). This means that the vertical distance between the ATC and AVC curves at any level of output will always be the corresponding level of AFC. Thus the vertical distance between ATC and AVC approaches infinity as output declines toward zero, and shrinks toward zero as output grows toward infinity. Note also in Figure 9.5 that the minimum point on the AVC curve occurs for a smaller unit of output than does the minimum point on the ATC curve. Because AFC declines continuously, ATC continues falling even after AVC has begun to turn upward.

EXAMPLE 9.2　　Determining Production Costs

Construct a table showing average fixed cost, average variable cost, average total cost, and marginal cost using the information in Table 9.1 for Zara's Cleaners. Then graph these average costs.

Outputs and Costs

Q	AFC	AVC	ATC	MC*
0	∞	—	∞	
				2.50
4	7.50	2.50	10.00	
				1.0
14	2.14	1.43	3.57	
				0.77
27	1.11	1.11	2.22	
				0.63
43	0.70	0.93	1.63	
				0.67
58	0.52	0.86	1.38	
				0.71
72	0.42	0.83	1.25	
				1.11
81	0.37	0.86	1.23	
				2.0
86	0.35	0.93	1.28	

*The marginal cost entries are placed between the lines of the table to indicate that each entry represents the cost per bag of moving from the preceding output level to the next.

FIGURE 9.6

Quantity vs. Average Costs

ATC is the sum of AVC and AFC. AFC is declining for all values of Q.

We calculate average fixed cost as fixed cost divided by quantity AFC = FC/Q, average variable cost as variable cost divided by quantity AVC = VC/Q, and average total cost as total cost divided by quantity ATC = TC/Q. We calculate marginal cost by finding the difference in total cost and dividing by the difference in quantity: MC = $\Delta TC/\Delta Q$ to fill in the table above. The average cost curves are illustrated in Figure 9.6.

SELF-TEST 9.2

If FC takes the value 20, what is the vertical distance between the ATC and AVC curves in Figure 9.5 when $Q = 10$?

In terms of its role in the firm's decision of how much output to produce, by far the most important of the seven cost curves is the *marginal cost curve*. The reason, as we will see in the coming chapters, is that the firm's typical operating decision involves the question of whether to expand or contract its current level of output. To make this decision intelligently, the firm must compare the relevant costs and benefits. The cost of expanding output (or the savings from contracting) is by definition equal to marginal cost.

Geometrically, marginal cost at any level of output may be interpreted as the slope of the total cost curve at that level of output. And since the total cost and variable cost curves are parallel, marginal cost is also equal to the slope of the variable cost curve. (Recall that the variable cost component is all that varies when total cost varies, which means that the change in total cost per unit of output must be the same as the change in variable cost per unit of output.)

Notice in the top panel in Figure 9.5 that the slope of the total cost curve decreases with output up to Q_1, and rises with output thereafter.[5] This tells us that the marginal cost curve, labeled MC in the bottom panel, will be downward-sloping up to Q_1 and upward-sloping thereafter. Q_1 is the point at which diminishing returns set in for this production function, and diminishing returns are what account for the upward slope of the short-run marginal cost curve.

At the output level Q_3, the slope of the total cost curve is exactly the same as the slope of the ray to the total cost curve (the ray labeled R_1 in the top panel in Figure 9.5). This tells us that marginal cost and average total cost will take precisely the same value at Q_3. To the left of Q_3, the slope of the total cost curve is smaller than the slope of the corresponding ray, which means that marginal cost will be smaller than average total cost in that region. For output levels in excess of Q_3, the slope of the total cost curve is larger than the slope of the corresponding ray, so marginal cost will be larger than average total cost for output levels larger than Q_3. These relationships are reflected in the average total

---

[5]A point at which the curvature change is called an *inflection point*.

cost and marginal cost curves shown in the bottom panel in Figure 9.5. Notice that the relationship between the MC and AVC curves is qualitatively similar to the relationship between the MC and ATC curves. One common feature is that MC intersects each curve at its minimum point. Both average cost curves have the additional property that *when MC is less than average cost (either ATC or AVC), the average cost curve must be decreasing with output; and when MC is greater than average cost, average cost must be increasing with output.*

Note also that both of these relationships are very much like the ones among marginal and average product curves discussed in Chapter 8. They follow directly from the definition of marginal cost. Producing an additional unit whose cost exceeds the average (either total or variable) cost incurred thus far has the effect of pulling the average cost up. Conversely, an extra unit whose cost is less than the average will necessarily pull down the average.

Finally, note in the bottom panel in Figure 9.5 that the units on the vertical axis of the marginal cost curve diagram are again dollars per unit ($/unit) of output, the same as for the three short-run average cost curves. All four of these curves can thus be displayed in a single diagram. But you must never, *ever,* attempt to place any of these four curves on the same axes with the total cost, variable cost, or fixed cost curves. The units measured along the vertical axes are simply not compatible.

EXAMPLE 9.3   Graphing Cost Curves

Suppose output is given by the production function $Q = 3KL$, where K denotes capital and L denotes labor. The price of capital is $2/machine-hr, the price of labor is $24/person-hr, and capital is fixed at 4 units in the short run (this is the same production function and input prices as in Example 9.1). Graph the ATC, AVC, AFC, and MC curves.

Recall from Example 9.1 that the total cost curve for this process is given by

$$TC_Q = 8 + 2Q. \tag{9.11}$$

Marginal cost is the slope of the total cost curve, which here is equal to $2/unit of output:

$$MC_Q = \frac{\Delta TC_Q}{\Delta Q} = 2. \tag{9.12}$$

Average variable cost is given by VC_Q/Q, which is also $2/unit of output:

$$AVC_Q = \frac{2Q}{Q} = 2. \tag{9.13}$$

When marginal cost is constant, as in this production process, it will always be equal to AVC.

Average fixed cost is given by

$$AFC_Q = \frac{8}{Q}, \tag{9.14}$$

and average total cost is given by

$$ATC_Q = 2 + \frac{8}{Q}, \tag{9.15}$$

in this example. The marginal and average cost curves are as shown in the bottom panel in Figure 9.7, where the top panel reproduces the corresponding total, variable, and fixed cost curves.

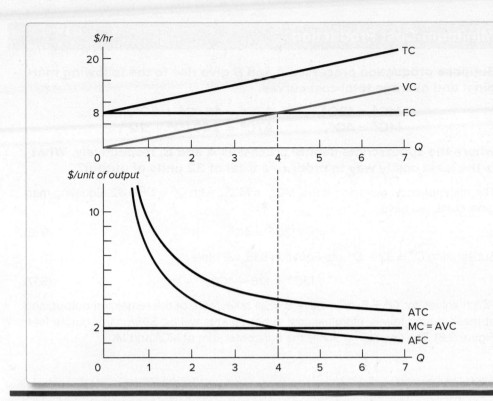

FIGURE 9.7

Cost Curves for a Specific Production Process

For production processes with constant marginal cost, average variable cost and marginal cost are identical. Marginal cost always lies below ATC for such processes.

ALLOCATING PRODUCTION BETWEEN TWO PROCESSES

In Chapter 8, we saw that the problem of allocating a fixed resource between two production activities is solved by equating the marginal product of the resource in each. A closely related problem can be solved with the cost concepts developed in this chapter. Here, the problem is to divide a given production quota between two production processes in such a way as to produce the quota at the lowest possible cost.

Let Q_T be the total amount to be produced, and let Q_1 and Q_2 be the amounts produced in the first and second processes, respectively. And suppose the marginal cost in either process at very low levels of output is lower than the marginal cost at Q_T units of output in the other (which ensures that both processes will be used).[6] *The values of Q_1 and Q_2 that solve this problem will then be the ones that result in equal marginal costs for the two processes.*

To see why, suppose the contrary—that is, suppose that the cost-minimizing allocation resulted in higher marginal cost in one process than in the other. We could then shift one unit of output from the process with the higher marginal cost to the one with the lower. Because the result would be the same total output as before at a lower total cost, the initial division could not have been the cost-minimizing one.

In Chapter 8 we saw that two production processes could have equal marginal products even though their average products differed substantially. Here, too, it is possible for two production processes to have equal marginal costs even though their average costs differ markedly. The cost-minimizing condition does not require average cost levels in the two processes to be the same, and indeed, in practice, they will often take substantially different values.

---

[6]Suppose the marginal cost at $Q = Q_T$ using production function A were less than the marginal cost at $Q = 0$ for production process B: $MC_{Q_T}^A < MC_0^B$. Then the cheapest way of producing Q_T would be to use only process A.

EXAMPLE 9.4   Minimum-Cost Production

Suppose production processes A and B give rise to the following marginal and average total cost curves:

$$MC^A = 12Q^A, \qquad ATC^A = 16/Q^A + 6Q^A,$$
$$MC^B = 4Q^B, \qquad ATC^B = 240/Q^B + 2Q^B,$$

where the superscripts denote processes A and B, respectively. What is the least costly way to produce a total of 32 units of output?

The minimum-cost condition is that $MC^A_{Q^A} = MC^B_{Q^B}$, with $Q^A + Q^B = 32$. Equating marginal costs, we have

$$12Q^A = 4Q^B. \qquad (9.16)$$

Substituting $Q^B = 32 - Q^A$ into Equation 9.16, we have

$$12Q^A = 128 - 4Q^A, \qquad (9.17)$$

which solves for $Q^A = 8$. $Q^B = 32 - 8 = 24$ takes care of the remaining output, and at these output levels, marginal cost in both plants will be \$96/unit of output (see Figure 9.8). The line $MC^T = 3Q^T$ is the horizontal sum of MC^A and MC^B.[7]

FIGURE 9.8

The Minimum-Cost Production Allocation

To produce a given total output at minimum cost, it should be allocated across production activities so that the marginal cost of each activity is the same.

The average total cost values that correspond to this allocation are $ATC^A = \$50$/unit of output and $ATC^B = \$58$/unit of output. From the average total cost curves we can deduce total cost curves in this example (just multiply ATC by Q).[8] They are given by $TC^A = 16 + 6(Q^A)^2$ and $TC^B = 240 + 2(Q^B)^2$. The cost-minimizing allocation results in $TC^A = \$400$ and $TC^B = \$1,392$, illustrating that the cost-minimizing allocation does not require equality of total costs either.

SELF-TEST 9.3

Same as Example 9.4 except the total output is 12.

THE RELATIONSHIP AMONG MP, AP, MC, AND AVC

In Chapter 8, we saw that the marginal product curve cuts the average product curve at the maximum value of the AP curve. And in this chapter, we saw that the marginal cost curve cuts the average variable cost curve at the minimum value of the AVC curve. There is a direct link between these relationships. To see the connection, note first that from the

---

[7]MC^T is found by solving $Q^T = Q^A + Q^B = MC/12 + MC/4 = MC/3$ for $MC^T = 3Q^T$.
[8]Note that $MC^A = dTC^A/dQ^A = d[16 + 6(Q^A)^2]/dQ^A = 12Q^A$ and $MC^B = dTC^B/dQ^B = d[240 + 2(Q^B)^2]/dQ^B = 4Q^B$.

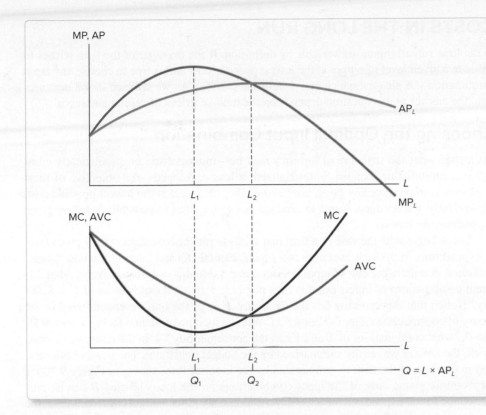

FIGURE 9.9

The Relationship among MP, AP, MC, and AVC
Normally, the MC and AVC curves are plotted with Q on the horizontal axis. In the bottom panel, they are shown as functions of L. The value of Q that corresponds to a given value of L is found by multiplying L times the corresponding value of AP_L. The maximum value of the MP curve, at $L = L_1$, top panel, corresponds to the minimum value of the MC curve, at $Q = Q_1$, bottom panel. Similarly, the maximum value of the AP curve, at $L = L_2$, top panel, corresponds to the minimum value of the AVC curve, at $Q = Q_2$, bottom panel.

definition of marginal cost we have $MC = \Delta VC/\Delta Q$. When labor is the only variable factor, $\Delta VC = \Delta wL$ so that $\Delta VC/\Delta Q$ is equal to $\Delta wL/\Delta Q$. If wage rates are fixed, this is the same as $w\Delta L/\Delta Q$. And since $\Delta L/\Delta Q$ is equal to $1/MP$, it follows that

$$MC = \frac{w}{MP} \qquad (9.18)$$

In similar fashion, note from the definition of average variable cost that $AVC = VC/Q = wL/Q$, and since L/Q is equal to $1/AP$, it follows that

$$AVC = \frac{w}{AP}. \qquad (9.19)$$

From Equation 9.18, we see that the minimum value of marginal cost corresponds to the maximum value of MP. Likewise, it follows from Equation 9.19 that the minimum value of AVC corresponds to the maximum value of AP. The top panel in Figure 9.9 plots the AP and MP curves as functions of L. The bottom panel uses Equations 9.18 and 9.19 to plot the corresponding MC and AVC curves as functions of L. (Normally, the MC and AVC curves are plotted as functions of Q. The value of Q that corresponds to a given value of L in the bottom panel may be calculated by multiplying L times the corresponding value of AP_L.) Note that the MP curve in the top panel takes its maximum value at $L = L_1$, and that the minimum value of the MC curve in the bottom panel occurs at the output level (Q_1) that corresponds to $L = L_1$. Note also that the AP curve in the top panel takes its maximum value at $L = L_2$, and that the minimum value of the AVC curve in the bottom panel occurs at the output level (Q_2) that corresponds to $L = L_2$.

SELF-TEST 9.4

For a production function at a given level of output in the short run, the marginal product of labor is greater than the average product of labor. How will marginal cost at that output level compare with average variable cost?

COSTS IN THE LONG RUN

In the long run all inputs are variable by definition. If the manager of the firm wishes to produce a given level of output at the lowest possible cost and is free to choose any input combination she pleases, which one should she choose? As we will see in the next section, the answer to this question depends on the relative prices of capital and labor.

Choosing the Optimal Input Combination

No matter what the structure of industry may be—monopolistic or atomistically competitive, capitalist or socialist, industrialized or less developed—the objective of most producers is to produce any given level and quality of output at the lowest possible cost. Equivalently, the producer wants to produce as much output as possible from any given expenditure on inputs.

Let us begin with the case of a firm that wants to maximize output from a given level of expenditure. Suppose it uses only two inputs, capital (K) and labor (L), whose prices, measured in dollars per unit of input per day, are $r = 2$ and $w = 4$, respectively. What different combinations of inputs can this firm purchase for a total expenditure of $C = \$200/$ day? Notice that this question has the same structure as the one we encountered in the theory of consumer behavior in Chapter 3 ("With an income of M, and facing prices of P_X and P_Y, what combinations of X and Y can the consumer buy?"). In the consumer's case, recall, the answer was easily summarized by the budget constraint. The parallel information in the case of the firm is summarized by the **isocost line,** shown in Figure 9.10 for the example given. Any of the input combinations on the locus labeled B can be purchased for a total expenditure of \$200/day. Analogously to the budget constraint case, the slope of the isocost line is the negative of the ratio of the input prices, $-w/r$.

isocost line a set of input bundles each of which costs the same amount.

SELF-TEST 9.5

If $w = 3$ and $r = 6$, draw the isocost lines that correspond to total expenditure of \$90 and \$180 per unit of time.

The analytic approach for finding the maximum output that can be produced for a given cost turns out to be similar to the one for finding the optimal consumption bundle. Just as a given level of satisfaction can be achieved by any of a multitude of possible consumption bundles (all of which lie on the same indifference curve), so too can a given amount of output be produced by any of a host of different input combinations (all of which lie on the same isoquant). In the consumer case, we found the optimum bundle by superimposing the budget constraint onto the indifference map and locating the

---

FIGURE 9.10

The Isocost Line

For given input prices ($r = 2$ and $w = 4$ in the diagram), the isocost line is the locus of all possible input bundles that can be purchased for a given level of total expenditure C (\$200 in the diagram). The slope of the isocost line is the negative of the input price ratio, $-w/r$.

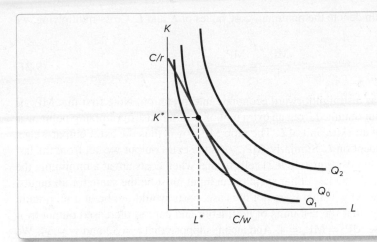

FIGURE 9.11

The Maximum Output for a Given Expenditure

A firm that is trying to produce the largest possible output for an expenditure of C will select the input combination at which the isocost line for C is tangent to an isoquant.

relevant point of tangency.[9] Here, we superimpose the isocost line onto the isoquant map. In Figure 9.11, the tangency point (L^*, K^*) is the input combination that yields the highest possible output (Q_0) for an expenditure of C.

As noted, the problem of producing the largest output for a given expenditure is solved in essentially the same way as the problem of producing a given level of output for the lowest possible cost. The only difference is that in the latter case we begin with a specific isoquant (the one that corresponds to the level of output we are trying to produce), then superimpose a map of isocost lines, each corresponding to a different cost level. In our first exercise, cost was fixed and output varied; this time, output is fixed and costs vary. As shown in Figure 9.12, the least-cost input bundle (L^*, K^*) corresponds to the point of tangency between an isocost line and the specified isoquant (Q_0).

Recall from Chapter 8 that the slope of the isoquant at any point is equal to $-\mathrm{MP}_L/\mathrm{MP}_K$, the negative of the ratio of the marginal product of L to the marginal product of K at that point. (Recall also from Chapter 8 that the absolute value of this ratio is called the marginal rate of technical substitution.) Combining this with the result that minimum cost occurs at a point of tangency with the isocost line (whose slope is $-w/r$), it follows that

$$\frac{\mathrm{MP}_{L^*}}{\mathrm{MP}_{K^*}} = \frac{w}{r},$$ (9.20)

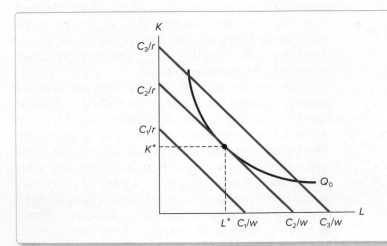

FIGURE 9.12

The Minimum Cost for a Given Level of Output

A firm that is trying to produce a given level of output, Q_0, at the lowest possible cost will select the input combination at which an isocost line is tangent to the Q_0 isoquant.

---

[9]Except, of course, in the case of corner solutions.

where K^* and L^* again denote the minimum-cost values of K and L. Cross-multiplying, we have

$$\frac{MP_{L^*}}{w} = \frac{MP_{K^*}}{r}. \qquad (9.21)$$

If you get a larger increase in output from the last dollar you spent on one input than from the last dollar you spent on another, you should be spending more on the first input and less on the second.

Equation 9.21 has a straightforward economic interpretation. Note first that MP_{L^*} is simply the extra output obtained from an extra unit of L at the cost-minimizing point. w is the cost, in dollars, of an extra unit of L. The ratio MP_{L^*}/w is thus the extra output we get from the last dollar spent on L. Similarly, MP_{K^*}/r is the extra output we get from the last dollar spent on K. In words, Equation 9.21 tells us that when costs are at a minimum, the extra output we get from the last dollar spent on an input must be the same for all inputs.

It is easy to show why, if that were not the case, costs would not be at a minimum. Suppose, for example, that the last units of both labor and capital increased output by 4 units. That is, suppose $MP_L = MP_K = 4$. And again, suppose that $r = \$2$ and $w = \$4$. We would then have gotten only 1 unit of output for the last dollar spent on L, but 2 units for the last dollar spent on K. We could reduce spending on L by a dollar, increase spending on K by only 50 cents, and get the same output level as before, saving 50 cents in the process. Whenever the ratios of marginal products to input prices differ across inputs, it will always be possible to make a similar cost-saving substitution in favor of the input with the higher MP/P ratio.[10]

More generally, we may consider a production process that employs not two but N inputs, $X_1, X_2, \ldots, X_N$. In this case, the condition for production at minimum cost is a straightforward generalization of Equation 9.21:

$$\frac{MP_{X_1}}{P_{X_1}} = \frac{MP_{X_2}}{P_{X_2}} = \cdots \frac{MP_{X_N}}{P_{X_N}}. \qquad (9.22)$$

Economic Naturalist 9.1

Why was gravel made by hand in Nepal but by machine in the United States?

Why is gravel made by hand in Nepal?

To model the production technology possibilities facing 1960s roadbuilders in Nepal and United States in the 1960s, let's suppose that capital (K) and labor (L) are employed to transform rocks into gravel. And suppose that any of the input combinations on the isoquant labeled $Q = 1$ ton in Figure 9.13 will yield 1 ton of gravel. Thus, the combination labeled ($L^*_{U.S.}$, $K^*_{U.S.}$) might correspond to the highly capital-intensive technique used in the United States and (L^*_{Nepal}, K^*_{Nepal}) to the highly labor-intensive technique used in Nepal.

The reason the chosen techniques differed between countries is not that the United States was richer, as I had originally thought when I taught in Nepal; rather, it is that the relative prices of labor and capital differed so dramatically in the two countries. In 1960s Nepal, labor *was* cheaper than in almost any other nation. While I was living there, I paid 10 cents for a haircut and chiropractic neck adjustment (both administered by the same person). Wages in the United States, by contrast, were (and remain) among the highest in the world. Construction equipment is traded in world

[10]Again, this statement is true except in the case of corner solutions.

FIGURE 9.13

Different Ways of Producing 1 Ton of Gravel

Countries where labor is cheap relative to capital will select labor-intensive techniques of production. Those where labor is more expensive will employ relatively more capital-intensive techniques.

markets and, aside from shipping costs, its price does not differ much from one country to another. Even if we ignore the high shipping costs to Nepal, and assume that the price of capital, r, was roughly the same in the two countries , it still follows from the much higher price of labor, w, in the United States that the isocost line was much flatter in Nepal. As shown in Figure 9.13, this fact alone would have been sufficient to account for the dramatic difference in production techniques.

Fast forward 50 years and, while unskilled labor wages in Nepal remain very low, the relative price of capital seems to have dropped. There are now stone-crushing plants and cement factories, along with 7,000 miles of paved roads, in Nepal. The country's strategic location has made it an important target of China's Belt and Road Initiative and Western-funded development agencies, with the result, as Broughton Coburn reports, that Nepal is on a road-building spree, which seeks to create a paved, gravel, or dirt road connection "to every town and size-able settlement in the country." Nepal may now buy as much new construction equipment as any country in South Asia.[11]

Does this mean the hand-crushing days are over? Not at all. Hand stone breaking persists in Nepal, but rather than being performed by gangs of road con-struction workers *in situ*, it seems to have increasingly moved off specific sites and into houses and farms along waterways, where whole families pound stones into gravel under contract to Nepal's now-very-active gravel transporters. It may be that as road-building "normalized" in Nepal, unskilled stonework was pushed out to the margins of the formal economy.[12]

SELF-TEST 9.6

Suppose capital and labor are perfect complements in a one-to-one ratio. That is, suppose that $Q = \min(L, K)$. Currently, the wage is $w = 5$ and the rental rate is $r = 10$. What is the minimum cost and method of producing $Q = 20$ units of output? Suppose the wage rises to $w' = 20$. If we keep total cost the same, what level of output can now be produced and what method of production (input mix) is used?

---

[11]Broughton Coburn, "Nepal's Road-Building Spree Pushes into the Heart of the Himalayas," *Yale Environment 360*, January 2, 2020, https://e360.yale.edu/features/paving-the-himalayas-a-road-building-spree-rolls-over-nepal.
[12]See International Labor Organization, "Nepal: The Lives of Young Stone Crushers," June 1, 2006, www.ilo.org/ipec/Informationresources/WCMS_IPEC_PUB_4167/lang--en/index.htm. See also Siddharth Kara, "On the Trail of Human Trafficking: Stone Breaking Industry in Nepal," *CNN*, September 30, 2010, www.cnn.com/2010/WORLD/asiapcf/09/13/kara.nepal.stone.breaking.labor/index.html. Kara reports that a family can break around 200 kilograms of river stones a day, enough to earn about $0.70 plus an in-kind food payment. This would put the entire family below the official Nepal minimum wage of $74 a month.

SELF-TEST 9.7

Repeat the previous exercise but now suppose capital and labor are perfect substitutes in a one-to-one ratio: $Q = K + L$.

Economic Naturalist 9.2

Why do unions support minimum wage laws so strongly?

Why do union members, who earn substantially more than the minimum wage, favor increasing the minimum wage?

American labor unions have historically been among the most outspoken proponents of minimum wage legislation. They favor not only higher levels of the minimum wage, but also broader coverage. Yet almost all members of the Teamsters, AFL-CIO, or United Auto Workers unions already earn substantially more than the minimum wage, and so are not directly affected by changes in the legislation. Why, then, do these unions devote such great effort and expense to lobbying in favor of minimum wages?

One reason might be that their members are genuinely concerned about the economic well-being of workers less fortunate than themselves. No doubt many do feel such concern. But there are other disadvantaged groups—many of them even more deserving of help than low-wage workers—on whose behalf the unions might also have lobbied. Why doesn't the AFL-CIO work just as hard, for example, trying to get extra benefits for homeless children or for the physically handicapped?

An understanding of the condition for production at minimum cost helps answer these questions. Note first that, on the average, union workers tend to be more skilled than nonunion workers. Unskilled labor and skilled labor are substitutes for one another in many production processes, giving rise to isoquants shaped something like the one shown in Figure 9.14. What mix of the two skill categories the firm chooses to use will depend strongly on relative prices. Figure 9.14 shows the least costly mix for producing $Q = Q_0$ both before and after the enactment of the minimum wage statute. The wage rate for skilled labor is denoted by w. The prelegislation price of unskilled labor is w_1, which rises to w_2 after enactment of the law. The immediate effect is to increase the absolute value of the slope of the

FIGURE 9.14

The Effect of a Minimum Wage Law on Employment of Skilled Labor

Unskilled labor and skilled labor are substitutes for one another in many production processes. When the price of unskilled labor rises, the slope of the isocost line rises, causing many firms to increase their employment of skilled (unionized) labor.

isocost line from w_1/w to w_2/w, causing the firm to increase its employment of skilled labor from S_1 to S_2, simultaneously reducing its employment of unskilled (nonunion) labor from U_1 to U_2.

Although most union workers are not affected directly by the minimum wage laws, these laws have the indirect consequence of increasing the demand for union labor.[13] Even if unions lacked their avowed concern for the well-being of unskilled, largely nonunion workers, there would thus be little mystery why unions devote so much of their resources in support of extensions of minimum wage legislation.

Economic Naturalist 9.3

Why would a bathroom equipment manufacturer bake the image of a housefly onto the center of its ceramic urinals?

The substitution of capital for labor is sometimes motivated not by a change in factor prices, but by the introduction of new ideas. Consider, for example, the "official toilet project" initiated by Jos van Bedaf, then head manager of cleaning for the Schiphol airport in Amsterdam.[14] His problem was that the airport men's rooms, which were used by more than 100,000 patrons a year, had a tendency to become messy and smelly despite frequent cleanings. Mr. van Bedaf's solution was not to intensify the efforts of maintenance crews but to make a minor change in the restroom equipment. Specifically, he requested that his sanitation equipment manufacturer supply the airport with urinals with the image of a housefly baked onto the center of each fixture's glazed ceramic surface. His theory was that the presence of this target would cause patrons to be much more accurate in their use of the facilities. The result? Dramatically cleaner facilities and a 20 percent reduction in cleaning costs. A national newspaper in the Netherlands rated the Schiphol facilities first on a list of clean restrooms.

How does the image of a housefly reduce airport maintenance costs?

The Relationship between Optimal Input Choice and Long-Run Costs

Given sufficient time to adjust, the firm can always buy the cost-minimizing input bundle that corresponds to any particular output level and relative input prices. To see how the firm's costs vary with output in the long run, we need only compare the costs of the respective optimal input bundles.

The curve labeled EE in Figure 9.15 shows the firm's **output expansion path.** It is the set of cost-minimizing input bundles when the input price ratio is fixed at w/r. Thus, when the price of K is r and the price of L is w, the cheapest way to produce Q_1 units of output is to use the input bundle S, which contains K_1^* units of K, L_1^* units of L, and costs TC_1. The bundle S is therefore one point on the output expansion path. In like fashion, the output level Q_2 is associated with bundle T, which has a total cost of TC_2; Q_3 is associated with U, which costs TC_3; and so on. In the theory of firm behavior, the long-run expansion path is the analog to the income-consumption curve in the theory of the consumer.

To go from the long-run expansion path to the long-run total cost curve, we simply plot the relevant quantity-cost pairs from Figure 9.15. Thus, the output level Q_1 corresponds to a

output expansion path the locus of tangencies (minimum-cost input combinations) traced out by an isocost line of given slope as it shifts outward into the isoquant map for a production process.

[13]Note that this example assumes that the firm will produce the same level of output after the minimum wage hike as before. As we will see in the next chapter, however, the firm will generally produce less output than before. If the output reduction is large enough, it could offset the firm's switch to skilled labor.
[14]This example is based on Stefan Verhagen, "Fly in the Pot," *Cornell Business*, April 21, 1992.

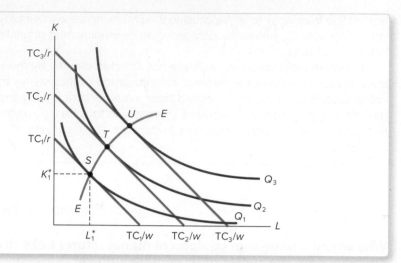

FIGURE 9.15

The Long-Run Expansion Path

With fixed input prices r and w, bundles S, T, U, and others along the locus EE represent the least costly ways of producing the corresponding levels of output

long-run total cost of TC_1, Q_2 to TC_2, and so on. The result is the curve labeled LTC in the top panel in Figure 9.16. In the long run there is no need to distinguish among total, fixed, and variable costs, since all costs are variable.

The LTC curve will always pass through the origin because in the long run the firm can liquidate all of its inputs. If the firm elects to produce no output, it need not retain, or pay for, the services of any of its inputs. The shape of the LTC curve shown in the top panel looks very much like that of the short-run total cost curve shown in Figure 9.2. But this need not always be the case, as we will presently see. For the moment, though, let us take the shape of the LTC curve in the top panel in Figure 9.16 as given and ask what it implies for the long-run average and marginal cost curves.

Analogously to the short-run case, long-run marginal cost (LMC) is the slope of the long-run total cost curve:

$$LMC_Q = \frac{\Delta LTC_Q}{\Delta Q}.$$ (9.23)

In words, LMC is the cost to the firm, in the long run, of expanding its output by 1 unit.

FIGURE 9.16

The Long-Run Total, Average, and Marginal Cost Curves

In the long run, the firm always has the option of ceasing operations and ridding itself of all its inputs. This means that the long-run total cost curve (top panel) will always pass through the origin. The long-run average and long-run marginal cost curves (bottom panel) are derived from the long-run total cost curves in a manner completely analogous to the short-run case.

FIGURE 9.17

The LTC, LMC, and LAC Curves with Constant Returns to Scale

(*a*) With constant returns, long-run total cost is strictly proportional to output. (*b*) Long-run marginal cost is constant and equal to long-run average cost.

Long-run average cost (LAC) is the ratio of long-run total cost to output:

$$LAC_Q = \frac{LTC_Q}{Q}. \tag{9.24}$$

Again, there is no need to discuss the distinctions among average total, fixed, and variable costs, since all long-run costs are variable.

The bottom panel in Figure 9.16 shows the LAC and LMC curves that correspond to the LTC curve shown in the top panel. The slope of the LTC curve is diminishing up to the output level Q_1 and increasing thereafter, which means that the LMC curve takes its minimum value at Q_1. The slope of LTC and the slope of the ray to LTC are the same at Q_3, which means that LAC and LMC intersect at that level of output. And again as before, the traditional average-marginal relationship holds: LAC is declining whenever LMC lies below it, and rising whenever LMC lies above it.

For a constant returns to scale production function, doubling output exactly doubles costs.[15] Tripling all inputs triples output and triples costs, and so on. For the case of constant returns to scale, long-run total costs are thus exactly proportional to output. As shown in Figure 9.17*a*, the LTC curve for a production function with constant returns to scale is a straight line through the origin. Because the slope of LTC is constant, the associated LMC curve is a horizontal line, and is exactly the same as the LAC curve (Figure 9.17*b*).

When the production function has decreasing returns to scale, a given proportional increase in output requires a greater proportional increase in all inputs and hence a greater proportional increase in costs. The LTC, LMC, and LAC curves for a production function with decreasing returns to scale are shown in Figure 9.18. For the particular LTC curve shown in Figure 9.18*a*, the associated LAC and LMC curves happen to be linear (Figure 9.18*b*), but this need not always happen. The general property of the decreasing returns case is that it gives rise to an upward-curving LTC curve and upward-sloping

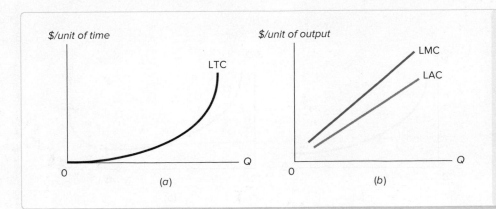

FIGURE 9.18

The LTC, LAC, and LMC Curves for a Production Process with Decreasing Returns to Scale

Under decreasing returns, output grows less than in proportion to the growth in inputs, which means that total cost grows more than in proportion to growth in output.

---

[15]Assuming, of course, that input prices remain the same as output varies.

FIGURE 9.19

The LTC, LAC, and LMC Curves for a Production Process with Increasing Returns to Scale

With increasing returns, the large-scale firm has lower average and marginal costs than the smaller-scale firm.

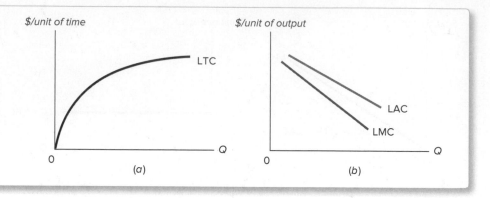

LAC and LMC curves. Note yet another application of the average-marginal relationship: the fact that LMC exceeds LAC ensures that LAC must rise with output.

Consider, finally, the case of increasing returns to scale. Here, output grows more than in proportion to the increase in inputs. In consequence, long-run total cost rises less than in proportion to increases in output, as shown in Figure 9.19*a*. The accompanying LAC and LMC curves are shown in Figure 9.19*b*. The distinguishing feature of the LAC and LMC curves under increasing returns to scale is not the linear form shown in this particular example, but the fact that they are downward-sloping.

The production processes whose long-run cost curves are pictured in Figures 9.17, 9.18, and 9.19 are "pure cases," exhibiting constant, decreasing, and increasing returns to scale, respectively, over their entire ranges of output. As discussed in Chapter 8, however, the degree of returns to scale of a production function need not be the same over the whole range of output.

LONG-RUN COSTS AND THE STRUCTURE OF INDUSTRY

As noted in the preview to this chapter, long-run costs are important because of their effect on the structure of industry. A detailed elaboration of this role will be the subject of the coming chapters. Here, a brief overview of the key issues will help set the stage for that discussion.

When, as in Figure 9.20*a*, there are declining long-run average costs throughout, the tendency will be for a single firm to serve the market. If two firms attempted to serve such a market, with each producing only part of the total output sold, each would have higher average costs than if one of them alone served the market. The tendency in such a market will be for the firm that happens to grow larger to have a cost advantage that

FIGURE 9.20

LAC Curves Characteristic of Highly Concentrated Industrial Structures

(*a*) LAC curves that slope downward throughout tend to be characteristic of natural monopolies. Unit costs are lowest when only one firm serves the entire market.
(*b*) U-shaped LAC curves whose minimum points occur at a substantial share of total market output are characteristic of markets served by only a small handful of firms.

FIGURE 9.21

LAC Curves Characteristic of Unconcentrated Industry Structures

The requirement for survival in any market is that a firm have the lowest possible unit costs. If the minimum point of a U-shaped LAC (Q_0 in panel *a*) occurs at a small fraction of market output, or if LAC is everywhere flat or rising (panels *b* and *c*, respectively), then small size and survival are compatible. Each firm will tend to produce only a small share of total market output.

enables it to eliminate its rival. Markets characterized by declining long-run average cost curves are for this reason often referred to as **natural monopolies.**

Consider now the LAC curve shown in Figure 9.20*b*. The minimum point on this curve occurs at the output level Q_0. At that output level, the firm achieves its lowest possible unit cost of production. The output level Q_0 may be called the *minimum efficient scale:* the level of production required for LAC to reach its minimum level. If Q_0 constitutes a substantial share of industry output—more than, say, 20 percent—the industry will tend to be dominated by a small handful of firms. As in the natural monopoly case, a large number of small firms would be unlikely to survive in such a market, since each would have much higher average costs than larger firms. By contrast to the natural monopoly case, however, the upturn in the LAC beyond Q_0 will make it difficult for a single firm to serve the entire market. Markets served by firms with LAC's like the one in Figure 9.20*b* are likely to be "highly concentrated," which means that a small number of firms will tend to account for the lion's share of all output sold.

The long-run average cost curve associated with a market served by many firms is likely to take one of the three forms shown in Figure 9.21. If Q_0, the minimum point on the U-shaped average cost curve in panel *a,* constitutes only a small fraction of total industry output, we expect to see an industry populated by numerous firms, each of which produces only a small percentage of total industry output. Small size is also not a disadvantage when the production process is one that gives rise to a horizontal LAC curve like the one shown in panel *b*. For such processes, all firms—large or small—have the same unit costs of production. For the upward-sloping LAC curve shown in panel *c* in Figure 9.21, small size is not only compatible with survival in the marketplace but positively required, since large firms will always have higher average costs than smaller ones. As a practical matter, however, it is very unlikely that there could ever be an LAC curve that is upward-sloping even at extremely small levels of output. (Imagine, for example, the unit costs of a firm that tried to produce $\frac{1}{100}$ of a pound of sugar.)

The relationship between market structure and the shape of the long-run average cost curve derives from the fact that, in the face of competition, market survival requires firms to have the lowest unit costs possible under existing production technology. Whether that happens at low or high levels of output depends entirely on the shape of the LAC curve.

natural monopoly an industry whose market output is produced at the lowest cost when production is concentrated in the hands of a single firm.

The Relationship between Long-Run and Short-Run Cost Curves

One way of thinking of the LAC curve is as an "envelope" of all the short-run average total cost (ATC) curves. Suppose the ATC curves that correspond to 10,000 different levels of *K* were drawn in a diagram like Figure 9.22. If we then took a string and molded

FIGURE 9.22

The Family of Cost Curves Associated with a U-Shaped LAC

The LAC curve is the "outer envelope" of the ATC curves. LMC = SMC at the Q value for which the ATC is tangent to the LAC. At the minimum point on the LAC, LMC = SMC = ATC = LAC.

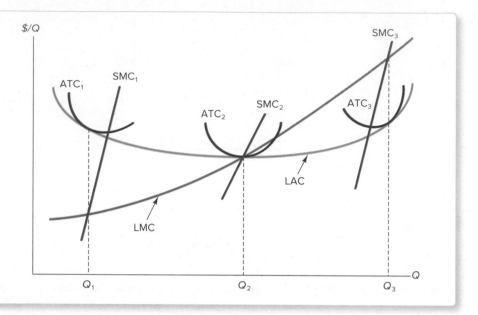

it to the outer contour of these ATC curves, it would trace out the shape of the LAC curve. In Figure 9.22, note that for the output level at which a given ATC is tangent to the LAC, the long-run marginal cost (LMC) of producing that level of output is the same as the short-run marginal cost (SMC). Thus, $LMC(Q_1) = SMC(Q_1)$, $LMC(Q_2) = SMC(Q_2)$, and $LMC(Q_3) = SMC(Q_3)$.[16] Note also that each point along a given ATC curve, except for the tangency point, lies above the corresponding point on the LAC curve. Note, finally, that at the minimum point on the LAC curve in Figure 9.22 ($Q = Q_2$), the long-run and short-run marginal and average costs all take exactly the same value.

Some intuition about the ATC-LAC relationship for a given ATC curve is afforded by noting that to the left of the ATC-LAC tangency, the firm has "too much" capital, with the result that its fixed costs are higher than necessary; and that to the right of the tangency, the firm has "too little" capital, so that diminishing returns to labor drive its costs up. Only at the tangency point does the firm have the optimal quantities of both labor and capital for producing the corresponding level of output.

The appendix to this chapter considers the relationship between long-run and short-run costs in greater detail. It also develops the calculus approach to cost minimization.

SUMMARY

- Of all the topics covered in an intermediate microeconomics text, students usually find the material on cost curves by far the most difficult to digest. And for good reason, since the sheer volume of specific concepts can easily seem overwhelming at first encounter. It is important to bear in mind, therefore, that all the various cost curves can be derived from the underlying production relationships in a simple and straightforward manner. *(LO1, LO2)*

- Short-run cost curves, for example, all follow directly from the short-run production function. All short-run production functions we have discussed involved one fixed factor and one variable factor, but the theory would be exactly the same in the case of more than one fixed input.

Short-run total costs are decomposed into fixed and variable costs, which correspond, respectively, to payments to the fixed and variable factors of production. Because of the law of diminishing returns, beyond some point we require ever larger increments of the variable input to produce an extra unit of output. The result is that short-run marginal cost, which is the slope of the short-run total cost curve, is increasing with output in the region of diminishing returns. Diminishing returns are also responsible for the fact that short-run average total and variable cost curves—which are, respectively, the slopes of the rays to the short-run total and variable cost curves—eventually rise with output. Average fixed costs always take

[16]These relationships are developed in greater detail in the appendix to this chapter.

the form of a rectangular hyperbola, approaching infinity as output shrinks toward zero, and falling toward zero as output grows increasingly large. *(LO2, LO3)*

- The problem of allocating a given production quota to two different production facilities is similar to the problem of allocating an available input across two different facilities. In the latter case, the goal is to maximize the amount of output that can be produced with a given amount of input. In the former, it is to produce a given level of output at the lowest total cost. The solution is to allocate the production quota so that the marginal cost is the same in each production process. This solution does not require that average costs be the same in each process, and in practice, they often differ substantially. *(LO4)*

- The optimal input bundle for producing a given output level in the long run will depend on the relative prices of the factors of production. These relative prices determine the slope of the isocost line, which is the locus of input bundles that can be purchased for a given total cost. The optimal input bundle will be the one that lies at the point of tangency between an isocost line and the desired isoquant. At the cost-minimizing point, the ratio of the marginal product of an input to its price will be the same for every input. Put another way, the extra output obtained from the last dollar spent on one input must be the same as the extra output obtained from the last dollar spent on any other input. Still another way of stating the minimum-cost condition is that the marginal rate of technical substitution at the optimizing bundle must be the same as the slope of the isocost line. *(LO6)*

- These properties of production at minimum cost help us understand why methods of production often differ sharply when relative factor prices differ sharply. We saw, for example, that it helps explain why developing countries often use labor-intensive techniques while their industrial counterparts choose much more capital-intensive

ones, and why labor unions often lobby on behalf of increased minimum wages, even though virtually all of their members earn more than the minimum wage to begin with. *(LO6)*

- For a given level of output, long-run total costs can never be larger than short-run total costs for the simple reason that we have the opportunity to adjust all inputs in the long run, only some of them in the short run. The slope of the long-run average cost curve is a direct reflection of the degree of returns to scale in production. When there are increasing returns, LAC declines with output. With decreasing returns, by contrast, LAC rises with output. And finally, constant returns in production give rise to a horizontal LAC. A U-shaped LAC is one that corresponds to a production process that exhibits first increasing, then constant, and finally decreasing returns to scale. No matter what its shape, the LAC curve will always be an envelope of the corresponding family of ATC curves, each of which will be tangent to the LAC at one and only one point. At the output levels that correspond to these points of tangency, LMC and the corresponding SMC will be the same. *(LO7)*

- The relationship between market structure and long-run costs derives from the fact that survival in the marketplace requires firms to have the lowest costs possible with available production technologies. If the LAC curve is downward-sloping, lowest costs occur when only one firm serves the market. If the LAC curve is U-shaped and its minimum point occurs at a quantity that corresponds to a substantial share of total market output, the lowest costs will occur when only a few firms serve the market. By contrast, if the minimum point on a U-shaped LAC curve corresponds to only a small fraction of total industry output, the market is likely to be served by many competing firms. The same will be true when the LAC curve is either horizontal or upward-sloping. *(LO7)*

KEY TERMS

average fixed cost (AFC)	isocost line	total cost (TC)
average total cost (ATC)	marginal cost (MC)	variable cost (VC)
average variable cost (AVC)	natural monopoly	
fixed cost (FC)	output expansion path	

REVIEW QUESTIONS

1. What is the relationship between the law of diminishing returns and the curvature of the variable cost curve? *(LO1)*

2. What is the relationship between the law of diminishing returns and the slope of the short-run marginal cost curve? *(LO2)*

3. In which production process is fixed cost likely to be a larger percentage of short-run total costs, book publishing or landscape gardening? *(LO1)*

4. Why does the short-run MC curve cut both the ATC and AVC curves at their minimum points? *(LO3)*

5. If the LAC curve is rising beyond some point, what can we say about the degree of returns to scale in production? *(LO7)*

6. Why should the production of a fixed amount of output be allocated between two production activities so that the marginal cost is the same in each? *(LO4)*

PROBLEMS

1. The Preservation Embalming Company's cost data have been partially entered in the table below. Following the sudden and unexpected death of the company's accountant, you are called on to fill in the missing entries. *(LO3)*

Bodies embalmed	Total cost	Fixed cost	Variable cost	ATC	AVC	AFC	MC
0	24			–	–	–	
1							16
2			50				
3	108						
4							52
5					39.2		
6					47		

2. Sketch the short-run TC, VC, FC, ATC, AVC, AFC, and MC curves for the production function *(LO3)*

$$Q = 3KL,$$

where K is fixed at 2 units in the short run, with $r = 3$ and $w = 2$.

3. When the average product of labor is the same as the marginal product of labor, how will marginal cost compare with average variable cost? *(LO3)*

4. A firm has access to two production processes with the following marginal cost curves: $MC_1 = 0.4Q$ and $MC_2 = 2 + 0.2Q$. *(LO4)*
   a. If it wants to produce 8 units of output, how much should it produce with each process?
   b. If it wants to produce 4 units of output?

5. A firm uses two inputs, K and L, in its production process and finds that no matter how much output it produces or how input prices vary, it always minimizes its costs by buying only one or the other of the two inputs. Draw this firm's isoquant map. *(LO6)*

6. A firm finds that no matter how much output it produces and no matter how input prices vary, it always minimizes its costs by buying half as many units of capital as of labor. Draw this firm's isoquant map. *(LO6)*

7. A firm purchases capital and labor in competitive markets at prices of $r = 6$ and $w = 4$, respectively. With the firm's current input mix, the marginal product of capital is 12 and the marginal product of labor is 18. Is this firm minimizing its costs? If so, explain how you know. If not, explain what the firm ought to do. *(LO6)*

8. A firm has a production function $Q = F(K, L)$ with constant returns to scale. Input prices are $r = 2$ and $w = 1$. The output-expansion path for this production function at these input prices is a straight line through the origin. When it produces 5 units of output, it uses 2 units of K and 3 units of L. How much K and L will it use when its long-run total cost is equal to 70? *(LO7)*

9. A firm with the production function $Q = F(K, L)$ is producing an output level Q^* at minimum cost in the long run. How will its short-run marginal cost when K is fixed compare with its short-run marginal cost when L is fixed? *(LO6)*

10. A firm employs a production function $Q = F(K, L)$ for which only two values of K are possible, K_1 and K_2. Its ATC curve when $K = K_1$ is given by $ATC_1 = Q^2 - 4Q + 6$. The corresponding curve for $K = K_2$ is $ATC_2 = Q^2 - 8Q + 18$. What is this firm's LAC curve? *(LO7)*

11. If a firm's LMC curve lies above its SMC curve at a given level of output, what will be the relationship between its ATC and LAC curves at that output level? *(LO7)*

12.* A firm has a long-run total cost function:

$$LTC(Q) = Q^3 - 20Q^2 + 220Q.$$

Derive expressions for long-run average cost and marginal cost, and sketch these curves. *(LO7)*

13.* For the long-run total cost function

$$LTC(Q) = Q^2 + 10,$$

sketch ATC, AVC, AFC, and MC. *(LO7)*

*These problems are most easily solved using the calculus definition of marginal cost.

ANSWERS TO SELF-TESTS

9.1 The variable cost curve is the same as before; the FC and TC curves are shifted upward by 8 units. (See the following graph.) *(LO1)*

9.2 The vertical distance between the ATC and AVC curves is AFC. So we have $\text{ATC}_{10} - \text{AVC}_{10} = \text{FC}/10 = 20/10 = 2$. *(LO1)*

9.3 Equating marginal costs, we have $12Q^A = 4Q^B$. Substituting $Q^B = 12 - Q^A$ yields $12Q^A = 48 - 4Q^A$, which solves for $Q^A = 3$. $Q^B = 12 - 3 = 9$ takes care of remaining output, and at these output levels, marginal cost in both plants will be \$36/unit of output. *(LO4)*

9.4 When marginal product lies above average product, marginal cost lies below average variable cost. (See Figure 9.9.) *(LO5)*

9.5

9.6 To produce 20 units of output, we will need $L = K = 20$. As $r = 10$ and $w = 5$, costs are

$$C = 10K + 5L = 200 + 100 = 300,$$

which may be rewritten as $K = 30 - \frac{1}{2}L$ in slope-intercept form. When the wage rises to $w = 20$, keeping costs at $C = 300$ requires that we find the point at which $K = L$ on the new isocost curve

$$C = 10K + 20L = 300,$$

which may be rewritten as $K = 30 - 2L$ in slope-intercept form. Setting $K = L$, we have

$$10K + 20L = 300 = 10L + 20L = 300 = 30L = 300, \text{ so } L = 10.$$

Thus, $L = K = 10$ and we produce $Q = 10$. *(LO6)*

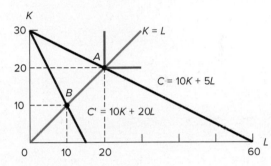

9.7 To produce 20 units of output, we will need $L = 20$ or $K = 20$. Since $r = 10$ and $w = 5$, costs are

$$C = \min\{10K, 5L\} = \min\{200, 100\} = 100.$$

When the wage rises to $w = 20$, keeping costs at $C = 100$ implies that

$$Q = \max\left\{ \frac{100}{r}, \frac{100}{w} \right\} = \max\{10, 5\} = 10.$$

Thus, we use no labor ($L = 0$), all capital ($K = 10$), and produce $Q = 10$. *(LO6)*

Mathematical Extensions of the Theory of Costs

THE RELATIONSHIP BETWEEN LONG-RUN AND SHORT-RUN COST CURVES

Let us consider first in greater detail the relationship between long- and short-run total costs. Recall that the LTC curve is generated by plotting the Q value for a given isoquant against the corresponding total cost level for the isocost line tangent to that isoquant. Thus, for example, in Figure 9A.1, $Q = 1$ is associated with a long-run total cost of LTC_1, $Q = 2$ with LTC_2, and so on.

When K is variable, as it and all other factors are in the long run, the expansion path is given by the line $0E$. Now suppose, however, that K is fixed at K_2^*, the level that is optimal for the production of $Q = 2$. The short-run expansion path will then be the horizontal line through the point $(0, K_2^*)$, which includes the input bundles X, T, and Z. The short-run total cost of producing a given level of output—say, $Q = 1$—is simply the total cost

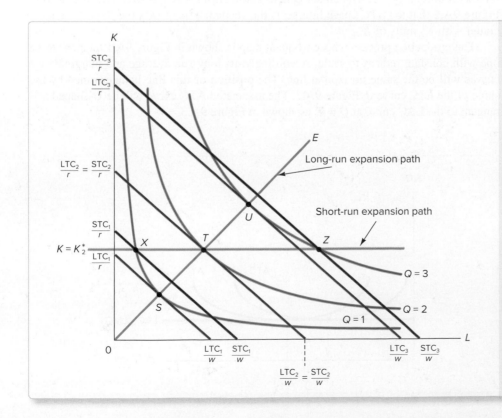

FIGURE 9A.1

The Short-Run and Long-Run Expansion Paths

The long-run expansion path is the line of $0E$. With K fixed at K_2^*, the short-run expansion path is a horizontal line through the point $(0, K_2^*)$. Because K_2^*, is the optimal amount of K for producing 2 units of output, the long-run and short-run expansion paths intersect at T. The short-run total cost of producing a given level of output is the cost associated with the isocost line that passes through the intersection of the relevant isoquant and the short-run expansion path. Thus, for example, STC_3 is the short-run total cost of producing 3 units of output.

FIGURE 9A.2

The LTC and STC Curves Associated with the Isoquant Map in Figure 9A.1

As Q approaches 2, the level of output for which the fixed factor is at its optimal level, STC_Q approaches LTC_Q. The two curves are tangent at $Q = 2$.

associated with the isocost line that passes through the intersection of the short-run expansion path and the $Q = 1$ isoquant (point X in Figure 9A.1), namely, STC_1.

Note in Figure 9A.1 that short- and long-run total costs take the same value for $Q = 2$, the output level for which the short- and long-run expansion paths cross. For all other output levels, the isocost line that passes through the intersection of the corresponding isoquant and the short-run expansion path will lie above the isocost line that is tangent to the isoquant. Thus, for all output levels other than $Q = 2$, short-run total cost will be higher than long-run total cost.

The short- and long-run total cost curves that correspond to the isoquant map of Figure 9A.1 are shown in Figure 9A.2. Note in Figure 9A.1 that the closer output is to $Q = 2$, the smaller the difference will be between long-run and short-run total cost. This property is reflected in Figure 9A.2 by the fact that the STC curve is tangent to the LTC curve at $Q = 2$: The closer Q is to 2, the closer STC_Q is to STC_2. Note also in Figure 9A.2 that the STC curve intersects the vertical axis at rK_2^*, the fixed cost associated with K_2^* units of K.

The production process whose isoquant map is shown in Figure 9A.1 happens to be one with constant returns to scale. Accordingly, its long-run average and marginal cost curves will be the same horizontal line. The position of this line is determined by the slope of the LTC curve in Figure 9A.2. The associated ATC curve will be U-shaped and tangent to the LAC curve at $Q = 2$, as shown in Figure 9A.3.

FIGURE 9A.3

The LAC, LMC, and Two ATC Curves Associated with the Cost Curves from Figure 9A.2

Short-run average cost is tangent to long-run average cost at the same output level for which the corresponding LTC and STC curves are tangent.

FIGURE 9A.4

The Family of Cost Curves Associated with a U-Shaped LAC

The LAC curve is the "outer envelope" of the ATC curves, LMC = SMC at the Q value for which the ATC is tangent to the LAC. At the minimum point on the LAC, LMC = SMC = ATC = LAC.

There are short-run cost curves not just for $K = K_2^*$, but for every other level of the fixed input as well. For example, the short-run average cost curve when K is fixed at K_3^* (the optimal amount of K for producing $Q = 3$) is shown in Figure 9A.3 as the curve labeled $ATC_{K=K_3^*}$. Like the ATC curve associated with K_2^*, it too is U-shaped, and is tangent to the LAC curve at $Q = 3$. The ATC curves will in general be U-shaped and tangent to the LAC curve at the output level for which the level of the fixed input happens to be optimal.

A similar relationship exists in the case of production processes that give rise to U-shaped LAC curves. For such a process, the LAC curve and three of its associated ATC curves are shown in Figure 9A.4. When the LAC curve is U-shaped, note that the tangencies between it and the associated ATC curves do not in general occur at the minimum points on the ATC curves. The lone exception is the ATC curve that is tangent to the minimum point of the U-shaped LAC (ATC_2 in Figure 9A.4). On the downward-sloping portion of the LAC curve, the tangencies will lie to the left of the minimum points of the corresponding ATC curves; and on the upward-sloping portion of the LAC curve, the tangencies will lie to the right of the minimum points.

In the text, we noted that one way of thinking of the LAC curve is as an "envelope" of all the ATC curves, like the one shown in Figure 9A.4. At the output level at which a given ATC is tangent to the LAC, the long-run marginal cost (LMC) of producing that level of output is the same as the short-run marginal cost (SMC). To see why this is so, recall that the tangency point represents the quantity level that is optimal for the fixed factor level that corresponds to the particular ATC curve. If we change output by a very small amount in the short run—by either increasing or reducing the amount of the variable input—we will end up with an input mix that is only marginally different from the optimal one, and whose cost is therefore approximately the same as that of the optimal mix. Accordingly, for output levels very near the relevant tangency point, SMC and LMC are approximately the same.

Note also in Figure 9A.4 that the SMC curves are always steeper than the LMC curve. The reason is implicit in our discussion of why LMC and SMC are nearly the same in a neighborhood of the tangency points. Starting at a tangency point—say, at Q_1 in Figure 9A.4—suppose we want to produce an extra unit of output in the short run. To do so, we will have to move from an input mix that is optimal to one that contains slightly more L and slightly less K than would be optimal for producing $Q_1 + 1$ in the long run. So the cost of that extra unit will be higher in the short run than in the long run, which is another way of saying $SMC_{Q_1+1} > LMC_{Q_1+1}$.

Now suppose that we start at Q_1 and want to produce 1 unit of output less than before. To do so, we will have to move to an input bundle that contains less L and more K than would be optimal for producing $Q_1 - 1$. In consequence, our cost savings will be smaller in the short run than they would be in the long run, when we are free to adjust both L and K. This tells us that $LMC_{Q_1-1} > SMC_{Q_1+1}$. To say that LMC exceeds SMC whenever output is less than Q_1, but is less than SMC when output is greater than Q_1, is the same thing as saying that the LMC curve is less steep than the SMC curve at Q_1.

SELF-TEST 9A.1

Consider a production function $Q = F(K, L)$ for which only two values of K are possible. These two values of K give rise to the ATC curves shown in the diagram. What is the LAC curve for this firm?

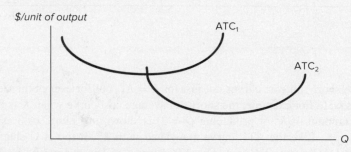

THE CALCULUS APPROACH TO COST MINIMIZATION

Using the Lagrangian technique discussed in the appendix to Chapter 3, we can show that the equality of MP/P ratios (Equation 9.22 in Chapter 9) emerges as a necessary condition for the following cost-minimization problem:

$$\min_{K, L} P_K K + P_L L \qquad \text{subject to } F(K, L) = Q_0. \tag{9A.1}$$

To find the values of K and L that minimize costs, we first form the Lagrangian expression:

$$\pounds = P_K K + P_L L + \lambda[F(K, L) - Q_0]. \tag{9A.2}$$

The first-order condition for a minimum is given by

$$\frac{\partial \pounds}{\partial K} = P_K + \frac{\lambda \partial F}{\partial K} = 0, \tag{9A.3}$$

$$\frac{\partial \pounds}{\partial L} = P_L + \frac{\lambda \partial F}{\partial L} = 0, \tag{9A.4}$$

and

$$\frac{\partial \pounds}{\partial \lambda} = F(K, L) - Q_0 = 0. \tag{9A.5}$$

Dividing Equation 9A.3 by Equation 9A.4 and rearranging terms, we have

$$\frac{\partial F / \partial K}{P_K} = \frac{\partial F / \partial L}{P_L}, \tag{9A.6}$$

which is the result of Equation 9.21 in Chapter 9. (As an exercise, derive the same result by finding the first-order conditions for a maximum level of output subject to a cost limit of *C*.)

An alternative to the Lagrangian technique is to solve the production function constraint in Equation 9A.1 for *K* in terms of *L*, then substitute the result back into the expression for total cost. To illustrate this alternative approach, consider the following example.

EXAMPLE 9A.1

For the production function $Q = F(K, L) = \sqrt{K}\sqrt{L}$ with $P_K = 4$ and $P_L = 2$, find the values of K and L that minimize the cost of producing 2 units of output.

Our problem here is to minimize $4K + 2L$ subject to $F(K, L) = \sqrt{K}\sqrt{L} = 2$. Here the production function constraint is $Q = 2 = \sqrt{K}\sqrt{L}$, which yields $K = 4/L$. So our problem is to minimize $4(4/L) + 2L$ with respect to L. The first-order condition for a minimum is given by

$$\frac{d[(16/L) + 2L]}{dL} = 2 - \frac{16}{L^2} = 0, \tag{9A.7}$$

which yields $L = 2\sqrt{2}$. Substituting back into the production function constraint, we have $K = 4/(2\sqrt{2}) = \sqrt{2}$.

PROBLEMS

Mc Graw Hill connect

1. A firm produces output with the production function

$$Q = \sqrt{K}\sqrt{L},$$

where *K* and *L* denote its capital and labor inputs, respectively. If the price of labor is 1 and the price of capital is 4, what quantities of capital and labor should it employ if its goal is to produce 2 units of output?

2. Sketch LTC, LAC, and LMC curves for the production function given in Problem 2. Does this production function have constant, increasing, or decreasing returns to scale?

3. Suppose that a firm has the following production function:

$$Q(K, L) = 2L\sqrt{K}.$$

   a. If the price of labor is 2 and the price of capital is 4, what is the optimal ratio of capital to labor?
   b. For an output level of $Q = 1,000$, how much of each input will be used?

4. A firm with the production function

$$Q(K, L) = 2L\sqrt{KL}$$

is currently utilizing 8 units of labor and 2 units of capital. If this is the optimal input mix, and if total costs are equal to 16, what are the prices of capital and labor?

5. For a firm with the production function

$$Q(K, L) = 3 \ln K + 2 \ln L,$$

find the optimal ratio of capital to labor if the price of capital is 4 and the price of labor is 6.

ANSWERS TO APPENDIX SELF-TEST

9A.1 The LAC curve (bottom panel) is the outer envelope of the two ATC curves (top panel).

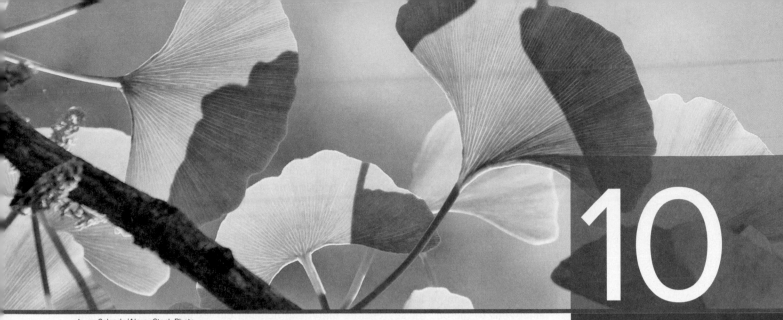

Perfect Competition

Imagine yourself a member of the Colorado state legislature. You have been asked to vote for a bill whose purpose is to alleviate poverty among farmers in a rural county. Farmers in that county rent their farmland from landowners and are allowed to keep the proceeds from the sale of the crops they grow. Because of limited rainfall, their crops are usually meager, resulting in very low incomes for the average worker. The bill under consideration would authorize public funds to construct an irrigation system that would double the crop yields on the land in the county.

You strongly favor the objective of the bill and are about to vote in favor of it when you meet with your legislative aide, an intern who majored in economics in college. She urges you in the strongest possible terms not to vote for the bill. She concedes that the project would double crop yields, and she too is sympathetic to the goal of providing improved conditions for farmers. Even so, she insists that the bill would have little or no long-run effect on the earnings of farmers. Your aide has given you sound advice on similar matters in the past, and you decide to hear her out.

CHAPTER PREVIEW

In this chapter, we'll develop the analytical tools necessary for our hypothetical state legislator to assess his aide's advice, including a model of price and output determination in perfectly competitive markets. We will begin with two provocative and seemingly contradictory assertions. The first is the competitive firm's objective is to earn the highest possible profit. The second is that under conditions of perfect competition firms earn no economic profit at all. To reconcile these claims, we will provide a definition of "economic profit" and explain how this concept differs from the accounting profits that are predicted by stock market analysts and reported by companies on quarterly and annual statements.

Profit maximization is clearly not the only goal a firm might pursue, but we'll discuss what profit includes in a behavioral sense and list several reasons firms might often behave as if profit was all they cared about. Just as we saw in our discussion of consumer choice, it simplifies the theory considerably to define firms as motivated by a single, clear goal.

We'll then consider the four conditions that define a perfectly competitive market: (1) the existence of a standardized product, (2) price-taking behavior on the part of firms, (3) perfect long-run mobility of factors of production, and (4) perfect information on the part of consumers and firms. We'll see that this highly simplified model often generates useful insights even when its structural preconditions are only approximately satisfied.

Having put the basic theoretical mechanisms in place, we'll derive the necessary condition for profit maximization in the short run, using the cost curves discussed in Chapter 9. The rule calls for the firm to produce an output level at which its short-run marginal cost is equal to the price of the product. We'll see that implementation of this rule fortunately does not require that firms have a detailed understanding of the economist's concept of marginal cost.

From the individual firm's supply decision, we'll move to the issue of industry wide supply. The technique for generating the industry supply schedule turns out to be closely analogous to the one for aggregating individual demand curves into a market demand curve: We simply add the individual firms' supply curves horizontally.

The industry short-run supply and demand curves interact to determine the short-run market price, which forms the basis for output decisions by individual firms. We'll see that a firm's short-run profitability acts as a signal governing the movement of resources into and out of the industry—more specifically, that profits prompt resources to enter while losses prompt them to leave.

We'll see that in the long run, if tastes and technology are unchanging, a competitive industry whose firms have U-shaped LAC curves will settle at an equilibrium price equal to the minimum value of the LAC curve. And we'll also see that, under certain conditions, it will not be possible in such a market for anyone to enter into additional transactions that would benefit some people without at the same time harming some others. One of the attractions of perfect competition is that the theory allows us to imagine the point at which, if we desire to change outcomes, we *must* turn from the question of how to enlarge the pie to the question of how to slice it.

THE GOAL OF PROFIT MAXIMIZATION

In taking up not only perfect competition but also a variety of other market structures, standard economic theory assumes that the firm's central objective is to maximize profit. Two things must be said about this assumption. The first is to clarify just what is meant by the term *profit*, and the second is to explain why it makes sense to assume that firms try to maximize it.

Profit—or, more precisely, *economic profit*—is defined as the difference between total revenue and total cost, where total cost includes all costs—both explicit and implicit—associated with resources used by the firm. This definition is significantly different from the one used by accountants and most noneconomists, which does not subtract opportunity or implicit costs from total revenue. *Accounting profit* is simply total revenue less all explicit costs incurred.

To illustrate the distinction, suppose a firm produces 100 units of output per week by using 10 units of capital and 10 units of labor. Suppose the weekly price of each factor is $10/unit and the firm *owns* rather than rents its 10 units of capital. If output sells for $2.50/unit, the firm's total revenue will be $250/wk.

To calculate the week's economic profit, we subtract from $250 the $100 spent on labor (an explicit cost) and the $100 opportunity cost of capital (an implicit cost), which leaves $50. The assumption here is that the firm could have rented its capital to some other firm at the weekly rate of $10/unit. The $100 opportunity cost is simply the earnings forgone by using the capital in its own operation. This reckoning of the opportunity cost of capital is critical, as we shall see, to the definition of perfect competition.

Now, note that, by contrast, the week's *accounting* profit for this firm is $150, the difference between the $250 total revenue and the $100 out-of-pocket expenditure for labor. Had the firm needed to rent its required 10 units of capital, its accounting and economic profits for the week would have been the same. Accounting profit may be thought

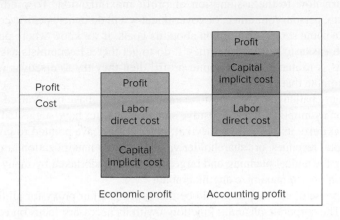

FIGURE 10.1

Economic vs. Accounting
Profit

of as the sum of two components: (1) "normal" profit, which is the implicit or opportunity cost of the resources owned by the firm (in this example, $100), and (2) economic profit, as defined above (here, $50). Economic profit is profit over and above the normal profit level. Figure 10.1 and Example 10.1 explore the differences between this firm's economic and accounting profit.

EXAMPLE 10.1   Economic vs. Accounting Profits

Using our earlier illustration, suppose a firm produces 100 units of output per week by using 10 units of capital and 10 units of labor. The weekly price of each factor is $10/unit, and the output sells for $2.50/unit. Now suppose that the firm owns half of its capital and rents its other 5 units of capital. What would be the firm's economic and accounting profit for the week?

What has changed is that we now have two capital costs items, one implicit and one direct, at $50 each. Previously, as you can see from Figure 10.1, all the capital costs were "above the line" as part of the profit number, now $50 will be "below the line," as part of the direct cost deduction. The result is that our accounting profit calculation is $250 of revenue, less $100 of labor cost and $50 of capital cost, for an accounting profit of $100. That is $50 less than before.

   What happens to the economic profit calculation? Nothing. On the economic profit side, the capital costs were already below the line, so our answer is the same as before, with the two $50 capital cost items adding up to a $100 deduction.

	Economic profit	Accounting profit
Gross receipts	$250	$250
Direct labor cost	($100)	($100)
Direct capital cost	($50)	($50)
Implicit capital cost	($50)	–
Profit	$50	$100

SELF-TEST 10.1

Suppose a firm has $250 of weekly revenue, $100 of weekly labor cost, and $150 of implicit weekly capital cost. What would be the firm's economic and accounting profit for the week?

Let's turn now to the assumption of profit maximization. To predict what any entity—a firm, person, committee, or government—will do under specific conditions, we need to make some sort of assumption about its goals. If we know where people want to go, it's much easier to predict what they'll do to get there. Economists assume that the goal of firms is to maximize economic profit; then they try to discover what specific behaviors promote that goal.

Numerous challenges—both positive and normative—have been raised to the profit-maximization assumption. On the positive side, some critics have suggested that a firm's goal is to maximize its chances of survival; other critics have pointed to profit margins, total sales, total revenues, or "shareholder value" as better maximization targets; and still others, citing the annual planning and targeting efforts undertaken by many firms, claim that firms don't try to maximize anything at all.

The response of economists would be that profit is a fair proxy for all the suggested substitutes. The corporate planning function—with its necessary focus on economic outlook, business mix, and product life cycles—may be a more detailed behavioral description of corporate goal setting than the economist's radically simplified model of the firm, but it is no sign that firms do not intend to use their assets to maximum effect.

And economists will also argue that for maximizing firm survival, nothing is more critical than profit. In the takeover-ridden world faced by corporations, fear may drive the profit motive nearly as much as greed, but neither may be required. On the contrary, a case can be made that, even in a world in which the actions of firms are initially random, a long-run tendency for profit-maximizing behavior will eventually dominate. Because profitability creates the resources that allow firms to invest in new opportunities and adapt to changing conditions, those firms with the highest profits are often considerably more likely to survive.[1]

On the normative side, constant demands are heard for corporations to take a broader view of their mission. And these calls do not always go unheard. In 2019, the Business Round table, while noting that each version of its Principles of Corporate Governance statement since 1997 had "endorsed principles of shareholder primacy—that corporations exist principally to serve shareholders," issued a new principles document asserting that companies, in addition to "generating long-term value for shareholders," should commit to delivering value to customers, dealing fairly and ethically with suppliers, investing in employees, supporting the communities in which they operate, and protecting the environment.[2]

But are such commitments credible? Writing at the end of the 2020 meeting of the Davos World Economic Forum, Jason Bordoff questioned how business leaders could make stronger emissions emissions-reduction targets, "yet still operate within a system in which oil, gas, and even coal use are still rising globally." In particular he noted how:

> Oil and gas companies face growing pressure to shift more of their capital budgets more quickly toward low-carbon energy sources, and yet risk being penalized in their share prices if they move too quickly in that direction because they can't earn the same returns and because oil and gas demand globally remains robust.[3]

It is the clarifying principle of profit maximization that allows a commentator such as Bordoff to recognize that, whatever its stated intentions, a major integrated oil and gas company cannot radically shift its business *on its own* toward zero-emission technology.

---

[1]For the evolutionary argument, see, for example, Armen Alchian, "Uncertainly, Evolution, and Economic Theory," *Journal of Political Economy*, 1950. A more detailed analysis of the evolutionary component of current economic and social issues can be found in Robert H. Frank, *The Darwin Economy: Liberty, Competition, and the Common Good*, Princeton: Princeton University Press, 2011.

[2]The Business Roundtable statement is at www.businessroundtable.org/business-roundtable-redefines-the-purpose-of-a-corporation-to-promote-an-economy-that-serves-all-americans.

[3]Jason Bordoff, "Letter from the Founding Director: Reflections on Davos 2020," Columbia/SIPA Center on Global Energy Policy, January 24, 2020, https://energypolicy.columbia.edu/letter-founding-director-reflections-davos-2020.

Without governmental and intergovernmental actions to change the incentives around energy investment for the entire industry, no single company can commit to a markedly less profitable business plan—and still hope to survive.

When we say that the goal of a firm is to maximize profit, we are not saying that firms should not have mission statements that include objectives around satisfaction and treatment of customers or its behavior as an employer or corporate citizen. These are worthwhile and important objectives. But we are saying that the firm must ultimately do well by doing good. The community standing, employee welfare, and customer loyalty that a firm achieves through its activities must ultimately show up as profit.

THE FOUR CONDITIONS FOR PERFECT COMPETITION

In describing perfect competition, it is useful to say what it is not. It is not, for example, just another expression for "supply and demand." Supply and demand are present and operative under many setups other than perfect competition. Likewise, perfect competition, although it assumes a market mechanism, is not a synonym for "free markets" or a description of a "market economy." The type of market that can satisfy the requirements of perfect competition is much more specific and precise than either of these terms, and it does not bring the same political connotation.

At the highest level, perfect competition is a theory of how competition benefits society through lower prices. At the technical level, the theory predicts how much output a firm will produce, under four conditions that define the existence of a perfectly competitive market. Let us consider each condition in turn.

1. **Firms Sell a Standardized Product** In a perfectly competitive market, the product sold by one firm is assumed to be a perfect substitute for the product sold by any other. Interpreted literally, this is a condition that is rarely if ever satisfied. Connoisseurs of fine wines, for example, insist that they can tell the difference between wines made from the same variety of grape grown on estates only a few hundred meters apart. It is also difficult to speak of a market commodity as shirts, because shirts come in so many different styles and quality levels. However, even though not every vendor at your local farmer's market will offer your favorite Arkansas Black apples, those that do are offering the same product. You can buy an Arkansas Black apple from any of them.

2. **Firms Are Price Takers** This means that the individual firm treats the market price of the product as given. More specifically, it must believe that the market price will not be affected by how much output it produces. This condition is likely to be satisfied when the market is served by a large number of firms, each one of which produces a negligible fraction of total industry output. At a large farmer's market (to repeat the previous example), one orchard is unlikely to drive up the price of apples by bringing fewer of them on a given Wednesday. But a large number of firms are not always necessary for price-taking behavior. Even with only two firms in the market, for example, each may behave as a price taker if it believes that other firms stand ready to enter its market at a moment's notice.

3. **Free Entry and Exit, with Perfectly Mobile Factors of Production in the Long Run** One implication of this condition is that if a firm perceives a profitable business opportunity at a given time and location, it will be able to hire the factors of production required to take advantage of it. Similarly, if its current venture no longer appears attractive in relation to alternative business ventures, it is free to discharge its factors of production, which will then move to industries in which opportunities are stronger. This movement can be headline grabbing.

Of course, no one believes that resources are perfectly mobile. Labor, in particular, is not likely to satisfy this condition. Much has been made of the decreasing *physical* mobility of labor in the United States in the last 30 years. Displaced

A standardized product. Watercolor of Arkansas Black apple, Deborah Griscom Passmore, 1895.

workers seem to be embedded in their communities not just for the usual "positive" reasons—attachment to home, community, and extended family—but also because they are deterred from moving by high housing and commuting costs in the new job clusters.

But frictionless *physical* mobility is not required for the condition to be satisfied. People do change jobs without moving, and mobility of workers between firms, especially in the great U.S. technological and financial hubs, can be very fluid. On the other side, firms change focus instead of location. Local farmers' markets facilitate mobility in the sense that they allow small farmers to withdraw their capital from commodity agricultural markets in which they cannot compete and redeploy it to far more attractive "luxury goods" markets, all without moving an inch. Of course, the market may be *so* attractive that farmers at greater and greater distances from the food hub will present themselves as "local," both demonstrating mobility and making the market more competitive. Here we see that It is the mobility assumption that tells us that profits will fall into the "normal" range in a relatively open farmers market—or any open market. The perfect mobility assumption, absurd at first glance, is often reasonably well satisfied in practice.

4. **Firms and Consumers Have Perfect Information** A firm has no reason to leave its current industry if it has no way of knowing about the existence of more profitable opportunities elsewhere. Similarly, a consumer has no motive to switch from a high-priced product to a lower-priced one of identical quality unless she knows about the existence of the latter. The role of markets becomes critical here since markets facilitate the follow of information as well as the exchange of commodities.

As an example, consider the Nagwon Musical Instrument Arcade. Visitors to Seoul, South Korea, often marvel how vendors of various product categories crowd into a couple of city blocks: Stores for men's shoes dominate one section of town, bridal shops another. At the Nagwon—a building on stilts in central Seoul—a consumer wanting a purple ukulele can circulate from vendor to vendor and compare price, appearance, and sound. At the same time, the vendors can keep an eye on consumers and each other. They can detect every ripple in prices, along with any shift in consumer tastes from guitars to saxophones.

Perfect information, of course, is context-dependent and not very portable. A consumer can't compare apples on the Internet the same way she can at a local market. Relevant points of comparison become unavailable as soon as we look at larger, more complex markets, but new ones also become available. If you search on Amazon for a used copy of this textbook, you will have to settle for a second-hand and perhaps unreliable description of a given copy's condition, but you will find price and availability information that you could never obtain from "walking around." As a practical matter, the assumption of perfect information is usually interpreted to mean that people can acquire most of the information that is most relevant to their choices without great difficulty. We will see that the state of knowledge is often sufficient to provide a reasonable approximation to the perfect information condition.

Are the assumptions underlying the model of perfect competition hopelessly restrictive? The farmers' market illustration we provided may seem a laughably throwback example. A great modern economy—dominated by large corporations, long supply chains, and increasing coordination among stakeholders—doesn't look much like a farmers market or the Nagwon arcade. Still, competition happens. The evidence is overwhelming that at the scale of the economy, the conditions for competition are met to a degree that both constrains prices and, by limiting profits on standard items, forces reallocation of resources in the direction of new goods and services. It is clear, then, that the competitive model can tell us something useful if we interpret it with care. In this chapter, we study competition in theory, if you will, the better to understand how it arises in practice, in the highly imperfect worlds of monopoly and monopolistic competition.

Robin Keefe/Getty Images

Need a purple uke? Choose among perfect competitors at the Nagwon Arcade.

THE SHORT-RUN CONDITION FOR PROFIT MAXIMIZATION

The first question we want our model of competitive firm behavior to be able to answer is, "How does a firm choose its output level in the short run?" Under the assumption that the firm's goal is to maximize economic profit, it will choose that level of output for which the difference between total revenue and total cost is largest.

Consider a firm with the short-run total cost curve labeled TC in the top panel in Figure 10.2. Like many of the firms we discussed in Chapter 9, this firm experiences first increasing, then decreasing, returns to its variable input, which produces the familiar pattern of curvature in its total cost curve. Suppose this firm can sell its output at a price of $P_0 = \$18$/unit. Its total revenue per week will then be \$18/unit of output times the number of units of output sold each week. For example, if the firm sells no output, it earns zero total revenue; if it sells 10 units of output per week, it earns \$180/wk; if it sells 20 units/wk, it earns \$360/wk; and so on. So for the perfectly competitive firm, which can sell as much or as little output as it chooses at a constant market price, total revenue is exactly proportional to output. For the firm in this example, the total revenue curve is the line labeled TR in the top panel in Figure 10.2. It is a ray whose slope is equal to the product price, $P_0 = 18$.

The bottom panel in Figure 10.2 plots the difference between TR and TC, which is the curve labeled Π_Q, the notation traditionally used in economics to represent economic profit. Here, Π_Q is positive for output levels between $Q = 4.7$ and $Q = 8.7$, and reaches a maximum at $Q = 7.4$. For output levels less than 4.7 or greater than 8.7, the firm is earning economic losses, which is simply another way of saying that its economic profits are negative for those values of Q.

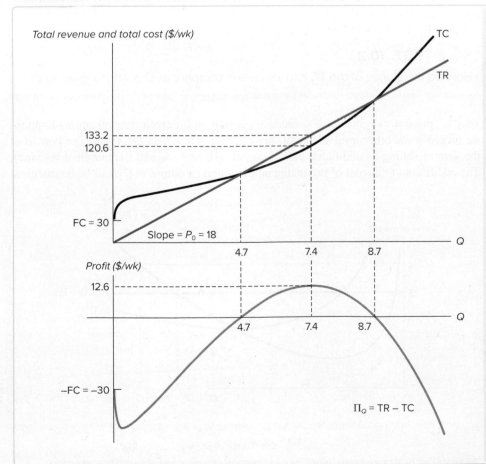

Total revenue and total cost ($/wk)

FC = 30
Slope = P_0 = 18

Profit ($/wk)

Π_Q = TR – TC

FIGURE 10.2

Revenue, Cost, and Economic Profit

The total revenue curve is the ray labeled TR in the top panel. The difference between it and total cost (TC in the top panel) is economic profit (Π_Q in the bottom panel). At $Q = 0$, $\Pi_Q = -FC = -30$. Economic profit reaches a maximum (\$12.60/wk) for $Q = 7.4$.

marginal revenue the change in total revenue that occurs as a result of a 1-unit change in sales.

In the bottom panel in Figure 10.2, note also that the vertical intercept of the profit curve is equal to −$30/wk, the negative of the firm's fixed cost. When the firm produces no output, it earns no revenue and incurs no variable cost but must still pay its fixed costs, so its profit when $Q = 0$ is simply −FC. If there were no positive output level for which the firm could earn higher profit than −FC, its best option would be to produce zero output in the short run.

The maximum profit point can also be characterized in terms of the relationship between output price and short-run marginal cost. Output price, which is equal to the slope of the total revenue curve, is also called **marginal revenue (MR)**.[4] Marginal revenue is formally defined as *the change in revenue that occurs when the sale of output changes by 1 unit.* In the cost-benefit language of Chapter 1, MR is the benefit to the firm of selling an additional unit of output. If the firm wants to maximize its profit, it must weigh this benefit against the cost of selling an extra unit of output, which is its marginal cost.

The short-run marginal and average variable cost curves that correspond to the TC curve in Figure 10.2 are shown in Figure 10.3, where we again suppose that the firm can sell its output at a price of $P_0 = \$18$/unit. To maximize its economic profit, the firm should follow this rule: Provided P_0 is larger than the minimum value of AVC (more on the reason for this condition below), *the firm should produce a level of output for which marginal revenue, $P_0 = 18$, is equal to marginal cost on the rising portion of the MC curve.* For the particular cost curves shown in Figure 10.3, $P_0 = 18$ is indeed larger than the minimum value of AVC, and is equal to marginal cost at the quantity level $Q^* = 7.4$. The requirement that marginal revenue intersect marginal cost on the rising portion of marginal cost implies that marginal revenue intersects marginal cost from above. Thus marginal revenue lies below marginal cost past this point of intersection, and the firm has no incentive to expand output beyond this point (additional units would reduce profits).

As the following exercise demonstrates, the definitions of MR and MC tell us something about the relative values of the slopes of the TR and TC curves at the maximum-profit point in Figure 10.2.

SELF-TEST 10.2

How do the slopes of the TC and TR curves compare at $Q = 7.4$ in Figure 10.2?

Why is "price = marginal cost" a necessary condition for profit maximization? Suppose we picked some other level of output, say, Q_1, that is less than $Q^* = 7.4$. The benefit to the firm of selling an additional unit of output will be $P_0 = \$18$ (its marginal revenue). The addition to total cost of producing an extra unit of output at Q_1 will be its marginal

---

FIGURE 10.3

The Profit-Maximizing Output Level in the Short Run

A necessary condition for profit maximization is that price equal marginal cost on the rising portion of the marginal cost curve. Here, this happens at the output level $Q^* = 7.4$.

cost at the level of output, MC_{Q1}, which in Figure 10.3 is clearly less than \$18. It follows that for any level of output on the rising portion of the MC curve to the left of $Q* = 7.4$, the benefit of expanding (as measured by marginal revenue) will be greater than the cost of expanding (as measured by marginal cost). This amounts to saying that profit will increase when we expand output from Q_1.

Now consider any level of output to the right of $Q* = 7.4$, such as Q_2. At Q_2, the benefit of contracting output by 1 unit will be the resulting cost savings, which is marginal cost at that level of output, namely, MC_{Q2}. (Note here that we are using the term "benefit" to refer to the avoidance of a cost.) The cost to the firm of contracting output by 1 unit will be its marginal revenue, $P_0 = 18$, the loss in total revenue when it sells 1 unit less. (Here, not getting a benefit is a cost.) Since $MC_{Q2} > \$18$, the firm will save more than it loses when it contracts output by 1 unit. It follows that for any output level greater than $Q* = 7.4$, the firm's profit will grow when it contracts output. The only output level at which the firm cannot earn higher profit by either expanding or contracting is $Q* = 7.4$, the level for which the cost of any move is exactly equal to its benefit.[5]

The Shutdown Condition

Recall that the rule for short-run profit maximization is to set price equal to marginal cost, provided price exceeds the minimum value of average variable cost. Why must price be greater than the minimum point of the AVC curve? The answer is that unless this condition is met, the firm will do better to shut down—that is, to produce no output—in the short run. To see why, note that the firm's *average revenue (AR)* per unit of output sold is simply the price at which it sells its product. (When price is constant for all levels of output, average revenue and marginal revenue are the same.)[6] If average revenue is less than average variable cost, the firm is taking a loss on each unit of output it sells. The firm's total revenue (average revenue times quantity) will be less than its total variable cost (AVC times quantity), and this means that it would do better by not producing any output at all. Shutting down in this context means simply to produce zero output in the short run. The firm will resume production if price again rises above the minimum value of AVC, the trigger point for its **shutdown condition.**

As we saw in Figure 10.2, a firm that produces zero output will earn economic profit equal to the negative of its fixed costs. If the price of its product is less than the minimum value of its average variable costs, it would have even greater economic losses if it produced a positive level of output.

The two rules—(1) that price must equal marginal cost on a rising portion of the marginal cost curve and (2) that price must exceed the minimum value of the average variable cost curve—together define the short-run supply curve of the perfectly competitive firm. The firm's supply curve tells how much output the firm wants to produce at various prices. As shown by the heavy red locus in Figure 10.4, it is the rising portion of the short-run marginal cost curve that lies above the minimum value of the average variable cost curve (which is \$12/unit of output in this example). Below $P = 12$, the supply

shutdown condition if price falls below the minimum of average variable cost, the firm should shut down in the short run.

---

[5]The firm's problem is to maximize $\Pi = PQ - TC_Q$, where TC_Q is the short-run total cost of producing Q units of output. The first-order condition for a maximum is given by

$$\frac{d\Pi}{dQ} = P - \frac{dTC_Q}{dQ} = P - MC_Q = 0,$$

which gives the condition $P = MC_Q$. The second-order condition for a maximum is given by

$$\frac{d^2\Pi}{dQ^2} = \frac{-dMC_Q}{dQ} < 0$$

or

$$\frac{dMC_Q}{dQ} > 0,$$

which tells us why we must be at a point on the rising portion of the marginal cost curve.
[6]Note that $AR = TR/Q = PQ/Q = P$.

FIGURE 10.4

The Short-Run Supply Curve of a Perfectly Competitive Firm

When price lies below the minimum value of average variable cost (here $12/unit of output), the firm will make losses at every level of output, and will keep its losses to a minimum by producing zero. For prices above min AVC, the firm will supply that level of output for which $P = MC$ on the rising portion of its MC curve.

curve coincides with the vertical axis, indicating that the firm supplies zero output when price is less than min AVC. For prices above 12, the firm will supply the output level for which $P = MC$. Thus, prices of 14 and 20 will cause this firm to supply 6.4 and 7.8 units of output, respectively. The competitive firm acts here as both a price taker and a profit maximizer: taking the market price as given, it chooses the level of output that maximizes economic profit at that price.

Note in Figure 10.4 that the firm supplies positive output whenever price exceeds min AVC, and recall that average variable cost is less than average total cost, the difference being average fixed cost. It follows that no matter how small AFC is, there will be a range of prices that lie between the AVC and ATC curves. For any price in this range, the firm supplies the level of output for which $P = MC$, which means that it will lose money because P is less than ATC. For example, the firm whose cost curves are shown in Figure 10.4 cannot cover all its costs at a price of $14. Even so, its best option is to supply 6.4 units of output per week, because it would lose even more money if it were to shut down. Being able to cover variable costs does not assure the firm of a positive level of economic profit. But it is sufficient to induce the firm to supply output in the short run.

Note also in Figure 10.4 that the firm's short-run supply curve is upward sloping. This is because the relevant portion of the firm's short-run marginal cost curve is upward sloping, which, in turn, is a direct consequence of the law of diminishing returns.

THE SHORT-RUN COMPETITIVE INDUSTRY SUPPLY

The short-run supply curve for a competitive industry is generated in a manner analogous to the one we used to generate the market demand curve in Chapter 5. In this case we simply announce a price and then add together the amounts each firm wishes to supply at that price. The resulting sum is industry supply at that price. Additional points on the industry supply curve are generated by pairing other prices with the sums of individual firm supplies at those prices.

Figure 10.5 illustrates the procedure for one of the simplest cases, an industry consisting of only two firms. At a price of $2/unit of output, only firm 1 (left panel) wishes to supply any output, and so its offering, $Q_1 = 2$ units of output per week, constitutes the entire industry supply at $P = 2$ (right panel). At $P = 3$, firm 2 enters the market (center panel) with an offering of $Q_2 = 4$. Added to firm 1's offering at $P = 3$—namely, $Q_1 = 3$—the resulting industry supply at $P = 3$ is $Q = 7$ (right panel). In like fashion, we see that industry supply at $P = 7$ is $Q = 7 + 8 = 15$. In Chapter 5, we saw that the market demand curve is the horizontal summation of the individual consumer demand curves. Here, we see that the market supply curve is the horizontal summation of the individual firm supply curves.

FIGURE 10.5

The Short-Run Competitive Industry Supply Curve

To get the industry supply curve (right panel), we simply add the individual firm supply curves (left and center panels) horizontally.

The horizontal summation of an individual firm's supplies into industry supply has a simple form when the firms in the industry are all identical. Suppose n firms each have supply curve $P = c + dQ_i$. To add up the quantities for the n firms into industry supply, we rearrange the firm supply curve $P = c + dQ_i$ to express quantity alone on one side: $Q_i = -(c/d) + (1/d)P$. Then industry supply is the sum of the quantities supplied Q_i by each of the n firms,

$$Q = nQ_i = n\left(-\frac{c}{d} + \frac{1}{d}P\right) = -\frac{nc}{d} + \frac{n}{d}P.$$

We can then rearrange industry supply $Q = -(nc/d) + (n/d)P$ to get it back in the form of price alone on one side: $P = c + (d/n)Q$. The intuition is that each one unit supplied by the industry is $1/n$ unit for each firm to supply. These calculations suggest a general rule for constructing the industry supply curve when firms are identical. If we have n individual firm supply curves $P = c + dQ_i$, then the industry supply curve is $P = c + (d/n)Q$.

EXAMPLE 10.2 Industry Supply Curve

Suppose an industry has 200 firms, each with supply curve $P = 100 + 1,000Q_i$. What is the industry supply curve?

First, we need to rearrange the representative firm supply curve $P = 100 + 1,000Q$ to have quantity alone on one side:

$$Q_i = -\frac{1}{10} + \frac{1}{1,000}P.$$

Then we multiply by the number of firms $n = 200$:

$$Q = nQ_i = 200Q_i = 200\left(-\frac{1}{10} + \frac{1}{1,000}P\right) = -20 + \frac{1}{5}P.$$

Finally, we rearrange the industry supply curve $Q = -20 + \left(\frac{1}{5}\right)P$ to have price alone on one side $P = 100 + 5Q$ to return to the slope-intercept form.

SELF-TEST 10.3

Suppose an industry has 30 firms, each with supply curve $P = 20 + 90Q_i$. What is the industry supply curve?

Short-Run Competitive Equilibrium

The individual competitive firm must choose the most profitable level of output to produce in response to a given price. But where does that price come from? As we saw in Chapter 2, it comes from the intersection of the supply and demand curves for the product. Recall that at the equilibrium price sellers are selling the quantity they wish to sell and buyers are buying the quantity they wish to buy.

In the left panel in Figure 10.6, the curve labeled D is the market demand curve for a product sold in a perfectly competitive industry. The curve labeled S is the corresponding short-run industry supply curve, the horizontal summation of the relevant portions of the individual short-run marginal cost curves.[7] These two curves intersect to establish the short-run competitive equilibrium price, here denoted $P^* = \$20$/unit of output. $P^* = 20$, in turn, is the price on which individual firms base their output decisions.

The conditions confronting a typical firm are shown in the right panel in Figure 10.6. The demand curve facing this firm is a horizontal line at $P^* = 20$. This means that it can sell as much or as little as it chooses at the market price of $20/unit. Put another way, any single firm can sell as much as it wants to without affecting the market price. If a firm charged more than $20, it would sell no output at all because buyers would switch to a competing firm that sells for $20. A firm could charge less than $20, of course, but would have no motive to do so if its objective were to maximize economic profit, since it can already sell as much as it wants to at $20. The result is that even though the market demand curve is downward sloping, the demand curve facing the individual firm is perfectly elastic. (Recall from the definition of price elasticity in Chapter 5 that a horizontal demand curve has infinite price elasticity, which is what "perfectly elastic" means.)

In the right panel in Figure 10.6, the representative firm maximizes its profit by equating $P^* = \$20$/unit to marginal cost at an output level of $Q_i^* = 80$ units/wk. At that output level its total revenue is $P^*Q_i^* = \$1,600$/wk and its total costs are $\text{ATC}_{Q_i^*} Q_i^* = (\$12$/unit$)$ (80 units/wk) = $960/wk. Its economic profit is the difference between total revenue and total cost, $1,600/wk/$960/wk = $640/wk, and is represented by the shaded rectangle denoted Π_i. Equivalently, profits can be calculated as the difference between price ($20/unit) and average total cost ($12/unit) times the quantity sold (80 units/week).

FIGURE 10.6

Short-Run Price and Output Determination under Pure Competition

The short-run supply and demand curves intersect to determine the short-run equilibrium price, $P^* = 20$ (left panel). The firm's demand curve is a horizontal line at $P^* = 20$ (right panel). Taking $P^* = 20$ as given, the firm maximizes economic profit by producing $Q_i^* = 80$ units/wk, for which it earns an economic profit of $\Pi_i = \$640$/wk (the shaded rectangle in the right panel).

[7]Here, the "relevant portions" are those that lie above the respective values of min AVC.

TABLE 10.1
Economic Profits versus Economic Losses

Q	ATC	MC	$\Pi(P=20)$	$\Pi(P=10)$
40	14	6	240	−160
60	12	10	480	−120
80	12	20	640	−160
100	15	31	500	−500

> At a price of 20, the firm earns economic profits, but at a price of 10, it suffers economic losses.

Recall that the opportunity cost of resources owned by the firm constitutes part of the cost included in its average total cost curve. This is why we say that total revenues over and above total costs constitute economic profit. If the firm's revenue were exactly equal to its total cost, it would earn only a normal profit—which is to say, zero economic profit.

Facing a price equal to average total cost implies that total cost equals total revenue, and the firm earns zero economic profits. Thus price equal to the minimum of average total cost can be called the breakeven point—the lowest price at which the firm will not suffer negative profits in the short run.

The situation portrayed in Figure 10.6 and Table 10.1 is one in which the short-run equilibrium price enables the firm to make a positive economic profit. Another possibility is that the short-run supply and demand curves will intersect at an equilibrium price that is sufficiently high to induce firms to supply output, but not high enough to enable them to cover all their costs. This situation is shown in Figure 10.7 and Table 10.1. In the left panel, supply and demand intersect at a price $P^* = \$10$/unit of output, which lies above the minimum value of the AVC curve of the firm shown in the right panel, but below that firm's ATC curve at the profit-maximizing level of output, $Q_i^* = 60$ units of output per week. The result is that the firm makes an economic loss of $P^*Q_i^* - \text{ATC}_{Q_i^*}Q_i^* = -\$120$/wk. This loss is shown in the right panel in Figure 11.7 by the shaded rectangle labeled Π_i. Note that this loss is less than $-\text{TFC}$, the value of economic profit when output is zero. Thus it makes sense to produce even when economic profit falls below zero in the short run.

Market   **Individual Firm**

Price ($/unit of output)   *Price ($/unit of output)*

$S = \Sigma MC$

$\Pi_i = -\$120$/wk

MC_i
ATC_i

12

$P^* = 10$ 10

$P = MR_i = 10$
AVC_i

D

Q

0   Q^*

0   60 Q_i

Units of output/wk

FIGURE 10.7

A Short-Run Equilibrium Price That Results in Economic Losses

The short-run supply and demand curves sometimes intersect to produce an equilibrium price $P^* = \$10$/unit of output (left panel) that lies below the minimum value of the ATC curve for the typical firm (right panel), but above the minimum point of its AVC curve. At the profit-maximizing level of output, $Q_i^* = 60$ units/wk, the firm earns an economic loss of $\Pi_i = -\$120$/wk.

SELF-TEST 10.4

If the short-run marginal and average variable cost curves for a competitive firm are given by MC = 2Q and AVC = Q, how many units of output will the firm produce at a market price of P = 12? At what level of fixed cost will this firm earn zero economic profit?

The Efficiency of Short-Run Competitive Equilibrium

allocative efficiency a condition in which all possible gains from exchange are realized.

One of the most attractive features of competitive markets is the fact that they result in **allocative efficiency,** which means that they fully exploit the possibilities for mutual gains through exchange. To illustrate, let us consider the short-run equilibrium pictured in the left panel of Figure 10.8, and suppose that the cost curves pictured in the right panel are the same for each of 1,000 firms in the industry.

In a competitive market in the short run, consumers give firms money, which firms use to buy variable inputs to produce the output that goes to consumers. To say that the competitive equilibrium leaves no room for further mutually beneficial exchange is the same thing as saying that there is no way for any producer and consumer to agree to a private transaction at any price other than $10. Of course, consumers would gladly pay less than $10 for an additional unit of output. But since $10 is equal to the value of the resources required to produce another unit (MC_i in the right panel of Figure 10.8), no firm would be willing to respond. Firms, for their part, would gladly produce an extra unit of output if the price were higher than $10. But with 100,000 units of output already in the market, there are no consumers left who are willing to pay more than $10 (left panel of Figure 10.8). At the short-run competitive equilibrium price and quantity, the value of the resources used to produce the last unit of output (as measured by short-run marginal cost) is exactly equal to the value of that unit of output to consumers (as measured by the price they are willing to pay for it). Firms may wish that prices were higher, and consumers may complain that prices are too high already. But two parties have no incentive to trade at any price other than the equilibrium price.

Producer Surplus

To say that a competitive market is efficient is to say that it maximizes the net benefits to its participants. In policy analysis, it is often useful to estimate the actual amount by which people and firms gain from their participation in specific markets. Suppose, for

FIGURE 10.8

Short-Run Competitive Equilibrium Is Efficient

At the equilibrium price and quantity, the value of the additional resources required to make the last unit of output produced by each firm (MC in the right panel) is exactly equal to the value of the last unit of output to buyers (the demand price in the left panel). This means that further mutually beneficial trades do not exist.

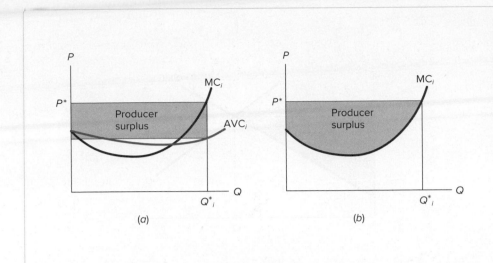

FIGURE 10.9

Two Equivalent Measures of Producer Surplus

The difference between total revenue and total variable cost is a measure of producer surplus, the gain to the producer from producing Q_i^* units of output rather than zero. It can be measured as the difference between $P^*Q_i^*$ and $AVC_{Q_i^*}Q_i^*$ (shaded rectangle, left panel), or as the difference between $P^*Q_i^*$ and the area under the marginal cost curve (upper shaded area, right panel).

example, that a Third World government knows it can open up new markets for seafood by building a road from its coast to an interior region. If its goal is to use the country's resources as efficiently as possible, its decision about whether to build the road will depend on whether the benefits people and firms reap from these new markets exceed the cost of building the road.

In Chapter 4 we discussed the concept of consumer surplus as a measure of the benefit to the consumer of engaging in a market exchange. An analogous measure exists for producers. Economists call it **producer surplus,** and it measures how much better off the firm is as a result of having supplied its profit-maximizing level of output. It may seem tempting to say that the firm's producer surplus is simply its economic profit, but surplus and profit often differ. To see why, first recall that in the short run if the firm produces nothing, it will sustain a loss equal to its fixed cost. If the price exceeds the minimum value of AVC, however, it can do better by supplying a positive level of output. How much better? The firm's gain compared with the alternative of producing nothing is the difference between total revenue and total variable cost at the output level where $P = MC$. Now recall that economic profit is the difference between total revenue and total cost and that total cost differs from variable cost by fixed cost; it follows that producer surplus is the sum of economic profit and fixed cost.[8] Diagrammatically, it is the area of the shaded rectangle shown in the left panel in Figure 10.9. In the short run, producer surplus is thus larger than economic profit, because the firm would lose more than its economic profit if it were prevented from participating in the market. In the long run, all costs are variable. So producer surplus is the same as economic profit in the long run.

The right panel in Figure 10.9 shows an equivalent way of representing producer surplus. The alternative measure makes use of the fact that variable cost at any level of output is equal to the area under the marginal cost curve (below the shaded area in the right panel). To see why this is so, note that the variable cost of producing 1 unit of output is equal to marginal cost at 1 unit, MC_1; VC for 2 units is the sum of MC_1 and MC_2, and so on, so that $VC_Q = MC_1 + MC_2 + \cdots + MC_Q$, which is just the area under the MC curve. Hence the difference between the total revenue and total variable cost may also be expressed as the upper shaded area in the right panel in Figure 10.9.

Which of the two ways of measuring producer surplus is most useful will depend on the specific context at hand. If we are interested in the change in an existing producer surplus, the method shown in the right panel in Figure 10.9 will usually be easiest to

producer surplus the dollar amount by which a firm benefits by producing a profit-maximizing level of output.

---

[8]If $\Pi = TR - TC$ and $TC = VC + FC$, then producer surplus $= TR - VC = TR - TC + FC = \Pi + FC$.

FIGURE 10.10

Aggregate Producer Surplus When Individual Marginal Cost Curves are Upward Sloping Throughout

For any quantity, the supply curve measures the minimum price at which firms would be willing to supply it. The difference between the market price and the supply price is the marginal contribution to aggregate producer surplus at that output level. Adding these marginal contributions up to the equilibrium quantity Q^*, we get the shaded area, which is aggregate producer surplus.

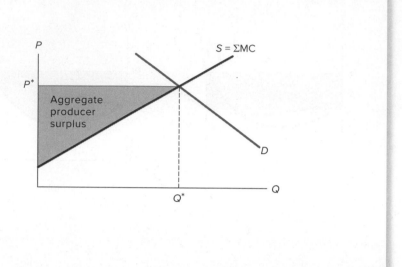

work with. But when we want to measure total producer surplus, it will often be easier to calculate the surplus by using the method shown in the left panel.

To measure aggregate producer surplus for a market, we simply add the producer surplus for each firm that participates. In cases where each firm's marginal cost curve is upward sloping for the bulk of its range, aggregate producer surplus will be well approximated by the area between the supply curve and the equilibrium price line, P^*, as shown in Figure 10.10.

Recall from Chapter 4 that a rough approximation of consumer surplus for the market as a whole is given by the area between the demand curve and the equilibrium price line, as indicated by the shaded upper triangle in Figure 10.11.[9] The total benefits from exchange in the marketplace may be measured by the sum of consumer and producer surpluses.

FIGURE 10.11

The Total Benefit from Exchange in a Market

The sum of aggregate producer surplus (shaded lower triangle) and consumer surplus (shaded upper triangle) measures the total benefit from exchange.

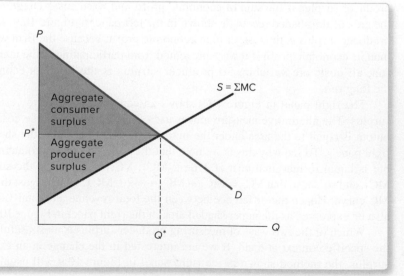

[9]Recall that this measure of consumer surplus is most accurate when income effects are small.

EXAMPLE 10.3   Consumer and Producer Surplus

Suppose there are two types of users of fireworks: careless and careful. Careful users never get hurt, but careless ones sometimes injure not only themselves, but also innocent bystanders. The short-run marginal cost curves of each of the 1,000 firms in the fireworks industry are given by MC = 10 + Q, where Q is measured in pounds of cherry bombs per year and MC is measured in dollars per pound of cherry bombs. The demand curve for fireworks by careful users is given by P = 50 − 0.001Q (same units as for MC). Legislators would like to continue to permit careful users to enjoy fireworks. But since it is impractical to distinguish between the two types of users, they have decided to outlaw fireworks altogether. How much better off would consumers and producers be if legislators had the means to effect a partial ban?

If the entire fireworks market is banned completely, the total of consumer and producer surplus will be zero. So to measure the benefits of a partial ban, we need to find the sum of consumer and producer surplus for a fireworks market restricted to careful users. To generate the supply curve for this market, we simply add the marginal cost curves of the individual firms horizontally, which results in the curve labeled S in Figure 10.12. The demand curve for careful users would intersect S at an equilibrium price of $30 and an equilibrium quantity of 20,000 lb/yr.

By outlawing the sale of fireworks altogether, legislators eliminate producer and consumer surplus values given by the areas of the two shaded triangles in Figure 10.12, which add to $400,000/yr. In the language of cost-benefit analysis, this is the cost imposed on producers and careful users. The benefit of the ban is whatever value the public assigns to the injuries prevented (net of the cost of denying careless users the right to continue). It is obviously no simple matter to put a dollar value on the pain and suffering associated with fingers blown off by cherry bombs. In Chapter 14, we will discuss how at least rough estimates have been attempted in similar situations. But even in the absence of a formal quantitative measure of the value of injuries prevented, the public can ask itself whether the forgone surplus of $400,000/yr is a reasonable price to pay. Because virtually every state legislature has enacted a ban on the private sale and use of fireworks, the answer to this question seems to be an emphatic yes.

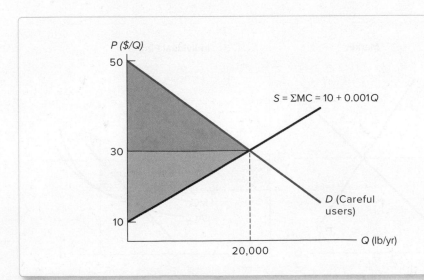

FIGURE 10.12

Producer and Consumer Surplus in a Market Consisting of Careful Fireworks Users

The upper shaded triangle is consumer surplus ($200,000/yr). The lower shaded triangle is producer surplus ($200,000/yr). The total benefit of keeping this market open is the sum of the two, or $400,000/yr.

Adjustments in the Long Run

The firm's objective, in both the long run and the short run, is to earn the highest economic profit it can. In the preceding section we saw that a firm will sometimes find it advantageous to continue supplying output in the short run even though it is making economic losses. In the long run, however, a firm would prefer to go out of business if it could not earn at least a normal profit in its current industry.

Suppose that industry supply and demand intersect at the price level $P = 10$, as shown in the left panel in Figure 10.13. The cost curves for a representative firm are shown in the right panel in Figure 10.13. At $Q = 200$, the price of $10/unit of output exceeds ATC_2, with the result that the firm earns economic profit of $600 each time period. This profit is indicated by the shaded rectangle.

The situation depicted in Figure 10.13 is inherently unstable. The reason is that positive economic profit creates an incentive for outsiders to enter the industry. Recall that the average total cost curves already include the opportunity cost of the capital that a firm requires to do business. This means that an outsider can buy everything needed to duplicate the operations of one of the existing firms in the industry, and in the process earn an economic profit of $600 each time period.

As additional firms enter the industry, their short-run marginal cost curves are added to those of existing firms, which shifts the industry supply curve to the right. If only one firm entered the industry, there would be no significant effect on price. And with price virtually the same as before, each firm in the industry would continue to earn economic profits of $600 per time period. These profits will continue to act as a carrot to lure additional firms into the industry, and the accumulating rightward supply shift will gradually cause price to fall.

The left panel in Figure 10.14 portrays the rightward shift in industry supply that results from a significant amount of entry. The new supply schedule, S', intersects the demand schedule at $P = 8$, and this lower price level gives firms an incentive to readjust their capital stocks. In the right panel in Figure 10.14, note that the amount of capital that gives rise to the short-run cost curves ATC_3 and SMC_3 is optimal for the price level $P = 8$.

FIGURE 10.13

A Price Level That Generates Economic Profit

At the price level $P = \$10$/unit, the firm has adjusted its plant size so that $SMC_2 = LMC = 10$. At the profit-maximizing level of output, $Q = 200$, the firm earns an economic profit equal to $600 each time period, indicated by the area of the shaded rectangle

FIGURE 10.14

A Step along the Path toward Long-Run Equilibrium

Entry of new firms causes supply to shift rightward, lowering price from 10 to 8. The lower price causes existing firms to adjust their capital stocks downward, giving rise to the new short-run cost curves ATC_3 and SMC_3. As long as price remains above short-run average cost (here, $ATC_3 = 5$), economic profits will be positive ($\Pi = \$540$ per time period), and incentives for new firms to enter will remain.

Note also that the profit-maximizing level of output for $P = 8$ is $Q = 180$, and that this results in an economic profit of 540 per time period, as indicated by the shaded rectangle.

Note that the adjustment by existing firms to the lower price level shifts each of their short-run marginal cost curves to the left. In terms of its effect on the industry supply curve, this adjustment thus works in the opposite direction from the adjustment caused by the entry of new firms. But the *net* effect of the two adjustments must be to shift industry supply to the right. If it were not, price wouldn't have fallen in the first place, and there would have been no reason for existing firms to reduce their capital stocks.

Even after the adjustments described above take place, new and existing firms in the industry continue to earn positive economic profits. The new profit level is lower than before, but still acts as an incentive for additional entry into the industry. Further entry sets off yet another round of adjustment, as the continuing fall in price renders existing capital stocks too large. For industries whose firms have U-shaped long-run average cost curves, entry, falling prices, and capital stock adjustment will continue until these two conditions are met: (1) Price reaches the minimum point on the LAC curve (P^* in the right panel in Figure 10.15), and (2) all firms have moved to the capital stock size that gives rise to a short-run average total cost curve that is tangent to the LAC curve at its minimum point (ATC^* in the right panel in Figure 10.15). Note in the right panel in Figure 10.15 that once all firms have reached this position, economic profit for each will

FIGURE 10.15

The Long-Run Equilibrium under Perfect Competition

If price starts above P^*, entry keeps occurring and capital stocks of existing firms keep adjusting until the rightward movement of the industry supply curve causes price to fall to P^*. At P^*, the profit-maximizing level of output for each firm is Q_i^*, the output level for which $P^* = SMC^* = LMC = ATC^* = LAC$. Economic profits of all firms are equal to zero.

be zero. The short-run marginal cost curve in the right panel is like the short-run marginal cost curve of all other firms in the industry, and when these curves are added horizontally, we get the industry supply curve shown in the left panel, which intersects the market demand curve at the long-run equilibrium price of P^*. This is the long-run competitive equilibrium position for the industry. Once it is reached, there will be no further incentive for new firms to enter the industry, because existing firms will all be earning an economic profit of zero.

In discussing the movement toward long-run competitive equilibrium, we began with an initial situation in which price was above the minimum value of long-run average cost and existing firms were all earning an economic profit. Suppose we had instead started with a situation in which price was below the minimum value of LAC. In that case, existing firms would be earning negative economic profits (that is, economic losses), which would be an incentive for some of them to leave the industry. The exodus would shift the supply curve leftward, causing an increase in price and movements by existing firms to adjust their capital stocks upward. This process would continue until all firms have once again settled into the long-run equilibrium position portrayed in the right panel in Figure 10.15.

THE INVISIBLE HAND

▶ Visit your instructor's Connect© course and access your eBook to view this video.

Why do supermarket checkout lines all tend to be roughly the same length?

As Adam Smith saw clearly more than two centuries ago, it is the invisible hand of the self-interest motive—in particular, the carrot of economic profit, or the stick of economic losses—that drives competitive industries to their respective long-run equilibrium positions. But even though no firm consciously intends to promote the general social welfare, there are some remarkably attractive features of long-run competitive equilibrium. Thus, as Smith described the actions of an industrialist,

> he intends only his own security; and by directing that industry in such a manner as its produce may be of the greatest value, he intends only his own gain; and he is in this, as in many other cases, led by an invisible hand to promote an end which was no part of his intention. Nor is it always the worse for the society that it was no part of it. By pursuing his own interest, he frequently promotes that of the society more effectually than when he really intends to promote it.[10]

In what sense is the long-run equilibrium in competitive markets attractive from the perspective of society as a whole? For one thing, price is equal to marginal cost, both long-run and short-run, which means that the equilibrium is efficient in the sense previously discussed: it exhausts all possibilities for mutually beneficial trades. The last unit of output consumed is worth exactly the same to the buyer as the resources required to produce it. Moreover, price is equal to the minimum point on the long-run average cost curve, which means that there is no less costly way of producing the product. Finally, all producers earn only a normal rate of profit, which is the opportunity cost of the resources they have invested in their firms. The public pays not a penny more than what it cost the firms to serve them.

Even more remarkable than these efficiency properties is the sheer volume of activity that is coordinated by the market mechanism. Throughout the dead of Ithaca winters, a food truck sits parked outside the Cornell dormitories all night, so that at 3 AM any student can take a few steps outside and purchase a fresh cup of coffee for a dollar. No students had to instruct the operator of that truck to be there, or tell him where to buy paper cups or propane gas for his portable stove. A store near my house will sell me a new cartridge for my printer at a moment's notice, or a new carbide-tipped blade for the radial arm saw that sits in my

[10]Adam Smith, *The Wealth of Nations,* Chapter 2, www.online-literature.com/view.php/wealth_ nations/24? term=invisible%20hand.

garage. The butcher shop at my supermarket has fresh rabbit on Fridays and Saturdays, and a truck arrives each morning at dawn carrying fresh swordfish caught in the waters off the coast of Maine. On only a few hours' notice, several airlines stand ready to carry me to New York, Los Angeles, or Cedar Rapids, Iowa. All this activity, and much, much more, takes place without any central coordination at all, the result of a multitude of economic agents each striving to earn an economic profit.

In controlled economies, resources are allocated not by markets but by central planning committees. Because of natural limits on the amount of information such committees can process, they are unable to specify in exact detail the characteristics of the goods called for by their plans. Workers and managers in controlled economies are therefore often able to interpret their production orders in self-serving ways.

The famous Russian cartoon, for example, shows the response of the manager of a roofing nail factory who was called on by the plan to deliver 10,000 pounds of roofing nails for the month of August. He alertly discovered that the easiest way to fulfill his quota was to produce a single 10,000-pound nail.

Whatever other faults it may have, the market system cannot be accused of producing products that people don't want to buy. In the market system, the consumer is sovereign, and firms that fail to provide what consumers want face economic extinction.[11] The question of whether central plans are more efficient than market incentives was a hotly debated issue for most of the twentieth century. But no longer. Before their demise in the late 1980s, controlled economies all over the globe introduced marketlike incentives in a desperate attempt to revive their lagging production totals.

This is not to say that competitive markets lead to the best possible outcome in every instance. On the contrary, in later chapters we will see that market systems fall short in a variety of ways.

Moreover, the efficiency claims on behalf of competitive allocations are conditional on the initial distribution of resources among members of society. Markets are efficient at producing what people demand in the marketplace, and what gets produced depends on how much income specific people have. If you do not believe that the underlying distribution of resources is fair, there is no compelling reason for you to approve of the pattern of goods and services served up by competitive markets. But one need not take a naively optimistic view of the competitive process to appreciate its truly awesome power to draw order from complexity.

Application: The Cost of Extraordinary Inputs

The Irrigation Project

We are in a position now to return to the question with which we began this chapter, namely, whether a state-supported irrigation system that doubles crop yields will raise the incomes of poor farmers. Recall that the farmers in question live in an isolated county and rent their farm parcels from landowners.

First, let's consider the current situation in which no irrigation system exists. Farmers here may be viewed as the operators of small competitive firms. They rent land, supply their own labor, and keep the proceeds from selling their grain in a market so large that their own offerings have no appreciable effect on the price of grain, which is, say, $10/bushel. For the sake of simplicity, let us ignore the cost of seed, tools, and other minor inputs.

Suppose that an individual farmer can farm 40 acres and that without irrigation the land will yield 30 bushels of grain per acre per year. Her total revenue from the sale of her grain will then be $12,000/yr, from which she must deduct the rent for her land. How will that rent be determined?

---

[11]The late Harvard economist John Kenneth Galbraith challenged this view. We will consider his arguments in Chapter 12.

Suppose the alternative to working as a farmer is to work in a factory for $6,000/yr, and that factory work is generally regarded as neither more nor less pleasant than farming. If the land rent were only, say, $5,000/yr for a 40-acre parcel, then all the county's workers would prefer farming to working in the factories, because their net earnings would be $7,000 instead of $6,000. Assuming that there are many more factory workers than could farm the county's limited supply of farmland, there would be excess demand for farm parcels at a rental price of $5,000/yr. Factory workers would bid against one another, and the bidding would continue until the rental price for a 40-acre parcel reached $6,000/yr. At that price, a farmer would have $6,000 left over from the sale of her crops, which would leave her indifferent between the options of farming and factory work. The land rent could never exceed $6,000 for long under these conditions, for if it did, net farm incomes would fall below $6,000/yr, and everyone would want factory work instead of farming.

Now let's see what happens with the introduction of the irrigation project. With grain yields now 60 bushels/acre instead of 30, a 40-acre farm will produce $24,000 in annual total revenue instead of $12,000. If the land rent remained at its original $6,000/yr level, a farmer would earn $18,000/yr instead of $6,000. Indeed, it was the prospect of such a dramatic rise in farm incomes that has attracted so much support for the irrigation bill in the first place.

What supporters of the bill have failed to recognize, however, is that land rents will not remain at $6,000/yr after the introduction of the irrigation system. Needless to say, factory workers would bid vigorously for an opportunity to rent a farm parcel that would raise their income from $6,000 to $18,000/yr. In the face of this bidding pressure, the rental price of farmland will continue to rise until it reaches a level of $18,000/yr. (If it were only $17,000, for example, a factory worker could switch to farming and raise his annual income from $6,000 to $7,000.) Once the annual rent for a 40-acre parcel reaches $18,000, the balance between farm and factory opportunities is restored.

Recall that our hypothetical state legislator's aide recommended against the irrigation project on the grounds that it would not raise the incomes of farmers in the long run. She perceived correctly that the beneficiaries of the state-supported irrigation project would be not the impoverished farmers but the owners of the land. On the view that these owners already have high incomes, there is no social purpose served by spending tax dollars to increase their incomes further.[12]

This example illustrates the important idea that strong forces tend to equalize the average total costs of different firms in a competitive industry. Here, land prices adjusted to bring the average costs of the irrigated farms into balance with the average costs of growing crops elsewhere.

An Efficient Manager

Suppose one firm is like all others except that it employs an extraordinarily efficient manager. This manager is so efficient that the firm earns $500,000 of economic profit each year in an industry in which the economic profit of the other firms hovers close to zero. Because this manager receives the same salary as all other managers, the firm that employs her has much lower costs than all other firms in the industry. But that creates a strong incentive for some other firm to bid this manager away by offering her a higher salary.

Suppose a new firm offered her $300,000 more than her current annual salary and she accepted. That new firm would then earn an economic profit of $200,000/yr. That's not as good as an economic profit of $500,000/yr, but it is $200,000/yr better than the normal profit her original employer will earn without her.

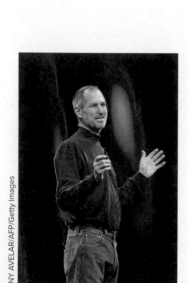

The late Apple co-founder and long-time CEO Steve Jobs was often described as the main reason for the firm's financial success. Was he compensated accordingly?

TONY AVELAR/AFP/Getty Images

---

[12]Of course, the irrigation project would still be attractive if its cost were less than the value of the extra grain that resulted.

Still other firms would have an incentive to offer even more for this manager. Theory tells us that the bidding should continue until the cost savings for which she is responsible are entirely incorporated into her salary—that is, until her salary is $500,000/yr higher than the salary of an ordinary manager. And once her salary is bid up to that level, the firm that hires her will no longer enjoy a cost advantage over the other firms in the industry. The existence of such competitive bidding for inputs makes it plausible to assume that all the firms in a competitive industry have roughly the same average total costs in equilibrium.

SELF-TEST 10.6

Suppose all firms in an industry have "competent" managers and earn zero economic profit. The manager of one of the firms suddenly leaves and the firm finds that only incompetent applicants respond when the position is advertised at the original salary of $50,000/yr (which is the going rate for competent managers in this industry). Under an incompetent manager paid this salary, the firm will experience an economic loss of $20,000/yr. At what salary would it make sense for this firm to hire an incompetent manager?

THE LONG-RUN COMPETITIVE INDUSTRY SUPPLY CURVE

We saw that the short-run supply curve for a perfectly competitive industry is the horizontal summation of the short-run marginal cost curves of its individual firms. But the corresponding long-run supply curve for a competitive industry is not the horizontal summation of the long-run marginal cost curves of individual firms. Our task in the next sections is to derive the long-run supply curve for competitive industries operating under a variety of different cost conditions.

Long-Run Supply Curve with U-Shaped LAC Curves

What does the long-run supply curve look like in an industry in which all firms have identical U-shaped long-run average cost (LAC) curves? Suppose, in particular, that these LAC curves are like the one labeled LAC_i in the right panel in Figure 10.16. Suppose the demand curve facing the industry is initially the one labeled D_1 in the left panel. Given this demand curve, the industry will be in long-run equilibrium when each firm installs the capital stock that gives rise to the short-run marginal cost curve labeled SMC_i in the right panel. The number of firms in the industry will adjust so that the short-run supply

FIGURE 10.16

The Long-Run Competitive Industry Supply Curve

When firms are free to enter or leave the market, price cannot depart from the minimum value of the LAC curve in the long run. If input prices are unaffected by changes in industry output, the long-run supply curve is S_{LR}, a horizontal line at the minimum value of LAC.

curve, denoted S_{SR} in the left panel, intersects D_1 at a price equal to the minimum value of LAC_i. (If there were more firms than that or fewer, each would be making either an economic loss or a profit.)

Now suppose demand shifts rightward from D_1 to D_2, intersecting the short-run industry supply curve at the price P_2. The short-run effect will be for each firm to increase its output from Q_{i1}^* to Q_{i2}^*, which will lead to an economic profit measured by the shaded rectangle in the right panel in Figure 10.16. With the passage of time, these profits will lure additional firms into the industry until the rightward supply shift (to S^* in the left panel) again results in a price of min LAC. The long-run response to an increase in demand, then, is to increase industry output by increasing the number of firms in the industry. As long as the expansion of industry output does not cause the prices of capital, labor, and other inputs to rise, there will be no long-run increase in the price of the product.[13]

If demand had shifted to the left from D_1, a parallel story would have unfolded: Price would have fallen in the short run, firms would have adjusted their offerings, and the resulting economic losses would have induced some firms to leave the industry. The exodus would shift industry supply to the left until price had again risen to min LAC. Here again the long-run response to a shift in demand is accommodated by a change in the number of firms. With U-shaped LAC curves, there is no tendency for a fall in demand to produce a long-run decline in price.

In summary, the long-run supply curve for a competitive industry with U-shaped LAC curves and constant input prices is a horizontal line at the minimum value of the LAC curve. In the long run, all the adjustment to variations in demand occurs not through changing prices but through variations in the number of firms serving the market. Following possibly substantial deviations in the short run, price shows a persistent tendency to gravitate to the minimum value of long-run average cost.

Industry Supply When Each LAC Curve Is Horizontal

As in the case of U-shaped LAC curves, the long-run industry supply curve when each firm's LAC curve is horizontal will again be a horizontal line (again assuming that input prices do not change with changes in industry output). But there is one salient difference between the two cases: When firms have identical U-shaped LAC curves, we can predict that each firm will produce the quantity that corresponds to the minimum point on its LAC curve. We thus get an industry composed of firms that all produce the same level of output.

With horizontal LAC curves, by contrast, there is simply no unique minimum-cost point. LAC is the same at any level of output, which leads to an indeterminacy not present in the earlier case. We just cannot predict what the size distribution of firms will look like in the case of horizontal LAC curves. There may be a handful of large firms, many small ones, or a mixture of different sizes. All we can say with confidence is that price in the long run will gravitate toward the value of LAC.

How Changing Input Prices Affect Long-Run Supply

In our analysis of cost curves in Chapter 9, which forms the basis of our analysis of supply under perfect competition, an important assumption was that input prices do not vary with the amount of output produced. For a single firm whose input purchases constitute only a small fraction of the total input market, this assumption is plausible. In many cases, moreover, even the entire industry's demands for inputs constitute only a small share of the overall input market. For example, even if the insurance industry issues 20 percent more policies this year than last, it employs such a small percentage of the total available supplies of secretaries, computers, executives, and other inputs that the prices of these inputs should not be significantly affected. So here too we may reasonably assume that input prices do not depend on output.

---

[13]More follows on what happens when changes in industry output cause changes in input prices.

FIGURE 10.17

Long-Run Supply Curve for an Increasing Cost Industry

When input prices rise with industry output, each firm's LAC curve will also rise with industry output (left panel). Thus the firm's LAC curve when industry output is Q_2 lies above its LAC curve when industry output is Q_1 (left panel). Firms will still gravitate to the minimum points on their LAC curves (Q_i^*, left panel), but because this minimum point depends on industry output, the long-run industry supply curve (S_{LR}, right panel) will now be upward sloping.

But there are at least some industries in which the volume of inputs purchased constitutes an appreciable share of the entire input market. The market for commercial airliners, for example, consumes a significant share of the total amount of titanium sold each year. In such cases, a large increase in industry output will often be accompanied by significant increases in input prices.

When that happens, we have what is known as a **pecuniary diseconomy,** a bidding up of input prices when industry output increases.[14] Even though the industry can expand output indefinitely without using more inputs per unit of output, the minimum point on each firm's LAC curve is nonetheless a rising function of industry output. For example, note in the left panel in Figure 10.17 that the firm's LAC curve for an industry output of Q_2 lies above its LAC curve for an industry output of $Q_1 < Q_2$, and that the LAC curve for an industry output of $Q_3 > Q_2$ lies higher still. To each industry output level there corresponds a different LAC curve, because input prices are different at every level of industry output. The long-run supply curve for such an industry will trace out the minimum points of these LAC curves. Thus, on the long-run industry supply curve (S_{LR}, right panel), Q_1 corresponds to the minimum point on the firm's LAC curve when industry output is Q_1 (left panel); Q_2 corresponds to the minimum point for the LAC curve for Q_2; and so on. With pecuniary diseconomies, the long-run supply curve will be upward sloping even though each individual firm's LAC curve is U-shaped. Pecuniary diseconomies also produce an upward-sloping industry supply curve when each firm's LAC curve is horizontal. Competitive industries in which rising input prices lead to upward-sloping supply curves are called *increasing cost industries.*

There are also cases in which the prices of inputs may fall significantly with expanding industry output. This will happen, for example, if inputs are manufactured using technologies in which there are substantial economies of scale. A dramatic increase in road building, for example, might facilitate greater exploitation of economies of scale in the production of earthmoving equipment, resulting in a lower price for that input. Such cases are called *pecuniary economies,* and give rise to a downward-sloping long-run industry supply curve, even where each firm's LAC curve is either horizontal or U-shaped. Competitive industries in which falling input prices lead to downward-sloping supply curves are called *decreasing cost industries.*

pecuniary diseconomy a rise in production cost that occurs when an expansion of industry output causes a rise in the prices of inputs.

[14]A *pecuniary diseconomy* thus implies that input prices will fall when industry output contracts.

Economic Naturalist 10.1

Why do color photographs cost less than black-and-white photographs?

When I was a boy, color photographs were a luxury, costing several times as much as black and white. Decades later, the photo-processing shop near my house charged $15 to develop and print a 36-exposure roll of black-and-white film, but only $7 for the same size roll of color film. This fall in the relative price of color photos has occurred despite the fact that the color process remained more complex than the one for black and white.

Why do color photos cost less than black-and-white ones?

If color processing was more complex than black and white, why did it cost less? The answer is in part because of economies of scale in the production of the machinery used to make both types of prints. When color photography was in its infancy, film was expensive and the colors tended to fade rapidly, so most people used black and white. The high volume of black-and-white photo processing, in turn, made it possible to produce processing machines cheaply because of economies of scale. As the price of color film declined over time and its quality rose, more people began to use it and the demand for color-processing equipment gradually grew. And again because of economies of scale in the production of processing equipment, this led to a fall in the cost of an important input for color print-making—a pecuniary economy. At the same time, the decline in production of black-and-white processing equipment led to an increase in its price—a pecuniary diseconomy.

FIGURE 10.18

Pecuniary Economies and the Price of Color and Black-and-White Photos

Because of economies of scale in the production of equipment used to process film, the long-run supply curves of both color and black-and-white prints are downward sloping. In 1955, when the quality of color film was poor, most people demanded black and white, resulting in lower prices. Fifty years later, in 2005, by contrast, demand for color is much greater than for black and white. The result is that color prints are now less expensive than black and white, even though color-processing equipment remains more complicated.

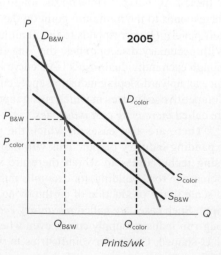

The resulting changes in the equilibrium prices and quantities of the two types of prints were roughly as shown in Figure 10.18. Note that the relative positions of the two supply curves were the same for both years. This means that the print-making industry would have been willing to supply any given total quantity of black-and-white prints for a lower price than for the same quantity of color prints in both years. It is the change in demand patterns, together with downward-sloping supply curves in both markets, that explains the observed reversal in relative prices.

With the rise in digital photography, the use of both black-and-white and color film has now all but disappeared. Kodak, once the premiere supplier of film world-wide, filed for bankruptcy in 2012, a year in which more photographs were taken with an iPhone than with any other type of camera.

This last reversal-of-fortune story was driven, like the first, by economies of scale. Apple can spread the cost of improved photo technology over far more phones than Nikon or Olympus can over their slower-selling cameras. And while iPhones themselves are not getting cheaper, taking and sharing pictures is. Services like Instagram allow friends to share photos over the same phones that took the pictures. Printing is completely optional.

The Elasticity of Supply

In Chapter 5 we defined the price elasticity of demand as a measure of the responsiveness of the quantity demanded to variations in price. An analogous concept exists for measuring the responsiveness of the quantity supplied to variations in price. Naturally, it is called the **price elasticity of supply.** Suppose we are at a point (Q, P) on the industry supply curve shown in Figure 10.19, where a change in price of ΔP gives rise to a change of ΔQ in the quantity supplied. The price elasticity of supply, denoted ϵ^s, is then given by

$$\epsilon^s = \frac{\Delta Q}{\Delta P} \frac{P}{Q} \text{ (see footnote 15 below).} \tag{10.1}$$

price elasticity of supply the percentage change in quantity supplied that occurs in response to a 1 percent change in product price.

As in the case of elasticity of demand, supply elasticity has a simple interpretation in terms of the geometry of the industry supply curve. When ΔP is small, the ratio $\Delta P/\Delta Q$ is the slope of the supply curve, which means that the ratio $\Delta Q/\Delta P$ is the reciprocal of

FIGURE 10.19

The Elasticity of Supply

At point A, the elasticity of supply is given by $\epsilon^s = (\Delta Q/\Delta P)(P/Q)$. Because the short-run supply curve is always upward sloping, the short-run elasticity of supply will always be positive. In the long run, elasticity of supply can be positive, zero, or negative.

[15]In calculus terms, supply elasticity is defined by

$$\epsilon^s = \frac{P}{Q} \frac{dQ}{dP}.$$

that slope. Thus the price elasticity of supply may be interpreted as the product of the ratio of price to quantity and the reciprocal of the slope of the supply curve:

$$\epsilon^s = \frac{P}{Q}\frac{1}{\text{slope}}. \tag{10.2}$$

Because of the law of diminishing returns, the short-run competitive industry supply curve will always be upward sloping, which means that the short-run elasticity of supply will always be positive. For industries with a horizontal long-run supply curve, the long-run elasticity of supply is infinite. Output can be expanded indefinitely without a change in price. Because of pecuniary economies and diseconomies, long-run competitive industry supply curves may also be either downward or upward sloping in specific cases. The corresponding long-run elasticities of supply in these cases will be either negative or positive.

As noted earlier, most industries employ only a relatively small share of the total volume of inputs traded in the marketplace, which means that modest variations in industry output should have no significant effect on input prices in most industries. In practical applications of the competitive model, therefore, most economists adopt the working hypothesis that long-run supply curves are horizontal. Of course, this hypothesis can always be modified when there is evidence that pecuniary economies or diseconomies are important.

APPLYING THE COMPETITIVE MODEL

As noted earlier in the chapter, economists recognize that no industries strictly satisfy the four requirements for perfect competition—a standardized product, firms as price takers, perfect factor mobility, and perfect information. For practical purposes, the important question is how far an industry can fall short of these conditions before general tendencies of the competitive model fail to apply. Unfortunately, there are no hard-and-fast rules for making this judgment. In industries where entry and exit are especially easy—such as the airline industry—a firm may behave as a price taker even in a market in which it is the only competitor.[16] In industries in which entry and exit are more difficult, even the existence of a relatively large number of established firms does not guarantee price-taking behavior. In the short run, especially, firms may be able to work out tacit agreements to restrain price competition even when there are extra-normal profits.

Despite this difficulty, experience has shown that many of the most important long-run properties of the competitive model apply in most industries, with the notable exception of those where the government erects legal barriers to entry (for example, by requiring a government license in order to participate in a market, as used to be the case in the airline industry).

By way of illustration, let's consider three brief applications that highlight some of the insights afforded by the perfectly competitive model.

Price Supports as a Device for Saving Family Farms

At the beginning of the twentieth century, more than 20 percent of the U.S. labor force earned its living by farming. Today, the corresponding figure is less than 3 percent. This change is obviously not the result of a dramatic decline in food consumption. Rather, it is one of the many consequences of farming methods having become vastly more productive over the course of a century.

As farm machinery has grown larger and more sophisticated, the size of land parcels at which long-run average cost curves cease declining has grown ever larger. Where family farms of fewer than 100 acres were once common in the American heartland, large corporate farms with several thousand acres have increasingly become the norm.

---

[16]At a limited number of large airports, entry is difficult even in the airline industry. For these airports to accommodate carriers, new capacity will have to be built, which could take years or even decades.

FIGURE 10.20

Cost Curves for Family and Corporate Farms

With the availability of modern farming methods, large farms have much lower unit costs than small ones. A price that covers cost for large corporate farms will produce large economic losses for family farms.

In terms of the competitive model developed in this chapter, the family farm may be thought of as a firm whose capital stock gives rise to the short-run cost curves denoted ATC_F and SMC_F in Figure 10.20. The corresponding cost curves for the corporate farm are denoted ATC_C and SMC_C. Competition has the effect of driving the long-run equilibrium price toward P^*, the minimum point on the LAC curve. At P^*, corporate farms earn a normal profit while family farms, with their higher costs, earn economic losses of Π_F, as measured by the shaded rectangle in Figure 10.20.

Despite the intense determination of many family farmers to remain on the land, large losses are simply not sustainable over a period of many years. Most farmers remain well past the time they are no longer able to earn a profit equal to the opportunity cost of their land. Many remain even long after they have ceased to earn the opportunity cost of their own labor. And a substantial number hang on by borrowing away most of the value of their only significant asset, their farmland. But credit cannot be extended without limit, and in the absence of government intervention, the long-run tendency has been for family farmers to leave the industry, selling whatever land they still own to the more efficient corporate farms.

Contrary to the stylized assumptions of the model of perfect competition, this process of resource mobility is far from perfect. Family farming is a way of life, one that people do not readily abandon when the terms of trade turn against them. There is great sympathy among American voters for the plight of family farmers. We don't like to witness scenes on the nightly news of families huddled tearfully together as the auctioneer sells off the last of their possessions. We appreciate that these families have worked hard all their lives in an era when many others earn their living by selling crack or robbing convenience stores. Our sympathy for the family farmers has been translated by Congress into legislative programs designed to enable them to remain on their farms.

Price supports for agricultural products are among the most important of these programs. The details of the support programs are highly complex, but for the purpose of our analysis it will suffice to say that the government announces a price for a given product and then stands ready to buy whatever private buyers fail to purchase.[17] One of the most important, if not always explicitly stated, goals of the price support programs is to keep prices high enough to prevent small family farms from going bankrupt.

Sad to say, these programs have failed miserably. Sadder still, even the most cursory understanding of competitive market dynamics would have made clear to Congress why this outcome was inevitable. To illustrate, suppose the price support is set at P_G in a

---

[17]Recent agricultural price support programs, such as the loan deficiency program, work by paying farmers the difference between a specified target price and the actual market price. Under these programs, the price paid by buyers can actually be lower than the unregulated equilibrium price.

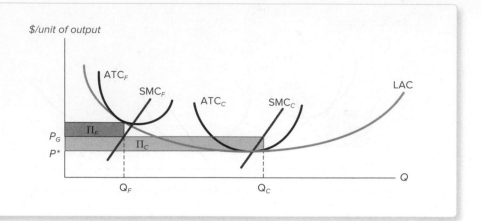

market in which the unsupported price would have been P^*. In Figure 10.21, we see that the short-run effect is to cause family farms to increase their output to Q_F, and to cause corporate farms to increase theirs to Q_C. At these output levels, family farms will earn an economic loss indicated by the light green rectangle labeled Π_F in Figure 10.21, while corporate farms earn an economic profit indicated by the shaded rectangle Π_C.

In the short run, to the extent the new loss is smaller than the previous loss suffered by family farmers, the price support has had the intended effect of helping the family farmer. But the relief is destined to be transitory. To see why, note first that the same price support that reduces the short-run losses of family farms generates positive profits for corporate farms. We know, however, that positive profits are not sustainable in an industry with freedom of entry. They will lure outsiders to bid for farmland so that they too may earn more than a normal rate of return. The effect of this bidding will be to cause land prices to rise to the point where corporate farms no longer earn economic profits. But with land prices higher than before, the cost curves of all farms, corporate and family, shift upward. For owners, some of the sting of these economic losses is mitigated by the greater implicit value of their land. But for the many farm families who rent their land, there is no such compensation.

As technology continues to advance, and with it the scale of the most efficient farms, the stage is now set for another round of distress for family farms and the attendant pressure to increase the government price support level. A treadmill has been set in motion whereby the price support keeps escalating, only to set off another round of escalation in land prices. As a policy for protecting the long-term economic viability of family farms, the agricultural price support program could hardly have been more ill conceived.

Economists are not in a position to tell Congress whether trying to preserve the existence of the family farm is a worthwhile goal. That is a political question. But given that Congress has decided to pursue this objective, economists can give advice about what policies are most likely to be effective. The price supports failed because of the competitive bidding for land that was induced by them. Their long-run effect was to drive up the price of land, while doing little to ensure the survival of small family farms. A much more direct and efficient way to aid family farmers would be to reduce their income taxes; or, in the case of more extreme need, to give them outright cash grants.

The Illusory Attraction of Taxing Business

As noted in Chapter 2, political leaders often find it easier to propose new taxes on business than to collect additional taxes from individuals. Proposals to tax business usually include statements to the effect that "wealthy corporations can better afford to pay extra taxes than struggling workers can." But as we saw in Chapter 2, a tax placed on the product sold by an industry will in general be passed on, at least in part, to consumers.

FIGURE 10.22

The Effect of a Tax on the Output of a Perfectly Competitive Industry

A tax of T dollars per unit of output raises the LAC and SMC curves by T dollars (right panel). The new long-run industry supply curve is again a horizontal line at the minimum value of LAC (left panel). Equilibrium price rises by T dollars (left panel), which means that 100 percent of the tax is passed on to consumers.

Let us examine a perfectly competitive industry in which individual firms have identical U-shaped LAC curves like the one labeled LAC_i in the right panel in Figure 10.22. In the most common case, moderate variations in the industry's output will have no appreciable effect on its input prices, with the result that the long-run supply curve for this industry will be a horizontal line at the minimum point of LAC_i (the curve labeled S_{LR} in the left panel). If D is the market demand curve, then the equilibrium price will be P^*.

Now suppose a tax of T dollars is collected on each unit of output sold in the market. The effect of this tax is to shift the LAC and SMC curves of each firm upward by T dollars (right panel in Figure 10.22). The new long-run industry supply curve is again a horizontal line at the minimum value of the LAC curve—this time the curve $S_{LR} + T$ in the left panel in Figure 10.22. The effect of the tax is to increase the price of the product by exactly T dollars. Industry output contracts from Q_1^* to Q_2^* (left panel), and this contraction is achieved by firms leaving the industry.

Thus we see that, for competitive industries whose firms have U-shaped LAC curves, and whose input prices are fixed (the most empirically relevant case), the burden of a tax on output falls entirely on consumers. As we will see in later chapters, there are a variety of legitimate reasons for taxing the output of specific industries. But the claim that corporations have more money than people do is simply not one of these reasons. Claims to the contrary are fraudulent, and an economically literate population would be unlikely to reelect politicians who defend taxing business on this ground.

If constant-cost competitive industries are able to pass on 100 percent of taxes to buyers, why do industry lobbyists oppose taxes so strongly? Note in Figure 10.22 that one effect of a tax is to reduce total industry output. This reduction is achieved by some firms going out of business. Bankruptcy is never a pleasant experience for the owners of a firm, and on this account it is far from surprising that industry trade associations are so strongly opposed to new taxes.

The Adoption of Cost-Saving Innovations

The economist's emphasis on the competitive firm as a price taker sometimes creates the impression that competitive firms do little more than passively respond to impersonal price signals served up by the environment. This impression is deeply misleading. While it is true, for example, that an individual trucker can do little to affect trucking rates set in the open market, there is a great deal he can and must do to ensure his continued survival.

The short-run response to the dramatic fuel price increases of the 1970s automatically led to just the sorts of adjustments predicted by the competitive model: short-term losses, exit from the industry, gradually rising prices, and a gradual restoration of profitability for surviving firms. But the change in the environment also created opportunities that some firms actively exploited to their own advantage. A case in point is illustrated in the following Economic Naturalist.

Economic Naturalist 10.2

Why did 18-wheel cargo trucks suddenly begin using airfoils in the mid-1970s?

Before 1970, the profile of the typical 18-wheel semi tractor-trailer truck was like the one shown in the margin drawing. The broad, flat expanse of the top of the trailer was directly exposed to the force of the oncoming wind, which at highway speeds was substantial. But diesel fuel cost only $0.30/gal in 1970, and so the penalty from having to run the engine a little harder was not large in those days.

With diesel prices over $1/gal by the early 1980s, however, that penalty became much more important—so much so that entrepreneurs devised ways of reducing it. One of the most successful innovations was the simple airfoil that now adorns the cab of virtually every large truck on the road. Shown in the bottom drawing, its purpose is to deflect the wind to the top of the trailer. The profile of today's semi is still no aerodynamic masterpiece, but truckers estimate that the reduced wind resistance increases their mileage by 15 percent at highway speeds.

Why did airfoils suddenly appear on large trucks in the mid-1970s?

The truckers who were first to install the airfoils did so at a time when the industry price level was determined by the higher costs of running trucks that lacked them. As a result, these early adopters earned economic profits from their efforts. As time passed, however, more and more trucks began to sport the devices, and the industry price level gradually declined in response to the lower costs they made possible. At this point in history, it is rare to see an 18-wheeler that lacks an airfoil. By now it is safe to assume that the resultant cost savings have been fully reflected in lower trucking rates. The result is that the owner of a truck must now install an airfoil merely to be able to earn a normal rate of profit. Those who fail to install them pay the penalty of earning economic losses.

The lesson of this example is that the entrepreneur who earns economic profits is the one who adopts cost-saving innovations ahead of the competition. It is the search for such innovations that keeps even the price-taking firm from being merely a passive reactor to economic forces beyond its control.

SUMMARY

- The assumed objective of the firm is to maximize its economic profit. Competitive pressures in the marketplace may render this a plausible assumption, even though it seems to impute an unrealistically high degree of purposefulness to the actions of many managers. Economic profit is the difference between total revenue and cost—both explicit and implicit—of all resources used in production. Economic profit is not to be confused with accounting profit, which is the difference between total revenue and the explicit cost of resources used. *(LO1)*

- The economic model of perfect competition assumes a standardized product, price-taking behavior on the part of the firms, perfect mobility of resources, and perfect

information on the part of buyers and firms. The model describes idealized conditions that are rarely if ever met in practice. Still, it generates useful predictions and explanations of events we observe in the world. *(LO2)*

- The rule for profit maximization in the short run is to produce the level of output for which price is equal to short-run marginal cost on the rising portion of that curve. If price falls below the minimum value of average variable cost, the firm does best to produce no output in the short run. The individual firm's short-run supply curve is thus the rising portion of its short-run marginal cost curve that lies above the minimum point of its average variable cost curve. *(LO3)*

- The short-run industry supply curve is the horizontal summation of the individual firms' supply curves. It intersects the industry demand curve to determine the short-run equilibrium price. The individual competitive firm's demand curve is a horizontal line at the equilibrium price. If that price happens to lie above the minimum value of the long-run average cost curve, each firm will earn positive economic profits. If price is less than that value, each will suffer economic losses. *(LO4)*

- Long-run adjustments consist not only of alterations in the size of existing firms' capital stocks, but also of entry and exit of firms. Where firms have identical U-shaped LAC curves, the long-run equilibrium price will be the minimum value of that LAC curve, and each firm will produce the corresponding quantity. *(LO6)*

- Both long-run and short-run equilibrium positions are efficient in the sense that the value of the resources used in making the last unit of output is exactly equal to the value of that output to the buyer. This means that the equilibrium position exhausts all possibilities for mutually beneficial exchange. The long-run equilibrium has two additional attractive features: (1) Output is produced at the lowest possible unit cost, and (2) the seller is paid only the cost of producing the product. No economic profit is extracted from the buyer. *(LO5)*

- Under perfect competition with constant input prices, the long-run industry supply curve is a horizontal line, not only when LAC curves are horizontal, but also when they are U-shaped. When input prices are an increasing function of industry output, the industry supply curves in both cases will be upward sloping. When input prices decline with industry output, the competitive industry supply curve will be downward sloping. *(LO6)*

- The effect of competition for the purchase of unusually high-quality inputs is to raise the price of those inputs until they no longer enable the firm that employs them to earn an economic profit. This is an extremely important part of the long-run adjustment process, and failure to account for it lies behind the failure of many well-intended economic policies. *(LO7)*

- Even price-taking firms must actively seek out means of reducing their costs of doing business. To the early adopters of cost-saving innovations goes a temporary stream of economic profit, while late adopters must suffer through periods of economic losses. *(LO7)*

KEY TERMS

allocative efficiency	pecuniary diseconomy	producer surplus
marginal revenue	price elasticity of supply	shutdown condition

REVIEW QUESTIONS

1. What is the difference between economic profit and accounting profit, and how does this difference matter for actual business decisions? *(LO1)*

2. Under what conditions will we expect firms to behave as price takers even though there are only a small number of other firms in the industry? *(LO2)*

3. Would the market for dry cleaning be perfectly competitive in large cities such as San Francisco or New York City? Why or why not? How about in a small city such as Athens, Ohio, or Meredith, New Hampshire? *(LO2)*

4. A firm's total revenue curve is given by $TR = aQ - 2Q^2$. Is this a perfectly competitive firm? Explain why or why not. *(LO2)*

5. Does the fact that a business manager may not know the definition of marginal cost contradict the theory of perfect competition? *(LO1)*

6. *True or false:* If marginal cost lies below average fixed cost, the firm should shut down in the short run. Explain. *(LO3)*

7. What do economists mean when they say that the short-run competitive equilibrium is efficient? *(LO3)*

8. *True or false:* In a constant-cost industry, a tax of a constant, fixed amount on each unit of output sold will not affect the amount of output sold by a perfectly competitive firm in the long run. Explain. *(LO3)*

9. Suppose all firms in a competitive industry are operating at output levels for which price is equal to long-run marginal cost. *True or false:* This industry is necessarily in long-run equilibrium. *(LO6)*

10. *True or false:* Consumer surplus is the area between the demand curve and the price line. For a perfectly competitive firm the demand curve equals the price line. Thus, a perfectly competitive industry produces no consumer surplus. *(LO5)*

11. Why are pecuniary economies and diseconomies said to be the exception rather than the rule? *(LO2)*

12. Would you expect a firm that adopts cost-saving innovations faster than 80 percent of all firms in its industry to earn economic profits? If so, will there be any tendency for these profits to be bid away? *(LO7)*

PROBLEMS

1. A competitive firm has the cost structure described in the following table. Graph the marginal cost, average variable cost, and average total cost curves. How many units of output will it produce at a market price of 32? Calculate its profits and show them in your graph. *(LO3)*

Q	ATC	AVC	MC
1	44	4	8
2	28	8	16
4	26	16	32
6	31	24	48
8	37	32	64

2. If the short-run marginal and average variable cost curves for a competitive firm are given by $SMC = 2 + 4Q$ and $AVC = 2 + 2Q$, how many units of output will it produce at a market price of 10? At what level of fixed cost will this firm earn zero economic profit? *(LO3)*

3. Each of 1,000 identical firms in the competitive peanut butter industry has a short-run marginal cost curve given by

$$SMC = 4 + Q.$$

If the demand curve for this industry is

$$P = 10 - \frac{2Q}{1,000},$$

what will be the short-run loss in producer and consumer surplus if an outbreak of aflatoxin suddenly makes it impossible to produce any peanut butter? *(LO4)*

4. Assuming the aflatoxin outbreak in Problem 3 persists, will the long-run loss in producer and consumer surplus be larger than, smaller than, or the same as the short-run loss? *(LO5)*

5. A perfectly competitive firm faces a price of 10 and is currently producing a level of output at which marginal cost is equal to 10 on a rising portion of its short-run marginal cost curve. Its long-run marginal cost is equal to 12. Its short-run average variable cost is equal to 8. The minimum point on its long-run average variable cost curve is equal to 10. Is this firm earning an economic profit in the short run? Should it alter its output in the short run? In the long run, what should this firm do? *(LO6)*

6. All firms in a competitive industry have long-run total cost curves given by

$$LTC_Q = Q^3 - 10Q^2 + 36Q,$$

where Q is the firm's level of output. What will be the industry's long-run equilibrium price? *(Hint: Use either calculus or a graph to find the minimum value of the associated long-run average cost curve.)* What will be the long-run equilibrium output level of the representative firm? *(LO6)*

7. Same as Problem 6, except now

$$LTC_Q = Q^2 + 4Q.$$

Could any firm actually have this particular LTC curve? Why or why not? *(LO6)*

8. The marginal and average cost curves of taxis in Metropolis are constant at \$0.20/mile. The demand curve for taxi trips in Metropolis is given by $P = 1 - 0.00001Q$, where P is the fare, in dollars per mile, and Q is measured in miles per year. If the industry is perfectly competitive and each cab can provide exactly 10,000 miles/yr of service, how many cabs will there be in equilibrium and what will be the equilibrium fare? *(LO6)*

9. Now suppose that the city council of Metropolis decides to curb congestion in the downtown area by limiting the number of taxis to 6. Applicants participate in a lottery, and the six winners get a medallion, which is a permanent license to operate a taxi in Metropolis. What will the equilibrium fare be now? How much economic profit will each medallion holder earn? If medallions can be traded in the marketplace and the rate of interest is 10 percent/yr, how much will the medallions sell for? *(Hint: How much money would you have to deposit in a bank to earn annual interest equal to the profit made by a taxi medallion?)* Will the person who buys a medallion at this price earn a positive economic profit? *(LO6)*

10. Amada is like all other managers in a perfectly competitive industry except in one respect: Because of her great sense of humor, people are willing to work for her for half the going wage rate. All other firms in the industry have short-run total cost curves given by

$$STC_Q = M + 10Q + wQ^2 \text{ (see footnote 18)},$$

where M is the salary paid to ordinary managers and w is the going wage rate for the industry. If all firms in the industry face an output price of 28, and if $w = 2$, how much more will Amada be paid than the other managers in the industry? *(LO7)*

11. You are the owner/manager of a small competitive firm that manufactures house paints. You and all your 1,000 competitors have total cost curves given by

$$TC = 8 + 2Q + 2Q^2,$$

and the industry is in long-run equilibrium.

[18] The associated marginal cost curve is $dSTC_Q/dQ = MC_Q = 10 + 2wQ$.

Now you are approached by an inventor who holds a patent on a process that will reduce your costs by half at each level of output. *(LO7)*

a. What is the most you would be willing to pay for the exclusive right to use this invention?

b. Would the inventor be willing to sell at that price?

12. In the short run, a perfectly competitive firm produces output using capital services (a fixed input) and labor services (a variable input). At its profit-maximizing level of output, the marginal product of labor is equal to the average product of labor. *(LO3)*

a. What is the relationship between this firm's average variable cost and its marginal cost? Explain.

b. If the firm has 10 units of capital and the rental price of each unit is $4/day, what will be the firm's profit? Should it remain open in the short run?

13. A firm in a competitive industry has a total cost function of TC = $0.2Q^2 - 5Q + 30$, whose corresponding marginal cost curve is MC = $0.4Q - 5$. If the firm faces a price of 6, what quantity should it sell? What profit does the firm make at this price? Should the firm shut down? *(LO3)*

14. The demand for gasoline is P = $5 - 0.002Q$ and the supply is P = $0.2 + 0.004Q$, where P is in dollars and Q is in gallons. If a tax of $1/gal is placed on gasoline, what is the incidence of the tax? What is the lost consumer surplus? What is the lost producer surplus? *(LO4)*

15. Suppose that bicycles are produced by a perfectly competitive, constant-cost industry. Which of the following will have a larger effect on the long-run price of bicycles: (1) a government program to advertise the health benefits of bicycling, or (2) a government program that increases the demand for steel, an input in the manufacture of bicycles that is produced in an increasing cost industry? *(LO6)*

16. Suppose a representative firm in a perfectly competitive, constant-cost industry has a cost function TC = $4Q^2 + 100Q + 100$. *(LO6)*

a. What is the long-run equilibrium price for this industry?

b. If market demand is given by the function Q = $1,000 - P$, where P denotes price, how many firms will operate in this long-run equilibrium?

c. Suppose the government grants a lump-sum subsidy to each firm that manufactures the product. If this lump-sum subsidy equals 36, what would be the new long-run equilibrium price for the industry?

17. The domestic supply and demand curves for Jolt coffee beans are given by P = $10 + Q$ and P = $100 - 2Q$, respectively, where P is the price in dollars per bushel, and Q is the quantity in millions of bushels per year. The United States produces and consumes only a trivial fraction of world Jolt bean output, and the current world price of $30/bushel is unaffected by events in the U.S. market. Transportation costs are also negligible. *(LO6)*

a. How much will U.S. consumers pay for Jolt coffee beans, and how many bushels per year will they consume?

b. How will your answers to part (a) change if Congress enacts a tariff of $20/bushel?

c. What total effect on domestic producer and consumer surplus will the tariff have? How much revenue will the tariff raise?

18. An Australian researcher has discovered a drug that weakens a sheep's wool fibers just above the sheep's skin. The drug sharply reduces the cost of shearing (cutting the wool off) sheep because the entire coat pulls off easily in one piece. The world wool market is reasonably close to the model of perfect competition in both the product and factor sides. Trace out all of the effects of the introduction of this new drug. *(LO6)*

ANSWERS TO SELF-TESTS

10.1 The firm's economic profit would be $0, while its accounting profit would remain at $150. As will be seen, zero economic profits is the theoretically expected outcome under perfect competition.

10.2 Marginal cost is the slope of the total cost curve, and marginal revenue is the slope of the total revenue curve. At the maximum profit point, Q = 7.4, the slopes of these two curves are exactly the same. *(LO3)*

10.3 First, we need to rearrange the representative firm supply curve P = $20 + 90Q_i$ to have quantity alone on one side.

$$Q_i = -\frac{2}{9} + \frac{1}{90}P.$$

Then we multiply by the number of firms n = 30.

$$Q = nQ_i = 30Q_i = 30\left(-\frac{2}{9} + \frac{1}{90}P\right) = -\frac{20}{3} + \frac{1}{3}P.$$

Finally, we rearrange the industry supply curve Q = $-\frac{20}{3} + \frac{1}{3}P$ to have price alone on one side, P = $20 + 3Q$, to return to slope-intercept form. *(LO4)*

10.4 Short-run profit maximization for a perfectly competitive firm occurs at the quantity where price equals marginal cost, P = MC, provided P > min AVC (otherwise, the firm shuts down). Since marginal cost is MC = $2Q$, the market price P = 12 equals marginal cost 12 = $2Q$ at quantity Q = 6. Note that min AVC = 0 here. We can express profits (with fixed costs separated out) as $\pi = (P - AVC)Q - FC$. Since average variable cost is $AVC = Q = 6$, the firm would earn profits of

$$\pi = (12 - 6)6 - FC = 36 - FC.$$

Thus, with fixed cost FC = 36, the firm would earn zero profits. *(LO3)*

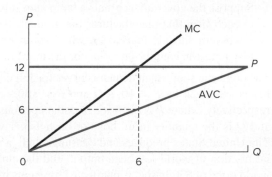

10.5 Total surplus is equal to the sum of the two shaded triangles shown below, which is $100,000/yr. *(LO5)*

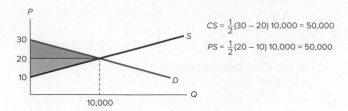

10.6 If the firm pays an incompetent manager only $30,000, it will continue to earn zero economic profit. It cannot pay any more than that without suffering an economic loss. *(LO7)*

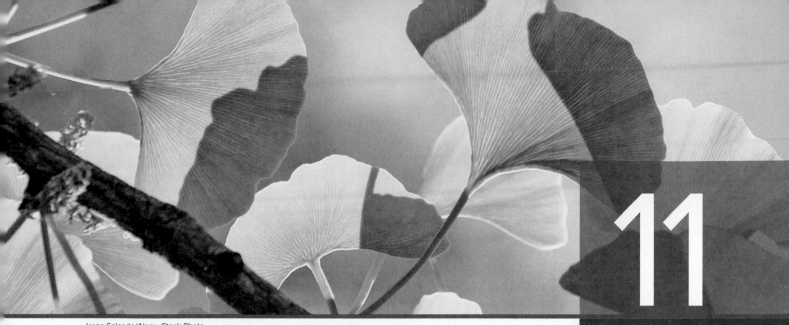
Jorge Salcedo/Alamy Stock Photo

Monopoly

11

Virtually every movie theater charges different admission prices to moviegoers who belong to different groups. Students pay one price, adults another, senior citizens still another. Some theaters sell "ten-packs" of movie tickets at a lower unit price than the tickets they sell at the door. And people who attend showings at the dinner hour sometimes pay much less than those who attend evening showings. None of these practices would be expected under our model of perfect competition, which holds that all buyers pay a single price for a completely standardized product (the so-called *law of one price*).

The same theater operators who charge different ticket prices to different groups follow quite another practice when it comes to the sale of concession items. Here, the law of one price almost always prevails. Students, adults, senior citizens, major league baseball players, the clergy, service station attendants, and all other patrons pay exactly the same price for their popcorn. The same observation applies to the prices of soft drinks and candy. These prices, however, are usually much higher than we see for the same items sold in grocery stores and other retail establishments, certainly far greater than any reasonable measure of the marginal cost of providing them.

Both behaviors—charging differential admission prices on the one hand and uniformly high concession prices on the other—are, as we will see, perfectly consistent with what the economic model predicts about the single seller of a good or service.

CHAPTER PREVIEW

In this chapter, our task will be to examine the market structure that least resembles perfect competition—namely, *monopoly,* a market served by a single seller of a product with no close substitutes. We'll discuss five factors that lead to this market structure: (1) control over key inputs, (2) economies of scale, (3) patents, (4) network economies, and (5) government licenses. We'll then see that the monopolist's rule for maximizing profits in the short run is the same as the one used by perfectly competitive firms. The monopolist will expand output if the gain in revenue exceeds the increase in costs, and will contract output if the loss in revenue is smaller than the reduction in costs.

Next, we'll examine the monopolist's behavior when confronted with the options of selling in several separate markets. Here again, the logic of cost-benefit analysis will provide a convenient framework for analyzing the firm's decision about whether to alter its current behavior.

Our next step will be to examine the efficiency properties of the standard monopoly equilibrium. Unlike the perfectly competitive case, the monopoly equilibrium does not exhaust the potential gains from exchange. In general, the value to society of an additional unit of output will exceed the cost to the monopolist of the resources required to produce it. This finding has often been interpreted to mean that monopoly is less efficient than perfect competition. But this interpretation, we will see, is of only limited practical significance because the conditions that give rise to monopoly are rarely compatible with those required for perfect competition.

Our policy focus in the chapter will be on the question of how the government should treat natural monopolies—markets characterized by downward-sloping long-run average cost curves. We'll consider five policy alternatives: (1) state ownership; (2) private ownership with government price regulation; (3) competitive bidding by private firms for the right to be the sole provider of service; (4) vigorous enforcement of antitrust laws designed to prevent monopoly, and finally; (5) a complete *laissez-faire,* or hands-off, policy. Because problems are inherent in each alternative, the best policy generally will be different in different circumstances.

DEFINING MONOPOLY

Monopoly is a market structure in which a single seller of a product with no close substitutes serves the entire market. This definition could hardly appear any simpler, and yet it turns out to be exceedingly difficult to apply in practice. Consider the example of movie theaters with which the chapter began. Is a local movie house a monopoly under our definition? In smaller cities, at least, it is likely to be the only one showing a given film at a given time. Whether it is a monopoly obviously depends on what we mean by a close substitute. If, for example, the theater is currently showing *Halloween Part 12,* there are likely to be a rich variety of close substitutes for its product. Indeed, literally hundreds of low-grade blood-and-gore films are released each year, and the potential patrons of such films generally do not have to look far if they are dissatisfied with the films available at any particular theater.

But what about a theater that is in the midst of an exclusive first-run engagement of the latest *Wonder Woman* film? For many fans of this series, there is really no close substitute. They do not want to wait to "see it on Netflix." People who want to see the film while the excitement level surrounding its release is still high have only one seller to deal with.

The key feature that differentiates the monopoly from the competitive firm is the price elasticity of demand facing the firm. For the perfectly competitive firm, recall, price elasticity is infinite. If a competitive firm raises its price only slightly, it will lose all its sales. A monopoly, by contrast, has significant control over the price it charges.

Empirically, one practical measure for deciding whether a firm enjoys significant monopoly power is to examine the cross-price elasticity of demand for its closest substitutes. In one famous antitrust case, the DuPont Corporation was charged with having an effective monopoly on the sale of cellophane. Even though the company sold more than 80 percent of all cellophane traded, it was able to defend itself against this charge by arguing that the cross-price elasticities between cellophane and its close substitutes—at the time, mainly waxed paper and aluminum foil—were sufficiently high to justify lumping all of these flexible-wrap products into a single market. DuPont sold less than 20 percent of total industry output under this broader market definition. In a controversial decision, the court deemed that small enough to sustain effective competition.

This is not to say, however, that cross-price elasticity provides a clear, unambiguous measure that distinguishes a product with close substitutes from one without. While there may not be anything quite like the latest *Wonder Woman* movie, there have always been lots of alternative ways to entertain oneself for 2 hours. For the person whose heart is set on seeing *Wonder Woman,* the theater operator is a monopolist, but for the person merely out in search of a good movie, the same theater operator faces stiff competition. The difference between perfect competition and monopoly often boils down to the question of which of these two types of buyers is more numerous. And, of course, the choices faced by both types of buyers are subject to change. On the seller side, having seen their customers successively tempted by videos, DVDs, and now by streaming services, theater owners can testify that "monopoly" does not connote permanent advantage. The task of distinguishing between competition and monopoly, when both are always in flight, remains as much art as science—an art in which definitions based on economic theory may diverge from those based in law or politics.

Note carefully that the distinction between monopoly and competition does not lie in any difference between the respective price elasticities of the *market* demand curves for the two cases. On the contrary, the market price elasticity of demand for products supplied by competitive firms is often much smaller than the price elasticity of demand facing a monopolist. The price elasticity of demand is smaller for wheat than for a copyrighted J.K. Rowling novel, even though wheat is produced under more competitive conditions while Rowling's copyright makes her the only legal seller of her book. *The important distinction between monopoly and competition is that the demand curve facing the individual competitive firm is horizontal (irrespective of the price elasticity of the corresponding market demand curve), while the monopolist's demand curve is simply the downward-sloping demand curve for the entire market.*

FIVE SOURCES OF MONOPOLY

How does a firm come to be the only one that serves its market? Economists discuss five factors, any one or combination of which can enable a firm to become a monopoly. Let's consider these factors in turn.

1. Exclusive Control over Important Inputs The Perrier Corporation of France sells bottled mineral water. It spends millions of dollars each year advertising the unique properties of this water, which are the result, it says, of a once-in-eternity confluence of geological factors that created their mineral spring. In New York State, the Adirondack Soft Drink Company offers a product that is essentially tap water saturated with carbon dioxide gas. I am unable to tell the difference between Adirondack Seltzer and Perrier. But others feel differently, and for many of them there is simply no satisfactory substitute for Perrier. Perrier's monopoly position with respect to these buyers is the result of its exclusive control over an input that cannot easily be duplicated.

A similar monopoly position has resulted from the De Beers Diamond Mines' exclusive control over most of the world's supply of raw diamonds. Synthetic diamonds have now risen in quality to the point where they can occasionally fool even an experienced jeweler. But for many buyers, the preference for a stone that was mined from the earth is not a simple matter of greater hardness and refractive brilliance. They want *real* diamonds, and De Beers is the company that has them.

Exclusive control of key inputs is not a guarantee of permanent monopoly power. The preference for having a real diamond, for example, is based largely on the fact that mined diamonds have historically been genuinely superior to synthetic ones. But assuming that synthetic diamonds eventually do become completely indistinguishable from real ones, there will no longer be any basis for this preference. And as a result, De Beers' control over the supply of mined diamonds will cease to confer monopoly power. New ways are constantly being devised of producing existing products, and the exclusive input that generates today's monopoly is likely to become obsolete tomorrow.

2. Economies of Scale When the long-run average cost curve (given fixed input prices) is downward sloping, the least costly way to serve the market is to concentrate production

FIGURE 11.1

Natural Monopoly

When the LAC curve is declining throughout, it is always cheaper for a single firm to serve the entire industry.

in the hands of a single firm. In Figure 11.1, for example, note that a single firm can produce an industry output of Q^* at an average cost of LAC_{Q^*}, while with two firms sharing the same market, average cost rises to $LAC_{Q^*/2}$. A market that is most cheaply served by a single firm is called a *natural monopoly*.

Recall from Chapter 10 that it is possible for the LAC curve to be downward sloping even in the absence of economies of scale. This can happen, for example, if the price of an important input falls significantly when industry output expands (a *pecuniary economy,* in the language of Chapter 10). Note carefully, however, that this case is *not* one that gives rise to natural monopoly. Input prices here depend on the level of industry output, not on the output of any one firm. Pecuniary economies will apply with equal force whether one or many firms serve the market.

Strictly speaking, then, it is the degree of returns to scale, not the slope of the LAC curve, that determines whether we have a natural monopoly. With fixed input prices, of course, there is always a one-to-one relationship between returns to scale and the slope of the LAC curve (see Chapter 9).

A long-cited-but-now-disrupted example of natural monopoly was telephone landlines. Today, of course, your cable provider will be happy to include telephone services in your package. But note that this competition emerged only as it became possible to provide very high value services through a wire. The revenue-rich combination of telephone services, TV programming, Internet bandwidth, and now captive streamed offerings has made the "last mile" investment in landlines less of a barrier. Indeed, the high value of content services provides an incentive, through satellite and wireless technologies, to bypass the "last mile" altogether and substitute on-property installations.

3. Patents Most countries protect inventions through some sort of patent system. A patent typically confers the right to exclusive benefit from all exchanges involving the invention to which it applies. There are costs as well as benefits to patents. On the cost side, the monopoly it creates usually leads, as we will see, to higher prices for consumers. On the benefit side, the patent makes possible a great many inventions that would not otherwise occur. Although some inventions are serendipitous, most are the result of long effort and expense in sophisticated research laboratories. If a firm were unable to sell its product for a sufficiently high price to recoup these outlays, it would have no economic reason to undertake research and development in the first place. Without a patent, competition would force price down to marginal cost, and the pace of innovation would be slowed dramatically since the protection from competition afforded by a patent is what makes it possible for the firm to recover its costs of innovation. In the United States, the life of a patent is 17 years, a compromise figure that is too long for many inventions, too short for many others. The prescription drug industry has argued that patent life should be extended since the current drug testing and approval process consumes all but a few years of patent protection. On the other side, critics have pointed to the many pharmaceutical industry–sponsored legislative restrictions that, combined with existing patent protection, have served to make U.S. drug prices a multiple of those in most other developed countries.[1]

4. Network Economies On the demand side of many markets, a product becomes more valuable as greater numbers of consumers use it.[2] We see this today in the search and social network advantages enjoyed by Google and Facebook, among others. But an early illustration involving physical products was the VHS technology's defeat of the competing Beta format in home video recorders. The attraction of VHS over the initial versions of Beta was that it permitted longer recording times. Beta later corrected this deficiency, and on most important technical dimensions became widely regarded by experts as superior to VHS. Yet the initial sales advantage of VHS proved insuperable. Once the fraction of consumers owning VHS passed a critical threshold, the reasons for choosing it became compelling—variety and availability of tape rentals, access to repair facilities, the capability to exchange tapes with friends, and so on.

In extreme cases, such *network economies* function like economies of scale as a source of natural monopoly. Microsoft's Windows operating system, for example, achieved its dominant market position on the strength of powerful network economies. Because Microsoft's initial sales advantage gave software developers a strong incentive to write for the Windows format, the inventory of available software in the Windows format quickly became vastly larger than for any competing operating system. And although general-purpose software such as word processors and spreadsheets continued to be available for multiple operating systems, specialized professional software and games usually appeared first in the Windows format and often only in that format. This software gap gave many people a good reason for choosing Windows, even if, as in the case of many Apple Macintosh users, they believed a competing system was otherwise superior. The end result was that at one point, more than 90 percent of the world's personal computers ran the Microsoft's Windows operating system. If that wasn't a pure monopoly, it came awfully close.

5. Government Licenses or Franchises In many markets, the law prevents anyone but a government-licensed firm from doing business. At rest areas on the Massachusetts Turnpike, for example, not just any fast-food restaurant is free to set up operations. The Turnpike Authority negotiates with several companies, chooses one, and then grants it an exclusive license to serve a particular area. As someone who likes Whoppers better than Big Macs, I am happy that the MassPike chose Burger King over McDonald's. But their choice is bound to disappoint many other buyers. The Turnpike's purpose in restricting access in the first place is that there is simply not room for more than one establishment in these locations. In such cases, the government license as a source of monopoly is really a scale economy acting in another form. But government licenses are also required in a variety of other markets, such as the one for taxis, where scale economies do not seem to be an important factor. Of course, in this case, the rise of Uber and Lyft reminds us that a government-issued "medallion" brings no assurance that a monopoly franchise will be permanent.

Government licenses are sometimes accompanied by strict regulations that spell out what the licensee can and cannot do. Where the government gives a chain restaurant an exclusive license, for example, the restaurant will often be required to charge prices no more than, say, 10 percent higher than it charges in its unregulated outlets. In other cases,

---

[1]On the "long run-up" to drug approval and its effects on new drug introduction, see Henry G. Grabowski and John W. Vernon, *Drug Regulation and Innovation: Balancing the Benefits and Risks*, Washington, DC: American Enterprise Institute, 1983 (www.aei.org/researchproducts/book/the-regulation-of-pharmaceuticals-balancing-the-benefits-and-risks/); and the follow-up by the same authors, "Longer Patents for Lower Imitation Barriers: The 1984 Drug Act, *AEA Papers and Proceedings*, 1986. A more recent study of the long run-up problem is Erika Lietzan, "The Drug Innovation Paradox." *Missouri Law Review* 83, 2018, 39. For a survey of recent articles around competition and pricing in the pharmaceutical industry, see Timothy Taylor, "The Market for US Prescription Drugs," May 17, 2017, http://conversableeconomist.blogspot.com/search?q=pharmaceutical.

[2]See, for example, Joseph Farrell and Garth Saloner, "Standardization, Compatibility, and Innovation," *Rand Journal of Economics*, 16, 1985: 70–83; and M. L. Katz and Carl Shapiro, "Systems Competition and Network Effects," *Journal of Economic Perspectives*, Spring 1994, 93–115.

the government simply charges an extremely high fee for the license, virtually forcing the licensee to charge premium prices. This is the practice of some airport authorities, who essentially auction their terminal counter space to the highest bidders. Your annoyance at having to pay $5 for a hot dog in LaGuardia Airport is thus more properly focused on the Port Authority of New York than on the vendor.

By far the most important of the five factors for explaining monopolies that endure is economies of scale. Production processes change over time, which makes exclusive control over important inputs only a transitory source of monopoly. Patents too are inherently transitory. Network economies, once firmly entrenched, can be as persistent a source of natural monopoly as economies of scale. Strictly speaking, network economies work through the demand side of the market by affecting what buyers are willing to pay for a product. But they may be equivalently conceptualized on the supply side as yet another feature of product quality. The more people who own the product, the higher its effective quality level. It may thus be said of a product that benefits from network economies that any given quality level can be produced at lower cost as sales volume increases. Viewed in this way, network economies are just another form of economies of scale in production, and that's how we shall view them in the discussion that follows. Government licenses can persist for extended periods, but many of these licenses are themselves merely an implicit recognition of scale economies that would lead to monopoly in any event.

Information as a Growing Source of Economies of Scale

In 1984, at the dawn of the personal computing age, approximately 80 percent of the cost of a personal computer was accounted for by its hardware, only 20 percent by its software. Only six years later, those percentages were exactly reversed. Now all but a tiny fraction of the total costs of bringing a personal computer to market are associated in one way or another with the production of information. Although this transformation has been especially dramatic in the case of personal computers, similar ones have been occurring for most other products as well.

The distinctive feature about information is that virtually all costs associated with the production of it are fixed—in contrast to hardware, for which a large share of production costs are roughly proportional to the volume of production. The upshot is that the production of information-rich products is often characterized by enormous economies of scale.

Because the concept of economies of scale refers to the long run by definition, the preceding paragraph's reference to economies of scale and fixed costs in the same breath might seem inconsistent. After all, fixed costs are expenditures associated with fixed inputs, and as we saw in Chapter 8, no inputs are fixed in the long run.

As a practical matter, however, large one-time costs, including product research and other costs associated with generating information, are often incurred before a product is launched. Typically these costs never recur, even during a product life cycle spanning several decades. Strictly speaking, these costs are not fixed, since the inputs used for generating the information could be varied in principle. Yet when the product is launched, there is simply no economic reason for varying them. So for practical purposes these costs are essentially fixed. In any case, the important point is that the firm's long-run average cost curve is likely to be downward sloping whenever a substantial share of its total cost is associated with initial investments in information.

A case in point is the microprocessor that powers personal computers and a growing array of other products. The fixed investment required to produce the latest Intel chip is roughly $2 billion. Once the chip has been designed and the manufacturing facility built, however, the marginal cost of producing each chip is very small. It is hardly a surprise, therefore, that Intel currently supplies more than 80 percent of all microprocessors in servers sold today.

Economies of scale have always been an important feature of the modern industrial landscape. But as more and more of the value embedded in products consists of information, the importance of economies of scale can only grow further.

With this brief overview of the causes of monopoly in mind, let's turn now to the question of what the consequences of monopoly are. In order to do this, we'll proceed in much the same fashion as we did in our study of the competitive firm. That is, we'll examine the firm's output decision and ask whether it leads to a situation in which all possible gains from exchange are exhausted. The answer is generally no. But in formulating a government policy to improve on the results of unregulated monopoly, we'll see that it is critical to understand the original source of monopoly.

THE PROFIT-MAXIMIZING MONOPOLIST

As in the competitive case, we assume that the monopolist's goal is to maximize economic profit. And again as before, in the short run this means to choose the level of output for which the difference between total revenue and short-run total cost is greatest. The case for this motive is less compelling than in the case of perfect competition. After all, the monopolist's survival is less under siege than the competitor's, and so the evolutionary argument for profit maximization applies with less force in the monopoly case. Nonetheless, we will explore just what behaviors follow from the monopolist's goal of profit maximization.

The Monopolist's Total Revenue Curve

The key difference between the monopolist and the perfect competitor is the way in which total, and hence marginal, revenue varies with output. Recall from Chapter 10 that the demand curve facing the perfect competitor is simply a horizontal line at the short-run equilibrium market price—call it P^*. The competitive firm is a price taker, typically because its own output is too small to have any discernible influence on the market price. Under these circumstances, the perfectly competitive firm's total revenue curve is a ray with slope P^*, as shown in Figure 11.2.

Now consider a monopolist with the downward-sloping demand curve $P = 80 - \left(\frac{1}{5}\right)Q$ pictured in the top panel in Figure 11.3. For this firm as well, total revenue is the product of price and quantity. At point A on its demand curve, for example, it sells 100 units of output per week at a price of $60/unit, giving a total revenue of $6,000/wk. At B, it sells 200 units at a price of $40, so its total revenue at B will be $8,000/wk, and so on. The difference between the monopolist and the competitor is that for the monopolist to sell a larger amount of output, it must cut its price—not only for the marginal unit but for all preceding units as well. As we saw in Chapter 5, the effect of a downward-sloping demand curve is that total revenue is no longer proportional to output sold. As in the competitive case, the monopolist's total revenue curve (middle panel in Figure 11.3) passes through the origin, because in each case selling no output generates no revenue. But as price falls, total revenue for the monopolist does not rise linearly with output. Instead, it reaches a maximum value at the quantity corresponding to the midpoint of the demand curve (B in the top panel), after which it again begins to fall. The corresponding values of the price elasticity of demand are shown in the bottom panel in Figure 11.3. Note that total revenue reaches its maximum value when the price elasticity of demand is unity.

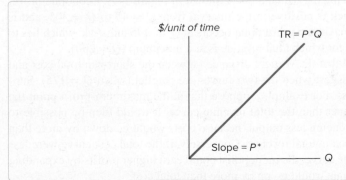

$/unit of time

TR = P*Q

Slope = P*

Q

FIGURE 11.3

Demand, Total Revenue, and Elasticity

For the monopolist to increase sales, it is necessary to cut price (top panel). Total revenue rises with quantity, reaches a maximum value, and then declines (middle panel). The quantity level for which the price elasticity of demand is unity corresponds to the midpoint of the demand curve, and at that value total revenue is maximized.

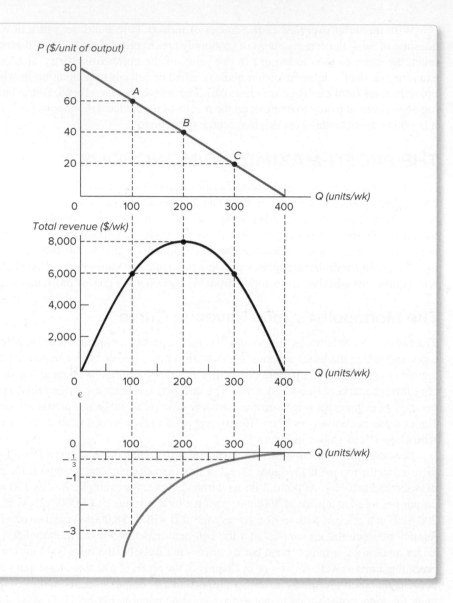

The top panel in Figure 11.4 portrays the short-run total cost curve and total revenue curve for a monopolist facing the demand curve shown in Figure 11.3. Economic profit, plotted in the bottom panel, is positive in the interval from $Q = 45$ to $Q = 305$, and is negative elsewhere. The maximum profit point occurs at $Q^* = 175$ units/wk, which lies to the left of the output level for which total revenue is at a maximum ($Q = 200$).

Notice in Figure 11.4 that the vertical distance between the short-run total cost and total revenue curves is greatest when the two curves are parallel (when $Q = 175$). Suppose this were not the case. For example, suppose that at the maximum-profit point the total cost curve were steeper than the total revenue curve. It would then be possible to earn higher profits by producing less output, because costs would go down by more than the corresponding reduction in total revenue. Conversely, if the total cost curve were less steep than the total revenue curve, the monopolist could earn higher profits by expanding output, because total revenue would go up by more than total cost.

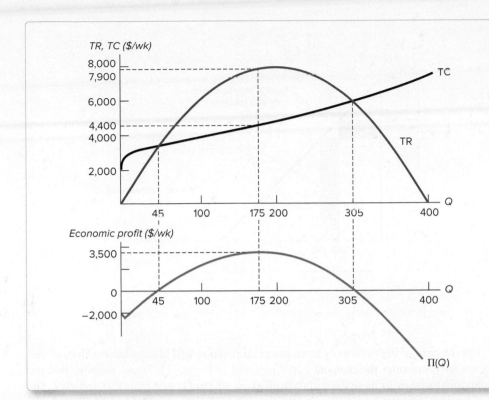

FIGURE 11.4

Total Cost, Revenue, and Profit Curves for a Monopolist

Economic profit [$\Pi(Q)$ in the bottom panel] is the vertical distance between total revenue and total cost (TR and TC in the top panel). Note that the maximum-profit point, $Q^* = 175$, lies to the left of the output level at which TR is at a maximum ($Q = 200$).

Marginal Revenue

The slope of the total cost curve at any level of output is by definition equal to marginal cost at that output level. By the same token, the slope of the total revenue curve is the definition of *marginal revenue*.[3] As in the case of the perfectly competitive firm, we can think of marginal revenue as the change in total revenue when the sale of output changes by 1 unit. More precisely, suppose ΔTR_Q is the change in total revenue that occurs in response to a small change in output, ΔQ. Marginal revenue, denoted MR_Q, is then given by

$$MR_Q = \frac{\Delta TR_Q}{\Delta Q}. \tag{11.1}$$

Using this definition, a profit-maximizing monopolist in the short run will choose that level of output Q^* for which

$$MC_{Q^*} = MR_{Q^*} \text{ (see footnote 4),} \tag{11.2}$$

provided marginal revenue intersects marginal cost from above. Equation 11.2 defines the **optimality condition for a monopolist.** The monopolist wants to sell all units for which marginal revenue exceeds marginal cost, so marginal revenue should lie above marginal cost prior to the intersection (for some cost structures, marginal cost may decline initially and then increase, leading to two intersections of marginal cost and marginal revenue).

Recall that the analogous condition for the perfectly competitive firm is to choose the output level for which price and marginal cost are equal. Recalling that marginal revenue and price (P) are exactly the same for the competitive firm (when such a firm expands output by 1 unit, its total revenue goes up by P), we see that the profit-maximizing condition for the perfectly competitive firm is simply a special case of Equation 11.2.

optimality condition for a monopolist a monopolist maximizes profit by choosing the level of output where marginal revenue equals marginal cost.

---

[3] In calculus terms, marginal revenue is defined as the derivative dTR/dQ.
[4] This condition can also be justified by noting that the first-order condition for maximum profit is given by

$$\frac{d\Pi}{dQ} = \frac{d(TR - TC)}{dQ} = MR - MC = 0$$

The area of rectangle *A* ($1,000/wk) is the loss in revenue from selling the previous output level at a lower price. The area of rectangle *B* ($2,500/wk) is the gain in revenue from selling the additional output at the new, lower price. Marginal revenue is the difference between these two areas ($2,500 − $1,000 = $1,500/wk) divided by the change in output (50 units/wk). Here MR equals $30/unit, which is less than the new price of $50/unit.

In the case of the monopoly firm, marginal revenue will always be less than price.[5] To see why, consider the demand curve pictured in Figure 11.5, and suppose that the monopolist wishes to increase output from $Q_0 = 100$ to $Q_0 + \Delta Q = 150$ units/wk. His total revenue from selling 100 units/wk is ($60/unit) (100 units/wk) = $6,000/wk. To sell an additional $\Delta Q = 50$ units/wk, he must cut his price to $60 − \Delta P = $50/unit, which means his new total revenue will be ($50/unit)(150 units/wk), which is equal to $7,500/wk. To calculate marginal revenue, we simply subtract the original total revenue, $6,000/wk, from the new total revenue, and divide by the change in output, $\Delta Q = 50$ units/wk. This yields $\mathrm{MR}_{Q_0 = 100} = ($7,500/wk − $6,000/wk)/(50 units/wk) = $30/unit, which is clearly less than the original price of $60/unit.

Another useful way of thinking about marginal revenue is to view it as the gain in revenue from new sales minus the loss in revenue from selling the previous output level at the new, lower price. In Figure 11.5, the area of rectangle *B* ($2,500/wk) represents the gain in revenue from the additional sales at the lower price. The area of rectangle *A* ($1,000/wk) represents the loss in revenue from selling the original 100 units/wk at $50/unit instead of $60. Marginal revenue is the difference between the gain in revenue from additional sales and the loss in revenue from sales at a lower price, divided by the change in quantity. This yields ($2,500/wk − $1,000/wk)/(50 units/wk), which is again equal to $30/unit.

To explore how marginal revenue varies as we move along a straight-line demand curve, consider the demand curve pictured in Figure 11.6, and suppose that the monopolist wishes to increase output from Q_0 to $Q_0 + \Delta Q$ units. His total revenue from selling Q_0 units is $P_0 Q_0$. To sell an additional ΔQ units, he must cut his price to $P_0 − \Delta P$, which means his new total revenue will be $(P_0 − \Delta P)(Q_0 + \Delta Q)$, which is equal to $P_0 Q_0 + P_0 \Delta Q − \Delta P Q_0 − \Delta P \Delta Q$. To calculate marginal revenue, simply subtract the original total revenue, $P_0 Q_0$, from the new total revenue, and divide by the change in output, ΔQ. This leaves $\mathrm{MR}_{Q_0} = P_0 − (\Delta P/\Delta Q)Q_0 − \Delta P$, which is clearly less than P_0. As ΔP approaches zero, the expression for marginal revenue thus approaches[6]

$$\mathrm{MR}_{Q_0} = P_0 - \frac{\Delta P}{\Delta Q} Q_0. \tag{11.3}$$

---

[5]There is actually one exception to this claim, namely, the case of the perfectly discriminating monopolist, discussion of which follows.

[6]Note that when ΔP shrinks toward zero, the corresponding ΔQ does so as well. Because ΔP and ΔQ are both positive here, the ratio $\Delta P/\Delta Q$ is simply the negative of the slope of the demand curve.

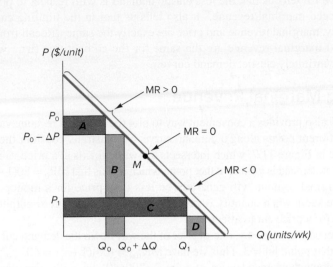

FIGURE 11.6

Marginal Revenue and Position on the Demand Curve

When Q is to the left of the midpoint (M) of a straight-line demand curve (for example, $Q = Q_0$), the gain from added sales (area B) outweighs the loss from a lower price for existing sales (area A). When Q is to the right of the midpoint (for example, $Q = Q_1$), the gain from added sales (area D) is smaller than the loss from a lower price for existing sales (area C). At the midpoint of the demand curve, the gain and the loss are equal, which means marginal revenue is zero.

Equation 11.3 makes intuitive sense if we think of ΔQ as being a 1-unit change in output; P_0 would then be the gain in revenue from the sale of that extra unit, and $(\Delta P/\Delta Q)Q_0 = \Delta P Q_0$ would be the loss in revenue from the sale of the existing units at the lower price. We see again in Equation 11.3 that marginal revenue is less than price for all positive levels of output.

The fact that area B is larger than area A in Figure 11.6 means that marginal revenue is positive at Q_0. Once output moves past the midpoint (M in Figure 11.6) on a straight-line demand curve, however, the marginal revenue of a further expansion will be negative. Thus, the area of rectangle C is larger than the area of rectangle D in Figure 11.6, which means that marginal revenue at the output level Q_1 is less than zero.

Marginal Revenue and Elasticity

Yet another useful relationship links marginal revenue to the price elasticity of demand at the corresponding point on the demand curve. Recall from Chapter 5 that the price elasticity of demand at a point (Q, P) is given by

$$\epsilon = \frac{\Delta Q}{\Delta P}\frac{P}{Q}. \tag{11.4}$$

In Equation 11.4, the terms ΔQ and ΔP have opposite signs, because the demand curve is downward sloping. By contrast, recall that the ΔQ and ΔP terms in Equation 11.3, which also represent changes in P and Q as we move along the demand curve, are both positive. Suppose we redefine ΔQ and ΔP from Equation 11.4 so that both of these terms are positive. That equation then becomes

$$|\epsilon| = \frac{\Delta Q}{\Delta P}\frac{P}{Q}. \tag{11.5}$$

The purpose of making both ΔQ and ΔP positive is to be able to relate Equation 11.5 back to Equation 11.3. If we now solve Equation 11.5 for $\Delta P/\Delta Q = P/(Q|\epsilon|)$ and substitute into Equation 11.3, we get

$$\mathrm{MR}_Q = P\left(1 - \frac{1}{|\epsilon|}\right). \tag{11.6}$$

Equation 11.6 tells us that the less elastic demand is with respect to price, the more price will exceed marginal revenue.[7] It also tells us that in the limiting case of infinite price elasticity, marginal revenue and price are exactly the same. (Recall from Chapter 10 that price and marginal revenue are the same for the competitive firm, which faces a horizontal, or infinitely elastic, demand curve.)

Graphing Marginal Revenue

Equation 11.6 also provides a convenient way to plot the marginal revenue values that correspond to different points along a demand curve. To illustrate, consider the straight-line demand curve in Figure 11.7, which intersects the vertical axis at a price value of $P = 80$. The elasticity of demand is infinite at that point, which means that $MR_0 = 80(1 - 1/|\epsilon|) = 80$. Although marginal revenue will generally be less than price for a monopolist, the two are exactly the same when quantity is zero. The reason is that at zero output there are no existing sales for a price cut to affect.

Now suppose we move, say, one-quarter of the way down the demand curve to point A, $(100, 60)$. At that point, $|\epsilon| = 3$. Thus we have $MR_{100} = (60)(1 - \frac{1}{3}) = 40$.

Halfway down the demand curve, at point B, $(200, 40)$, $|\epsilon| = 1$, which gives us $MR_{200} = (40)(1 - \frac{1}{1}) = 0$. This confirms our earlier finding (Chapter 5) that total revenue is at a maximum at the midpoint of a straight-line demand curve, where elasticity is unity.

Finally, consider point C, $(300, 20)$, which is three-fourths of the way down the demand curve. Here $|\epsilon| = \frac{1}{3}$, so we have $MR_{300} = (20)[1 - (1/\frac{1}{3})] = (20)(-2) = -40$. Thus, at $Q = 300$, the effect of selling an extra unit of output is to reduce total revenue by \$40/wk.

Filling in additional points in the same fashion, we quickly see that the marginal revenue curve associated with a straight-line demand curve is itself a straight line, one whose slope is twice that of the demand curve. The marginal revenue curve cuts the horizontal axis just below the midpoint of the demand curve, and for all quantities larger than that marginal revenue is negative. Note that all points to the right of the midpoint of the demand curve have price elasticity values less than 1 in absolute value. The fact that

FIGURE 11.7

The Demand Curve and Corresponding Marginal Revenue Curve

For the case of a straight-line demand curve, the corresponding marginal revenue curve is also a straight line. It has the same vertical intercept as the demand curve, and its horizontal intercept is half that of the demand curve.

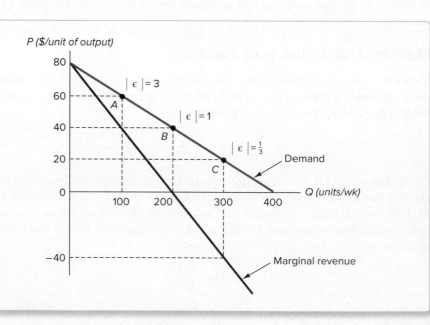

[7]Equation 11.6 can be derived using calculus as follows:

$$MR = \frac{dTR}{dQ} = \frac{d(PQ)}{dQ} = P + Q\frac{dP}{dQ} = P\left(1 + \frac{Q}{P}\frac{dP}{dQ}\right) = P\left(1 + \frac{1}{\epsilon}\right) = P\left(1 - \frac{1}{|\epsilon|}\right).$$

marginal revenue is negative in this region thus fits our observation from Chapter 5 that a cut in price will reduce total revenue whenever demand is inelastic with respect to price.

EXAMPLE 11.1   Marginal Revenue Curve

Find the marginal revenue curve that corresponds to the demand curve $P = 12 - 3Q$.

The marginal revenue curve will have the same intercept as and twice the slope of the demand curve, which gives us $MR = 12 - 6Q$, as plotted in Figure 11.8.

The general formula for a linear demand curve is $P = a - bQ$, where a and b are positive numbers. The corresponding marginal revenue curve will be $MR = a - 2bQ$ (see footnote 8).

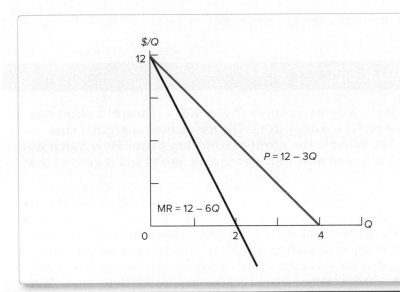

FIGURE 11.8

A Specific Linear Demand Curve and the Corresponding Marginal Revenue Curve

The marginal revenue curve has the same vertical intercept and twice the slope of the corresponding linear demand curve.

SELF-TEST 11.2

Sketch demand and marginal revenue curves for a monopolist whose market demand curve is given by $P = 100 - 2Q$.

Graphical Interpretation of the Short-Run Profit Maximization Condition

Recall from Chapter 10 the graphical representation of the maximum-profit point for the competitive firm in the short run. An analogous graphical representation exists for the monopolist. Consider a monopolist with the demand, marginal revenue, and short-run cost curves pictured in Figure 11.9. The profit-maximizing level of output for this firm is Q^*, the one for which the marginal revenue and marginal cost curves intersect. At that quantity level, the monopolist can charge a price of P^*, and by so doing will earn an economic profit equal to the shaded rectangle labeled Π.

---

[8]Note that total revenue for the demand curve $P = a - bQ$ is given by $TR = aQ - bQ^2$. The corresponding marginal revenue curve is

$$MR = \frac{dTR}{dQ} = a - 2bQ.$$

FIGURE 11.9

The Profit-Maximizing Price and Quantity for a Monopolist

Maximum profit occurs at the output level Q^*, where the gain in revenue from expanding output (or loss in revenue from contracting output), MR, is exactly equal to the cost of expanding output (or the savings from contracting output), SMC. At Q^*, the firm charges P^* and earns an economic profit of Π.

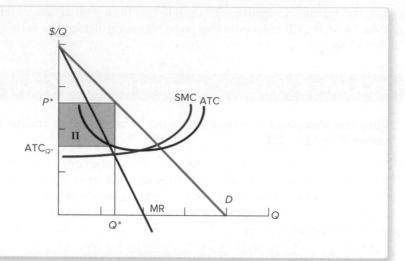

EXAMPLE 11.2   Profit Maximization

A monopolist faces a demand curve of $P = 100 - 2Q$ and a short-run total cost curve of $TC = 640 + 20Q$. The associated marginal cost curve is $MC = 20$. What is the profit-maximizing price? How much will the monopolist sell, and how much economic profit will it earn at that price?

The marginal revenue curve for this demand curve is $MR = 100 - 4Q$. Marginal cost is the slope of the total cost curve, which is constant at 20 in this example. Setting $MR = MC$, we have $100 - 4Q = 20$, which yields the profit-maximizing quantity, $Q^* = 20$. Plugging $Q^* = 20$ back into the demand curve, we get the profit-maximizing price, $P^* = 60$. This solution is shown graphically in Figure 11.10, which also displays the average total cost curve for the monopolist. Note that at Q^* the ATC is 52, which means the monopolist earns an economic profit of $60 - 52 = 8$ on each unit sold. With $Q^* = 20$, that makes for a total economic profit of 160.

FIGURE 11.10

The Profit-Maximizing Price and Quantity for Specific Cost and Demand Functions

---

Note in Figure 11.10 that the monopolist's fixed cost was irrelevant to the determination of the profit-maximizing output level and price. This makes sense intuitively, because fixed cost has no bearing on the gains and losses that occur when output changes.

A Profit-Maximizing Monopolist Will Never Produce on the Inelastic Portion of the Demand Curve

If a monopolist's goal is to maximize profits, it follows directly that she will never produce an output level on the inelastic portion of her demand curve. If she were to increase her price at such an output level, the effect would be to increase total revenue. The price increase would also reduce the quantity demanded, which, in turn, would reduce the monopolist's total cost. Since economic profit is the difference between total revenue and total cost, profit would necessarily increase in response to a price increase from an initial position on the inelastic portion of the demand curve. The profit-maximizing level of output must therefore lie on the elastic portion of the demand curve, where further price increases would cause both revenue and costs to go down.

The Profit-Maximizing Markup

The profit-maximization condition MR = MC can be combined with Equation 11.6, which says $MR = P[1 - (1/|\epsilon|)]$, to derive the profit-maximizing markup for the monopolist:

$$\frac{P - MC}{P} = \frac{1}{|\epsilon|}, \tag{11.7}$$

which is the difference between price and marginal cost, expressed as a fraction of the profit-maximizing price. For example, if the price elasticity of demand facing a monopolist were equal to -2, the profit-maximizing markup would be $\frac{1}{2}$ which implies that the profit-maximizing price is twice marginal cost. Equation 11.7 tells us that the profit-maximizing markup grows smaller as demand grows more elastic. In the limiting case of infinitely elastic demand, the profit-maximizing markup is zero (which implies $P = MC$), the same as in the perfectly competitive case.

The Monopolist's Shutdown Condition

In the case of the perfectly competitive firm, we saw that it paid to shut down in the short run whenever the price fell below the minimum value of average variable cost (AVC). The analogous condition for the monopolist is that there exists no quantity for which the demand curve lies above the average variable cost curve. The monopolist whose demand, marginal revenue, SMC, and AVC curves are shown in Figure 11.11, for example, has no positive level of output for which price exceeds AVC, and so the monopolist does best by

FIGURE 11.11

A Monopolist Who Should Shut Down in the Short Run

Whenever average revenue (the price value on the demand curve) is lower than average variable cost for every level of output, the monopolist does best to cease production in the short run.

ceasing production in the short run. He will then sustain a short-run economic loss equal to his fixed costs, but he would do even worse at any positive level of output.

Another way of stating the shutdown condition for a monopolist is to say that he should cease production whenever average revenue is less than average variable cost at every level of output. Average revenue is simply another name for price—the value of P along the monopolist's demand curve.[9]

Figure 11.11 also illustrates the important point that MR = MC is a necessary, but not sufficient, condition for maximum profit. Note in the figure that marginal revenue is equal to marginal cost at the output level Q_0. Why isn't this the maximum-profit point? Recall that in the case of the perfectly competitive firm, the maximum-profit condition called for price to equal marginal cost on a rising portion of the marginal cost curve, above the minimum point on the AVC curve. A somewhat different condition applies in the case of the monopolist. In Figure 11.11, note that at Q_0 the MR curve intersects the MC curve from below.[10] This means not only that Q_0 is not the maximum-profit point, but that it actually corresponds to a *lower* profit level than any of the other output levels nearby. For example, consider an output level just less than Q_0. At any such output level the gains from contracting output (MC) will exceed the losses (MR), so the firm does better to contract from Q_0. Now consider an output level just slightly larger than Q_0. For such an output level, the gains from expanding (MR) exceed the costs (MC), so the firm does better to expand. Thus, when the firm is at Q_0, it can earn higher profits by either contracting *or* expanding. Q_0 is called a *local minimum* profit point.[11]

Note also in Figure 11.11 that the MR curve intersects the MC curve a second time at the output level Q_1. This time the intersection occurs from above, and you can easily show as an exercise that Q_1 yields higher profits than any of the other output levels close by. (The argument runs exactly parallel to the one in the preceding paragraph.) We refer to points like Q_1 as *local maximum* profit points. But although Q_1 yields more profit than any nearby output level, the firm fails to cover its average variable cost at the level of output, and so does better simply to produce nothing at all. The point Q^* we saw earlier in Figure 11.9 is both a local maximum profit point and a *global maximum* profit point, the latter designation indicating that no other output level, including zero, yields higher profit. For a monopolist, a global maximum profit point might occur either on the rising or on the falling portion of the MC curve. But it must be at a point where the MR curve intersects the MC curve from above.

SELF-TEST 11.4

Find the optimal price and quantity for the monopolist described by the information in the following table.

Q	P	MR	SMC	AVC
0	100	100	150	150
15	86	71	71	107
25	75	50	41	84
34	66	33	33	72
50	50	0	63	63

To recapitulate briefly, we have seen that the monopolist behaves like a perfectly competitive firm in the sense that each chooses an output level by weighing the benefits of expanding (or contracting) output against the corresponding costs. For both the perfect

[9]More formally, note that average revenue = $TR/Q = PQ/Q = P$.
[10]To "intersect from below at Q_0" means that as Q approaches Q_0 from the left, MR lies below MC and then crosses MC when $Q = Q_0$.
[11]The second-order condition for maximum profit is given by

$$\frac{d(\text{MR} - \text{MC})}{dQ} = \frac{d\text{MR}}{dQ} - \frac{d\text{MC}}{dQ} < 0,$$

which says simply that the slope of the marginal revenue curve must be less than the slope of the marginal cost curve.

competitor and the monopolist, marginal cost is the relevant measure of the cost of expanding output. Fixed costs are irrelevant for short-run output decisions in both cases. For both the monopolist and the perfect competitor, the benefits of expanding output are measured by their respective values of marginal revenue. For the competitor, marginal revenue and price are one and the same. For the monopolist, by contrast, marginal revenue is less than price. The competitor maximizes profit by expanding output until marginal cost equals price. The monopolist maximizes profit by expanding output until marginal cost equals marginal revenue, and thus chooses a lower output level than if he had used the competitor's criterion. Both the monopolist and the perfect competitor do best to shut down in the short run if price is less than average variable cost for all possible levels of output.

A MONOPOLIST HAS NO SUPPLY CURVE

As we saw in Chapter 10, the competitive firm has a well-defined supply curve. It takes market price as given and responds by choosing the output level for which marginal cost and price are equal. At the industry level, a shifting demand curve will trace out a well-defined industry supply curve, which is the horizontal summation of the individual firm supply curves.

There is no similar supply curve for the monopolist. The reason is that the monopolist is not a price taker, which means that there is no unique correspondence between price and marginal revenue when the market demand curve shifts. Thus, a given marginal revenue value for one demand curve can correspond to one price, while the same value of marginal revenue for a second demand curve corresponds to a different price. As a result, it is possible to observe the monopolist producing Q_1^* and selling at P^* in one period, and then selling Q_2^* at P^* in another period.

To illustrate, consider a monopolist with a demand curve of $P = 100 - Q$ and with the same cost curves as in Example 11.2, in particular with MC = 20. The marginal revenue curve for this monopolist is given by MR = $100 - 2Q$, and equating MR to MC yields a profit-maximizing output level of $Q^* = 40$. The corresponding profit-maximizing price is $P^* = 60$. Note that this is the same as the profit-maximizing price we saw for the monopolist in Example 11.2, even though the demand curve here lies to the right of the earlier one.

When the monopolist's demand curve shifts, the price elasticity of demand at a given price generally will also shift. But these shifts need not occur in the same direction. When demand shifts rightward, for example, elasticity at a given price may either increase or decrease, and the same is true when demand shifts leftward. The result is that there can be no unique correspondence between the price a monopolist charges and the amount she chooses to produce. And hence we say that the monopolist has no supply curve. Rather, she has a *supply rule,* which is to equate marginal revenue and marginal cost.

Adjustments in the Long Run

In the long run, the monopolist is of course free to adjust all inputs, just as the competitive firm is. What is the optimal quantity in the long run for a monopolist with a given technology? The best the monopolist can do is to produce the quantity for which long-run marginal cost is equal to marginal revenue. In Figure 11.12, that will mean choosing a capital stock that gives rise to the short-run average and marginal cost curves labeled ATC* and SMC*. For that level of capital stock, the short-run marginal cost curve passes through the intersection of the long-run marginal cost and marginal revenue curves. Q^* will be the profit-maximizing quantity in the long run, and it will sell at a price of P^*. For the conditions pictured in Figure 11.12, the long-run economic profit level, P, will be positive, and is indicated by the area of the shaded rectangle.

As we saw in Chapter 10, economic profits tend to vanish in the long run in perfectly competitive industries. This tendency will sometimes be present for monopoly. To the extent that the factors that gave rise to the firm's monopoly position come under attack in the long run, there will be downward pressure on its profits. For example, competing firms may develop substitutes for important inputs that were previously under the control of the monopolist. Or in the case of patented products, competitors may develop close substitutes that do not infringe on existing patents, which are in any event only temporary.

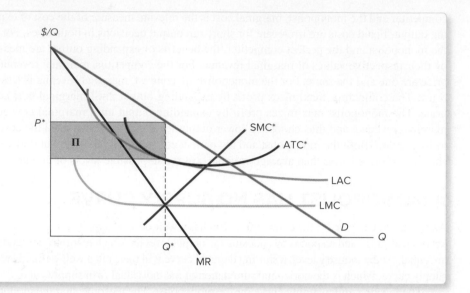

FIGURE 11.12

Long-Run Equilibrium for a Profit-Maximizing Monopolist

The profit-maximizing quantity in the long run is Q^*, the output level for which LMC = MR. The profit-maximizing price in the long run is P^*. The optimal capital stock in the long run gives rise to the short-run marginal cost curve SMC*, which passes through the intersection of LMC and MR.

But in other cases there may be a tendency for monopoly profits to persist. The firm shown in Figure 11.12, for example, has a declining long-run average cost curve, which means that it may enjoy a persistent cost advantage over potential rivals. In such natural monopolies, economic profits may be highly stable over time. And the same, of course, may be true for a firm whose monopoly comes from having a government license. Persistent economic profits are indeed one of the major policy concerns about monopoly, as we will discuss later in the chapter.

PRICE DISCRIMINATION

Our discussion thus far has assumed that the monopolist sells all its output at a single price. In reality, however, monopolists often charge different prices to different buyers, a practice that is known as *price discrimination*. The movie theater discount tickets discussed at the beginning of this chapter constitute one example. In the following sections, we analyze how the profit-maximizing monopolist behaves when it is possible to charge different prices to different buyers. When price discrimination is possible, a monopolist can transfer some of the gains from consumers into its own profits. However, we will see that not all the higher profits under price discrimination come at the expense of consumers. Efficiency is enhanced as the monopolist expands output toward the level at which demand intersects marginal cost.

Sale in Different Markets

Suppose the monopolist has two completely distinct markets in which she can sell her output. Perhaps she is the only supplier in the domestic market for her product, and the only one in a foreign market as well. If she is a profit maximizer, what prices should she charge and what quantities should she sell in each market?

Suppose the demand and marginal revenue curves for the two markets are as given in the left and middle panels in Figure 11.13. First note that if the monopolist is maximizing profit, her marginal revenue should be the same in each market. (If it weren't, she could sell 1 unit less in the market with lower MR and 1 unit more in the market with higher MR, thereby increasing her profit.) Given that MR in the two markets must be the same, the profit-maximizing total quantity will be the one for which this common value is the same as marginal cost. Graphically, the solution is to add the marginal revenue curves horizontally across the two markets, and produce the level of output for which the resulting curve intersects the marginal cost curve. In the right panel in Figure 11.13, the optimal total output is indicated by $Q^* = 10$ units. $Q_1^* = 4$ of it is sold in market 1 at a price of P_1^*, and the remaining $Q_2^* = 6$ in market 2 at a price of P_2^*.

FIGURE 11.13

The Profit-Maximizing Monopolist Who Sells in Two Markets

For a monopolist who sells in two markets, the profit-maximizing output level is where the ΣMR curve intersects the MC curve, here, $Q^* = 10$. Marginal revenue in each market will be the same when $Q_1^* = 4$ and $Q_2^* = 6$ are sold in markets 1 and 2, respectively.

EXAMPLE 11.3   Profits in Two Different Markets

A monopolist has marginal costs MC = Q and home market demand P = 30 − Q. The monopolist can also sell to a foreign market at a constant price $P_F = 12$. Find and graph the quantity produced, quantity sold in the home market, quantity sold in the foreign market, and price charged in the home market. Explain why the monopolist's profits would fall if it were to produce the same quantity but sell more in the home market.

The linear demand curve $P = 30 - Q$ has associated marginal revenue $MR = 30 - 2Q$. The profit-maximizing level of output for a monopolist selling to segmented markets occurs where ΣMR = MC. The horizontal sum of the marginal revenues across markets is the home marginal revenue function MR_H up to home output where $MR_F = MR_H$, and then the foreign marginal revenue function $MR_F = 12$ for any further units (see Figure 11.14). Total marginal revenue equals marginal cost at $MR_F = MC$, which solves for $Q = 12$. Marginal cost for this level of output equals home marginal revenue at $30 - 2Q_H = 12$, so $Q_H = 9$, with the remaining units sold abroad:

$$Q_F = Q - Q_H = 12 - 9 = 3.$$

In the home market, the monopolist charges

$$P_H = 30 - Q_H = 30 - 9 = 21.$$

FIGURE 11.14

A Monopolist with a Perfectly Elastic Foreign Market

The curve ΣMR overlays MR_H as long as $MR_H \geq MR_F$, and then overlays MR_F. The profit-maximizing output level is where the ΣMR curve intersects the MC curve, here $Q^* = 12$.

Any further units sold at home would yield marginal revenue less than 12. Since sales to the foreign market yield a constant marginal revenue of 12, shifting sales to the home market would decrease profits due to the lost marginal revenue for each unit shifted.

SELF-TEST 11.5

Suppose a monopolist sells in two separate markets, with demand curves given by $P_1 = 10 - Q_1$ and $P_2 = 20 - Q_2$, respectively. If her total cost curve is given by TC = 5 + 2Q (for which the associated marginal cost curve is given by MC = 2), what quantities should she sell and what prices should she charge in the two markets?

Note in Self-Test 11.5 that the monopolist who sells in two markets charges a higher price in the market where demand is less elastic with respect to price.[12] Charging different prices to buyers in completely separate markets is often referred to as *third-degree price discrimination*. There is no special significance to the term "third-degree" beyond the fact that this type of price discrimination happened to have been the third one that appeared in an early taxonomy.

Examples of third-degree price discrimination abound. This textbook, for instance, is also offered in an international student edition that sells for about one-third the price of the domestic edition. Because the incomes of students are generally much lower in foreign markets than in the United States, the price elasticity of demand tends to be much higher in foreign than in U.S. markets. The price that maximizes profits in the U.S. market would discourage most Third World students from buying.

Economic Naturalist 11.1

Why do some doctors and lawyers offer discounts to people with low incomes?

Why do doctors often set lower fees for poor patients?

In medicine, law, dentistry, and other professions, many practitioners set their fees on a "sliding scale"—in effect, selling their services to low-income consumers at significant discounts. This practice is often said to stem from professionals' concerns about the economic hardships confronting the poor. Such concerns are no doubt often heartfelt. But note also that the services offered by these professionals are normal goods, which means that the demand curves of low-income customers lie well below those of their wealthier counterparts. Sliding-scale fees may thus also be viewed as attempts by professionals to increase their profits by tailoring their prices to elasticity differences among different groups of buyers. A similar pattern is observed in the market for movie tickets, in which it is common for theater owners to set lower prices for students, senior citizens, and other groups believed to have higher price elasticities of demand.

---

[12]This result follows from Equation 11.6, which says that MR = $P(1 - 1/|\epsilon|)$. Setting $MR_1 = MR_2$ yields $P_1/P_2 = (1 - 1/|\epsilon_2|)/(1 - 1/|\epsilon_1|)$. Hence the higher price will be charged to customers with the lower price elasticity of demand.

Notice also that price discrimination is feasible only when it is impossible, or at least impractical, for buyers to trade among themselves. If students in other lands could trade with those in the United States, for example, it would not be possible to sell essentially the same book for $30 in Calcutta and $100 in New York. Entrepreneurial students would buy $30 books abroad and sell them to U.S. students for, say, $95; others, hoping to get in on the action, would cut price even further, and eventually the price differential would vanish. Buying at a low price from one source and reselling at a higher price is often called **arbitrage.** Where arbitrage is practical, large price differentials for a single product cannot persist. Arbitrage ensures, for example, that the price of gold in London can never differ significantly from the price of gold in New York.

arbitrage the purchase of something for costless risk-free resale at a higher price.

Economic Naturalist 11.2

Why do theater owners offer student discounts on admission tickets but not on popcorn?

Arbitrage is practical in some cases but not in others. Student discounts on tickets enable theater operators to segment their markets because it is not possible for one person to see a movie at a low price and then sell the experience to someone else at a higher price. By the same token, it is practical for lawyers and doctors to charge different people different prices on the basis of differences in price elasticity of demand. But such market segmentation is more difficult for products like popcorn. If the-

Why do theater owners give student discounts on tickets but not on snacks?

ater operators attempted to sell popcorn for $1 to students and for $3 to adults, some enterprising student would seize the arbitrage opportunity, selling popcorn to disgruntled adults for only $2. And under the pressure of competition from other arbitrageurs, the price differential would fall until the price differential was barely sufficient to make it worth the students' while to engage in the transaction.

The Perfectly Discriminating Monopolist

First-degree price discrimination is the term used to describe the largest possible extent of market segmentation. To illustrate, suppose a monopolist has N potential customers, each one of whom has a downward-sloping demand curve like the one labeled D_i in Figure 11.15. What is the most revenue the monopolist could extract from the sale of Q' units of output to such a customer? If the monopolist had to sell all units at the same price, the best he could do would be to charge P', which would yield a total revenue of $P'Q'$. But if he can charge different prices for different units of output, he can do much

FIGURE 11.15

Perfect Price Discrimination

If the monopolist can sell each unit of output at a different price, he will charge the maximum the buyer is willing to pay for each unit. In this situation, the monopolist captures all the consumer surplus.

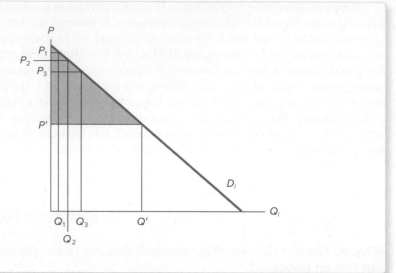

better. For example, he can sell the first Q_1 units at a price of P_1, the next $Q_2 - Q_1$ units at a price of P_2, and so on. If the intervals into which the monopolist can partition the product are arbitrarily small, this form of pricing will augment total revenue by the area of the shaded triangle in Figure 11.15.

How much output will a profit-maximizing, perfectly discriminating monopolist produce? As always, the rule is to equate marginal revenue to marginal cost. Figure 11.16 portrays the demand, short-run marginal, and average total cost curves for a perfectly discriminating monopolist. But what is the marginal revenue curve for this monopolist? *It is exactly the same as his demand curve.* Because he can discriminate perfectly, he can lower his price to sell additional output without having to cut price on the output originally sold. Price and marginal revenue are one and the same, just as in the case of perfect competition. The best this firm can do is to produce Q^* units of output, each of which it sells at the highest price each of its buyers is willing to pay.

FIGURE 11.16

The Perfectly Discriminating Monopolist

The marginal revenue curve for the monopolist who can discriminate perfectly is exactly the same as his demand curve. The profit-maximizing output is Q^*, the one for which the SMC and demand curves intersect. Economic profit (Π) is given by the shaded area.

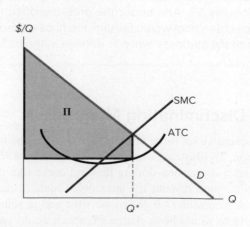

There are two salient points of comparison between the perfectly discriminating monopolist and the monopolist who cannot discriminate at all. The first is that the perfect discriminator produces a higher level of output because he need not be concerned with the effect of a price cut on the revenue from output produced thus far. He can cut price to the people who would not otherwise buy, and maintain higher prices to those who are willing to pay them.

A second important difference is that there generally is positive consumer surplus under the nondiscriminating monopolist, but none under the perfect discriminator. Because the nondiscriminator must charge the same price to all buyers, there is pressure on him not to set his price too high. If he sets it at the level the least elastic demanders are willing to pay, he will lose the patronage of all others. As a result, the monopolist will not do this, and the least elastic demanders end up paying a price well below their respective reservation prices—hence the consumer surplus.

Perfect price discrimination is a never-attained theoretical limit. If a customer's demand curve were tattooed on his forehead, it might be possible for a seller to tailor each price to extract the maximum possible amount from every buyer. But in general, the details of individual demand are only imperfectly known to the seller. Merchants often estimate individual elasticity on the basis of information known about groups to which the individual belongs. A catalog merchant, for example, may print special editions with higher prices for mailing into high-income zip codes like 90210 (Beverly Hills, California). The practice suggests that when an online-only retailer asks to know your location, prior to your making a product selection, you may wish to think how the information will be used.

Perhaps the closest thing we see to an in-depth assessment of individual elasticities is in the behavior of merchants in bazaars in the Middle East. The shrewd camel trader has had many years of experience in trying to assess how much a buyer with a given demographic and psychological profile is willing to pay. His stock in trade is to interpret the incongruous gesture, the furtive eye movement. But even here, the wily buyer may know how to conceal his eagerness to own the camel.

Second-Degree Price Discrimination

Yet another form of price discrimination is the practice by which many sellers post not a single price, but a schedule along which price declines with the quantity you buy. Thus, many electric utilities employ what are called *declining tail-block rate structures* by which the first, say, 300 kilowatt-hours per month are billed at 10 cents each, the next 700 at 8 cents, and all quantities over 1,000 kilowatt-hours/mo at 5 cents each. Such rate structures are a form of *second-degree price discrimination.*

Figure 11.17 illustrates the effect of such a rate structure for a consumer with the demand curve labeled D_i. In comparison with the alternative of charging a price of P_3 for every unit, the quantity discount scheme increases the consumer's total payment by an amount equal to the shaded area.

Second-degree price discrimination is like first-degree in that it tries to extract consumer surplus from each buyer. The two principal differences are these: (1) The same rate structure is available to every consumer under second-degree schemes, which means that they make no attempt to tailor charges to elasticity differences among buyers; and (2) the limited number of rate categories tends to limit the amount of consumer surplus that can be captured under second-degree schemes. First-degree schemes get the whole triangle, whereas Figure 11.17 shows that second-degree schemes capture only part of it.

The Hurdle Model of Price Discrimination

Every seller would like to practice perfect price discrimination. The difficulty, as noted earlier, is that sellers lack the information on individual demand curves necessary to do so. Yet another important form of price discrimination consists of a technique whereby

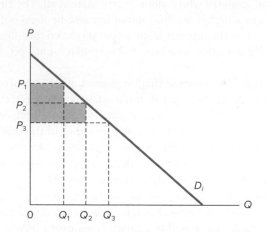

FIGURE 11.17

Second-Degree Price Discrimination

The seller offers the first block of consumption (0 to Q_1) at a high price (P_1), the second block (Q_1 to Q_2) at a lower price (P_2), the third block (Q_2 to Q_3) at a still lower price (P_3), and so on. Even though second-degree price discrimination makes no attempt to tailor rates to the characteristics of individuals or specific groups, it often enables the monopolist to capture a substantial share of consumer surplus (the shaded area).

the firm induces the most elastic buyers to identify themselves. This is the *hurdle model of price discrimination*. The basic idea is that the seller sets up a hurdle of some sort and makes a discount price available to those buyers who elect to jump over it. The logic is that those buyers who are most sensitive to price will be more likely than others to jump the hurdle.

One example of a hurdle is a rebate form included in the product package. Here, jumping over the hurdle means filling in the form, finding a stamp and an envelope, and then getting to the post office to mail it in. The firm's hope is that people who don't care much about price will be less likely than others to bother going through this process. If so, then people whose demands are less elastic end up paying the "regular" price, while those with more elastic demands pay the lower discount price.

It is a rare product whose seller does not use the hurdle model of differential pricing. Booksellers offer only high-priced hardback editions in the first year of publication. Buyers who don't care strongly about price buy these editions when they first come out. Others wait a year or two and then buy the much less expensive softcover edition. Here, the hurdle is having to endure the wait, although, given that publishers now face almost immediate competition from the "used" market, the wait may be getting shorter. Appliance sellers offer regular "scratch-'n-dent" sales at which machines with trivial cosmetic imperfections are sold for less than half their regular price. Here, there are two common hurdles: having to find out when and where the sale takes place and having to put up with a scratch or dent (which most of the time will be out of sight). Airlines offer "super-saver" discounts of up to half off the regular coach fare. Here also there are two common hurdles: having to make reservations a week or more in advance and having to stay over a Saturday night. Many retailers include discount coupons in their media ads. Here, the hurdles are having to read the ads, clip the physical coupons or copy the online discount codes, and use them before they expire. Some sellers post signs behind the counter saying "Ask about our special low price." Here, the hurdle is merely having to do the asking. But even this trivial hurdle can be remarkably effective, because many well-heeled buyers would find asking about a special price too unseemly even to contemplate.

Why might an appliance retailer hammer dents into the sides of its stoves and refrigerators?

None of these schemes perfectly segregates high-elasticity from low-elasticity buyers. For instance, there are some people who wait for the January white sales to buy their towels even though they would buy just as many if the sales weren't offered. But on the whole, the hurdles seem to function much as intended. A perfect hurdle would be one that imposes only a negligible cost on the buyers who jump it, yet perfectly separates buyers according to their elasticity of demand. Analytically, the effect of such a hurdle is portrayed in Figure 11.18, where P_H represents the "regular" price and P_L represents the discount price. With a perfect hurdle, none of the people who pay the discount price has a reservation price greater than or equal to the regular price, which means that all of them would have been excluded from the market had only the regular price been available.

The hurdle model need not be limited to the two-price version depicted in Figure 11.18. On the contrary, many sellers have developed it into a highly complex art form involving literally dozens of price-hurdle combinations. On its Los Angeles–Honolulu route alone, for example, United Airlines offers dozens of different fares, each with its own set of restrictions. But no matter how simple or complex the scheme may be, its goal is the same—to give discounts to customers who would not otherwise buy the product.

The hurdle model is like first-degree price discrimination in that it tries to tailor prices to the elasticities of individual buyers. The principal difference is that even in its most sophisticated form, the hurdle model cannot hope to capture all the consumer surplus.

THE EFFICIENCY LOSS FROM MONOPOLY

Recall from Chapter 10 the claim that perfect competition led to an efficient allocation of resources. This claim was based on the observation that in long-run competitive equilibrium, there are no possibilities for additional gains from exchange. The value to buyers of the last unit of output is exactly the same as the market value of the resources required to produce it.

How does the long-run equilibrium under monopoly measure up by the same criteria? Not very well, it turns out. To illustrate, consider a monopolist with constant long-run average and marginal costs and the demand structure shown in Figure 11.19. The profit-maximizing quantity for this monopolist is Q^*, which he will sell at a price of P^*. Note that at Q^*, the value of an additional unit of output to buyers is P^*, which is greater than the cost of producing an additional unit, LMC. This means that the single-price monopolist does not exhaust all possible gains from exchange. As we saw earlier, if it were possible for the monopolist to charge different prices to every buyer, output would expand to Q_C, which is the same amount we would see in a perfectly competitive industry under the same demand and cost conditions. If output did expand from Q^* to Q_C because

FIGURE 11.19

The Welfare Loss from a Single-Price Monopoly

A monopolist who charges a single price to all buyers will produce Q^* and sell at P^*. A competitive industry operating under the same cost conditions would produce Q_C and sell at P_C. In comparison with the perfectly competitive outcome, single-price monopoly results in a loss of consumer surplus equal to the area of $\Pi + S_1$. Since the monopolist earns Π, the cost to society is S_1—called the deadweight loss from monopoly.

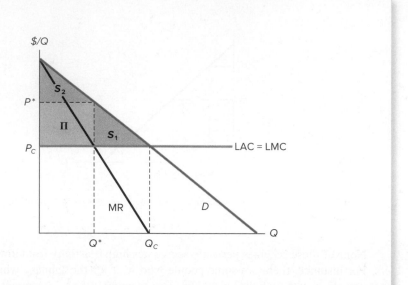

of perfect price discrimination, the gain in producer surplus would be equal to the combined areas of the triangles labeled S_1 and S_2. Under perfect competition, the triangle S_1 would be part of consumer surplus. The cost to society of having such an industry served by a single-price monopolist, rather than by perfectly competitive sellers, will be the loss of that consumer surplus.

Thus, in pure efficiency terms, the perfectly discriminating monopolist and the perfectly competitive industry lead to the same result. The difference is that in the former case all the benefit comes in the form of producer surplus, in the latter case all in the form of consumer surplus. The efficiency loss from monopoly is the result of failure to price discriminate perfectly. This loss (the area of triangle S_1 in Figure 11.19) is called the *deadweight loss from monopoly.*

In the preceding analysis, it made sense to speak of the welfare loss from having monopoly rather than competition because the cost structure was one that is compatible with the existence of perfect competition. But with that kind of cost structure, only legal barriers could prevent the emergence of competition. The existence of economic profits (P in Figure 11.19) would lure competitors into the industry until price and quantity were driven to P_C and Q_C, respectively.

Suppose the reason for having a monopoly with a flat LAC curve is that the firm enjoys patent protection for its product. Can we now say that the welfare loss from having a single-price monopoly is equal to the lost consumer surplus measured in Figure 11.19? Before answering, we must first ask, "What is the alternative to the current situation?" If it is a society without patent protection, we may well have never gotten the product in the first place, so it hardly makes sense to complain that, compared with pure competition, monopoly produces a welfare loss. True enough, the patent-protected single-price monopoly does not exhaust all possible gains from trade. But with the patent-protected monopoly, we do get a consumer surplus plus producer surplus of $S_2 + \Pi$, whereas we might have gotten nothing at all without the patent protection.

PUBLIC POLICY TOWARD NATURAL MONOPOLY

These observations make clear that the relevant question is not whether monopoly is efficient in comparison with some unattainable theoretical ideal, but how it compares with the alternatives we actually confront. This question is nowhere more important than in the case of natural monopoly.

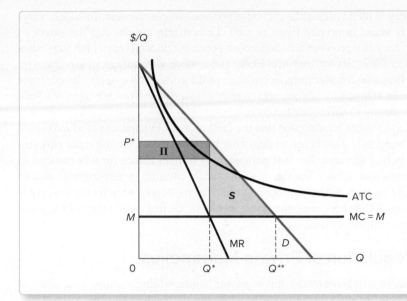

FIGURE 11.20

A Natural Monopoly
The two main objections to single-price natural monopoly are that it earns economic profit (Π) and that it results in the loss of consumer surplus (S).

To keep the analysis simple, consider a technology in which total cost is given by

$$TC = F + MQ, \tag{11.8}$$

where Q is the level of output. And suppose the demand and marginal revenue curves for a single-price monopolist producing with this technology are as shown in Figure 11.20. The theoretical ideal allocation for this market would be to produce a quantity of Q^{**} and sell it at marginal cost, which here is equal to M. By contrast, the single-price monopoly produces only Q^* and sells it for P^*.

There are basically two objections to the equilibrium price-quantity pair of the single-price natural monopoly: (1) the *fairness objection,* which is that the producer earns an economic profit (Π); and (2) the *efficiency objection,* which is that price is above marginal cost, resulting in lost consumer surplus (S).

Policymakers may respond in a variety of ways to the fairness and efficiency objections. The five options considered below account for the most important alternatives.

1. State Ownership and Management

Efficiency requires that price be equal to marginal cost. The difficulty this creates is that, for natural monopoly, marginal cost is below average total cost. Because private firms are not able to charge prices less than average cost and remain in business in the long run, the single-price firm has no alternative but to charge more than marginal cost. An option for getting around this particular difficulty is to have the state take over the industry. The attractive feature of this option is that the government is not bound, the way a private firm is, to earn at least a normal profit. It would thus be able to set a price equal to marginal cost, and absorb the resulting economic losses out of general tax revenues.

But there are also unattractive features of state ownership. Foremost among them is the fact that it often seems to weaken incentives for cost-conscious, efficient management. As the late Harvard University economist Harvey Leibenstein emphasized, an organization's costs depend not just on its technology, but also on the vigor with which it pursues efficiency. In Leibenstein's phrase, an organization that does not act energetically to curb costs is said to exhibit **X-inefficiency.**[13]

X-inefficiency a condition in which a firm fails to obtain maximum output from a given combination of inputs.

[13]Harvey Leibenstein, "Allocative Efficiency vs. X-Efficiency," *American Economic Review,* June 1966, 392–415.

X-inefficiency is by no means the exclusive province of government. In widely varying degrees, it is found in private firms as well. Leibenstein argued that the extent to which X-inefficiency is a problem will depend on economic incentives, which suggests a theoretical reason for believing that it is likely to be more widespread in government. When a private firm cuts a dollar from its costs, its profit goes up by a dollar. By contrast, when the person in charge of a government agency cuts a dollar from her agency's budget, the effect is merely to shrink her fiefdom.

Several noted scholars have argued that the goal of most bureaucrats is to maximize their operating budgets.[14] This is not to deny that bureaucrats are for the most part sincere, dedicated public servants. But it is perhaps only human nature for a bureaucrat to think that her particular agency has the most important mission in government, and to lobby accordingly on its behalf. State-operated natural monopoly may be the best solution in some cases.[15] But there are other policy alternatives that offer many of the same benefits with fewer apparent costs.

2. State Regulation of Private Monopolies

One such alternative is to leave ownership in private hands, while providing guidelines or regulations that limit pricing discretion. The stereotypical example of this approach is public regulation of private companies that provide electricity, water, and telephone service.

The main form of government price regulation employed in the United States is known as *rate-of-return regulation,* in which prices are set to allow the firm to earn a predetermined rate of return on its invested capital. Ideally, this rate of return would allow the firm to recover exactly the opportunity cost of its capital, which is to say, it would ideally be the same as the competitive rate of return on investment.

In practice, however, regulatory commissions can never be certain what the competitive rate of return will be in any period. If the rate they set lies below the competitive return, the firm will have an incentive to reduce the quality of its service, and eventually to go out of business. By contrast, if regulators set too high a rate of return, prices will be higher than necessary and the firm will earn an extra-normal profit. Neither of these outcomes is attractive, but regulatory commissions have traditionally decided that the problems caused by an insufficient rate of return are far more serious than those caused by an excessive one.

Harvey Averch and Leland Johnson were the first to explore in detail the consequences of a regulatory rate of return set higher than the cost of capital.[16] Their conclusion, in a nutshell, is that this practice gives the firm an incentive to substitute capital for other inputs in a way that inflates the cost of doing business. If the regulated utility's goal is to maximize profit, the behavioral path it will follow will be to make its "rate base"—the invested capital on which it earns the allowed rate of return—as large as possible. If the regulated monopolist can borrow capital at 8 percent/yr and is allowed to earn 10 percent/yr on each dollar invested, it can clear $20,000 of extra profit for every extra $1,000,000 of borrowed funds it invests.

At least two important distortions follow from the discrepancy between the allowed rate of return and the actual cost of capital. The first we may call the *gold-plated water cooler effect.* It refers to the fact that the regulated monopolist has an incentive to purchase more capital equipment than is actually necessary to produce any given level of output. Faced with a choice between buying a regular water cooler, for example, and a

[14]See, for example, William Niskanen, *Bureaucracy and Representative Government,* Chicago: Aldine-Atherton, 1971; and Gordon Tullock, *The Politics of Bureaucracy,* Washington, DC: Public Affairs Press, 1965. But for a contrasting view, see Albert Breton and Ronald Wintrobe, *The Logic of Bureaucratic Conduct,* Cambridge: Cambridge University Press, 1982.
[15]See Elliott D. Sclar, *You Don't Always Get What You Pay For,* Ithaca, NY: Cornell University Press, 2000.
[16]Harvey Averch and Leland Johnson, "Behavior of the Firm under Regulatory Constraint," *American Economic Review,* December 1962, 1052–1069. See also R. M. Spann, "Rate of Return Regulation and Efficiency in Production: An Empirical Test of the Averch-Johnson Thesis," *Bell Journal of Economics,* Spring 1974, 38–52.

more expensive gold-plated one, the regulated monopolist has an incentive to opt for the latter. To illustrate, suppose that the allowed rate of return on capital were 10 percent a year and the actual cost of capital only 8 percent. If a gold-plated water cooler costs $1,000 more than a regular one, the monopolist would then earn $20 higher profit each year by installing the more expensive water cooler. Regulatory commissions try to prevent the purchase of unnecessary equipment, but the complexities of day-to-day operations are too great to allow every decision to be monitored carefully.

A second distortion induced by rate-of-return regulation is peculiar to the monopolist who serves more than one separate market, and we may call it the *cross-subsidy effect*. Because the allowed rate of return exceeds the cost of capital, such a monopolist has an incentive to sell below cost in the more elastic market, and cross-subsidize the resulting losses by selling above cost in the less elastic market. The idea is that the below-cost price in the elastic market boosts sales by more than the above-cost price in the less elastic market curtails them. The resulting increase in output increases the requirements for capital to produce it, and hence increases the profits allowed by regulation.

To illustrate, consider the regulated monopolist whose demand and cost curves for two markets are shown in Figure 11.21. The ATC curves are constructed to include the allowed rate of profit, which exceeds the cost of capital. Thus, when the monopolist is earning a zero profit in terms of the cost curves shown in Figure 11.21, he is really earning

$$\Pi = (r^a - r^c)K, \tag{11.9}$$

where r^a is the allowed rate of return, r^c the actual cost of capital, and K the size of the total capital stock. To maximize profit, the monopolist thus wants to make K as big as possible, which in turn means making the sum of the outputs sold in the two markets as large as possible. To do that, he will set MR = MC in the market with the less elastic demand (market 1 in panel a) and use the profits earned in that market (Π_1) to subsidize a price below average cost in the market with more elastic demand (market 2 in panel b). The aim, again, is to boost sales in the latter market by more than they are curtailed in the former. By selling the largest possible output, the monopolist is able to employ the largest possible capital stock, and thereby is able to earn the largest possible profit.

Regulatory pitfalls have not prevented governments in virtually every part of the world from continuing to intervene in the price and output decisions of important natural monopolies like electric utilities and local telephone service. Whether these interventions

FIGURE 11.21

Cross-Subsidization to Boost Total Output

A regulated monopolist is generally allowed to earn a rate of return that exceeds the actual cost of capital, which provides an incentive to acquire as much capital as possible. To increase output (thereby to increase the required capital stock), the monopolist can sell above cost in his less elastic market (market 1 in panel a) and use the resultant profits ($\Pi_1 > 0$) to subsidize the losses ($\Pi_2 < 0$) sustained by selling below cost in his more elastic market.

do more good than harm, in purely economic terms, remains an unsettled question. But they clearly seem to serve an important psychological function on behalf of a public that feels understandably uncomfortable about not having a buffer between itself and the sole supplier of a critical good or service.

3. Exclusive Contracting for Natural Monopoly

Rural-Metro, a private, for-profit company, has provided fire protection services in Scottsdale, Arizona, since 1952.

In the title of a widely quoted article, UCLA economist Harold Demsetz asked the disarmingly simple question, "Why Regulate Monopoly?"[17] His point was that even though cost conditions may dictate that a market be served by a single supplier, there can still be vigorous competition to see who gets to *be* that supplier. In Demsetz's proposal, the government would specify in detail the service it wanted provided—fire protection, garbage collection, postal delivery, whatever—and then call for private companies to submit bids to supply the service. And to the low bidder would then go the contract.

This scheme has been tried with success in a number of different municipalities. The city of Scottsdale, Arizona, for example, has its fire protection services provided by a private contractor selected in this fashion. And the residents of Oakland, California, have their garbage collected each week not by municipal garbage workers but by the Oakland Scavenger Company, a private, profit-seeking firm. In both instances, the costs incurred in providing service are approximately half the cost of comparable services provided directly by municipal governments. In the fire protection case, moreover, there is hard evidence that the cost reductions are not achieved through reductions in the quality of service. Profit-seeking fire insurance companies, whose survival depends on their ability to assess risks accurately, charge no more for fire insurance in Scottsdale than they do in communities with municipal fire departments.[18] The advantage of private contracting for the provision of natural monopoly services is that it takes production out of the hands of bureaucrats, who are often not very good at keeping costs down.

The political scientist Elliott Sclar cautions, however, that the advantages of contracting for public services are often more apparent than real (see footnote 15). Most contracts with private suppliers, for example, contain contingency clauses that allow higher fees in the event of unforeseen changes in circumstances. The government employees who monitor the implementation of private contracts may be unable to keep these extra fees under tight control. Added to that is the problem of corruption. Public contracts in practice may often go not to the firm that submits the lowest bid but to the one that pays the highest bribe.

Even if we abstract from these problems, private contracting may not be an attractive option in many cases. Because the contract must specify the details of the service to be provided, it must go into extraordinary detail in the case of a complex service, such as telecommunications. Moreover, it must make provisions for how new contractors are to be selected. In the case of electric utilities, changing contractors necessarily involves the transfer of a vast, complex array of generation and distribution equipment. At what price should this equipment be sold? By the time all the *i*'s are dotted and the *t*'s crossed, the exclusive contracts for providing monopoly service may be so detailed as to be indistinguishable from direct economic regulation.

4. Vigorous Enforcement of Antitrust Laws

A major element in the policy arsenal for dealing with monopoly is the nation's antitrust laws. The most important of these are the Sherman Act (1890), which makes it illegal "to monopolize, or attempt to monopolize . . . any part of the trade or commerce among the several States . . . ," and the Clayton Act (1914), one of whose provisions prevents

[17]Harold Demsetz, "Why Regulate Monopoly?" *Journal of Law and Economics,* April 1968, 55–65.
[18]For an extended survey of studies comparing private costs and public costs, see E. S. Savas, *Privatizing the Public Sector,* Chatham, NJ: Chatham House Publishers, 1982.

Rural Metro Fire

corporations from acquiring shares in a competitor where the effect would be to "substantially lessen competition or create a monopoly."

In interpreting the antitrust laws, the U.S. Justice Department has developed guidelines that prohibit mergers between competing companies whose combined market share would exceed some predetermined fraction of total industry output. These guidelines are applied with highly varying degrees of zeal under different political administrations. As a general rule, Democrats have been far less tolerant of mergers than Republicans have.

In the case of industries with declining long-run average cost curves, the cost of production will be much higher if we are served by many firms rather than by only a few. The most vigorous supporters of the antitrust laws insist that the laws will not impede the formation of natural monopolies. But as we will see in Chapter 12, they may substantially postpone the time when economies of scale are fully realized.

One response to this difficulty would be to apply the antitrust laws to prevent only those mergers where significant cost savings would not be realized. The government is not in a good position, however, to distinguish one type of case from another. Congress was well aware of this, and explicitly ruled out consideration of cost savings as a rationale for allowing mergers. The result is that antitrust policy impedes all consolidations, even those that would lead to substantial reductions in cost.

5. A Laissez-Faire Policy toward Natural Monopoly

As a fifth and final alternative for dealing with natural monopoly, let us consider the possibility of laissez faire, or doing nothing—just letting the monopolist produce whatever quantity she chooses and sell it at whatever price the market will bear. The obvious objections to this policy are the two we began with, namely, the fairness and efficiency problems. In this section, however, we will see that there may be at least some circumstances in which these problems are of only minimal importance.

Consider, in particular, a natural monopolist who uses the hurdle model of differential pricing. To keep the discussion simple, let's suppose she charges a regular price and also a discount price, the latter available to customers who clear some hurdle, such as mailing in a rebate form. How does the presence of this differential pricing device affect the fairness and efficiency objections to natural monopoly?

Consider first the efficiency objection. Recall that the problem is that the single-price monopolist charges a price above marginal cost, which excludes many potential buyers from the market, ones who value the product more highly than the value of the resources required to produce it.

For illustrative purposes, let's examine a natural monopolist with a total cost curve given by $F + MQ$ and a linear demand curve given by $P = A - BQ$. Figure 11.22a shows the demand and marginal cost curves for such a monopolist. If she is a single-price

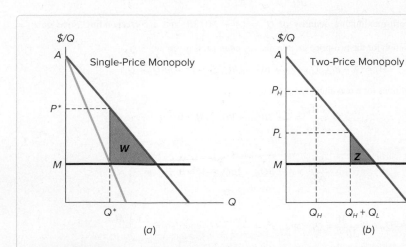

(a)   (b)

FIGURE 11.22

The Efficiency Losses from Single-Price and Two-Price Monopoly

By being able to offer a discount price to the most elastic portion of the demand curve, the two-price monopolist (panel b) expands the market, thereby causing a much smaller efficiency loss (area Z, panel b) than in the case of the single-price monopolist (area W, panel a).

profit maximizer, she will produce Q^* and sell for P^*. But if she is able to charge one price to the buyers along the upper part of the demand curve and a lower price to all other buyers (Figure 11.22*b*), her profit-maximizing strategy will be to sell Q_H at the price P_H and Q_L at the price P_L.[19]

Note that the efficiency loss associated with the two-price monopolist (lost consumer surplus, which is the area of triangle Z in panel *b*) is much smaller than the corresponding loss for the single-price monopolist (the area of triangle W in panel *a*).

In general, the more finely the monopolist can partition her market under the hurdle model, the smaller the efficiency loss will be. As noted earlier, it is common in most firms to see not one but a whole menu of different discount prices, each with a different set of restrictions (the deeper the discount, the more stringent the restriction). Given the wide latitude many firms have to expand their markets through hurdle pricing, the efficiency problem of natural monopoly will often be of only secondary importance.

What about the fairness problem? First, what *is* this problem? The popular perception of it is that the monopolist transfers resources from people who desperately need them (namely, poor consumers) to others who have more than they need to begin with (namely, wealthy shareholders). We will see below that, defined in this particular way, the problem is sometimes less serious than it appears.

The more general question of what constitutes a fair distribution of society's resources is a deep philosophical one, well beyond the scope of our discussion here. At the very least, however, we can say that no firm is entitled to acquire, through force or coercion, the power to extract excessive resources from other persons. But suppose the monopolist has become the lone seller in her market through completely benevolent means. This is not implausible. As a natural monopolist, her costs are by definition lower than if other firms also served the same market. And perhaps her cheerful and courteous service has also helped entrench her position. Does she then create an injustice by charging prices in excess of marginal cost?

Certainly consumers would be happier to pay only the marginal cost of production. But marginal cost is less than average cost in a natural monopoly, and so it is not possible for *everyone* to pay marginal cost and have the supplier remain in business. At best, *some* consumers can pay prices close to marginal cost, but others will have to pay substantially more. Even so, if the monopolist is earning an economic profit, we know that buyers are

---

[19]For the single-price monopolist the profit function is given by

$$\Pi_1 = (A - BQ)Q - F - MQ.$$

The first-order condition for a maximum is given by

$$\frac{d\Pi_1}{dQ} = A - 2BQ - M = 0,$$

which yields a profit-maximizing quantity of $Q' = (A - M)/2B$, and a corresponding price of $P' = (A + M)/2$.

The profit function for the two-price monopolist, by contrast, is given by

$$\Pi_2 = (A - BQ_H)Q_H + (A - BQ_H - BQ_L)Q_L - F - M(Q_H + Q_L).$$

The first-order conditions for a maximum are given by

$$\frac{\partial \Pi_2}{\partial Q_H} = A - 2BQ_H - BQ_L - M = 0$$

and

$$\frac{\partial \Pi_2}{\partial Q_L} = A - BQ_H - 2BQ_L - M = 0,$$

which can be solved for

$$Q_H = \frac{A - M}{3B} = Q_L \quad \text{and} \quad P_L = \frac{A + 2M}{3} \quad \text{and} \quad P_H = \frac{2A + M}{3}.$$

paying more, on the average, than the cost of the resources required to serve them. How can this be defended in the name of fairness?

Earlier we saw that hurdle pricing makes the monopoly allocation more efficient. It would be an exaggeration to say that the same hurdle model makes the existence of monopoly profits seem completely fair. But it does help mitigate some of the most serious objections to them.

Consider first the source of a given dollar of monopoly profit. From which buyers does this dollar come? It is straightforward to show that it cannot have come from the discount price buyer. Typical discount prices range from 15 to 50 percent off the so-called regular price, and seldom do more than half of all buyers pay the discount price. Taking an illustrative case in which the discount is 30 percent and half of all buyers receive it, we see that the monopolist's revenue would fall by 15 percent if everyone paid the discount price. Very few firms would remain profitable in the face of a 15 percent decline in total revenue.

It follows that if the monopolist is earning economic profit, the source of that profit is the buyer who pays the regular price. The fact that this buyer could have paid a discount price if he had been willing to jump the requisite hurdle tells us that the burden imposed on him is no greater than the trouble of jumping the hurdle. This is obviously not the same as saying that the regular-price buyer makes a voluntary charitable contribution to the monopolist. But it does take at least some of the sting out of the notion that the monopolist's customers are being cruelly victimized.

So much for the source of monopoly profit. What about its disposition? Who gets it? If we assume a corporate income tax rate of 40 percent, 40 cents of each dollar of monopoly profits goes to the U.S. Treasury. The remainder is paid out to shareholders, either directly through dividends or indirectly by reinvesting it into the company. Granted, the average income of shareholders is greater than that of citizens as a whole. But there are many low-income shareholders in the United States. Most employee pension funds, for example, are invested in the stock market, as are the private insurance holdings of many low-income individuals. So a considerable fraction of any dollar of monopoly profit will wind up in the hands of low-income shareholders.

But to take the worst possible case from a distributional point of view, let us suppose that what is left of the dollar of monopoly profit goes entirely to the wealthiest resident of Manhattan. Assume that she pays federal income tax at the rate of 33 percent on the 60 cents that the federal government hasn't already taken, leaving 40 cents. State and local income and sales taxes will claim an additional 7 cents, leaving only 33 cents in the hands of our wealthy shareholder.

To summarize, then, the source of a dollar in monopoly profit is the regular-price buyer, someone who could have paid a discount price had he but taken a little extra trouble. Of that dollar, 60 cents goes to the federal treasury and another 7 cents to state and local governments. The disposition of more than two-thirds of the dollar is thus subject to governmental control. The remainder becomes income in the hands of shareholders, at least some of whom have low incomes to begin with. So it is by no means clear that the economic profit associated with natural monopoly creates distributional inequities of the sort commonly perceived.

Hurdles, of course, are seldom perfect. Inevitably they screen out some buyers who will not buy at the regular price. And much of the time, real resources must be expended in order to jump over these hurdles. Mailing in a rebate coupon may not take a lot of time, but the time it takes could certainly be better spent. And in at least some cases, tax avoidance will keep the government from collecting as much as the tax tables specify.

So what are we to conclude from this brief analysis of the five policy options for dealing with natural monopoly? The short answer is that each has problems. None completely eliminates the difficulties that arise when a single seller serves the market. Sometimes the least costly solution will be competitive contracting, other times direct state ownership. Regulation will continue to play a role in specific industries, particularly the traditional public utilities. And despite their many shortcomings, antitrust laws serve the public well by discouraging price-fixing and other anticompetitive practices. But in some cases, particularly those in which the monopolist has devised means of richly segmenting the market, the best option may be simply not to intervene at all.

Does Monopoly Suppress Innovation?

One of the most enduring topics of conversation among economic conspiracy buffs is the notion that monopolists deprive consumers of a spectrum of enormously valuable technological innovations. Who has not heard, for example, of how the lightbulb manufacturers have conspired to prevent revolutionary new designs for long-lasting lightbulbs from reaching the market?

Is the suppression of innovation yet another cost of monopoly that we ought to have considered in our analysis of public policy options? As the following example will make clear, the logic of profit maximization suggests that monopolists may not always be so eager to suppress innovation.

EXAMPLE 11.4	The Impact of Innovation on Profits

Suppose the current lightbulb design lasts 1,000 hours. Now the lightbulb monopolist discovers how to make a bulb that lasts 10,000 hours for the same per-bulb cost of production. Will the monopolist introduce the new bulb?

Suppose we measure the quantity produced by the monopolist not as lightbulbs per se, but as the number of bulb-hours of lighting services. Thus, if the cost of producing the current design is, say, $1.00/bulb-hr, then the cost of the new design is only $0.10/bulb-hr. In Figure 11.23, D represents the market demand curve for lighting and MR the associated marginal revenue curve.

Note that the profit-maximizing price and quantity for the current design, whose marginal cost is $1/bulb-hr, are P_1 and Q_1, respectively. For the new design, whose marginal cost is $0.10/bulb-hr, the profit-maximizing price and quantity are P_2 and Q_2. The monopolist's profit under the current design is the area of the rectangle $ABCE$. For the new design, the corresponding profit value is the area of the rectangle $FGHK$. And because the monopolist's profit is higher under the new design, it has every incentive to make that design available. Indeed, as some of you may recall, the availability of just such an efficient new lightbulb was announced several years ago.

FIGURE 11.23

Does Monopoly Suppress Innovation?

The cost of producing the new, efficient lightbulb, at $0.10/bulb-hr, is only one-tenth the cost of producing the current design, $1/bulb-hr. Because the monopolist's profits with the efficient design (area of $FGHK$) exceed its profits with the current design (area of $ABCE$), it will offer the new design.

This example does not imply that the monopolist's incentives to introduce innovations will always and everywhere be the same as a competitive firm's. But it should caution us against uncritical acceptance of claims that monopolists always deprive consumers of the benefits of the latest available technology.

SUMMARY

- Monopoly is the name given to the market structure in which a single firm serves the entire market. Five factors, acting alone or in combination, give rise to monopoly: (1) control over key inputs, (2) economies of scale, (3) patents, (4) network economies, and (5) government licenses. In the long run, by far the most important of these is economies of scale, in part because it also helps explain network economies and government licenses. *(LO1, LO2)*

- Because the monopolist is the only seller in the market, his demand curve is the downward-sloping market demand curve. Unlike the perfect competitor, who can sell as much as he chooses at the market price, the monopolist must cut price in order to expand his output. The monopolist's rule for maximizing profits is the same as the one used by perfectly competitive firms. It is to expand output if the gain in revenue (marginal revenue) exceeds the increase in costs (marginal cost), and to contract if the loss in revenue is smaller than the reduction in costs. The pivotal difference is that marginal revenue is less than price for the monopolist, but equal to price for the perfect competitor. *(LO3)*

- When the monopolist can sell in several separate markets, he distributes output among them so that marginal revenue is the same in each. Here again, the familiar logic of cost-benefit analysis provides a convenient framework for analyzing the firm's decision about whether to alter its current behavior. *(LO3)*

- Unlike the perfectly competitive case, the monopoly equilibrium generally does not exhaust the potential gains from exchange. In general, the value to society of an additional unit of output will exceed the cost to the monopolist of the resources required to produce it. This finding has often been interpreted to mean that monopoly is less efficient than perfect competition. But this interpretation is of only limited practical significance, because the conditions that give rise to monopoly—in particular, economies of scale in production—are rarely compatible with those required for perfect competition. *(LO4)*

- Monopolists have an incentive to offer price discounts if they can be limited to customers who wouldn't otherwise purchase the product. One effective technique is to make discounts available only to those who are willing to jump some form of hurdle, such as mailing in rebate coupons. *(LO5)*

- Our policy focus in the chapter was on the question of how the government should treat natural monopolies—markets characterized by downward-sloping long-run average cost curves. We considered five policy alternatives: (1) state ownership, (2) private ownership with government price regulation, (3) competitive bidding by private firms for the right to be the sole provider of service, (4) vigorous enforcement of antitrust laws designed to prevent monopoly, and finally (5) a complete laissez-faire, or hands-off, policy. Problems arise with each of these alternatives, and the best policy will in general be different in different circumstances. The laissez-faire stance is most attractive in markets where the monopolist is able to employ the hurdle model of differential pricing. Allowing buyers to decide for themselves whether to become eligible for a discount price softens both the efficiency and fairness objections to natural monopoly. *(LO6)*

KEY TERMS

arbitrage	optimality condition for a monopolist	X-inefficiency

REVIEW QUESTIONS

1. What five factors give rise to monopoly? In the long run, why is economies of scale the most important factor? *(LO2)*

2. If the United States has thousands of cement producers but a small town has only one, is this cement producer a monopolist? Explain. *(LO1, LO2)*

3. When is marginal revenue less than price for a monopolist? Explain. *(LO3)*

4. Why does a profit-maximizing monopolist never produce on an inelastic portion of the demand curve? Would a revenue-maximizing monopolist ever produce on the inelastic portion of the demand curve? *(LO3)*

5. Why is an output level at which MR intersects MC from below never the profit-maximizing level of output? *(LO3)*

6. What effect will the imposition of a 50 percent tax on economic profit have on a monopolist's price and output decisions? *(Hint:* Recall that the assumed objective is to choose the level of output that maximizes economic profit.) *(LO3)*

7. Suppose the elasticity of demand is $\epsilon = -3$. By how much will a profit-maximizing monopolist's price exceed marginal cost? How does this markup of price over marginal cost compare with perfect competition? *(LO3)*

8. *True or false:* A lump-sum tax on a monopolist will always increase the price charged by the monopolist and lower the quantity of output sold. *(LO3)*

9. *True or false:* If a monopolist faces a perfectly horizontal demand curve, then the deadweight loss to the economy is zero. *(LO4)*

10. What forces work against X-inefficiency in privately owned monopolies? *(LO4)*

11. How does the hurdle method of price discrimination mitigate both the efficiency and fairness problems associated with monopoly? *(LO5)*

PROBLEMS

1. You are a self-employed profit-maximization consultant specializing in monopolies. Five single-price, profit-maximizing monopolies are currently seeking your advice, and although the information they have supplied to you is incomplete, your expert knowledge allows you to go back and make a definite recommendation in each case. Select one of the following recommendations for each firm in the short run: *(LO3)*
   a. Remain at the current output level.
   b. Increase output.
   c. Reduce output.
   d. Shut down.
   e. Go back and recalculate your figures because the ones supplied can't possibly be right.

2. A monopolist has a demand curve given by $P = 100 - Q$ and a total cost curve given by $TC = 16 + Q^2$. The associated marginal cost curve is $MC = 2Q$. Find the monopolist's profit-maximizing quantity and price. How much economic profit will the monopolist earn? *(LO3)*

3. Now suppose the monopolist in Problem 2 has a total cost curve given by $TC = 32 + Q^2$. The corresponding marginal cost curve is still $MC = 2Q$, but fixed costs have doubled. Find the monopolist's profit-maximizing

quantity and price. How much economic profit does the monopolist earn? *(LO3)*

4. Now suppose the monopolist in Problem 2 has a total cost curve given by $TC = 16 + 4Q^2$. The corresponding marginal cost curve is now $MC = 8Q$, and fixed costs are back to the original level. Find the monopolist's profit-maximizing quantity and price. How much economic profit does the monopolist earn? *(LO3)*

5. Now suppose the monopolist in Problem 2 also has access to a foreign market in which he can sell whatever quantity he chooses at a constant price of 60. How much will he sell in the foreign market? What will his new quantity and price be in the original market? *(LO3)*

6. Now suppose the monopolist in Problem 2 has a long-run marginal cost curve of $MC = 20$. Find the monopolist's profit-maximizing quantity and price. Find the efficiency loss from this monopoly. *(LO3, LO4)*

7. Suppose a perfectly discriminating monopolist faces market demand $P = 100 - 10Q$ and has constant marginal cost $MC = 20$ (with no fixed costs). How much does the monopolist sell? How much profit does the monopolist earn? What is the maximum per-period

Firm	P	MR	TR	Q	TC	MC	ATC	AVC	Your recommendation
A	3.90	3.00		2,000	7,400	2.90		3.24	
B	5.90			10,000		5.90	4.74	4.24	
C		9.00	44,000	4,000		9.00	11.90	10.74	
D	35.90	37.90		5,000		37.90	35.90		
E	35.00		3,990	1,000	3,300	at min value	23.94		

license fee the government could charge the firm and have the firm still stay in business? *(LO5)*

8. The demand by senior citizens for showings at a local movie house has a constant price elasticity equal to -4. The demand curve for all other patrons has a constant price elasticity equal to -2. If the marginal cost per patron is \$1 per showing, how much should the theater charge members of each group? *(LO3)*

9. During the Iran–Iraq war, the same arms merchant often sold weapons to both sides of the conflict. In this situation, a different price could be offered to each side because there was little danger that the country offered the lower price would sell arms to its rival to profit on the difference in prices. Suppose a French arms merchant has a monopoly of Exocet air-to-sea missiles and is willing to sell them to both sides. Iraq's demand for Exocets is $P = 400 - 0.5Q$ and Iran's is $P = 300 - Q$, where P is in millions of dollars. The marginal cost of Exocets is $MC = Q$. What price will be charged to each country? *(LO3)*

10. If you have ever gone grocery shopping on a weekday afternoon, you have probably noticed some elderly shoppers going slowly down the aisles checking their coupon book for a coupon that matches each of their purchases. How is this behavior explained by the hurdle model of price discrimination? *(LO5)*

11. A monopolist's price is \$10. At this price the absolute value of the elasticity of demand is 2. What is the monopolist's marginal cost? *(LO3)*

12. Suppose the government imposed a price ceiling on a monopolist (an upper bound on the price the monopolist can charge). Let $\bar{P}$ denote the price ceiling, and suppose the monopolist incurs no costs in producing output. *True or false:* If the demand curve faced by the monopolist is inelastic at the price $\bar{P}$, then the monopolist would be no better off if the government removed the price ceiling. *(LO3)*

13.* Crazy Harry, a monopolist, has a total cost curve given by $TC = 5Q + 15$. He sets two prices for his product, a regular price, P_H, and a discount price, P_L. Everyone is eligible to purchase the product at P_H. To be eligible to buy at P_L, it is necessary to present a copy of the latest Crazy Harry ad to the salesclerk. Suppose the only buyers who present the ad are those who would not have been willing to buy the product at P_H. *(LO5)*
   a. If Crazy Harry's demand curve is given by $P = 20 - 5Q$, what are the profit-maximizing values of P_H and P_L?
   b. How much economic profit does Harry make?
   c. How much profit would he have made if he had been forced to charge the same price to all buyers?
   d. Are buyers better or worse off as a result of Harry's being able to charge two prices?

14. An author has signed a contract in which the publisher promises to pay her \$10,000 plus 20 percent of gross receipts from the sale of her book. *True or false:* If both the publisher and the author care only about their own financial return from the project, then the author will prefer a higher book price than will the publisher. *(LO3)*

15. A film director has signed a contract in which the production studio promises to pay her \$1,000,000 plus 5 percent of the studio's rental revenues from the film, all of whose costs of production and distribution are fixed. *True or false:* If both the director and the studio care only about their own financial return from the project, then the director will prefer a lower film rental price than will the studio. *(LO3)*

ANSWERS TO SELF-TESTS

11.1 *(LO3)*

11.2 *(LO3)*

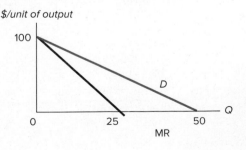

*This problem is most easily solved using the calculus method described in footnote 19.

11.3 $MC = 40 = 100 - 4Q$, which solves for $Q^* = 15$, $P^* = 100 - 2Q^* = 70$. *(LO3)*

11.4 The profit-maximizing level of output for a single-price monopolist occurs where MR = MC. Marginal revenue equals marginal cost at both $Q = 15$ and $Q = 34$, but $Q = 34$ has marginal revenue intersect from above and thus is the maximal one. However, even at $Q = 34$, price does not cover average variable cost ($66 = P <$ AVC $= 72$). The average variable cost curve lies everywhere above the demand curve (see figure), so the firm can do no better than earn profits equal to negative of the fixed costs. Thus, the optimal quantity is $Q = 0$: the firm should shut down! *(LO3)*

11.5 $MR_1 = 10 - 2Q_1$ (left panel), and $MR_2 = 20 - 2Q_2$ (center panel), so the horizontal summation of the MR curves is given by ΣMR (right panel). The profit-maximizing quantity is 13, 4 of which should be sold in market 1, the remaining 9 in market 2. The profit-maximizing prices are $P_1^* = 6$ and $P_2^* = 11$. *(LO3)*

Jorge Salcedo/Alamy Stock Photo

12

A Game-Theoretic Approach to Strategic Behavior

LEARNING OBJECTIVES

After reading this chapter, you should be able to:

LO1 Identify the three basic elements of a game as the players, their possible strategy choices, and the individual payoffs that accrue to each combination of choices.

LO2 Identify a dominant strategy as one that yields a higher payoff, and a dominated strategy as one that yields a lower payoff, regardless of the choices made by other players.

LO3 List the conditions of a prisoner's dilemma and explain why it is a powerful metaphor for situations in which individual and group interests are in conflict.

LO4 Define a Nash equilibrium of a game.

LO5 Employ game trees to represent the payoffs in games for which the order in which players choose is important.

LO6 Employ evolutionary game theory to explain how the effects of specific preferences depend on the proportion of players who have them.

The story is told of three lawyers and three economists who meet one morning as they arrive at the 30th Street Station in Philadelphia to catch the Acela for New York, where they are scheduled to attend the annual meetings of the Law and Economics Association. Each lawyer buys a one-way ticket. To their surprise, however, they notice that the economists standing in the adjacent ticket line buy only a single ticket among them. "What are they up to?" one of the lawyers wonders aloud to his colleagues as the six men take their seats on the train.

Shortly after the train pulls out, the lawyers notice the conductor punching tickets in the car ahead. At this point, the three economists quickly crowd into one of the lavatories at the back of the car. Presently, the conductor comes by and collects each lawyer's ticket and, on his way to the next car, knocks on the door of the occupied lavatory, saying "Tickets, please." The door opens a crack, and a hand reaches out to present a ticket, which the conductor dutifully punches and returns.

Four days later, the men arrive at Penn Station for their return journey. Inspired by the economists, the lawyers buy only a single ticket, cackling to themselves at their cleverness. But this time they are puzzled to notice that the economists don't buy any tickets at all.

The six men board the train, and at first sight of the approaching conductor, the three lawyers hurriedly sequester themselves in one of the lavatories. At this, the three economists get up and proceed to the rear of the car. Two of them go into the other lavatory while the third knocks on the door of the lawyers' lavatory, saying, "Tickets please." One of the lawyers holds their ticket out the door, which the economist collects and then joins his colleagues.

CHAPTER PREVIEW

As the parable of the lawyers and the economists illustrates, the payoff to an action often depends not only on the action itself, but also on how it relates to actions taken by others in the same environment. In previous chapters, we viewed economic decision makers as confronting an environment that was essentially passive. In the perfectly competitive environment of Chapter 10, for example, firms were assumed to ignore the actions of their adversaries. And in the monopoly environment of Chapter 11, the firm simply had no rivals to worry about. Both perfect competition and monopoly represent idealized forms. They are useful for generating insights about general tendencies but are rarely, if ever, encountered in practice.

Our task in this chapter is to develop a theoretical framework for thinking about situations in which individuals and firms know that the outcomes of their own choices depend on the choices taken by others. We'll begin by introducing some elementary concepts from the mathematical theory of games. Next we'll apply these concepts to predict and explain what decisions people will make in strategic settings. We'll see that in many situations, the choices that appear most attractive to each individual often lead to outcomes that are unattractive from the perspective of broader groups. Finally, we'll examine how evolutionary game theory can provide a more secure foundation for thinking about the origins of people's preferences.

THE PRISONER'S DILEMMA: AN INTRODUCTION TO THE THEORY OF GAMES

At the market equilibrium price, worldwide demand for coffee is inelastic with respect to price. Thus, when a frost destroys half the crop in a country that exports a large share of the world's coffee, the price of coffee may rise so much that local farmers actually earn higher profits than if there had been no frost. If coffee growers could earn more by selling less coffee, why do they need to wait for a frost to kill half their crop? Why not just plant less coffee in the first place?

The answer, of course, is that while it might be in the interests of farmers as a whole to curtail production, no individual farmer would ever have an incentive to do so. Each individual farmer, after all, does best if all others *except* him cut back. That way he gets to sell the same quantity as before at the new higher price. In a competitive industry like coffee farming, the existence of many small independent producers makes it difficult to organize conspiracies to curtail output.

Such collusion might seem less difficult to accomplish among oligopolists—that is, in industries served by only a small number of firms. But although successful collusion sometimes does work to the benefit of firms in such industries, it usually turns out to be surprisingly difficult to sustain. Indeed, a recurring theme in the economics of oligopoly is that what it pays each firm to do individually often turns out to be harmful to the interests of firms taken as a whole.

The basic problem confronting colluding oligopolists has the same structure as a game known as the prisoner's dilemma. In the original story used to illustrate the prisoner's dilemma, two prisoners are held in separate cells for a serious crime that they did in fact commit. The prosecutor, however, has only enough hard evidence to convict them of a minor offense, for which the penalty is, say, a year in jail. Each prisoner is told that if one confesses while the other remains silent, the confessor will go scot-free while the other spends 20 years in prison. If both confess, they will get an intermediate sentence, say, 5 years. These payoffs are summarized in Table 12.1. The two prisoners are not allowed to communicate with one another.

Situations like the prisoner's dilemma may be analyzed using the mathematical theory of games developed by John von Neumann and Oskar Morgenstern during the 1940s.[1] This theory begins by describing the three elements common to all games: (1) the players, (2) the list of possible strategies, and (3) the payoffs that correspond to each combination of strategies. In Table 12.1, the two players in the game are prisoner X and prisoner Y. Each player has two strategies: confess and remain silent. The payoffs to each combination

---

[1]See John von Neumann and Oskar Morgenstern, *Theory of Games and Economic Behavior,* 3rd ed., Princeton, NJ: Princeton University Press, 1953.

TABLE 12.1
The Prisoner's Dilemma

		Prisoner Y	
		Confess	**Remain silent**
Prisoner X	**Confess**	5 years for each	0 years for X 20 years for Y
	Remain silent	20 years for X 0 years for Y	1 year for each

> The dominant strategy for each prisoner is to confess. Yet when each confesses, each does worse than if each had remained silent.

of strategies are the sentences they receive, which are summarized in the *payoff matrix* shown in Table 12.1.

Some games, like the prisoner's dilemma, have a **dominant strategy,** which means a strategy that produces better results no matter what strategy the opposing player follows. The dominant strategy in the prisoner's dilemma is to confess. No matter what Y docs, X gets a lighter sentence by speaking out: if Y too confesses, X gets 5 years instead of 20; and if Y remains silent, X goes free instead of spending a year in jail. The payoffs are perfectly symmetric, so Y also does better to confess, no matter what X does. The difficulty is that when each behaves in a self-interested way, both do worse than if each had shown restraint. Thus, when both confess, they get 5 years, instead of the 1 year they could have gotten by remaining silent.

In general, a game will be a prisoner's dilemma if it satisfies two simple conditions.

1. Each player must have a dominant strategy.

2. When both players choose their dominant strategy, each gets a smaller payoff than if each had chosen their dominant strategy.

The prisoner's dilemma thus describes situations in which the rational pursuit of individual self-interest does not yield favorable outcomes from the perspective of players as a group.

To illustrate the analogy between the prisoner's dilemma and the problem confronting oligopolists who are trying to collude, let us consider two firms that are the sole providers of mineral water in a given market. Suppose the market demand curve takes the specific form $P = 20 - Q$, and that each firm can produce mineral water from its own spring at zero marginal cost. Suppose the two firms are considering a collusive agreement under which each produces half the monopoly output and offers it for sale at the monopoly price. For the specific demand curve assumed, the monopoly quantity (that is, the quantity for which $MR = MC = 0$) is 10, and the monopoly price is also 10. If the firms enter into and abide by this agreement, each will sell 5 units at a price of 10, giving each an economic profit of 50. On a strict profit criterion, there is no possibility for each firm to do better than that.

Yet this does not assure that each firm will abide by the agreement. Note that the payoff to each firm depends on the combination of behaviors they choose. Each firm has two options—namely, to abide by the agreement or to defect. For the sake of discussion, suppose that to defect means to cut price by 1 unit, from 10 to 9. If one firm abides by the agreement while the other defects, what will happen? Since the two firms are selling identical products, the defecting firm will capture the entire market because of its lower price. Selling 11 units at a price of 9, it will earn a profit of 99; the trusting cooperator sells no output and thus earns zero profit.

If both firms defect, they will end up splitting the 11 units of output sold at a price of 9, and each will make an economic profit of 49.50. Since each firm has two options—(1) cooperate, by charging 10 as agreed; and (2) defect, by charging 9—there are four possible

dominant strategy the strategy in a game that produces better results irrespective of the strategy chosen by one's opponent.

TABLE 12.2
Profits to Cooperation and Defection

		Firm 1	
		Cooperate (P = 10)	Defect (P = 9)
Firm 2	Cooperate (P = 10)	$\Pi_1 = 50$ $\Pi_2 = 50$	$\Pi_1 = 99$ $\Pi_2 = 0$
	Defect (P = 9)	$\Pi_1 = 0$ $\Pi_2 = 99$	$\Pi_1 = 49.50$ $\Pi_2 = 49.50$

> The dominant strategy is for each firm to defect, for by so doing it earns higher profit no matter which option its rival chooses. Yet when both defect, each earns less than when each cooperates.

combinations of behavior. These combinations, and the profits that result from each, are summarized in Table 12.2.

Note in the table that it is a dominant strategy for each firm to defect. That is, each firm gets a higher payoff by defecting, no matter which option the other firm chooses. To illustrate, consider the choice facing firm 2. It says to itself, "Suppose firm 1 cooperates; which choice is best for me?" By cooperating when firm 1 cooperates, the firms end up in the upper left cell of the profit matrix in Table 12.2, which means each earns 50. But if firm 2 defects, the result will be the lower left cell, where it would end up earning 99. Now firm 2 says, "Suppose firm 1 defects. Which choice is best for me this time?" If firm 2 cooperates, we get the upper right cell of the profit matrix, where it earns 0. But if firm 2 defects, it earns 49.50. Thus, no matter which choice firm 1 makes, firm 2 earns higher profit by defecting.

By exactly parallel reasoning, defection is also a dominant strategy for firm 1. Note, however, that when each firm defects, each does worse than if each had cooperated. In this situation, behavior that is in the interest of each individual firm adds up to a result that is not in the interest of firms generally.

As this example is set up, the firms don't do much worse when each defects than when each cooperates. But firms that find it in their interest to defect once are likely to find it in their interest to do so again. If one now charges 8 while the other remains at 9, for example, the former will earn a profit of 96, while the latter earns 0. A firm need not feel a compelling desire to outdo its rival in order for defection to be an attractive option. On the contrary, its motive may be purely self-protective, motivated by the rational fear that its rival will defect. The resulting process of competitive price-cutting will terminate only when price has plummeted all the way down to marginal cost. At that point, neither firm earns any profit at all. So the cost of failing to abide by a cooperative agreement can be high indeed.

Oligopolists compete not only along the price dimension, but through the use of advertising as well. And here too the interests of an individual firm often conflict with the interests of firms taken as a whole, as Economic Naturalist 12.1 illustrates.

▶ Visit your instructor's Connect© course and access your eBook to view this video.

Why do people shout at parties?

Economic Naturalist 12.1

Why do cigarette companies advertise "too much"?

When a firm advertises its product, its demand increases for two reasons. First, people who never used that type of product before learn about it, leading some to buy it. Second, other people who already consume a different brand of the same product may switch brands because of advertising. The first effect boosts

TABLE 12.3
Advertising as a Prisoner's Dilemma

		Firm 1	
		Don't advertise	**Advertise**
	Don't advertise	$\Pi_1 = 500$ $\Pi_2 = 500$	$\Pi_1 = 750$ $\Pi_2 = 0$
Firm 2			
	Advertise	$\Pi_1 = 0$ $\Pi_2 = 750$	$\Pi_1 = 250$ $\Pi_2 = 250$

> When advertising's main effect is brand switching, the dominant strategy is to advertise heavily (lower right cell), even though firms as a whole would do better by not advertising (upper left cell).

sales for the industry as a whole. The second merely redistributes existing sales among firms.

The American cigarette industry is one in which the most important effect of advertising is believed to be brand switching. In such industries, the decision whether to advertise often confronts individual firms with a prisoner's dilemma. Table 12.3 shows the profits to a hypothetical pair of cigarette producers under the four possible combinations of their advertise/don't advertise decisions. If both firms advertise (lower right cell), each earns a profit of only 250, as compared with a profit of 500 each if neither advertises (upper left cell). So it is clearly better for neither firm to advertise than for both to advertise.

Yet note the incentives confronting the individual firm. Firm 1 sees that if firm 2 doesn't advertise, firm 1 can earn higher profits by advertising (750) than by not advertising (500). Firm 1 also sees that if firm 2 does advertise, firm 1 will again earn more by advertising (250) than by not advertising (0). It is thus a dominant

Why do cigarette companies advertise so much?

strategy for firm 1 to advertise. And because the payoffs are symmetric, it is also a dominant strategy for firm 2 to advertise. So here too when each firm does what is rational from its own point of view, firms as a group do worse than if they had acted in concert.

Congress passed a law forbidding the advertising of cigarettes on television as of January 1, 1971. Its stated purpose was to protect people from messages that might persuade them to consume a product that has been proved hazardous to human health. The law seems to have achieved this purpose, at least in part, as evidenced by the subsequent decline in the proportion of Americans who smoke. But the law has also had an unintended effect, which was to solve—at least temporarily—the prisoner's dilemma confronting American cigarette manufacturers. In the year before the law's enactment, cigarette manufacturers spent more than $300 million advertising their products. The corresponding figure for the following year was more than $60 million smaller, and much of that difference translated into higher profits for the industry. The advertising ban thus accomplished for the cigarette manufacturers what the imperatives of individual profit seeking could not—an effective way of limiting the advertising arms race. In the succeeding years, however, competitive pressures have led cigarette manufacturers to increase their expenditures on forms of advertising that remain legal, thereby eroding their profit windfall.

SELF-TEST 12.1

Consider a game between two players, Makenna and Tamika, where each has two strategies: Tamika can choose between going up or down and Makenna can choose between going left or right. If the payoff matrix is as shown, for what range of values of A would this game be a prisoner's dilemma?

		Makenna	
		Left	Right
Tamika	Up	2 for Tamika 2 for Makenna	1 for Tamika 5 for Makenna
	Down	5 for Tamika 1 for Makenna	A for Tamika A for Makenna

The Nash Equilibrium Concept

When, as in the prisoner's dilemma, both parties have a dominant strategy in a game, the equilibrium for the game occurs when each plays the dominant strategy. But there are many games in which not every player has a dominant strategy. Consider, for example, the variation on the advertising game shown in Table 12.4. No matter what firm 2 does, firm 1 does better to advertise; so advertise is the dominant strategy for firm 1. But now the same cannot be said of firm 2. If firm 1 advertises, firm 2 does best also to advertise. But if firm 1 does not advertise, firm 2 does best not to advertise. In contrast to the prisoner's dilemma, here the best strategy for firm 2 depends on the particular strategy chosen by firm 1.

Even though firm 2 does not have a dominant strategy in this game, we can say something about what is likely to happen. In particular, firm 2 is able to predict that firm 1 will advertise because that is a dominant strategy for firm 1. And since firm 2 knows this, it knows that its own best strategy is also to advertise. In this game, the lower right cell is called a **Nash equilibrium**,[2] which is defined as a combination of strategies such that each player's strategy is the best he can choose given the strategy chosen by the other player. Thus, at a Nash equilibrium, neither player has any incentive to deviate from its current strategy. Note that when each player follows his dominant strategy in a prisoner's dilemma, the result is a Nash equilibrium. But as we have seen, a Nash equilibrium does not require both players to have a dominant strategy.

Nash equilibrium the combination of strategies in a game such that neither player has any incentive to change strategies given the strategy of his opponent.

TABLE 12.4
A Game in Which Firm 2 Has No Dominant Strategy

		Firm 1	
		Don't advertise	Advertise
Firm 2	Don't advertise	$\Pi_1 = 500$ $\Pi_2 = 400$	$\Pi_1 = 750$ $\Pi_2 = 100$
	Advertise	$\Pi_1 = 200$ $\Pi_2 = 0$	$\Pi_1 = 300$ $\Pi_2 = 200$

Firm 1's dominant strategy is to advertise. But firm 2 has no dominant strategy. If firm 1 advertises, firm 2 does best also to advertise, but if firm 1 does not advertise, firm 2 does best not to advertise.

[2]After John F. Nash, the American mathematician who introduced the concept in 1951.

A good rule of thumb for assessing whether a particular combination of strategies constitutes a Nash equilibrium is to ask whether either player has any incentive to choose a different strategy. Consider, for example, the combination of strategies in the upper left cell of Table 12.4. Does either player have an incentive to choose differently?

To answer this question, note first that each player has the option of moving to only one other cell in the table. Firm 2, for example, can choose only the top row or the bottom row, and so it cannot move to a cell in a different column. If it wants to move from the upper left cell, its only option is the lower left cell. But since its profit (0) would be lower there than in the upper left cell (400), it would not want to make that move.

Similarly, firm 1 can choose only the left column or the right column, and so it cannot move to a cell in a different row. Starting from the upper left cell, then, firm 1's only option would be to move to the upper right cell. And since its profit in that cell (750) would be higher than in the upper left cell (500), it would want to move. Thus, if we start in the upper left cell, at least one player (firm 1) would want to move, which means that the upper left cell cannot be a Nash equilibrium.

In contrast, consider the lower right cell of Table 12.4. Firm 2, which chooses only the row, can move only to the upper right cell, which it would not want to do because its profits there (100) would be lower than in the lower right cell (200). Similarly, firm 1, which chooses only the column, can move only to the lower left cell, which it would not want to do because its profit there (200) would be lower than in the lower right cell (300). And since neither firm would want to move from the lower right cell of Table 12.4, that combination of strategies satisfies the definition of a Nash equilibrium.

SELF-TEST 12.2

Does either firm have a dominant strategy in the game below? Does the game have a Nash equilibrium?

		Firm 1	
		High research budget	Low research budget
Firm 2	High research budget	$\Pi_1 = 200$ $\Pi_2 = 40$	$\Pi_1 = 60$ $\Pi_2 = 100$
	Low research budget	$\Pi_1 = 0$ $\Pi_2 = 30$	$\Pi_1 = 40$ $\Pi_2 = 80$

The Maximin Strategy

In the game shown in Table 12.4, we saw that if firm 1 follows its dominant strategy by advertising, firm 2 will also do better by advertising. So if firm 2 believes that firm 1 will act rationally, firm 2's best option is to advertise. But firm 2 may not be sure that firm 1 will choose rationally. In that case firm 2 might want at least to consider the possibility that firm 1 will choose not to advertise. In that case, if firm 2 advertises it will earn a profit of 0, far worse than the 400 it would earn by not advertising.

When firm 2 does not have a dominant strategy of its own and is uncertain about firm 1's choice, what should it do? The answer depends on both the likelihood it assigns to firm 1's possible choices and how its own payoffs are affected by those choices. Under the circumstances, it is extremely difficult to predict what firm 2 will do.

Suppose, however, that firm 2 takes an extremely cautious approach when confronted with such uncertainty. It might then choose to follow what is called the **maximin strategy**, which means to choose the option that maximizes the lowest possible value of its own payoff. Referring again to Table 12.4, note that if firm 2 chooses not to advertise, the lowest payoff it can receive is 100 (which will happen if firm 1 advertises). But if

maximin strategy choosing the option that makes the lowest payoff one can receive as large as possible.

firm 2 chooses to advertise, the lowest payoff it can receive is 0 (which will happen if firm 1 chooses not to advertise). So if we know that firm 2 follows the maximin strategy in this situation, we can predict that it will choose not to advertise.

Strategies for Repeated Play in Prisoner's Dilemmas

Games discussed thus far have involved only two players. But these games are easily extended to cover multiple players. In the multi-player prisoner's dilemma, for example, the two strategy choices are again cooperate and defect, and defecting is again a dominant strategy for every player. And the defining condition of the game continues to be that each player receives a higher payoff when each cooperates than when each defects.

To say that the costs of failing to cooperate are high in prisoner's dilemmas is simply another way of saying that there are powerful financial incentives to find some way to hold collusive agreements together. What the potential participants in a collusive agreement need is some way to penalize those who defect, thereby making it in their material interests not to do so. When a prisoner's dilemma confronts parties who will interact only once, this turns out to be very difficult to achieve. But when the participants expect to interact repeatedly in the future, new possibilities emerge.

Experimental research in the 1960s identified a very simple strategy that proves remarkably effective at keeping potential defectors in check.[3] The strategy is called *tit-for-tat,* and it works as follows: The first time you interact with someone, you cooperate. In each subsequent interaction you simply do what that person did in the previous interaction. Thus, if your partner defected on your first interaction, you would then defect on your next interaction with her. If she then cooperates, your move next time will be to cooperate as well.

Tit-for-tat is described as a "nice" strategy because of the propensity of players to cooperate on the first interaction. If two tit-for-tat players interact together over a long period of time, the result will be cooperation in each and every interaction. Tit-for-tat is also a "tough" strategy, however, because those who follow it always stand ready to punish defectors in the next interaction. Finally, it is a "forgiving" strategy, in the sense that a player is willing to cooperate with a former defector once she shows evidence of willingness to cooperate.

University of Michigan political scientist Robert Axelrod conducted an extensive analysis of how well the tit-for-tat strategy performs against other strategies for playing the repeated prisoner's dilemma game.[4] In an early round of Axelrod's computer simulations, tit-for-tat was the most successful strategy, in the sense that people who followed it earned more, on the average, than those using any of the other strategies tested. Axelrod then published this finding and invited experts from all over the world to try to design a better strategy. His challenge produced a host of ingenious responses. Axelrod found, however, that even these strategies, many of which had been put together for the specific purpose of defeating tit-for-tat, did not survive against it.

The success of tit-for-tat requires a reasonably stable set of players, each of whom can remember what other players have done in previous interactions. It also requires that players have a significant stake in what happens in the future, for it is only the fear of retaliation that keeps people from defecting. When these conditions are met, cooperators can identify one another and discriminate against defectors.

The conditions called for by the tit-for-tat strategy are often met in human populations. Many people do interact repeatedly, and most keep track of how others treat them. Axelrod has

---

[3]See Anatol Rapoport and A. Chammah, *Prisoner's Dilemma,* Ann Arbor: University of Michigan Press, 1965.
[4]Robert Axelrod, *The Evolution of Cooperation,* New York: Basic Books, 1984.

assembled persuasive evidence that these forces help explain how people actually behave. Perhaps the most impressive of all this evidence comes from accounts of the "live-and-let-live" system that developed in the trench warfare in Europe during World War I. In many areas of the war, the same enemy units lay encamped opposite one another in the trenches over a period of several years. Units were often closely matched, with the result that neither side had much hope of quickly defeating the other. Their choices were to fight intensively, with both sides sustaining heavy casualties, or to exercise restraint.

The conditions of interaction described by historian Tony Ashworth in his account of the trench fighting closely resemble those required for the success of tit-for-tat.[5] The identities of the players were more or less stable. Interactions between them were repeated, often several times daily, for extended periods. Each side could easily tell when the other side defected. And each side had a clear stake in keeping its future losses to a minimum.

There is little doubt that tit-for-tat often did emerge as the strategy of choice for both Allied and German fighting units in World War I. Although strongly discouraged as a matter of official policy, restraint was sometimes conspicuously apparent. Referring to night patrol squads operating out of the trenches, Ashworth writes:

> both British and Germans on quiet sectors assumed that should a chance face-to-face encounter occur, neither patrol would initiate aggression, but each would move to avoid the other. Each patrol gave peace to the other where aggression was not only possible, but prescribed, provided, of course, the gesture was reciprocated, for if one patrol fired so would the other.[6]

In the words of one of the participants in the conflict:

> We suddenly confronted, round some mound or excavation, a German patrol. . . . We were perhaps twenty yards from one another, fully visible. I waved a weary hand, as if to say, what is the use of killing each other? The German officer seemed to understand, and both parties turned and made their way back to their own trenches.[7]

Often, bombardments would occur only at specified times of day and would be directed away from the most vulnerable positions. Mealtimes and hospital tents, for example, were usually tacitly off limits.

The conditions discussed by Axelrod help to explain not only when people will cooperate, but also when they are most likely to *refrain* from cooperation. For example, he notes that mutual restraint in trench warfare began to break down once the end of the war was clearly in sight.

As in warfare, so, too, in the world of business. Companies pay their bills on time, Axelrod suggests, not because it is the right thing to do but because they require future shipments from the same suppliers. When future interactions appear unlikely, this tendency to cooperate often breaks down: "[An] example is the case where a business is on the edge of bankruptcy and sells its accounts receivable to an outsider called a 'factor.' This sale is made at a very substantial discount because

> once a manufacturer begins to go under, even his best customers begin refusing payment for merchandise, claiming defects in quality, failure to meet specifications, tardy delivery, or what-have-you. The great enforcer of morality in commerce is the continuing relationship, the belief that one will have to do business again with this customer, or this supplier, and when a failing company loses this automatic enforcer, not even a strong-arm factor is likely to find a substitute.[8]

[5]Tony Ashworth, *Trench Warfare: The Live and Let Live System,* New York: Holmes and Meier, 1980.
[6]Ibid., p. 103.
[7]Herbert Read, quoted in ibid., p. 104.
[8]Mayer, quoted in Axelrod, op. cit., pp. 59, 60.

One additional requirement for the success of tit-for-tat is that there not be a known, fixed number of future interactions. Indeed, if players know exactly how many times they will interact, then mutual cooperation on every move cannot be a Nash equilibrium. To see why, suppose each firm knew it was going to interact with its rival for, say, exactly 1,000 more times. Each would then know that the other would defect on the last interaction, because there would be no possibility of being punished for doing so. But since each firm realizes that, it will also have no reason not to defect on the 999th interaction. After all, a defection will occur on the 1,000th interaction no matter what it does on the round before. The same argument can be applied step-by-step back to the first interaction, with the result that the tit-for-tat strategy completely unravels.

The unraveling problem does not arise if there is not a known, fixed number of interactions.[9] If we suppose, for example, that there is always some positive probability that a further interaction will ensue, then no interaction can ever be identified as being the last one, which means the threat of future punishment will always have at least some force. In the situations in which most firms find themselves (an exception being the bankruptcy case cited earlier), it seems plausible to assume that there will always be some probability of interaction in the future.

Is it inevitable, then, that the tit-for-tat strategy will produce widespread collusion among firms? By no means. One difficulty is that tit-for-tat's effectiveness depends on there being only two players in the game. In competitive and monopolistically competitive industries there are generally many firms, and even in oligopolies there are often several. When there are more than two firms, and one defects this period, how do the cooperators selectively punish the defector next period? By cutting price? That will penalize everyone, not just the defector. Even if there are only two firms in an industry, the problem remains that some other firm may enter the industry. So the would-be cooperators have to worry not only about each other, but also about the entire list of firms that might decide to compete with them. Each firm may see this as a hopeless task and decide to defect now, hoping to reap at least some extra-normal profit in the short run.

We will consider the threat of potential entry in greater detail in the sections to follow. For the moment, we may note that, as a purely empirical matter, cartel agreements and other forms of collusion have occurred frequently in the past but have tended to be highly unstable. Apparently the practical problems involved in implementing tit-for-tat in the environments confronting firms make it very difficult to hold collusive agreements together for long.

SEQUENTIAL GAMES

The games we have considered so far have been ones in which both players must pick their strategies simultaneously. Each player had to choose his strategy knowing only the incentives facing his opponent, not the opponent's actual choice of strategy. But in many games, one player moves first, and the other is then able to choose his strategy with full knowledge of the first player's choice. This description roughly fits the circumstances in which the United States and the former Soviet Union (USSR) found themselves during much of the cold war.

At that time, the military strategies of both nations were based on the doctrine of mutually assured destruction (MAD). The idea behind MAD was simple: Both sides maintained sufficiently large and well-defended nuclear arsenals to ensure that each would be able to retaliate if the other launched a first strike. The prospect of a devastating counterstrike, according to the MAD theory, is what prevented each side from even considering a first strike.

---

[9]Another way the unraveling problem is avoided is if there is some positive probability that others will follow the tit-for-tat strategy even though, strictly speaking, it is not rational for them to do so. See David Kreps, Paul Milgrom, John Roberts, and Robert Wilson, "Rational Cooperation in Finitely Repeated Prisoner's Dilemmas," *Journal of Economic Theory*, 27, 1982, 245–252.

The fact that neither side ever launched a first strike is interpreted by some people as evidence that the MAD strategy must have worked. And yet there is an apparent logical flaw in the strategy, one that suggests the real source of restraint must lie elsewhere. To appreciate the problem, put yourself in the shoes of a U.S. president who has just learned that the Russians have launched a first strike. At that moment, you know that the MAD strategy has already failed. For whatever reason, the threat of a counterstrike did not in fact deter the Russian first strike. Do you now order a counterstrike anyway? You realize that to do so will only increase the likelihood of total world destruction. True enough, American interests have been grievously damaged by the attack. But at that point, a counterstrike will only damage them further.

The logical difficulty with MAD is thus that each side knows perfectly well that once a first strike has already been launched, it will not be in the other side's interest to retaliate. And since each party knows this, the threat of a counterstrike loses all power to deter.

Or at least so it seems in theory. Perhaps the threat deters because each side fears the other might not respond rationally once it is the victim of a first strike. (A casual review of the American and Soviet leaders of the post–World War II period lends at least some credence to this interpretation.) But whether or not MAD is an effective defense strategy, its apparent flaw is troubling. The same logic that exposed this flaw suggests a simple way to repair it. It is to install a so-called doomsday machine—a tamper-proof device that will *automatically* retaliate once a first strike has been launched. Once each side became aware the other had such a device in place, the MAD strategy would be complete and a first strike truly would become unthinkable.

To see how economists treat sequential games analytically, suppose the former Soviet Union (the USSR) was considering whether to launch a nuclear strike against the United States. This decision may be portrayed in a "game tree" diagram like the one shown in Figure 12.1. If the first move is the USSR's, the game starts at point A. The first two branches of the game tree represent the USSR's alternatives of attacking and not attacking. If it attacks, then the United States finds itself at point B on the top branch of the game tree, where it must decide whether or not to strike back. If the United States retaliates, we end up at point D, where the payoffs are −100 for each country. If the United States does not retaliate, we end up at point E, where the payoffs are 100 for the USSR and −50 for the United States. (The units of these payoffs are purely arbitrary. The values chosen are intended to reflect each country's hypothetical relative valuation of the different outcomes.) The bottom half of the game tree represents

FIGURE 12.1

Nuclear Deterrence as a Sequential Game

If the USSR attacks, the best option for the United States is not to retaliate (point E). If the USSR doesn't attack, the best option for the United States is also not to attack (point G). Since the USSR gets a higher payoff at E than at G, it will attack. If the United States is believed to be a payoff maximizer, its threat to retaliate against a first strike will not be credible.

the alternative in which the USSR does not attack. If the USSR chooses this alternative, the United States finds itself at point *C,* where it again faces a decision about whether or not to launch missiles at the USSR. For argument's sake, suppose that the payoffs to the two countries under each alternative are shown on the bottom two branches of the game tree at points *F* and *G,* respectively. Given the assumed payoffs for each of the four possible outcomes of the game tree, the USSR can analyze what the United States will do under each alternative. If the USSR attacks (point *B*), the best option open to the United States is not to retaliate (point *E*). If the USSR does not attack (point *C*), the best option for the United States is also not to attack (point *G*). The USSR thus knows that if the United States is a payoff maximizer, the game will end at point *E* if the USSR attacks, and at point *G* if the USSR does not attack. And since the USSR has a higher payoff at point *E,* it does best to attack. The United States may threaten to retaliate, but as long as its adversaries believe it is a payoff maximizer, such threats will lack credibility.

Now suppose that the United States could install a "doomsday machine"—a device that would automatically retaliate in the event of an attack by the USSR. The effect would be to eliminate the bottom half of the top branch of the game tree in Figure 12.1. The USSR would then know that if it attacked, the game would end at point *D,* where the USSR gets a payoff of −100. And since this is worse than the outcome if the USSR does not attack (point *G*), the best option open to the USSR would then be to leave its missiles in their silos.

Economic Naturalist 12.2

Why might a company make an investment it knew it would never use?

At 1,451 feet, the Willis Tower—still called the Sears Tower by many—was, until 2014, the tallest building in the United States and remains the tallest building in Chicago. This status endows the building with a special form of prestige, enabling its owners to command higher rents than in otherwise similar office buildings. Now, suppose that Company *X* is considering whether to build an even taller building. Suppose it knows that any firm that has permanent ownership of the tallest building in Chicago will earn a large economic profit. Its concern, naturally, is that a rejuvenated Sears (or some other firm) may build a still taller building, which would substantially diminish Company *X*'s payoff.

Both Sears and Company *X* realize that they are participants in a sequential game of the type pictured in Figure 12.2. The game starts at point *A,* where *X* must decide whether to enter with a taller building. If it does not, Sears will receive a payoff of 100, *X* a payoff of 0. If *X* enters, however, the game moves to point *B,* where Sears must decide whether to build higher or stand pat. Suppose that if Sears builds higher, its payoff will be 30, while *X* will earn a payoff of −50; and that if Sears does not build higher, its payoff will be 40, while *X* will get a payoff of 60. Sears naturally wants *X* not to enter. It may even announce its intention to build a taller building in the event that *X* enters. But as long as *X* knows the payoffs facing Sears, it can conclude that the best option open once *X* enters is for Sears to stand pat. The Nash equilibrium of this sequential game is point *E,* where *X* enters and Sears stands pat.

Now suppose that before Sears had originally built its tower, it had the option of building a platform atop the building on which it could build an addition that would make the building taller. Building this platform costs 10 units, but reduces the cost of building a taller building by 20 units. If Sears had installed this

FIGURE 12.2

The Decision to Build the Tallest Building

If company X builds a skyscraper taller than the Sears (Willis) Tower, Sears must decide whether to build higher (point D) or yield its status as the tallest building (point E). Because Sears earns a higher payoff at E than at D, it will not build higher. And since X knows that, it will enter the market despite Sears's threat to build a taller building.

platform, the sequential game between it and company X would then be as portrayed by the game tree in Figure 12.3. Sears's payoff at point D is now 40 (it saves 20 on building costs less the 10-unit cost of the platform). Its payoffs at C and E are each 10 units less than in Figure 12.2 (reflecting the cost of the platform). Despite the small magnitude of these changes in payoffs, the presence of the platform dramatically alters the outcome of the game. This time X can predict that if it enters with the tallest building, it will be in Sears's interest to add to its existing building, which means that X will receive a payoff of −50. As a result, X will not find it worthwhile to enter this market, and so the game will end at point C. The payoff to Sears at C is 90 (the original 100 minus the 10-unit cost of building the platform). Its 10-unit investment in the platform thus increases its net payoff by 50 (the difference between the 90-unit payoff it receives with the platform and the 40-unit payoff it would have received without it).

The platform investment just discussed is an example of what economists call *strategic entry deterrence*. When such investments are effective, it is because they change potential rivals' expectations about how the firm will respond when its market position is threatened.

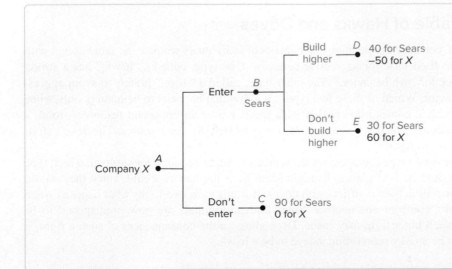

FIGURE 12.3

Strategic Entry Deterrence

Had it originally built a platform atop its building at a cost of 10 units, Sears would have reduced the cost of building a taller building by 20 units. Then company X would have calculated that it would not be worthwhile to build a taller building, because it then would have been in Sears's interest to respond with an addition. The Nash equilibrium of the altered game occurs at point C.

Economic Naturalist 12.3

Why would a firm build a factory with more capacity than it would ever need?

Why might a firm build a bigger factory than it needed?

Larger production facilities typically have higher fixed costs and lower marginal costs than smaller ones. So the question can be rephrased as follows: Why might it be in a firm's interest to have a factory with very low marginal cost, even if the result were to make its total cost higher than for a smaller facility?

A possible answer is that the larger factory constitutes another example of strategic entry deterrence. If potential entrants knew that an incumbent firm had extremely low marginal cost, they could predict that it would be in the incumbent's interest to remain in business even at a price level too low for entrants to earn a normal profit. In that case, it would not be rational for rivals to enter the market. And their absence, in turn, would enable the incumbent to charge a price sufficiently high to cover the costs of the larger facility.

THE EVOLUTION OF STRATEGIC PREFERENCES

In Chapter 7, we discussed the concept of strategic preferences, ones that help people solve problems of social interaction. "Evolutionary game theory," a branch of game theory, provides a structured way of thinking about how strategic preferences might have emerged. An early example comes from the biological literature's approach to the origin of a preference for aggressive behavior. Careful examination of the biologist's model for the evolution of this preference will help us think more fruitfully about some of the other nonstandard preferences discussed in Chapter 7.

A Parable of Hawks and Doves

To begin, consider a population that consists of individuals who are the same except with respect to their taste for aggressive behavior. One type, called a "hawk," has a strong preference for such behavior.[10] The other type, called a "dove," prefers to avoid aggressive behavior. Which of these two types an individual happens to be matters only when that individual comes into conflict with another over an important resource—food, a mate, whatever. The hawk's strategy is always to fight for the resource. The dove's strategy is never to fight.

If these two types compete for the scarce resources required for survival, which type will win out? At first glance, it might seem as if the hawks would, since they would always prevail in their conflicts with doves. But this view overlooks what happens when two hawks confront one another. Since both individuals are now predisposed to be aggressive, a bitter fight may ensue. Depending on the consequences of such a fight, it may thus be a risky proposition indeed to be a hawk.

[10]The names "hawk" and "dove" are used metaphorically here to describe members of the same species who have different tastes for aggressive behavior.

The potential disadvantage of being a hawk becomes even clearer when we examine what happens when two doves confront one another over an important resource. In these encounters, the costs of a bloody battle are avoided, and the doves share the resource.

In our hypothetical population, pairs of individuals interact with one another at random, and there are three possible pairings: (1) two doves, (2) two hawks, and (3) a hawk and a dove. To see how this population will evolve, we need to know the payoffs for each of these three types of interaction. To make our analysis manageable, let's assume that a biologist has gathered data that enable us to express these payoffs in units of some common measure—say, calories. Suppose the conflict involves food that contains 12 calories. When two doves interact, they share the food, so that each receives a payoff of 6 calories. When a hawk and a dove interact, the dove defers to the hawk, so the hawk gets 12 calories, the dove none. Finally, when two hawks interact, the winner of the ensuing fight gets the 12 calories, the loser none. The fight itself, however, consumes 10 calories for each hawk, which means that the net payoff is $12 - 10 = 2$ calories for the winning hawk, and -10 calories for the losing hawk. Over the course of many encounters between hawks, any given hawk can expect to win half the time and lose half the time. Thinking of hawks as a whole, then, the average payoff for each participant in a hawk-hawk encounter is $(2 - 10)/2 = -4$ calories.

If we let X and Y represent two individuals from the population, the average payoffs for the different combinations of interactions are summarized in Table 12.5.

As biologists view the matter, the question of whether it is better to be a hawk or to be a dove is answered by computing which type gets more calories on the average. To do this, we must first know the likelihood of each type of interaction. To illustrate, suppose that half the population initially consists of hawks, the other half of doves. Then, half of each individual's interactions would be with hawks, the other half with doves. For a hawk, then, the average payoff, denoted P_H, would be a weighted average of the two payoff values:

$$P_H = \left(\tfrac{1}{2}\right)(-4) + \left(\tfrac{1}{2}\right)(12) = 4. \tag{12.1}$$

The corresponding average payoff for a dove, denoted P_D, would be

$$P_D = \left(\tfrac{1}{2}\right)(0) + \left(\tfrac{1}{2}\right)6 = 3. \tag{12.2}$$

The implicit assumption in the biologist's view of the competition between hawks and doves is that whichever type garners a larger number of calories will tend to raise larger families and will thus make up an increasing share of the total population. We have just seen that in a population initially split 50-50 between the two types, the hawks will get more calories than the doves, which means that the hawks' share of the total population will grow.

Suppose we use h to denote the fraction of the population that consists of hawks (so that, in the example just considered, we had $h = \tfrac{1}{2}$). Since the population shares of the two types must sum to 1, $1 - h$ will be the fraction of the population that consists of

TABLE 12.5
The Hawk-Dove Payoff Matrix

		Individual Y	
		Hawk	**Dove**
Individual X	**Hawk**	−4 calories for each	12 calories for X 0 calories for Y
	Dove	0 calories for X 12 calories for Y	6 calories for each

Two individuals are in conflict over food worth 12 calories. When two hawks meet, a fight ensues that consumes 10 calories each, leaving an average net payoff of −4 calories per hawk. When doves and hawks meet, doves defer, so hawks get 12 calories, doves 0. When two doves meet, they share the food, so each gets 6 calories.

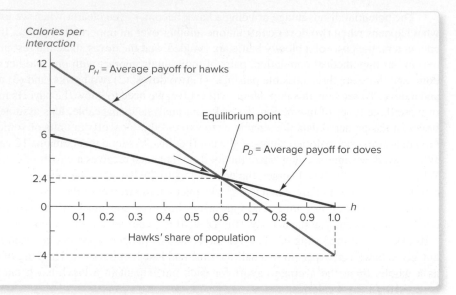

FIGURE 12.4

Average Payoffs for Hawks and Doves

The average payoffs for both hawks and doves are declining functions of the share of the population consisting of hawks. The mixture of the two types is in equilibrium when the average payoffs are the same for the two types.

doves. For such a population, the average payoff for hawks is again a weighted average of the two types of hawk payoffs, where now the weights are the respective population shares, h and $(1 - h)$:

$$P_H = (h)(-4) + (1 - h)(12) = 12 - 16h. \tag{12.3}$$

The corresponding general expression for the average payoff for doves is

$$P_D = (h)(0) + (1 - h)6 = 6 - 6h. \tag{12.4}$$

For example, if the share consisting of hawks were four-fifths, hawks would encounter other hawks in their interactions four-fifths of the time, doves the remaining one-fifth of the time, making the average payoff for hawks $P_H = \left(\frac{4}{5}\right)(-4) + \left(\frac{1}{5}\right)(12) = -0.8$. The corresponding average for doves would be $P_D = \left(\frac{4}{5}\right)(0) + \left(\frac{1}{5}\right)(6) = 1.2$. So when hawks make up four-fifths of the population, their average payoff will be smaller than the average payoff for doves, and this means that the hawks' share of the population will begin to fall.

To see whether the population shares will settle at some equilibrium, we plot the average payoff curves for the two types and look for a point at which they cross. As shown in Figure 12.4, this occurs when $h = 0.6$. This means that when 60 percent of the population consists of hawks, the remaining 40 percent of doves, each type will receive an average payoff of 2.4 calories per interaction. With equal average payoffs, the two types will tend to have equally many offspring, which implies that their respective shares of the population will remain unchanged.

Note that the equilibrium point identified in Figure 12.4 is stable: If the population share of hawks were ever to deviate from 0.6, there would immediately be forces pulling it back to 0.6. For example, if the share of hawks for some reason dipped to 0.5, the average payoff curves in Figure 12.4 show that the average payoff for hawks would exceed the average payoff for doves, and this would cause the hawks' population share to rise. Conversely, if the share of hawks somehow rose to 0.7, then the hawks' average payoff would be smaller than the doves', and this would cause the hawks' population share to fall.

SELF-TEST 12.3

In the example discussed above, suppose now that the payoffs are altered as follows: When two doves interact, each earns 3 units; when two hawks interact, each earns 1 unit; and when a dove and a hawk interact, the former gets a payoff of 2 units, the latter a payoff of 6 units. What will be the equilibrium population share of each type?

The hawks and doves example illustrates how the usefulness of a preference for a certain mode of behavior depends on the frequency with which others in the population also prefer that behavior. Being a hawk (preferring aggression) can be advantageous, but only up to a point. For once hawks become sufficiently numerous, it then becomes advantageous to be a dove. The population is in equilibrium only when the average payoffs for the two tastes are the same.

The hawks and doves example also illustrates an important property of evolution by natural selection, which is that traits are often favored for their effects on *indi-*

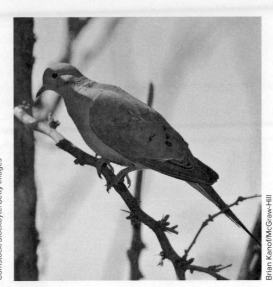

The population as a whole fares best when all individuals are doves. But in such a population, an individual hawk would fare better than a dove.

vidual payoffs, not for their effects on the payoffs of populations as a whole. Note in Figure 12.4 that the population as a whole would be better off if there were no hawks at all ($h = 0$), or in a population consisting only of doves, all individuals would receive 6 calories per interaction, a dramatic improvement over the equilibrium value of 2.4. But a population consisting only of doves would not be stable. A hawk could invade such a population and make rapid headway because of its success when interacting with doves.

The rational choice model introduced in Chapter 3 regards the consumer's tastes as given, a set of goals the consumer strives to fulfill. Ecological models like the hawks and doves example take a step back and ask where those tastes come from. These models view preferences not as ends in themselves but as a means by which individuals achieve important material objectives (in the hawks and doves case, the acquisition of calories needed to survive and reproduce).

With the workings of the hawks and doves model firmly in mind, we are now in a position to analyze how a variety of other tastes might have emerged. In particular, we will focus on how certain unselfish motives often help people solve an important class of problems that arise in economic and social interaction.

The Commitment Problem

As noted, the pursuit of self-interest is self-defeating in the prisoner's dilemma.

The dominant strategy in the prisoner's dilemma is to confess. As we saw earlier, each prisoner gets a lighter sentence by speaking out, no matter what his partner does. The difficulty is that when each behaves in a self-interested way, both do worse than if each had shown restraint.

Although the prisoners are not allowed to communicate with one another, it would be a mistake to assume that this is the real source of difficulty. Their problem is rather a lack of *trust*. A simple promise not to confess does not change the material payoffs of the game. (If each could promise not to confess, each would *still* do better if he broke his promise.)

The prisoner's dilemma is an example of a broader class of problems called *commitment problems*. The common feature of these problems is that people can do better if they can commit themselves to behave in a way that will later be inconsistent with their own material interests. In the prisoner's dilemma, for example, if the prisoners could commit themselves to remain silent, they would do better than if left free to pursue their narrow material interests.

The late economist Thomas Schelling[11] provided another vivid illustration of a commitment problem. Schelling described a kidnapper who suddenly gets cold feet. He wants to set his victim free but is afraid he will go to the police. In return for his freedom, the victim gladly promises not to do so. The problem, however, is that both realize it will no longer be in the victim's interest to keep this promise once he is free. And so the kidnapper reluctantly concludes that he must kill him. The kidnapper's belief that the victim will act in a rational, self-interested way spells apparent doom for the victim.

Schelling suggested the following way out of the dilemma: "If the victim has committed an act whose disclosure could lead to blackmail, he may confess it; if not, he might commit one in the presence of his captor, to create a bond that will ensure his silence."[12] (Perhaps the victim could allow the kidnapper to photograph him in the process of committing some unspeakably degrading act.) The blackmailable act serves here as a **commitment device,** something that provides the victim with an incentive to keep his promise. Keeping it will still be unpleasant for him once he is freed, but clearly less so than not being able to make a credible promise in the first place.

In everyday economic and social interaction, we often encounter commitment problems like the prisoner's dilemma, or like the one confronting Schelling's kidnapper and victim. The solution Schelling suggested tries to eliminate the problem by altering the relevant material incentives. Unfortunately, however, this approach will not always be practical.

An alternative approach is to alter the psychological rewards that govern behavior—in economic terms, to have preferences that lead people to behave in ways contrary to narrow self-interest. Suppose, for example, the kidnap victim was known to be a person who would feel bad if he broke a promise. Such a feeling, if sufficiently strong, would deter him from going to the police even after it became in his material interests to do so. Knowing this would enable the kidnapper to set him free.

commitment device a device that commits a person to behave in a certain way in the future, even though he may wish to behave otherwise when the time comes.

Illustration: The Cheating Problem

The functional role of unselfish motives can be seen more clearly with the help of an example of a simple ecology in which egoists are pitted against nonegoists in a struggle to survive. The commitment problem they face arises in joint business ventures, each of which consists of a pair of individuals. In these ventures each person can behave in either of two ways: He can "cooperate," which means to deal honestly with his partner, or he can "defect," which means to cheat his partner. The payoffs to each of two representative partners, Smith and Jones, depend on the combination of behaviors chosen in the manner shown in Table 12.6. These payoffs confront the partners with a monetary version of the prisoner's dilemma. Note that Jones gets a higher payoff by defecting, no matter what Smith does, and that the same is true for Smith. If Jones believes Smith will behave in a

TABLE 12.6
Monetary Payoffs in a Joint Venture

		Smith	
		Defect	**Cooperate**
Jones	**Defect**	2 for each	0 for Smith 6 for Jones
	Cooperate	6 for Smith 0 for Jones	4 for each

> The payoffs in the table have the same structure as the payoffs in the prisoner's dilemma. Holding the other player's behavior fixed, each player does best by defecting. Yet when each defects, each gets only 2, whereas each gets 4 when both cooperate.

[11]Thomas Schelling, *The Strategy of Conflict,* Cambridge, MA: Harvard University Press, 1960.
[12]Ibid., pp. 43–44.

self-interested way, he will predict that Smith will defect. And if only to protect himself, he may feel compelled to defect as well. When both defect, each gets only a 2-unit payoff. The frustration, as in all dilemmas of this sort, is that both could have done better. Had they cooperated, each would have gotten a 4-unit payoff.

Now suppose we have not just Smith and Jones but also a large population. Pairs of people again form joint ventures and the relationship between behavior and payoffs for the members of each pair is again as given in Table 12.6. Suppose further that everyone in the population is of one of two types—cooperator or defector. A cooperator is someone who, possibly through intensive cultural conditioning, has developed a heritable capacity to experience a moral sentiment that predisposes him to cooperate. A defector is someone who either lacks this capacity or has failed to develop it.

In this scheme, cooperators are altruists in the sense that they refrain from cheating even when there is no possibility of being detected. Viewed in the narrow context of the choice at hand, this behavior is clearly contrary to their material interests. Defectors, by contrast, are pure opportunists. They always make whatever choice will maximize their personal payoffs. As in the hawks and doves example considered earlier, our task here is to determine what will happen when people from the two groups are thrown into a survival struggle against one another. As we will see, the answer depends critically on how easily the two types may be distinguished from one another. We will consider several possibilities in turn.

Population Movements When Cooperators and Defectors Look Alike

Suppose, for argument's sake, that cooperators and defectors look exactly alike, thus making it impossible to distinguish between the two types. In this hypothetical ecology, this means that individuals will pair at random, as in the hawks and doves example. Naturally, cooperators (and defectors, for that matter) would like nothing better than to pair with cooperators, but they have no choice in the matter. Because everyone looks the same, they must take their chances. The expected payoffs to both defectors and cooperators therefore depend on the likelihood of pairing with a cooperator, which in turn depends on the proportion of cooperators in the population.

Let c denote the fraction of the population that consists of cooperators. If a cooperator interacts with a randomly chosen person from the population, the probability of that person also being a cooperator will be c. The probability of that person being a defector is $1 - c$. Since a cooperator gets 4 when he interacts with another cooperator and zero when he interacts with a defector, the expected, or average, payoff for each cooperator in this case can be written as

$$P_C = c(4) + (1 - c)(0) = 4c. \qquad (12.5)$$

Thus, when half of the population consists of cooperators $\left(c = \frac{1}{2}\right)$, a cooperator has a 50-50 chance of interacting with another cooperator, in which case he will get 4 units, and a 50-50 chance of interacting with a defector, in which case he will get 0 units. His expected payoff here is a weighted average of these two outcomes, namely, 2 units.

SELF-TEST 12.4
What is a cooperator's average payoff when $c = 0.97$?

The corresponding expression for the average payoff for defectors is given by

$$P_D = 6c + 2(1 - c) = 2 + 4c. \qquad (12.6)$$

The average payoff relationships for the monetary values assumed in this illustration are shown in Figure 12.5.

FIGURE 12.5

Average Payoffs When Cooperators and Defectors Look Alike

The expected payoffs for both cooperators and defectors increase with the percentage of cooperators in the population. But no matter what the initial population share of cooperators is, cooperators earn a lower average payoff than defectors. This means that cooperators are destined for extinction.

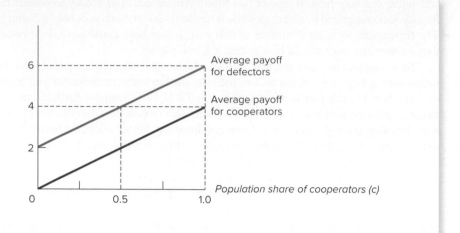

When cooperators and defectors look exactly the same, how will the population evolve over time? As in the hawks and doves example, the rule here is that each individual reproduces in proportion to its average payoff: Those with larger material payoffs have the resources necessary to raise larger numbers of offspring.[13] Recall that in the hawks and doves example the average payoff curves for the two types intersected, resulting in a stable population share for each type. In the current case, however, the average payoff curves do not intersect. Since defectors always receive a higher average payoff, their share of the population will grow over time. Cooperators, even if they make up almost the entire population to begin with, are thus destined for extinction. When cooperators and defectors look alike, genuine cooperation cannot emerge. In a crude way, this case provides the underlying rationale for the self-interest model's assumption of egoistic behavior.

Note in Figure 12.5 that in a population consisting only of cooperators ($c = 1.0$), everyone's payoff would be 4, or twice as much as everyone gets in the equilibrium consisting only of defectors. As in the hawks and doves example, we see in this case too that tastes evolve according to their effect on individual, not group, payoffs.

Population Movements When Cooperators Are Easily Identified

Now suppose everything is just as before except that cooperators and defectors are perfectly distinguishable from each other. For concreteness, suppose that sympathy is the emotion that motivates cooperation, and that there is an observable symptom present in people who experience this emotion (perhaps a "sympathetic manner"). Defectors lack this observable symptom; or, more generally, they may try to mimic it, but fail to get it exactly right.

If this symptom is observable at a glance, the tables are completely turned. Cooperators can now interact selectively with one another and be assured of a payoff of 4. No cooperator need ever interact with a defector. Defectors are left to interact with one another, for which they get a payoff of only 2.

Since all element of chance has been removed from the interaction process, payoffs no longer depend on the proportion of cooperators in the population (see Figure 12.6). Cooperators always get 4, defectors always get 2.

This time the cooperators' larger payoffs enable *them* to raise larger families, which means they will make up an ever growing share of the population. When cooperators can be easily identified, it is the defectors who face extinction.

---

[13]In very recent times, of course, there has been a *negative* relationship between income and family size. But if preferences were forged by natural selection, the relationship that matters is the one that existed during most of evolutionary history. And that relationship was undisputedly positive: Periods of famine were frequent and individuals with greater material resources saw many more of their children reach adulthood. Moreover, most early societies were polygynous—their wealthiest members usually claimed several wives, leaving many of the poor with none.

FIGURE 12.6

Average Payoffs When Cooperators and Defectors Are Perfectly Distinguishable

When cooperators can be identified at a glance, they can always interact with one another and get a payoff of 4. Defectors are left to interact with each other, and get a payoff of 2. In this case, it is the defectors who become extinct.

Mimicry without Cost or Delay

The defectors need not give up without a fight, however. Suppose a mutant strain of defectors emerges, one that behaves exactly like other defectors but in which each individual has precisely the same symptoms of trustworthiness as cooperators. Since this particular strain of defectors looks exactly the same as cooperators, it is impossible for cooperators to discriminate against them. Each impostor is therefore just as likely to interact with a cooperator as a genuine cooperator is. This, in turn, means that the mutant defectors will have a higher expected payoff than the cooperators.

The nonmutant defectors—those who continue to look different from cooperators—will have a lower payoff than both of these groups and, as before, are destined for extinction. But unless the cooperators adapt in some way, they too face the same fate. When defectors can perfectly mimic the distinguishing feature of cooperators with neither cost nor delay, the feature loses all power to distinguish. Cooperators and the surviving defectors again look exactly alike, which again spells doom for the cooperators.

Imperfect Mimicry and the Costs of Vigilance

Defectors, of course, have no monopoly on the power to adapt. If random mutations alter the cooperators' distinguishing characteristic, the defectors will be faced with a moving target. Imagine that symptoms by which cooperators originally managed to distinguish themselves can be imperfectly mimicked by defectors. If the two types could be distinguished at a glance, defectors would again be doomed. But suppose it requires effort to differentiate between a cooperator and a defector. For concreteness, suppose inspection costs 1 unit. Paying this cost is like buying a pair of special contact lenses that enable cooperators and defectors to be distinguished at a glance. For those who do not pay, the two types remain perfectly indistinguishable.

To see what happens this time, suppose the payoffs are again as given in Table 12.6, and consider the decision facing a cooperator who is trying to decide whether to pay the cost of vigilance. If he pays it, he can be assured of interacting with another cooperator and will thus get a payoff of $4 - 1 = 3$. If he does not, his payoff is uncertain. Cooperators and defectors will look exactly alike to him and he must take his chances. If he happens to interact with another cooperator, he will get 4. But if he interacts with a defector, he will get zero. Whether it makes sense to pay the 1-unit cost of vigilance thus depends on the likelihood of those two outcomes.

Suppose the population share of cooperators is 90 percent. By not paying the cost of vigilance, a cooperator will interact with another cooperator 90 percent of the time, with a defector only 10 percent. His payoff will thus have an average value of $(0.9)(4) + (0.1)(0) = 3.6$. Since this is higher than the 3-unit net payoff he would get if he paid the cost of vigilance, it is clearly better not to pay it.

Now suppose the population share of cooperators is not 90 percent but 50 percent. If our cooperator does not pay the cost of vigilance, he will now have only a 50-50 chance of interacting with a cooperator. His average payoff will thus be only 2, or 1 less than if he had paid the cost. On these odds, it would clearly be better to pay it.

The numbers in this example imply a "breakeven point" obtained by solving the following equation for c:

$$4c = 3, \tag{12.7}$$

which yields $c = 0.75$. Thus, when the population share of cooperators is 75 percent, a cooperator's expected payoff if he does not pay the cost of vigilance ($4c$) is exactly equal to his certain payoff if he does (3). A cooperator who does not pay the cost has a 75 percent chance at a payoff of 4, and a 25 percent chance of getting zero, which means an average payoff of 3, the same as if he had paid the cost. When the population share of cooperators is below 75 percent, it will always be better for him to pay the cost of vigilance. When the population share of cooperators is above 75 percent, it will never be better for him to pay this cost.

SELF-TEST 12.5

In a population with 60 percent cooperators and a cost of vigilance equal to 1.5, should a cooperator pay the cost of vigilance?

With the breakeven rule in mind, we can now say something about how the population will evolve over time. When the population share of cooperators is below 75 percent, cooperators will all pay the cost of vigilance and get a payoff of 3 units by cooperating with one another. It will not be in the interests of defectors to bear this cost, because the vigilant cooperators would not interact with them anyway. The defectors are left to interact with one another and get a payoff of only 2 units. Thus, if we start with a population share of cooperators less than 75 percent, the cooperators will get a higher average payoff, which means that their share of the population will grow.

In populations that consist of more than 75 percent cooperators, the tables are turned. Now it no longer makes sense to pay the cost of vigilance. Cooperators and defectors will thus interact at random, which means that defectors will have a higher average payoff. This difference in payoffs, in turn, will cause the population share of cooperators to shrink.

For the values assumed in this example, the average payoff schedules for the two groups are plotted in Figure 12.7. As noted, the cooperators' schedule lies above the defectors' for shares smaller than 75 percent, but below it for larger shares. The sharp discontinuity in the defectors' schedule reflects the fact that, to the left of 75 percent, all cooperators pay for vigilance, while to the right of 75 percent, none of them does. Once the population share of cooperators passes 75 percent, defectors suddenly gain access to their victims. The evolutionary rule, once again, is that higher relative payoffs result in a growing population share. This rule makes it clear that the population in this example will stabilize at 75 percent cooperators.

Now, there is obviously nothing magic about this 75 percent figure. Had the cost of vigilance been lower than 1, for example, the population share of cooperators would have been larger.

SELF-TEST 12.6

What will be the equilibrium population share of cooperators if the cost of vigilance is 0.5?

An increase in the payoff when cooperators pair with one another would also increase the equilibrium population share of cooperators. The point of the example is that when there are costs of vigilance, there will be pressures that pull the population toward

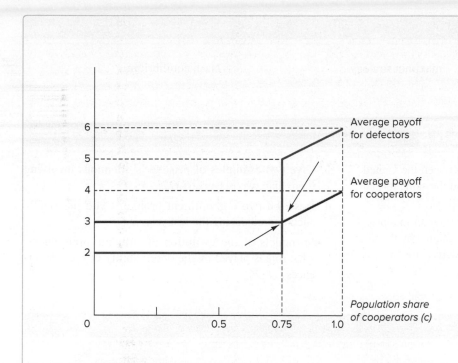

FIGURE 12.7

Average Payoffs with Costs of Vigilance

When the share of cooperators exceeds 75 percent, it does not pay cooperators to bear the cost of vigilance. As a result, the expected payoff for defectors exceeds the expected payoff for cooperators, and the share of cooperators declines. When the share of cooperators is less than 75 percent, cooperators pay the cost of vigilance and thereby avoid interaction with defectors. In this region the cooperators receive higher payoffs than defectors, and the share of cooperators increases as a result. From any starting point, the population eventually stabilizes at 75 percent cooperators.

some stable mix of cooperators and defectors. As in the hawks and doves example considered earlier, once the population settles at this mix, members of both groups have the same average payoff and are therefore equally likely to survive. There is an ecological niche, in other words, for both groups. This result stands in stark contrast to the view that only opportunism can survive in a bitterly competitive material world.

The central assumption behind the claim that certain nonegoistic motives or preferences can help solve commitment problems is that the presence of these motives can somehow be discovered by others. As discussed in Chapter 7, psychologists have confirmed Charles Darwin's claim that certain facial expressions are characteristic of specific emotions. These expressions, which are the result of complex combinations of facial muscle movements, convey, credible information about others' emotional states.

SUMMARY

- Situations in which people's choices are known to affect one another can often be analyzed fruitfully with the mathematical theory of games. The three basic elements of any game are the players, the set of possible strategies, and the payoff matrix. A Nash equilibrium occurs when each player's choice is optimal given the other player's choice. *(LO1, LO4)*

- A strategy is called dominant if it is optimal no matter what strategy other players choose. A dominated strategy is one that yields a lower payoff no matter what other players choose. *(LO2)*

- A prisoner's dilemma is a game defined by two features: each player has a dominant strategy; and when each plays that strategy, each gets a lower payoff than if each

had played the dominated strategy. Strategies like tit-for-tat are often effective in eliciting cooperative behavior when prisoner's dilemmas are repeated. *(LO3)*

- The timing of players' choices strongly shapes the outcomes of many games. It is often useful to summarize the payoff structure of such games by means of a game tree. *(LO5)*

- Incumbent firms may sometimes act strategically to deter potential rivals from entering their markets. Often this involves incurring higher costs than would otherwise be necessary. *(LO5)*

- Evolutionary game theory sheds light on why it might be advantageous to hold preferences that motivate unselfish behavior, such as cooperating in one-shot prisoner's dilemmas. *(LO6)*

KEY TERMS

commitment device
dominant strategy

maximin strategy

Nash equilibrium

REVIEW QUESTIONS

1. Explain how the military arms race between the United States and the former Soviet Union had the same formal structure as a prisoner's dilemma. *(LO3)*

2. Suppose A and B know that they will interact in a prisoner's dilemma exactly four times. Explain why the tit-for-tat strategy will not be an effective means for assuring cooperation. *(LO3)*

3. Give two examples of prisoner's dilemmas involving more than two players. *(LO3)*

4. Describe two commitment problems you personally encountered during the last year. *(LO5)*

5. In models of the evolution of strategic preferences, what role is played by the observability of such preferences? *(LO6)*

PROBLEMS

_{Mc Graw Hill} connect

1. While grading a final exam a professor discovers that two students have virtually identical answers. She talks to each student separately and tells them that she is sure that they shared answers, but she cannot be sure who copied from whom. She offers each student a deal—if they both sign a statement admitting to the cheating, each will be given an F for the course. If only one signs the statement, that student will be allowed to withdraw from the course and the other nonsigning student will be expelled from the university. Finally, if neither signs the statement they will both get a C for the course because the professor does not have enough evidence to prove that cheating has occurred. Assuming the students are not allowed to communicate with one another, set up the relevant payoff matrix. Does each student have a dominant strategy? *(LO3)*

2. Kiplinger and Intuit are two rival firms in the tax-software industry. Each faces a choice for the coming year between developing a simple tax-advice program or a comprehensive one. The matrix below shows how the profits of each firm depend on the combination of choices made by the two. *(LO2, LO4)*

a. Identify the Nash equilibria of this game, if any exist.

b. Suppose a uniquely talented programmer exists who would enable her employer to bring its product to market before the employer's rival even had a chance to choose its development strategy. Either firm's failure to hire this programmer will result in her being hired by the other. If the programmer's decision rule is to work for the highest bidder and both firms are rational profit-maximizers, for whom will the programmer work, and how much will she be paid?

3. Firm 1 and firm 2 are automobile producers. Each has the option of producing either a big car or a small car. The payoffs to each of the four possible combinations of choices are as given in the following payoff matrix. Each firm must make its choice without knowing what the other has chosen. *(LO2, LO4)*

a. Does either firm have a dominant strategy?

b. There are two Nash equilibria for this game. Identify them.

	Kiplinger	
	Simple	Comprehensive
Intuit Simple	$\Pi_I = 120$ $\Pi_K = 50$	$\Pi_I = 110$ $\Pi_K = 200$
Comprehensive	$\Pi_I = 220$ $\Pi_K = 80$	$\Pi_I = 50$ $\Pi_K = 100$

	Firm 1	
	Big car	**Small car**
Firm 2 **Big car**	$P_1 = 400$ $P_2 = 400$	$P_1 = 800$ $P_2 = 1{,}000$
Small car	$P_1 = 1{,}000$ $P_2 = 800$	$P_1 = 500$ $P_2 = 500$

4. Suppose we have the same payoff matrix as in Problem 3 except now firm 1 gets to move first and knows that

firm 2 will see the results of this choice before deciding which type of car to build. *(LO5)*

a. Draw the game tree for this sequential game.

b. What is the Nash equilibrium for this game?

5. Rohan and Zuri are roommates who are taking the same economics class. This morning Rohan wakes up and is trying to decide whether to go to class or not. He knows that if Zuri is going to go to class he will hear her fixing herself breakfast. Zuri knows that Rohan may or may not go to class depending on what she does. The timing of their decisions and their respective payoffs are as represented by the diagram below, where choosing the upper path means go to class and choosing the lower path means don't go to class. Zuri makes her decision first and Rohan waits to see what she has decided before making his decision. If the payoffs for each are as shown, what is the equilibrium of this game? *(LO5)*

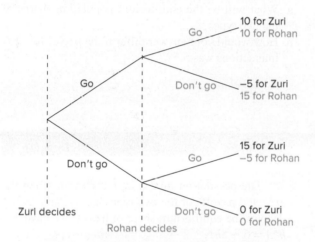

6. Taylor and Chris have arranged to meet for a date tonight and have sent e-mails to one another proposing locations for their meeting: Taylor suggests Rulloff's and Chris suggests Joe's. Before they can agree on a location, satellites are knocked out so email and phone reception go down, so they each have to choose their meeting place without further communication. Their payoffs for each potential outcome are as given in the matrix below. If each is rational and self-interested, and each knows the other's payoffs and understands the theory of games, what will happen? *(LO2, LO4)*

	Chris	
	Rulloff's	Joe's
Taylor Rulloff's	20 for Taylor 10 for Chris	0 for Taylor 15 for Chris
Joe's	5 for Taylor 5 for Chris	10 for Taylor 20 for Chris

7. Netflix and Hulu compete in offering streamed content subscriptions. Both companies are considering whether to offer an initially discounted subscription to attract new customers. Their payoffs depend as follows on the combinations of strategies chosen:

> If both companies offer discounted subscriptions, then each company loses $8 million.
>
> If Netflix offers a discounted subscription and Hulu does not, then Netflix makes a profit of $15 million and Hulu suffers a loss of $12 million.
>
> If Hulu offers a discounted subscription and Netflix does not, then Hulu makes a profit of $5 million and Netflix suffers a loss of $6 million.
>
> If neither company offers an initially discounted subscription, each makes a profit of $6 million.

Which of following statements is true? *(LO2, LO3, LO4)*

a. The dominant strategy for Netflix is to offer a discounted subscription.

b. Only one Nash equilibrium pair of strategies exists.

c. If Netflix offers an initially discounted subscription, the best strategy for Hulu is not to offer a such a discounted service.

d. This game is a prisoner's dilemma.

e. None of the above statements are true.

8. A traveler dines at a restaurant along an interstate highway. Both she and the restaurant server are rational and self-interested in the narrow sense. The server must first choose between providing good service or bad service, whereupon the diner must choose between leaving the customary tip or leaving no tip at all. The payoffs for their interaction are as summarized on the accompanying game tree. What is the most the diner would be willing to pay for the right to make a binding commitment (visible to the server) to leave the customary tip at the end of the meal in the event of having received good service? *(LO5)*

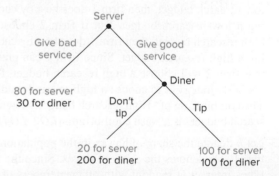

9. Raj and Adhira can each choose only one of two locations to search for gold. The payoffs to each for each possible combination of choices are as given in the payoff matrix below. Which of the following statements is true? *(LO4)*

Adhira

		Go to A	Go to B
Raj	Go to A	5 for Raj 3 for Adhira	8 for Raj 2 for Adhira
	Go to B	4 for Raj 6 for Adhira	7 for Raj 7 for Adhira

a. The upper-left cell of the payoff matrix is a Nash equilibrium.

b. The upper-right cell of the payoff matrix is a Nash equilibrium.

c. The lower-right cell of the payoff matrix is a Nash equilibrium.

d. The lower-left cell of the payoff matrix is a Nash equilibrium.

e. This game has no Nash equilibrium or it has more than one Nash equilibrium.

10. A population consists of two types, "friendlies" and "aggressives." Each individual interacts with a ran-domly chosen member of the population. When two friendlies interact, each earns 3 units. When two aggressives interact, each earns 0 units. When a friendly and an aggressive interact, the former gets a payoff of 1 unit, the latter a payoff of 5 units. The growth rate of each type is proportional to its average payoff. What will be the equilibrium population shares of each type? *(LO6)*

11. Consider a population with two types of people, C's and D's. Interactions among various combinations of the two types produce the following payoffs:

   C-C: 6 each
   C-D: 8 for D, 0 for C
   D-D: 4 each

Invisible contact lenses are available at a cost of 1 unit that enable the wearer to identify each person's type with certainty. Without the lenses the two types are in-distinguishable. *(LO6)*

a. What will be the equilibrium population shares of the two types?

b. How would your answer differ if the payoff for *D-D* interactions was 5.5?

ANSWERS TO SELF-TESTS

12.1 For values of A greater than 1 but less than 2, Tamika's dominant strategy is to play down and Makenna's is to play right, and each gets a lower payoff when they play those strategies than if each had played her dom-inated strategy. *(LO2)*

12.2 Regardless of firm 1's strategy, firm 2 does best with a big research budget. The choice of a big research budget is thus a dominant strategy for firm 2. Firm 1 does not have a dominant strategy. If firm 2 chooses a low research budget, then firm 1 does best by choos-ing a low research budget. But if firm 2 chooses a high research budget, then firm 1 does best by choos-ing a high research budget. Since firm 1 can predict that firm 2 will choose a high research budget, firm 1's best strategy is to choose a high research budget. The combination of "High research budget—High re-search budget" is a Nash equilibrium. *(LO2, LO4)*

12.3 Let h denote the share of hawks in the population, so that $1 - h$ denotes the share of doves. Since the two types interact at random with other members of the population, the expected payoff for doves is given by

$$P_D = 3(1 - h) + 2(h) = 3 - h.$$

The corresponding expected payoff for hawks is

$$P_H = 6(1 - h) + 1(h) = 6 - 5h.$$

The population mix is in equilibrium when the expected payoffs of the two types are the same. If h^* denotes the equilibrium share of hawks, we have $3 - h^* | = 6 - 5h^*$,
   which solves for $h^* = \frac{3}{4}$.

The equilibrium share of doves is $1 - h^* = \frac{1}{4}$. *(LO6)*

12.4 $P_C = 0.9(4) = 0.1(0) = 3.6.$ *(LO6)*

12.5 If all cooperators pay the cost of vigilance, each will get a payoff of $4 - 1.5 = 2.5$. If none pays the cost of vigilance, the expected payoff will be

$$P_C = 0.6(4) + 0.4(0) = 2.4,$$

which is less than 2.5. So they should pay the cost of vigilance. *(LO6)*

12.6 The payoff net of the cost of vigilance is now $4 - 0.5 = 3.5$. If C's do not pay the cost of vigilance, their expected payoff is again given by $P_C = 4c$. To find the breakeven level of c, we solve $4c' = 3.5$, which yields $c' = \frac{7}{8}$.

   For $c < \frac{7}{8}$, the C's have a higher expected payoff if they pay the cost. For $c > \frac{7}{8}$, they have a higher expected payoff if they simply take their chances. For $c < \frac{7}{8}$, the D's will be forced to interact with one an-other, which gives the D's a payoff of 2. Once $c > \frac{7}{8}$, however, the C's stop paying the cost and the expected payoff for the D's becomes

$$P_D = c6 + (1 - c)2 = 2 + 4c.$$

The expected payoff functions for the C's and D's are now as shown in the diagram:

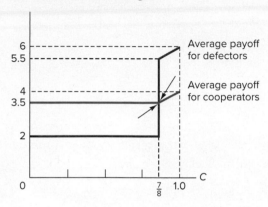

Note that the average payoff for C's is greater than for D's whenever $c < \frac{7}{8}$, while the expected payoff for D's exceeds that of C's whenever $c > \frac{7}{8}$. The result is that if we start with $c > \frac{7}{8}$, the population share of C's will shrink to $\frac{7}{8}$ because the growth rate of D's will be faster than that of C's. If we start with $c < \frac{7}{8}$, the population share of C's will grow to $\frac{7}{8}$. *(LO6)*

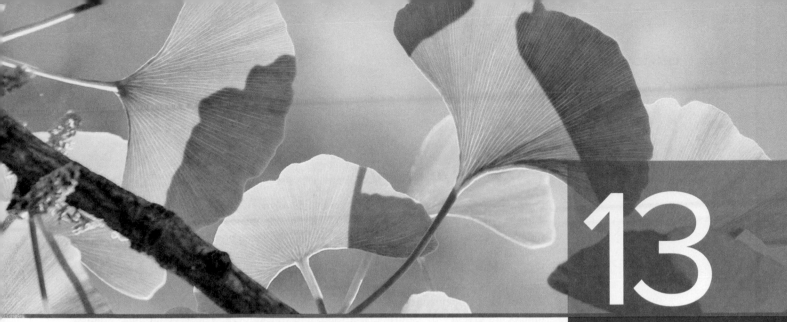

13

Oligopoly and Monopolistic Competition

A local gas station sells 200,000 gallons of gasoline a year at a price of $3 per gallon. It has just announced plans to increase its price to $3.06 per gallon next year, even though all other stations have committed to maintain their current prices at $3.

Now suppose someone offered you the following bet: If the station's sales fall to zero next year as a result of the price change, you win $1,000; but if its sales remain above 100,000 gallons, you lose $1,000. Would you take that bet?

As we saw in Chapter 10, the theory of the perfectly competitive firm predicts that if the firm in question was selling its product in a perfectly competitive market, the price elasticity of demand for its product would be infinite, implying that even a small price increase would cause its sales to plummet to zero.

Do local gas stations sell in perfectly competitive markets? On the surface, at least, they seem to satisfy the conditions traditionally said to define such markets: Their product is highly standardized. There are many small sellers, each serving only a tiny fraction of the market. Entry into and exit from the industry are essentially unrestricted. And consumers are generally well informed about gasoline prices and availability.

Yet only someone who had taken an economics course and was utterly devoid of common sense might be foolish enough to accept this bet. In no city on earth would a 2 percent rise in a station's gas price cause its sales to shrink by even half, much less fall all the way to zero.

Even if all consumers knew with certainty that identical gasoline was sold in all stations, at least some would ignore a small price increase rather than switch to another station. Perhaps they're in the habit of buying from a station conveniently located on their way home from work, which might make them willing to remain loyal even in the face of a much larger price increase.

The simple fact is that there is no such thing as the perfectly competitive firm described in economics textbooks. Nor are there any pure monopolies. For virtually every

LEARNING OBJECTIVES

After reading this chapter, you should be able to:

LO1 Describe how oligopolists differ from pure monopolists and how monopolistically competitive firms differ from perfectly competitive ones.

LO2 Compare and contrast the predictions of the Cournot, Bertrand, and Stackelberg oligopoly firms.

LO3 Describe how increasing returns to scale in production affects the structure of competition.

LO4 Describe the properties of short- and long-run equilibrium in the Chamberlin model.

LO5 Describe the trade-off that exists between greater product variety and lower prices in locational models of monopolistic competition.

LO6 Derive the optimal degree of product variety when consumers are assumed to care only about a single dimension of product quality.

LO7 Describe methods employed by firms to eliminate the costs of greater variety among different buyers.

LO8 Critically evaluate the claim that product advertising generally makes consumers worse off.

product, there are substitutes of one kind or another, and there is always the option of nonconsumption. In short, virtually every good we buy is sold by a firm located somewhere between the two extreme cases of perfect competition and pure monopoly.

CHAPTER PREVIEW

Our task in this chapter is to explore the hybrid forms of industrial organization we deal with on a daily basis—namely, oligopoly and monopolistic competition. Oligopolies are industries served by only a small number of sellers whose product offerings will in some cases be highly standardized but may sometimes be sharply differentiated. Monopolistically competitive industries are much like the perfectly competitive ideal except that product offerings differ across firms along at least some dimensions.

We'll begin with a review of several early models, including those introduced in the nineteenth century by Cournot, Bertrand, and Stackelberg. Those economists studied competition between oligopolists selling identical products. The predictions that emerge from their models, as we'll see, differ according to the specific assumptions they made about how firms react to one another's choices.

Next we'll consider the Chamberlin model of monopolistic competition, which assumed that firms matched rivals' price cuts but ignored their price increases. Then we'll examine more recent attempts to examine how firms compete when their buyers focus on a specific dimension of product quality, such as the location of retail outlets. We'll conclude with a brief discussion of product advertising.

SOME SPECIFIC OLIGOPOLY MODELS

If a firm is considering a change in its output level or selling price, there are many possible assumptions it could make about the reactions of its rivals. It could assume, for example, that its rivals will continue producing at their current levels of output. Alternatively, it could assume that they would continue to charge their current prices. Or it could assume that they would react in various specific ways to its own price and output changes. In the sections that follow, we explore the implications of each alternative assumption.

The Cournot Model

Cournot model oligopoly model in which each firm assumes that rivals will continue producing their current output levels.

We begin with the simplest case, the so-called **Cournot model,** in which each firm assumes that its rivals will continue producing at their current levels of output. Named for the French economist Auguste Cournot, who introduced it in 1838, this model describes the behavior of two firms that sell bottled water from mineral springs. A two-firm oligopoly is called a *duopoly,* and the Cournot model is sometimes referred to as the *Cournot duopoly model,* although its conclusions can easily be generalized to more than two firms.

The central assumption of the Cournot model is that each duopolist treats the other's quantity as a fixed number, one that will not respond to its own production decisions. This is a weak form of interdependence, indeed, but we will see that even it leads to an outcome in which the behavior of each firm substantially affects its rival.

Suppose the total market demand curve for mineral water is given by

$$P = a - b(Q_1 + Q_2), \tag{13.1}$$

where a and b are positive numbers and Q_1 and Q_2 are the outputs of firms 1 and 2, respectively. Cournot assumed that the water could be produced at zero marginal cost, but this assumption is merely for convenience. Essentially similar conclusions would emerge if each firm had a constant positive marginal cost.

Let us look first at the profit-maximization problem facing firm 1. Given its assumption that firm 2's output is fixed at Q_2, the demand curve for firm 1's water is given by

$$P_1 = (a - bQ_2) - bQ_1, \tag{13.2}$$

which is rewritten to emphasize the fact that firm 1 treats Q_2 as given.

FIGURE 13.1

The Profit-Maximizing Cournot Duopolist

The Cournot duopolist's demand curve is obtained by shifting the vertical axis rightward by the amount produced by the other duopolist (Q_2 in the diagram). The portion of the original market demand curve that lies to the right of this new vertical axis is the demand curve facing firm 1. Firm 1 then maximizes profit by equating marginal revenue and marginal cost, the latter of which is zero.

As Equation 13.2 shows, we get the demand curve for firm 1 by subtracting bQ_2 from the vertical intercept of the market demand curve. The idea is that firm 2 has skimmed off the first Q_2 units of the market demand curve, leaving firm 1 the remainder to work with.

If Q_2 were equal to zero, firm 1 would have the entire market demand curve to itself, as is indicated by D in Figure 13.1. If Q_2 is positive, we get firm 1's demand curve by shifting the vertical axis of the demand diagram rightward by Q_2 units. Firm 1's demand curve is that portion of the original demand curve that lies to the right of this new vertical axis, and for this reason it is sometimes called a *residual demand curve*. The associated marginal revenue curve is labeled MR_1. Firm 1's rule for profit maximization is the same as for any other firm that faces a downward-sloping demand curve, namely, to equate marginal revenue and marginal cost. Marginal cost in this example is assumed to be zero, so the profit-maximizing level of output for firm 1 is that level for which its marginal revenue curve takes the value of zero.

The equilibrium outputs for a Cournot duopoly can be deduced from the residual demand diagram. Given that firm 2 is producing Q_2, firm 1 maximizes its profits by producing where marginal revenue equals marginal cost. Marginal revenue for firm 1 is given by $MR_1 = (a - bQ_2) - 2bQ_1$. Marginal revenue has twice the slope as demand, so marginal revenue intersects zero marginal cost at half the distance from the $Q_1 = 0$ axis to the horizontal intercept of the demand curve. By symmetry (the two firms are identical so they must behave the same), $Q_2 = Q_1$, which means that each of the three segments shown on the horizontal axis in Figure 13.1 has the same length. And this implies that each firm produces output equal to one-third of the distance from the origin to the horizontal intercept of the demand curve. The demand curve $P = a - bQ$ has a horizontal intercept of $Q = a/b$; hence, $Q_1 = Q_2 = a/(3b)$. A more general approach is to set marginal revenue equal to marginal cost and solve for the output of firm 1 in terms of the output of firm 2.[1]

$$Q_1^* = \frac{a - bQ_2}{2b}.$$ (13.3)

---

[1]For example, this more general approach is needed if firms are asymmetric (not identical) and thus would not produce the same level of output.

FIGURE 13.2

Reaction Functions for the Cournot Duopolists

The reaction function for each duopolist gives its profit-maximizing output level as a function of the other firm's output level. The duopolists are in a stable equilibrium at the point of intersection of their reaction functions.

reaction function a curve that tells the profit-maximizing level of output for one oligopolist for each amount supplied by another.

Economists often call Equation 13.3 firm 1's **reaction function,** and denote it by $Q_1^* = R_1(Q_2)$. This notation is suggestive because the reaction function tells how firm 1's quantity will react to the quantity level offered by firm 2.

Because the Cournot duopoly problem is completely symmetric, firm 2's reaction function has precisely the same structure:

$$Q_2^* = R_2(Q_1) = \frac{a - bQ_1}{2b}. \tag{13.4}$$

The two reaction functions are plotted in Figure 13.2. To illustrate the workings of the reaction function concept, suppose firm 1 initially produced a quantity of Q_1^0. Firm 2 would then produce the level of output that corresponds to Q_1^0 on its reaction function. Firm 1 would respond to that output level by picking the corresponding point on its own reaction function. Firm 2 would then respond by picking the corresponding point on its reaction function, and so on. The end result of this process is a stable equilibrium at the intersection of the two reaction functions. When both firms are producing $a/3b$ units of output, neither wants to change.[2] These output levels thus constitute a Nash equilibrium for the Cournot duopolists.

How profitable are the Cournot duopolists? Since their combined output is $2a/3b$, the market price will be $P = a - b(2a/3b) = a/3$. At this price, each will have total revenue equal to $(a/3)(a/3b) = a^2/9b$. And since neither firm has any production costs, total revenues and economic profits here are one and the same.

EXAMPLE 13.1 **The Cournot Model**

Cournot duopolists face a market demand curve given by $P = 56 - 2Q$, where Q is total market demand. Each can produce output at a constant marginal cost of 20/unit. Graph their reaction functions and find the equilibrium price and quantity.

Figure 13.3a shows the residual demand curve facing firm 1 when firm 2 produces Q_2 units. Firm 1's marginal revenue curve has the same vertical intercept as its

---

[2]To solve algebraically for firm 1's equilibrium level of output, we substitute $Q_1^* = Q_2^*$ into its reaction function and solve:

$$R_1(Q_2^*) = \frac{a - bQ_2^*}{2b} = \frac{a - bQ_1^*}{2b} = Q_1^*,$$

which yields $Q_1^* = a/3b$.

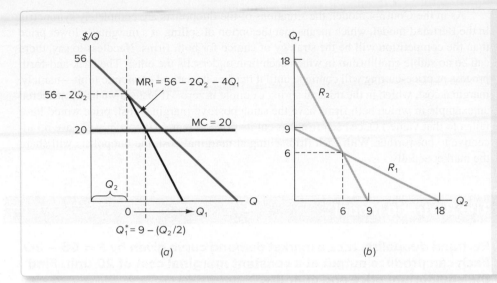

FIGURE 13.3

Deriving the Reaction Functions for Specific Duopolists

Panel *a* shows the profit-maximizing output level for firm 1 (Q_1^*) when firm 2 produces Q_2. That and the parallel expression for firm 2 constitute the reaction functions plotted in panel *b*.

demand curve and is twice as steep. Thus the equation for firm 1's marginal revenue curve is $MR_1 = 56 - 2Q_2 - 4Q_1$. Equating MR_1 to marginal cost (20), we solve for firm 1's reaction function, $Q_1^* = R_1 = 9 - (Q_2/2)$. By symmetry, firm 2's reaction function is $R_2 = 9 - (Q_1/2)$. The two reaction functions are shown in Figure 13.3*b*, where they intersect at $Q_1 = Q_2 = 6$. Total market output will be $Q_1 + Q_2 = 12$. Consulting the market demand curve, we see that the market price will be $P = 56 - 2(12) = 32$.

SELF-TEST 13.1

Repeat Example 13.1 with the two firms facing a market demand curve of $P = 44 - Q$.

You may be wondering why the Cournot duopolists assume that their own production decisions will be ignored by their rivals. If so, you have asked a penetrating question, the same one posed by Cournot's critic, the French economist Joseph Bertrand. Let's now consider his alternative solution to the duopoly problem.

The Bertrand Model

Bertrand's insight was that from the buyer's perspective, what really counts is how the prices charged by the two firms compare. Since the duopolists are selling identical mineral water, every buyer will naturally want to buy from the seller with the lower price. The **Bertrand model** proposed that each firm chooses its price on the assumption that its rival's price would remain fixed. On its face, this assumption seems no more plausible than Cournot's, and since prices and quantities correspond uniquely along market demand curves, it may seem natural to wonder whether Bertrand's assumption even leads to a different outcome. On investigation, however, the outcomes turn out to be very different indeed.

To illustrate, suppose the market demand and cost conditions are the same as in the Cournot example. And suppose firm 1 charges an initial price of P_0^1. Firm 2 then faces essentially three choices: (1) it can charge more than firm 1, in which case it will sell nothing; (2) it can charge the same as firm 1, in which case the two firms will split the market demand at that price; or (3) it can sell at a marginally lower price than firm 1, in which case it will capture the entire market demand at that price. The third of these options will always be by far the most profitable.[3]

Bertrand model oligopoly model in which each firm assumes that rivals will continue charging their current prices.

---

[3]In the case of a price only infinitesimally smaller than firm 1's price, firm 2's profit will be virtually twice as large under option 3 as under option 2.

As in the Cournot model, the situations of the duopolists are completely symmetric in the Bertrand model, which means that the option of selling at a marginally lower price than the competition will be the strategy of choice for both firms. Needless to say, there can be no stable equilibrium in which each firm undersells the other. The back-and-forth process of price-cutting will continue until it reaches its natural economic limit—namely, marginal cost, which in the mineral spring example is zero. (If instead we had considered an example in which both firms have the same positive marginal cost, price would have fallen to that value.) Once each firm has cut its price to marginal cost, it will have no incentive to cut further. With each firm selling at marginal cost, the duopolists will share the market equally.

EXAMPLE 13.2   **The Bertrand Model**

Bertrand duopolists face a market demand curve given by $P = 56 - 2Q$. Each can produce output at a constant marginal cost of 20/unit. Find the equilibrium price and quantity.

The solution is both firms price at marginal cost $P = MC = 20$. Industry output is determined by market demand: $20 = 56 - 2Q$ implies $Q = 18$. The firms split the market equally, so each firm produces half of industry output $Q_1 = Q_2 = Q/2 = 9$.

> **SELF-TEST 13.2**
>
> If the market demand curve facing Bertrand duopolists is given by $P = 10 - Q$ and each has a constant marginal cost of 2, what will be the equilibrium price and quantity for each firm?

So we see that a seemingly minor change in the initial assumptions about firm behavior—that each duopolist takes its rival's price, not quantity, as given—leads to a sharply different equilibrium. Now we consider how another small change in the initial assumptions about firm behavior can lead to yet another equilibrium.

The Stackelberg Model

In 1934, the German economist Heinrich von Stackelberg asked the simple but provocative question, "What would a firm do if it knew its only rival were a naive Cournot duopolist?" The answer is that it would want to choose its own output level by taking into account the effect that choice would have on the output level of its rival.

Returning to the Cournot model, suppose firm 1 knows that firm 2 will treat firm 1's output level as given. How can it make strategic use of that knowledge? To answer this question, recall that firm 2's reaction function is given by $Q_2^* = R_2(Q_1) = (a - bQ_1)/2b$. Knowing that firm 2's output will depend on Q_1 in this fashion, firm 1 can then substitute $R_2(Q_1)$ for Q_2 in the equation for the market demand curve, which yields the following expression for its own demand curve:

$$P = a - b[Q_1 + R_2(Q_1)] = a - b\left(Q_1 + \frac{a - bQ_1}{2b}\right) = \frac{a - bQ_1}{2}. \tag{13.5}$$

This demand curve and the associated marginal revenue curve are shown as D_1 and MR_1 in Figure 13.4. Since marginal cost is assumed to be zero in the mineral spring example, firm 1's profit-maximizing output level will be the one for which MR_1 is zero, namely, $Q_1^* = a/2b$. The market price will be $a/4$.

FIGURE 13.4

The Stackelberg Leader's Demand and Marginal Revenue Curves

When firm 1 knows firm 2 is a Cournot duopolist, it can take account of the effect of its own behavior on firm 2's quantity choice. The result is that it knows exactly what its demand curve will be.

EXAMPLE 13.3   The Stackelberg Model

A Stackelberg leader and follower face a market demand curve given by $P = 56 - 2Q$. Each can produce output at a constant marginal cost of 20/unit. Find the equilibrium price and quantity.

The solution is found by substituting firm 2's reaction function $Q_2 = 9 - Q_1/2$ into the demand facing firm 1, $P = (56 - 2Q_2) - 2Q_1$, to find $P = 38 - Q_1$ with corresponding marginal revenue $MR_1 = 38 - 2Q_1$. Setting marginal revenue equal to marginal cost yields firm 1's output $Q_1 = 9$. Inserting firm 1's output into firm 2's reaction function yields firm 2's output $Q_2 = \frac{9}{2}$. Total industry output is $Q = Q_1 + Q_2 = \frac{27}{2}$, with price $P = 56 - 2Q = 56 - 27 = 29$.

SELF-TEST 13.3

The market demand curve for a Stackelberg leader and follower is given by $P = 10 - Q$. If each has a marginal cost of 2, what will be the equilibrium price and quantity for each?

For obvious reasons, firm 1 is referred to as a *Stackelberg leader. Stackelberg follower* is the term used to describe firm 2. To help place the Stackelberg leader's behavior in clearer perspective, let's again consider the graph of the two firms' Cournot reaction functions, reproduced here as Figure 13.5. As we saw in Figure 13.4, $a/2b$ is the best output for firm 1 to produce once it takes into account that firm 2 will respond to its choice according to the reaction function $R_2(Q_1)$. Once firm 1 produces $a/2b$, firm 2 will consult R_2 and respond by producing $a/4b$. Now here is the crucial step. If firm 1 thought that firm 2 would stay at $a/4b$ no matter what, its best bet would be to consult its own reaction function and produce the corresponding quantity, namely, $3a/8b$. By doing so, it would earn more than by producing $a/2b$. The problem is that firm 1 realizes that if it cuts back to $3a/8b$, this will elicit a further reaction from firm 2, culminating in a downward spiral to the intersection point of the two reaction functions. Firm 1 would do better to move to $3a/8b$ if it could somehow induce firm 2 to remain at $a/4b$. But it cannot. The best option open to firm 1 is therefore to grit its teeth and stay put at $a/2b$.

FIGURE 13.5

The Stackelberg Equilibrium

In the Stackelberg model, firm 1 ignores its own reaction function from the Cournot model. It chooses its own quantity to maximize profit, taking into account the effect that its own quantity will have on the quantity offered by firm 2.

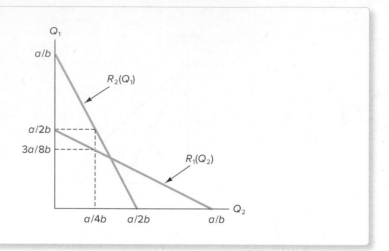

Comparison of Outcomes

Now that we have considered three different types of behavior for duopolists, let's compare the outcomes of the different models. A monopoly confronting the same demand and cost conditions as Cournot duopolists would have produced $a/2b$ units of output at a price of $a/2$, earning an economic profit of $a^2/4b$ (see Figure 13.6). The interdependence between the Cournot duopolists thus causes price to be one-third lower and total quantity to be one-third higher than the corresponding values in the monopoly case.[4] Whereas the equilibrium price and quantity in the Cournot model differed by only a factor of one-third from those in the monopoly case, in the Bertrand model they are precisely the same as in the competitive case.[5]

How well should the Stackelberg duopolists do? Naturally, the leader fares better since it is the one strategically manipulating the behavior of the follower. Referring to Figure 13.4 we see that firm 1's profit is $a^2/8b$, which is twice that of firm 2. As it happens, this is exactly what firm 1 would have earned had it and firm 2 colluded to charge the monopoly price, $a/2$, and split the market evenly (see Figure 13.6). The combined

FIGURE 13.6

Comparing Equilibrium Price and Quantity

The monopolist would maximize profit where marginal revenue equals zero, since there are no marginal production costs. The equilibrium price will be higher, and the equilibrium quantity lower, than in the Cournot case.

[4]As a fraction of the output for a perfectly competitive industry, industry output under a Cournot duopoly is $N/(N + 1)$ with N firms. As the number of firms N becomes large, the Cournot industry output (and therefore price and profit) approaches that of a perfectly competitive industry. In this sense, Cournot duopoly is truly between monopoly and perfect competition.

[5]If firms choose capacity and then price, the outcome matches the Cournot equilibrium. See David Kreps and Jose Scheinkman, "Quantity Precommitment and Bertrand Competition Yield Cournot Outcomes," *Bell Journal of Economics,* 14, 1983, 326–337.

TABLE 13.1
Comparison of Oligopoly Models

Model	Industry output Q	Market price P	Industry profit Π	
Shared monopoly	$Q_m = a/(2b)$	$P_m = a/(2)$	$\Pi_m = a^2/(4b)$	All four models assume a market demand curve of $P = a - bQ$ and marginal cost equal to zero. (Of course, if marginal cost is not zero, the entries will be all different from the ones shown.)
Cournot	$(4/3)Q_m$	$(2/3)P_m$	$(8/9)\Pi_m$	
Stackelberg	$(3/2)Q_m$	$(1/2)P_m$	$(3/4)\Pi_m$	
Bertrand	$2Q_m$	0	0	
Perfect competition	$2Q_m$	0	0	

output of the two firms in the Stackelberg case is $3a/4b$, which is slightly higher than in the Cournot case, with the result that the market price, $a/4$, is slightly lower than in the Cournot case ($a/3$). The results of the four possibilities considered thus far are summarized in Table 13.1.

The Stackelberg model represents a clear improvement over the Cournot and Bertrand models in that it allows at least one of the firms to behave strategically. But why should only one firm behave in this fashion? If firm 1 can make strategic use of its rival's reaction function, why can't firm 2 do likewise? Suppose, in fact, that both firms try to be Stackelberg leaders. Each will then ignore its own reaction function and produce $a/2b$, with the result that total industry output and price will be a/b and 0, respectively, the same as in the Bertrand model. From the standpoint of consumers, this is a very desirable outcome, of course. But for the owners of the firms, universal strategic behavior leads to the worst possible outcome.

COMPETITION WHEN THERE ARE INCREASING RETURNS TO SCALE

Consider an example of a duopoly in an industry with increasing returns to scale. How would two firms survive in such an industry, whose cost conditions make it a natural monopoly? It is easy enough to imagine two firms starting out at an early stage of a new product's development, each serving a largely different segment of the market. But now suppose the industry has matured, and a single, nationwide market exists for the product. Should we expect that one firm will drive the other out of business and take over the role of natural monopolist? And if so, what price will it charge?

To make our discussion concrete, suppose that the technology is one with constant marginal cost and declining average total cost, as shown in Figure 13.7. For simplicity, suppose that the size of the total market is fixed at Q_0. With two firms in the industry, each producing half that amount, average cost is AC'. If there were only one firm, its average cost would be only AC_0. By what process do we expect that one firm might eliminate the other?

FIGURE 13.7

Sharing a Market with Increasing Returns to Scale

With two firms in the market, costs are higher than with one. Yet there may be no tendency for one firm to drive the other out of business.

The obvious strategy for the two firms would be to merge. The difficulty is that Justice Department antitrust guidelines do not permit mergers between firms whose combined share of the market exceeds a small fraction of total market output. Here, the combined share would be 100 percent, making approval all but impossible.

A second alternative is that one of the firms will announce a preemptive price cut, hoping to drive the other out of business. Suppose, for example, that it charges AC_0, what its average cost would be if in fact its strategy proved successful. How will its rival respond? It can either match the price cut and again split the market or refuse and sell nothing. Since its marginal cost is less than AC_0, it will do better by matching. At that price, however, both firms will lose money; and if the price holds, it is just a matter of time before one of them goes out of business. It might take a long time, though, and even the surviving firm could suffer substantial losses in the interim.

More important, from the perspective of the firm considering whether to initiate a price cut, there is no assurance that it would be the one to survive. So if we view the decision from the point of view of the firm, initiating a price war looks like a very risky proposition indeed. Without the threat of entry, it is easy to see why a live-and-let-live strategy might be compellingly attractive.

But let us suppose, for the sake of discussion, that one firm does somehow manage to capture the entire market, and suppose further that potential entrants face substantial sunk costs if they enter this market. Will the surviving firm then be free to charge the monopoly price?

For the same reasons a duopolist would be reluctant to initiate a price war, an outsider would be wary about entering the industry to face a possibly ruinous battle with the incumbent firm. It may be possible, though, for an outside firm to write contracts with buyers. If it offered a lower price than the incumbent firm, it could then assure itself of the entire market. But an outside firm realizes that it would be in the interest of the incumbent to match or beat any price it could offer. The potential entrant, after all, must charge enough to cover its prospective sunk costs if entry into the market is to be profitable, whereas the incumbent need only cover its variable costs. Of course, the incumbent would be delighted to cover *all* its costs. But rather than be driven from the market, it would be rational for the incumbent to accept a price that just barely covered its variable costs.

Because of this asymmetry, it will never pay a new firm to take the initiative to enter a natural monopolist's market (unless the new firm happens, for some reason, to have a substantial cost advantage). Any money it spent on market surveys, contract negotiations, and the like would be lost as soon as the incumbent made a better offer, which it would always be in the incumbent's interest to do.

There is one remaining avenue along which the threat of entry might serve to discipline an incumbent natural monopolist. Although it would never pay a potential entrant to incur expenses to try to penetrate this type of market, it might very well pay *buyers* in the market to bear the expense of approaching a potential entrant. If the buyers absorb this expense, they can again expect that the incumbent will agree to offer a competitive price on the product. (If the incumbent does not, they can simply sign an agreement to buy from the outside firm.) So if it is practical for buyers to act collectively at their own expense to negotiate with potential entrants, even an incumbent natural monopolist may be forced to sell at close to a competitive price. By way of illustration, most local governments act as purchasing agents for their communities by negotiating contracts with potential monopoly suppliers of community services.

In markets for privately sold goods, buyers are often too numerous to organize themselves to act collectively in this fashion. Few people want to go to a town meeting every night to discuss negotiations with potential suppliers of countless different products. Where it is impractical for buyers to organize direct collective action, it may nonetheless be possible for private agents to accomplish much the same objective on their behalf.

Certain department stores, for example, might be interpreted as acting in this role. The Sears, Roebuck chain built its early success by delivering on its slogan, "Quality at a fair price." Its function was to act as a purchasing agent for the community, negotiating contracts with single-source suppliers. It earned a reputation for driving hard bargains with these suppliers and for passing the savings along to its customers. Why should it and other department stores pass such savings along in the form of lower prices? Merchants are in competition with one another not only for the sale of products produced by natural monopolists, but for an enormous list of competitively produced products as well. To have a reputation for delivering quality merchandise at reasonable prices is an essential element in the marketing strategies of many of these merchants, and consumers are the ultimate beneficiaries.

MONOPOLISTIC COMPETITION

Monopolistic competition, a market structure that is close to perfect competition, occurs if many firms serve a market with free entry and exit, but in which one firm's products are not perfect substitutes for the products of other firms. The degree of substitutability between products then determines how closely the industry resembles perfect competition.

The Chamberlin Model

The traditional economic model of monopolistic competition was developed independently during the 1930s by Edward Chamberlin and Joan Robinson. It begins with the assumption of a clearly defined "industry group," which consists of a large number of producers of products that are close, but imperfect, substitutes for one another. The market for men's dress shirts provides a convenient illustration. Shirts made by Brooks Brothers serve essentially the same function as those made by Men's Wearhouse or Ralph Lauren. And yet, for many consumers, it is hardly a matter of indifference which brand they buy.

Two important implications follow from these assumptions about industry structure. The first is that because the products are viewed as close substitutes, each firm will confront a downward-sloping demand schedule. Someone who has a particular liking for Brooks Brothers shirts would be willing to pay more for one than for a shirt from some other manufacturer. But let Brooks Brothers raise its price sufficiently and even these buyers will eventually switch to another brand. The second implication, which follows from the assumption of a large number of independent firms, is that each firm will act as if its own price and quantity decisions have no effect on the behavior of other firms in the industry. And because the products are close substitutes, this in turn means that each firm perceives its demand schedule as being highly elastic.

A fundamental feature of the Chamberlin model is the perfect symmetry of the position of all firms in the industry. In metaphorical terms, the Chamberlinian firm may be thought of as one of many fishing boats, each of which has a number of fishing lines in the water. If any one boat were to set its hooks with a more alluring bait while others used the same bait as before, the effect would be for the innovator to increase its share of the total catch by a substantial margin. After all, its lines have become more attractive not only in absolute terms, but also relative to the lines of other boats. Because the situation is perfectly symmetric, however, if it makes sense for one boat to use more attractive bait, so will it for others. Yet when all use better bait, the innovator's lines are no more attractive in relative terms than before. Accordingly, the addition to its total catch will be much smaller than if others had held to their original behavior.

The analogy between the fishing example and pricing behavior by the Chamberlinian monopolistically competitive firm is complete. In contemplating the demand for its own product, the firm assumes that its competitors do not respond in any way to its price and quantity decisions. Like the operators of the fishing boats, the firm is correct in assuming that a change in its own behavior will not *cause* others to change theirs. Yet the symmetry between firms assures that if it makes sense for one firm to alter its price, it will make sense for all others to do likewise.

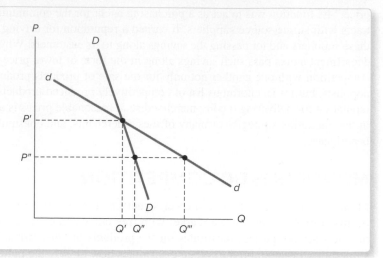

The result is that the firm really confronts two different demand curves—one that describes what will happen when it alone changes its price and a second that describes what will happen when all prices change in unison. Thus, for example, the curve *dd* in Figure 13.8 represents the demand curve facing the Chamberlinian firm if it alone varies its price; the curve *DD* is the demand curve when all firms change prices together. At an initial situation in which all firms charge *P'*, each will sell *Q'*. If only one firm lowers its price to *P"*, it will sell *Q'''*. But if others match its price cut, each will sell only *Q"*.

It is important to stress that individual firms need not fail to realize that the prices of similarly situated firms tend to move together. On the contrary, each firm may be perfectly aware of that. But it also realizes that its own price movements are not what *cause* other firms to change their behavior. When it is thinking about the consequences of a price move, therefore, it is forced to think in terms of movements along *dd,* not along the demand curve that describes what happens when all prices change in unison (*DD*).[6]

Chamberlinian Equilibrium in the Short Run

For illustrative purposes, let us consider the monopolistically competitive firm whose demand (the *dd* curve), marginal revenue, average total cost, and short-run marginal cost curves are portrayed in Figure 13.9. Following precisely the same argument we employed in the case of the pure monopoly, we can easily show that the short-run profit-maximizing quantity is *Q**, the one for which the marginal revenue curve intersects the short-run marginal cost curve. The profit-maximizing price is *P**, the value that corresponds to *Q** on the demand curve *dd*.

In Figure 13.9, note also that the demand curve *DD* intersects the demand curve *dd* at the profit-maximizing price, *P**. This is yet another consequence of the fundamental symmetry that exists within Chamberlinian firms. The *DD* curve, recall, is the locus along which each firm's quantity would move with price if the prices of all firms moved in unison. The *dd* curve, by contrast, is the locus along which the firm's quantity will move with price when the prices of all other firms are fixed. Because the situation confronting each firm is the same, if *P** is the profit-maximizing price for one, it must also be for the rest. The price level at which other firms' prices are fixed along *dd* is thus *P**, which implies that at *P** on *dd,* the price of *every* firm will be *P**. And this is why *dd* intersects *DD* at *P**.

---

[6]The issue here is much the same as the one confronting participants in the prisoner's dilemma. Each person may know that it is rational for the other person to defect and may therefore expect him to do so. But each person also knows that his own behavior will not affect what the other person does.

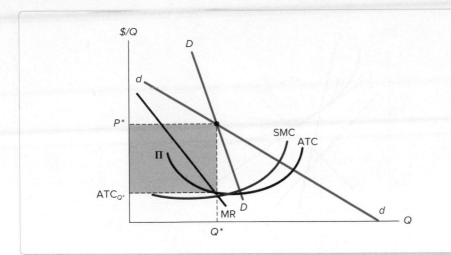

FIGURE 13.9

Short-Run Equilibrium for the Chamberlinian Firm

The Chamberlinian monopolistically competitive firm maximizes economic profit in the short run by equating marginal revenue and short-run marginal cost. Economic profit is Π, the area of the shaded rectangle.

Chamberlinian Equilibrium in the Long Run

As in the perfectly competitive case, the fact that there are economic profits in the short run will have the effect of luring additional firms into the monopolistically competitive industry. What is the effect of the entry of these firms? In the competitive case, we saw that it was to shift the industry supply curve rightward, causing a reduction in the short-run equilibrium price. Put another way, the effect of entry in the perfectly competitive model is to cause each firm's horizontal demand curve to shift downward. In the Chamberlin model, the analogous effect is to shift each firm's demand curve to the left. More precisely, on the assumption that each firm competes on an equal footing for a share of total industry demand, the effect of entry is to cause an equal proportional reduction in the quantity that each firm can sell at any given price. Each firm in the market essentially claims an equal share of industry demand, and with more firms in the industry, that share necessarily declines.

SELF-TEST 13.4

Each of 20 firms in a Chamberlinian monopolistically competitive industry faces a *dd* curve given by $P = 10 - 0.001Q$. What will each firm's *dd* curve be following the entry of five new firms?

Following the leftward shift in demand caused by entry, each firm has the opportunity to readjust the size of its capital stock and to choose its new profit-maximizing level of output. If extra-normal profit still remains, entry will continue.

The long-run equilibrium position is one in which the demand curve *dd* has shifted left to the point that it is tangent to the long-run average cost curve (and tangent as well to the associated short-run average cost curve). Note in Figure 13.10 that Q^*, the profit-maximizing level of output by the MR = MC criterion, is exactly the same as the output level for which the *dd* curve is tangent to the long- and short-run average cost curves. This is no mere coincidence. We can argue independently of the MR = MC condition that the tangency point must be the maximum-profit point. At that point, the firm earns zero economic profit, while at any other output level, average cost would exceed average revenue, which means that economic profit would be negative.

Note again in Figure 13.10 that the demand curve *DD* intersects *dd* at the equilibrium price P^* for the reasons discussed earlier. If all firms raised price from P^*, each would move upward along *DD,* and each would earn an economic profit. But in the absence of a binding collusive agreement, it would not be in the interest of any firm to maintain its price above P^*, because at any such price its marginal revenue (along the

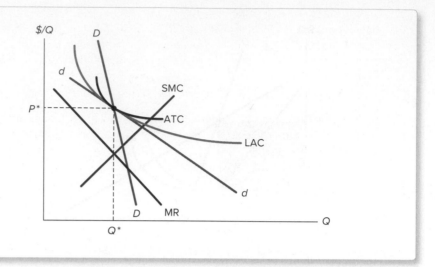

FIGURE 13.10

Long-Run Equilibrium in the Chamberlin Model

Entry occurs, shifting *dd* leftward until it becomes tangent to the LAC curve. The firm produces Q*, sells for P*, and earns zero economic profit.

MR curve associated with *dd*) would exceed its marginal cost. At any price above P*, it could earn higher profits by cutting price and selling more output. The only stable outcome is the tangency point shown in Figure 13.10.

Perfect Competition versus Chamberlinian Monopolistic Competition

There are several obvious points of comparison between the long-run equilibrium positions of perfect competition and Chamberlinian monopolistic competition. First, competition meets the test of allocative efficiency, while monopolistic competition does not. Under competition, price is exactly equal to long-run marginal cost, which means that there are no unexploited possibilities for mutual gains through exchange. Under monopolistic competition, by contrast, price will exceed marginal cost, even in the long run. This means that there will be people in society who value an additional unit of output more highly than the value of the resources required to produce it. If monopolistic competitors could come up with a way to cut price to such buyers without cutting price on existing sales, they would gladly do so, making everyone better off in the process. As we saw in the case of the monopolist, such selective price cutting is sometimes possible. But it is inherently imperfect, and on this account monopolistic competition is destined to fall short of perfect competition on the narrow efficiency standard.

Some economists also argue that monopolistic competition is less efficient than perfect competition because in the former case firms do not produce at the minimum points of their long-run average cost (LAC) curves. This is not a very telling comparison, however, because other aspects of the two cases are so different. The relevant question is whether people who currently buy from monopolistic competitors would be happier if all products were exactly the same and cost a little less. This is not an easy question, and, lacking an answer to it, we cannot conclude that monopolistic competition is inefficient merely because firms don't produce at the minimum points of their LAC curves.

There is at least one important sense, related to the discussion in the preceding paragraph, in which the Chamberlin model is strikingly more realistic than the competitive model. In the perfectly competitive case, recall, price and marginal cost are the same in equilibrium. This implies that the firm should react with indifference to an opportunity to fill a new order at the current market price. In the monopolistically competitive case, by contrast, price exceeds marginal cost, which implies that the firm should greet a new order at the current market price with enthusiasm. Periods of temporary shortages apart, we know of very few instances of the former reaction. Almost every businessperson who ever lived is delighted to accept new orders at the current market price.

In terms of long-run profitability, finally, the equilibrium positions of both the perfect competitor and the Chamberlinian monopolistic competitor are precisely the same. Freedom of entry in each case holds long-run economic profit at zero. By the same token, freedom of exit assures that there will be no long-run economic losses in either case.

Criticisms of the Chamberlin Model

The late Nobel laureate George Stigler and others criticized the Chamberlin model on a variety of grounds. First of all, there is the difficulty of defining what is meant by the amorphous concept of "industry group." The Chamberlinian concept envisions a group of products that are different from one another in some unspecified way, yet equally likely to appeal to any given buyer. Stigler complained that it is impossible, as a practical matter, to draw operational boundaries between groups of products in this fashion. Viewed from one perspective, a product like Coca-Cola is unique unto itself. (Thus buyers reacted angrily when Coke made a slight alteration in its traditional formula, which led the company to reintroduce "Coke Classic.") Viewed slightly differently, however, Coke is a substitute for Pepsi, which is a substitute for milk, which in turn is a substitute for ice cream. But ice cream is a substitute for chocolate cake, which certainly doesn't *seem* like a substitute for Coca-Cola. Pushed to its logical extreme, Stigler argued, the Chamberlinian product group quickly expands to include virtually every consumer product in the economy.

From a methodological perspective, Stigler joined his University of Chicago colleague Milton Friedman in arguing that a theory should be judged not by the descriptive accuracy of its assumptions, but by its ability to predict responses to changes in the economic environment. Stigler believed that Chamberlin's theory significantly complicates the theory of perfect competition, without appreciably altering its most important predictions.[7] There are certainly cases where the above criticism holds, where it is simpler and clearer to analyze an issue in terms of perfect competition because the predictions obtained will be similar to those of a monopolistic competition model and where the special concerns of the latter are not salient. That said, the Stigler-Friedman criticism has obviously had only limited effect on the teaching of economics; this text, like virtually every other introductory or intermediate microeconomics text, contains a discussion of monopolistic competition.

Criticisms of the Chamberlin model can just as easily be made from the opposite direction—that it does not depart *enough* in the direction of realism from the competitive model to depict consequences of market and product segmentation in a complete or convincing way. For that reason, in recent years, research on the theory of monopolistic competition has focused on models that incorporate the specific features of a product that make buyers choose it over all others. In contrast with the Chamberlin model, these models produce conclusions that often differ sharply with those of the perfectly competitive model. To this alternative way of thinking about monopolistic competition we now turn.

A SPATIAL INTERPRETATION OF MONOPOLISTIC COMPETITION

As noted earlier, the extent to which one monopolistically competitive firm's product is an effective substitute for another's determines how closely their industry will resemble perfect competition. One concrete way of thinking about lack of complete substitutability is distance. Gasoline sold across town is not a perfect substitute for gasoline sold at the nearest corner, especially when your tank is nearly empty.

---

[7]See "Monopolistic Competition in Retrospect," in George Stigler, *Five Lectures on Economic Problems*, London and New York: Longmans, Green, 1949. Stigler's statement that "it is not true that a theory which is realistic in its assumptions ... is necessarily realistic in its implications" (p. 14) reemerged as a central tenet of the "The Methodology of Positive Economics" chapter in Milton Friedman's *Essays in Positive Economics* (Chicago: University of Chicago Press, 1953). Friedman, however (with the pool player example we mentioned in Chapter 1), also underscored a subtly different and more broadly accepted point: that assumptions need not be realistic to generate correct predictions.

Imagine yourself a resident of a small island nation with a large lake in the middle of it. Business activity there is naturally restricted to the doughnut-shaped piece of land that constitutes the island's periphery. There is considerable specialization of labor on your island. People toil all day at their respective tasks and then take their evening meals at restaurants. People on your island lack the customary preference for culinary diversity. Instead, you and your neighbors prefer to eat baked potatoes and grilled beefsteak every night. Meals in any given restaurant are produced under increasing returns to scale—the more meals produced, the lower the average cost per meal.

How many restaurants should there be in this island nation? We are tempted to say only one, thereby keeping the cost per meal to a minimum. If the circumference of the island were, say, only 300 yards, this would almost surely be the correct answer. But for a much larger island, the direct cost of meals is not likely to be the only concern to you and your fellow residents. You will also care about the cost of getting to and from the nearest restaurant. If the island were 300 miles around, for example, the cost savings from having only a single restaurant could hardly begin to compensate for the travel costs incurred by those who live on the far side of the island.

The market for evening meals on this island is in one respect the same as the markets we have considered in earlier chapters: A single, standardized meal is served in every restaurant. But the type of food served is not the only important characteristic of a meal. Buyers care also about *where* the meal is served. When products differ along one or more important dimensions—location, size, flavor, quality, and so on—we immediately confront the general question of how much product diversity there should be. Should an economy have 5 different brands of cars, 10, or 50? How many different kinds of tennis racquets should there be?

To help fix ideas, suppose there are initially four restaurants evenly spaced around the periphery of the island, as represented by the heavy green squares in Figure 13.11. Suppose the circumference of the island is 1 mile. The distance between adjacent restaurants will then be $\frac{1}{4}$ mile, and no one can possibly live more than $\frac{1}{8}$ mile away from the nearest restaurant, the one-way trip length required for someone who lives exactly halfway between two restaurants.

To fill out the structure of the environment, suppose there are L consumers scattered uniformly about the circle, and suppose the cost of travel is t dollars per mile. Thus, for example, if t were equal to \$24/mile, the transportation cost incurred by someone who lives $d = \frac{1}{16}$ mile from the nearest restaurant would be the product of the round-trip distance ($2d$) and the unit travel cost (t): $2td = 2(\$24/\text{mile})(\frac{1}{16}\text{mile}) = \$3$.

Suppose further that each consumer will eat exactly 1 meal/day at the restaurant for which the total price (which is the price charged for the meal plus transportation costs) is lowest. And suppose, finally, that each restaurant has a total cost curve given by

$$TC = F + MQ. \tag{13.6}$$

FIGURE 13.11

An Industry in Which Location Is the Important Differentiating Feature

Restaurants (heavy green squares) are the same except for their geographic location. Each person dines at the restaurant closest to home. If the circumference of the loop is 1 mile, this means that the distance between restaurants will be $\frac{1}{4}$ mile, giving rise to a maximum one-way trip length of $\frac{1}{8}$ mile.

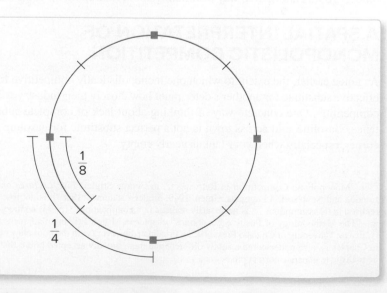

Recall from earlier chapters that the total cost curve in Equation 13.6 is one in which there is a fixed cost F and a constant marginal cost M. Here, F may be thought of as the sum of equipment rental fees, opportunity costs of invested capital, and other fixed costs associated with operating a restaurant; and M is the sum of the labor, raw material, and other variable costs incurred in producing an additional meal.

Recall also that average total cost (ATC) is simply total cost divided by output. With a total cost function given by $TC = F + MQ$, average total cost is thus equal to $F/Q + M$. This means that the more customers that are served in a given location, the lower the average total cost will be.

Suppose, for example, that each of our four restaurants has a total cost curve, measured in dollars per day, given by $TC = 50 + 5Q$, where Q is the number of meals it serves each day. If the population, L, is equal to 100 persons, each restaurant will serve $(100/4) = 25$ meals/day, and its total cost will be given by $TC = 50 + 5(25) = \$175$/day. Average total cost in each restaurant will be $TC/25 = (\$175/\text{day})/(25 \text{ meals/day}) = \$7$/meal. By comparison, if there were only two restaurants, each would serve 50 meals/day and have an average total cost of only \$6/meal.

What will be the average cost of transportation when there are four restaurants? This cost will depend on unit transportation costs (t) and on how far apart the restaurants are. Recall that the distance between adjacent restaurants will be $\frac{1}{4}$ mile when there are four restaurants. Some people will live right next door to a restaurant, and for these people the transportation cost will be zero. With four restaurants, the farthest someone can live from a restaurant is $\frac{1}{8}$ mile, the one-way distance for a person who lives halfway between two adjacent restaurants. For this person, the round-trip will cover $\frac{1}{4}$ mile; and if t is again equal to \$24/mile, the travel cost for this patron will be $(\$24/\text{mile})(\frac{1}{4}\text{ mile}) = \$6$. Since people are uniformly scattered about the loop, the average round-trip will be halfway between these two extremes; it will thus cover a distance of $\frac{1}{8}$ mile, and its cost will be \$3.

The *overall average cost per meal* is the sum of average total cost (\$7/meal in the four-restaurant example) and average transportation cost (here, \$3/meal), which comes to \$10/meal.

The Optimal Number of Locations

If unit transportation cost (t) were zero, it would then clearly be optimal to have only a single restaurant, because that would minimize the overall average cost per meal. But if transportation cost were sufficiently high, a single restaurant would not be optimal because the average patron would have to travel too great a distance. The optimal number of locations is thus the result of a trade-off between the start-up and other fixed costs (F) of opening new locations, on the one hand, and the savings from lower transportation costs, on the other.

What is the best number of outlets to have? Our strategy for answering this question will be to ask whether the overall average cost per meal served (average total cost plus average transportation cost) would decline if we had one more restaurant than we have now. If so, we should add another restaurant and ask the same question again. Once the overall average cost stops declining, we will have reached the optimal number of restaurants.

To illustrate, suppose we increase the number of restaurants in our earlier example from four to five. How will this affect overall average cost? Again supposing that the restaurants are evenly spaced around the loop, each will now attract only one-fifth of the island's 100 inhabitants, which means that each will serve 20 meals/day. The ATC for each restaurant will thus be $[50 + 5(20)]/20 = \$7.50$/meal, up \$0.50/meal from the previous value. (Recall that ATC with four restaurants was \$7/meal.) The distance between adjacent restaurants is $\frac{1}{5}$ mile when there are five restaurants. This means that the average one-way trip with five restaurants is $\frac{1}{20}$ mile, which in turn means that the average round-trip length is $\frac{1}{10}$ mile. Average transportation cost is thus $(\frac{1}{10}\text{ mile})(\$24/\text{mile}) = \$2.40$. Note that this is \$0.60 less than the previous average transportation cost of \$3, reflecting the decline in average trip length. Adding average total cost and average transportation cost, we see that the overall average cost with five restaurants is $\$7.50 + \$2.40 = \$9.90$/meal.

Your calculation in Self-Test 13.5 demonstrates that overall average cost per meal goes up when we increase the number of restaurants from five to six. And since the overall average cost declined when we moved from four to five, this means the optimal number of restaurants for our island nation is five.

We can make the preceding analysis more general by supposing that there are N outlets around the loop, as shown by the heavy green squares in Figure 13.12. Now the distance between adjacent outlets will be $1/N$, and the maximum one-way trip length will be half that, or $1/2N$. If we again suppose that people are uniformly distributed around the loop, it follows that the average one-way distance to the nearest outlet is $1/4N$ (which is halfway between 0, the distance of the person closest to a given outlet, and $1/2N$, the distance of the person farthest from it). The average round-trip distance is twice the average one-way distance, and is thus equal to $1/2N$.

Because the distance between restaurants declines as the number of restaurants grows, the total transportation cost, denoted C_{trans}, will be a decreasing function of the number of outlets. Since transportation cost is t dollars per person per mile traveled, total transportation cost will be the product of the cost per mile (t), population (L), and the average round-trip length $\left(\frac{1}{2N}\right)$:

$$C_{trans} = tL\frac{1}{2N}. \tag{13.7}$$

The total cost of meals served, denoted C_{meals}, also depends on both population and the number of outlets. It is given by

$$C_{meals} = LM + NF, \tag{13.8}$$

where the first term on the right reflects the fact that each of the L people eats a meal whose marginal cost is M, and the second term is the total fixed cost for N outlets. The object is to choose N to minimize the sum of the two types of costs, $C_{trans} + C_{meals}$.

The two cost functions and their sum are shown graphically in Figure 13.13, where N^* denotes the cost-minimizing number of outlets.[8]

FIGURE 13.12

Distances with _N_ Outlets

With N outlets, the distance between adjacent outlets will be $1/N$. The farthest a person can live from an outlet is $1/2N$. And the average one-way distance people must travel to reach the nearest outlet is $1/4N$. The average round-trip distance is $1/2N$.

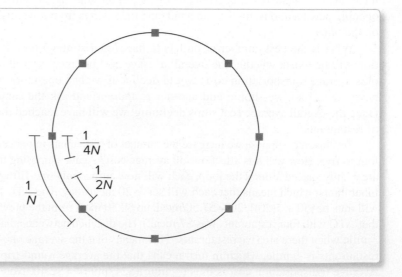

[8]These functions are plotted as if N were a continuous variable, not an integer. For industries involving large numbers of firms, the continuous approximation will introduce only minimal error.

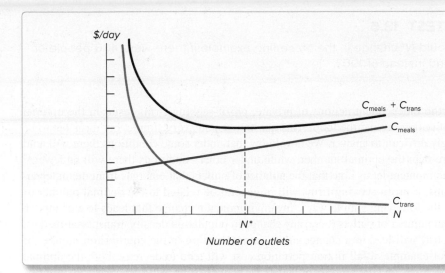

FIGURE 13.13

The Optimal Number of Outlets

Total transportation cost (C_{trans}) declines with the number of outlets (N), while total cost of meals served (C_{meals}) increases with N. The optimal number of outlets (N*) is the one that minimizes the sum of these costs.

The slope of the C_{meals} curve is equal to F, which represents the cost of an additional outlet. The slope of the C_{trans} curve is equal to $-tL/2N^2$ and represents the savings in transportation cost from adding an additional outlet.[9] If the slope of C_{meals} is less than the absolute value of the slope of C_{trans}, the reduction in transportation cost from adding another outlet will more than compensate for the extra fixed cost from adding that outlet. The optimal number of outlets, N^*, is the one for which the slope of the C_{meals} curve is the same as the absolute value of the slope of the C_{trans} curve. N^* must thus satisfy

$$\frac{tL}{2N^{*2}} = F, \tag{13.9}$$

which yields

$$N^* = \sqrt{\frac{tL}{2F}}. \tag{13.10}$$

This expression for the optimal number of outlets has a straightforward economic interpretation. Note first that if transportation cost rises, N^* will also rise. This makes sense because the whole point of adding additional outlets is to economize on transportation costs. Note that N^* also increases with population density, L. The more people there are who live on each segment of the loop, the more people there are who will benefit if the average distance to the nearest outlet becomes shorter. And note, finally, that N^* declines with F, the start-up cost of an additional outlet, which is also just as expected.

Applying Equation 13.10 to our restaurant example in which $L = 100$, $t = 24$, and $F = 50$, we get $N^* = \sqrt{(2400/100}} = 4.9$. Needless to say, it is impossible to have 4.9 restaurants, so we choose the integer nearest 4.9, namely, 5. And indeed, just as our earlier calculations indicated, having five restaurants results in a lower overall average cost than does having either four or six.

[9]This slope is found by taking the derivative

$$\frac{d(C_{trans})}{dN} = \frac{-tL}{2N^2},$$

again treating N as if it were continuously variable. Students who haven't had calculus can convince themselves that this expression is correct by letting ΔN be, say, 0.001 and then calculating the resulting change in C_{trans},

$$\Delta C_{trans} = \frac{tL}{2(N + 0.001)} - \frac{tL}{2N} = \frac{-0.001tL}{2N(N + 0.001)}.$$

The ratio $\Delta C_{trans}/\Delta N$ is thus

$$\frac{\Delta C_{trans}}{0.001} = \frac{-tL}{2N(N + 0.001)} \approx \frac{-tL}{2N^2}.$$

SELF-TEST 13.6

How would N^* change in the preceding example if there were 400 people on the island instead of 100?

Will the independent actions of private, profit-seeking firms result in the optimal number of outlets around the loop? This question sounds very simple, but turns out to be exceedingly difficult to answer. We now know that under some conditions there will tend to be more than the optimal number, while under other conditions there will be fewer.[10] But for the moment let us note that the number of outlets that emerges from the independent actions of profit-seeking firms will in general be related to the optimal number of outlets in the following simple way: Any environmental change that leads to a change in the optimal number of outlets (here, any change in population density, transportation cost, or fixed cost) will lead to a change in the same direction in the equilibrium number of outlets. For example, a fall in transportation cost will tend to decrease both the optimal number of outlets and the number of outlets we actually observe in practice.

Economic Naturalist 13.1

Why are there so many fewer grocery stores in most cities now than there were in 1930? And why do residential neighborhoods in New York City have more grocery stores than residential neighborhoods in Los Angeles?

Why are grocery stores closer together in New York City than in Los Angeles?

Grocery retailing, like other forms of retailing, is characterized by strong economies of scale. It thus confronts the usual trade-off between direct production cost, on the one hand, and transportation cost, on the other. Throughout this century, changing patterns of automobile ownership have affected the pattern of grocery store size and location in the United States. In 1920, most families did not own cars and had to do their shopping on foot. In terms of our expression for the optimal number of outlets (Equation 13.10), this meant a high value of t, unit transportation cost. Today, of course, virtually every family has a car, which has led people to take advantage of the lower prices that are possible in larger stores. One exception to this general pattern is Manhattan. Even today, most Manhattan residents do not own cars. Moreover, population density is extremely high there, which means a high value of L in Equation 13.10. The combined effect of high values of L and t is that very few Manhattan residents have to walk more than two blocks to get to their nearest grocery store. The total population in Los Angeles is also very high, but it is spread out over a much larger area, and most families own at least one automobile. As a result, Los Angeles grocery stores are both larger and farther apart than their New York City counterparts.

---

[10]A detailed technical discussion of some of the relevant issues can be found in Avinash Dixit and Joseph Stiglitz, "Monopolistic Competition and Optimal Product Diversity," *American Economic Review,* 1977, 297–308; and A. Michael Spence, "Product Selection, Fixed Costs, and Monopolistic Competition," *Review of Economic Studies,* 1976, 217–235.

FIGURE 13.14

A Spatial Interpretation of Airline Scheduling

In a market with four flights per day, there is no traveler for whom there is not a flight leaving within 3 hours of his most preferred departure time.

The Analogy to Product Characteristics

The power of the spatial interpretation of monopolistic competition is that it can be applied not only to geographic location, but also to a variety of other product characteristics. Consider, for example, the various airline flights between any two cities on a given day. People have different preferences for traveling at various times of day, just as they have different preferences about where to eat or shop. Figure 13.14 depicts an air-travel market (for example, Kansas City to Minneapolis) with four flights per day, scheduled at midnight, 6 AM, noon, and 6 PM. With the choice of an airline flight, just as with the choice of a place to dine, people will tend to select the alternative that lies closest to their most preferred option. Thus, a person who would most prefer to go at 7 PM will probably choose the 6 PM flight. In terms of our spatial model, having to wait for a flight is the analog of having to travel a certain distance in order to get to a store.

Why not have a flight leaving every 5 minutes, so that no one would be forced to travel at an inconvenient time? The answer again has to do with the trade-off between cost and convenience. The larger an aircraft is, the lower its average cost per seat is. If people want frequent flights, airlines are forced to use smaller planes and charge higher fares. Conversely, if people didn't care when they traveled, the airline could use the largest possible aircraft (in today's fleet, the 853-seat Airbus A380) and fly at whatever interval was required to accumulate enough passengers to fill the plane. (In the Paducah, Kentucky–Klamath Falls, Oregon, market, that would mean one flight every other February 29!) But most passengers have schedules to keep and are willing to pay a little extra for more conveniently timed flights. The result is the same sort of compromise we saw in the restaurant and grocery store examples.

Virtually every consumer product can be interpreted fruitfully within the context of the spatial model. In the automobile market, for example, the available permutations of turbo versus nonturbo, automatic versus standard, coupe versus convertible, sedan versus station wagon, two doors versus four doors, bucket seats versus bench seats, air conditioned versus not air conditioned, metallic indigo versus forest green, and so on, lead to an extraordinarily large number of possibilities. It would be considerably cheaper, of course, if we had only a single standard model. But people are willing to pay a little extra for variety, just as they are willing to pay a little extra for a more conveniently located store. In the parlance of the spatial model, car manufacturers are said to "locate" their models in a "product-space." Their aim is to see that few buyers are left without a choice that lies "close" to the car that would best suit them. Similar interpretations apply to cameras, stereos, vacations, bicycles, wristwatches, wedding bands, and virtually every other good for which people have a taste for variety.

Paying for Variety

Variety, as we have seen, is costly. Many critics claim that market economies serve up wastefully high degrees of product variety. Wouldn't the world be a better place, these critics ask, if we had a simpler array of products to choose from, each costing less than the highly specific models we see today? The extra costs of product variety may indeed seem an unnecessary burden imposed on consumers who neither desire nor can easily afford it. In a slightly more detailed model of spatial competition, however, these problems appear much less serious.

In our simple model, we assumed that each buyer faced the same unit transportation cost. This assumption is unrealistic even in models where the only dimension of variety is geographic location. Buyers who own automobiles, for example, will have much lower transportation costs than those who don't; likewise, buyers whose time is worth little, in opportunity cost terms, have lower transportation costs than those whose time is more valuable. The issue is the same for product variety. Those who care a lot about special product features will have higher "transport costs" than those who do not, which means simply that people in the former group are willing to pay more than others for a product whose special features suit their particular tastes.

It is also true, as a general proposition, that the demand for variety increases sharply with income. In the language of Chapter 5, variety is a luxury, not a necessity. The association between income and the demand for variety plays a pivotal role in the way most producers market their products. To illustrate, consider the array of automobiles offered by General Motors, ranging from the small Chevrolet Sonic hatchback to the full-sized Cadillac Escalade. All these cars incorporate a variety of specialized features, which are the result of costly research and development. The research and development costs are largely fixed, which gives rise to a substantial scale economy in the production of cars. If GM (or any other company) could sell more cars in a given year, it could produce each of them at a lower cost.

When marginal cost lies below average cost, it is not possible to charge each buyer a price equal to marginal cost and still earn a normal profit. (Recall from Chapter 9 that a firm's average cost includes a normal rate of profit.) As we saw in Chapter 11, the firm with a scale economy has an incentive to expand its market by setting price close to marginal cost if it can do that without altering its prices on existing sales. But we also saw that if some buyers pay prices below average cost, others must pay prices above it.

The car manufacturer's response to this situation is to set the prices of its better models above average cost, while pricing its lesser models below average cost. Panels *a* and *b* in Figure 13.15, for example, show the cost and demand conditions for Chevrolets and Cadillacs, respectively. The marginal cost of producing a Cadillac is only slightly higher than that of producing a Chevrolet. The basic design innovations are available to the company for both cars, and the hardware produced for the Cadillac is only slightly more costly than that used in the Chevrolet. But because the buyers who care most about variety are willing to pay much more for a Cadillac than for a Chevrolet, the company can set sharply different prices for the two models. In an average year, the surplus of total

FIGURE 13.15

Distributing the Cost of Variety

The buyers who care most about variety will generally choose the model with premium features. By pricing its models differently, the seller recovers most of the extra costs of variety from the buyers who are most responsible for their incurrence.

revenue above variable cost for all models (which is the sum of the two shaded rectangles in Figure 13.15) is just about enough to cover the company's research and development and other fixed costs.

Variety is costly, just as the critics claim. But the cost of variety is not distributed evenly among all buyers. In the example above, it was paid by the buyers of Cadillacs, not by the buyers of Chevrolets. By the same token, people who buy the BMW 328i enjoy almost all the important advantages of the extensive BMW research program for about $6,000 less than the people who buy the BMW 330i, which differs from the 328i only in having a slightly more powerful engine. Even by the yardstick used by critics of the market system, this seems a better outcome than the one they urge, which is that all buyers have a standardized "people's car." Under current marketing arrangements, people who don't place high value on variety get to enjoy it at the expense of those who care most about having it. The alternative would be to deny variety to the people who care most about it, without producing real cost savings for the buyers who would be satisfied with a standardized product. Even Volkswagen, which once touted the virtues of a single, standardized model, now offers several dozen versions of its Golf, Jetta, and Passat lines.

Similar pricing strategies affect recovery of the costs of variety in virtually every industry. Consider again the restaurant industry. In a city in which most people have cars, which is to say in virtually every city, the cheapest way to provide restaurant meals would be to have a single restaurant with only one item on the menu. An army of chefs would labor over gigantic cauldrons of peas and mashed potatoes, while others operated huge ovens filled with roasting chickens. But people don't want the same meal every night, any more than they all want the same kind of car. Even in small cities like Ithaca, New York, we have Indian, Mexican, Thai, Chinese, Japanese, Korean, Greek, Italian, French, Cajun, Vietnamese, and Spanish restaurants in addition to the usual domestic fare and fast-food chains.

How are the extra costs of all this variety apportioned? Most restaurants price the different items on their menus in differing multiples of marginal cost. Alcoholic beverages, desserts, and coffee, in particular, are almost always priced at several times marginal cost, whereas the markup on most entrees is much smaller. Most restaurants also offer some sort of daily specials, entrees that are priced very close to marginal cost. The result is that the diner who wants to economize on the cost of eating out, either because he has low income or for whatever other reason, will order only the basic meal, taking before-dinner drinks and dessert and coffee at home (or doing without those extras). Such diners end up paying a price not much more than the marginal cost of being served. Other diners who are willing or able to do so will purchase the more costly option of having the entire package at the restaurant. The diners who pursue the latter strategy are much more likely than others to be the ones who feel strongly about variety (again, because the demand for variety is strongly linked to income). Under current marketing arrangements, they are the ones who end up paying most of its cost. Those who care less about variety are still able to enjoy a lamb vindaloo dinner one night and Szechuan chicken the next; and if they don't order drinks and dessert, they pay little more than they would have to in a standardized soup kitchen.

As a final illustration of how the costs of variety are apportioned in monopolistically competitive markets, consider the case of airline ticket pricing. As discussed earlier, the important dimension of variety here is the timing of flights. Not all travelers have equally pressing demands for frequently scheduled flights. Some are willing to pay substantially extra for a slightly earlier departure time, while others would wait a week rather than pay even $5 more. To the extent that airlines use smaller, more costly (per seat) aircraft in order to offer more frequent flights, it is to accommodate the needs of the former group.

Who pays the added costs of the smaller flights? Virtually every airline employs the hurdle model of differential pricing described in Chapter 11. The particular variant the airlines use offers discounts of approximately 50 percent to passengers who satisfy two restrictions: (1) they must buy their tickets in advance, usually at least 7 days before flight time; and (2) their journey must include a Saturday night. The effect of these two restrictions together is to eliminate most travelers who demand maximum travel flexibility. In particular, business travelers, whose schedules tend to be much tighter than those of vacation travelers, almost always end up paying the regular coach fare under the current marketing system. By contrast, very few vacation travelers fail to qualify for at least some form of discount.

If it is largely the scheduling demands of business travelers that dictate the use of smaller, more costly aircraft, this apportioning of the costs appears not only fair but also efficient. Discount tickets enable airlines to attract passengers who would not fly otherwise, and these passengers make possible the use of larger, less costly aircraft. Business travelers end up getting the frequent service they want, and leisure travelers are not forced to pay the added costs of it.[11]

Historical Note: Hotelling's Hot Dog Vendors

▶ Visit your instructor's Connect© course and access your eBook to view this video.

Why do we often see convenience stores located an adjacent street corners?

In Harold Hotelling's seminal paper on the spatial model of monopolistic competition,[12] he discussed the problem of two hot dog vendors who are free to position themselves wherever they wish along a stretch of beach. Suppose the beach is 1 mile long and bounded at each end by some natural obstacle. Suppose also that the vendors charge the same price, customers are evenly distributed along the beach, and each customer buys one hot dog from the nearest vendor. If the vendors' goal is to sell as many hot dogs as possible, where should they position themselves?

Suppose, as in Figure 13.16, that vendor 1 stands at point A and vendor 2 stands at point B, where both A and B are $\frac{1}{4}$ mile from the midpoint of the beach located at C. In this configuration, all customers to the left of C are closest to vendor 1 and will buy from him, while those to the right of C will buy from vendor 2. Each vendor thus gets half the market. The greatest one-way distance any customer has to travel is $\frac{1}{4}$ mile, and the average one-way distance between customers and their nearest vendor is half that, or $\frac{1}{8}$ mile.

Mathematically inclined readers can verify that A and B are in fact the locations that minimize average travel distance for all consumers. And yet these locations are clearly not optimal from the perspective of either vendor. To see why, suppose vendor 1 were to move 10 steps toward B. The customers to the left of C would continue to find him the closest vendor. But now those customers less than 5 steps to the right of C—people who used to be closest to vendor 2—will suddenly find themselves switching to vendor 1. Moving farther to the right will increase vendor 1's sales still further. Vendor 1 will maximize his sales by positioning himself as close as he can get to vendor 2 on the side of vendor 2 that is closer to the center of the beach.

Vendor 2, of course, can reason in the same fashion, so his strategy will be perfectly symmetric: He will try to get as close to vendor 1 on the side of vendor 1 that is closest to the center. And when both vendors behave in this fashion, the only stable outcome is for each to locate at C, the center of the beach. At C, each gets half of the market, just as he did originally. But the average distance that customers must travel is now $\frac{1}{4}$ mile, twice what it was when the vendors were located at A and B.

FIGURE 13.16

The Hot Dog Vendor Location Problem

Each hot dog vendor does best by positioning himself at the center of the beach, even though that location does not minimize the average distance that their customers must travel.

[11]For a more detailed discussion of this issue, see R. Frank, "When Are Price Differentials Discriminatory?" *Journal of Policy Analysis and Management,* 2, Winter 1983, 238–255.
[12]Harold Hotelling, "Stability in Competition," *The Economic Journal,* 39, 1929, 41–57.

Having both vendors at the middle of the beach is thus not optimal from the vantage point of customers, and yet neither vendor would be better off if he were to move unilaterally. The hot dog vendor location problem is thus not one of those cases in which Adam Smith's invisible hand guides resources so as to produce the greatest good for all.

Which Model Applies?

All these considerations of location and product variety take us back to the farmers' market example that we used to illustrate the idea of perfect competition in Chapter 10. Is it correct to say that farmers use these facilities to locate and compete for "upmarket" consumers who desire luxury food products? Or are consumers, in identifying local production with freshness and quality,[13] essentially granting monopoly status to the limited number of farmers that can qualify as "local"? Our answer must stress that both perfect competition and monopolistic competition are theoretical descriptions of *competition*. In both models the opportunity for economic profits attracts new entrants and creates downward pressure on prices. In both models consumers play a critical role in establishing equilibrium. Whether a given market is more competitive or monopolistic may come down to the rules that govern vendor access and product eligibility.[14]

CONSUMER PREFERENCES AND ADVERTISING

In perfectly competitive markets it would never pay a producer to advertise her product. Being only one of many producers of identical products, the firm that advertised would attract only an insignificant share of any resulting increase in demand. In monopolistically competitive and oligopolistic markets, the incentives are different. Because products are differentiated, producers can often shift their demand curves outward significantly by advertising.

How does advertising affect the efficiency with which markets allocate resources? In the description of the world offered by rational choice theory, producers are essentially agents of consumers. Consumers vote with their purchase dollars, and producers are quick to do their bidding. This description has been called the *traditional sequence,* and the late Harvard economist John Kenneth Galbraith is one of its most prominent critics. In its place, he proposed a *revised sequence* in which the producer, not the consumer, sits in the driver's seat. In Galbraith's scheme, the corporation decides which products are cheapest and most convenient to produce, and then uses advertising and other promotional devices to create demand for them.

Galbraith's revised sequence recasts Adam Smith's invisible hand in an unflattering new light. Smith's story, recall, was that producers motivated only by self-interest would provide the products that best meet consumers' desires. Those who did not would fail to attract customers and go out of business. If Galbraith is correct, however, this story is turned on its head: It is like saying the all-too-visible hand of Madison Avenue guides consumers to serve the interests of large corporations.

Galbraith's revised sequence is not without intuitive appeal. Many people are understandably skeptical, for example, when an economist says that the purpose of advertising is to make consumers better informed. The plain fact, after all, is that this is often anything but its intent. For example, the celebrity milk mustache is surely not part of a process whereby we become more knowledgeable about the nutritional merits of milk consumption.

[13]Economists are prominent among these consumers. Tyler Cowen asked 2019 Nobel laureate Abhijit Banerjee, "Why is the quality of vegetables so much higher in India than anywhere else?" Banerjee's response was that "[P]eople really pull out the vegetables in the morning and bring them to the market . . . [F]reshness is such an enormous part of taste, and also not designing food for durability. In the U.S., tomatoes are designed for durability, and that takes away from other things." https://conversationswithtyler.com/episodes/abhijit-banerjee/.
[14]Note that while many farmers' markets are strictly "producers only," some do allow vendors, upon review and approval, to fill out their offerings with goods purchased directly from remote farmers or even, occasionally, purchased wholesale. The intent is both to assure alternatives are available in all product categories and to extend the periods that specialized vendors can participate in the market. The effect, certainly, is to increase competition.

But for all the obvious hype in advertising messages, the Galbraith view of the process overlooks something fundamental: It is easier to sell a good product than a bad one. All an advertisement can reasonably hope to accomplish is to induce the consumer to *try* the product. If it is one she tries and likes, she will probably buy it repeatedly. She will also recommend it to friends. If it is one she doesn't like, however, the process usually ends there. Even if a firm were to succeed in getting *everyone* to try it once, it still wouldn't be able to maintain a profitable, ongoing venture.

Imagine two alternative products, one that meets real human needs but is costly to produce, and another that meets no real need but is somewhat cheaper. Which of these two types would a profit-hungry producer do best to advertise? Given the importance of repeat business and word-of-mouth endorsements, the first will generally be more attractive, often by a compelling margin. The fact that it costs more to produce will not deter consumers unless its extra benefits do not justify those extra costs.

New products go through extensive market testing before they ever land on the shelves. Millions of dollars are spent analyzing test subjects' reactions to them. In the end, most products that enter this testing process never see the light of day. Only when a firm has concrete evidence that a product is likely to be well received does it dare to commit the millions of dollars required for an intensive national advertising campaign.

Firms that fail to adopt this posture often pay sharp penalties. In 1985, the Lotus software company, for example, spent more than $10 million advertising *Jazz*, its spreadsheet program for the then-new Apple Macintosh, even though it had clear evidence that the program lacked specific features that many users deemed vital. The Lotus ads were incredibly sophisticated, and no doubt succeeded in selling a fair number of programs. And yet *Jazz*'s main rival, Microsoft's *Excel,* a much better product, quickly captured the market with only a small fraction of Lotus's advertising outlays.

Advertising and other efforts to persuade consumers are best viewed as part of a pump-priming process. Given the enormous costs, it usually pays to promote only those products that consumers are likely to want to purchase repeatedly, or to speak well of to their friends. And in fact there is clear evidence that most firms follow precisely this strategy. Frozen-dinner producers advertise their fancy ethnic entrees, not their chicken pot pies. Publishers advertise books that seem likely to become best-sellers, not their titles with more limited appeal. Motion picture studios tout the movies they hope will become blockbusters, not their low-budget films.

Because producers have an incentive to advertise only those products that consumers are most likely to find satisfying, the so-called traditional sequence is more plausible than Galbraith and other critics make it out to be. True enough, where the quality differences between competing goods are small, advertising may have a significant influence on which brand a consumer chooses. But as a first approximation, it still makes sense to assume that consumers have reasonably well-defined notions of what they like, and that producers spend much effort on trying to cater to those notions.

This is not to say, however, that market incentives lead to the amount of advertising that is best from society's point of view. As we saw earlier in this chapter, strategic competition between rivals leads firms to spend excessively on advertising.

SUMMARY

- The characteristic feature of oligopolistic markets is interdependence among firms. Predictions about how oligopolists will behave depend heavily on specific assumptions about the nature of this interdependence. *(LO1)*

- The incentives facing firms who attempt to collude are similar to the ones facing participants in the prisoner's dilemma. The difficulty in holding cartels together is

that the dominant strategy for each member is to cheat on the agreement. Repeated interactions between a very small number of firms can support collusive behavior under circumstances in which strategies like tit-for-tat are effective. *(LO2)*

- There is not always a strong tendency for natural monopoly to emerge from the interaction of a small number of firms, each of which produces under sharply increasing returns to scale. Here the role of sunk costs turns out to be important. It may sometimes be necessary for buyers to take certain initiatives if they are to secure the least costly of the potentially available options. *(LO3)*

- In the Cournot model, each firm takes the *quantities* produced by its rivals as given; in the Bertrand model, by contrast, each firm takes its rivals' *prices* as given. Although the behavioral orientation of firms sounds very much the same in these two cases, the results are strikingly different. The Cournot model yields a slightly lower price and a slightly higher quantity than we would see if the firms colluded to achieve the monopoly outcome. By contrast, the Bertrand model leads to essentially the same outcome we saw under perfect competition. *(LO2)*

- A slightly more sophisticated form of interdependence among firms is assumed in the Stackelberg model, in which one firm plays a leadership role and its rivals merely follow. This model is similar in structure to the Cournot model, except that where the Cournot firms take one another's quantities as given, the Stackelberg leader strategically manipulates the quantity decisions of its rivals. *(LO2)*

- Monopolistic competition is defined by two simple conditions: (1) the existence of numerous firms each producing a product that is a close, but imperfect, substitute for the products of other firms; and (2) free entry and exit of firms. In the spatial model of monopolistic competition, customers have particular locations or product characteristics they most prefer. The result is that firms tend to compete most intensively for the consumers of products most similar to their own. *(LO1, LO4)*

- A central feature of the spatial model of monopolistic competition is the trade-off between the desire for lower cost, on the one hand, and greater variety or locational convenience, on the other. The optimum degree of product diversity depends on several factors. Greater diversity is expected with greater population density and higher transportation costs (where, in the general case, "transportation costs" measure willingness to pay for desired product features). Optimal product diversity is negatively related to the start-up costs of adding new product characteristics or locations. The market metes out a certain rough justice in that the costs of additional variety tend to be borne most heavily by those to whom variety is most important. *(LO5, LO6, LO7)*

KEY TERMS

Bertrand model	Cournot model	reaction function

REVIEW QUESTIONS

1. What is the fundamental difference among the Cournot, Bertrand, and Stackelberg models of oligopoly? *(LO2)*

2. How is the problem of oligopoly collusion similar in structure to the prisoner's dilemma? *(LO2)*

3. What is the difficulty with the tit-for-tat strategy as a possible solution to the oligopoly collusion problem? *(LO2)*

4. Does the equilibrium in the Cournot model satisfy the definition of a Nash equilibrium? *(LO2)*

5. Describe the trade-off between cost and variety. *(LO5)*

6. How is the optimal degree of product variety related to population density? To transportation cost? To the fixed costs of offering new products? *(LO5, LO6)*

PROBLEMS

McGraw Hill connect

1. The market demand curve for mineral water is given by $P = 15 - Q$. If there are two firms that produce mineral water, each with a constant marginal cost of 3 per unit, fill in the entries for each of the four duopoly models indicated in the table. (In the Stackelberg model, assume that firm 1 is the leader.) *(LO2)*

Model	Q_1	Q_2	$Q_1 + Q_2$	P	Π_1	Π_2	$\Pi_1 + \Pi_2$
Shared monopoly							
Cournot							
Bertrand							
Stackelberg							

2. The market demand curve for a pair of Cournot duopolists is given as $P = 36 - 3Q$, where $Q = Q_1 + Q_2$. The constant per unit marginal cost is 18 for each duopolist. Find the Cournot equilibrium price, quantity, and profits. *(LO2)*

3. Solve the preceding problem for Bertrand duopolists. *(LO2)*

4. The market demand curve for a pair of duopolists is given as $P = 36 - 3Q$, where $Q = Q_1 + Q_2$. The constant per unit marginal cost is 18 for each duopolist. Find the equilibrium price, quantity, and profit for each firm, assuming the firms act as a Stackelberg leader and follower, with firm 1 as the leader. *(LO2)*

5. Because of their unique expertise with explosives, the Zambino brothers have long enjoyed a monopoly of the U.S. market for public fireworks displays for crowds above a quarter of a million. The annual demand for these fireworks displays is $P = 140 - Q$. The marginal cost of putting on a fireworks display is 20. A family dispute broke the firm in two. Alfredo Zambino now runs one firm and Luigi Zambino runs the other. They still have the same marginal costs, but now they are Cournot duopolists. How much profit has the family lost? *(LO2)*

6. The state has announced its plans to license two firms to serve a market whose demand curve is given by $P = 100 - Q$. The technology is such that each can produce any given level of output at zero cost, but once each firm's output is chosen, it cannot be altered. *(LO2)*
   a. What is the most you would be willing to pay for one of these licenses if you knew you would be able to choose your level of output first (assuming your choice was observable by the rival firm)?
   b. How much would your rival be willing to pay for the right to choose second?

7.* Firm 1 and firm 2 are competing for a cable television franchise. The present value of the net revenues generated by the franchise is equal to R. Each firm's probability of winning the franchise is given by its proportion of the total spent by the two firms on lobbying the local government committee that awards the franchise. That is, if I_1 and I_2 represent the lobbying expenditures of firms 1 and 2, respectively, then firm 1's probability of winning is given by $I_1/(I_1 + I_2)$, while firm 2's probability of winning is $I_2/(I_1 + I_2)$. If each firm assumes that the other firm's spending is independent of its own, what is the equilibrium level of spending for each firm? *(LO2)*

8. State whether true or false and briefly explain why: If a business owner is delighted to accept additional orders at the current price, he or she cannot have been a profit-maximizing, perfectly competitive producer. *(LO3)*

9. A toll road commission is planning to locate garages for tow trucks along a 100-mile circular highway. Each garage has a fixed cost of $5,000 per day. Towing jobs are equally likely along any point of the highway, and cost per mile towed is $50. If there were 5,000 towing jobs per day, what number of garages would minimize the sum of the fixed costs and towing costs? *(LO3)*

10. The 1,000 residents of Great Donut Island are all fishermen. Every morning they go to the nearest port to launch their fishing boats and then return in the evening with their catch. The residents are evenly distributed along the 10-mile perimeter of the island. Each port has a fixed cost of $1,000/day. If the optimal number of ports is 2, what must be the per mile travel cost? *(LO6)*

ANSWERS TO SELF-TESTS

13.1 *(LO2)*

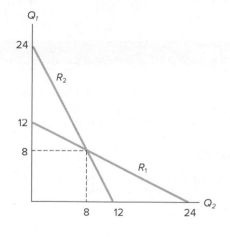

*This problem requires the use of calculus maximization techniques.

13.2 Price will settle at marginal cost, and so $P = 2$. The corresponding market demand, $Q = 8$, will be shared equally by the two firms: $Q_1 = Q_2 = 4$. *(LO2)*

13.3 Firm 2's marginal revenue curve is given by $10 - Q_1 - 2Q_2$. Setting MR = MC = 2, we have firm 2's reaction function, $R_2(Q_1) = Q_2^* = 4 - (Q_1/2)$. Substituting into firm 1's demand function, we get $P_1 = 10 - Q_1 - 4 + (Q_1/2) = 6 - (Q_1/2)$, and the corresponding marginal review curve, $MR_1 = 6 - Q_1$. $MR_1 = MC = 2$ solves for $Q_1^* = 4$. This means that Q_2 will be 2 units, for a total market output of 6 units. The market price will be $10 - 6 = 4$. *(LO3)*

13.4 Each firm initially got $\frac{1}{20} = 5$ percent of total demand, but will now get only $\frac{1}{25} = 4$ percent. This means that at every price, the quantity demanded will be 20 percent lower than before (see the graph below). The new *dd* curve is $P = 10 - 0.00125Q$. *(LO4)*

13.5 With six restaurants the average round-trip distance is $\frac{1}{12}$ mile, which yields an average transportation cost of $2. On average, each restaurant will attract 100/6 people per day, which yields an ATC of [50 + 5(100/6)]/(100/6) = $8/day. Overall average cost with six restaurants is thus $10/day. *(LO6)*

13.6 N^* will now be $\sqrt{[(24)(400)/100]} \approx 9.8$, so there should now be 10 restaurants. *(LO6)*

Labor

During the 1931 season, Yankee slugger Babe Ruth was the highest-paid player in baseball at an annual salary of $85,000. Asked how he felt about earning more than President Herbert Hoover, Ruth responded with characteristic bravado that he deserved it. "I had a much better year than Hoover," he explained.

Productivity differences, however, are not always sufficient to account for pay differences among workers. For example, there is widespread movement of employees between the public and private sectors, and from watching what happens in these moves, we know that highly productive persons almost always earn dramatically less in the public sector. Thus, former Federal Reserve Board Chair Alan Greenspan, who occupied perhaps the most important post in the U.S. government, earned less than a tenth of the salary he used to command on Wall Street.

Why do people accept top positions in government at such a huge sacrifice in pay? By all accounts, the attraction for the high-level bureaucrat is the power and public attention such posts command. Greenspan went on to a consulting firm, again earning many times what he earned in government. But his daily decisions no longer affected the lives of millions. The eager audience for his views and opinions evaporated overnight. Greenspan took the Fed chairmanship, and the sharp reduction in pay that went with it, because the post carried benefits that no other employer could offer. The package, taken as a whole, was attractive to him.

Jobs that provide a high degree of public visibility do not always entail a cut in pay. Major league pitcher Gerrit Cole, who signed with the New York Yankees in the 2019–2020 off season, will (barring injury) be the center of attention every 5 days, in one of the world's most intense media markets, for 6 months a year. Yet, with a guaranteed salary of $36 million a year, Cole hardly seems to have made a real economic sacrifice for this position of prominence. There are plenty of people, including me, who would be willing to do Cole's job for less. Indeed, Cole himself would surely be willing to perform for a subsistence wage rather than work in lifelong obscurity in some anonymous job elsewhere in the private sector.

His lofty salary is the result of two important factors: (1) He can do valuable things that the rest of us can't; and (2) there is more than one employer who can provide Cole with a place in the spotlight. Note that only the first of these factors applied in Alan Greenspan's case. If you want to be Chair of the Board of Governors of the Federal Reserve System of the United States, the U.S. government is the only employer you can work for. If you want to be a Major League Baseball player, however, 30 different teams can bid for your services. In Cole's case, if the Yankees didn't pay him such a high salary, some other team gladly would. Thousands of extra fans are drawn to the ballpark by the prospect of seeing perhaps the best all-around player in the game. The Yankees management knows it could hire me for much less than it pays Cole. But they are smart enough also to know that, even for free, I would be a bad bargain.

CHAPTER PREVIEW

Our goal in this chapter is to examine the economic forces that govern wages and other conditions of employment. Relatively simple models of the labor market shed light on a variety of interesting questions, such as: How much will a worker with a given set of skills earn? Why do working conditions differ from one occupation to another? What do unions do? And so on.

We'll begin by deriving the demand curve for labor in both the short run and the long run. We'll then approach the supply side of the labor market from the standpoint of an individual worker trying to decide how much to work at a given wage rate.

Our next step will be to take up the issue of compensating wage differentials, differences in wage payments that reflect differences in the environments in which people work. The general result is that the attractiveness of the overall compensation package—wages and environmental factors taken as a whole—tends to equalize across jobs that employ workers of a given skill level. As a further illustration of the concept of compensating differentials, we will then examine the question of safety levels in the workplace.

We'll also apply the economic theory of labor markets to such topics as discrimination and minimum wage laws. We'll conclude, finally, by looking at why differences in pay sometimes seem to overstate differences in productivity while at other times seeming to understate them.

THE PERFECTLY COMPETITIVE FIRM'S DEMAND FOR LABOR

Short-Run Demand

Consider a firm that produces output by the use of two inputs, capital (K) and labor (L). Suppose that in the short run, its capital stock is fixed. If this firm sells all its output in a perfectly competitive market at the going market price, and if it can hire any quantity of labor it wishes at a wage rate of $12/hr, how many units of labor should it hire?

If the manager of the firm is thinking like an economist, she will reason as follows: "The benefit of hiring an extra unit of labor will be the amount for which I can sell the extra output I will get. The cost will be the wage rate. Thus I should hire an extra unit of labor as long as the former exceeds the latter. If the latter exceeds the former, however, I should reduce the amount of labor I hire."

This reasoning is easily translated into a simple graphical hiring rule. Figure 14.1*a* shows the marginal product curve for the labor input when capital is fixed (see Chapter 8). The marginal product curve, recall, tells how much extra output the firm will get when it hires an extra unit of labor. For example, when there are 40 units of labor employed, hiring an extra unit will yield 8 units of output. The downward slope of the marginal product curve reflects the law of diminishing returns.

value of marginal product (VMP) the value, at current market price, of the extra output produced by an additional unit of input.

Figure 14.1*b* simply multiplies the marginal product curve by the price of output, here $P = \$2$. The product of output price and marginal product, $P \times \text{MP}_L$, is called the **value of the marginal product of labor**—denoted **VMP$_L$**, which is the extra revenue

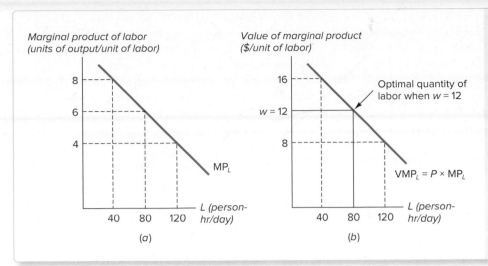

FIGURE 14.1

The Competitive Firm's Short-Run Demand for Labor

When the wage rate is $12/unit of labor (panel *b*), the perfectly competitive firm will hire 80 units of labor, the amount for which VMP_L and the wage rate are the same.

the firm will get by selling the extra output produced by the extra unit of labor. *The hiring rule for the firm is to choose that amount of labor for which the wage rate is equal to the VMP_L.* In Figure 14.1*b*, the rule thus tells the firm it should hire 80 units of labor when the wage rate is $12.

To illustrate the logic of the rule, suppose that the firm had instead hired only 40 units of labor. At that level of employment, the value of extra output produced by an extra worker ($16) is greater than the cost of hiring the worker ($12), and so the firm can increase its profit by hiring more workers. Alternatively, suppose that the firm had hired 120 units of labor. VMP_L at $L = 120$ is only $8, which is less than the wage rate of $12, and so the firm can increase its profit by discharging workers. Only at $L = 80$ will the firm be unable to take additional steps to increase its profit.[1] Figure 14.1*a* is drawn for $MP_L = 10 - \left(\frac{1}{20}\right)L$. When $P = 2$, the value of the marginal product of labor, depicted in Figure 14.1*b*, is

$$VMP_L = P(MP_L) = 2(10 - \tfrac{1}{20}L) = 20 - \tfrac{1}{10}L.$$

If the wage is $w = 12$, then the quantity of labor demanded by the firm will be

$$w = VMP_L \Rightarrow 12 = 20 - \tfrac{1}{10}L \Rightarrow 8 = \tfrac{1}{10}L \Rightarrow L^* = 80.$$

SELF-TEST 14.1

At a wage rate of $12/unit of labor, how many units of labor would the firm shown in Figure 14.1 hire if its product sold not for $2/unit but for $3/unit?

Long-Run Demand for Labor

In the short run, the only way for the firm to respond to a reduction in the wage rate is to hire more labor. In the long run, however, all inputs are variable. As we saw in Chapter 8, a reduction in the price of labor will cause the firm to substitute labor for capital, reducing its marginal cost still further. This additional cost reduction will cause an even greater expansion of output than before. It follows that the firm's long-run hiring response to a

---

[1]There is one important limitation to the application of the $w = VMP_L$ rule. Suppose the wage rate were above the value of the average product of labor, which is the product of price and the average product of labor, denoted VAP_L. If the firm pays a wage higher than VAP_L, it will be paying out more than the total value of what workers produce, which means that it will earn a loss on each worker it hires. For values of w above VAP_L then, the perfectly competitive firm will demand no labor at all.

FIGURE 14.2

Short- and Long-Run Demand Curves for Labor

The demand for labor is more elastic in the long run because the firm has the opportunity to substitute labor for capital. In the short run, its only avenue of response is to increase output.

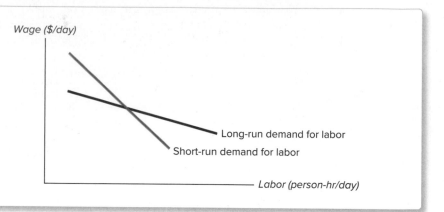

change in the wage rate will be larger than its short-run response. The relationship between the two labor demand curves is portrayed in Figure 14.2.

The firm's demand for labor will also tend to be more elastic the more elastic the demand is for its product. If a price reduction stimulates a large increase in the quantity of the product demanded, it will also stimulate a large increase in the amount of labor required to produce it. Finally, the firm's demand for labor will tend to be more elastic the more it is able to substitute the services of labor for those of other inputs. Other things equal, the firm with L-shaped isoquants will have the least elastic demand curve for labor.

The Market Demand Curve for Labor

Recall from Chapter 5 that the technique for deriving a market demand curve for a product is to add the individual consumer demand curves horizontally. The technique for generating the market demand curve for labor is similar except for one important difference. In Figure 14.3, the curve labeled $\Sigma VMP_L, P = P_1$ is the horizontal summation of the individual VMP_L curves when the output price is equal to P_1. At that value of the price of output, firms taken as a whole demand L_1 units of labor per time period when the wage rate is equal to w_1. Now let the wage rate fall to w_2. Each firm will hire more labor, in the process moving downward along its own individual demand curve for labor. As each firm responds in this way, it offers more of its product for sale in the market. Such action by any one firm in a competitive market would leave the price of output unchanged. But the effect of all firms acting in concert is to produce a downward movement along the industry product demand curve.

FIGURE 14.3

The Market Demand Curve for Labor

When the wage rate falls from w_1 to w_2, each firm hires more labor and produces more output. The increase in output causes output price to fall, which reduces the value of labor's marginal product. The market demand curve for labor is thus more steep than the horizontal summation of the individual demand curves.

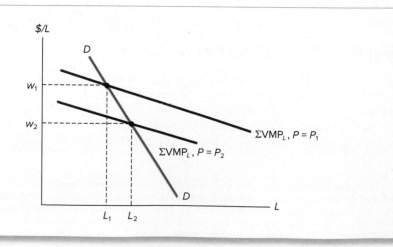

This increase in output will necessarily involve a reduction in output price. And in turn this will cause the VMP_L curve for each firm to shift downward. If output price falls from P_1 to P_2, the aggregate demand for labor will be given by the point that corresponds to w_2 on the curve labeled ΣVMP_L, $P = P_2$. By this reasoning, we see that the market demand curve for labor (the curve labeled DD) will be steeper than the horizontal summation of the VMP_L curves.

The preceding discussion implicitly assumed that there is only one type of labor and that all of it is employed by a single competitive industry. In the real world, of course, matters are more complicated. There are almost countless categories of labor—carpenters, electricians, physicists, attorneys, high school teachers, and so on—and any one type finds employment in many different industries. Thus, electricians are employed in the residential construction, automobile, commercial office building, steel, computer, and fishing industries, to name but a small sample. The market demand curve for electricians is therefore made up of the individual demands of firms in not just one industry but many.

Suppose the payments to electricians by firms in each separate industry constitute only a small fraction—say, 0.1 percent—of their respective total costs. A small change—say, 10 percent—in the wage paid to electricians would then produce an all but imperceptible change—namely, 0.01 percent—in each industry's total costs, and hence no appreciable effect on their respective output prices. Under these circumstances, the demand for electricians will be closely approximated by the horizontal summation of the various individual firm demand curves, and the complication discussed in connection with Figure 14.3 may be ignored.

AN IMPERFECT COMPETITOR'S DEMAND FOR LABOR

Our discussion of the demand for labor has assumed that the firm faces a perfectly elastic demand for its product. Any additional output produced by additional workers could be sold at the same price as existing output. With an imperfect competitor, of course, this will not be so. Such firms face downward-sloping demand curves, and if they hire additional workers, they must cut their prices in order to sell the additional output.

We saw that with a perfect competitor, the value of the extra output obtained by hiring an extra worker is the product of price and the marginal product of labor. With an imperfect competitor, by contrast, it is the product of marginal revenue and marginal product. This product is called the **marginal revenue product of labor,** and is denoted $\mathbf{MRP_L}$. In terms of the definitions of marginal revenue and marginal product, MRP_L is thus given by

marginal revenue product (MRP) the amount by which total revenue increases with the employment of an additional unit of input.

$$MRP_L = \frac{\Delta Q}{\Delta L}\frac{\Delta TR}{\Delta Q}, \tag{14.1}$$

which reduces to

$$MRP_L = \frac{\Delta TR}{\Delta L}. \tag{14.2}$$

VMP_L and MRP_L are alike in that each represents the addition to total revenue that results from the addition of a unit of labor. The difference between them is that the MRP_L takes into account that the sale of additional output requires a cut in price for the imperfect competitor. VMP_L values the extra output at the existing product price, which is unaffected by variations in the perfect competitor's output. MRP_L values the additional output at its marginal revenue, which is less than its price.

How much labor will a firm hire if it faces a downward-sloping demand curve for its output? The answer is that it will hire that quantity for which the wage rate and MRP_L are equal. The argument for this claim is essentially similar to the one offered for the $w = VMP_L$ condition for the perfect competitor.

In the case of the perfectly competitive firm, the short-run demand for labor is downward sloping because of the law of diminishing returns. The more labor the firm hires, the lower the MP_L will be and hence the lower the VMP_L will be. For the monopolist, too, the law of diminishing returns causes the short-run demand curve for labor to be downward sloping. But there is an additional reason in the case of the monopolist, which is that its marginal revenue curve is also downward sloping.

For the same reasons discussed in the perfectly competitive case, the monopolist's long-run demand for labor will be more elastic than his short-run demand. But we need not make any additional adjustments to the MRP_L curve when moving from the firm to the industry demand curve, in either the long run or the short run. The monopolist's demand for labor *is* the industry demand for labor. It already takes account of the fact that extra output means a lower product price.

THE SUPPLY OF LABOR

For simplicity, let's again imagine that there is only one category of labor and that the choice confronting each worker is how many hours to work each day. The alternative to working is to spend time in "leisure activities," which here include play, sleep, eating, and any other activity besides paid work in the labor market. If the worker is paid at a constant rate of $10 for each hour she works, how many hours should she work?

On reflection, this turns out to be a simple consumer choice problem of the same sort we took up in Chapter 3. The choice in this context is between two goods we may call "income" and "leisure." As in the standard consumer choice problem, the individual is assumed to have preferences over the two goods that can be summarized in the form of an indifference map. In Figure 14.4, the curves labeled I_1, I_2, and I_3 represent three such curves for a hypothetical worker.

The line labeled B in the same diagram represents the individual's budget constraint. If she spent the entire day in leisure activities, she would earn no income, which says that the point $(24, 0)$ must be the horizontal intercept of B. Alternatively, if she worked 24 hr/day at the wage rate of $w_0 = \$10/hr$, her daily income would be $24w_0 = \$240$, which tells us that the point $(0, 240)$ must be the vertical intercept of B. The remainder of B is the straight line that joins these two points. Its equation is $M = w(24 - h) = 10(24 - h) = 240 - 10h$, where M is daily income in dollars. The slope of B is simply the negative of the hourly wage rate, $-w_0 = -10$.

Given her preferences and budget constraint, the best this hypothetical consumer can do is point A in Figure 14.4, the tangency between B and the indifference curve

FIGURE 14.4

The Optimal Choice of Leisure and Income

The optimal amount of leisure is $h^* = 15$ hr/day, which corresponds to a point of tangency between the budget constraint (B) and the indifference curve I_2. The corresponding amount of paid labor is $24 - h^* = 9$ hr/day, which yields a daily wage income of $(24 - h^*)w_0 = \$90/day$.

I_2. Here, the optimal bundle corresponds to spending $h^* = 15$ hr/day in leisure, the remaining $24 - h^* = 9$ hr in paid work. The consumer's daily income in dollars will be $(24 - h^*)w_0 = 90$. At A, the marginal rate of substitution between leisure and income is exactly w_0, the hourly wage rate. This means that at the optimal bundle, the marginal value of an extra hour of leisure is exactly equal to the opportunity cost of acquiring it—namely, the $10 the consumer would have earned had she worked that extra hour.

SELF-TEST 14.2

Suppose the wage is $w = \$20$/hr. Find the equation for the income/leisure budget constraint and graph it. Suppose that, facing this wage, an individual chooses $h = 14$ hr of leisure. Find the worker's income M per day for this amount of leisure.

To generate a worker's supply curve of labor, we simply ask how the optimal amount of paid work varies as the wage rate varies. Figure 14.5 looks at the optimal leisure choices for three different hourly wage rates, $w = \$4$, $w = \$10$, and $w = \$14$. The supply of labor corresponding to $w = \$4$ is $24 - h_1^* = 6$ hr; to $w = \$10$, $24 - h_2^* = 9$ hr; and to $w = \$14$, $24 - h_3^* = 7$ hr.

Figure 14.6 plots the relationship between the wage rate and the hours of work supplied by the hypothetical worker whose indifference map is shown in Figure 14.5. Calling this person the ith worker of many, we see that her supply curve is the line denoted S_i. When compared with the other supply curves we have encountered, the salient feature of S_i is that it is not everywhere upward sloping.[2] In particular, it is "backward bending" for values of w larger than 10/hr, which is another way of saying that, in that region, higher wages lead to fewer hours of work supplied.

Colonialists who employed unskilled labor in less developed countries once thought it a sign of backwardness that their employees worked fewer hours whenever their wages rose. But as the following example makes clear, such behavior is consistent with the rational pursuit of a perfectly coherent objective.

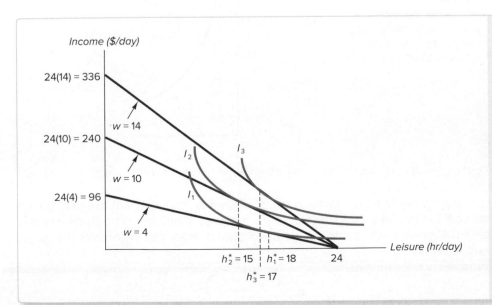

FIGURE 14.5

Optimal Leisure Choices for Different Wage Rates

When the hourly wage rises from $4 to $10, the optimal amount of leisure falls from 18 to 15 hr/day. But when the wage rises still further to $14, the optimal amount of leisure rises to 17 hr/day.

---

[2]Recall from Chapter 5 that we saw a similar supply curve in the case of savings.

FIGURE 14.6

The Labor Supply Curve for the *i*th Worker

For this worker, an increase in the wage elicits greater labor supply when the wage is less than $10/hr, but smaller labor supply when the wage is above $10/hr.

EXAMPLE 14.1   Labor Supply Curve

Annika wants to earn $200/day because with that amount she can live comfortably and meet all her financial obligations. Graph Annika's labor supply curve.

If L^S denotes the number of hours per day Annika chooses to work, it must satisfy $wL^S = 200$, where w is Annika's hourly wage rate in dollars. Annika's supply curve will thus be given by $L^S = 200/w$, which is shown in Figure 14.7.

FIGURE 14.7

The Labor Supply Curve for a Worker Seeking a Target Level of Income

The higher her hourly wage rate, the fewer hours Annika has to work to earn her daily target of $200.

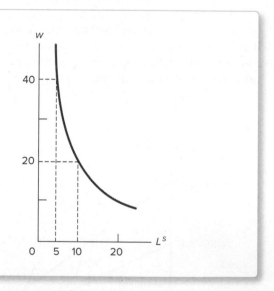

Attempting to earn a target level of income is obviously not the only goal a rational person might pursue. But there is certainly nothing retrograde about it either. A person who holds this goal will always work less whenever the wage rate rises.

SELF-TEST 14.3

Draw the labor supply curve for a person with a daily target income of $120.

Economic Naturalist 14.1

Why is it so hard to find a taxi on rainy days?

It was a long-standing observation in New York, Chicago, and other large U.S. cities that it was as hard to find a taxi on rainy days as it was easy in bright sunshine. Perhaps the most obvious reason is that many people who would be willing to walk short distances during good weather prefer to take a cab when it rains. But why don't more taxis appear to meet the lucrative additional demand? Several studies[3] have produced answers that conform—or not—with the "target income" theory we outlined in Example 14.1.

In 1997, economists Linda Babcock, Colin Camerer, George Loewenstein, and Richard Thaler concluded that many drivers work only as long as necessary to reach a target level of income each day. On sunny days, it took drivers much longer to reach their target income level because they spent much of their day waiting in cab stands or cruising for passengers. They reached the same target more quickly on high-demand rainy days—and went home early.

Not so fast (almost literally), countered Princeton economist Henry Farber in 2015. After analyzing an enormous database of New York City trip records, Farber concluded

Why do many taxis disappear when it starts raining?

that taxi drivers did not earn more per hour when it rains. The reason is that bad weather creates traffic congestion; the increased taxi utilization was offset by the increased time required per trip. Overall, drivers seemed to target working hours as much dollars, and if drivers worked slightly fewer hours on rainy days, this was likely due to deep unpleasantness of urban driving under such conditions.

But many readers of this text, we suspect, will spend their lives without hailing a traditional taxi. Has the rise of Uber and Lyft made rides more available on urban rainy days? To a degree, it appears, the answer is yes. Also looking at New York City data, Abel Brodeur and Kerry Nield of the University of Ottawa noted that while taxi rides increased about 5 percent in rainy hours, Uber rides increased over 18 percent. Uber's "dynamic pricing," which pays drivers more for working high-demand hours, mazy explain the difference. Although competition from Uber and similar firms has significantly reduced overall taxi utilization in New York City, Brodeur and Nield estimate that the combined presence of Uber, Lyft, and traditional taxi services has served to reduce the wait times on rainy days.

SELF-TEST 14.4

Suppose that a cab driver does target earnings, but for each week rather than each day. The driver also prefers to drive no more hours than necessary to reach his target, and in his city it always rains two days each week. How would this driver's hours driven on rainy days compare with his hours driven on sunny days?

[3]L. Babcock, C. Camerer, G. Loewenstein, and R. Thaler, "Labor Supply of New York City Cab Drivers: One Day at a Time," *Quarterly Journal of Economics*, 111, 1997, 408–441; Henry S. Farber, "Why You Can't Find a Taxi in the Rain and Other Labor Supply Lessons from Cab Drivers," *Quarterly Journal of Economics* 130, 2015, 1975–2026, cited in Annie Lowrey, "Why You Can't Get a Taxi When It's Raining," *New York Magazine*, November 11, 2014, http://nymag.com/intelligencer/2014/11/why-you-cant-get-a-taxi-when-its-raining.html; Abel Brodeur and Kerry Nield, "Has Uber Made It Easier to Get a Ride in the Rain," University of Ottawa Working Paper 1708, 2017, https://socialsciences.uottawa.ca/economics/sites/socialsciences.uottawa.ca.economics/files/working_paper_1708e.pdf.

Not all individuals exhibit backward-bending supply curves. An increase in the wage has both an income and a substitution effect on the quantity of leisure demanded. By making leisure more expensive, a wage increase leads people to consume less of it, and hence to work more—the substitution effect. But an increase in the wage also gives people more real purchasing power and, on the plausible assumption that leisure is a normal good, causes them to demand more of it—the income effect. If the income effect dominates the substitution effect over some range of wage rates, we see a backward-bending labor supply curve over that range. Otherwise, the labor supply curve will be everywhere upward sloping.

EXAMPLE 14.2   Leisure Demand

Find the optimal leisure demand for wage $w = \$20$/hr for someone who views income and leisure as perfect complements in a 10-1 ratio (who requires 1 hr of leisure for every $10 of income).

The income/leisure budget constraint is

$$M = w(24 - h) = 20(24 - h) = 480 - 20h.$$

Since the individual requires 1 hr of leisure for every $10 of income, the consumption point must lie on the line $M = 10h$. The intersection of the budget constraint and this consumption line (see Figure 14.8) yields the leisure demand:

$$480 - 20h = 10h \Rightarrow 480 = 30h \Rightarrow h = 16 \text{ hr/day.}$$

FIGURE 14.8

When Leisure and Income Are Perfect Complements

If income and leisure are perfect complements in a 10-1 ratio, an individual will consume leisure at a point on the budget constraint that satisfies $M = 10h$.

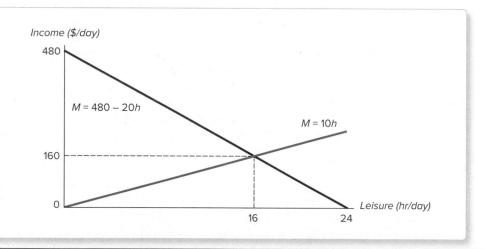

SELF-TEST 14.5

Find the optimal leisure demand for wage $w = \$20$/hr for someone who views income and leisure as perfect substitutes in a 10-1 ratio (willing to sacrifice 1 hr of leisure for $10 of income). *Hint:* This person's indifference curves are straight lines with the equation $M = a - 10h$ for various values of a.

For many people, the wage rate varies with the number of hours they work, as in the case of a higher wage for overtime. People who have the opportunity to earn premium pay by working overtime face a kinked budget constraint as illustrated in Self-Test 14.6.

Often we can judge whether a change in income possibilities leaves people better off or worse off without detailed information about their preferences. Knowing their two budget constraints, before and after, and their initial choice of leisure can suffice. If the initial choice of leisure lies on the new budget constraint but the wage at that point has changed, the individual must be better off. The individual can be no worse off since she can still afford the same leisure and income. Now, the worker can adjust leisure choice (more leisure if her wage fell, less leisure if her wage rose) to reach a higher indifference curve. This line of reasoning will help you work through Self-Test 14.6.

> ## SELF-TEST 14.6
>
> Mayra can work as many hours as she chooses. In her current job, Mayra is paid $5/hr for the first 8 hours she works and $20 for each hour over 8. Faced with this payment schedule, Mayra chooses to work 12 hours a day. If Mayra is offered a new job that pays $10 for every hour she works, will she take the new job? Explain.

For the U.S. labor market taken as a whole, there has been a steady tendency for the average workweek to decline over time, while at the same time real wages have been rising. Manufacturing production workers, for example, worked 20 percent fewer hours in 1980 than in 1914, even though their real wage was more than four times as high in 1980 as in 1914. This negative correlation between wage rates and average hours naturally does not establish that rising wages are the sole cause of shorter workweeks. But given our theory of individual labor supply, it seems plausible to suppose that they have played a role. This interpretation is reinforced by the observation that a modest decline in manufacturing wages since 1985 has been accompanied by a small increase in average weekly hours.

The theory of labor supply played a crucial role in the "welfare reform" debates of the 1990s, just as it does in current discussions around poverty and income equality that weigh proposed remedies such as a universal basic income (UBI), a jobs guarantee, and an increased minimum wage. The question that is always raised around "welfare" programs is whether they will weaken incentives to work. While many studies have explored—often with contrary results—the effects of specific programs, standard theory suggests that lump-sum transfers are more likely to reduce labor supply than wage subsidies because transfers invoke a greater income effect relative to the substitution effect in labor supply.

> ## SELF-TEST 14.7
>
> Consider the following two antipoverty programs: a payment of $24/day or a payment of 40 percent of wage income. Assume that persons who qualify for the first program also are able to find work at $5/hour. Show how each program would affect the budget constraint of a representative participant. Which program would be most likely to reduce the number of hours worked?

Is Leisure a Giffen Good?

In the standard consumer choice problem considered in Chapter 3, we saw that the individual demand curve for a product is downward sloping except in the anomalous case of the Giffen good. Here we have seen that the supply curve of labor can be backward bending, which is just another way of saying that the demand curve for leisure can be upward sloping. Does this mean that in such cases leisure is a Giffen good?

The answer is no. Recall that a Giffen good is typically a strongly inferior good for which there are attractive but higher-priced substitutes. For such a good, if we hold money income constant and increase price, the quantity demanded increases, because the income effect outweighs the substitution effect. In the case of leisure, by contrast, an increase in the wage rate constitutes not just an increase in the price (or opportunity cost) of leisure, but also an increase in money income (for any given number of hours worked). As with any other good, the substitution effect of a higher relative price of leisure is to reduce the quantity of leisure demanded. But if leisure is a normal good, the added income increases the demand for leisure. The labor supply curve can be backward bending only when the income effect of the wage increase outweighs the substitution effect. So if leisure is an inferior good, the labor supply curve can never be backward bending. If the labor supply curve *is* backward bending, then leisure cannot be an inferior good. And since only inferior goods can be Giffen goods, leisure cannot be a Giffen good.

The Noneconomist's Reaction to the Labor Supply Model

Seeing the economic model of labor supply for the first time, many noneconomists consider it a most unrealistic description of the way people actually allocate their time between labor and leisure. Most jobs, after all, offer little choice in the number of hours to work each day. One can of course choose between part-time and full-time work, but the jobs in the part-time category are often so unattractive that many workers view this as a choice not even worth considering.

In part, such criticism of the labor supply model is based on too narrow an understanding of it. The model does not say that people literally choose the number of hours they work each day. Critics are correct that this is simply not a choice open to most workers. But over the span of several months or years, people have considerably more say over the amount of time spent at work. Law school graduates, for example, can go to work for fast-track law firms where associates routinely put in 14-hour days 7 days a week; or they can choose firms where everyone is out by 5 PM. People can choose jobs, such as teaching, that offer summers off. They can moonlight. And they can change jobs frequently, taking time off in between.

Even allowing for all these possible sources of flexibility, however, it is still fair to say that the options for most people are limited. If firms could offer complete flexibility with no loss in productivity, it would be to their advantage to do so. But most firms hire groups of workers who must interact, and things begin to break down if people are not all on the premises during the same hours of the day. This still leaves the possibility of different firms having workdays of different lengths, which, as noted, we do see to some extent. But even here there are often limits. If the workers in one firm need to interact with those in other firms, even if only to exchange information over the telephone, there has to be a common span of time when people are reliably at their desks.

So for many people the amount of time spent at work is probably more a result of the constraints imposed by employers than of any deliberate choices of their own. The need for coworker interaction explains the existence of a common workweek, but not why that workweek is 40 hours long instead of 30. This is the question that the economic model of labor supply really helps us to answer. The model says that the workweek is 40 hours long because, on the average, that's how long workers want it to be. If most people found an extra hour of leisure much more valuable than an extra hour's wage, profit-seeking employers would have an immediate incentive to reduce the length of the workweek. Here again we see the power of a simple theory to help explain what people do, even when they themselves correctly perceive that the proximate reasons for their actions are forces beyond their control.

THE MARKET SUPPLY CURVE

The market supply curve for any given category of labor is obtained by horizontally adding the individual supply curves for the potential suppliers of labor in that category. Even though many individuals may have backward-bending supply curves—indeed, even though the nation as a whole may have a backward-bending supply curve—the supply curve for any particular category of labor is nonetheless almost certain to be upward sloping. The reason is that wage increases in one category of labor not only change the number of hours worked by people already in that category, but also lure people into that category from other categories. Just as an increase in the price of soybeans causes many cotton farmers to switch to soybeans, an increase in the wages of hair stylists causes file clerks, department store salespersons, and others to try their hand at cutting hair.

EXAMPLE 14.3   Market Supply

Rising enrollments in MBA programs have increased the demand for economics faculty in business schools. If most economists are currently teaching in liberal arts schools, how will this increase in business school demands affect salaries and employment of economists in the two environments?

The right panel in Figure 14.9 shows the market supply curve of economists as the line labeled S. It is upward sloping on the assumption that higher wage rates for economists will induce some people to choose economics over other professions. The demand curve for economists by liberal arts colleges is shown in the left panel. In the center panel, the original and new demand curves for economists by business schools are labeled D_{B1} and D_{B2}, respectively. Adding the liberal arts and business school demand curves horizontally (on the assumption that the salaries paid to economists are too small a share of total university costs to affect tuition significantly), we get both the original and new total demand curve for economists in the right panel, labeled $D_A + D_{B1}$ and $D_A + D_{B2}$, respectively.

Note that the increased demand by business schools causes the wage rate for economists in both environments to rise from w_1 to w_2. To see how employment in the two environments is affected, we simply trace w_2 leftward to the respective demand curves. The increase in business school employment of economists is $Q_{B2} - Q_{B1}$, while the reduction in liberal arts employment is $Q_{A1} - Q_{A2}$. The gain in business school employment will be equal to the sum of the movements out of liberal arts positions ($Q_{A1} - Q_{A2}$) and the overall movement into the economics profession from the outside ($Q_2 - Q_1$).

This example illustrates two points of particular interest. First is the tendency of salaries for workers in a given occupation to equalize across sectors of the economy that employ that occupation. If the demand for carpenters goes up because of a boom in commercial construction projects, the homeowner who wants to add a

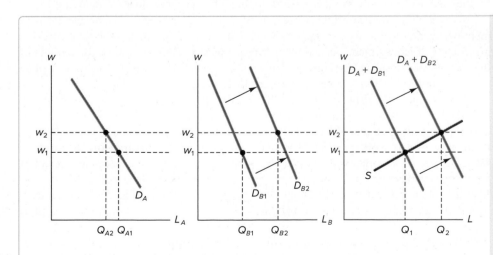

FIGURE 14.9

An Increase in Demand by One Category of Employer

The demand for economists to teach in business schools rises (center panel), causing the total market demand curve for economists to rise (right panel). Employment at the new higher wage is determined by consulting the respective demand curves of the liberal arts sector (left panel) and business school sector (center panel).

recreation room in her basement soon finds herself paying more as well. The idea here is simple: Unless the wages of carpenters employed in residential construction also rose, many of them would leave that sector for commercial construction. Provided that work in the two environments is in other respects equally desirable, the only stable outcome is for the wage to be the same in each.

The second point suggested by the example is that a small occupational subsector can experience a large proportional rise in demand without appreciably bidding up wages throughout the occupation. Because business schools employed only a small fraction of the total number of academic economists to begin with, these schools could increase their employment substantially without having to pay dramatically higher wages. The general rule is that the effective elasticity of supply to any small occupational subsector will be much higher than to the occupational market taken as a whole.

As a strictly empirical matter, economists who teach in business schools earn about 20 percent higher salaries than those who teach in liberal arts colleges. This is a large enough difference to suggest that something must be missing from our theory that calls for equal wages in each sector. It is not sufficient merely to observe that business schools are "richer" and therefore can afford to pay more. The question is why they should have to pay more if the economist's only other alternative is to work at a liberal arts salary.

The implicit assumption in our model most likely to be invalid is that economists regard the two working environments as being equally attractive. For reasons we will explore later in the chapter, it seems to be necessary to pay economists a premium to induce them to move from a liberal arts to a business school environment.

MONOPSONY

The classic illustration of a single-employer labor market is the so-called company town. Workers either cannot or will not leave the area, and new firms cannot enter. A firm in this position is called a *monopsonist*—for "sole buyer"—in its labor market. Does it follow that a monopsonist will exploit its workers by paying them too little and offering them too little safety?

Let's consider first the question of wages. A firm that hires labor in a perfectly competitive labor market faces a supply curve of labor that is a horizontal line at the market wage. Its own hiring decisions have essentially no effect on the market wage. For the monopsonist, by contrast, the labor supply curve is the market supply curve itself. Suppose, for the sake of discussion, that it is upward sloping, like the curve labeled *S* in Figure 14.10. *S* is also called the **average factor cost,** or **AFC,** curve, because it tells the average payment per worker necessary to achieve any given level of employment. The total cost of a given level of employment—called **total factor cost,** or **TFC**—is simply the product of that employment level and the corresponding value of AFC. Thus, the total factor cost of an employment level of 100 workers/hr in Figure 14.10 is equal to $100 \times \$4 = \$400$/hr.

Now suppose the firm already has 100 workers and is considering the cost of adding the 101st. To increase its employment by 1 unit, it must raise its wage by $0.04/hr, not only for the additional unit of labor it hires, but for the current 100 units as well. The total factor cost of 101 workers is $\$4.04 \times 101 = \$408.04$. The **marginal factor cost,** or **MFC,** of the 101st worker is the amount by which total factor cost changes as a result of hiring that worker:

$$MFC = \frac{\Delta TFC}{\Delta L}.$$ (14.3)

For the example given in Figure 14.10, we thus have MFC = $408.04 − $400 = $8.04/hr. The MFC of the 101st worker is the sum of the $4.04/hr she is paid directly and the

average factor cost (AFC) another name for the supply curve for an input.

total factor cost (TFC) the product of the employment level of an input and its average factor cost.

marginal factor cost (MFC) the amount by which total factor cost changes with the employment of an additional unit of input.

FIGURE 14.10

Average and Marginal Factor Cost

When the supply curve (S) facing a monopsonist is upward sloping, the cost of hiring an additional unit of labor (MFC) is no longer merely the wage she must be paid. To that wage must be added the additional payment that must be made to existing workers (shaded rectangle).

extra \$4/hr that must be divided among the existing 100 workers. Because hiring an extra worker always means paying more to existing workers, the MFC curve will always lie above the corresponding AFC curve. If the AFC curve is a straight line with the formula $AFC = a + bL$, then the corresponding MFC curve will be a straight line with the same intercept and twice the slope as the AFC curve: $MFC = a + 2bL$ (see footnote 4).

Figure 14.11 describes the equilibrium wage and employment levels for a monopsonist. A monopsonist's demand curve for labor is constructed the same way as any firm's. If it is a perfect competitor in its product market, its demand for labor will be VMP_L. If its product demand curve is downward sloping, its demand for labor will be MRP_L. Given its demand curve, its optimal level of employment is the level for which MFC and the demand for labor intersect, L^* in Figure 14.11. At that level of employment, it must pay a wage given by the value on its supply curve, namely, w^*.

The argument that L^* is the profit-maximizing level of employment takes much the same form as the one we saw in the other labor market structures. The demand curve for

FIGURE 14.11

The Profit-Maximizing Wage and Employment Levels for a Monopsonist

At L^*, the cost of expanding or contracting employment is exactly equal to the benefit. Both exceed the profit-maximizing wage of w^*.

---

[4]In calculus terms, MFC is defined as

$$MFC = \frac{d(TFC)}{dL}.$$

Thus, if $AFC = a + bL$, then $TFC = AFC \times L = aL + bL^2$, which yields $MFC = a + 2bL$.

labor, recall, represents the increase in the firm's total revenue that results from hiring an additional unit of labor, while the MFC curve represents the corresponding addition to its total costs. To the left of L^*, the former exceeds the latter, so the firm's profit will rise if it expands employment. To the right, the latter exceeds the former, so it will do better if it contracts.

SELF-TEST 14.8

A monopsonist's demand for labor is given by $w = 12 - L$. If her AFC curve is given by $w = 2 + 2L$, with corresponding MFC $= 2 + 4L$, what wage rate will she offer and how much labor will she hire?

How do the wage and employment levels under monopsony compare with those in competitive labor markets? If the same overall demand were the result of hiring by not one but many firms, the level of employment would rise to L^{**}, the point at which demand intersects the supply curve in Figure 14.12. The wage rate, too, would rise, from w^* to w^{**}.

In comparison with this competitive norm, the monopsony equilibrium is inefficient in much the same sense that the monopoly equilibrium in the product market is inefficient—it does not exhaust all potential gains from trade. Note in Figure 14.12 that when the employment level is L^*, workers would be willing to supply an additional hour of labor for a payment of only w^*, whereas the extra revenue that would be produced by that extra unit is MFC*. If the firm could somehow increase total employment by 1 unit without paying its existing workers more, both it and the extra worker would be better off. To the extent that such exchanges are blocked by the calculus of profit maximization, the monopsony structure is less efficient than the competitive ideal.

For the monopsony firm, then, wages will indeed be lower than under competition, lending force to the critics' claims of exploitation. What about other elements of compensation, such as safety equipment? Here, too, there will be a tendency for the monopsonist to offer less, for exactly parallel reasons. It does not follow, however, that employees of a monopsonist would be made better off by a regulation requiring additional safety equipment. The monopsonist's incentives cause it to offer a compensation package—consisting of wages, safety equipment, and other fringe benefits—that is worth less than the corresponding package under competition. But the monopsonist's incentives are to allocate the total amount spent on compensation within that package in exactly the way that workers would want. Suppose, for example, a safety device was worth $10/wk to each worker and cost only $9/wk per worker to install and operate. This device would meet the standard cost-benefit test, and the monopsonist would earn higher profits by installing it. Workers,

FIGURE 14.12

Comparing Monopsony and Competition in the Labor Market

Because the monopsonist takes into account the effect of employment expansions on wages paid to existing workers, it will employ less and pay less than the corresponding values under competition.

after all, would tolerate up to a $10/wk pay cut rather than do without the device. Alternatively, suppose the device cost $11/wk. Then both the firm and the workers would do better by not installing it.

The firm's incentives regarding the distribution of total compensation are exactly the same as the workers'. A regulation requiring the firm to install the device will diminish wages even further. And if the monopsonist's wages are too low to begin with, workers will not necessarily regard this as an attractive solution.

How important is the problem of monopsony? Recall that the requirement for perfect competition in the labor market is that workers be freely mobile. Many workers, especially older ones, have commitments—networks of friends, mortgage payments, children in school, and so on—that make it difficult to move. It is far less clear, however, that this confers the power to exploit. At the entry level, most workers are relatively free to move, and most shop carefully for the jobs they ultimately accept. The late Stephen Marston estimated that between 1970 and 1978 alone, intercity migration flows exceeded 25 percent of the urban population. While current U.S. Census data suggest that the overall U.S. mobility rate has fallen by 50 percent since the 1970s, it remains true that no firm can survive for long without a steady inflow of new workers; and without a competitive compensation package, it would be difficult to attract entry-level workers.[5]

To this observation, critics often respond that firms offer competitive terms to entry-level workers but then cut wages and benefits (or have them grow insufficiently) once these workers have put down roots. But firms develop reputations in the labor market, much as they do in the product market. Other things the same, a firm with a reputation for paying competitive wages to all its workers will be able to lure the best entry-level workers away from firms with reputations for exploiting older workers.

But even if *no* workers were willing or able to move, firms might still not be able to exploit their workers in the long run. If firms in a labor market area paid much less than the value of what their workers produce, new firms could move into the area to compete for the services of those workers. Thus, many engineering firms moved to the Seattle area in the 1970s in the wake of the aerospace industry recession that had left thousands of technical employees out of work.

The most compelling argument against the allegation of widespread exploitation is that the profit rates we observe in practice are too low to be compatible with a significant degree of monopsony power. If we assume that the monopsonist holds wages down by only 10 percent of the level paid in competitive labor markets, it follows that the rate of return for the monopsonist will be roughly 50 percent higher than the competitive rate of return.[6] Yet few firms consistently earn profit rates as high as that.

---

[5]See Stephen T. Marston, "Two Views of the Geographic Distribution of Unemployment," *Quarterly Journal of Economics,* 1985. For a visualization by the U.S. Census of historical U.S. geographical mobility, see: www.census.gov/library/visualizations/time-series/demo/historic.html.

[6]To illustrate this claim, consider the case of a firm that hires labor in a competitive market at an annual wage rate w, and that can borrow at an annual interest rate r. If L denotes this firm's employment level and K the size of its capital stock, and these are its only factors of production, then its total costs, TC, are given by

$$TC = wL + rK.$$

Suppose that $r = 0.10$ and that labor costs are 70 percent of total costs. Then

$$TC = 0.7TC + 0.1K,$$

from which it follows that $K = 3TC$ (in words, that the value of the firm's capital stock is three times its annual total production costs).

Now consider a firm identical to the one above except that its monopsony power in the labor market enables it to pay its workers only 90 percent of the competitive wage level. Let Π denote the excess profit it receives as a result of its monopsony power. To calculate Π, note first that the monopsonist's total revenue (which will be the same as the competitor's total costs, TC) will equal its total costs plus its extra-normal profit. Thus we solve

$$(0.9)(0.7)TC + (0.1)3TC + \Pi = TR = TC$$

for Π, which yields $\Pi = 0.07TC$. Suppose half of the firm's capital stock (1.5TC) is owned by stockholders; the other half is financed by loans. Its rate of return will then be the sum of the competitive return on capital ($0.10 \times 1.5TC = 0.15TC$) and the excess return ($0.07TC$) divided by the capital it owns (1.5TC), which yields $0.22TC/1.5TC \approx 0.147$, a 47 percent premium over the competitive rate of return.

More important, those industries that do have higher than average rates of return almost always turn out to be high-wage rather than low-wage industries. Empirical studies have repeatedly found that wage rates are positively, not negatively, influenced by profit rates.[7] To be sure, the West Virginia coal miner in a one-mine town earns a low wage. But the mine that employs him probably exists on the margin of economic profitability. To say that exploitation is the cause of the miner's low wages seems strange if the consequence of paying higher wages would be to force the mine into bankruptcy.

The profitability argument does not say that firms never face upward-sloping supply curves for labor. But it does suggest that such conditions in the labor market are not an important mechanism whereby the owners of capital take unfair advantage of their workers. And it clearly does not provide a compelling justification for regulating safety procedures in the workplace. (We'll consider an alternative rationale for safety regulation in Chapter 17, one that does not involve market power on the part of employers.)

MINIMUM WAGE LAWS

In 1938 Congress passed the Fair Labor Standards Act, one of whose provisions established a minimum wage for all covered employees. Coverage was initially limited to workers in large firms involved in interstate commerce but now has become almost universal. The intent of the legislation was to elevate the wages of unskilled workers sufficiently to lift them from poverty. Economists have long been skeptical, however, about the power of government to legislate the price of anything. And indeed the minimum wage laws seem to have had a variety of unintended, undesired consequences.

Figure 14.13 shows the demand and supply curves for unskilled labor, which intersect at an equilibrium real wage of w_0, at which employment is L_0. If the statutory minimum wage is set at w_m, the effect is to reduce employment to D_m, while increasing the quantity of labor supplied to S_m. The difference, $S_m - D_m$, is the unemployment that results from the minimum wage.

According to the simple model in Figure 14.13, there are both winners and losers from the imposition of the minimum wage. The unskilled workers who retain their jobs earn more as a result. Those who lose their jobs obviously earn less. Whether the net effect is to increase the amount of income earned by unskilled workers depends on the elasticity of demand for that category of labor. If it exceeds 1, earnings will fall; if it is less than 1, they will rise.

FIGURE 14.13

A Statutory Minimum Wage

The effect of the minimum wage is to reduce employment of unskilled labor from L_0 to D_m, while increasing supply from L_0 to S_m. The resulting difference, $S_m - D_m$, is the unemployment attributable to the minimum wage.

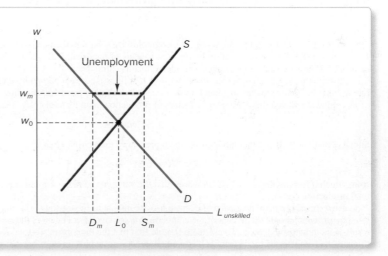

[7]See, for example, George J. Stigler, "The Economics of Minimum Wage Legislation," *American Economic Review,* 36, 1946, 358–365; Laurence Siedman, "The Return of the Profit Rate to the Wage Equation," *Review of Economics and Statistics,* 61, 1979, 139–142; and Alan Kreuger and Lawrence Summers, "Reflections on the Interindustry Wage Structure," *Econometrica,* 1987.

Proponents of the minimum wage implicitly assume that the demand curve for unskilled labor is nearly vertical. Opponents, by contrast, tend to describe it as highly elastic. Empirical estimates turn out to be highly variable, but for the most part lie slightly below 1, suggesting that the net effect is to increase wage payments to unskilled labor.[8] Some studies even suggest that minimum wage laws may not raise overall unemployment at all.[9]

There is a strong consensus, however, that minimum wage legislation has reduced the employment of teenagers. The size of any group's employment reduction will depend not only on the elasticity of demand, but also on the extent to which the minimum wage exceeds the market-clearing level. Teenagers as a group are much less productive than adults, if only because they have less education and experience, and so the statutory minimum creates a much larger employment gap for them than for other groups. There have been recent proposals in Congress to eliminate teenagers from minimum wage coverage altogether, or else to have a much lower "subminimum" wage apply to them. Opponents of these proposals fear that they will cause some firms to substitute teenagers for adult workers, but the proposals have nonetheless gained substantial support.

An interesting exception exists to the general proposition that minimum wages imply a reduction in employment. Figure 14.14 shows the case of a monopsony firm that without a minimum wage would hire L^* workers at a wage of w^*. Confronted with a minimum wage of w_m, its marginal factor cost curve suddenly becomes horizontal over the region from 0 to L_1. No matter how much labor it hires in that region, the marginal cost of an additional worker is constant at w_m. If it wants to expand employment beyond L_1, it must offer a higher wage than w_m, as indicated along the original supply curve. With the minimum wage in effect, the monopsonist's demand curve for labor intersects its new MPC curve at L_m. The effect of the law is thus to increase both the wage and the employment level for the monopsonist.

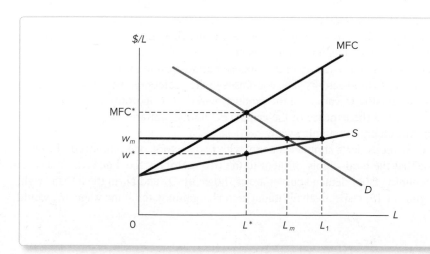

FIGURE 14.14

The Minimum Wage Law in the Case of Monopsony

The effect of a minimum wage at w_m is to make the monopsonist's MFC curve horizontal in the region from 0 to L_1, which increases employment from L^* to L_m.

[8]See, for example, Daniel Hamermesh, "Economic Studies of Labor Demand and Their Applications to Public Policy," *Journal of Human Resources,* Fall 1976, 507–525; Edward M. Gramlich, "Impact of Minimum Wages on Other Wages, Employment, and Family Incomes," *Brookings Papers on Economic Activity,* 2, 1976; Jacob Mincer, "Unemployment Effects of Minimum Wages," *Journal of Political Economy,* August 1976; Sar Levitan and Richard Belous, *More Than Subsistence: Minimum Wages for the Working Poor,* Baltimore: Johns Hopkins University Press, 1979; and Finis Welch, *Minimum Wages: Issues and Evidence,* Washington, DC: American Enterprise Institute, 1978. For a review, see Chapter 4 in Ronald Ehrenberg and Robert S. Smith, *Modern Labor Economics,* Glenview, IL: Scott, Foresman, 1982.

[9]For this conclusion, see one of the mostly hotly debated economics papers in recent history: David Card and Alan B. Krueger, "Minimum Wages and Employment: A Case Study of the Fast-Food Industry in New Jersey and Pennsylvania: Reply," *American Economic Review,* 90, 2000. It should be noted that Alan Krueger, who died in 2019, did not take these findings to be an indication that the minimum wage could be raised to some arbitrary level without adverse employment effects. See "The Minimum Wage: How Much is Too Much?" *The New York Times,* October 9, 2015, https://www.nytimes.com/2015/10/11/opinion/sunday/the-minimum-wage-how-much-is-too-much.html.

Minimum wages will not always increase employment in monopsony labor markets. If the minimum wage were set above MFC*, for example, the effect would be to reduce employment. And no matter where the minimum wage is set in the region above $w*$, the effect will be to reduce the monopsonist's overall rate of return on investment. If the monopsonist's profit were close to normal to begin with, the long-run effect would thus be to induce him to leave the market. Needless to say, this too would result in a reduction of employment for unskilled workers.

SELF-TEST 14.9

A monopsonist's demand curve for labor is given by $w = 12 - L$. If she originally faced an AFC curve given by $w = 2 + 2L$, with corresponding MFC $= 2 + 4L$, how will her wage and employment offers be affected by the passage of a law requiring $w \geq 8$? A law requiring $w \geq 10$?

Minimum wage legislation was once a much more hotly debated topic than it is today because inflation has so reduced the real value of the minimum wage that it is below the equilibrium wage level in many unskilled labor markets. In the Boston area, for example, entry-level employees in fast-food restaurants are paid roughly twice the minimum wage. Unless and until Congress enacts a substantial increase in the minimum wage, interest in the subject is likely to continue to wane.

LABOR UNIONS

About one in six workers in the nonfarm sector of the U.S. economy is a member of a labor union. The primary difference between unionized and nonunionized employment is simple. Unionized workers bargain collectively over the terms and conditions of employment; to nonunionized workers, the firm simply announces its offer, which the workers can either accept or reject, by staying with or leaving the firm. Unions may also facilitate communication between labor and management.

For much of this century, economists focused almost exclusively on the collective bargaining aspect of union activity. The consensus in the profession was that unions were the labor market analog to cartels in the product market, serving only to enhance their members' interests at the expense of the general economic welfare. The basic argument in support of this claim is straightforward.

To illustrate, consider a simple economy with two sectors, one unionized, the other not. Suppose that the total supply of labor to the two sectors is fixed at S_0, and that the union and nonunion labor demand curves are as shown by D_U and D_N in the left and right panels of Figure 14.15, respectively. Without union bargaining, the same wage, w_0, would

---

FIGURE 14.15

The Allocative Effects of Collective Bargaining

Without collective bargaining, the same wage, w_0, prevails in each sector. With the union wage pegged at w_u, employment falls in the union sector. The displaced workers seek employment in the nonunion sector, driving wages down there. The result is a reduction in national output.

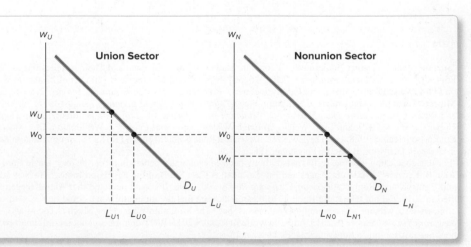

prevail in each sector, and employment levels in the two sectors would be L_{U0} and L_{N0}, respectively, where $L_{U0} + L_{N0} = S_0$.

Collective bargaining fixes the wage in the union sector at $w_U > w_0$. The demand for labor is downward sloping, and this causes firms in the union sector to reduce employment from L_{U0} to L_{U1}. The displaced workers in the union sector are then forced to seek employment in the nonunion sector, which drives the wage down to w_N in that sector.

At first glance, the process resembles a zero-sum game, one in which the gains of the union workers are exactly offset by the losses of nonunion workers. On closer inspection, however, we see that the process actually reduces the value of total output. Recall from Chapter 8 that the condition for output maximization with two production processes is for the value of the marginal product of the resource to be the same in each process. With the wage set initially at w_0 in both sectors, that condition was satisfied. But with the divergence in wages caused by the collective bargaining process, the value of total output can no longer be at a maximum. Note that if a worker is taken out of the nonunion sector, the reduction in the value of output there will be only w_N, which is less than w_U, the gain in the value of output when that same worker is added to the union sector.

The economic distortion implied by the analysis in Figure 14.15 is exaggerated. If the union firm is required to pay a higher wage, it will attract an excess supply of workers. In practice, the skill levels of workers differ a great deal, and the natural response of the union firm will be to select the most qualified of its job applicants. The other side of the same coin is that nonunion firms will be left to hire workers who are less productive than average. Empirical studies have shown that the union premium not accounted for by differences in worker quality is only about 10 percent. This means that the gain from shifting workers from the nonunion to the union sector will be smaller than it first appeared.

Even if the union wage premium is only 10 percent, however, we should be puzzled about the ability of union firms to compete successfully against their nonunion counterparts. Of course, the nonunion firms sometimes do manage to drive the union firms out of business, as happened when the textile industry moved to the South to escape the burden of high union wages in New England. But much of the time union and nonunion firms compete head-to-head for extended periods. If their costs are significantly higher, how do the union firms manage to survive?

Researchers have discovered a variety of ways in which unions may actually boost productivity.[10] The revisionist view stresses their role in communicating worker preferences to management. When channels of communication between labor and management do not flow freely, the only option open to a dissatisfied worker is to leave the firm to search for a better situation. The union's role, in the revisionist account, is to offer the worker a voice as an alternative to leaving. The organization of formal grievance procedures, combined with the higher level of monetary compensation, boosts morale among union workers, which in turn leads to higher productivity. Quit rates in union firms, for example, are significantly lower than in nonunion firms, enabling them to economize on hiring and training costs. Recent empirical work suggests that union productivity may be sufficiently high, in fact, to compensate for the premium in union wages. That is to say, even though monetary wages are higher in union firms, labor costs per unit of output may not be. If this conclusion is correct, it resolves the paradox of how union firms survive in competition with their nonunion rivals.

But in so doing, it raises an even more troubling question: If unions lead to higher morale and increased wages, and don't raise unit labor costs, why don't all firms have unions? The trend in union membership in this country has been declining during the post–World War II era, precisely the opposite of what the revisionist theory would lead us to expect. From the record, it is tempting to conclude that unions may enhance productivity enough to offset wage increases in some industries but not in others. Much more research needs to be done, however, before we have a clear picture of just what unions do.

---

[10]See, in particular, Albert O. Hirschman, *Exit, Voice, and Loyalty,* Cambridge, MA: Harvard University Press, 1973; and Richard B. Freeman and James Medoff, *What Do Unions Do?,* New York: Basic Books, 1985.

DISCRIMINATION IN THE LABOR MARKET

One of the most emotionally volatile issues in all of economics is the phenomenon of discrimination in the labor market. Discussions of it almost always begin by noting the large disparities in earnings that exist between different groups in the labor force. For example, the average earnings of black males are roughly 70 percent of those for white males. The corresponding ratio for females and males is approximately the same.

▶ Visit your instructor's Connect© course and access your eBook to view this video.

Why do female models earn so much more than male models?

Everyone recognizes that at least some components of these differentials have nothing to do with discrimination by employers. Part of the black-white differential, for example, reflects the fact that the median age of black males is almost a decade lower than for white males. Since earnings rise with experience, white males earn more in part simply because they are older. By the same token, part of the male-female differential reflects the historical pattern by which females' labor force participation was always much more intermittent than males'. Salaries increase most sharply when a worker follows the orderly career progression characteristic of male employment patterns. The traditional female pattern was to drop out of the labor force several times in connection with childrearing, which often meant starting over each time at the bottom of the employment ladder. Recent research has added the disappointing result that structured "family leave" programs, for all their benefits to participants, do not alter the income penalty incurred by women who take time off from work for child-rearing.[11]

Each effect is almost surely the result of *some* sort of discrimination against the affected groups. Median ages of black males are lower in part, for example, because blacks so often grow up in poverty, without the education or health care resources to achieve the same life expectancy as whites. No one denies that these conditions are rooted in society's history of discrimination against blacks. Nor do many people deny that the asymmetric distribution of child care responsibilities between the sexes is at least in part the result of discriminatory social attitudes about sex roles. For present purposes, however, it is important to emphasize that from any individual employer's point of view, such effects are examples of *nonmarket* discrimination—effects that lower productivity before job applicants even make contact with the employer. The wage differences for which nonmarket discrimination is responsible cannot logically be attributed to the employer's current hiring behavior. A completely nondiscriminatory employer would have to pay similar wage differentials on the basis of these effects, or else be forced out of business by competitors who did.

Our concern here is with that portion of the wage differentials that cannot be attributed to nonmarket discrimination. In particular, we are concerned with the case in which a firm pays a lower wage to a black, female, Hispanic, or other minority group member than it would to an equally productive white male (or, in the more extreme case, simply refuses to hire members of those groups). There have been numerous theories offered to explain why firms might behave in this fashion.

One theory is that the firm's customers do not wish to deal with minority employees. So-called *customer discrimination* has special force in the vivid examples of segregation in southern lunch counters before the mid-1960s. Any southern lunch counter operator who moved unilaterally to break the color barrier risked losing the bulk of his business to competitors who maintained the tradition of an all-white staff. The Civil Rights Act of 1964 made such discrimination illegal, ensuring that no firm could maintain an advantage over its rivals by refusing to hire blacks.

When employment discrimination is the result of attitudes of the firm's customers, collective action through legislation is one logical way, perhaps even the only practical way, to end the impasse. The reason is that, without the legislation, discrimination may be the only strategy open to firms that is consistent with profit maximization, and hence

[11]Henrik Kleven, Camille Landais, and Jakob Egholt Søgaard, "Children and Gender Inequality: Evidence from Denmark," *American Economic Journal: Applied Economics*, 11(4), 2019, 181–209.

with survival. Black staff may have been just as productive as white staff at preparing and serving food. But from the standpoint of a lunch counter's bottom line, blacks were less productive because of the racial bias of the customers.

Similar considerations may apply to a law firm's decision about whether to hire female lawyers. If clients, or even judges, are less likely to take advice from a female attorney seriously, the law firm's position is completely analogous to that of the southern lunch counter owner. The law firm might believe firmly that clients and judges would change their minds about female attorneys if given enough experience in dealing with them. But if it hires female attorneys while its competitors do not, its business may suffer in the short run. Here again, legislation requiring equal treatment in hiring may be the only effective way to end the impasse.

Lunch counter segregation protest. Many owners of southern restaurants welcomed laws requiring them to serve customers of all races. They said they wanted to desegregate their lunch counters, but were fearful their white customers would desert them.

Customer discrimination is a powerful explanation of employment discrimination in cases such as these. But it cannot account for wage differentials in the cases of workers—such as manufacturing production workers—who never come in contact with customers. Wage differentials in such cases have sometimes been explained as the result of *coworker discrimination.* White workers who feel uneasy about working with blacks, for example, may prefer employment in firms that hire only white workers. Or the fragile egos of some males may be unable to deal with the idea of taking orders from a female supervisor.

Such preferences imply employment segregation, but not a pattern of wage differentials for equally productive workers. Blacks may work together in some firms or plants, while whites work together in others. Or males may tend to work in separate environments from females. Segregation of just this sort is sometimes observed, and this option makes it difficult for the coworker discrimination theory to explain any significant part of observed wage differentials. An employer in an all-black or all-female establishment who paid lower wages than were received by white males of the same productivity would have lower costs, and hence higher profits, than the all-white-male employers. This would provide an incentive for a new firm to bid for that employer's workers, an incentive that should persist until all wage differentials had been eliminated.

Employer discrimination is the term generally used to describe wage differentials that arise from an arbitrary preference by the employer for one group of worker over another. Since this is the type envisioned by popular accounts of discrimination in the labor market, let us examine it in some detail. To describe the process formally, let us suppose that there are two labor force groups, the Ms and the Fs, and that there are no productivity differences between them. More specifically, suppose that the values of their respective marginal products are the same:

$$\text{VMP}_F = \text{VMP}_M = V_0, \tag{14.4}$$

and that discriminating employers pay a wage of V_0 to Ms, but only $V_0 - d$ to Fs.

Labor costs for a discriminating employer will be a weighted average of V_0 and $V_0 - d$, where the weights are the respective shares of the two groups in the employer's work force. Thus, the more Ms the employer hires, the higher his costs will be.

Apart from the isolated cases in which customer discrimination might be a relevant factor, a consumer will be unwilling to pay more for a product produced by an F. If product price is unaffected by the composition of the work force that produces the product, a firm's profit will be smaller the more Ms it employs. The most profitable firm will be one that employs only Fs.

Given our initial assumption that Ms are paid the value of their marginal product, firms that employ only Ms will earn a normal profit, while those that hire a mix will earn a positive economic profit. The initial wage differential provides an opportunity for employers who hire mostly Fs to grow at the expense of their rivals. Indeed, because such firms make an extra-normal profit on the sale of each unit of output, their incentive is to expand as rapidly as they possibly can. And to do that, they will naturally want to continue hiring only Fs.

But as profit-seeking firms continue to pursue this strategy, the supply of Fs at the wage rate $V_0 - d$ will not be adequate for further expansion. The short-run solution is to offer the Fs a slightly higher wage. But this strategy works only if other firms do not pursue it. Once they too start offering a higher wage, Fs will again be in short supply. In the end, of course, the only solution is for the wage of Fs to be bid up all the way to V_0, thereby eliminating further opportunities for profitable expansion by hiring additional Fs.

Any employer who wants to voice a preference for hiring Ms must now do so by paying Ms a wage in excess of V_0. Employers can discriminate against Fs if they want to, but only if they are willing to pay premium wages to the Ms out of their own profits. Earlier we saw that if a monopsonist paid its workers 10 percent less than the going wage (or VMP_L), it would earn roughly 50 percent more than the competitive rate of return on investment. A parallel calculation reveals that a firm that paid its workers 10 percent more than the VMP_L would earn roughly 50 percent less than the competitive rate of return. Few firms could continue to attract capital for long at profit rates that much below normal.

The competitive labor market model suggests that the persistence of significant employer discrimination requires the owners of the firm to supply capital at a rate of return substantially below what they could earn by investing their money elsewhere. The theory of competitive labor markets tells us that unless we can come up with a plausible reason to suppose they might do so, we should concentrate our search for the sources of wage differentials on factors other than employer discrimination. Or else we should look for additional ways in which the theory of competitive labor markets provides an incomplete description of reality.

Statistical Discrimination

In Chapter 6 we saw how insurance companies employed data on average claims by various groups to arrive at differential rates for policyholders whose individual claim records were identical. A similar kind of statistical discrimination is pervasive in the labor market. The theory of competitive labor markets tells us that workers will be paid the values of their respective marginal products. But an employee's marginal product is not like a number tattooed on his forehead, there for everyone to observe at a glance. On the contrary, because people often work together in complicated team activities, it is often exceedingly difficult, even after many years on the job, to estimate what any one worker contributes. The problem of estimating the productivity of job applicants, with whom the employer has had no direct experience, is obviously even more difficult.

Still, the task is not hopeless. Just as insurance companies know from long experience that adolescent males are much more likely than other drivers to file accident claims, so too do employers know that applicants from certain groups are likely to be much more productive than others. The average college graduate, for example, will be more productive than the average high school graduate, even though many high school graduates are much more productive than their college counterparts.

In the insurance case, we saw that even when two people had identical driving records, competitive pressures led to different rates if they happened to belong to groups with differing accident records. We see closely analogous results in the labor market. Even when the employer's information indicates that two individuals have exactly the same productivity, there will be competitive pressure to pay higher wages to the person who belongs to the group with higher average productivity. The problem is, unless the employer's information about individual productivity is perfect, group membership conveys relevant information about likely productivity differences, information a firm can ignore only at its peril.

To illustrate how group membership influences the estimation of individual productivity, consider a labor market group—call it group A—the VMPs of whose members are

On average, teenage males are more likely to have accidents than other drivers. Because insurance companies lack good ways of assessing individual driver safety, even teenage males who are very safe drivers end up paying high insurance premiums.

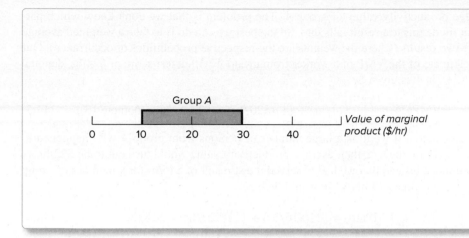

FIGURE 14.16

A Hypothetical Uniform Productivity Distribution
The productivity values for members of this group are uniformly distributed between $10/hr and $30/hr. This means that the VMP of a person chosen at random from the group is equally likely to be any number from $10/hr to $30/hr. The average VMP for members of this group is $20/hr.

uniformly distributed between $10/hr and $30/hr, as shown in Figure 14.16. This means that if we were to choose a person at random from group *A*, the value of his marginal product would be equally likely to be any number from $10/hr to $30/hr. If we knew nothing about this person other than that he was from group *A*, the expected value of his productivity would simply be the average for members of that group, which is $20/hr.

If there were no practical way to learn anything about a specific individual's productivity, and if the productivity distribution of his group were known, competitive pressures would require that members of group *A* be paid $20/hr (see footnote 12). Suppose an employer offered less—say, $15/hr—perhaps in the fear that he would be unlucky and hire the least productive member of group *A*. This employer would not be able to retain his workers because a competing firm could offer $16/hr and lure them away. And since group *A* workers are worth an average of $20/hr each, this competing firm would augment its expected profits by $4/hr for each worker it hired. But for the same reason, it too would eventually lose the workers to yet another competing firm.

Alternatively, consider a firm that paid $25/hr to workers from group *A*, perhaps because it felt bad about underpaying the more productive members of that group. This firm would lose an average of $5/hr for every worker from group *A* it hired, and unless it had some source of extra-normal profits, it would sooner or later be forced out of business.

If individual productivity values cannot be measured, the only competitively stable outcome is for members of group *A* to be paid $20/hr. Some of them will end up being paid more than they are worth, others less. But the firms that hire at this rate will cover all their costs, on the average, and can expect to remain in business. Any other policy will result in failure.

Now suppose that employers have a productivity test. This test is not perfect, but it does provide information about individual productivity values. To keep the analysis simple, suppose that the test is 100 percent accurate half of the time, but has no value at all the other half of the time (that is, it yields a random number drawn from the group's productivity distribution); and suppose that employers have no way of knowing when the test is accurate.

Suppose further that the test is administered to a worker from group *A* and yields a value of $24/hr. What is our best estimate of this worker's true productivity? The test is 100 percent accurate half of the time, and if we knew this was one of those times, the answer would, of course, be $24. Alternatively, if we knew that this was one of the times the test was worthless, our best estimate would be the expected value of a random number drawn from the uniform distribution between $10/hr and $30/hr, namely, $20/hr, the

[12]This analysis ignores the complication of compensating wage differences for internal rank, discussed in the next section.

average productivity value for group *A*. The problem is that we don't know which particular mode this test result falls into. So the best we can do is to take a weighted average of the two results (where the weights are the respective probabilities of occurrence). Our best estimate of the VMP of a worker from group *A* with a test score of $24/hr, denoted VMP(24), is thus given by

$$VMP(24) = \left(\tfrac{1}{2}\right)(\$24/hr) + \left(\tfrac{1}{2}\right)(\$20/hr) = \$22/hr \text{ (see footnote 13).} \qquad (14.5)$$

This means that if we took a large number of persons from group *A* who happened to score $24/hr on the test, their average productivity value would turn out to be $22/hr.

Suppose instead that we had observed a test result of $16/hr for a member of group *A*. Our best estimate of his VMP would then be

$$VMP(16) = \left(\tfrac{1}{2}\right)(\$16/hr) + \left(\tfrac{1}{2}\right)(\$20/hr) = \$18/hr. \qquad (14.6)$$

This time note that the effect of the uncertainty in the test causes us to revise upward the estimate of the individual's productivity. *In general, the rule is that when a test is less than completely accurate, our best estimate of a worker's productivity will lie between his actual test score and the average productivity of the group to which he belongs.* And again, the prediction of competitive labor market theory is that any firm that did not pay its workers according to the best available estimates of their respective VMPs would eventually be driven from the market by the forces of competition.

SELF-TEST 14.10

In the example above, what is the best available estimate of the VMP of a person with a test score of 12?

Now suppose an employer confronts job applicants not only from group *A*, but also from group *B*. And suppose the VMP distribution for group *B* is uniform between $20/hr and $40/hr, as shown in Figure 14.17. Suppose, finally, that two applicants come in one morning, one from group *A*, the other from group *B*, and that each gets a score of 28 on the test (the same test as before). What are the employer's best estimates of their respective productivity values?

FIGURE 14.17

Productivity Distributions for Two Groups

The VMP values of members of group *A* are uniformly distributed between $10/hr and $30/hr, while those of members of group *B* are uniformly distributed between $20/hr and $40/hr. If we know only the groups to which people belong, our best estimates of an individual's VMP would be the average VMP for his or her group—$20/hr for group *A*, $30/hr for group *B*.

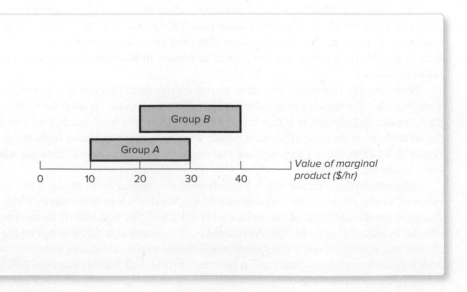

---

[13]Note the similarity of this adjustment procedure to the one discussed in Chapter 8, whereby we estimated the probability that a given shy person was a librarian.

In both cases, the imperfection in the test calls for an adjustment toward the relevant group average. Specifically, the best estimate of the VMP for the worker from group A, denoted $VMP_A(28)$, is

$$VMP_A(28) = \left(\tfrac{1}{2}\right)(\$28/\text{hr}) + \left(\tfrac{1}{2}\right)(\$20/\text{hr}) = \$24/\text{hr}, \quad\quad (14.7)$$

while the corresponding estimate for the worker from group B is

$$VMP_B(28) = \left(\tfrac{1}{2}\right)(\$28/\text{hr}) + \left(\tfrac{1}{2}\right)(\$30/\text{hr}) = \$29/\text{hr}. \quad\quad (14.8)$$

Thus, even though the two workers earn exactly the same score on the test, the employer adjusts downward in one case, upward in the other. And again, note that if the firm fails to pay its workers according to the best available estimates of their VMPs, it is in danger of extinction. It is a cruel understatement to say that such competitive imperatives have caused great pain for both employees and employers. The many talented and productive members of group A cannot help but feel chagrined when their group identity causes them to be treated differently from the members of other groups. And surely there cannot be many employers who feel comfortable offering different salaries to people whose records look just the same.

Note carefully that statistical discrimination is the result, not the cause, of average productivity differences between groups. Its sole effect is to reduce wage variation within each group. If employers suddenly switched to a policy of setting wages strictly on the basis of individual-specific information, the average wage differential between groups would remain the same as before.

THE INTERNAL WAGE STRUCTURE

On first examination, the wage structure within many private firms seems much more egalitarian than would be warranted under our marginal productivity theory of wages. Many firms, for example, follow strict salary formulas based on experience, education, and length of tenure within the firm, even when there are large visible differences in the productivity of workers paid the same under these formulas. Indeed, pay patterns of the sort predicted by the marginal productivity theory are virtually never observed in practice.

A simple amendment to our theory helps to square it with the wage distributions we observe in practice.[14] The amendment rests on two plausible assumptions: (1) Most people prefer high-ranked to low-ranked positions among their coworkers, and (2) no one can be forced to remain in a firm against his wishes.

By the laws of simple arithmetic, not everyone's preference for high rank in the wage distribution of his firm can be satisfied. After all, only 50 percent of the members of any group can be in the top half. But if people are free to associate with whomever they please, why are the lesser-ranked members of groups content to remain? Why don't they all leave to form new groups of their own in which they would no longer be near the bottom? Many workers undoubtedly do precisely that. And yet we also observe many stable, heterogeneous groups. Not all accountants at General Motors are equally talented; and in every law firm, some partners attract much more new business than others. If everyone prefers to be near the top of his group of coworkers, what holds these heterogeneous groups together?

The apparent answer is that their low-ranked members receive extra compensation. If they were to leave, they would gain by no longer having to endure low status. By the same token, however, the top-ranked members would lose; they would no longer enjoy high status. If their gains from having high rank are larger than the costs borne by members with low rank, it does not make sense for the group to disband. Everyone can do better if the top-ranked workers induce their lesser-ranked colleagues to remain by sharing some of their pay with them.

---

[14]For a more complete development of the argument to follow, see R. Frank, *Choosing the Right Pond*, New York: Oxford University Press, 1985.

FIGURE 14.18

The Wage Structure When Local Status Matters

The higher the average productivity level of a firm, the lower a given worker's rank will be. Workers who choose high-ranked positions (A) must share some of their pay with their lower-ranked coworkers. Those who choose low-ranked positions (C) receive compensating payments from their coworkers.

Of course, not everyone assigns the same value to having high rank. Those who care relatively less about it will do best to join firms in which most workers are more productive than themselves. As lesser-ranked members in these firms, they will receive extra compensation. People who care most strongly about rank, by contrast, will want to join firms in which most other workers are less productive than themselves. For the privilege of occupying top-ranked positions in those firms, they will have to work for less than the value of what they produce.

Workers can thus sort themselves among a hierarchy of firms in accordance with their demands for within-firm status. Figure 14.18 depicts the menu of choices confronting workers whose productivity takes a given value, M_0. The colored lines represent the wage schedules offered by three different firms. They tell how much a worker with a given productivity would be paid in each firm. The average productivity level is highest in firm 3, next highest in firm 2, and lowest in firm 1. The problem facing persons with productivity level M_0 is to choose which of these three firms to work for.

Workers who care most about status will want to "purchase" high-ranked positions such as the one labeled A in firm 1. In such positions, they work for less than the value of what they produce. By contrast, those who care least about status will elect to receive wage premiums by working in low-ranked positions such as the one labeled C in firm 3. Workers with moderate concerns about local rank will be attracted to intermediate positions such as the one labeled B in firm 2, for which they neither pay nor receive any compensation for local rank.

Note also in Figure 14.18 that even though not every worker in each firm is paid the value of what he produces, workers taken as a group nonetheless do receive the value of what they produce. The extra compensation received by each firm's low-ranked workers is exactly offset by the shortfall in pay of its high-ranked workers.

How large are the compensating wage differentials for rank within the firm? The answer will be different for different occupations. In occupations in which coworkers do not associate closely with one another, people will not be willing to pay much for a high-ranked position. After all, the comparisons that most matter are those between people who interact most intensively. The price paid for high rank (and received for low rank) will be highest in occupations in which coworkers work closely together for extended periods.

The extended marginal productivity model predicts that the wage will rise by less than a dollar for each extra dollar of value produced, and that the difference between productivity and pay will increase with the extensiveness of interaction between coworkers. The predictions of the original model are contrasted with those of the extended model in Figure 14.19.

FIGURE 14.19

Wage Schedules and the Intensity of Interaction

The more intensively coworkers interact, the higher should be the compensating wage differential for rank in the internal wage distribution.

Table 14.1 presents estimates of the rates at which earnings rise with productivity for three occupations. The occupations are listed in increasing order of closeness of interaction. Real estate salespersons, who have the least intensive contact, pay the lowest amounts for high-ranked positions. At the other end of the spectrum, research chemists, who work together in close-knit groups for extended periods, pay very large sums indeed. In the sample studied, the most productive chemists accounted for over $200,000 more in revenues each year than their least productive colleagues, yet received only slightly higher salaries.[15] Auto salespersons do not associate nearly as intensively as chemists, but unlike real estate salespersons, they do spend their working hours together in the same locations. Just as predicted, the price of high-ranked positions for auto salespersons lies between those of the other two occupations.

The entries in Table 14.1 suggest that, for some occupations at least, compensating wage differentials for internal rank are substantial. Taking these compensating differentials into account, the egalitarian wage structure within private firms appears perfectly consistent with the marginal productivity theory of wages. Here again, it appears that critics have written off the economic model prematurely.

The role of concerns about rankings in the internal wage distribution helps shed light on the example we considered earlier in which economists working in business schools often earn 20 percent more than their counterparts working in liberal arts colleges. Business schools have to pay their other faculty members—accountants, marketers, financial analysts, and the like—high salaries because of the high earnings opportunities available in these fields in the private sector. (A dean is reported to have

TABLE 14.1

Pay versus Productivity for Three Occupations

| | Extra Earning Per Extra Dollar of Production | |
Occupation	Actual	Predicted by original model
Real estate sales	$0.70	$1
Automobile sales	$0.24	$1
Research chemists	<$0.09	$1

> Compensating wage differentials for internal rank are largest in those occupations in which coworkers interact most intensively.

[15]Ibid., Chap. 4.

said to a classics professor who complained about the high salaries in the law school, "If you're not happy, why don't you go out and start a classics consulting firm?") Economists who accept jobs in a business school find themselves at the bottom of the pay scale among their coworkers. The premium salaries they receive in comparison with economists in liberal arts colleges may be interpreted in part as a compensating differential for occupying a low-ranked position.

WINNER-TAKE-ALL MARKETS

In this section we will see that differences in rank sometimes cause small differences in ability to translate into large differences in the values of marginal products.[16] The essence of the idea is captured in the following simple example. Imagine that your company, General Motors, has been sued by Ford for $1 billion for patent infringement. On the merits, the case is so close that it is certain to be decided in favor of the side that hires the better lawyer. Suppose Day and Jones are the top two lawyers in the country, and that while they are almost equally talented in every respect, Jones is just perceptibly better.

Naturally, both Ford and GM will want to hire Jones, and so both start bidding vigorously for her services. How much will the winner have to pay her? On a moment's reflection, it should be clear that the answer must be $1 billion. If Ford offered only $999 million, it would be in GM's interest to bid still higher because the alternative is to lose the lawsuit. But then Ford will respond by raising its own bid, for its alternative too is to lose the lawsuit. Unless Ford and GM can collude successfully, the only stable outcome is for Jones to be paid $1 billion. Day's value, even though she is only a shade less talented, is exactly zero, for by assumption, the side that hires her will lose the lawsuit.

The example is a caricature, but it captures the flavor of what happens in a variety of labor market contexts. Consider, for example, the pay structure in professional tennis. Given the limited amount of time most people are willing to spend watching tennis matches on television, it is practical to see only a handful of players in action during any given year. And given a choice, most fans would be willing to pay a little extra to see the top-ranked players play. The result is that the demand for tennis players ranked in the top 10 is hundreds of times greater than for players ranked around 100. And yet the differences in playing ability between the two categories are often very small. Let the 101st-ranked player meet the 102nd-ranked player and fans will see almost as exciting a match as when the 1st-ranked player meets the 2nd-ranked player. The problem, from the perspective of the lower-ranked pair, is that most fans have time to watch only a single match and would naturally prefer to see the top-ranked pair. The result is that top-ranked players earn millions each year, while those in the second tier earn barely enough to cover their expenses on the tour.

Similar *superstar effects* are observed in virtually every professional sport, in the world of entertainment, and even in the ordinary workings of business. Regulated companies spend vast sums bidding for the services of a handful of expert witnesses. A small number of actors and actresses have their pick of all the best roles.

For the superstar effect to occur, there must be a winner-take-all effect somewhere in the production process. In tennis it is that the top players capture virtually the entire viewing audience. In the lawsuit example, it was that the better lawyer wins the suit. For the superstar effect to be important, the stakes in the contest must be high, as they are in each of these examples.

The marginal productivity theory of pay determination has been criticized on the grounds that workers with nearly identical abilities are often paid vastly different amounts. At first glance, such observations do indeed seem to contradict the theory. But

[16]The discussion in this section draws on R. Frank, "The Economics of Buying the Best," Cornell University Department of Economics Working Paper, 1978; Sherwin Rosen, "The Economics of Superstars," *American Economic Review,* September 1981; and R. Frank and P. Cook, *The Winner-Take-All Society,* New York: The Free Press, 1995.

on a closer look, we see that critics may have been too hasty to condemn the model. The difficulty, as we have seen, is that small differences in ability sometimes translate into very large differences in the values of marginal products.

The appendix to this chapter examines compensating wage differentials for safety and the effect of concerns about relative income on safety choices.

SUMMARY

- Our goal in this chapter was to examine the economic forces that govern wages and other conditions of employment. The perfectly competitive firm's hiring rule in the short run is to keep hiring until the value of what the last worker produces—the VMP_L—is exactly equal to the wage rate. In the long run, the firm's demand curve for labor is more elastic than in the short run, because the firm faces the additional possibility of substituting labor for capital. *(LO1)*

- To aggregate the individual firm demand curves into an industry demand curve for labor involves more than a simple horizontal summation of the individual firm demand curves. An adjustment has to be made for the fact that increasing industry output brings a lower product price. *(LO4)*

- The demand curve for labor for a monopolist in the product market is constructed by comparing the wage not with the value of the output the worker produces, but with the amount by which the worker's output will change total revenue—MRP_L. Unlike the perfectly competitive firm, monopolists must take into account that an increase in output requires them to sell existing output at a lower price. *(LO3)*

- We began our approach to the supply side of the labor market by considering the individual worker's decision of how much to work at a given wage rate. The more she works, the more she will earn, but the less time she will have available for other activities. The result is a standard consumer choice problem of the kind we examined in Chapter 3. In the consumer case, a price increase of a product is accompanied by a reduction in the quantity demanded (except in the case of the anomalous Giffen good). By contrast, in the labor supply context, it is not uncommon for people to supply fewer hours of labor when wage rates rise. To generate the market supply curve, we add the individual supply curves horizontally. The market supply and demand curves intersect to determine the industry wage level and total volume of industry employment. *(LO3, LO4)*

- The conventional view of labor unions is that they increase labor's bargaining power vis-à-vis management, thereby increasing labor's share of a fixed economic pie. Recent research, however, suggests that unions may actually improve the productivity of workers, thereby enlarging not only their slice of the economic pie but also management's. *(LO7)*

- Proponents of minimum wage laws say they are needed to protect workers from being exploited by employers with excessive market power. Whether the legislation actually serves this goal, however, turns out to be a difficult empirical question. There is a case, however, to be made on behalf of exempting teenagers from the minimum wage laws. *(LO6)*

- Critics claim that many firms pay members of certain groups—notably blacks and females—less than they pay white males with the same productivity. Such charges pose a fundamental challenge to the very core of microeconomic theory, for they imply that firms are passing up opportunities to enhance their profits. We saw several reasons, including discrimination by institutions other than firms, that people in the affected groups appear to earn lower salaries. *(LO8)*

- An apparent anomaly is the fact that people whose abilities differ only slightly sometimes earn vastly different salaries. This time the key to resolving the contradiction is to observe that in many contexts, the value of what someone produces depends not only on the absolute level of his or her skills, but on how those skills compare with others'. In arm wrestling, being just a little stronger than your opponent means you win just about every time. In the labor market as well, being just a little better than the competition sometimes means earning vastly more than they do. *(LO9)*

KEY TERMS

average factor cost (AFC)	marginal revenue product (MRP)	value of marginal product (VMP)
marginal factor cost (MFC)	total factor cost (TFC)	

REVIEW QUESTIONS

1. What is the difference between the perfect competitor's VMP_L curve and the imperfect competitor's MRP_L curve? *(LO1, LO2)*

2. If a monopolist bought all the firms in a formerly competitive industry and acquired the legal right to exclude entry, how would the quantity of labor employed be affected? *(LO5)*

3. Why might local employers pay workers the value of what they produce even if workers are unable or unwilling to move to another area to accept a better job? *(LO1)*

4. Why does economic theory lead us to place more emphasis on discrimination by persons and institutions other than employers as a cause of wage differences that exceed productivity differences? *(LO8)*

PROBLEMS

1. Given the information in the following table, fill in the value of the marginal product of labor for price $P = 4$. Find the perfectly competitive firm's optimal labor demand for a wage $w = \$4/hr$. *(LO1)*

L	MP	VMP
0	4	
10	3	
20	2	
30	1	
40	0	

2. Given the information in the table below, graph the budget constraint (depicted for $w = \$6/hr$, where h is hours of leisure per day and M is income per day). Find and graph the new budget constraint (income per day = M') for $w = \$12/hr$. How do the slopes of the two budget constraints compare, and why? *(LO3)*

h	M	M'
0	144	
6	108	
12	72	
18	36	
24	0	

3. Given the information in the following table, find the monopsonist's optimal labor demand and wage paid. *(LO5)*

L	AFC	TFC	MFC	VMP
0	0	0	0	16
10	2	20	4	12
20	4	80	8	8
30	6	180	12	4

4. A perfectly competitive firm has $MP_L = 22 - L$. Find and graph its value of the marginal product of labor at a product price of $P = 5$. Find its optimal quantity demanded of labor at a wage of $w = \$10/hr$. *(LO1)*

5. In her current job, Asmee can work as many hours per day as she chooses, and she will be paid $\$1/hr$ for the first 8 hours she works, $\$2.50/hr$ for each hour over 8. Faced with this payment schedule, Asmee chooses to work 12 hr/day. If Asmee is offered a new job that pays $\$1.50/hr$ for as many hours as she chooses to work, will she take it? Explain. *(LO3)*

6. Consider the following two antipoverty programs: (1) A payment of $\$10/day$ is to be given this year to each person who was classified as poor last year; and (2) each person classified as poor will be given a benefit equal to 20 percent of the wage income he earns each day this year. *(LO3)*
   a. Assuming that poor persons have the option of working at $\$4/hr$, show how each program would affect the daily budget constraint of a representative poor worker during the current year.
   b. Which program would be most likely to reduce the number of hours worked?

7. A monopsonist's demand curve for labor is given by $w = 12 - 2L$, where w is the hourly wage rate and L is the number of person-hours hired. *(LO5)*
   a. If the monopsonist's supply (AFC) curve is given by $w = 2L$, which gives rise to a marginal factor cost curve of $MFC = 4L$, how many units of labor will she employ and what wage will she pay?
   b. How would your answers to part (a) be different if the monopsonist were confronted with a minimum wage bill requiring her to pay at least $\$7/hr$?
   c. How would your answers to parts (a) and (b) be different if the employer in question were not a monopsonist but a perfect competitor in the market for labor?

8. Acme is the sole supplier of security systems in the product market and the sole employer of locksmiths in the labor market. The demand curve for security systems is given by $P = 100 - Q$, where Q is the number of systems installed per week. The short-run production function for security systems is given by $Q = 4L$, where L is the number of full-time locksmiths employed per week. The supply curve for locksmiths is given by $W = 40 + 2L$, where W is the weekly wage for each locksmith. How many locksmiths will Acme hire, and what wage will it pay? *(LO2, LO5)*

9. The demand curve for labor facing a monopsonist is given as $W = 35 - 6L$; the supply curve (AFC) for this monopsonist is $W = 3 + L$, with corresponding MFC $= 3 + 2L$, where W represents the hourly wage rate and L is the number of person-hours hired. *(LO5)*
   a. Find the optimal quantity of labor and wage rate for this profit-maximizing monopsonist.
   b. Suppose a minimum wage law imposed a $17/hr minimum wage. How would this affect the quantity of labor demanded by this firm?

10. A monopolist can hire any quantity of labor for $10/hr. If her marginal product of labor is currently 2, and her current product price is $5/unit, should she increase or decrease the amount of labor hired? *(LO6)*

11. The Ajax Coal Company is the only employer in its area. Its only variable input is labor, which has a constant marginal product equal to 5. Because it is the only employer in the area, the firm faces a supply curve for labor given by $W = 10 + L$, where W is the wage rate and L is the number of person-hours employed. This supply curve yields the marginal factor cost curve MFC $= 10 + 2L$. Suppose the firm can sell all it wishes at a constant price of 8. *(LO1, LO5)*
   a. How much labor does the firm employ, how much output does it produce, and what is the wage?
   b. Suppose now the firm sells a special kind of coal such that it faces a downward-sloping demand curve for its output. In particular, assume that Ajax faces the demand curve given by $P = 102 - 1.96Q$. How much labor does the firm employ, how much output does it produce, what price does it set for the output, and what is the wage?
   c. Assume that Ajax still faces the demand curve $P = 102 - 1.96Q$, but now further assume that Ajax has five laborers under contract to produce coal at a wage of 15. If Ajax has the option of hiring additional laborers at a higher wage without increasing the wage to the five laborers already under hire, will Ajax increase its labor force? Explain.

12. Suppose vacation time comes in 1-week intervals, and that the total willingness to pay for total vacation time by younger and older workers in a competitive industry is as given in the following table: *(LO1)*

Total vacation time, weeks	Total Willingness to Pay	
	Younger workers	Older workers
1	300	500
2	475	800
3	600	1,050
4	700	1,250
5	750	1,400

Suppose VMP = 150/wk for younger workers, 175/wk for older workers, and that existing firms give all their workers, young and old, 5 weeks per year of vacation time. Can these firms be maximizing their profits? If so, explain why. If not, say what changes they should make, and how much extra profit will result.

13. Members of two groups, the blues and the greens, have productivity values that range from $5 to $15/hr. The average productivity of the blues is $6/hr and the corresponding average for the greens is $12/hr. A costless productivity test is known to have the property that it gives the correct productivity value with probability $1/3$, and a random productivity value drawn from the relevant group distribution with probability $2/3$. *(LO8)*
   a. Assuming labor markets are competitive, how much will a blue with a test value of 9 be paid?
   b. How much will a green with the same test value be paid?
   c. Is it correct to say that statistical discrimination accounts for why the greens, as a group, are paid more than the blues?

14. A firm has a task to carry out that involves opportunities to shirk with little probability of detection. If it can hire a nonshirking employee for this task, it will make a lot of money. Its strategy for finding a nonshirker is to pay a very low wage at first, then increase the wage gradually each year so that, by the time the worker has been with the firm for 10 years, he will be earning more than he could elsewhere. The present value of the wage premiums in the later years is larger than the present value of the shortfall in the early years. *(LO8)*
   a. Explain how this strategy helps to attract a nonshirking employee. Would the same strategy work if the probability of detecting shirking were zero?
   b. Explain why the ability of the firm to implement this strategy might depend to an extent on its own reputation in the labor market.

15. Consider a two-sector economy that employs a total of 80 units of a single input, labor. N_1 of these units are allocated to sector 1, where the wage is 100 for the top five workers in that sector and zero for all others. (Both the wage for the top workers and the number who receive that wage are invariant to changes in N_1.) The remaining $N_2 = 80 - N_1$ units of labor serve in sector 2,

where every worker receives a wage of 10. All workers in sector 1 have an equal probability of being among the top five workers, $5/N_1$, and all workers are risk neutral. *(LO9)*

a. How many workers will work in sector 1?

b. What will be the value of GNP for the economy?

c. How would your answers differ if there were a 50 percent tax on the earnings of workers in sector 1?

16.* A firm produces output according to the production function $Q = K^{1/2}L^{1/2}$. If it sells its output in a perfectly competitive market at a price of 10, and if K is fixed at 4 units, what is this firm's short-run demand curve for labor? *(LO1)*

17.* How would your answer to the Problem 16 be different if the employer in question sold his product according to the demand schedule $P = 20 - Q$? *(LO2)*

ANSWERS TO SELF-TESTS

14.1 When the product price rises to $3, the VMP_L curve is as shown in panel *b* of the diagram below. The new quantity of labor demanded at $w = \$12$ is 120 units.

The value of the marginal product is

$$\text{VMP}_L = P(\text{MP}_L) = 3\left(10 - \tfrac{1}{20}L\right) = 30 - \tfrac{3}{20}L.$$

The optimal quantity of labor is found by solving

$$w = \text{VMP}_L \Rightarrow 12 = 30 - \tfrac{3}{20}L \Rightarrow 18 = \tfrac{3}{20}L \Rightarrow L^* = 120. \text{ (LO1)}$$

Marginal product of labor (units of output/unit of labor)

(a)

Value of marginal product ($/unit of labor)

(b)

14.2 With $w = \$20/\text{hr}$, the income/leisure budget constraint is

$$M = w(24 - h) = 20(24 - h) = 480 - 20h.$$

At leisure $h = 14$ hr/day, income per day is

$$M = 20(24 - h) = 20(24 - 14) = 20(10) = \$200. \text{ (LO3)}$$

14.3 *(LO3)*

*This question requires the calculus definition of the marginal product of labor: MPL $= \partial Q/\partial L$.

14.4 The answer depends upon whether, in the city in question, the driver earns more than his normal take per hour during periods when it rains. If so, the driver can reach his weekly income target in fewer total hours per week if he works longer hours during the rainy days and shorter hours during the nonrainy days. If not, all else being equal, the driver should focus on predictable peak-earning periods if he wishes to minimize the total hours worked. *(LO3)*

14.5 The budget constraint remains $M = 480 - 20h$. As the individual is willing to sacrifice 1 hour of leisure for $10 of income, indifference curves are straight lines of the general form $M = a - 10h$ provided in the hint. The highest indifference curve that shares a point with the income/leisure constraint is $M = 480 - 10h$, with optimal leisure demand $h = 0$. This form of preferences exhibits extreme substitution effects (will consume no leisure for any $w > 10$ and all leisure for any $w < 10$). *(LO3)*

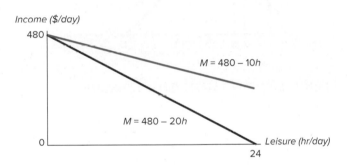

14.6 Under his current job, Mayra's maximum income from working all 24 hours is the sum of 8 hours at $5/hr and the remaining 16 hours at $20/hr:

$$8(5) + 16(20) = 40 + 320 = \$360/\text{day}.$$

Each hour of leisure requires sacrifice of $20 up to $h = 16$ hr, but only $5 beyond 16 hr. Consuming $h = 16$ hr of leisure and working $24 - h = 24 - 16 = 8$ hr yields $8(5) = 40$ income (at the kink in the budget constraint). Mayra's original budget constraint is thus

$$M_1 = \begin{cases} 360 - 20h; & 0 \leq h \leq 16 \\ 40 - 5h; & 16 \leq h \leq 24 \end{cases}.$$

The budget constraint has two pieces reflecting the two wages (regular and overtime). If Mayra works 12 hours, then she enjoys $h_1 = 12$ hr of leisure per day, and thus with the original budget constraint earns income

$$M_1 = 360 - 20h = 360 - 20(12) = 360 - 240 = \$120/\text{day}.$$

Under her potential new job, Mayra's maximum income from working all 24 hours is $24(10) = \$240$.

An hour of leisure requires sacrifice of $10 income up to 24 hours. Mayra's new budget constraint is

$$M_2 = 240 - 10h.$$

Here the budget constraint is a simple straight line. Mayra's original optimal labor supply choice would still be feasible with the new budget constraint: Mayra could earn the same income with the same amount of leisure time under the new budget constraint

$$M_2 = 240 - 10h = 240 - 10(12) = 240 - 120 = \$120/\text{day}.$$

Thus, Mayra can be no worse off with the new budget constraint. However, Mayra will have an opportunity cost of leisure time of $w = 10$ with the new budget constraint rather than $w = 20$ with the old budget constraint. Therefore, Mayra must optimally adjust her labor supply toward more leisure. Mayra will be happier at her new optimal labor supply choice: She reaches a higher indifference curve (I_2) between income and leisure, so she will accept the new job. *(LO3)*

14.7 The original budget constraint is

$$M_0 = w(24 - h) = 5(24 - h) = 120 - 5h.$$

The first program yields a budget constraint

$$M_1 = S + w(24 - h) = 24 + 5(24 - h) = 144 - 5h.$$

The second program yields a budget constraint

$$M_2 = (1 + s)w(24 - h) = (1 + 0.4)5(24 - h)$$
$$= 7(24 - h) = 168 - 7h.$$

The first program is more likely to reduce hours worked because it increases income but leaves the opportunity cost of leisure unchanged: assuming leisure is a normal good, higher income leads to more leisure consumed. In contrast, the second program increases the opportunity cost of leisure: for low levels of wages, an increase in the wage generally increases labor supply as the substitution effect dominates the income effect. Thus, participants will likely work less under the first program and more under the second program. *(LO3)*

14.8   *Wage, MFC ($/unit of labor)*

(LO5)

14.9   When the minimum wage is 8, the monopsonist's MFC curve is the heavy locus with the discontinuity at $L = 3$. The demand curve for labor passes through this discontinuity, which means that the monopsonist will hire 3 units of labor at a wage of 8. When the minimum wage is 10, the firm will pay $w = 10$ and hire 2 units of labor, the same quantity she would have hired in the absence of a minimum wage. *(LO6)*

14.10 $\text{VMP}(12) = \left(\frac{1}{2}\right)(\$12/\text{hr}) + \left(\frac{1}{2}\right)(\$20/\text{hr}) = \$16/\text{hr}.$
(LO8)

The Economics of Workplace Safety

COMPENSATING WAGE DIFFERENTIALS: THE CASE OF SAFETY

Noneconomists in Congress and elsewhere often speak as if every situation should be made as safe as possible, regardless of costs. "The safety of human beings is simply not a matter of economics," such people are fond of saying. But the notion that costs should play no role in safety decisions fails to withstand even the most casual scrutiny. To see what a truly curious notion it is, we need only look at some of the conclusions that follow from it.

Consider, for example, the question of automobile safety. At any moment, there is some small probability of a brake failure occurring in any given automobile. When such an event happens, the consequences are often dire. The likelihood of being killed in an auto accident could be reduced if people had their brakes tested thoroughly by a trained mechanic once each day. Yet no one would dream of having his brakes tested that often, because the costs would be so high in relation to the likely benefits. Most people take their cars in for checkups once or twice a year, and no one seriously asserts that there is any more reasonable course of action available.

Safety is something that most people value. To obtain it, real resources must be expended. Just like any other question involving resource use, how much safety there ought to be is best settled by comparing the relevant costs and benefits.

Both the costs of safety and the benefits are likely to be viewed differently by different people. Someone who is terrified of being struck by lightning, for example, will experience more peace of mind from installing a lightning rod than will someone who thinks thunderstorms are exciting. The optimal amount of this specific form of safety will be higher for the former person than for the latter.

The issues are fundamentally the same when it comes to decisions involving safety in the workplace. Many production activities entail risks to health and safety. These risks can usually be reduced by safety devices and procedures. Such modifications involve additional costs, and in most cases it will be simply impossible to eliminate risk altogether. Whether the modifications should be made, and if so, to what extent, depends on how their value compares with their cost.

To help make our discussion more concrete, let us consider the case of a coal mine that is considering whether to install filters to eliminate coal dust from the air. The cost of installing and operating these filters is $50/wk per miner. With the filters in place, the life expectancy of miners is the same as for people who work at desk jobs, but without them it is 10 years shorter. The question of whether the filters should be installed reduces to a question of whether miners value the enhanced life expectancy more highly than $50/wk. If so, the devices should be installed; otherwise they should not. Suppose, for example, that miners value the extra 10 years at only $40/wk. A mine operator who installed the filters would have to pay his workers $50/wk less in order to cover his added costs (on the assumption that coal buyers are not willing to pay extra for coal from mines with filters). By assumption, however, the miners would rather have the $50 than the protection afforded by the filters.

FIGURE 14A.1

The Optimal Wage-Safety Combination

Risk takers (people with low marginal rates of substitution of wages for survival probability) will choose riskier jobs with higher wages (point *A*). Risk averters will choose safer jobs with lower wages (point *C*).

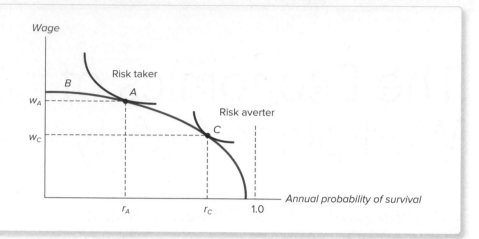

As a practical matter, of course, some miners are likely to find the filters an attractive proposition while others are not. Suppose, for example, that 30 percent of the miners value the filters at $60/wk, while the remaining 70 percent value them at $40. The tendency in the marketplace will then be for 30 percent of the mines to install filters and the remaining 70 percent to go without. The mines that install them will offer a wage that is $50/wk less than the wage paid in the other mines. The miners who value the filters at $60/wk will choose jobs in the mines with air filters, while the remaining miners will gravitate toward those without.

More generally, the choice will involve more than just two alternatives. The line labeled *B* in Figure 14A.1 shows a continuum of technically feasible wage-safety pairs. The horizontal axis measures safety as the annual probability of survival in the workplace. (A perfectly safe job would be one for which that probability is 1.0.) The vertical axis measures the hourly wage rate. *B* has a negative slope because resources must be expended in order to enhance safety. The downward curvature of *B* results from the fact that we install the cheapest, most effective safety devices first, and only then move on to more costly ones. The near-vertical slope of *B* as survival probability approaches 1.0 tells us that no matter how much we spend on safety, we cannot absolutely guarantee survival.

Given this set of technically feasible jobs, the right job for a given worker depends on how he or she feels about the trade-off between risk and material goods. Someone who strongly dislikes risk will have indifference curves that are relatively steep, reflecting his willingness to accept a large cut in wages in return for a boost in his probability of survival. Such a person's optimal job choice is represented by the tangency at *C* in Figure 14A.1.

By contrast, someone who is less concerned about risk will have more gently sloped indifference curves, reflecting his lower willingness to give up wage income for extra safety. The optimal job choice for this person is represented by the tangency at *A*.

The theory of compensating wage differentials clearly predicts that, other things equal, the more dangerous a job is, the higher its wage rate will have to be. Cornell labor economist Robert S. Smith has reviewed eight different empirical studies that examine the relationship between wage rates and the riskiness of jobs.[1] All these studies, each of which was based on a different data set, found a positive association between wage rates and the probability of being killed on the job.

Estimates of the size of the compensating wage differentials varied from $20/yr to $300/yr for every 1-in-10,000 increase in the annual probability of dying on the job. To put this probability in perspective, 1 in 10,000 steelworkers dies on the job each year, as compared with 10 in 10,000 loggers. Suppose, for the sake of illustration, that workers

[1]Robert S. Smith, "Compensating Wage Differentials and Public Policy. A Review," *Industrial and Labor Relations Review,* 32, April 1979, 339–352.

value a 1-in-10,000 reduction in the probability of death at \$100/yr, on the average. This implies that the compensating wage differential for safety should be \$900/yr greater for loggers than for steelworkers because the logger's annual probability of dying is 9/10,000 higher. Of course, the overall wage differential between any two occupations is the result of many differences other than the risk of death or injury, and so the wage difference between steelworkers and loggers may be either more or less than \$900/yr. The theory tells us that if logging could somehow be made just as safe as working in a steel mill, the wage paid to loggers would go down by \$900/yr.

I once attended a conference in which an economist discussed the concept of compensating wage differentials for safety. A sociologist in the audience reacted angrily at the very mention of this notion. He announced triumphantly that "the theory is completely invalid because, as everyone knows, the most dangerous and otherwise disagreeable jobs are always occupied by the lowest-paid workers." The most dangerous jobs do indeed tend to be occupied by low-income workers, but this observation does nothing whatever to invalidate the theory. The claim of the theory, again, is that, *other factors equal,* wages will be higher in less agreeable jobs. When we look at a large sample of American workers, other factors are by no means the same across workers. In particular, the levels of education, intelligence, experience, and energy all vary enormously, and with them, the capacity to earn income from the sale of labor in the marketplace. On the plausible assumption that safety is a normal good, it follows that workers with high earning power will choose jobs in which both wage rates and safety levels are high. By the same token, workers with the lowest productivity will choose jobs with lower safety levels, with wages that are also lower. But by choosing such jobs, their wages are higher than they would have been had they instead chosen safer jobs.

The preceding argument is easily translated into the graphical framework for representing optimal wage-safety choices. The line labeled B_1 in Figure 14A.2 represents the set of technically feasible wage-safety combinations available to a worker with high productivity. The lower line, B_2, is the corresponding set for a worker with much lower productivity. B_1 and B_2 play the role of budget constraints in the analysis, and the highly productive worker's is farther out from the origin. If the two workers have identical indifference curves and safety is a normal good, it then follows that the optimal job for the more productive worker (A) will have both a higher wage and a higher survival probability than the optimal job for the less productive worker (C).

Many economists have argued that the existence of compensating wage differentials for safety makes safety regulation unnecessary in competitive labor markets. To illustrate this argument, consider again the logging and steel mill example. Suppose there were steps

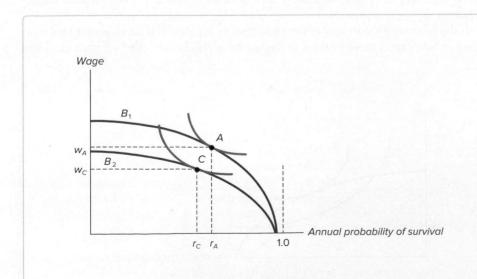

FIGURE 14A.2

The Effect of Productivity on the Optimal Safety Choice

The budget constraint confronting highly productive workers (B_1) presents a more favorable set of options than the one confronting less productive workers (B_2). If safety is a normal good, more productive workers will tend to choose jobs with higher wages and more safety (A) than the jobs chosen by less productive workers (C). But for any given productivity level, there is still a trade-off between wages and safety.

(buying safer equipment, enforcing stricter safety rules, and so on) that could be taken to reduce the annual probability of death in logging to only 1 in 10,000, the same rate as in steel mills. Assuming that workers are willing to pay $100/yr for each 1-in-10,000 reduction in the probability of death, this means that logging workers would be willing to give up as much as $900/yr in wages to see these additional safety steps taken. Profit-maximizing logging companies would thus have an incentive to implement these steps if their cost were less than $900/yr per worker. If the cost of the actions were greater than $900/yr per worker, however, neither the company nor the workers would stand to gain by them. True enough, the actions would make logging safer, but at a cost the loggers themselves would consider too high to be worth it.

The Occupational Safety and Health Act (OSHA), passed by Congress in 1970, mandates strict safety standards in the workplace. Its stated goal is to "insure the highest degree of health and safety protection for the employee." Many economists have been critical of OSHA on the grounds that it forces many workers to purchase more safety than they would choose to purchase on their own. Consider, for example, the worker who would have chosen the job at *A* in Figure 14A.3 had he been left to his own devices. And now suppose that OSHA requires all jobs to have an annual survival probability of at least r_c. The effect of the requirement will be to force the worker to abandon the job at *A* in favor of the one at *C*. But the job at *C*, even though safer, puts this worker on a lower indifference curve. At *C* the amount he is willing to spend for an increment in safety is less than the cost of providing that increment. If we accept the worker's own valuation of the alternatives, the safety requirement seems to make him worse off.

Supporters of health and safety regulations sometimes respond that the economist's criticism of OSHA would be justified in a perfectly informed, highly competitive labor market. They add, however, that these conditions are rarely, if ever, satisfied in practice. With respect to health issues in general, and the effects of toxic substances in particular, workers are often completely uninformed and so cannot make intelligent choices between different compensation packages. On this view, the workers empower government administrators to act as expert advisors on their behalf, to protect them against risks they find too complicated to assess intelligently for themselves.

This response by supporters of health and safety regulations seems sufficient to justify intervention in many cases. But it does not seem to explain many other instances. Consider again the case of the coal miner's choice between a dusty and a clean mine. Virtually every miner is aware that the likely consequence of working in a dusty mine is that he will eventually contract pneumoconiosis—coal miner's black lung disease—a seriously debilitating and sometimes fatal ailment. Since every miner is likely to have several people in his immediate family afflicted with black lung disease, ignorance of the consequences of working in a dusty mine seems an implausible rationale for requiring filters.

If the economist's criticism of health and safety regulation is on target for coal miners, we should expect these workers to oppose these regulations. And yet such measures

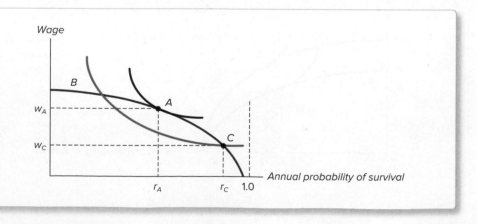

FIGURE 14A.3

A Safety Requirement That Reduces Utility

Left to his own devices, the worker in the diagram would choose the job at *A*. When there is a minimum survival probability of r_C, however, he must choose the job at *C*, which puts him on a lower indifference curve than the job at *A*.

appear to command widespread and enthusiastic support from the workers affected by them. This poses the puzzling question of why profit-seeking mine owners didn't simply install filters on their own to attract the miners who insist they want mines to have them (and who are willing to accept wage reductions sufficient to pay for them).

An alternative rationale for regulating safety and other specific terms of the labor contract is that labor markets may not, in fact, be workably competitive. Proponents of this view argue that workers lack the freedom of mobility necessary to have a range of job choices, and are thus vulnerable to exploitation by their employers.

SAFETY CHOICES AND RELATIVE INCOME

One other possible rationale for safety regulation is that the choices workers make as individuals may simply differ from those they would make collectively. Suppose, in particular, that miners care not only about safety and the absolute amount of income they earn, but also about how their incomes compare with those of others in the community. Perhaps their goal is to send their children to a good school, and they realize that to buy a house in one of the best school districts requires them to have more purchasing power than most other people have.

For simplicity, consider a community consisting of two identical workers, Jones and Smith, each of whom faces a choice between a clean mine that pays $200/wk and a dusty mine that pays $250/wk. The $50/wk differential reflects the cost per worker of filtering out the dust. Because relative income matters, the attractiveness of each choice depends on the choice made by the other person. Suppose the four possible combinations of choices are ranked as in Table 14A.1.

Note first how the two jobs compare when both workers choose the same type of job—that is, when the combination of choices results in the same income level for each worker. The upper left cell of the table corresponds to both choosing the safe mine, and this alternative is rated higher (second best for each) than the lower right cell, which corresponds to both choosing the unsafe mine (third best for each). This says merely that, concerns about relative income aside, the additional safety is worth more than $50/wk to each worker.

But suppose Smith chooses a job in the safe mine. The best outcome available to Jones will then be to work in the unsafe mine. By so doing, he gives up safety that is worth more than $50/wk to him for a reward of only $50/wk. In the process, however, he earns more income than Smith. According to Jones's preference ranking, this more than compensates for the loss in safety, because he can now send his children to the best schools.

Alternatively, suppose that Smith had chosen the unsafe mine. Jones again does better to choose the unsafe mine. By so doing, he gets his third best alternative, whereas the safe mine would have led to the worst possible combination. In short, no matter what Smith does, Jones gets a better outcome by choosing the unsafe mine.

TABLE 14A.1
Job Safety Choices When Relative Income Matters

		Smith	
		Safe mine, $200/wk	Unsafe mine, $250/wk
Jones	Safe mine, $200/wk	Second best for each	Worst for Jones Best for Smith
	Unsafe mine, $250/wk	Best for Jones Worst for Smith	Third best for each

No matter what the other person does, each party does better to choose the unsafe mine. And yet when each chooses the unsafe mine, each gets a worse outcome than if each had chosen the safe mine.

The incentives confronting Smith are exactly the same. He too does better by picking the unsafe mine, no matter what Jones does. The result is that each person picks the unsafe mine, which is worse than if each had chosen the safe mine. The choice confronting these workers is a prisoner's dilemma, just like the ones we saw in Chapter 12. The difficulty, as in all prisoner's dilemmas, is that it does not pay either player, acting alone, to choose the alternative that would be better for both. In this situation, it is easy to see why Jones and Smith might want to enter a binding agreement to work in the safe mine.

It is also easy to see why analysts who ignore concerns about relative income might conclude that a mine safety regulation makes each person worse off. Before the regulation, they would argue, each person freely chose to work in the unsafe mine. From that choice it seems to follow that additional safety was worth less than $50/wk to each worker. The apparent conclusion, finally, is that a safety regulation harms the workers by making them purchase safety that is worth less to them than its cost.

This argument strikes a resonant chord in the hearts of many freedom-loving people. Where it goes wrong, however, is in assuming that individual choices always reveal underlying preferences. When relative income matters, the structure of the problem is such that individual choices simply do not tell us how people feel about the aggregate results of their choices.

PROBLEM

Mc Graw Hill connect

1. *A* and *B* face the choice of working in a safe mine at $200/wk or an unsafe mine at $300/wk. The wage differential between the two mines reflects the costs of the safety equipment in the safe mine. The only adverse consequence of working in the unsafe mine is that life expectancy is shortened by 10 years. *A* and *B* have utility functions of the form $U_i[X_i, S_i, R(X_i)] = X_i + S_i + R(X_i)$ for $i = A, B$, where

$X_i = i$'s income per week in dollars,
$S_i = 200$ if i's mine is safe, 0 if unsafe,
$R(X_i) = 200$ if $X_i > X_j$, 0 if $X_i = X_j$,
$\qquad -250$ if $X_i < X_j$ $(i, j = A, B; j \neq i)$.

a. If the two choose independently, which mine will they work in? Explain. (*Hint:* Use the utility function to construct a payoff matrix like the one described in the text.)

b. If they can negotiate binding agreements costlessly with one another, will their choice be the same as in part a? Explain.

Jorge Salcedo/Alamy Stock Photo

Capital

Fortune magazine once conducted a survey in which business leaders were asked to identify the "best managed companies in America." Respondents were requested not to name their own firms, and there was considerable overlap in the lists they submitted. Some firms, such as Procter & Gamble, appeared on virtually every list.

The people surveyed were probably the most knowledgeable observers to whom such a question could have been put, and there is every reason to believe that the companies they named are indeed among the most well managed. And yet a follow-up study discovered that people who bought stock in these companies after publication of the survey actually earned slightly less on their investments than the average return for the stock market taken as a whole.

We see a similar pattern with respect to the investment advice published in investment newsletters. These newsletters are compiled by the country's leading financial analysts, and often sell for several hundred dollars per year. Their subscription lists include some of the most sophisticated members of the investment community. And yet the stocks recommended in most of these newsletters perform no better, on the average, than the stocks picked by a monkey throwing darts at the financial page.

As anomalous as these patterns may appear at first glance, we'll see that they are just what a careful analysis of the capital market would have predicted. Indeed, with investment newsletters, the real anomaly is not that the stocks they recommend do no better than others, but that people continue to pay such high prices for this kind of advice.

CHAPTER PREVIEW

In this chapter we'll examine the market for services of capital inputs. In many respects, the results from our study of labor inputs will carry forward intact. One feature that often sets capital apart from other inputs is that whereas other inputs are usually hired on a period-by-period basis, capital equipment is often owned outright by the firm. In our first exercise we'll examine the factors that govern the firm's decision to buy a piece of capital equipment.

We'll then examine the distinction between real and nominal rates of interest. This distinction will help make clear why the interest rates charged by banks and other lenders tend to rise hand in hand with the overall rate of inflation.

Next we'll see how interest rates are determined in the market for loanable funds. A topic of special focus will be the market for stocks and bonds and the apparent anomalies mentioned in the chapter introduction. Additional items on our agenda include economic rent and peak-load pricing.

FINANCIAL CAPITAL AND REAL CAPITAL

financial capital money or some other paper asset that functions like money.

real capital productive equipment that generates a flow of services; also called *physical capital*.

When people use the term "capital," they usually mean one of two very different things. They may have in mind **financial capital,** which essentially means money or some other form of paper asset that functions like money. Or they may mean **real capital** (or **physical capital**), which means a piece of productive equipment, such as a lathe or printing press, that generates a flow of productive services over time. When we refer to capital as a factor of production, we are almost always talking about real capital.[1] When people talk about the "capital market," they generally mean the market for financial capital, such as bank loans, corporate stocks, and bonds. Our direct concern in this chapter is with real capital, but because firms require financial capital to purchase real capital, we must consider markets for financial capital as well.

The Demand for Real Capital

Our theory of the individual firm's demand for labor developed in Chapter 14 applies without modification to the demand for other inputs. In the short run, if the firm can acquire the services of as much capital as it wishes at a constant rental rate of r/yr, it should employ capital up to the point at which its marginal revenue product (MRP_K) is exactly equal to the rental rate:

$$MRP_K = MR \times MP_K = r, \tag{15.1}$$

where MR is the firm's marginal revenue and MP_K is the marginal product of capital.

If the firm happens to be a perfect competitor in its product market, so that its marginal revenue is the same as its product price, then Equation 15.1 reduces to the simpler form:

$$VMP_K = P \times MP_K = r, \tag{15.2}$$

where VMP_K denotes the value of the marginal product of capital and P is the price of the firm's output.

For firms in a perfectly competitive industry, aggregation of individual firm demand curves into an industry demand curve for capital involves essentially the same complication we saw for labor. We must take into account that an expansion of industry output involves a reduction in the product price, with attendant moderations in the quantities of capital demanded. Again as before, this effect is already accounted for in the monopolist's demand curve for capital.

One salient difference between capital and labor markets is that whereas workers tend to specialize in particular types of activities, new sources of capital (financial capital) are almost completely fungible. Thus, a given sum can just as easily fund the construction of a machine to make soft ice cream as it can a printing press, or the production of an animated cartoon. Once financial capital has been used to purchase real capital, however, the firm's flexibility is limited. Whereas labor can, at some expense, be retrained to perform new tasks when conditions change, it is much more difficult to transform a drill press into a sewing machine.

---

[1]The exception is what we call "working capital," money the firm keeps on hand to facilitate timely payment of debts when current revenues fall short. By allowing the firm to function more efficiently, this working capital is no less a factor of production than labor and machines are.

THE RELATIONSHIP BETWEEN THE RENTAL RATE AND THE INTEREST RATE

How is the rental price of a unit of real capital equipment related to the interest rate at which money can be borrowed? To answer this question, put yourself in the position of a firm whose business is to rent machines. Suppose the purchase price of a particular machine is $1,000 and the interest rate is 5 percent/yr. To cover just the opportunity cost of the $1,000 you have tied up in the machine, you would have to charge $50/yr for it. But in general there will be additional costs as well. Suppose the machine requires $100/yr worth of maintenance. Your breakeven rental will then have risen to $150/yr. Finally, you must consider changes in the future price of the machine.

A rental car company must charge its customers enough to cover maintenance, depreciation, and forgone interest on the purchase price of the car.

For simplicity, suppose that the overall level of prices in the economy is stable. (More below on what happens when we relax this assumption.) Even a well-maintained machine will lose some of its value each year. Indeed, if newer, more efficient machines are being designed each year, an existing machine may lose its economic value overnight, even though it continues to function exactly as it did when new. This phenomenon is called **technological obsolescence.** If the net result of these factors—physical wear and tear and technological obsolescence—is for the price of the machine in our example to fall by $100/yr, the total cost of supplying it will then be $250/yr—$50 in forgone interest, $100 in maintenance, and $100 in lost market value. Any additional costs you incur as a rental business—such as wages for your staff—would have to be added to that figure.

Let m stand for annual maintenance expenses, expressed as a fraction of the price of the capital good, and let ∂ stand for physical and technological depreciation, similarly expressed. If i denotes the market rate of interest, expressed in decimal form, then the annual rental rate of capital, k, will be the sum of i, m, and ∂:

$$k = i + m + \partial. \tag{15.3}$$

Sometimes a machine will actually grow, rather than depreciate, in value over time. This can happen, for example, when a key input used in making the machine becomes more expensive. In such cases, the term ∂ in Equation 15.3 would be negative. For example, if the rental firm from our earlier example expected the price of a machine to go *up* by $100 in the year to come, it could break even at a rental fee of only $50, $200 lower than if the price of the machine went down by $100. Expectations of asset price increases appear to explain why, when housing prices are rising rapidly, rents are often lower than the corresponding mortgage payments.

technological obsolescence the process by which a good loses value not because of physical depreciation, but because improvements in technology make substitute products more attractive.

SELF-TEST 15.1

Suppose the purchase price of a Coke machine is $5,000. If the annual interest rate is 0.08, the maintenance rate is 0.02, and the rate of physical and technological depreciation is 0.10, how much will the machine's annual rental fee be?

THE CRITERION FOR BUYING A CAPITAL GOOD

Another factor that sets capital apart from labor is that firms have the option of purchasing capital equipment. Professional athletes are sometimes bought and sold as if they were no different from machines, but even they cannot be forced to play for a team indefinitely against their wishes. Labor contracts in general permit workers to move whenever the terms of employment are no longer attractive, the primary reason being that it is impractical to make a disgruntled employee work effectively on the firm's behalf. The machine, of course, enjoys no such latitude. It goes to the highest bidder.

What factors govern a firm's decision about whether to buy a given piece of capital equipment? As always, the firm will weigh the benefits of owning the machine against its costs. On the benefit side, the machine will bolster the firm's rate of production not only in the current period, but also in the future. Suppose the extra output made possible by the machine will enhance the firm's total revenue by R for each of the next N years. Suppose further that the machine costs M each year to maintain, and that at the end of N years it has a scrap value of S dollars. And suppose, finally, that the firm is given this machine and expects to operate it for N years, at which point it will sell it for scrap. By how much will the present value of the firm's stream of profits go up?

To answer this question, we must translate net revenues the firm will receive in the future into an equivalent present value. As we saw in Chapter 6, the present value of a dollar to be received 1 year from now is $\$1/(1 + i)$, where i denotes the market rate of interest. The present value of a dollar to be received 2 years from now is $\$1/(1 + i)^2$. (To see this, ask yourself, "How much money would I have to put in the bank today at an interest rate of i per year in order for my account to be worth \$1 two years from now?") The net present value of the stream of returns produced by the machine, including the proceeds from sale for scrap, is therefore given by

$$\text{PV} = \frac{R - M}{1 + i} + \frac{R - M}{(1 + i)^2} + \cdots + \frac{R - M}{(1 + i)^N} + \frac{S}{(1 + i)^N}. \tag{15.4}$$

The cost of the machine is simply its purchase price, P_K. The firm should buy the machine if and only if PV is greater than or equal to P_K. We see from Equation 15.4 that PV is inversely related to the market rate of interest. Thus, as with the firm that rents its equipment, the firm that owns its capital will want to employ more of it the lower the market rate of interest is.

SELF-TEST 15.2

Suppose a machine generates \$121 worth of revenue at the end of each of the next 2 years, at which time it can be sold to a salvage company for \$242. If the annual rate of interest is 0.10, what is the maximum amount a business would pay for this machine?

INTEREST RATE DETERMINATION

To recapitulate, a firm's demand for capital equipment depends on the rate of interest, the purchase price of capital, and the rates of technological and physical depreciation. Interest rates, in turn, are determined by the intersection of the supply and demand curves for loanable funds. Because financial capital is perfectly fungible, the market for loanable funds is an almost literal embodiment of the ideal of a perfectly homogeneous, standardized product. The result is a national—indeed international—market for loanable funds in which the interest rate charged to a given type of borrower is virtually the same everywhere.

How is the demand for loanable funds related to the demand for capital? A firm's demand for capital tells us how much capital it would like to employ at any given rental rate of capital, k. If it is a firm that has already been in operation for some time, it presumably has already acquired much of the capital it needs.

For simplicity, let us assume that in the current year the firm wishes to bridge the entire gap between the amount of capital it has and the amount it would like to have. This gap then constitutes its demand for loanable funds. At the industry level, similarly, the demand for loanable funds is the difference between the amount of capital firms as a whole would like

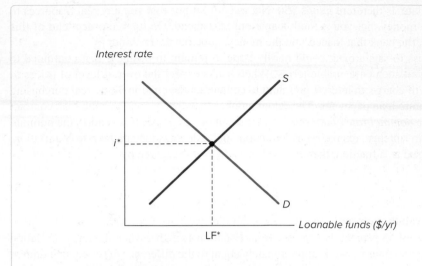

Interest rate

i^*

S

D

LF*

Loanable funds ($/yr)

FIGURE 15.1

Equilibrium in the Market for Loanable Funds

The quantity of loanable funds demanded at any interest rate (*D*) is the difference between the desired stock of capital at that interest rate and the amount of capital stock already in place. The supply of loanable funds (*S*) comes from consumers, firms, and international lenders. The growing importance of foreign lenders assures that the supply curve of loanable funds will be upward sloping.

to have and the amount they already do have. The price that is used to ration money in the loanable funds market is the interest rate.

Firms are not the only borrowers in the loanable funds market. Consumers borrow to finance the purchase of houses and other goods. Governments borrow to build roads and schools and to finance general budget deficits. The demand curve for loanable funds is the horizontal summation of the demands from all these sources.

On the supply side, there are also multiple sources of loanable funds. Consumer savings supplement funds made available by firms out of profits. And of growing importance in recent years has been the active participation of foreign lenders in the American market for loanable funds. The theory of consumer behavior tells us that a rise in interest rates may either raise or lower consumer savings. The total effect is the net result of off-setting income and substitution effects, and theory alone does not tell us which will dominate. Empirical studies suggest that in fact the elasticity of consumer savings with respect to interest rates is sometimes positive, sometimes negative, but in any event almost certainly very small.

For savings by private firms, there is no analog to the income effect in the consumer case, so the quantity of loanable funds supplied by firms will respond positively to interest rates. Most foreign lenders are happy to supply funds to U.S. borrowers whenever the interest rate meets or exceeds what they can earn at home. Adding all sources of supply horizontally, we obtain the aggregate supply curve of loanable funds. The large size of foreign lending in recent years suggests that this source is responsible for most of the elasticity we see in the supply curve of loanable funds. The intersection of this curve with the aggregate demand curve for loanable funds, shown in Figure 15.1, determines both the market rate of interest, i^*, and the total volume of funds exchanged, LF*.

REAL VERSUS NOMINAL INTEREST RATES

Suppose you borrow $1,000 from a bank, which you agree to repay in a year's time at 5 percent interest. And suppose that once the year passes, the overall price level in the economy has risen by 10 percent (as, for example, would happen if each and every price rose by 10 percent). What has been the real cost to you of your loan?

To answer this question, imagine that when you first borrowed the money, you used it to buy 100 oz of silver at $10/oz. Because the price of silver, like every other price, is assumed to be rising at 10 percent/yr, this means you can sell your silver for $11/oz when your loan comes due. The proceeds from this sale will be $1,100, or $50 more than the $1,050 you need to repay the bank. The real cost to you of the loan, measured in dollars on its due date, is therefore *minus* $50. Not only did it not cost you any real resources to borrow the money, but you actually came out $50 ahead. On the reciprocal end of this transaction, the bank that loaned you the money came out $50 behind.

Needless to say, a bank could hardly hope to remain in business if it continued to loan money at such unfavorable terms. When banks expect the overall level of prices to rise, they will charge an interest premium to counteract the erosion of the real purchasing power of future loan payments. The actual number that appears on the bank loan contract is called the *nominal rate of interest*—5 percent in our example. If n denotes the nominal annual rate of interest, expressed as a fraction, and q denotes the annual rate of inflation, also expressed as a fraction, then the *real rate of interest* is given by

$$i = \frac{n - q}{1 + q}. \tag{15.5}$$

Using the values from our hypothetical example, we have $i = (0.05 - 0.10)/1.10 = -0.0455$, or -4.55 percent. We can see from Equation 15.5 that when the rate of inflation is small, the real interest rate is approximately equal to the difference between the nominal rate of interest and the rate of inflation, $n - q$. In all our prior examples, the interest rate has been implicitly assumed to be the real interest rate. In its investment decisions, the firm wants to compare the real costs of capital against the real benefits, and proceed only if the latter exceeds the former.

THE MARKET FOR STOCKS AND BONDS

One common method by which firms raise money for new investments is by issuing corporate bonds. A bond is essentially a promissory note issued by the firm. An investor gives the firm some money—say, $10,000—and in return the firm hands the investor a handsomely engraved certificate that promises to pay the investor a fixed rate of interest—say, 10 percent—for a specified time. The *face value* of the bond is the amount for which it was sold to the investor who bought it from the firm. The lifetimes of corporate bonds vary considerably. *Short-term bonds* often promise to return their face value in full within 90 days. Many *long-term bonds* reach maturity only after 30 years, and some have even longer lifetimes.

Once bought, a bond may be traded in the open market. If it is a short-term bond, its price will almost always be close to its face value. For longer-term bonds, however, the price fetched in the open market can differ substantially from face value.

To see why, suppose the market rate of interest is 10 percent when an investor buys a $10,000 bond from a corporation; the bond promises to pay her $1,000/yr interest for the next 30 years and then return her $10,000 in full. As long as the interest rate remains 10 percent, the bond will continue to be "worth" $10,000 in the sense that its $1,000 annual interest payment fully compensates the investor for the opportunity cost of doing without her money. But suppose the interest rate suddenly falls to 5 percent. Now the opportunity cost of doing without $10,000 suddenly falls from $1,000/yr to only $500/yr. The investor who holds a bond that promises to give her $1,000/yr would not be willing to sell it for only $10,000, because with the interest rate at 5 percent, she would need $20,000 in order to earn the $1,000/yr interest she will get by keeping the bond.

The price of the bond in this example will not rise all the way to $20,000, however, because the new buyer knows that the bond will be worth only $10,000 when it reaches maturity. If the due date is imminent, the price will be close to $10,000 no matter what the interest rate is. But the farther away the maturity date of the bond is, the less its face value will affect its current market price. Indeed, there is a particular type of bond, called a **perpetual bond** or **consol,** for which the face value does not matter at all. A perpetual bond is a promise to pay its bearer a fixed sum of money each year forever. As a close approximation, the current market price of a consol is the amount of money that would be needed, at the current interest rate, to generate the same amount of interest as is paid by the consol. Thus, for example, a consol that promises to pay $1,000/yr will be worth $10,000 when the interest rate is 10 percent, and $20,000 when the interest rate

perpetual bond a bond that pays a fixed payment each year in perpetuity; also called a *consol.*

is 5 percent. More generally, if I represents the consol's annual payment and i is the market rate of interest, then the price of the consol, P_C, will be given by

$$P_C = \frac{I}{i}. \tag{15.6}$$

SELF-TEST 15.3

Consider a perpetual bond that pays \$120/yr to its owner. By how much would the price of this bond rise if the interest rate fell from 10 to 5 percent?

Corporations are not the only institutions that issue bonds. Governments at the federal, state, and local level do so as well. The examples discussed earlier implicitly assumed that there is a single, uniform market rate of interest at any moment, but in fact there are many different interest rates. The general rule is that the greater the risk is that a borrower will not repay a loan, the greater the interest rate that borrower will pay. United States government bonds carry the lowest risk of default available in the bond market, and the government therefore pays lower rates of interest than do the issuers of other bonds. Suppose, for example, that 30-year, \$10,000 General Motors Corporation bonds pay 8 percent annual interest, while the same type of bond issued by the federal government pays only 5 percent. The 3 percent interest rate differential is called a **risk premium,** and it compensates the investor for the fact that General Motors has a higher likelihood of not repaying its loan than does the federal government.

risk premium a payment differential necessary to compensate the supplier of a good or service for having to bear risk.

Someone who owns a corporate bond does not have an ownership share in the corporation. The bondholder's financial position is similar to that of a bank that has issued the corporation a loan. The corporation's stockholders are the people who actually own it. A firm that wants to raise money to invest in capital equipment can hire a broker to arrange a new issue of stock certificates. The broker then prepares a description of the firm's investment proposal and, with the cooperation of a network of other brokers, offers the new stock for sale to the public.

If a firm sells 1,000,000 shares of stock, each share constitutes a claim against $\frac{1}{1,000,000}$ of the current and future profits of the firm. Profits may be distributed to shareholders directly in the form of dividends, or they may be reinvested in the company, which will increase the value of the company's future profits.

What price will each share of stock command? Suppose the present value of the current and future profits of our 1,000,000-share hypothetical company is known with certainty to be \$500 million. Its stock should then trade at exactly \$500/share. At a price any lower than that, investors could increase their wealth immediately by buying it. And at any price above \$500, no one would have any economic incentive to own it.

Seldom, if ever, is a company's future profit stream known with certainty. The price people are willing to pay for shares depends on their best estimates of the firm's prospects. For new firms, or for firms that are moving into uncharted territory, the risk of low earnings can be very substantial indeed. If a genetic engineering company comes up with a way to clone an otherwise harmless protein that destroys the AIDS virus, its profits will be virtually unbounded. But many companies are struggling to be first in that race, and the destiny of most of them is to fail.

In other areas of the economy, the economic prospects of a company are easier to predict. Hertz has been in the business of renting cars for many decades now, and no major surprises appear to be on the horizon. Hertz stands almost no chance of hitting a big jackpot. But by the same token, its odds of continuing to survive are relatively high.

Consider two firms with the same expected value of current and future profits. The present value of firm 1's profit stream is \$100 million with certainty. The present value of firm 2's profit stream, by contrast, has a 50-50 chance of being either \$200 million or zero. If the stock prices of the two firms were the same, which one would you prefer to buy? If you are like most investors, you are risk averse (see Chapter 6) and therefore prefer firm 1, the safer of the two.

FIGURE 15.2

The Trade-Off between Safety and Expected Return

Because most investors are averse to risk, they will not buy a risky stock unless its expected return is greater than that of less risky stocks. Which type of stock to buy depends on the buyer's preferences. Relatively cautious investors will prefer safer stocks like *C*. Less cautious investors will give up some safety for the greater expected return on investments like *A*.

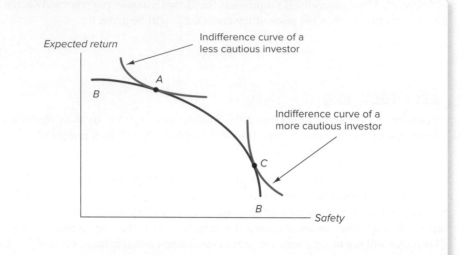

Because most people have this preference, the stocks of firms with risky future earnings generally sell at lower prices, just as riskier bonds generally must pay higher interest rates. As an investor confronting the stock market, you face a budget constraint something like the curve labeled *BB* in Figure 15.2. Along *BB*, the safer the investment, the lower its expected return. Investors with relatively low marginal rates of substitution between return and safety will choose risky investments such as *A*, which offer relatively high expected returns. Those with higher marginal rates of substitution between return and safety will choose safer investments such as *C*. Virtually everyone would like to own stocks with high expected returns *and* high safety. But the terms available in the market force people to choose between these attributes.

The Efficient Markets Hypothesis

Most economists believe the stock market is efficient. By this we mean that the price of a stock embodies all available information that is relevant to its current and future earnings prospects. To illustrate, consider a hypothetical example involving Genentech, a highly successful genetic engineering company. Suppose that on the strength of its earnings prospects, the current value of a share of Genentech is $100. Now suppose that one of Genentech's researchers suddenly stumbles onto a miracle cure for cancer. The discovery is simple and easy to patent. The company is certain to win government approval for its discovery, at which point its revenues will soar dramatically. But because of bureaucratic red tape, the approval process never takes less than 3 years. You read in *Newsweek* about Genentech's discovery and decide to buy stock in the company. Is this a shrewd move on your part?

The answer is almost certainly no, but not because the company does not have the rosy future that has been forecast for it. The difficulty, according to the efficient markets hypothesis, is that the value of the new discovery will be almost instantaneously bid into the market price of its stock. By the time you hear about it, the rise in price for which it is responsible will have long since occurred.

Critics of the efficient markets hypothesis often object that it refers to a frictionless ideal world. In the real world, they argue, it may take considerable time for new information to disseminate, and so its effect on stock prices may be gradual and protracted. Thus, they conclude, if the news of the Genentech discovery is only a few weeks old, there will still be plenty of room for stock prices to keep growing on the strength of it.

This view is almost certainly wrong. The difficulty is a confusion that arises because new information often comes not in the very sure form assumed in the example, but in highly uncertain form. In practice it would be much more common for the market to learn at first only that a Genentech researcher had a promising lead on a cure for cancer. This more limited information would justify a much smaller boost in the company's stock price, which would then be followed by further increases if the development continued to show promise. But it would be followed by a plunge in stock prices if the development were to fizzle. In either event, however, the full value of the information at hand would be reflected in the stock price of the moment. But because information about new profit opportunities usually emerges gradually, many observers erroneously conclude that the market's response to the new information is also gradual.

Unlike the conditions in our hypothetical example, in the real world it is usually hard to quantify exactly what information becomes available at specific times. Moreover, there is almost always latitude for differences in interpretation of any given piece of information. For these reasons, it is extremely difficult to verify the efficient markets hypothesis empirically. Nonetheless, most economists believe that it is correct. If the hypothesis is impossible to verify directly, what accounts for the strength of economists' commitment to it?

The answer is that the alternative hypothesis—namely that stock prices *don't* embody all the available information—leads to conclusions that we find so difficult to accept. To illustrate, consider our cancer cure example again, and suppose the market did not immediately bid up the price of the stock to reflect the higher future profits implied by the new discovery. Then you or I could simply pick up the phone and instruct our stockbrokers to buy as many shares in Genentech as we could afford. We could then sit back and wait for the market to bid up our shares to their full market value, reaping a substantial gain in the process.

The one belief that economists hold more deeply than any other is that the only way to reap such gains is by some combination of talent, hard work, and luck. But if we deny the efficient markets hypothesis, there can be cash just sitting on the table for the taking. We need no talent; we needn't do any hard work; and because the information is certain, we don't even need to be lucky. We just call our brokers and wait for the money to roll in. There is an ample supply of people who would be delighted to earn their livings in this painless way. That it seems generally impossible to do so is all the confirmation most economists need for the efficient markets hypothesis.

Does the efficient markets hypothesis imply that stocks will never be generally overpriced or underpriced? Some economists favor a strict version of the hypothesis with this implication. But most favor a less strict version, one that admits the possibility that waves of optimism or pessimism can cause stock prices to depart for extended periods from the valuations implied by long-run earnings prospects.

The important feature common to all versions of the efficient markets hypothesis is that individual stock pickers can't beat the market except through the aforementioned combination of talent, hard work, and luck. Suppose, for example, that a wave of optimism has caused stocks to become generally overvalued, as apparently happened in the late 1990s and again prior to the financial crisis that began in 2007. Should people who are holding stocks sell them? That might be the best move, but prices might continue rising faster than expected for several more years, in which case they would do better to hold on a little longer before selling.

Alternatively, suppose a wave of pessimism has caused most stocks to sell for prices lower than their companies' long-run earnings prospects would seem to imply. Should you buy stocks? You might do well if you did, but it's also possible that the wave of pessimism will persist, in which case you would have done better to hold government bonds for the time being.

In short, turning points in the market are extremely difficult to predict. The financial landscape is littered with bankrupt investors who thought they could beat the market by buying and selling at the right times. The efficient markets hypothesis suggests that trying to time the turning points in market sentiment is an ill-advised strategy, because frequent buying and selling entails such high transaction costs. A more prudent strategy is to invest in a diversified portfolio of stocks and bonds, and then stick with it for an extended period. Following that strategy, you'll earn a rate of return close to the overall long-run market average, which has been pretty good. Over the long haul, it's unlikely that market timers will do better, and quite likely that they'll do worse.

Economic Naturalist 15.1

Why is owning stock in a monopoly no better than owning stock in a perfectly competitive firm?

Are stocks in monopoly firms a good deal?

Many people believe that it is better to buy stock in a highly profitable company than in one with only an average profit level. An important implication of the efficient markets hypothesis, however, is that this belief is wrong. To see why, consider two firms identical in all respects except that one is a monopoly and earns twice the profit earned by the other. If the prices of the two stocks were the same, everyone would naturally want to own stock in the monopoly. But for that very reason, the prices of the two stocks cannot be the same. The excess profit of the monopoly will result in its stock selling for twice the price of the other firm's stock. From the perspective of the person buying the stock, therefore, the rate of return will be exactly the same for the two firms. True enough, the monopoly is twice as profitable, but its stock will cost twice as much to acquire.

Economic Naturalist 15.1 helps us explain one of the apparent anomalies mentioned at the outset of the chapter. Recall that shares in the best-managed companies performed no better than the stock market taken as a whole. Indeed, they even performed slightly worse. We can now see that this does not mean that the best-managed companies are no more profitable than others (although this may be so). If they do have higher profits because they are better managed, and if investors already know that, then their stock prices will have been high to begin with. There is no reason to expect them to grow more rapidly than the stock prices of other firms.

The Anomaly of the Investment Newsletter

I am always amused at how often I am asked to give or receive expert advice on the stock market. For example, when people at parties first learn that I am an economist, they often ask me which stocks they should buy. I tell them that if I knew the answer to that question, I wouldn't have to work for a living.

Stockbrokers who don't know that I am an economist often get my name from various mailing lists and then have their assistants call me to ask whether I would like to receive investment advice from their bosses. Here again, I am forced to decline, and certainly not because I already know which stocks will do well.

Because of their faith in the efficient markets hypothesis, most economists believe that it is generally fruitless to act on investment advice. The one important exception to this general rule occurs when the advice is based on information not available to other investors. Suppose, for example, that your sister was the Genentech researcher who came up with the miracle cure for cancer. You know that she has been working on this problem in her office in the house you share, and you can tell by the spring in her step that she has just solved it. And because you have learned this before anyone else did, you can be sure of making a lot of money by buying Genentech stock. But note that even this example does not violate the rule that substantial gains require talent, hard work, or luck. Here, it is simply your good fortune to have learned of the discovery before anyone else could act on it.

But generally the information we get about new profit opportunities is days, weeks, or even months old. It is very hard to see how information of that vintage could have any residual economic value. And yet ostensibly sophisticated investors frequently behave as if old news is worth acting upon.

One of the most puzzling examples of such behavior is the investment newsletter. Most major stock brokerages employ analysts to keep abreast of industry developments. The findings of these analysts are periodically distilled into investment newsletters that are then mailed to subscribers. Typically, subscriptions to these newsletters, which come out as infrequently as once a month, cost several hundred dollars a year. To economists, the disturbing question is why anyone would think the advice that comes in these newsletters could be worth acting on.

To illustrate the problem, consider an analyst who on June 1 discovers in his research that faulty accounting procedures have understated the profits of some company. Because investors thought the company was less profitable than in fact it was, its stock sold for too low a price. The analyst discusses this finding with his colleagues and superiors, who do some additional digging and confirm his conclusion. On June 15, the researcher writes up his findings in an article for the company's newsletter. The newsletter goes to the typesetter on June 22, and comes back for proofreading by July 6. Errors are corrected, and the printer returns the finished copies by July 20. The staff prepares the newsletters for mailing, and they are in subscribers' hands by the first of August.

During the nearly 2 months that have elapsed between the initial discovery of the information and the time it reaches subscribers, numerous people are in a position to act on it. The entire staff of the brokerage house, for example, has nearly 60 days in which to purchase shares of the undervalued stock. With the ample pools of resources into which large brokerages can tap, 60 minutes would be sufficient to capitalize fully on the discovery. Of course, many newsletters come out more frequently than once a month, but even with a daily newsletter the problem remains essentially the same. Even on the instantaneous Internet, you are unlikely to be the first to come upon an update; after all, someone had to write the web page.

Why would anyone think it possible to make money from information in a newsletter? And why, therefore, would anyone part with several hundred dollars a year to buy a subscription to this kind of information? Perhaps many investors buy the newsletters not for investment advice but in order to keep themselves informed of industry developments. The buying and selling of assets in the capital markets involves transactions among real people. In the social and business gatherings that take place in the investment industry, people naturally find it advantageous to appear well informed, and the newsletters may help them achieve this goal. But it is difficult to see how anyone could make money following their investment advice.

Sound Advice for Investors

The preceding discussion may make it appear that investment advisers serve no purpose. On the contrary, there is a clear role for professional investment advice, only of a different sort than many investors hope for. The efficient markets hypothesis suggests that investment advisers will not be able to tell you how to pick stocks that do better than the market as a whole. But they can tell you how to select the kinds of stocks that best suit your investment objectives. More specifically, they can help you decide intelligently about what combination of risk and expected return best suits your purposes. If you are a young person trying to save for retirement, it will usually make sense for you to acquire a portfolio of riskier stocks with higher than average returns. They may perform poorly during some periods, but if your real concern is to obtain the highest growth over the long run, this is the best mix for you.

If, by contrast, you are a person nearing retirement, a competent adviser will probably tell you to choose stocks that are safer but have lower expected returns because in this situation your primary concern is not to obtain long-term growth but to make sure your savings are protected against a large drop in value.

When you go out in the world, you will receive calls from stockbrokers who will tell you they can help you beat the market. Politely decline their services and seek out an adviser with a more realistic sense of what can be accomplished. Fortunately, some parts of the investment management industry have changed in the last few years to reflect the findings of the efficient markets hypothesis. Most large firms now offer low-cost index funds that seek to mirror market returns and that allow investors to manage their allocation between high- and low-risk investments. Some firms even offer "robo" accounts that are automatically rebalanced when gains or losses in one area pull the account out of sync with the target allocation. None of this changes the need for investors—young and old— to watch out for "beat the market" claims.

Tax Policy and the Capital Market

The government's tax policy toward the income earned from investments often has strong effects on how people allocate their resources. One example is the exemption from federal income tax that applies to the interest earned by holders of municipal bonds. A municipal bond is in most respects like a corporate bond, except that it is issued by a local government, not a corporation. An investor gives the government some money—say, $10,000—and the city pays the investor a fixed rate of interest—say, 5 percent—for a specified period, often 10 years, and then returns the $10,000.

To make it easier for local governments to raise money, Congress has exempted the interest earned on municipal bonds from the federal income tax. The holder of the bond in the example would thus receive $500 of tax-free interest each year. The interest earned on federal government bonds, by contrast, is fully taxable, as is the interest on bonds issued by corporations.

Hearing about this government policy for the first time, you may wonder why anyone ever buys any kind of bond other than a municipal bond. Why buy a federal or corporate bond and pay tax on the interest? People would indeed purchase only municipal bonds if the terms they offered were in other respects the same as those of federal or corporate bonds. Naturally, however, their terms will not be the same. In particular, local governments quickly discovered that they didn't have to pay as high an interest rate as the issuers of other bonds. Thus, a 10-year Treasury bill (a common federal bond) might pay 6 percent interest, while a 10-year Iowa City bond pays only 5 percent.

Which kind of bond you should buy depends on the marginal rate at which your income is taxed. Suppose you are taxed at the 33 percent rate on any extra income you earn. A federal bond that pays $600/yr interest will leave you with only $400/yr of interest after taxes. You would do better to purchase the municipal bond with its smaller, but tax-free, interest of $500/yr. Alternatively, suppose you pay tax at the marginal rate of only 10 percent. Your after-tax earnings for the federal bond ($540) would then be higher than for the municipal bond (again, $500).

Tax policy also affects the firm's decision whether to buy or lease its capital equipment. Under federal tax law, firms are granted a depreciation allowance for all capital equipment they own. The details of this allowance are complex, but a simple example will help make the essential point. If a firm owns a machine with, say, a 10-year life span, it is permitted to deduct 10 percent of the purchase price of the machine from its corporate profit each year in reflection of the machine's depreciation in value. By so doing, it avoids having to pay tax on that portion of its profit. This makes good economic sense because wear and tear on equipment is a legitimate operating expense for the firm. It should no more have to pay tax on such an expense than on its expenses for labor, paper, or any other input.

The depreciation allowance reduces the firm's income tax only if it has to pay income tax in the first place. If a firm experiences not a profit but a loss, or if it is a non-profit firm, then it owes no tax to the federal government, and its depreciation allowance essentially goes unclaimed. This fact has opened up an opportunity for entrepreneurs who start companies to lease capital equipment to firms that owe little or no corporate income tax. Because the leasing company can claim the full value of the depreciation allowance, it can essentially supply capital to its clients more cheaply than they can supply it to themselves. From the point of view of society as a whole, however, there is no savings in resources. What the companies save under this arrangement, the government loses in tax revenue. Indeed, the net effect is almost certainly to reduce the total value of output, since additional resources are expended to organize the leasing companies.

Corporations expend real resources in a variety of other ways to reduce their corporate income taxes. This waste could be eliminated if the tax on corporate profits were simply eliminated. The effect would be for more income to be transferred to the shareholders of corporations, where it could be taxed at whatever rate the government saw fit.

ECONOMIC RENT

In everyday usage, the term "rent" refers to the payment received by a landlord, a rental car company, or some other owner in return for the use of a real economic asset. In economic analysis, however, the term has taken on a slightly different definition. **Economic rent** is the difference between the payment actually received by the owner of a factor of production and his or her reservation price (the minimum amount necessary to induce him or her to employ it in its current use). For example, if a landlord would rather see her land lie fallow than let someone else farm it for a payment of less than $100/mo, then only $150 of the $250 monthly payment she currently gets for her land is economic rent.

If an input is supplied perfectly inelastically (that is, if its owner would supply it no matter how low the price), then the entire payment to the owner is economic rent. This situation is shown in Figure 15.3a. Suppose, however, that the owner of an input has an upward-sloping supply curve, which intersects the demand curve for the input at a price of r_1^*, as shown in Figure 15.3b. If buyers of the input could collude and make the owner a take-it-or-leave-it offer for K_1^* units of the input, the lowest amount the owner would accept is equal to the area under the supply curve up to K_1^* (the lower shaded area in panel b). But if buyers do not collude, the owner receives a price of K_1^* on each unit sold, and thus receives more than this minimum amount. Her economic rent is the shaded area above the supply curve.

Economic rent is the factor market analog of producer surplus in the goods market. Producer surplus, recall, is the revenue in excess of the minimum required to call forth a given supply of output in the goods market. As with producer surplus, economic rent will be greater, other things equal, the more inelastic the supply curve of the product.

Whether the payment to a factor of production constitutes an economic rent depends in part on the vantage point from which the transaction is viewed. Consider, for example, the parcel of land on which the McGraw Hill headquarters sits. From the landowner's point of view, no portion of McGraw Hill's monthly payment for the site is an economic rent. After all, if the company paid any less than it did for the site, the landowner could rent it for the same amount to some other company. In this sense,

economic rent the difference between what a factor of production is paid and the minimum amount necessary to induce it to remain in its current use.

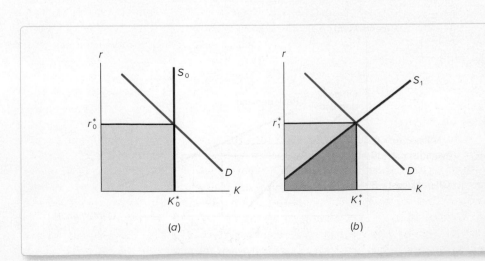

FIGURE 15.3

Economic Rent

(a) When an input is supplied perfectly inelastically, the entire payment it receives is an economic rent. (b) The economic rent received by an input with an upward-sloping supply curve is the shaded area above the supply curve.

McGraw Hill is not paying a penny more than necessary. But if we view the same transaction from the point of view of the economy as a whole, virtually the entire payment is an economic rent, because the owner of that land will offer it to *someone,* no matter how low the price falls.

Though rent is strongly associated in the public mind with payments to the owners of capital inputs, economic rents are often of even greater importance in the labor market. Recall, in particular, our discussion of the economics of winner-take-all markets in Chapter 14. People of rare talent or ability often command exceptionally high salaries, even though, in many instances, they would be willing to perform their services for next to nothing. The multimillion-dollar salaries of top entertainers and professional athletes, for example, are for the most part economic rent, not compensation for the inconvenience of sacrificing leisure.

PEAK-LOAD PRICING

A firm's demand for capital will depend not only on the rental rate of capital, but also on how it apportions the costs of its capital equipment among the buyers of its product. To illustrate the nature of this relationship, and at the same time to help shed light on an extremely important policy issue, let us consider the case of an electric utility whose demands differ sharply at different hours of the day. The historical pattern has been for such companies to be regulated by the state, which has instructed them to charge a single, uniform price for electricity sold at different times of the day or year. This price was generally pegged at a level sufficient to enable the company to cover its labor, equipment, fuel, and other costs, plus a normal return on its investment.

Recently, however, regulatory commissions have begun to alter this policy, implementing rate structures in which prices are directly related to the intensity of overall usage at the time of consumption. For example, a company whose loads are heaviest during business hours may be instructed to charge a higher price for electricity used between 8 AM and 8 PM than for electricity used during other hours. Such rate structures are commonly referred to as **peak-load pricing.**

peak-load pricing the practice whereby higher prices are charged for goods or services during the periods in which they are consumed most intensively.

To illustrate the effects of peak-load pricing, consider an electric utility that uses only two inputs, generators and fuel. Suppose that customer demands for electricity in the short run vary by time of day according to the pattern shown in Figure 15.4. The demand curve during business hours is labeled "Peak demand." The demand curve during the rest of the day is labeled "Off-peak demand." Suppose the company initially sells all its power at the same rate, 10 cents/kWh, and that its revenues at that rate exactly cover all its costs. Note in the diagram that when all power sells for 10 cents/kWh, peak demand is 250 MWh/mo.

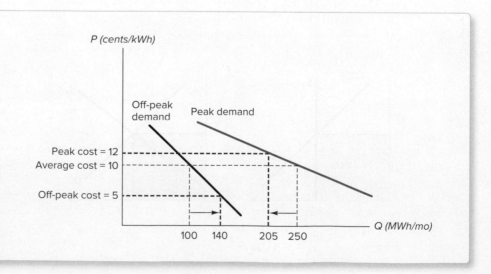

FIGURE 15.4

The Effect of Peak-Load Pricing

By charging higher prices during the peak hours ($P = 12$) and lower prices during the off-peak hours ($P = 5$), utilities give their customers an incentive to shift consumption onto off-peak hours. The resulting fall in peak-period usage enables the utility to serve its customers with a significantly smaller stock of generating equipment.

If the average cost of production is 10 cents/kWh, we know that the marginal cost of serving off-peak users must be less than 10 cents/kWh, while the marginal cost of serving peak users must be more. This follows because we can serve an extra off-peak user without having to add any more generating equipment, whereas we must add new generators to serve additional peak users. The only cost of serving an off-peak user will be the extra fuel required to run some of the generating capacity that would otherwise be idle during that period. Suppose this off-peak marginal cost is 5 cents/kWh. The extra cost during the peak period will include not only the cost of fuel, but also the cost of the required extra capital. For purposes of illustration, suppose that these peak-period costs add to 12 cents/kWh.

And suppose, finally, that the utility charges 12 cents/kWh to peak-period users and only 5 cents/kWh to off-peak users. Note in Figure 15.4 that the effect is to reduce peak-period consumption by 45 MWh/mo, most of which shifts to the off-peak period. The shift is achieved in a variety of ways. For example, people may buy timers that operate water heaters, air conditioners, and space heaters only during off-peak hours. Similarly, they may avoid using dishwashers, washing machines, and clothes dryers during the peak period. The net result of such consumption shifts is that a utility can serve its customers with much smaller generating capacity. The resulting cost savings represent a real increase in customer living standards.

Peak-load pricing is by no means limited to the electric utility industry. Airlines employ peak-load pricing, canceling some or all of their discount seats during heavy travel periods. Many ski areas have higher lift prices on major holiday weekends. Seasonal price differences are a common practice among resort hotels. The Washington metro charges its riders higher ticket prices during rush hours. And as noted in Chapter 11, many movie theaters charge lower prices during the dinner hour. Experience with these pricing practices tells us that when capital costs are assigned to the users responsible for their incurrence, the overall level of capital required can be reduced significantly.

EXHAUSTIBLE RESOURCES AS INPUTS IN PRODUCTION

In addition to man-made machines and other equipment, natural resources are also important inputs in many production processes. Microeconomic analysis affords insights of particular interest in the case of exhaustible resources. An exhaustible resource is one that cannot be replenished by people. Oil, gold, titanium, and aluminum are examples. Once the earth's stock of these substances runs out, we will have to do the best we can without them. How does a competitive market allocate exhaustible resources?

The owner of an exhaustible resource has two options: (1) he can hold the resource for the time being, or (2) he can sell it. The opportunity cost implicit in the first option is the interest that could have been earned had the resource been sold and the proceeds deposited in a bank (or used to purchase a stock or bond). The only economic reason the owner of an exhaustible resource would have for holding it is the expectation that its price will rise relative to the prices of other goods and services. Suppose you are the owner of several million barrels of oil, which sells at a current price of $60/bbl. If the real interest rate is 5 percent, how much will the price of oil have to rise in the next year for you to be willing to hold at least some of your oil? Suppose the price rises to $66/bbl. If you sold all your oil now and deposited the proceeds in an account at 5 percent, your total wealth would grow by 5 percent during the next year. If instead you hold on to your oil, your total wealth will grow by 10 percent. Since the second option is obviously more attractive, the likelihood is that you will not sell any of your oil. By contrast if the price of oil were expected to rise to only $61.50/bbl in the next year, your best bet would be to unload all of your oil now and invest the proceeds at 5 percent. A $1.50 rise in the price of a $60 barrel oil means that oil you hold will grow by only 2.5 percent in value.

FIGURE 15.5

The Equilibrium Price Path for an Exhaustible Resource

When the market for an exhaustible resource is in equilibrium, its price will grow at the real rate of interest.

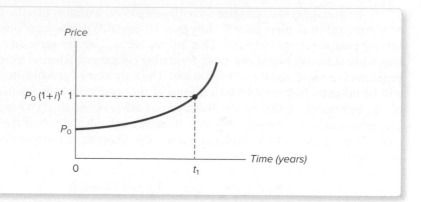

It should be clear from this example that for the market for an exhaustible resource to be in equilibrium, its price must be rising at precisely the real rate of interest. A growth in price any smaller than that would result in *all* owners trying to sell. And one any higher would result in a complete shutdown of trading. Suppose P_0 denotes the current price of an exhaustible resource—say, oil. If this price grows at the rate of i per year, then the mathematical expression for the price after t years will be given by[2]

$$P_t = P_0(1 + i)^t, \tag{15.7}$$

a plot of which is shown in Figure 15.5.

Two important conclusions follow from the fact that exhaustible resource prices will tend to grow at the real rate of interest. First, because the demand curves for exhaustible resources are downward sloping like any others, the gradual rise in price will cause a gradual reduction in the quantity of the resource demanded. This, in turn, means that the initial stock of the resource will be used up gradually, not precipitously. As less and less of the original stock remains, higher prices will slow down further the rate at which the resource is drawn upon.

A second important effect of rising prices is to stimulate the production of substitutes for the exhaustible resource. Sooner or later, the world is going to run out of oil. The activities we use oil for today will someday have to be done using some other means, or else not be done at all. As oil gets more expensive, entrepreneurs will have strong incentives to discover alternative ways of carrying out the activities that require oil.

Despite uncertainty about the volume of existing oil reserves and about the future costs of alternative technologies, markets for oil and other exhaustible resources function remarkably smoothly most of the time. Severe disruptions are usually the result of politically related cutbacks in supply. Apart from supply interruptions of this sort, perhaps the greatest threat to the functioning of these markets is policies that attempt to restrain the natural growth of exhaustible resource prices.

In an attempt to maintain affordable supplies of energy for the poor, the Carter administration implemented a complex system of fuel price controls during the late 1970s. By keeping energy prices well below their equilibrium values, we jeopardize the gradual transition between energy sources that is characteristic of the market allocation. Far better to let energy prices be governed by market forces and find some other way of easing the burden on the poor.

The appendix to this chapter discusses the use of exhaustible resources in more detail.

---

[2]If the growth in price is continuous, the exact relationship will be

$$P_t = P_0 e^{it},$$

where e denotes the constant, 2.7183. Equation 15.7 provides a close approximation to this relationship.

SUMMARY

- Our task in this chapter was to examine the market for services of capital inputs. Many of the results from our study of labor inputs apply to capital as well. Thus, a firm's demand for the services of a capital input is the marginal revenue product of that input—which, in the case of the perfectly competitive firm, is the same as the value of capital's marginal product. *(LO1)*

- One feature that often sets capital apart from other inputs is that while other inputs are usually hired on a period-by-period basis, capital equipment is often owned outright by the firm. In considering whether to purchase a machine, the firm must ask how much its output will increase not only in the current period, but also in future periods. The firm's decision rule is to acquire the machine if and only if the present value of the current and future increases in revenue made possible by the machine exceeds its purchase price. This rule illustrates the factors that determine the rental rate of capital. These include the interest rate, or opportunity cost, of borrowed funds, the rates of physical and technological depreciation, and expected future movements in the price of the capital. *(LO3)*

- The real rate of interest measures interest in terms of equivalent quantities of real goods or services. If, for example, a bank lends 100 oz of gold and requires a repayment of 105 oz after 1 yr, the real interest rate would be 5 percent. When the rate of inflation is small, the nominal rate of interest is approximately equal to the real rate of interest plus the rate of inflation. This relationship helps make clear why the interest rates charged by banks and other lenders tend to rise hand in hand with the overall rate of inflation. *(LO5)*

- A firm's demand for borrowed money depends on how the amount of capital equipment it would like to have compares with the amount it actually does have. The supply of loanable funds is highly responsive to interest rates because of the importance of foreign lenders in this market. The market interest rate and equilibrium level of borrowing are determined by the intersection of the supply and demand curves for loanable funds. *(LO4)*

- The market for stocks and bonds is one of the principal sources of funds to finance new capital equipment. A corporate bond is essentially a loan from the purchaser of the bond to the corporation. As a bond nears maturity, its price must converge to its face value. But for bonds that are far from maturity, there will be a significant inverse relationship between current interest rates and the price of the bond. The price of a given stock is the present value, suitably discounted for risk, of the current and future profits to which it provides a claim. *(LO6)*

- The "efficient markets hypothesis" says that, holding risk constant, all available information about current and future earnings of a firm is immediately incorporated into the price of its stock. The implication is that an investor should do equally well no matter which stocks he or she purchases. The efficient markets hypothesis thus helps explain why the investment tips of "experts" are of little or no value.

- Tax policy has numerous effects on capital market decisions. The fact that municipal bonds are tax-free helps explain why their interest rates are generally lower than for bonds with taxable interest. Tax policy also sometimes induces firms to lease, rather than buy, their capital equipment. *(LO6)*

- The term "rent" as used by economists has a somewhat different meaning from the one familiar from everyday usage. It is the payment to a factor of production in excess of the minimum value required to keep that factor in its current use. A significant share of the payments received by owners of capital constitutes economic rent under this definition. Rents often constitute a large share of incomes generated in the labor market as well. *(LO7)*

- In peak-load pricing schemes, firms and regulatory agencies must decide how much to charge for the use of capital equipment when the intensity of demand varies greatly. As ever, the rule for efficient allocation is to set prices on the basis of marginal cost. Peak-load pricing enables firms to serve their markets while using significantly smaller amounts of capital equipment. *(LO8)*

- In competitive markets for exhaustible resources, such as petroleum or titanium, prices tend to rise at the real rate of interest. This not only curtails the rate at which exhaustible resources are used, but also stimulates the rate at which new substitutes are developed. And it also assures a smooth transition between the use of an exhaustible resource and its eventual substitute. *(LO9)*

KEY TERMS

economic rent	perpetual bond	risk premium
financial capital	real capital	technological obsolescence
peak-load pricing		

REVIEW QUESTIONS

1. What is the difference between real capital and financial capital? Why does concern with one type of capital invariably involve concern with the other? *(LO1)*

2. Explain why depreciation is an economic cost just like any other. *(LO2)*

3. Why do higher interest rates make future events economically less important? *(LO6)*

4. Why do nominal interest rates rise approximately 1-for-1 with increases in inflation? *(LO5)*

5. Why are bond prices and interest rates inversely related? *(LO6)*

6. Why is published investment advice unlikely to be worth very much? *(LO6)*

7. Give three examples of peak-load pricing used in your community. *(LO8)*

8. Who will typically achieve a higher expected return on their investments: young investors or older investors with more immediate need for retirement income? *(LO6)*

PROBLEMS

Mc Graw Hill **connect**

1. You are deciding which of two computers to purchase. The interest rate is 0.09, and the maintenance rate of both machines is 0.01. The first computer costs $4,000 and has a rate of physical and technological depreciation of 0.10. The second computer, on the verge of obsolescence, has a rate of physical and technological depreciation of 0.30. If the annual rental payment for the two computers is the same, how much must the purchase price of the second computer be for you to be willing to buy it? *(LO3)*

2. A machine that costs $100 will yield returns of $30 at the end of each of the next 3 years, at which time it will be sold as scrap for $30. If the interest rate facing this firm is 10 percent, should it purchase this machine? *(LO3)*

3. Suppose a perpetual bond pays $3,000/yr to its owner. What is the price of the bond at 5 percent interest? At 6 percent? *(LO6)*

4. If everyone's marginal tax rate is 50 percent and if the interest rate on taxable government bonds is 8 percent, what will be the interest rate on nontaxable government bonds? *(LO6)*

5. If the interest rate on taxable government consols is 10 percent, what will happen to the price of an existing tax-exempt government consol if the government reduces everyone's marginal tax rate from 50 to 30 percent? *(LO6)*

6. Suppose a majority of investors do not care whether the companies whose stock they own do business in China. How, if at all, will the rate of return on stocks that do business in China differ from the rate of return on stocks that do not? *(LO6)*

7. Tony's barbershop has four chairs and four barbers. Most of the time at least one barber is idle, except on Saturday mornings when all four are continuously booked. Explain, in terms a noneconomist could understand, why the cost of providing a haircut on Saturday morning is higher than at other times of the week. *(LO8)*

8. Around 1890 the vineyards in Bordeaux were infected by Phylloxera, a louse that attacks the vine's roots. To preserve the original grape varieties, the Bordeaux vines were grafted onto roots taken from American grape plants. Since 1890 all Bordeaux wines have been made with vines grafted onto American roots. These wines do not taste the same as the wines made before the Phylloxera infection. A bottle of Bordeaux wine that was made before the infection sells for thousands of dollars. Suppose you had a bottle of pre-Phylloxera Bordeaux that you could sell today for $2,000 and you were interested only in its value as an investment. To make it worthwhile for you to hold on to your investment, what must be the expected price of the bottle in n years if the market rate of interest is i? *(LO6)*

ANSWERS TO SELF-TESTS

15.1 Since $k = i + m + \partial$, we have $k = 0.08 + 0.02 + 0.10 = 0.20$. So the annual rental payment will be $k(\$5,000) = \$1,000$. *(LO2)*

15.2 $PV = (121/1.1) + (121/1.1^2) + (242/1.1^2) = 110 + 100 + 200 = \$410$. *(LO6)*

15.3 The price at 10 percent is $\$120/0.10 = \$1,200$. At 5 percent the price will be $\$120/0.05 = \$2,400$, so the rise in price is $1,200. *(LO6)*

A More Detailed Look at Exhaustible Resource Allocation

NATURAL RESOURCES AS INPUTS IN PRODUCTION

In addition to man-made machines and other equipment, natural resources are also important inputs in many production processes. For purposes of analysis, it is common to partition natural resources into two distinct categories: (1) renewable resources, such as trees, and (2) exhaustible resources, ones that exist in finite quantities that cannot be replaced once expended. A common example of an exhaustible resource is oil. Let us consider each of these categories in turn.

Renewable Resources

To illustrate the economic issues that arise in connection with renewable resources as inputs, consider the case of a lumber company whose business it is to produce lumber from the trees grown on its own land. Its objective is to plant, care for, and harvest trees in such a way as to maximize the present value of its current and future profits.

An agricultural specialist advises the firm about how far apart to plant its trees, what fertilizers to apply, and so on. The economist's expertise lies in answering the question of when the trees should be harvested. Each year the firm must decide whether to cut a tree down or to let it grow another year. The benefit of cutting it down now is to get the revenue from selling it right away. If the firm waits a year, it loses the use of that revenue for the time being, but in the meantime the tree continues to grow.

Suppose trees grow over time according to the growth curve labeled B in Figure 15A.1. Suppose also that the price of lumber remains constant through time, and that the real market rate of interest, expressed as a fraction, remains constant at i/yr. At what age should a tree then be harvested for its lumber?

The revenue from the sale of the tree is proportional to the volume of lumber in it. The slope of the growth curve, $\Delta B/\Delta t$, tells us how much extra lumber the firm will get by waiting an additional Δt units. The rate at which revenue will grow if the tree is left alone is the extra lumber divided by the size of the tree, $(\Delta B/\Delta t)/B$. Thus, if Δt is 1 year and if $\Delta B = 0.10B$, then the rate at which lumber—and hence total revenue—grows will be 0.10/yr. Because the slope of the B curve eventually declines over time (see Figure 15A.1), it follows that the value of $(\Delta B/\Delta t)/B$ will also eventually decrease over time, as shown in Figure 15A.2.

If instead of letting the tree continue to grow, the firm cuts it down now and invests the proceeds at the market rate of interest, its revenue will grow at the rate of i/yr. It follows that the tree should be harvested as soon as

$$\frac{\Delta B/\Delta t}{B} = i, \tag{15A.1}$$

FIGURE 15A.1

The Growth Curve for a Tree

The curve labeled B tells the volume of lumber in the tree as a function of its age in years. The slope of the curve at a point is given by the ratio $\Delta B / \Delta t$.

FIGURE 15A.2

The Optimal Time of Harvest

The optimal harvest time, t^*, is when the growth rate of the tree, $(\Delta B / \Delta t)/B$, is exactly equal to the real rate of interest, i. At that point the extra revenue from leaving the tree in the ground for Δt longer is exactly equal to the interest that could be earned by harvesting the tree and investing the proceeds at i.

which will happen for $t = t^*$ in Figure 15A.2. For values of t to the left of t^*, the growth rate of the tree exceeds the growth rate of money deposited at i, which means that the firm should wait a little longer. For values of t greater than t^*, by contrast, money deposited at i will grow faster than the lumber in the tree, so the firm should harvest the tree a little sooner.

SELF-TEST 15A.1

The volume of lumber in a tree is given by $B = 80\sqrt{t}$, the slope of which curve at any point is given by $\Delta B / \Delta t = 40/\sqrt{t}$. If the annual interest rate is 0.02, at what age should the tree be harvested?

Note that the optimal time for harvesting a tree is not when it is as big as it will possibly get. On the contrary, it is still growing at the rate $i > 0$ at the optimal time of harvest. The company's objective is not to get the maximum possible quantity of lumber out of any one tree, but to maximize the net revenues that result from an ongoing process of growing trees. And this will necessarily mean clearing out slower-growing mature trees to make room for faster-growing young ones.

Many observers complain that lumber companies often harvest trees wastefully, even by the standard of Equation 15A.1. Where this has in fact been the case, the reason is generally that the trees were growing on land owned by someone other than the harvester. Where, for example, timber grows on commonly owned land and is free for the taking on a first-come, first-served basis, it is almost always harvested well before it reaches economic maturity. Each firm in this situation might want to let the trees grow a little longer. But each knows that a tree not harvested today by one firm will be harvested instead by another. And so, reluctantly, each firm harvests trees as soon as they are large enough to justify the costs of processing them. But if a tree is growing on land owned or controlled by the firm that will harvest it, there is every financial incentive not to harvest it too soon. For to do so would only reduce the present value of the firm's future earnings.

MORE ON EXHAUSTIBLE RESOURCES

All exhaustible sources of energy will eventually run out, at which point we will be forced to rely on renewable sources of energy. Our task in this section is to investigate in greater detail the process of transition from exhaustible to renewable energy sources.

Again for simplicity, assume that oil is the only exhaustible energy source and that when it is used up, we will switch to solar energy. Recall from the text that equilibrium in the oil market requires that the price of oil rise at the rate of interest. Figure 15A.3, in which D is the demand curve for oil, summarizes the effect of rising oil prices on the rate at which oil is consumed.

If we know how the price of oil will grow over time, and if we know the demand curve for oil, it is a simple matter to calculate the amount of oil that will be left at any moment in time. Suppose the current stock of oil is S_0 and its current price is P_0. Consulting the demand curve for oil (Figure 15A.3), we see that consumers will use Q_0 units of oil this year, leaving $S_0 - Q_0$ units remaining at the beginning of next year. At next year's price of P_1, they will use Q_1 units, leaving $S_0 - Q_0 - Q_1$ at the beginning of the following year, and so on. Plotting the quantity of oil remaining at each moment in time, we have the *stock exhaustion path*, shown in Figure 15A.4.

FIGURE 15A.3

The Effect of Rising Prices on the Use of an Exhaustible Resource

The demand curve for an exhaustible resource, like any other, is downward sloping. Gradually rising prices thus lead to gradual reductions in the quantities by which the stock is depleted each year.

FIGURE 15A.4

The Stock Exhaustion Path

In the current moment ($t = 0$), the stock of oil is S_0 units. Given its current price of P_0, we consult the demand curve (Figure 15A.3) to get this year's consumption (Q_0). The stock remaining at the beginning of next year ($t = 1$) will be $S_0 - Q_0$. At next year's price of $P_0(1 + i) = P_1$, consumption will be Q_1, which means that the stock remaining at the beginning of the following year will be $S_0 - Q_0 - Q_1$, and so on.

FIGURE 15A.5

Adjustment When Investors Expect to Be Stuck with Excess Oil

If investors believe they will still be holding some oil when its price reaches P^* (the price of solar energy), they will try to reduce their current holdings. This leads the current price to fall (bottom panel), which causes current and future use to increase. The increased rate of consumption is reflected in the downward shift of the stock exhaustion path (top panel).

Suppose that the price of solar energy is P^* per unit and is expected to remain constant through time. Suppose also that our current stock of oil embodies S_0 units of energy. We have already seen that the theory of exhaustible resource markets tells us that the price of energy in the form of oil will grow at the real rate of interest. But the theory also predicts that the last drop of oil will be used up at the very moment that its price (measured in dollars per unit of energy) reaches P^*, the level at which it becomes economical to use solar energy.

To see why this second prediction must be expected to hold, suppose that the owners of oil expected it not to. First, suppose they expect that when the price of oil reaches P^*, they will have some additional oil left. The locus labeled SEP_0 in the top panel of Figure 15A.5 depicts the stock exhaustion path corresponding to an initial stock of S_0, with an initial price of P_0. Starting at P_0, price rises at the real rate of interest over time, intersecting P^* when time $= t_1$ (bottom panel of Figure 15A.5). Note in the top panel that at t_1 there are S_1 units of oil remaining. But the owners of oil know that once its price reaches P^*, it can increase no further. After all, why should anyone be willing to pay more than P^* for oil if solar energy can be had for that price? If the owners have oil left over when the price reaches P^*, they will be able to sell it only at the rate at which people demand energy at that price. This means they will end up having to hold on to an asset—namely, what's left of their oil—whose price doesn't grow, and no investor wants to do that.

Individual owners can avoid that outcome by selling their oil right now. And since all owners face the same incentive to sell, it follows that the current price will fall—from P_0 to P'_0 in the bottom panel of Figure 15A.5. This fall in price will accomplish two things: (1) when price again grows at the real rate of interest, it will take longer than before to reach P^*, and (2) oil use levels will be higher, both now and in the future (because the demand curve for oil is downward sloping). In Figure 15A.5, the first effect is reflected in the fact that $t_2 > t_1$, the second in the fact that the new stock exhaustion locus (SEP_1) lies below the original one. Both effects will tend to reduce the amount of oil left over when the price reaches P^*. As Figure 15A.5 is drawn, the last drop of oil is used at the exact moment the new price path reaches P^*. If owners had still expected some to be left over at t_2, the current price would have fallen still further.

If oil is expected to run out before price reaches P^*, owners will conclude that they can earn more than the real rate of interest by holding on to their oil. This will cause current price to rise (bottom panel), which in turn will cause an upward shift in the stock exhaustion path (top panel). The upward price adjustment will continue until investors expect price to reach P^* at the moment all stocks are exhausted.

Alternatively, suppose owners think they will run out of oil before its price reaches P^*. That is, suppose, as in Figure 15A.6, that we start with an initial stock of S_0 and price of P_0, and that we run out of oil at t_1, before its price reaches P^*. Once oil runs out, people will have to pay P^* per unit of energy since solar energy will be the only source available. So owners can foresee that at t_1 they will be able to charge not P_{t_1} but P^* for their oil. This means that by holding on to their oil until t_1, they can earn more than the real rate of interest. So if the owners of oil expect it to run out before its price reaches P^*, they will have an immediate incentive to stop selling oil right now. This produces an increase in the current price of oil, from P_0 to P'_0 in the bottom panel of Figure 15A.6, which in turn causes an upward shift in the stock exhaustion path (top panel). The upward movement in price will continue until owners expect that the new price path will reach P^* at the exact moment the corresponding stock exhaustion path reaches zero.

The theory of exhaustible resource markets discussed above implicitly assumes that investors know how much oil remains in the ground at any moment. In practice, however, no one is really sure. Similarly, we don't know exactly how much solar energy will cost once we run out of oil, for that depends on technological developments that are difficult to foretell. In place of known values of oil reserves and known values of the prices of alternative energy sources, the market must rely on estimates. These estimates are often highly imprecise, and always subject to revision as we acquire new information. If someone discovers a massive new oil field, or a substantially cheaper method of harnessing solar energy, current energy prices may change dramatically, as the following example illustrates.

EXAMPLE 15A.1

Suppose that because of breakthroughs in superconductor technology, the price of solar energy falls by half, from P^* to $P^*/2$. Show how this affects the time path of oil prices and the time at which we switch from oil to solar power.

Suppose the original stock adjustment and price paths are as given in Figure 15A.7. With a solar energy price of P^*, the last drop of oil would be used when $t = t_1$, the

FIGURE 15A.7

Response to a Fall in the Price of Solar Energy

moment when the price of oil reaches P^*. If the price of oil continued on its original path after the price of solar energy fell, it would reach $P^*/2$ at $t = t'$, when there would be S'_t units of oil remaining. For the reasons discussed earlier, this would cause the current price of oil to fall. It would continue falling until it reached a level (P_0 in Figure 15A.7) for which the new price path reaches $P^*/2$ at the same moment the corresponding stock adjustment path reaches zero. As shown in the diagram, the effect of the price reduction in solar energy is to produce downward shifts in both the price and stock adjustment paths for oil. Whereas the age of solar power originally would have begun at $t = t_1$, it will now begin much sooner, at $t = t_2$.

SUMMARY

- In competitive markets for exhaustible resources, such as petroleum or titanium, prices tend to rise at the real rate of interest. This not only curtails the rate at which exhaustible resources are used, but also stimulates the rate at which new substitutes are developed. And it also assures a smooth transition between the use of an exhaustible resource and its eventual substitute.

REVIEW QUESTION

1. Why does equilibrium require the price of exhaustible resources to rise at the real rate of interest?

PROBLEMS

1. Suppose solar energy can be produced at a cost of $2 per unit of energy. Suppose the current price of oil is $1.80 per unit of energy and there is currently enough oil to last 100 more years at current use levels. If the real rate of interest is 0.05, what do you expect to happen to the current price of oil?

2. There are two remaining exhaustible energy sources, underground oil and offshore oil, with extraction costs

of \$2/barrel and \$6/barrel, respectively. There is also solar energy with the price of \$12 per energy equivalent of a barrel of oil. Everyone believes that there are currently S_1 barrels of underground oil and S_2 barrels of offshore oil remaining. How would the discovery of A additional barrels of underground oil affect the time and the gross price at which offshore oil will first be extracted? How will the discovery affect the length of the "offshore oil age," that is, the length of the time interval during which we use offshore oil?

3. Suppose a certain species of tree grows according to the function $B = 20\sqrt{t}$, where B is the volume of lumber in the tree, measured in board-feet, and t is the tree's age in years. If the interest rate is 0.05, at what age should the trees be cut if the goal is to maximize long-run profit?

4. Suppose there are two kinds of oil left, underground oil and shale oil. The cost of extracting a unit of underground oil is \$2/barrel, of shale oil \$10/barrel. Once extracted from the earth, the two kinds of oil are identical. Explain, in terms a noneconomist could understand, why it does not make sense to begin using the shale oil until all the underground oil has been exhausted.

ANSWER TO APPENDIX SELF-TEST

15A.1 $(\Delta B/\Delta t)/B = (40/\sqrt{t})/80\sqrt{t} = 1/2t = 0.02$, which solves for $t = 25$ years.

Jorge Salcedo/Alamy Stock Photo

Externalities, Property Rights, and the Coase Theorem

16

LEARNING OBJECTIVES

After reading this chapter, you should be able to:

LO1 Describe the reciprocal nature of externalities by noting that preventing an activity that causes harm to others also causes harm to the person thus restricted.

LO2 Explain why, if transaction costs render private negotiation impractical, the law should place responsibility for mitigating externalities on the party that can do so at lowest cost.

LO3 Explain why, if property rights were fully defined and transaction costs were negligible, people would be able to negotiate efficient solutions to problems caused by externalities.

LO4 Give an example of a positive externality.

LO5 Define positional externalities and explain why they often lead to inefficient allocations when private negotiation is impractical.

LO6 Explain why imposing taxes on activities that cause harm to others helps concentrate mitigation effort in the hands of those who can accomplish it at lowest cost.

At the corner of 22nd and M streets, NW, in Washington, D.C., there once stood a venerable restaurant called Blackie's House of Beef. During a real estate boom in the 1970s, this location emerged as a prime site for the construction of high-rise commercial buildings. With the passage of each month, the opportunity cost of continuing to operate a one-story restaurant on that site continued to soar. And yet the owners of Blackie's were of no mind to abandon their location. The restaurant had been the family business for many years, and the family was determined to see it continue.

Eventually they came up with a creative solution. They negotiated a multimillion-dollar agreement whereby, without disturbing a single brick in the restaurant, a high-rise structure would be constructed on stilts *above* the restaurant. Blackie's remained open until 2006, a quaint, old-world country inn nestled beneath a high-rise Marriott Hotel. In a similar multimillion-dollar transaction, a developer purchased the rights to build a new skyscraper astraddle the Museum of Modern Art in midtown Manhattan.

In most jurisdictions, owning a piece of property confers the right to exclude anyone from constructing a building in the airspace above it. But a similar right does not extend to all other forms of activity in the same airspace. For example, hundreds of thousands of American houses are located beneath commercial flight paths between major cities, and each day thousands of airliners use the airspace above these houses without paying a penny. This pattern of rights is not a matter of historical accident. It has emerged, as we'll see, as a means of making the most efficient use of property when it is difficult to negotiate agreements on a case-by-case basis.

CHAPTER PREVIEW

Our subjects in this chapter are externalities and property rights. We'll begin with a series of examples illustrating what happens when an action by one party harms another and the parties are able to negotiate costlessly with one another. Next we'll consider a related set of examples in which negotiation is costly. We'll then apply the principles that emerge from these examples to a variety of questions regarding the design of property rights. Should the owner of a dock be allowed to exclude a boater from tying up during a storm? When should a person be allowed to exclude others from walking across his land? Or from blocking his view? Should pastureland be owned privately or in common? Should a developer be allowed to construct an office building over someone else's property without her consent? Should airplanes be allowed to fly over houses? The answers to such questions, we'll see, depend on the kinds of accommodations people would reach among themselves if they were free to negotiate costlessly with one another.

Next we'll apply the theory of property rights and externalities to the topic of contests for relative position. We'll conclude this chapter with an examination of taxation as a possible solution to the problem of negative externalities.

THE RECIPROCAL NATURE OF EXTERNALITIES

In the first edition of this text (which went to press in 1990), I began this section with the following sentence:

> One of the great injustices of academic life is that Ronald H. Coase[1] has never been awarded the Nobel Prize in economics.

Ronald Coase, 1991 Nobel Laureate in economics.

I was thus delighted when I learned that Coase was at last awarded the prize in 1991. Now an emeritus professor at the University of Chicago Law School, Coase is the author of the most influential and widely cited economics paper of the postwar era. Titled "The Problem of Social Cost,"[2] this paper profoundly changed the way economists, legal scholars, political philosophers, and others think about externalities and the legal and social institutions that have evolved to deal with them.

Coase began with an example involving a doctor whose ability to examine patients was disrupted by the noise of machinery operated by a confectioner in an adjacent building. It is worth noting that Coase's disarmingly simply example was not as unrealistic in the 1950s as it might seem today. In that era, physicians were not located in serenely isolated medical office buildings. They would very commonly have had offices on the upper floors of old-style commercial buildings and been exposed to noise from neighboring businesses, streets, and alleys.

Historically, the economic and legal view toward such a situation was simple and clear: The candy maker's noise was harming the doctor and it ought to be restrained. Coase's seminal insight was that this view completely overlooks the reciprocal nature of the problem. True enough, the confectioner's noise does harm the doctor. *But if we prevent the noise, we harm the confectioner.* After all, the confectioner makes the noise, not for the purpose of harming the doctor, but in pursuit of his own livelihood. In such situations, there will be harm to *someone,* no matter what happens. Whether the harm caused to the doctor by the noise is greater than the harm that would be caused to the confectioner if he were prohibited from making it is strictly an empirical question. The common interest of each party, Coase recognized, is to avoid the larger of these two unpleasant outcomes.

The earlier, one-sided view of externalities led to a legal tradition in which the confectioner was generally held liable for any damage his noise caused to the doctor. Coase pointed out, however, that if the doctor and the confectioner were able to negotiate costlessly with one another, the most efficient outcome would occur regardless of whether the confectioner was liable. His simple and elegant argument in support of this claim is illustrated in the following series of numerical examples.

[1]Rhymes with "rose."
[2]*Journal of Law and Economics, 3,* 1960, 144–171.

EXAMPLE 16.1   Shut Down Decision (Part 1)

Suppose the benefit to the confectioner of continuing to make noise is 40, while the cost of the noise to the doctor is 60. Suppose also that these figures represent the present values of all current and future benefits to the parties in question.

If the confectioner's only alternative to making the noise is to produce nothing, what will happen if she is made liable for the noise damage? (To be liable for the damage means being required to compensate the doctor for any damage caused by the noise.)

The confectioner will examine her two options—shutting down or compensating the doctor—and choose the one that makes her best off. If she stays open, she will earn 40, but will have to pay 60 to the doctor, for a net loss of 20. If she shuts down, her net gain is 0, and since this is clearly better than losing 20, she will discontinue operation.

Alternatively, suppose the confectioner had not been liable for noise damage. That is, suppose the law grants her the right to continue operating without compensation to the doctor. Coase argued that in this case the doctor will pay the confectioner to shut down. If the confectioner stays open, she will gain only 40 while the doctor will lose 60. But the doctor can compensate the confectioner for the loss of shutting down and still have enough left over to be better off than if the confectioner had stayed open. Suppose, for example, the doctor pays the confectioner 50 to shut down. The confectioner's net gain will now be 10 more than if she had stayed open. And the doctor's net gain of 10 is 10 more than if the noise had continued.

If P denotes the payment the doctor makes to the confectioner to compensate her for shutting down, we know that P must be at least 40 (what the confectioner would get by staying open) and no larger than 60 (what the doctor would get if there were no noise). The net results under the two legal regimes (confectioner liable versus confectioner not liable) are summarized in Table 16.1.

TABLE 16.1
Outcome and Payoff Summary for Example 16.1

Legal regime	Outcome	Net Benefit		
		Doctor	Confectioner	Total
Liable	Confectioner shuts down to avoid liability payment	60	0	60
Not liable	Doctor pays confectioner P to shut down, $40 \leq P \leq 60$	$60 - P$	P	60

The gain to the confectioner from operating is 40. The loss to the doctor from the noise is 60. The efficient outcome is for the confectioner to shut down, and this happens under both legal regimes.

Note that because the gain to the confectioner of operating her machinery (40) is smaller than the noise damage it imposes on the doctor (60), the most efficient outcome is for the confectioner to shut down. Example 16.1 makes clear that if both the doctor and confectioner are rational and can negotiate costlessly with one another, this will happen regardless of whether the confectioner is liable for noise damage. On efficiency grounds, the legal regime is thus a matter of complete indifference here. On distributional grounds, however, the parties will be anything but neutral about liability. If the confectioner is not liable, her gain is $P \geq 40$, whereas she will be forced to shut down and earn nothing if she is liable. The doctor's net gain will be 60 if the confectioner is liable, but only $60 - P$ if the confectioner is not liable.

EXAMPLE 16.2   **Shut Down Decision (Part 2)**

Same as Example 16.1, except now the benefit to the confectioner of operating is 60, the benefit to the doctor in a noise-free environment only 40. Assume that the doctor must shut down if the noise continues.

This time the efficient outcome is for the confectioner to continue operating, since her gain exceeds the cost she imposes on the doctor. If she is not liable for noise damages, the confectioner will stay open and the doctor's best option will be to shut down. Alternatively, if the confectioner is liable for noise damage, she will again continue to operate and pay the doctor 40 to compensate her for her losses. The net results for this example are summarized in Table 16.2. Note that, as in Example 16.1, both legal regimes lead to the most efficient outcome, but have very different distributional consequences.

TABLE 16.2
Outcome and Payoff Summary for Example 16.2

Legal regime	Outcome	Net Benefit		
		Doctor	Confectioner	Total
Liable	Confectioner stays open and pays doctor 40	40	20	60
Not liable	Confectioner stays open; doctor shuts down	0	60	60

The gain to the confectioner from operating is 60. The loss to the doctor from the confectioner's noise is 40. The efficient outcome is for the confectioner to continue operating, and this happens under both legal regimes.

The preceding examples assumed that the only alternatives open to two parties were either to continue operations in the current form or to shut down entirely. In practice, however, one or both parties often face a broader range of alternatives. As the following examples will illustrate, here too the ability to negotiate costlessly leads to efficient outcomes.

EXAMPLE 16.3   **Efficient Negotiation (Part 1)**

Same as Example 16.1, except now the confectioner has access to a soundproofing device that will completely eliminate the noise from her machines. The cost of the device is 20, which means that if she installs it, her net gain from operating will fall from 40 to 20. As in Example 16.1, the doctor will gain 60 if there is no noise, 0 if there is noise.

If the confectioner is liable for noise damage, her best option will be to install the soundproofing. Her alternatives are either to shut down or to pay the doctor 60 in noise damages, and each of these is clearly worse. If the confectioner is not liable, it will be in the doctor's interest to pay the confectioner to install the soundproofing. Her alternative, after all, is to shut down or to endure the noise damage. The minimum payment that would be acceptable to the confectioner to install the soundproofing is 20, its cost. The most the doctor would be willing to pay for her to install it is 60, the amount the doctor would lose if it weren't installed. Again letting P denote the payment from the doctor to the confectioner, the outcomes and payoffs for the two legal regimes are as summarized in Table 16.3.

TABLE 16.3
Outcome and Payoff Summary for Example 16.3

Legal regime	Outcome	Net Benefit		
		Doctor	Confectioner	Total
Liable	Confectioner installs soundproofing at own expense	60	0	80
Not liable	Doctor pays confectioner P to install soundproofing, $20 \leq P \leq 60$	$60 - P$	$20 + P$	80

> The gain to the confectioner from operating without soundproofing is 40. Soundproofing costs 20. The loss to the doctor from the confectioner's noise is 60. The efficient outcome is for the confectioner to install soundproofing and to continue operating, and this happens under both legal regimes.

Let us now consider what happens when the doctor too has some adjustment he can make to escape the damage caused by the confectioner's noise.

EXAMPLE 16.4   Efficient Negotiation (Part 2)

Same as Example 16.3, except now the doctor can escape the noise damage by moving her examination room to the other side of her office. The noisy room in which she now examines patients could then be used for storage. The cost to the doctor of this rearrangement is 18.

With this new option available, the doctor is the one who is able to eliminate the noise damage at the lowest possible cost. If the confectioner is liable for noise damage, she will offer the doctor a payment P to compensate her for rearranging her office. The payment must be at least 18, or else the doctor would not make the accommodation. (Recall that, with the confectioner liable, the doctor has the option of being fully compensated for any noise damage.) And the payment cannot exceed 20, or else the confectioner could install soundproofing and solve the problem on her own. If the confectioner is not liable for noise damage, the doctor will rearrange her office at her own expense. The outcomes and payoffs for this example are summarized in Table 16.4. Note that we again get the efficient outcome no matter which legal regime we choose. Note also that the choice of legal regime again affects the distribution of costs and benefits, only this time by a much smaller margin than in Example 16.3. The difference is that each party now has a relatively inexpensive method for solving the noise problem unilaterally. In Example 16.3, the doctor lacked such an alternative, making the confectioner's bargaining power very strong when she was not liable for noise damage. In this example, by contrast, the confectioner cannot extract a large payment from the doctor for keeping quiet because the doctor can solve the noise problem on her own.

TABLE 16.4
Outcome and Payoff Summary for Example 16.4

Legal regime	Outcome	Net Benefit		
		Doctor	Confectioner	Total
Liable	Confectioner pays doctor P to rearrange her office, $18 \leq P \leq 20$	$42 + P$	$40 - P$	82
Not liable	Doctor rearranges her office at her own expense	42	40	82

> The gain to the confectioner from operating without soundproofing is 40. Soundproofing costs 20. The loss to the doctor from the confectioner's noise is 60. The doctor can rearrange her office to eliminate the noise problem at a cost of 18. The efficient outcome is for the doctor to rearrange her office, and this happens under both legal regimes.

The patterns revealed in the preceding examples may be stated formally as:

> **The Coase Theorem:** When the parties affected by externalities can negotiate costlessly with one another, an efficient outcome results no matter how the law assigns responsibility for damages.

In the wake of its publication, Coase's classic paper became a subject of great controversy. Many took him to be saying that there is no real role for government in solving problems related to pollution, noise, and other externalities.[3] By this interpretation, Coase's message seemed to be that if government stays out of the way, people will always come up with efficient solutions on their own. And yet Coase stated clearly that this conclusion holds only for a world in which parties can negotiate with one another at relatively low cost. He recognized that for many important externalities this assumption is not satisfied. At the simplest level, time and energy are required for negotiation, and when the potential benefits are small, it may simply not be worth it. Alternatively, there are situations in which a single polluter causes damage to a large number of people. Negotiating with large groups is inherently difficult and costly, and each person in the group faces strong incentives to escape these costs. Another serious barrier to negotiation is the problem of how to divide the surplus. Recall from Example 16.3 that the efficient outcome was for the doctor to pay the confectioner to install soundproofing. The minimum payment acceptable to the confectioner was 20, the cost of the soundproofing. The most the confectioner could hope to extract from the doctor was 60, the value to the doctor of eliminating the noise. The doctor would naturally like to pay only 20, and the confectioner would like to get 60. If each takes a hard line in the discussion, animosities may emerge and the possibility of a deal may break down altogether. For these and a host of other reasons, negotiations are often costly. When they are, it matters very much indeed which legal regime we choose, as the following examples will illustrate.

[3]For an amusing account of the naming and misinterpretation of the Coase Theorem, with George Stigler as the villain, see Deirdre McCloskey, "Other Things Equal: The So-Called Coase Theorem," *Eastern Economic Journal*, 24(3), 1998, 268–271. For Stigler's own version, see his *Theory of Price*, 3rd ed., New York: Macmillan, 1966.

EXAMPLE 16.5   Negotiation at a Cost

As in Example 16.2, suppose that the gain to the doctor in a noise-free environment is 40, while the gain to the confectioner from unfettered operations is 60. Suppose also that the confectioner has access to a soundproofing device that eliminates all noise damage at a cost of 20. And suppose, finally, that it costs the doctor and confectioner 25 to negotiate a private agreement between themselves. For negotiation to be a worthwhile alternative, they must be able to share this cost in some way that makes each of them better off than if they did not negotiate.

If the confectioner is made liable for noise damage, she will install the soundproofing. Her next-best alternative, after all, is to pay the doctor 40 in noise damages,[4] and the installation of soundproofing costs her only 20. Because being liable gives the confectioner an incentive to install the soundproofing on her own, there is no need for her to negotiate an agreement with the doctor, and thus no need to incur the cost of negotiation.

But now suppose that the confectioner is not liable for noise damage. If there were no costs of negotiation, the doctor would pay the confectioner P, where $20 \leq P \leq 40$, to install soundproofing. If it costs 25 to negotiate an agreement, however, then it is no longer possible for the doctor to compensate the confectioner for installing soundproofing. The soundproofing makes it possible for the doctor to gain 40, which is insufficient to cover both the cost of the soundproofing (20) and the cost of negotiating the agreement (25), which total 45. When it is costly to negotiate, we no longer get the efficient outcome irrespective of which legal regime we choose. In this example, for which the relevant data are summarized in Table 16.5, we get the most efficient result only if the confectioner is liable.

TABLE 16.5
Outcome and Payoff Summary for Example 16.5

Legal regime	Outcome	Net Benefit Doctor	Confectioner	Total
Liable	Confectioner installs soundproofing at her own expense	40	40	80
Not liable	Confectioner does not install soundproofing; doctor shuts down	0	60	60

The gain to the confectioner from operating without soundproofing is 60. Soundproofing costs 20. The loss to the doctor from the confectioner's noise is 40. The cost of negotiating a private agreement is 25. The efficient outcome is for the confectioner to install soundproofing, but this happens only when she is made liable for noise damage.

[4]For the confectioner to operate and pay noise damages to the doctor, it is not necessary for them to incur the cost of negotiating a private agreement.

In Example 16.5, the total gain for society as a whole is 80 if the confectioner is liable, only 60 if she is not liable. But as the following example will illustrate, the existence of barriers to negotiation does not guarantee that we will always get an efficient outcome by making parties liable for the damage caused by external effects.

EXAMPLE 16.6   Barriers to Negotiation

Same as Example 16.5, except the confectioner no longer has a soundproofing option; instead, the doctor has the option of avoiding the noise by rearranging her office, which will cost her 18.

If the confectioner is not liable for noise damage, this is exactly what the doctor will do. But if the confectioner is liable, the cost of negotiation now stands in the way of her paying the doctor to rearrange her office. The sum of negotiating costs (25) and rearrangement costs (18) comes to 43, which is 3 more than the 40 that will be saved by avoiding the noise. So if she is liable, the best option available to the confectioner is simply to continue operating and pay the doctor 40 for the noise damage.[5] Here, unlike Example 16.5, we get the efficient outcome when the confectioner is not liable. The data for Example 16.6 are summarized in Table 16.6.

TABLE 16.6
Outcome and Payoff Summary for Example 16.6

Legal regime	Outcome	Net Benefit		
		Doctor	Confectioner	Total
Liable	Confectioner operates and pays doctor 40 for noise damage	40	20	60
Not liable	Doctor rearranges her office at her own expense	22	60	82

> The gain to the confectioner from operating is 60. The loss to the doctor from the confectioner's noise is 40. The doctor can escape the noise by rearranging her office at a cost of 18. The cost of negotiating a private agreement is 25. The efficient outcome is for the doctor to rearrange her office, but this happens only when the confectioner is not liable for noise damage.

SELF-TEST 16.1

How would the entries in Table 16.6 be affected if the cost of negotiation were 20 instead of 25?

APPLICATION: EXTERNAL EFFECTS FROM NUCLEAR POWER PLANTS

Although Austria itself has had a law banning nuclear power plants since 1978, it is surrounded by countries that operate a total of 41 such plants. Two of these plants, located just 35 miles from the Austrian border with Slovakia, share important design features with the ill-fated Chernobyl plant that in 1986 experienced the worst nuclear accident in

[5]Again, making a liability payment does not require the parties to incur the costs of negotiation.

history. Thus the citizens of Austria were understandably concerned about their vulnerability to a similar mishap.

In a remarkably bold application of the reasoning Coase suggested, Austrian officials offered in January 1991 to provide Slovakia (then part of Czechoslovakia) with free electric power as an inducement to shut down the two Soviet-designed reactors.[6] Austrian Economics Minister Wolfgang Scheussel estimated that the cost of the replacement power would be about $350 million annually.

Czech Premier Marian Calfa expressed interest in the Austrian offer and pledged that a working group would study it. But no agreement was ever reached to implement it. As this experience illustrates, the costs of negotiation sometimes stand in the way even of agreements that would substantially benefit both parties.

Coase's observation that people will reach efficient outcomes when they can negotiate costlessly has widespread application. In many situations, after all, the costs of negotiation are small relative to the benefits of reaching agreements about externalities. But the more far-reaching implications of Coase's work lie in the pattern illustrated in Examples 16.5 and 16.6, where we find the seeds of a powerful theory of law and social institutions. Boiled down to its essence, the theory can be stated as the following rule:

> Efficient laws and social institutions are the ones that place the burden of
> adjustment to externalities on those who can accomplish it at least cost.

One of the immediate implications of this rule is that the best laws regarding harmful effects cannot be identified unless we know something about how much it costs different parties to avoid harmful effects. If, as in Example 16.5, the emitter of noise has lower costs, we get an efficient outcome by making him liable for damages. But if the person adversely affected by the noise has a lower cost of avoidance, as in Example 16.6, we do better by not making the noisemaker liable.

The efficiency rule finds application in a rich variety of situations, several of which we examine in the sections that follow.

PROPERTY RIGHTS

Private Property Laws and Their Exceptions

No free-market economy can function successfully without laws that govern the use of private property. Among other things, these laws describe how people can lawfully acquire different types of property—by inheriting it, purchasing it, or receiving it as a gift, but not by theft or other means that entail the use of force. In most cases, these laws grant owners of property the right to exclude others from using it without permission. Yet hosts of detailed exceptions sharply limit this right to exclude. As the following Economic Naturalist examples suggest, these exceptions are not random. Rather, they follow a systematic pattern, one that the insights of Coase help us to understand.

Economic Naturalist 16.1

Why does the law permit airlines to operate flights over private land without permission?

Think back to the discussion with which we began this chapter about the rights to use airspace over various parcels of land. For a developer to build a hotel in the airspace above my land, he must first secure my permission, which I will grant only in return for a substantial payment. But even in the aftermath of the terrorist attacks of September 11, 2001, the law permits commercial airliners to fly over my

[6]See Michael Z. Wise, "Prague Offered Payoff to Shut Nuclear Plant," *The Washington Post,* January 30, 1991.

Should commercial aircrafts be allowed to fly over private land without the property owner's permission?

land without payment whenever they choose. Why this distinction?

Note first that each case involves an externality—the visual blight and inconvenience of having a hotel overhead in the first case, the noise and possible danger from the airplanes in the second. The cost to me of the first externality is much larger than the second, but that alone cannot account for why we treat the two cases differently, since the benefits to the developer from erecting a building over my land are also likely to be great. The crucial distinction is that individual negotiation is much more practical in the case of the developer than in the case of the airlines. In the former case, there are only two parties involved, and the benefits from an efficient outcome are likely to be large enough to justify the costs of negotiation. So in this case, we can feel confident of achieving an efficient outcome most of the time if we define property rights to exclude developers from building in the airspace above our houses. In the airline case, by contrast, the benefits of flying over any single house are small, and in any event, the cost of negotiating with all the potentially affected parties would be prohibitive. Because the total benefits of overflight are large relative to the total costs imposed on homeowners, we get an efficient outcome here if property rights do not permit landowners to exclude planes from flying overhead.

There are exceptions to this general principle, however, and these too provide an illuminating illustration of the Coasian efficiency rule. The most conspicuous exception involves approach and takeoff lanes to and from airports near major metropolitan areas. Jets fly low to the ground just after takeoff and just before landing, and the noise that reaches property below is often deafening. In these situations, local ordinances commonly prohibit landings and takeoffs during the hours when it is most costly (difficult) for property owners to adjust to noise—namely, the hours when most of them are sleeping. Here again, negotiation on an individual basis is impractical, and the best we can do is to define rights to achieve the lowest cost of accommodation.

Economic Naturalist 16.2

Why does the law of trespass not apply along waterfront property?

In many cultures of the world, people regard a stranger walking across their land as an intrusion. The trespasser, in the economist's parlance, confers a negative externality on the property owner. Such externalities might be dealt with in a variety of ways. Most of my neighbors, for example, have built fences across their yards to prevent people from taking shortcuts across their property. Some even post signs saying to beware of violent dogs. In most jurisdictions, it is perfectly lawful to take such steps to exclude others from using your property. And yet the laws of my community do not afford the same rights to people who own cottages on the shore of nearby Cayuga Lake. On the contrary, they explicitly permit any citizen to walk across any parcel of land located along the lakeshore.

FIGURE 16.1

Lakeshore Property and the Law of Trespass
The cost of getting from *A* to *C* without crossing *B*'s property is much higher than by the direct route along the lakeshore. For this reason, the law does not allow lakeshore homeowners to exclude people from walking across their property.

This distinction exists not because the owners of lakeshore property value their privacy any less than others do. Rather, it is because the cost of not being able to cross a person's land along the lakeshore is so much higher than it is elsewhere. To illustrate, suppose that *A, B,* and *C* in Figure 16.1 are three lakeshore properties and that someone at *A* wants to visit someone at *C*. Access to lakeshore properties by road involves travel from the main highway down long, steep, often treacherous driveways. Lacking the ability to cross *B*'s property, *A* would have to ascend his driveway out to the main road, travel to *C*'s driveway, and then make the trip down it. Because the costs of this circuitous routing are so much larger than the costs of the direct path along the lakeshore, the law of trespass makes an exception for these properties. Their owners consider an occasional unwelcome disturbance a small price to pay for the additional convenience of being able to travel freely along the lakeshore.

By contrast, the right to cross someone's property in my neighborhood would be worth relatively little. The streets are all close together, so there is always a relatively easy way to get where you want to go without having to take shortcuts. With respect to potential trespass on both the lakeshore and other properties, negotiation is prohibitively costly on a case-by-case basis. So the law of property defines rights of access in the way that, on average, leads to an efficient outcome. It gives most property owners the right to exclude, but withholds that right from the owners of lakeshore property.

Should trespassing on waterfront property be permitted?

Economic Naturalist 16.3

Why are property laws often suspended during storms?

On the 13th day of November 1804, the Ploof family went sailing on Vermont's Lake Champlain. A sudden violent storm came up, making it impossible for them to get back to their home port. In desperation, they took refuge by tying up at a dock on an island in the lake. The dock was owned by a Mr. Putnam, who sent his

Does a property owner always have the right to exclude strangers from using his dock?

servant down to order the Ploofs off his property. The Ploofs cast off into the storm, and shortly thereafter their sloop was destroyed, injuring several family members. The Ploofs later filed a successful damage suit against Putnam. The court decided that although Putnam would ordinarily have the right to exclude people from using his dock, the circumstances of the storm created an exception. Note that in deciding the case this way, the Vermont court was mimicking the result that dock owners and boat owners would generally reach for themselves if it were possible to negotiate

costlessly and dispassionately during a storm. The value of the dock to a boater in distress is almost certainly higher than the value to the owner of being able to exclude him, and the Vermont court chose to define the state's laws of property with this observation in mind.

Economic Naturalist 16.4

Why do building height limits vary from city to city?

Consider the situation pictured in Figure 16.2. Resident A owns a house on a hillside overlooking the sea and places high value on being able to watch the sunset from her living room window. Now B purchases the property below A and is considering which of two houses to build. The first is a one-story house that would

FIGURE 16.2

The Value of an Unobstructed View

It is efficient for B to build a two-story house if and only if the extra value of the taller house to B is greater than the value to A of maintaining her view.

leave *A*'s view intact. The second is a two-story design that would completely block *A*'s view. Suppose the gain to *A* from an unobstructed view is 100, the gain to *B* from having a one-story house is 200, and the gain to *B* from a two-story house is 280. If the laws of property let people build houses of any height they chose, and if negotiation between property owners were costless, which of the two houses would *B* build?

To answer this question, first note that the increase in *B*'s gain from having the taller house is 80, which is 20 less than the cost to *A* from the loss of his view. The efficient outcome is thus for *B* to build the one-story house. And that is exactly what would happen if the two parties could negotiate costlessly. Rather than see *B* build the taller house, it will be in *A*'s interest to compensate *B* for choosing the shorter version. To do so, she will have to give *B* at least 80, for that is what *B* gives up by not having the two-story house. The most *A* would be willing to give *B* is 100, since that is all the view is worth to *A*. For some payment *P*, where $80 \leq P \leq 100$, *A* will get to keep her view.

Suppose, however, that negotiations between the two parties were impractical. *B* would then go ahead with the two-story house, since that is the version she

Why are zoning laws more strict in San Francisco than in most Midwest cities?

values most. By comparison with the one-story design, *B* would gain 80, but *A* would lose 100. The optimal structure of property rights in this particular example would be to prohibit any building that blocks a neighbor's view.

Of course, if the valuations assigned by the parties were different, a different conclusion might follow. If, for example, *B* valued the two-story house at 300 and *A*'s view were again worth 100, the optimal structure of property rights would be to allow people to build to whatever height they choose. In either case, the optimal structure of property rights is the one that places the burden of adjustment (either the loss of a view or the loss of a preferred building design) on the party that can accomplish it at the lowest cost.

As a practical matter, the laws of property in many jurisdictions often embody precisely this principle. In cities like San Francisco, where the views of the ocean and bay are breathtakingly beautiful, strict zoning laws regulate construction that blocks an existing building's line of sight. Zoning laws in cities where there is less to look at are generally much more liberal in the kinds of buildings they permit. But even in cities that have no special view to protect, zoning laws generally limit the fraction of the lot that can be occupied by man-made structures. Most people value access to at least some sunlight, and ordinances of this sort make it possible for them to get it.

As we have seen with other examples, however, there is no guarantee that relative valuations will remain stable over time. The high cost of housing in urban clusters has led to a YIMBY movement that asserts that access to housing for new residents should be given priority over the protection of existing residents' views.

Most people who grow up in market economies like the United States take the institution of private property rights for granted. But as the preceding examples have made clear, the details of our various property laws have a great deal of economic structure. They embody sophisticated, if often implicit, calculations about how to reach the most efficient solutions to practical problems involving externalities. Indeed, as the following section illustrates, the very existence of private property may be traced to early attempts to deal with externalities.

The Tragedy of the Commons

To explore the origins of the institution of private property, it is instructive to consider, as in the next example, what would happen in a society that lacked a well-developed institution of property rights.

EXAMPLE 16.7   **Tragedy of the Commons**

A village has six residents, each of whom has wealth of 100. Each resident may either invest his money in a government bond, which pays 12 percent per year, or use it to buy a year-old steer, which will graze on the village commons (there being no individually owned grazing land in this village). Year-old steers and government bonds each cost exactly 100. Steers require no effort to tend and can be sold for a price that depends on the amount of weight they gain during the year. Yearly weight gain, in turn, depends on the number of steers that graze on the commons. The prices of 2-year-old steers are given in Table 16.7 as a function of the total number of steers. If village residents make their investment decisions independently, how many steers will graze on the commons?

TABLE 16.7
Steer Prices as a Function of Grazing Density

Number of steers	Price per 2-year-old steer
1	120
2	118
3	114
4	111
5	108
6	105

> As more steers graze on the commons, each steer gains less weight, resulting in a lower price per steer.

As long as each villager cannot control access to the commons by cattle owned by others, the income-maximizing strategy will be to send an extra steer out onto the commons if and only if its price next year will be at least 112. (At that price, the gain from owning a steer is equal to the gain from buying a bond.) By this reckoning, there will be 3 steers sent onto the commons, and the rest of the villagers' money will be invested in government bonds. With this pattern of investment, village income from investment will be 14 from each of the 3 steers and 12 from each of the 3 bonds, for a total of 78.

Notice, however, that this is not the largest possible income the villagers could have earned. From the point of view of the village as a whole, the investment rule for steers should be: Send an extra steer onto the commons if and only if its marginal contribution to the value of the total herd after 1 year is greater than or equal to 112. Sending the third steer onto the commons resulted in a total herd worth $3 \times 114 = 342$, which is only 106 more than the value of a herd with only 2 steers ($2 \times 118 = 236$). Total village income is maximized by buying 4 bonds and sending 2 steers onto the commons. This pattern results in an income of 48 from bonds and 36 from steers, for a total of 84.

The reason that the invisible hand failed to produce the best social result here is that individual villagers ignored an important externality. Their criterion for deciding to send another steer was to look only at the price increase that would occur for that particular steer. They took no account of the fact that sending an extra steer would cause existing cattle to gain less weight. Pastureland is a scarce resource in this example, and the villagers failed to allocate it efficiently because they were allowed to use it for free.

The problem would be solved if individual villagers could own pastureland and exclude others from using it. Suppose, for example, the village government decided to put the pastureland up for auction. What price would it fetch? Anyone who buys the pastureland has the right to restrict the number of steers to 2, which is the income-maximizing amount. We saw that, if used in this way, the land will generate an annual income of 36 from an annual investment of 200 (the price of two steers). Had the 200 instead been used to purchase government bonds, only 24 would have been earned. Having control over the commons thus yields a surplus of 12/yr over the income available to a person able to buy only government bonds. It follows that the price of the pastureland at auction will be 100 (the price of a bond that pays an income of 12/yr). If the price of pastureland were any less than 100, all investors would want to buy it instead of buying government bonds. If it sold for more than 100, every investor could do better by buying government bonds. The village government could take the 100 raised from the auction of its pastureland and distribute it among the six villagers, for an average payment of $\frac{100}{6}$.

SELF-TEST 16.2

What grazing fee would solve the commons problem discussed in Example 16.7?

In early societies, it was a general practice for important resources such as pastureland and fisheries to be owned in common. The difficulty with such ownership schemes is that they lead to overexploitation of the resource. Figure 16.3 illustrates the problem of individual villagers who have the option of working in a factory at a wage of W/day, or of keeping all the fish they can catch from the village lake. The curve labeled AP shows how the average catch per fisherman varies with the number of

FIGURE 16.3

The Tragedy of the Commons

When a resource, such as a fishery or a pasture, is owned in common, each user gets to keep the average product of his own productive inputs he applies to the resource. Privately owned inputs will be applied to the resource until X', the point at which their average product equals their opportunity cost, W, resulting in an economic surplus of zero. The socially optimal allocation is X^*, the level of input for which W is equal to the marginal product of privately owned inputs, and results in an economic surplus of S^*.

fishermen, while MP shows the change in the total catch as a function of the number of fishermen. If fishermen get to keep whatever they catch, their decision rule will be to fish up to X', the point where AP = W. At X', the value of the total catch is exactly equal to the total income that the villagers who fished could have earned by working in the factory.

The socially optimal allocation is to fish only up to X^* in Figure 16.3, the point at which W = MP, and for all remaining villagers to work in the factory. At this allocation, the villagers who fish will earn a total of S^* (the shaded area) more than they could have earned by working in the factory.

If villagers are given free access to fish in the lake, the allocation that sends X^* out to fish will not be stable. Because each fisherman will be earning more than the villagers who work in the factory, factory workers will have an incentive to switch to fishing. Switching will stop only when X' have gone out to fish, making earnings in the two alternatives the same. As in the earlier pastureland example, the additional fishermen ignore the externality they impose on the existing fishermen. Each looks only at the size of his own catch, ignoring the fact that his presence makes everyone else's catch smaller.

In order to sustain the efficient allocation, something must be done to limit access to the lake. The simplest approach is to charge people for the right to go fishing. If the fishing fee were set at AP* − W (see Figure 16.3), the optimal allocation would result automatically from the income-maximizing decisions of individual villagers. Here, as in the pasture example, the problem was that individuals overutilized a productive resource they were allowed to use for free. The invisible hand mechanism can function properly only when all resources sell for prices that reflect their true economic value.

▶ Visit your instructor's Connect© course and access your eBook to view this video.

Why do blackberries in public parks get picked before they're completely ripe?

One of the continuing sources of inefficiency in modern economies involves the allocation of resources that no single nation's property laws can govern. For instance, several species of whales have been hunted to near extinction because no international laws of property exist to restrain individual incentives to kill whales. And the Mediterranean Sea has long had serious problems with pollution because none of the many nations that border it has an economic incentive to consider the effects of its discharges on other countries. As the world's population continues to grow, the absence of an effective system of international property rights will become an economic problem of increasing significance.

When we turn to the question of climate change, it becomes obvious that the lack of enforceable international coordination becomes a critical problem. Scientists now estimate that if carbon dioxide and other greenhouse gases continue to accumulate in the atmosphere at current rates, the earth's average temperature will rise by as much as 8 degrees Fahrenheit in this century—enough to melt the polar ice caps and flood thousands of square miles of coastal land, at the same time as countries are converting forests into tinder boxes and disrupting food production in ways that are still incalculable. If a single agency had the power to enact globally binding environmental legislation, it would be a straightforward, albeit costly, matter to reduce the buildup of greenhouse gases. But in our world of sovereign nations, this power does not exist.

Externalities, Efficiency, and Free Speech

As the following discussion illustrates, the Coasian principles of efficiency apply not only to the design of property rights but also to the design of constitutions. In particular, they shed light on the extent to which society has an interest in protecting the right to free speech.

The First Amendment to the U.S. Constitution protects most forms of speech and expression, even those that cause intensely painful effects on others. A man once wrote to a newspaper advice columnist to confess to a cruel act he had committed decades earlier, during his senior year in high school. He and his friends had leafed through the school yearbook and picked out the photograph of the girl they agreed was the ugliest in their class. The letter writer had then called the girl on the telephone to congratulate her on her selection. During the ensuing years, he had never been able to forget her anguished groan in response. He would give anything, he said, if he could turn back the clock and recant that phone call.

Given the choice between receiving such a telephone call and being hit sharply on the arm with a stick, many people would immediately choose the latter. Had the boys hit the girl with a stick, they could have been put in jail. And yet they were perfectly within their First Amendment rights to make that phone call.

Why does our Constitution prohibit one form of harm but not the other? In the Coasian framework, the first thing to recognize is that it is highly impractical to negotiate solutions case by case to either type of harmful effect. We just cannot imagine the boys and the girl dickering about what she would be willing to pay to avoid hearing a painful remark or, for that matter, to avoid being struck with a stick. The structure of the law must therefore be guided by a judgment about which structure of rights will generate the best outcome where case-by-case negotiation is impractical.

Most people would surely agree that the world would be better if speech like the telephone prank could be prohibited. The practical question is whether it is possible to frame a law that would prevent such speech without preventing other speech that we value highly. Sadly, the answer seems to be no. Any law that prevented people from making cruel remarks to others would almost surely prohibit a great deal of highly valuable speech as well. The fear of criticism keeps many an otherwise wayward person in line, much to society's benefit. If it were practical to write a law that would permit justified criticism but prohibit criticism that is unwarranted, or even merely unkind, we might be seriously tempted to implement it. But so far, no one has come up with such a law.

Even so, the First Amendment's protection of free speech is far from absolute. For example, it does not protect a person's right to yell "Fire" in a crowded theater. Nor does it permit people to shout profanities on public street corners. Nor are we permitted to advocate the overthrow of the government by violent means. In such cases, we seem willing to say that the benefits of free speech are too small to justify its external costs.

POSITIVE EXTERNALITIES

The Coase theorem applies not only to negative externalities but also to positive ones. When a beekeeper and an apple grower operate on adjacent properties, the activities of each confer positive externalities on the other. If the beekeeper adds an additional hive, the apple trees in the adjacent orchard will be more fully pollinated, ensuring a larger crop. If the orchard owner plants additional trees, the beekeeper's output of honey will rise. These positive externalities, if ignored, will result in suboptimally small levels of both apple and honey production. But if negotiation between them is costless, the beekeeper can offer to subsidize the orchard owner for planting more trees. The orchard owner, likewise, can offer payments to induce the beekeeper to enlarge her apiary. With either positive or negative externalities, inefficiencies result only if it is costly or otherwise impractical to negotiate agreements about how to correct them.

Gold medalist, Janet Evans

POSITIONAL EXTERNALITIES

In many areas of endeavor, rewards are determined not by our absolute performance, but by how we perform relative to others. To be a champion swimmer, for example, what counts is not how fast you swim in absolute terms, but how your times compare with others'. Swimmer Janet Evans won three gold medals in the 1988 Olympics, and yet her winning times would not even have qualified her for the 2020 American women's swimming team.

Situations in which rewards are determined by relative performance are often called contests. In virtually every contest, each contestant will take a variety of actions in an attempt to enhance his or her probability of winning. Indeed, to take such actions is the essence of what it means to be in a contest. Some of these actions entail only minimal costs. Swimmers, for example, sometimes shave the hair from their heads and bodies in order to glide more smoothly through the water.

But in every contest where something important is at stake, competitors almost always take much more costly steps to win. In the race for national political office, contestants spend hundreds of millions of dollars on advertising. In the race for military supremacy, nations invest billions developing and building new weapons.

Because the rewards in contests are distributed according to relative position, the laws of simple arithmetic tell us that any action that increases one contestant's chances of winning must necessarily reduce the chances of others. With this observation in mind, it is instructive to think of performance-enhancing actions as giving rise to *positional externalities*. If *A* and *B* are competing for a prize that only one of them can attain, anything that helps *A* will necessarily harm *B*.

The result is that when the stakes are high, unregulated contests almost always lead to costly *positional arms races*. In the absence of effective drug regulations, for example, many linemen in the National Football League apparently now feel compelled to enhance their size and strength by using anabolic steroids. It is easy to see why. In an arena where sheer physical bulk plays a central role, failure to use these dangerous hormones might obviously jeopardize a player's position on his team.

Like so many other arms races, however, the race to grow bigger and stronger yields few real benefits for the group of contestants as a whole. After all, the contest at the line of scrimmage can have only one winner, whether each team's linemen average 300 pounds or 240. At the same time, the race imposes substantial costs. Anabolic steroids have been linked to cancer of the liver and other serious health problems.

In hockey it is standard procedure for defensemen to throw their bodies to the ice to prevent an opponent's shot from going into the net. In NCAA hockey contests, this practice seldom causes serious injury anymore, because players are now required to wear helmets with heavy wire cages over the face openings. But before the appearance of these helmets, it was a risky proposition indeed. When a hockey puck traveling at more than 100 miles/hr makes contact with a human face, the results are ugly. On objective grounds, it seems utter folly for a player to risk mutilation by throwing his face in the path of the puck. And yet few players ever hesitated to do so when the chance arose. The urge to win—to do well in relative terms—is a powerful force of human nature. In situations where the material payoffs from winning are very large, this is hardly surprising. But even when the stakes are ostensibly low—as, for example, in a nonleague high school hockey game in upstate New York—people go to extreme lengths to enhance their chances.

When hockey helmets are not required, players almost never wear them. Yet most players favor a rule requiring helmets. Positional externalities explain the apparent paradox.

Given what is at stake, voluntary restraint is rarely an effective solution to positional arms races. And so governing bodies in many sports now require strict drug testing of all competing athletes. The NCAA's helmet rule, similarly, has been a face-saving solution, both literally and figuratively; without it, few players would have dared to wear a face cage on their own. (In the National Hockey League, which has no similar requirement, helmets with face cages are rarer than defensemen's front teeth.)

As a further illustration of collective restraint of positional externalities, consider the ancient practice of dueling. A gentleman once felt compelled to defend his honor by challenging the offending party to a duel with pistols at sunrise. Duelists, and the people who cared about them, soon recognized the unfettered duel as an unacceptably costly practice. Over time, rules evolved that reduced the mortality rate. For example, the distance at which the pistols were fired grew steadily longer. And pistols with spiral-grooved barrels were forbidden. (Such grooves impart a spin to the bullet, making its trajectory much more true.) With these restrictions in place, only 1 in 6 duelists was actually struck by a bullet, and only 1 in 14 died. This was still a steep price to pay, of course, and it eventually led to an outright prohibition against dueling. With firm legal sanctions in place, we are now able to maintain our honor in a variety of much less injurious ways.

One of the most important contests people face in life is the task of making sure their children enter the labor market with a good education. This task is a contest because a "good" education, like an "effective" lineman, is an inescapably *relative* concept. If an effective lineman is one who is bigger, stronger, and faster than most other linemen, a good education is one that is better than the education that most others receive. This relativistic aspect of our objective is what makes us vulnerable to a positional arms race of the sort we see elsewhere.

In the education context, what form does this arms race take? Because public schools are funded largely by local property taxes, educational quality and neighborhood quality are closely linked in our public school systems. Competition for position thus often involves trying to move to the best possible neighborhoods. It is common for families to endure many hardships—working long hours, accepting risky jobs, going without vacations, skimping on savings, and so on—in order to scrape together the cash needed to move into a better school district. Again, however, the laws of simple arithmetic remind us that it is not possible for *everyone* in society to move forward in relative terms. Only 10 percent of our children can occupy the top tenth of our school seats, no matter how valiantly everyone strives.

Even in contests with very low stakes, we have seen that people often accept considerable sacrifice and risk to enhance their chances of winning. The contest to launch our children well in life is a contest whose stakes are high. Any one family's efforts to move forward in relative terms impose a negative externality on others. In a variety of other contexts, we have seen that social institutions evolve to promote efficient solutions to externalities. Armed with this view, we can gain similar new insights into a variety of social institutions that restrain the positional arms race among families. The traditional explanations for many of these institutions, we will see, often raise more questions than they answer.

Limiting the Workweek

The Fair Labor Standards Act requires, among other things, that employers pay a 50 percent wage premium whenever people work more than 8 hours a day or 40 hours a week. This regulation sharply discourages overtime work, and has been defended on the grounds that, without it, monopsony employers would require unacceptably long hours.

Critics of overtime laws respond that if workers disliked working long hours, competition would result in an overtime premium even without a regulation. Alternatively, if workers wanted to work long hours, why would they support a law that discourages employers from having them do so? In the eyes of its detractors, the overtime law is either irrelevant or harmful.

Positional externalities suggest an alternative rationale for work hours regulation. If someone stays a few extra hours at work, she will increase her earnings, both in absolute and in relative terms. One result is that she will be able to afford a house in a better school district. But again, the problem is that one family's forward movement in relative terms means a backward movement for others. Rather than see their families fall behind, others will feel pressure to work longer hours themselves. In the end, these efforts are largely offsetting. As before, only 10 percent of our children can occupy seats in top-decile school districts.

By working until 8 PM each day, we can produce more and enjoy larger incomes than if we work only until 5 PM. But in the process, we have less time to spend with our families and friends. It is easy to see why people might prefer to live in communities where everyone quits work at 5 PM. And it is equally easy to see why there might be few such communities in the absence of overtime laws.

Savings

Many observers complain, correctly, that the Social Security system prevents them from deciding for themselves when and how much to save for retirement. On the traditional view that having more options is better than having fewer, it would appear better for participation in Social Security to be purely voluntary. Yet most societies have mandatory programs to supplement retirement incomes. Positional externalities may again help us to understand why.

The argument is essentially the same as in the case of hours regulation. A parent has the choice of saving some of her current income for retirement or spending that income now on a house in a better school district. As before, many parents find the second option compelling.

The aggregate effects of such choices, however, fall short of what parents intend. When everyone spends more on a house in a better school district, the result is merely to bid up the prices of those houses. In the process, no one moves forward in the educational hierarchy, and yet parents end up having too little savings for retirement. Acting as individuals, however, their only real alternative is to send their children to less desirable schools.

The Social Security system mitigates this dilemma by making a portion of each person's income unavailable for spending. It helps solve a related set of positional externalities as well. A job seeker, for example, is well advised to look as good as he or she possibly can for job interviews. Looking good, however, is not a simple matter of wearing clothes that are clean and mended. Like a good education, a tasteful appearance is a relative concept. To look good means to look better than others, and the most practical way to do that is to spend more than most others do on clothing. The rub is that this same calculus operates for everyone. In the end, we get a fruitless escalation in the amount a person has to spend on clothing merely to avoid looking shabby. Viewed from the perspective of the population as a whole, it would make sense to save more and spend less on clothing. But it would not pay any individual, acting alone, to take this step. The Social Security system, by sheltering a portion of our incomes, limits how much people spend in this and a variety of other analogous situations.

Workplace Safety

As a final illustration of positional externalities, consider the case of safety regulations in the workplace. As in the case of hours regulations, proponents of safety regulations often defend them by saying that monopsonists would otherwise force their workers to labor under unacceptably risky conditions. But as we saw in Chapter 14, this argument seriously underestimates the pressures of competition in the labor market. With these pressures in mind, critics of safety regulation say that it deprives workers of the right to decide for themselves how much safety they want to purchase in the workplace.

Once we take positional externalities into account, however, the institution of safety regulation appears less puzzling. One worker's choice of a riskier job makes it difficult for other workers to bid as effectively as before for houses in the best school districts. Feeling this pressure, they too are more likely to opt for riskier jobs. In positional terms, of course, these movements largely offset one another. People may prefer to neutralize this arms race by adopting laws that set minimum standards for workplace safety.[7]

---

[7]Whether such standards achieve their stated goal of making the workplace safer is strictly an empirical question. Some authors have argued that the bureaucratic inefficiencies of safety regulation have actually led to *reduced* safety levels. See Albert Nichols and Richard Zeckhauser, "Government Comes to the Workplace: An Assessment of OSHA," *The Public Interest*, 49, 1977, 39–69.

TAXING EXTERNALITIES

Before the appearance of Coase's 1960 paper, the economics profession was wedded to the view, pioneered by the British economist A. C. Pigou, that the best solution to negative externalities is to tax them. The idea is simple. If *A* carries out an activity that imposes a cost on *B*, then taxing *A* by the amount of that cost will provide him with the proper incentive to consider the externality in his production decisions. As Example 16.8

EXAMPLE 16.8   Taxing Externalities

Consider again the doctor and confectioner from Examples 16.1 through 16.6. Suppose that the doctor gains 60 by operating in a noise-free environment, and that the confectioner gains 40 by operating her noisy equipment. Suppose also that the doctor can eliminate the noise problem by rearranging her office at a cost of 18. And suppose, finally, that negotiation between the doctor and confectioner is prohibitively costly. The tax approach calls for a tax on the confectioner equal to the damage her activity would cause, which, in the absence of a response by the doctor, means a tax of 60. How will the outcome under such a tax compare with what would have happened in its absence?

If there were costless negotiation, the confectioner could pay the doctor to rearrange her office and then operate without paying the tax, since her operation would cause no noise damage. But since negotiation is impractical, the doctor has no reason to incur this cost on her own. She knows that by doing nothing, the confectioner will face a tax of 60 if she operates, which in turn means that the confectioner's best option is to shut down. After all, her operation generates a gain of only 40 to begin with. With the confectioner no longer in operation, the doctor will gain 60 and the confectioner 0.

With no tax, however, the confectioner would have continued operations, for a gain of 40. The doctor's best response would have been to rearrange her office at a cost of 18, leaving her with a net gain of 42. Without the tax, we thus get the most efficient outcome, whereas the total gain with the tax is considerably smaller. The relevant data for this example are summarized in Table 16.8.

TABLE 16.8
Outcome and Payoff Summary for Example 16.8

Legal regime	Outcome	Net Benefit		
		Doctor	Confectioner	Total
Tax of 60 on confectioner	Confectioner shuts down	60	0	60
No tax or liability	Doctor rearranges her office at her own expense	42	40	82

The gain to the confectioner from operating is 40. The loss to the doctor from the confectioner's noise is 60. The doctor can rearrange her office to eliminate the noise problem at a cost of 18. The efficient outcome is for the doctor to rearrange her office, and this happens only when there is no tax on the confectioner.

makes clear, however, such taxes sometimes make matters worse than if we did nothing at all. On the other hand, Example 16.9 will show that in the case of carbon emissions, taxing the harmful behavior is likely to be more efficient than placing blanket restrictions on all emitters.

As Example 16.8 amply demonstrates, a tax on pollution can leave us in a worse position than if there were no tax at all. This is not surprising once we recognize that a tax on pollution has essentially the same effect as making the polluter liable for pollution damages. But this same recognition implies that taxation will not *always* be inefficient. It happened to be inefficient in Example 16.8 because the doctor happened to be the party who was best able to deal with the noise problem and the tax removed all incentive for her to do so. Suppose, to the contrary, the doctor had not had some inexpensive means of escaping the noise damage. The tax still would have led the confectioner to shut down, but this would now be the most efficient outcome. (See Example 16.1.)

Alternatively, suppose the confectioner had had some inexpensive means of eliminating the noise problem. Suppose, for example, that he could have installed soundproofing for a cost of 10. Here, too, the tax would have led to the most efficient outcome. The confectioner would have installed the soundproofing to escape the tax, and the doctor would have operated without disturbance.

Carbon Tax or Direct Restrictions on Emissions?

When we turn from the rather artificial problem we addressed in Example 16.8 to the massive issues we face around greenhouse gas emissions, we have to reconsider classic Coase Theorem requirements. Our carbon-fueled world does not sort neatly into perpetrators and victims. Both firms and consumers harm the environment through carbon emissions, and both suffer harm (and can be expected to suffer future harm) as a result. In this situation, we can't expect to untangle the questions of liability. Even less can we wait for millions of present and future stakeholders to reach a negotiated solution. Collective action is clearly required. But what kind?

For simplicity, we will consider just the corporate side of the problem. (We looked at the individual side in the "Social Cost of Carbon" section in Chapter 5.) Let's say that drastic legislation to reduce corporate CO_2 emissions is under consideration. One option is to set direct limits on the amount of CO_2 that companies can discharge. Alternatively, we could adopt a carbon tax, which means to charge companies a fee for each unit of pollution they discharge. A Coase-like setup can help us determine how to get the most bang for the buck. As the following example will demonstrate, the tax option offers a compelling advantage over the option of direct regulation.

EXAMPLE 16.9   Regulation vs. Taxation

Two firms, *X* and *Y*, have access to five different production processes, each one of which has a different cost and gives off a different amount of CO_2 emissions. The daily costs of the processes and the corresponding number of tons of carbon are listed in Table 16.9. If emissions are unregulated, each firm will use *A*, the least costly of the five processes, and each will emit 4 tons of CO_2 emissions per day, for a total of 8 tons/day. The government wants to cut CO_2 emissions by half. To accomplish this, the government is considering two options. The first is to require each firm to curtail its emissions by half. The alternative is to set a tax of *T* on each ton of daily CO_2 emissions. How large would *T* have to be in order to curtail emissions by half? And how would the total costs to society compare under the two alternatives?

If each firm is required to cut CO_2 emissions by half, each must switch from process *A* to process *C*. The result will be 2 tons/day of carbon for each firm. The cost

TABLE 16.9

Cost and Emissions for Five Production Processes

Process (CO$_2$ emissions)	A (4 tons/day)	B (3 tons/day)	C (2 tons/day)	D (1 ton/day)	E (0 tons/day)
Cost to firm X	100	190	600	1200	2000
Cost to firm Y	50	80	140	230	325

Each firm has access to five alternative production processes, A–E, which vary both in cost and in the amount of CO$_2$ they produce.

of the switch for firm X will be 600/day − 100/day = 500/day. The cost to Y will be 140/day − 50/day = 90/day, which means a total cost for the two firms of 590/day.

How will each firm respond to a tax of T per ton of CO$_2$ emissions? First it will ask itself whether switching from process A to B will increase its costs by more or less than T/day. If by less, it will pay to switch, because process B, which yields 1 ton less carbon, will save the firm T/day in taxes. If process B's costs exceed A's by more than T, however, the firm will not switch. It will be cheaper to stick with A and pay the extra T in taxes. If the switch from B to C pays, the firm will then ask the same question about the switch from B to C. It will keep switching until the extra costs of the next process are no longer smaller than T.

To illustrate, suppose a tax of 50/ton were levied. Firm X would stick with process A because it costs 90/day less than process B and produces only 1 ton/day of extra carbon, and thus 50/day in extra taxes. Firm Y, by contrast, will switch to process B because it costs only 30/day more and will save 50/day in taxes. But firm Y will not continue on to C because it costs 60/day more than B and will save only an additional 50/day in taxes. With firm X staying with A and firm Y switching to B, we get a total reduction in emissions of 1 ton/day. A tax of 50/ton thus does not produce the desired 50 percent reduction.

The solution is to keep increasing the tax until we get the desired result. Consider what happens with a tax of 91/ton. This tax will lead firm X to adopt process B, firm Y to adopt process D. Total emissions will be the targeted 4 tons/day. The cost to firm X will be 190/day − 100/day = 90/day, and the cost to firm Y will be 230/day − 50/day = 180/day. The total cost for both firms is thus only 270/day, or 320/day less than the cost of having each firm cut CO$_2$ emissions by half. Note that the taxes paid by the firm are not included in our reckoning of the social costs of the tax alternative, because this money is not lost to society. It can be used to reduce whatever taxes would otherwise have to be levied on citizens.

The advantage of the tax approach is that it concentrates CO$_2$ emissions reduction in the hands of the firms that can accomplish it in the least costly way. The direct regulatory approach of requiring each firm to cut by half took no account of the fact that firm Y can reduce emissions much more cheaply than firm X can. Under the tax approach, note that the cost of the last ton of CO$_2$ reduction is the same for each firm.

More generally, suppose that there are two producers, firm X and firm Y, whose marginal costs of reduced carbon emissions are shown by the curves labeled MC$_X$ and MC$_Y$, respectively, in Figure 16.4. If the goal is to reduce total CO$_2$ emissions by $Q = Q_X^* + Q_Y^*$ tons/day, a tax of T^* will accomplish that goal in the least costly way. The characteristic feature of this solution is that the marginal cost of carbon emissions reduction would be exactly the same for all firms. If that were not the case, it would always be possible to reallocate the emissions reduction in such a way as to reduce total costs.

FIGURE 16.4

The Tax Approach to Reduce CO₂ Emissions

MC_X and MC_Y represent the marginal cost of carbon reduction for firms X and Y, respectively. When emissions are taxed at a fixed rate, each firm reduces its emissions up to the point where the marginal cost of further reduction is exactly equal to the tax. The result is the least costly way of achieving the corresponding aggregate reduction in CO₂ emissions.

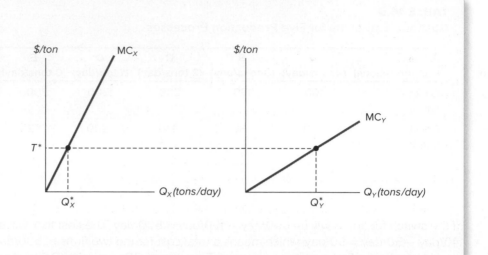

The direct regulatory approach (telling each firm how much to reduce emissions) could also achieve any given total pollution reduction at minimum costs if regulators knew each firm's marginal cost of reduction curve. They could then simply assign reduction quotas in such a way as to equate marginal reduction costs across firms. The difficulty is that regulatory officials will generally not have even the vaguest idea of what these curves look like. The compelling advantage of the tax approach is that it achieves efficiency without requiring any such knowledge on the part of regulators.

When the government places a tax on a product whose production does not generate externalities, the product will sell for a price that exceeds its marginal cost (see Chapter 2). And when price exceeds marginal cost, output falls short of the level that would maximize economic surplus. In contrast, when there is no tax on a product whose production generates negative externalities, output of that product exceeds the level that would maximize economic surplus. Thus, another advantage of taxing negative externalities is that it provides a means of raising government revenue that does not entail such efficiency losses. On the contrary, we have seen that the taxation of negative externalities can actually *increase* efficiency. Whether taxing negative externalities would yield enough revenue for government to carry out all its activities is an empirical question. If it would, then concerns about inefficiencies from taxation would no longer be a subject of concern.

Taxing Positional Externalities

There is considerable evidence that the utility that people get from consumption depends not only on absolute consumption levels, but on relative consumption levels as well. No one in the nineteenth century felt disadvantaged by not owning an automobile or a television set, and yet people who lack these items today are apt to feel strongly dissatisfied indeed. And their dissatisfaction is not merely a matter of envying the possessions of their neighbors. If no one owned a car, then I would not be required to have one to meet the minimal demands of social existence. But because almost everyone has a car today, it is extremely difficult to get along without one.

If relative consumption is important, it follows logically that each person's consumption imposes negative externalities on others. When any one person increases his consumption, he raises, perhaps imperceptibly, the consumption standard for others. As the British economist Richard Layard once stated, "In a poor society a man proves to his wife that he loves her by giving her a rose, but in a rich society he must give a dozen roses."

The fact that many forms of consumption generate negative externalities has important implications for tax policy. To illustrate, consider a young man's decision about how big a diamond to give his fiancée. Because the function of this gift is to serve as a token of commitment, the one he buys must necessarily cost enough to hurt. His jeweler will tell him that the custom in this country is to pay 2 months' salary for a stone and setting. If he makes $60,000/yr, he will have to come up with $10,000 or else feel like a cheapskate.

From the perspective of the economy as a whole, the outcome would be better if there were a 400 percent tax on jewelry. The after-tax price of what is now only a $2,000 diamond would then rise to $10,000. In buying this smaller diamond, the young man would incur the same economic hardship as before. And since this is the essence of the gift's function, his goal would not really be compromised by the tax. Nor would the young man's fiancée suffer any real loss. Because *everyone* would now be buying smaller diamonds, the smaller stone would provide much the same satisfaction as the larger one would have. On the plus side, the government gets an additional $8,000 to finance its expenditures or reduce other taxes. The only loser is the deBeers diamond cartel of South Africa, which would earn $8,000 less than before the tax.

The standards that define acceptable schools, houses, wardrobes, cars, vacations, and a host of other important budget items are inextricably linked to the amounts other people spend on them. Because individual consumers typically ignore positional externalities in their choices, the result is that such commodities appear much more attractive to individuals than to society as a whole. For the same reasons that it is often efficient to tax pollution, it will be efficient to tax many of these forms of consumption. On efficiency grounds, such taxes would be an attractive substitute for existing taxes that interfere with efficient resource allocation.

SUMMARY

- When an action by one party harms another and the parties are able to negotiate costlessly with one another, the negative externalities are dealt with efficiently regardless of whether the law makes people liable for the harmful effects of their actions. This result is known as the Coase theorem. *(LO3)*

- This general principle sheds light on a variety of questions regarding the design of property rights. It helps explain: why the owner of a dock may not legally exclude a boater from tying up during a storm; when people are allowed to exclude others from walking across their land or from blocking their view; why pastureland is more productive if owned privately rather than in common; why airplanes are allowed to fly over someone's property, while developers cannot build above it without permission. In each case, the laws of property are set up to mimic as closely as possible the kinds of accommodations people would reach for themselves if they were free to negotiate costlessly with one another. *(LO3)*

- Similar conclusions apply in situations that involve positive externalities. If negotiation is costless, people will forge agreements that result in efficient outcomes, even in cases in which one party's activities create indirect benefits to the other. And where negotiation is costly, institutions often tend to evolve that encourage activities with positive external effects. *(LO3, LO4)*

- Similar principles apply to a variety of other governmental restraints on behavior. In the case of free speech and other constitutional liberties, the best legal solutions turn out to be the ones that most closely resemble the solutions people would have negotiated among themselves, had it been practical to do so. *(LO4)*

- When negotiation is costly, it does matter how liability is assigned. In general, the most efficient outcome occurs when the law places the burden of avoiding harmful effects on the party that can accomplish it at the lowest cost. *(LO4)*

- In contests for relative position, as in all other contests, the efforts by one contestant confer a negative externality on other contestants: anything that increases one party's odds of winning necessarily reduces the odds of others. The effect is almost always to induce some form of arms race among contestants, in which the efforts of each party serve largely to offset one another. The theory of externalities and property rights sheds light on the laws by which citizens of modern societies restrict such arms races. *(LO6)*

- Taxation is one solution to the problem of negative externalities. Although it is not always an ideal answer, it does offer several important advantages over direct regulation in many situations. *(LO7)*

REVIEW QUESTIONS

1. When negotiation costs are negligible, why is the assignment of liability for externalities irrelevant for efficiency? *(LO1)*

2. Give three examples of the tragedy of the commons on your campus. *(LO3)*

3. Suppose you are the party who can avoid a particular external effect at the lowest cost. Why might you favor a general rule that assigns liability to whichever party can avoid damage at the lowest cost? *(LO4)*

4. Why do we permit airplanes but not real estate developers to use the airspace over private homes without prior consent? *(LO4)*

5. Why do most property laws limit private coastal property to the waterline at high tide? *(LO4)*

6. Does the assignment of liability matter for distributional reasons? *(LO4)*

PROBLEMS

1. Every November, Ushi and Kabir each face the choice between burning their leaves or stuffing them into garbage bags. Burning the leaves is much easier but produces noxious smoke. The utility values for each person, measured in utils, are listed in the table for each of the four possible combinations of actions: *(LO1, LO3)*

		Ushi	
		Burn	**Bag**
Kabir	**Burn**	Kabir: 4 Ushi: 4	Kabir: 8 Ushi: 2
	Bag	Kabir: 2 Ushi: 8	Kabir: 6 Ushi: 6

a. If Ushi and Kabir are utility maximizers and make their decisions individually, what will they do?

b. How will your answer to part (a) differ, if at all, if Ushi and Kabir can make binding agreements with each other?

Now suppose the payoff matrix is as follows:

		Ushi	
		Burn	**Bag**
Kabir	**Burn**	Kabir: 6 Ushi: 6	Kabir: 8 Ushi: 2
	Bag	Kabir: 2 Ushi: 8	Kabir: 4 Ushi: 4

c. What will they do this time if they can make binding agreements?

2. Ushi can produce with or without a filter on his smokestack. Production without a filter results in greater smoke damage to Kabir. The relevant gains and losses for the two individuals are listed in the table below: *(LO3)*

	With filter	Without filter
Gains to Ushi	$200/wk	$245/wk
Damage to Kabir	$35/wk	$85/wk

a. If Ushi is not liable for smoke damage and there are no negotiation costs, will he install a filter? Explain carefully.

b. How, if at all, would the outcome be different if Ushi were liable for all smoke damage and the cost of the filter were $10/wk higher than indicated in the table? Explain carefully.

3. Ushi can operate his sawmill with or without soundproofing. Operation without soundproofing results in noise damage to his neighbor Kabir. The relevant gains and losses for Ushi and Kabir are listed in the table: *(LO3, LO4)*

	Without soundproofing	With soundproofing
Gains to Ushi	$150/wk	$34/wk
Damage to Kabir	$125/wk	$6/wk

a. If Ushi is not liable for noise damage and there are no negotiation costs, will he install soundproofing? Explain.

b. How, if at all, would your answer differ if the negotiation costs of maintaining an agreement were $4/wk? Explain.

c. Now suppose Kabir can escape the noise damage by moving to a new location, which will cost him $120/wk. With negotiation costs again assumed to be zero, how, if at all, will your answer to part (a) differ? Explain.

4. Nimit and Gian are trying to decide whether to share an apartment. To live separately, each would have to pay $300/mo in rent. An apartment large enough to share

can be rented for $450/mo. Costs aside, they are indifferent between living together and living separately except for these two problems: Nimit likes to play his stereo late at night, which disturbs Gian's sleep; and Gian likes to sing in the shower at 6 AM, which awakens Nimit. Gian would sacrifice up to $80/mo rather than stop singing in the shower, and Nimit would sacrifice up to $155/mo rather than stop playing his stereo late at night. Nimit would tolerate Gian's singing and Gian would tolerate Nimit's stereo in return for compensation payments not less than $75/mo and $80/mo, respectively. *(LO3)*

a. Should they live together? If so, indicate how they can split the rent so that each does better than by living alone. If not, explain why no such arrangement is feasible.

b. Now suppose Nimit wins a free pair of stereo headphones. If he wears them late at night, Gian's sleep is not disturbed. Nimit likes the headphones well enough, but would be willing to pay $40/mo to keep on listening to late-night music through his speakers. How, if at all, does the existence of this new option affect your answer to part (a)? Explain carefully.

5. Sophia and Ava can live separately at a rent of $400/mo each, or together at a rent of $600. Each would be willing to give up $30/mo to avoid having to give up her privacy. In addition to the loss of privacy, joint living produces two other conflicts, namely, each has a particular behavior the other finds offensive: Ava is a trumpet player, and Sophia smokes cigarettes. Ava would be willing to pay $60/mo rather than tolerate smoking in her house and $120/mo to continue playing her trumpet. Sophia, for her part, would pay up to $100/mo to continue smoking and up to $90/mo to avoid listening to trumpet music. Will they live together? Explain carefully. Would your answer be different if Sophia didn't mind giving up her privacy? *(LO3)*

6. Kenya and Dionne live on adjacent plots of land. Each has two potential uses for their land, the present values of each of which depend on the use adopted by the other, as summarized in the table. All the values in the table are known to both parties. *(LO3, LO4)*

	Kenya	
	Apple growing	Pig farming
Dionne Rental housing	Kenya: $200 Dionne: $700	Kenya: $450 Dionne: $400
Bee keeping	Kenya: $400 Dionne: $650	Kenya: $450 Dionne: $500

a. If there are no negotiation costs, what activities will the two pursue on their land?

b. If there are negotiation costs of $150, what activities will the two pursue on their land?

c. What is the maximum net income Kenya can earn in parts (a) and (b) above?

7. A village has six residents, each of whom has $1,000. Each resident may either invest his money in a government bond, which pays 11 percent/yr, or use it to buy a year-old steer, which will graze on the village commons. Year-old steers and government bonds each cost exactly $1,000. Steers require no effort to tend and can be sold for a price that depends on the amount of weight they gain during the year. Yearly weight gain, in turn, depends on the number of steers that graze on the commons. The prices of 2-yr-old steers are given in the table as a function of the total number of steers. *(LO3)*

Number of steers	Price per 2-year-old steer
1	$1,200
2	1,175
3	1,150
4	1,125
5	1,100
6	1,075

a. If village residents make their investment decisions independently, how many steers will graze on the commons?

b. How many steers would graze on the commons if investment decisions were made collectively?

c. What grazing fee per steer would result in the socially optimal number of steers?

8. A competitive fishing industry consists of five independently owned and operated fishing boats working out of the port of Ithaca. Assume that no other fishermen fish Cayuga Lake, and that the MC of operating a boat for 1 day is equivalent to 70 pounds of fish. (A boat left idle generates no costs.) The total catch per shoreline, in pounds, is given in the following table as a function of the number of boats fishing the east and west shores of the lake: *(LO3, LO4)*

	Total catch	
Number of boats per side	East shore	West shore
1	100	85
2	180	150
3	255	210
4	320	260
5	350	300

a. If each boat owner decides independently which side of the lake to fish and all boats are in plain view of each other, how many boats would you expect to find fishing each shore on any given day? What is the net catch (that is, the total catch from both shores, less operating costs)?

b. Is this distribution of fishing craft optimal from the social point of view? If so, explain why. If not, what is the socially optimal distribution and the corresponding net catch?

9. Two firms, X and Y, have access to five different production processes, each one of which gives off a different amount of carbon. The daily costs of the processes and the corresponding number of tons of CO_2 are listed in the table: *(LO6)*

Process (CO_2)	A (4 tons/ day)	B (3 tons/ day)	C (2 tons/ day)	D (1 ton/ day)	E (0 tons/ day)
Cost to firm X	100	120	140	170	220
Cost to firm Y	60	100	150	255	375

a. If emissions are unregulated, which process will each firm use, and what will be the total daily CO_2 emissions?

b. The government wants to cut CO_2 emissions by half. To accomplish this, it requires a permit for each ton of CO_2 emitted and limits the number of permits to the targeted level of emissions. The permits are then auctioned off to the highest bidders. If X and Y are the only emitters, how much will each permit cost? How many permits will X buy? How many will Y buy?

c. Compare the total cost to society of this permit auction procedure to the total cost of having each firm reduce emissions by half.

10. Suppose the government attempts to restrict greenhouse gas emissions by mandating a maximum emission level for each firm. In general, this will result in a higher cost for pollution control than is necessary. Explain why. *(LO6)*

11* A small village has six people. Each can either fish in a nearby lagoon or work in a factory. Wages in the factory are $4/day. Fish sell in competitive markets for $1 apiece. If L persons fish the lagoon, the total number of fish caught is given by $F = 8L - 2L^2$. People prefer to fish unless they expect to make more money working in the factory. *(LO4)*

a. If people decide individually whether to fish or work in the factory, how many will fish? What will be the total earnings for the village?

b. What is the socially optimal number of fishermen? With that number, what will the total earnings of the village be?

c. Why is there a difference between the equilibrium and socially optimal numbers of fishermen?

12. Once a week Latrell purchases a six-pack of cola and puts it in his refrigerator for his two children to drink later. He invariably discovers that all six cans get drunk the first day. Jabari also purchases a six-pack of cola once a week for his two children, but unlike Latrell, he tells them that each may drink no more than three cans. Explain why the cola lasts much longer at Jabari's house than at Latrell's. *(LO3)*

13. Suppose Krisha owns and works in a bakery located next to an outdoor café owned by Amoli. The patrons of the outdoor café like the smell that emanates from the bakery. When Krisha leaves her windows open, the café faces the demand curve $P_C = 30 - 0.2Q_C$, while when the windows are closed, demand is given by $P_C = 25 - 0.2Q_C$. However, Krisha doesn't like the street noise she hears when her windows are open, and in particular, the disutility she receives has a monetary value of 5. Assume that the café has a constant marginal cost of 10, and that integration (merger) is not a possibility because each owner greatly enjoys owning and operating her own establishment. *(LO3)*

a. In the absence of a contract between the parties, do the firms behave in an efficient fashion? If not, describe the range of contracts that might emerge in response to the externality problem present in the environment. In answering this question, assume Krisha understands how the bakery odor affects demand at the café, and Amoli knows how much Krisha dislikes street noise.

b. Suppose now everything is the same as above, except that given the current seating arrangement in the café, the café does not face a higher demand when the bakery windows are open. To realize this higher demand, Amoli needs to make a sunk investment of 50, which moves the tables closer to the bakery. Is it wise for Amoli to make this investment prior to Krisha and Amoli signing a contract? Explain.

c. Go back to the initial setup, but now assume that Krisha's disutility from street noise equals 50 rather than 5. Further, suppose that prior to the parties agreeing on a contract Amoli becomes the mayor and grants to herself the property rights concerning

---

*This problem is most easily solved by making use of the calculus definition of marginal product given in the appendix to Chapter 8.

whether the bakery windows are left open or closed. Does this have an effect on whether the parties reach an efficient outcome? Explain.

14. Rashida and Maya face the choice of driving to work early or late. If they both drive to work at the same time, each gets in the way of the other on the road, and so their daily commute takes longer and is more irritating. The monetary payoffs for each person are listed in the table on the next page for each of the four possible combinations of actions: *(LO3)*
    a. If Rashida and Maya are payoff maximizers and make their decisions individually, what will they do?
    b. If Rashida and Maya can make binding agreements with each other, what will they do?

		Rashida	
		Early	**Late**
Maya	**Early**	Maya: 30 Rashida: 30	Maya: 50 Rashida: 20
	Late	Maya: 20 Rashida: 50	Maya: 10 Rashida: 10

15. Same as Problem 14, except now the payoff values of each person are as follows: *(LO3)*

		Rashida	
		Early	**Late**
Maya	**Early**	Maya: 30 Rashida: 30	Maya: 50 Rashida: 20
	Late	Maya: 20 Rashida: 60	Maya: 10 Rashida: 10

    a. If Rashida and Maya are payoff maximizers and make their decisions individually, what will they do?
    b. If Rashida and Maya can make binding agreements with each other, what will they do?
    c. How do your answers differ from Problem 14 and why?

16. Nora loves dogs and has a pair of West Highland terriers. Ivy has an incredible fear of dogs and cannot stand to be within sight of them. Nora and Ivy are deciding whether to live in Arlington or Bexley. If they end up living in the same part of town, Ivy will run into Nora out walking the Westies and get frightened. Thus, Ivy prefers to be physically separated from Nora. The payoffs for each person are listed in the table below for each of the four possible combinations of actions: *(LO3)*

		Nora	
		Arlington	**Bexley**
Ivy	**Arlington**	Ivy: 0 Nora: 800	Ivy: 500 Nora: 900
	Bexley	Ivy: 800 Nora: 800	Ivy: 0 Nora: 900

    a. If Nora and Ivy are payoff maximizers and make their decisions individually, what will they do?
    b. If Nora and Ivy can make binding agreements with each other, what will they do?

		Nora	
		Arlington	**Bexley**
Ivy	**Arlington**	Ivy: 0 Nora: 800	Ivy: 500 Nora: 1,000
	Bexley	Ivy: 600 Nora: 800	Ivy: 1,000 Nora: 900

17. Same as Problem 16, except now payoff values of each person are *(LO3)*
    a. If Nora and Ivy are payoff maximizers and make their decisions individually, what will they do?
    b. If Nora and Ivy can make binding agreements with each other, what will they do?
    c. How do your answers differ from Problem 16 and why?

ANSWERS TO SELF-TESTS

16.1 With a negotiation cost of only 20, it is now practical for the confectioner to pay the doctor to rearrange her office when the confectioner is liable. But note in the table below that it is still more efficient for the confectioner not to be liable: *(LO4)*

Legal regime	Outcome	Net Benefit		
		Doctor	Confectioner	Total
Liable	Confectioner operates and pays doctor $18 \leq P \leq 20$ to rearrange office	$22 + P$	$40 - P$	62
Not liable	Doctor rearranges her office at her own expense	22	60	82

16.2 Recall that the optimal number of steers is two. The grazing fee must be more than 2 to prevent a third steer from being sent out to graze. The fee cannot be more than 6 without keeping the second steer from being sent out. *(LO7)*

Jorge Salcedo/Alamy Stock Photo

General Equilibrium and Market Efficiency

Barbers earn more today than they did 50 years ago, not because they cut hair any faster than they did then but because productivity has grown so rapidly in the other occupations they could have chosen. By the same token, $8.5'' \times 11''$ paper now sells in much greater quantities, not because we have discovered a cheaper way to produce it but because so many more people now own their own printers and copying machines. And we know that when a frost kills half the coffee crop in Brazil, the price of tea grown in Darjeeling usually rises substantially.

In the preceding chapters we saw occasional glimpses of the rich linkages between markets in the real world. But for the most part, we ignored these linkages in favor of what economists call *partial equilibrium analysis*—the study of how individual markets function in isolation. One of our tasks in this chapter is to investigate the properties of an interconnected system of markets. This is called *general equilibrium analysis,* and its focus is to make explicit the links that exist between individual markets. It takes into account, for example, the fact that inputs supplied to one market are unavailable for any other and that an increase in demand in one market implies a reduction in demand in others.

CHAPTER PREVIEW

We will begin with one of the simplest forms of **general equilibrium analysis,** a pure exchange economy with only two consumers and two goods. We will see that for any given initial allocation of the two goods between the two consumers, a competitive exchange process always exhausts all possible mutually beneficial gains from trade.

Next we will add the possibility of production, again using one of the simplest possible models, one with only two inputs whose total supply is fixed. We will see that here too competitive trading exploits all mutually beneficial gains from exchange.

general equilibrium analysis
the study of how conditions in each market in a set of related markets affect equilibrium outcomes in other markets in that set.

We will then add the possibility of international trade, assuming that prices are given externally in world markets. We will see that even though trade leaves domestic production possibilities unchanged, its immediate effect is to increase the value of goods available for domestic consumption.

From trade, we will move to the question of how taxes affect the allocation of resources. We will conclude with a brief discussion of factors that interfere with the efficient allocation of resources.

A SIMPLE EXCHANGE ECONOMY

Imagine a simple economy in which there are only two consumers—Aaliyah and Bahjat—and two goods, food and clothing. Food and clothing are not produced in this economy. Rather, they arrive in fixed quantities in each time period, just like manna from heaven. To help fix ideas, suppose there is a total of 100 units of food each time period and a total of 200 units of clothing. An *allocation* is defined as an assignment of these total amounts between Aaliyah and Bahjat. An example is the allocation in which Aaliyah receives 70 units of clothing and 75 units of food, with the remaining 130 units of clothing and 25 units of food going to Bahjat. In general, if Aaliyah receives F_A units of food and C_A units of clothing, then Bahjat will get $100 - F_A$ units of food and $200 - C_A$ units of clothing. The amounts of the two goods with which Aaliyah and Bahjat begin each time period are called their *initial endowments*.

In the next section we'll have more to say about where these initial endowments come from, but for now let's take them as externally determined. The question before us here is "What will Aaliyah and Bahjat do with their initial endowments?" One possibility is that they might simply consume them, but only in rare circumstances will that be the best option available. To see why, it is helpful to begin by portraying the initial endowments diagrammatically. Consider again the case in which Aaliyah receives 70 units of clothing and 75 units of food, with the remaining 130 units of clothing and 25 units of food going to Bahjat. From earlier chapters, we know how to represent these initial endowments as bundles in two separate food-clothing diagrams. The same allocation can also be represented as a point in a single rectangular diagram—namely, point R in Figure 17.1. The height of the rectangle corresponds to the total amount of food available per time period, 100 units. Its width is equal to the total amount of clothing, 200 units. O^A is the origin for Aaliyah, and the left and bottom sides of the rectangle are the axes that measure her quantities of food and clothing, respectively. O^B is the origin for Bahjat, and movements to the left from O^B correspond to increases in his amount of clothing. Downward movements from O^B correspond to increases in Bahjat's amount of food.

Because of the special way the rectangle is constructed, every point that lies within it corresponds to an allocation that exactly exhausts the total quantities of food and clothing

---

FIGURE 17.1

An Edgeworth Exchange Box

Aaliyah's quantity of food at any point is measured by how far the point lies above O^A. Aaliyah's clothing is measured by how far the point lies to the right of O^A. Bahjat's clothing is measured leftward from O^B, and his food downward from O^B. At any point within the Edgeworth box, the individual quantities of food and clothing sum to the total amounts available.

available. Thus, point R is 70 units to the right of O^A and 130 units to the left of O^B, which means 70 units of clothing for Aaliyah and 130 units for Bahjat, for a total of 200. R also lies 75 units above O^A and 25 units below O^B, which means 75 units of food for Aaliyah and 25 for Bahjat, for a total of 100. The rectangular diagram in Figure 17.1 is often referred to as an **Edgeworth exchange box,** after the British economist Francis Y. Edgeworth, who introduced it.

Edgeworth exchange box a diagram used to analyze the general equilibrium of an exchange economy.

SELF-TEST 17.1

Suppose point S in Figure 17.1 lies 25 units above O^A and 25 units to the right of O^A. Verify that Bahjat's initial endowment at S is 75 units of food and 175 units of clothing.

If Aaliyah and Bahjat have the initial endowments represented by R, what will they do with them? Their possibilities are either to consume what they already have or to engage in exchange with one another. Exchange is purely voluntary, so trades can take place only if they make both parties better off.

Our criterion for saying an exchange makes someone better off is very simple: It must place him on a higher indifference curve. In the Edgeworth box in Figure 17.2, Aaliyah's indifference map has the conventional orientation, while Bahjat's is rotated 180°. Thus the curves labeled I_{A1}, I_{A2}, and I_{A3} are representative curves from Aaliyah's indifference map, while I_{B1}, I_{B2}, and I_{B3} play the corresponding role for Bahjat. Aaliyah's satisfaction increases as we move to the northeast in the box; Bahjat's as we move to the southwest.

Because we assume that preference orderings are complete, we know that each party will have an indifference curve passing through the initial endowment point R. In Figure 17.2 these curves are labeled I_{A2} and I_{B2}. Note that Aaliyah's MRS between food and clothing at R (that is, the slope of her indifference curve) is much larger than Bahjat's (where the MRS for Bahjat is measured with respect to his own food and clothing axes). Suppose, for example, that Aaliyah requires 2 units of food in order to be willing to part with a unit of clothing, while Bahjat requires only $\frac{1}{2}$ unit of food to make the same exchange. Both parties will then be better off if Aaliyah gives Bahjat a unit of food in exchange for a unit of clothing. Indeed, any point in the lens-shaped shaded region in Figure 17.2 is one for which each party lies on a higher indifference curve than at R. Point T, at which Aaliyah has 65 units of food and 85 units of clothing, is one such point. The two parties can move from R to T by having Aaliyah give Bahjat 10 units of food in exchange for 15 units of clothing.

FIGURE 17.2

Gains from Exchange

By moving from R to T, each party attains a higher indifference curve.

FIGURE 17.3

Further Gains from Exchange

Any point in the shaded region lies on a higher indifference curve for both parties than the ones that pass through *T.*

But the movement from *R* to *T* does not exhaust all possible gains from exchange. Note in Figure 17.3 that there is an additional, albeit smaller, lens-shaped region enclosed by the indifference curves that pass through *T* by both parties.

Through a process of repeated exchange, Aaliyah and Bahjat will finally reach a point at which further mutual gains from trade are no longer possible. The indifference curves for the two parties that pass through any such point will necessarily be tangent to one another, as at point *M* in Figure 17.4. (If they were not tangent, they would necessarily enclose yet another lens-shaped region in which further gains from exchange would be possible.) Note that at *M* the marginal rates of substitution of Aaliyah and Bahjat are exactly the same. It was a difference in these rates that provided the original basis for exchange, and once they are the same, all voluntary trading will cease.

One allocation is said to be *Pareto preferred* or **Pareto superior** to another if at least one party prefers it and the other party likes it at least as well. Allocations like the one at *M* are called **Pareto optimal.** A Pareto-optimal allocation is one for which there is no other feasible reallocation that is preferred by one party and liked at least equally well by the other party. The concept of Pareto optimality was introduced by the nineteenth-century Italian economist Vilfredo Pareto. Pareto-optimal allocations are essentially ones from which further mutually beneficial moves are impossible.

Pareto superior allocation an allocation that at least one individual prefers and others like at least as well.

Pareto optimal allocation the term used to describe situations in which it is impossible to make one person better off without making at least some others worse off.

FIGURE 17.4

A Pareto-Optimal Allocation

At the allocation *M,* no further mutually beneficial exchange is possible. The marginal rate of substitution of food for clothing is the same for both parties at *M.*

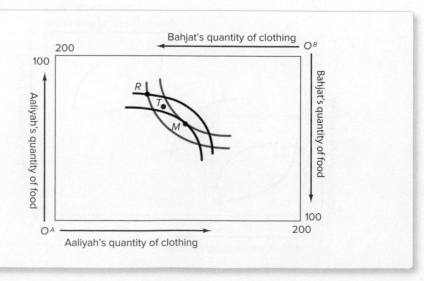

SELF-TEST 17.2

Suppose Aaliyah has an initial allocation of 50 units of food and 100 units of clothing in Figure 17.4. She regards food and clothing as perfect, 1-for-1 substitutes. Bahjat regards them as perfect, 1-for-1 complements, always wanting to consume 1 unit of clothing for every unit of food. Describe the set of allocations that are Pareto preferred to the initial allocation.

In any Edgeworth exchange box, there will be not one but an infinite number of mutual tangencies, as illustrated in Figure 17.5. The locus of these tangencies is called the **contract curve,** a name that was chosen because it describes where all final, voluntary contracts between rational, well-informed persons must lie. Put another way, the contract curve identifies all the efficient ways of dividing the two goods between the two consumers.

contract curve a curve along which all final, voluntary contracts must lie.

Where Aaliyah and Bahjat end up on the contract curve naturally depends on the initial endowments with which they start. Suppose they start with the one labeled F in Figure 17.6. We can then say that they will end up somewhere on the contract curve between points U and V. Given that they are starting from F, the best possible outcome from Aaliyah's point of view is to end up at V. Bahjat, of course, would most prefer U. Whether they end up closer to U or to V depends on the relative bargaining skills of the two traders. Had they instead started at the allocation G, they would have ended up between W and Z on the contract curve.

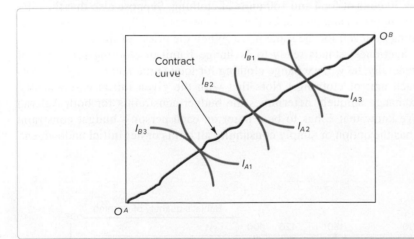

FIGURE 17.5

The Contract Curve

The locus of mutual tangencies in the Edgeworth exchange box is called the contract curve. Any point that does not lie on the contract curve cannot be the final outcome of a voluntary exchange because both parties will always prefer a move from that point in the direction of the contract curve.

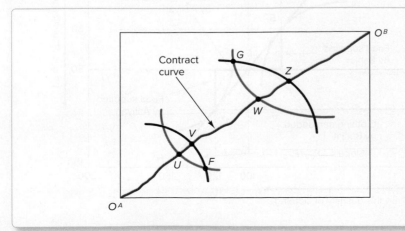

FIGURE 17.6

Initial Endowments Constrain Final Outcomes

Starting from F, traders will move to a point on the contract curve between U and V. They will land closer to V the better Aaliyah's bargaining skills are relative to Bahjat's. If they start at G, they will end up between W and Z on the contract curve.

The uses and limitations of the two Pareto criteria—Pareto preferred and Pareto optimal—can be seen by an examination of some of the points in Figure 17.6. Note, for example, that both W and Z are Pareto preferred to the original allocation G. This follows because W is better than G from Bahjat's point of view and no worse from Aaliyah's; and similarly, Z is better from Aaliyah's point of view and no worse from Bahjat's. Note that both points are also Pareto optimal. The two Pareto criteria are essentially relative in nature. Thus, when we say that U is Pareto preferred to F, or even when we say that U is Pareto optimal, we are not saying that U is good in any absolute sense. On the contrary, Aaliyah is hardly likely to find U very attractive, and it is certainly much worse, from her standpoint, than an allocation like G, which is neither Pareto optimal nor even Pareto preferred to U. If Aaliyah is starving to death in a tattered coat at U, she will not take much comfort in being told that U is Pareto optimal.

The Pareto criteria thus have force only in relation to the allocation with which the two players begin. Rather than remain at an initial allocation, both will always agree to move to one that is Pareto preferred and, indeed, to keep on moving until they reach one that is Pareto optimal.

In the simple, two-person economy described above, exchange took place through a process of personal bargaining. In market economies, by contrast, most exchanges have a much more impersonal character. People have given endowments and face given prices, and then decide how much of the various goods and services they want to buy and sell. We can introduce market-type exchange into our simple economy by the simple expedient of assuming that there is a third person who plays the role of an auctioneer. His function is to keep adjusting relative prices until the quantities demanded of each good match the quantities supplied.

Suppose Aaliyah and Bahjat start with the allocation at E in Figure 17.7, in which each has 50 units of food and 100 units of clothing. Suppose also that the ratio of food to clothing prices announced by the auctioneer is $P_{C0}/P_{F0} = 1$, meaning that food and clothing both sell for the same price. When the prices of the two goods are the same, the auctioneer stands ready to exchange 1 unit of clothing for 1 unit of food. (More generally, he will exchange clothing for food at the rate of P_{C0}/P_{F0} units of food for each unit of clothing.) Note that with the given initial endowments, this rate of exchange uniquely determines the budget constraints for both Aaliyah and Bahjat. We know that E has to be a point on each person's budget constraint because each has the option of simply consuming all of his or her initial endowment.

FIGURE 17.7

A Disequilibrium Relative Price Ratio

At the price ratio $P_{C0}/P_{F0} = 1$, both Aaliyah and Bahjat want to sell 20 units of food and buy 20 more units of clothing. But in general equilibrium, the amount sold by one party must equal the amount bought by the other. Both the food and clothing markets are out of equilibrium here.

But suppose that Aaliyah wants to sell some food and use the proceeds to buy more clothing. She can do this by moving downward from E along the line labeled HH'. Alternatively, if she wants to sell clothing to buy more food, she can move upward along HH'. The same HH', seen from Bahjat's point of view, constitutes the budget constraint for Bahjat.

Given their budget constraints and preferences, Aaliyah and Bahjat face a simple choice problem of the sort we discussed in Chapter 3. The optimal bundle for Aaliyah on the budget HH' is the one labeled A_0^* in Figure 17.7, in which she consumes 30 units of food and 120 units of clothing. The corresponding bundle for Bahjat is labeled B_0^*, and it too contains 30 units of food and 120 units of clothing. Note that by choosing A_0^*, Aaliyah indicates that she wants to sell 20 units of her initial endowment of food in order to buy 20 units of additional clothing. Similarly, by choosing B_0^*, Bahjat indicates that he too wants to sell 20 units of food and buy 20 more units of clothing.

This creates a problem, however. There are only 200 units of clothing to begin with, and the initial endowments of clothing at E add to precisely that amount. It is thus mathematically impossible for each person to have more clothing. By the same token, it is not possible for each person to sell food. The auctioneer in this exercise is a figment, a hypothetical person who calls out relative prices in the hope of stimulating mutually beneficial exchange. He acts as a middleman, arranging for clothing to be exchanged for an equivalent value of food. But if *everyone* wants to sell food and buy clothing, there is no such exchange he can arrange.

At the price ratio $P_{C0}/P_{F0} = 1$, there is excess demand for clothing and excess supply of food. At this price ratio the markets are not in general equilibrium. The solution to this problem is straightforward: The auctioneer simply calls out a new price ratio in which the price of clothing relative to food is higher than before. If there is still excess demand for clothing, he calls out a still higher price ratio, and so on, until the excess demand in each market is exactly zero.[1] Starting with the allocation at E, the price ratio $(P_C/P_F)^*$ that produces general equilibrium is shown in Figure 17.8. On the budget line through E with slope $(P_C/P_F)^*$, the highest attainable indifference curves for Aaliyah and Bahjat are

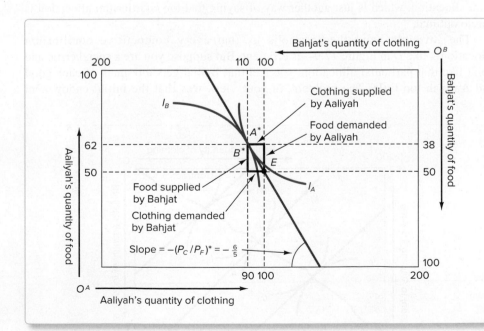

FIGURE 17.8

General Equilibrium

A simple exchange economy is in equilibrium when excess demands for both products are exactly equal to zero. At the price ratio $(P_C/P_F)^* = \frac{6}{5}$, Aaliyah wants to buy 12 units of food, which is exactly the amount Bahjat wants to sell; also, Aaliyah wants to sell 10 units of clothing, which is exactly the amount Bahjat wants to buy.

[1]In advanced courses, we show that a competitive equilibrium will exist in a simple exchange economy if the sum of all individual excess demands is a continuous function of relative prices. This will always happen whenever individual indifference curves have the conventional convex shape.

tangent. In order to move from E to the bundle $A*$, Aaliyah must purchase exactly the quantity of food (12 units) that Bahjat wishes to sell. And for Bahjat to move from E to the bundle $B*$, he must purchase exactly the quantity of clothing (10 units) that Aaliyah wishes to sell. In this illustration, excess demands for both products are exactly equal to zero at the price ratio $(P_C/P_F)* = \frac{6}{5}$.

Only Relative Prices Are Determined

From the information given in our simple exchange model, note that we are able to determine only the *ratio* of clothing to food prices, not the actual value of individual prices. If, for example, $P_C = 6$ and $P_F = 5$ produce a budget constraint with the slope shown in Figure 17.8, then so will the prices $P_C = 12$ and $P_F = 10$, or indeed any other pair of prices whose ratio is $\frac{6}{5}$. Doubling or halving all prices will double or halve the dollar value of each consumer's initial endowment. In real terms, such price movements leave budget constraints unchanged.

THE INVISIBLE HAND THEOREM

We are now in a position to consider one of the most celebrated claims in intellectual history, namely, Adam Smith's *theorem of the invisible hand.* In the context of our simple exchange economy, the theorem can be stated as follows:

> An equilibrium produced by competitive markets will exhaust all possible
> gains from exchange.

The invisible hand theorem is also known as the *first theorem of welfare economics,* and an alternative way of stating it is that *equilibrium in competitive markets is Pareto optimal.* To see why this must be so, recall that at the general equilibrium allocation, the optimizing indifference curves are tangent to one another. The possible allocations that Aaliyah regards as better than the equilibrium allocation all lie beyond her budget constraint, and the same is true for Bahjat. And since the two budget constraints coincide in the Edgeworth box, this means that there is no allocation that both prefer to the equilibrium allocation, which is just another way of saying that the equilibrium allocation is Pareto optimal.

The invisible hand theorem tells us that every competitive equilibrium allocation—like D in Figure 17.9—is efficient. But suppose you are a social critic and don't like that particular allocation; you feel that Bahjat gets too much of each good and Aaliyah too little. The problem, in your view, was that the initial endowment

FIGURE 17.9

Sustaining Efficient Allocations

If indifference curves are convex, any efficient allocation can be sustained through a suitable choice of initial endowments and relative prices. To sustain E, for example, we announce a relative price ratio equal to the slope of HH', the mutual tangent to I_{A2} and I_{B2}, and give consumers an initial endowment bundle that lies anywhere on HH', such as M.

point—J in the diagram—is unjustly favorable to Bahjat. Suppose there is some other allocation on the contract curve—such as E—that you find much more equitable. Is there a set of initial endowments and relative prices for which E will be a competitive equilibrium? The *second theorem of welfare economics says* that, under relatively unrestrictive conditions:

> *Any* allocation on the contract curve can be sustained as a competitive equilibrium.

The basic condition that assures this result is that consumer indifference curves be convex when viewed from the origin. We know that an allocation like E, or any other efficient allocation, lies at a point of tangency between indifference curves. In Figure 17.9, the locus HH' is the mutual tangent between I_{A2} and I_{B2}. If the difference curves are convex, any initial endowment along HH'—such as M—will lead to a competitive equilibrium at E. If we redistribute the initial endowments from J to M, and announce a price ratio equal to the slope of HH', Aaliyah and Bahjat will then be led by the invisible hand to E. Indeed, any point along the contract curve can be reached in this fashion by a suitable choice of initial endowments and relative prices.

In the context of this simple, two-good, two-person exchange economy, it may not seem like a major accomplishment to be able to sustain all efficient allocations in the manner described by the second welfare theorem. After all, if we are free to redistribute initial endowments, why not simply redistribute them so as to achieve the desired final outcome directly? Why even bother with the intermediate steps of announcing prices and allowing people to make trades? If we are free to move from J to M in Figure 17.9, then we ought to be able to move directly to E and cut out the intervening steps.

The difficulty in practice is that the social institutions responsible for redistributing income have little idea of the shapes and locations of individual consumer indifference curves. People know their own preferences much better than governments do. And for an initial endowment of given value, they will generally achieve a much better result if they are free to make their own purchase decisions. *The significance of the second welfare theorem is that the issue of equity in distribution is logically separable from the issue of efficiency in allocation.* As the nineteenth-century British economist John Stuart Mill saw clearly, society can redistribute incomes in accordance with whatever norms of justice it deems fitting, at the same time relying on market forces to assure that those incomes are spent to achieve the most good.

EFFICIENCY IN PRODUCTION

In our simple exchange model, the total supply of each good was given externally. In practice, however, the product mix in the economy is the result of purposeful decisions about the allocation of productive inputs. Suppose we now add a productive sector to our exchange economy, one with two firms, each of which employs two inputs—capital (K) and labor (L)—to produce either of two products, food (F) or clothing (C). Suppose firm C produces clothing and firm F produces food. In order to keep the model simple, suppose that the total quantities of the two inputs are fixed at $K = 50$ and $L = 100$, respectively. Suppose, finally, that the production processes employed by the two firms give rise to conventional, convex-shaped isoquants.

Just as the Edgeworth exchange box provided a convenient way to summarize the conditions required for efficiency in consumption, a similar analysis serves an analogous purpose in the case of production. Figure 17.10 is called an *Edgeworth production box*. O^C represents the origin of the clothing firm's isoquant map, O^F the origin of the food firm's isoquant map. Any point within the box represents an allocation of the total inputs to firm C and firm F. Firm C's isoquants correspond to increasing quantities of clothing as we move to the northeast in the box; firm F's correspond to increasing quantities of food as we move to the southwest.

FIGURE 17.10

An Edgeworth Production Box

Firm *C*'s quantity of capital at any point is measured by how far the point lies above O^C. Firm *C*'s quantity of labor is measured by how far the point lies to the right of O^C. The corresponding values of firm *F*'s inputs are measured downward and leftward, respectively, from O^F. At any point within the Edgeworth production box, the separate input allocations to the two firms add up to the total amounts available, $K = 50$ for capital, $L = 100$ for labor. The contract curve is the locus of tangencies between isoquants.

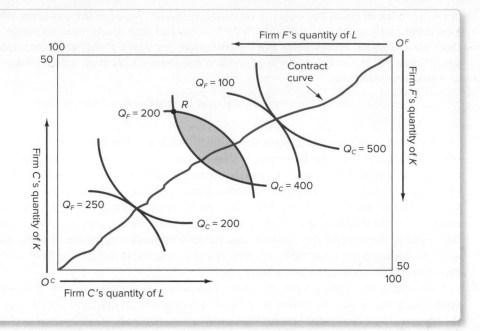

Suppose the initial allocation of inputs is at point *R* in Figure 17.10. We know that this allocation cannot be efficient because we can move to any point within the shaded lens-shaped region and obtain both more food and more clothing. As in the consumption case, the contract curve is the locus of efficient allocations, which here is the locus of tangencies between isoquants. Recalling from Chapter 8 that the slope of an isoquant at any point is called the marginal rate of technical substitution (MRTS) at that point, it is the ratio at which labor can be exchanged for capital without altering the total amount of output. Note that the MRTS between *K* and *L* must be the same for both firms at every point along the contract curve.

Suppose the equilibrium food and clothing prices are P_F^* and P_C^*, respectively. Suppose also that the two firms hire labor and capital in perfectly competitive markets at the hourly rates of *w* and *r*, respectively. If the firms maximize their profits, is there any reason to suppose that the resulting general equilibrium will satisfy the requirements of efficiency in production? That is, is there any reason to suppose that the MRTS between capital and labor will be the same for each firm? If both firms have conventional, convex-shaped isoquants, the answer is yes.

To see why, first note that a firm that maximizes its profits must also be minimizing its costs. Recall from Chapter 9 that the following conditions must be satisfied if the firms are minimizing costs:

$$\frac{\text{MPL}_C}{\text{MPK}_C} = \frac{w}{r} \tag{17.1}$$

and

$$\frac{\text{MPL}_F}{\text{MPK}_F} = \frac{w}{r}, \tag{17.2}$$

where MPL_C and MPK_C are the marginal products of labor and capital in clothing production and MPL_F and MPK_F are the corresponding marginal products in food production. Recall, too, that the ratio of marginal products of the two inputs is equal to the marginal rate of technical substitution. Since both firms pay the same prices for labor and capital, Equations 17.1 and 17.2 tell us that the marginal rates of technical substitution for the two firms will be equal in competitive equilibrium. And this tells us, finally, that competitive general equilibrium is efficient, not only in the allocation of a given endowment of consumption goods, but also in the allocation of the factors used to produce those goods.

SELF-TEST 17.3

For an economy like the one described above, suppose the price per unit of labor and the price per unit of capital are both equal to $4/hr. Suppose also that in clothing production we have $MPL_C/MPK_C = 2$ and that in food production we have $MPL_F/MPK_F = \frac{1}{2}$. Is this economy efficient in production? If not, how should it reallocate its inputs?

EFFICIENCY IN PRODUCT MIX

An economy could be efficient in production and at the same time efficient in consumption and yet do a poor job of satisfying the wants of its members. This could happen if, for example, the economy for some reason devoted almost all its resources to producing clothing, almost none to food. The tiny quantity of food that resulted could be allocated efficiently. And the inputs could be allocated efficiently in the production of this lopsided product mix. But everyone would be happier if there were less clothing and more food. There is thus one additional efficiency criterion of concern, namely, whether the economy has an efficient mix of the two products.

To define an efficient product mix, it is helpful first to translate the contract curve from the Edgeworth production box into a **production possibilities frontier,** the set of all possible output combinations that can be produced with given quantities of capital and labor. Every point along the contract curve gives rise to specific quantities of clothing and food. Suppose $F_C(K, L)$ and $F_F(K, L)$ denote the production functions for clothing (firm C) and food (firm F), respectively. Point O^C in the top panel in Figure 17.11 represents what happens when we allocate all the inputs (50 units of capital, 100 units of labor) to food production and none to clothing. If $F_F(50, 100) = 275$, then the product mix to which this allocation gives rise has zero units of clothing and 275 units of food, and is shown by point O^C in the bottom panel. Point O^F in the top panel in Figure 17.11 represents what happens when we allocate all the inputs to clothing production and none to food. If $F_C(50, 100) = 575$, then the product mix to which this allocation gives rise has 575 units of clothing and zero units of food, and is shown by point O^F in the bottom panel. The product mix corresponding to point E in the top panel has $F_C(14, 30) = 200$ units of clothing and $F_F(36, 70) = 250$ units of food, and is shown by point E in the bottom panel. Similarly, the product mix at F in the top panel has $F_C(22, 53) = 400$ units of clothing and $F_F(28, 47) = 200$ units of food, and corresponds to F in the bottom panel. Likewise, G in the top panel has $F_C(38, 76) = 500$ units of clothing and $F_F(12, 24) = 100$ units of food, and corresponds to G in the bottom panel. By plotting other correspondences in like fashion, we can generate the entire production possibilities frontier shown in the bottom panel.

production possibilities frontier the set of all possible output combinations that can be produced with a given endowment of factor inputs.

SELF-TEST 17.4

In the economy shown in Figure 17.11, suppose that a technical change occurs in the clothing industry that makes any given combination of labor and capital yield twice as much clothing as before. Show the effect of this change on the production possibilities frontier.

As we move downward along the production possibilities frontier, we give up food for additional clothing. The slope of the production possibilities frontier at any point is called the **marginal rate of transformation (MRT)** at that point, and it measures the opportunity cost of clothing in terms of food. For the economy shown, the production possibilities frontier bows out from the origin, which means that the MRT increases as we move to the right. As long as both production functions have constant or decreasing returns to scale, the production possibilities frontier cannot bow in toward the origin.

marginal rate of transformation (MRT) the rate at which one output can be exchanged for another at a point along the production possibilities frontier.

FIGURE 17.11

Generating the Production Possibilities Frontier

Each point on the contract curve in the Edgeworth production box (top panel) gives rise to specific quantities of food and clothing production. The food-clothing pairs that lie along the contract curve are plotted in the bottom panel, and their locus is called the production possibilities frontier. Movements to the northeast along the contract curve correspond to movements downward along the production possibilities frontier.

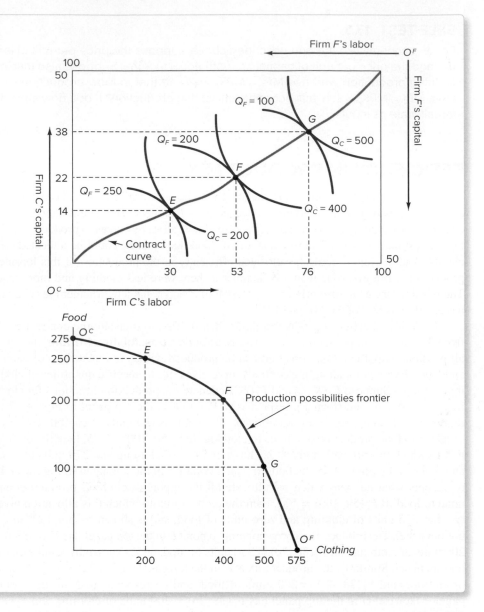

In order for an economy to be efficient in terms of its product mix, it is necessary that the marginal rate of substitution for every consumer be equal to the marginal rate of transformation. To see why, consider a product mix for which some consumer's MRS is greater or less than the corresponding MRT. The product mix Z in panel a in Figure 17.12, for instance, has an MRT of 1, while Aaliyah's consumption bundle at W in panel b shows that her MRS is 2. This means that Aaliyah is willing to give up 2 units of food in order to obtain an additional unit of clothing, but that an additional unit of clothing can be produced at a cost of only 1 unit of food. With the capital and labor saved by producing 2 fewer units of food for Aaliyah, we can produce 2 additional units of clothing. We can give 1.5 units of this extra clothing to Aaliyah and the remaining 0.5 unit to Bahjat, making both parties better off. It follows that the original product mix cannot have been efficient (where, again, efficient means Pareto optimal).

We are now in a position to ask, finally, whether a market in general competitive equilibrium will be efficient in terms of its product mix. Here, too, the answer turns out to be yes, provided the production possibilities frontier bows out from the origin. Let P_F^* and P_C^* again denote competitive equilibrium prices for food and clothing. As we have already seen in the case of the simple exchange economy, the MRS of every

FIGURE 17.12

An Inefficient Product Mix

At the product mix Z (panel a) the MRT is smaller than Aaliyah's MRS at W (panel b). By producing 2 fewer units of food, we can produce 2 additional units of clothing. If we give 1.5 of these extra units to Aaliyah and the remaining 0.5 unit to Bahjat, both parties will be better off. Efficiency requires that every consumer's MRS be exactly equal to the economy's MRT.

consumer in equilibrium will be equal to the ratio of these prices, P_C^*/P_F^*. What we must show is that the MRT will also be equal to P_C^*/P_F^*.

To do this, note first that the MRT at any point along the production possibilities frontier is equal to the ratio of the marginal cost of clothing (MC_C) to the marginal cost of food (MC_F). Suppose, for example, that MC_C at point Z in Figure 17.13 is \$100/unit of clothing and that MC_F is \$50/unit of food. The marginal rate of transformation at Z is $\Delta F/\Delta C$, the amount of food we have to give up to get an extra unit of clothing. Since MC_C is \$100, we need \$100 worth of extra labor and capital to produce an extra unit of clothing. And since MC_F is \$50, we have to produce 2 fewer units of food in order to free up \$100 worth of labor and capital. MRT at Z is therefore equal to 2, which is exactly the ratio of MC_C to MC_F.

$$MRT = \frac{MC_C}{MC_F}. \tag{17.3}$$

We also know that the equilibrium condition for competitive food and clothing producers is that product prices be equal to the corresponding values of marginal cost:

$$P_F^* = MC_F \tag{17.4}$$

and

$$P_C^* = MC_C. \tag{17.5}$$

FIGURE 17.13

MRT Equals the Ratio of Marginal Costs

At Z, to produce an extra unit of clothing requires MC_C worth of labor and capital. Each unit less of food we produce at Z frees up MC_F worth of labor and capital. To get an extra unit of C, we must give up MC_C/MC_F units of food, and so the marginal rate of transformation is equal to MC_C/MC_F.

Dividing Equation 17.5 by Equation 17.4, we have

$$\frac{P_C^*}{P_F^*} = \frac{MC_C}{MC_F},$$ (17.6)

which establishes that the equilibrium product price ratio is indeed equal to the marginal rate of transformation.

To summarize, we have now established that an economy in competitive general equilibrium will, under certain conditions, be simultaneously efficient (Pareto optimal) in consumption, in production, and in the choice of product mix. As we have already seen, a society with a Pareto-optimal allocation of resources is not necessarily a good society. The final equilibrium in the marketplace depends very strongly on the distribution of initial endowments, and if this distribution isn't fair, we have no reason to expect the competitive equilibrium to be fair. Even so, it is truly remarkable to be able to claim, as Adam Smith did, that each person, merely by pursuing his own interests, is "led by an invisible hand to promote an end which was no part of his intention"—namely, the exploitation of all gains from exchange possible under given initial endowments.

GAINS FROM INTERNATIONAL TRADE

In our simple model of exchange and production, we saw why efficiency requires that every consumer's MRS be equal to the economy's MRT. This same requirement must be satisfied even for an economy that is free to engage in foreign trade. To illustrate, consider an economy just like the one we discussed, and suppose that its competitive general equilibrium in the absence of international trade occurs at point V in Figure 17.14. Now suppose that country opens its borders to international trade. If the country is small relative to the rest of the world, output prices will no longer be determined in its own internal markets, but in the much larger international markets. Suppose, in particular, that world prices for food and clothing are P_F^w and P_C^w, respectively. The best option available to this economy will no longer be to produce and consume at V. On the contrary, it should now produce at Z, the point on its production possibilities frontier at which the MRT is exactly equal to the international price ratio, P_C^w/P_F^w. Z is the point that maximizes the value of its output in world markets. Having produced at

FIGURE 17.14

Gains from International Trade

Without international trade, the economy's competitive equilibrium was at V. With the possibility of buying or selling in world markets, the economy maximizes the total value of its output by producing at Z, where its MRT is equal to the international price ratio, P_C^w/P_F^w. Along BB', the international budget constraint, it then chooses the consumption allocation for which every consumer's MRS is equal to P_C^w/P_F^w. If this occurs at T, the country will export $C^* - C^{**}$ units of clothing and import $F^{**} - F^*$ units of food.

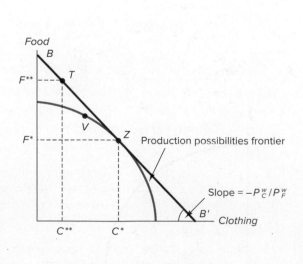

Z, the country is then free to choose any point along its "international budget constraint," BB'. Since the original competitive equilibrium point, V, lies within BB', we know that it is now possible for every person in the economy to have more of each good than before.

Which of the infinitely many bundles along BB' should be chosen? The best outcome is the one for which P_C^w/P_F^w is equal to every consumer's MRS. We know that without international trade the common value of MRS was equal to the MRT at V, which is smaller than the MRT at Z. Since there is more clothing and less food at Z than at V, it follows that the MRS at Z will be smaller than the MRT at V. This means that people will be better off moving to the northwest from Z. Suppose T is the combination of food and clothing that equates everyone's MRS to P_C^w/P_F^w. This economy will then do best by exporting $C^* - C^{**}$ units of clothing and using the proceeds to import $F^{**} - F^*$ units of food.

As noted, the fact that the international budget constraint contains the original competitive equilibrium point means that it is possible to make everyone better off than before. But the impersonal workings of international trading markets provide no guarantee that every single person will in fact be made better off by trade. In the illustration given, international trading possibilities led the economy to produce more clothing and less food than it used to. The effect will be to increase the demand for factors of production used in clothing production and to reduce the demand for those used in food production. If food production is relatively intensive in the use of labor and clothing production is relatively intensive in the use of capital, the shift in product mix would drive up the price of capital and drive down the price of labor. In this case, the primary beneficiaries from trade would be the owners of capital. People whose incomes come exclusively from the sale of their own labor would actually do worse than before, even though the value of total output is higher. What our general equilibrium analysis shows is that trade makes it *possible* to give everyone more of everything. It does not prove that everyone necessarily *will* get more.

EXAMPLE 17.1 The Trade Decision

You are the president of a small island nation that has never engaged in trade with any other nation. You are considering the possibility of opening the economy to international trade. The chief economist of the island's only labor union, to which every worker belongs, tells you that free trade will reduce the real purchasing power of labor, and you have no reason to doubt him. You are determined to remain in office and need the union's support in order to do so. The union will never support a candidate whose policies adversely affect the welfare of its members. Does this mean you should keep the island closed to trade?

The answer is yes only if there is no way to redistribute the gains that trade will produce. Our general equilibrium analysis establishes that trade will increase the total value of output, which makes it possible for everyone to do better. If the alternative is for the island to remain closed, the owners of capital should readily agree to transfer some of their gains to labor. The only president who would fail to open the island's economy is one who is too lazy or unimaginative to negotiate an agreement under which every party ends up with more of everything than before.

Much has been written about the agonizing trade-off between equity and efficiency, the notion that greater distributional fairness requires some sacrifice in efficiency. The lesson in Example 17.1 is that when people are able to negotiate costlessly with one another, there is in fact no conflict between equity and efficiency. When the total size of the economic pie grows larger, it is always possible for everyone to have a larger slice than before. Efficiency is achieved when we have made the economic pie as large as possible. Having done that, we are then free to discuss what constitutes a fair division of the pie.

TAXES IN GENERAL EQUILIBRIUM

Suppose we are back in our simple production economy without the added complication of international trading opportunities. The economy is in competitive general equilibrium at point V in Figure 17.15, where the marginal rate of transformation is equal to the competitive equilibrium product price ratio, P_C^*/P_F^*. Now suppose the government decides to raise revenue by taxing food at the rate of t/dollar. Every time a producer sells a unit of food for P_F^*, she gets to keep only $(1 - t)P_F^*$. How will such a tax affect resource allocation?

The immediate effect of the tax is to raise the relative price ratio, as seen by producers, from P_C^*/P_F^* to $P_C^*/(1 - t)P_F^*$. Producers who were once content to produce at V on the production possibilities frontier will now find that they can increase their profits (or reduce their losses) by producing more clothing and less food than before. Suppose that, in the end, the effect is to cause producers to relocate at point Z along the production possibilities frontier. Recall that the MRT at V was equal to the common value of MRS at V. Since Z has more clothing and less food than V, the MRS at Z will be smaller than at V. It follows that the MRT will be higher than the MRS at Z, which means that the economy will no longer have an efficient product mix. The original allocation at V was Pareto optimal. The new allocation has too much clothing, too little food.

Note that a tax on food does not alter the fact that consumers will all have a common value of MRS in equilibrium. Nor does it alter the fact that producers will all have a common value of MRTS. Even with such a tax, the economy remains efficient in consumption and production. The real problem created by the tax is that it causes producers to see a different price ratio from the one seen by consumers. Consumption decisions are based on *gross prices*—that is, on prices inclusive of taxes. Production decisions, by contrast, are guided by *net prices*—the amount producers get to keep after the tax has been paid. When producers confront a different price ratio from the one that guides consumers, the MRS can never be equal to the MRT in equilibrium. By driving a wedge between the price ratios seen by producers and consumers, the tax leads to an inefficient product mix.

Subsidies, like taxes, upset the conditions required for efficiency. The problem with a taxed product is that it appears too cheap to its producer. By contrast, the problem with a subsidized product is that it appears too expensive. In general equilibrium, we get too much of the subsidized product and too little of the unsubsidized one.

The distortionary effects of taxes and subsidies identified by our simple general equilibrium analysis form the cornerstone of the so-called supply-side school of economic

FIGURE 17.15

Taxes Affect Product Mix

A tax on food causes a shift away from food toward clothing consumption. If the original allocation was Pareto optimal, the new one will not be. The marginal rate of transformation will exceed the marginal rate of substitution. There will be too much clothing and too little food.

policy. As supply-siders are ever ready to testify, taxes almost always lead to some sort of inefficiency in the allocation of resources.

Does it then follow that the world would be better off if we simply *abolished* all taxes? Hardly, for in such a world there could be no goods or services provided by government, and as we will presently see, there are many valuable goods and services that are unlikely to be provided in any other way. The practical message of general equilibrium analysis is that care should be taken to design taxes that keep distortions to a minimum. Note that in our simple model, the problem would have been eliminated had we taxed not just food but also clothing at the same rate *t*. Relative prices would then have stayed the same, and producers and consumers would again be motivated by a consistent set of price signals.

In more realistic general equilibrium models, however, even a general commodity tax would have distortionary effects. A tax on all commodities is essentially the same as a tax on income, including the income earned from the sale of one's own labor. In our simple model, the supply of labor was assumed to be fixed, but in practice it may be sensitive to the real, after-tax wage rate. In a fuller model that included this relationship, a general commodity tax might thus lead to a distortion in decisions about the allocation of time between labor and leisure—for example, people might work too little and consume too much leisure.

From the standpoint of efficiency, a better tax would be a *head tax* (also called a *lump-sum tax*), one that is levied on each person irrespective of his or her labor supply decisions. The problem with this kind of tax is that many object to it on equity grounds. If we levied the same tax on every person, the burden of taxation would fall much more heavily on the poor than it does under our current system, which collects taxes roughly in proportion to individual income. On efficiency grounds, the very best tax of all is one levied on activities of which there would otherwise be too much. And as we will see below, there are many such activities—more than enough, perhaps, to raise all the tax revenue we need.

OTHER SOURCES OF INEFFICIENCY

Monopoly

Taxes are but one of many factors that stand in the way of achieving Pareto optimality in the allocation of resources. One other source of inefficiency is monopoly. The general equilibrium effects of monopoly are closely analogous to those of a commodity tax. Consider again our simple production economy with two goods, and suppose that food is produced by a monopolist, clothing by a price taker. The competitive producer selects an output level for which marginal cost is equal to the price of clothing; the monopolist, as we saw in Chapter 11, selects one for which marginal cost is equal to marginal revenue. Because price always exceeds marginal revenue along a downward-sloping demand curve, this means that price will exceed marginal cost for the monopolist.

From the standpoint of efficiency, this wedge between price and marginal cost functions exactly like a tax on the monopolist's product. The marginal rate of transformation, which is the ratio of the marginal cost of clothing to the marginal cost of food, will no longer be equal to the ratio of product prices. Producers will be responding to one set of incentives, consumers to another. The result is that too few of the economy's resources will be devoted to the production of food (the monopolized product) and too many to the production of clothing (the competitive product).

The general equilibrium analysis of the effect of monopoly adds an important dimension to our partial equilibrium analysis from Chapter 11. The partial analysis called our attention to the fact that there would be too little output produced by the monopolist. The general equilibrium analysis forcefully reminds us that there is another side of this coin, which is that the resources not used by the monopolist will be employed by the competitive sector of the economy. Thus, if monopoly output is too small, competitive output is too big. The additional competitive output does not undo the damage caused by monopoly, but it partially compensates for it. Viewed within the framework of general equilibrium analysis, the welfare costs of monopoly are thus smaller than they appeared from our partial equilibrium analysis.

Externalities

Another source of inefficiency occurs when production or consumption activities involve benefits or costs that fall on people not directly involved in the activities. As discussed in Chapter 16, such benefits and costs are usually referred to as externalities. A standard example of a *negative externality* is the case of pollution, in which a production activity results in emissions that adversely affect people other than those who consume the product. The planting of additional apple trees, whose blossoms augment the output of honey in nearby beehives, is an example of a *positive externality*. And so is the case of the beekeeper who adds bees to his hive, unmindful of the higher pollination rates they will produce in nearby apple orchards.

Externalities are both widespread and important. The problem they create for efficiency stems from the fact that, like taxes, they cause producers and consumers to respond to different sets of relative prices. When the orchard owner decides how many trees to plant, he looks only at the price of apples, not at the price of honey. By the same token, when the consumer decides how much honey to buy, he ignores the effects of his purchases on the quantity and price of apples.

In the case of negative externalities in production, the effect on efficiency is much the same as that of a subsidy. In deciding what quantity of the product to produce, the producer equates price and his own private marginal cost. The problem is that the negative externalities impose additional costs on others, and these are ignored by the producer. As with the subsidized product, we end up with too much of the product with negative externalities and too little of all other products. With positive externalities, the reverse occurs. We end up with too little of such products and too much of others.

Taxes as a Solution to Externalities and Monopoly

As noted earlier, the best tax from an efficiency standpoint is one levied on an activity there would otherwise be too much of. This suggests that the welfare losses from monopoly can be mitigated by placing an excise tax on the good produced in the competitive sector. Properly chosen, such a tax could exactly offset the wedge that is created by the disparity between the monopolist's price and marginal cost.

In the case of negative externalities, the difficulty is that individuals regard the product as being cheaper than it really is from the standpoint of society as a whole. By taxing the product with negative externalities at a suitable rate, the efficiency loss can be undone. For products accompanied by positive externalities, the corresponding solution is a subsidy.

Public Goods

One additional factor that stands in the way of achieving efficient allocations through private markets is the existence of *public goods*. As we will discuss in Chapter 18, a pure public good is one with two specific properties: (1) *nondiminishability,* which means that one person's use of the good does not diminish the amount of it available for others, and (2) *nonexcludability,* which means that it is either impossible or prohibitively costly to exclude people who do not pay from using the good. In the days before the invention of channel scramblers, broadcast television signals were an example of a pure public good. My tuning in to a movie on channel 11, for example, does not make that movie less available to anyone else. And before the advent of scramblers and cable TV, there was no practical way to exclude anyone from making use of a television signal once it was broadcast. National defense is another example of a pure public good. The fact that Smith enjoys the benefits of national defense does not make those benefits any less available to Jones. And it is exceedingly difficult for the government to protect some of its citizens from foreign attack while denying the same protection to others.

There is no reason to presume that private markets will supply optimal quantities of pure public goods. Indeed, if it is impossible to exclude people from using the good, it might seem impossible for a profit-seeking firm to supply any quantity of it at all. But profit-seeking firms often show great ingenuity in devising schemes for providing pure public goods. Commercial broadcast television, for example, covers its costs by charging advertisers for access to the audience it attracts with its programming. But even in these cases, there is no reason to suppose that the amount and kind of television programming we get under this arrangement is economically efficient.

The problem is less acute in the case of goods that have the nondiminishability but not the nonexcludability property. Once every household is wired for cable TV, for example, it will be possible to prevent people from watching any given program if they do not pay for it. But even here, there are likely to be inefficiencies. Once a TV program has been produced, it costs society nothing to let an extra person see it. If there is a positive price for watching the program, however, all those who value seeing it at less than that price will not tune in. It is inefficient to exclude these viewers, since their viewing the program would not diminish its usefulness for anyone else.

SUMMARY

- One of the simplest possible general equilibrium models is a pure exchange economy with only two consumers and two goods. For any given initial allocation of the two goods between the two consumers in this model, a competitive exchange process will always exhaust all possible mutually beneficial gains from trade. This result is known as the invisible hand theorem and is also called the first theorem of welfare economics. *(LO1)*

- If consumers have convex indifference curves, any efficient allocation can be sustained as a competitive equilibrium. This result is known as the second theorem of welfare economics. Its significance is that it demonstrates that the issues of efficiency and distributional equity are logically distinct. Society can redistribute initial endowments according to accepted norms of distributive justice, and then rely on markets to assure that endowments are used efficiently. *(LO1, LO3)*

- An economy is efficient in production if the marginal rate of technical substitution is the same for all producers. In the

input market, too, competitive trading exploits all mutually beneficial gains from exchange. *(LO4)*

- Even though international trade leaves domestic production possibilities unchanged, its immediate effect is to increase the value of goods available for domestic consumption. With a suitable redistribution of initial endowments, a free-trade economy will always be Pareto superior to a non-free-trade economy. *(LO1, LO6)*

- Taxes often interfere with efficient resource allocation, usually because they cause consumers and producers to respond to different price ratios. The practical significance of this result is to guide us in the search for taxes that minimize distortions. The best tax, from an efficiency standpoint, is one levied on an activity that would otherwise be pursued too intensively. *(LO7)*

- Monopoly, externalities, and public goods are three other factors that interfere with the efficient allocation of resources. *(LO7)*

KEY TERMS

contract curve
Edgeworth exchange box
general equilibrium analysis

marginal rate of transformation
   (MRT)
Pareto optimal allocation

Pareto superior allocation
production possibilities frontier

REVIEW QUESTIONS

1. Why does efficiency in consumption require the MRS of all consumers to be the same? *(LO1)*

2. Distinguish among the terms "Pareto superior," "Pareto preferred," and "Pareto optimal." *(LO7)*

3. Why might voters in a country choose a non-Pareto-optimal allocation over another that is Pareto optimal? *(LO2)*

4. How do the initial endowments constrain where we end up on the contract curve? *(LO1)*

5. In general equilibrium, can there be excess demand for every good? *(LO1)*

6. How might a social critic respond to the claim that governmental involvement in the economy is unjustified because of the invisible hand theorem? *(LO2, LO7)*

7. Why is the slope of the production possibilities frontier equal to the ratio of marginal production costs? *(LO4)*

8. How might a critic respond to the claim that taxes always make the allocation of resources less efficient? *(LO7)*

PROBLEMS

Mc Graw Hill connect

1. Bert has an initial endowment consisting of 10 units of food and 10 units of clothing. Ernie's initial endowment consists of 10 units of food and 20 units of clothing. Represent these initial endowments in an Edgeworth exchange box. *(LO1)*

2. Bert regards food and clothing as perfect 1-for-1 substitutes. Ernie regards them as perfect complements, always wanting to consume 3 units of clothing for every 2 units of food. *(LO1)*
   a. Describe the set of allocations that are Pareto preferred to the one given in Problem 1.
   b. Describe the contract curve for that allocation.
   c. What price ratio will be required to sustain an allocation on the contract curve?

3. How will your answers to Problem 2 differ if 5 units of Ernie's clothing endowment are given to Bert? *(LO1)*

4. Consider a simple economy with two goods, food and clothing, and two consumers, A and B. For a given initial endowment, when the ratio of food to clothing prices in an economy is 3/1, A wants to buy 6 units of clothing while B wants to sell 2 units of food. Is $P_F/P_C = 3$ an equilibrium price ratio? If so, explain why. If not, state in which direction it will tend to change. *(LO1)*

5. How will your answer to Problem 4 change if A wants to sell 3 units of clothing and B wants to sell 2 units of food? *(LO1)*

6. Suppose Sarah has an endowment of 2 units of X and 4 units of Y and has indifference curves that satisfy our four basic assumptions (see Chapter 3). Suppose Brian has an endowment of 4 units of X and 2 units of Y, and has preferences given by the utility function $U(X, Y) = \min \{X, Y\}$, where

$$\min(X, Y) = \begin{cases} X \text{ if } X \leq Y \\ Y \text{ if } Y \leq X \end{cases}.$$

On an Edgeworth box diagram, indicate the set of Pareto-superior bundles. *(LO1, LO2)*

7. A simple economy produces two goods, food and clothing, with two inputs, capital and labor. Given the current allocation of capital and labor between the two industries, the marginal rate of technical substitution between capital and labor in food production is 4, while the corresponding MRTS in clothing production is 2. Is this economy efficient in production? If so, explain why. If not, describe a reallocation that will lead to a Pareto improvement. *(LO4)*

8. Given the current allocation of productive inputs, the marginal rate of transformation of food for clothing in a simple two-good economy is equal to 2. At the current allocation of consumption goods, each consumer's marginal rate of substitution between food and clothing is 1.5. Is this economy efficient in terms of its product mix? If so, explain why. If not, describe a reallocation that will lead to a Pareto improvement. *(LO5)*

9. Chun can make 5 units of food per day if he devotes all his time to food production. He can make 10 units of clothing if he spends the whole day at clothing production. If he divides his time between the two activities, his output of each good will be proportional to the time spent on each. The corresponding figures for Friday are 10 units of food and 15 units of clothing. Describe the production possibilities frontier for their economy. *(LO5)*

10. If Chun and Friday regard food and clothing as perfect 1-for-1 substitutes, what should each produce? *(LO5)*

11. Now suppose a trading ship visits the island each day and offers to buy or sell food and clothing at the prices $P_F = 4$, $P_C = 1$. How, if at all, will the presence of this ship alter the production and consumption decisions of Chun and Friday? *(LO6)*

12. How will your answers to Problems 9, 10, and 11 differ if Friday's maximum production figures change to 20 units of food and 50 units of clothing? *(LO5, LO6)*

13. There are two industries in a simple economy, each of which faces the same marginal cost of production. One of the industries is perfectly competitive, the other a pure monopoly. Describe a reallocation of resources that will lead to a Pareto improvement for this economy. *(LO7)*

14. Suppose capital and labor are perfect substitutes in production for clothing: 2 units of capital *or* 2 units of labor produce 1 unit of clothing. Suppose capital and labor are perfect complements in production for food: 1 unit

of capital *and* 1 unit of labor produce 1 unit of food. Suppose the economy has an endowment of 100 units of capital and 200 units of labor. Describe the set of efficient allocations of the factors to the two sectors (determine the contract curve in an Edgeworth production box). *(LO4)*

15. Construct the production possibilities frontier for the economy described in Problem 14. What is the opportunity cost of food in terms of clothing? *(LO5)*

16. Construct the production possibilities frontier for an economy just like the one described in Problem 14, except that its endowment of capital is 200 units. *(LO5)*

ANSWERS TO SELF-TESTS

17.1 Bahjat's endowment of food = 100 − Aaliyah's endowment = 75. Bahjat's endowment of clothing = 200 − Aaliyah's endowment = 175. *(LO1)*

17.2 Let M denote the initial allocation. Aaliyah's indifference curve through M is a straight line with slope = −1. Bahjat's indifference curve through M is right-angled, as shown in the following diagram. The set of Pareto-superior allocations is indicated by the shaded triangle. *(LO1, LO2)*

17.3 Here, $P_L/P_K = 1$, which is half as big as $\text{MPL}_C/\text{MPK}_C$:

$$\frac{P_L}{P_K} = \frac{1}{2}\frac{\text{MPL}_C}{\text{MPK}_C},$$

from which it follows that

$$\frac{\text{MPK}_C}{P_K} = \frac{1}{2}\frac{\text{MPL}_C}{P_L}.$$

In words, this says that the last dollar spent on capital in clothing production produces only half as much extra output as does the last dollar spent on labor in clothing production. It follows that clothing producers can get more output for the same cost by hiring less capital and more labor. Parallel reasoning tells us that food producers can increase food production at no extra cost by hiring less labor and more capital. Only when these producers have reached a cost-minimizing input mix characteristic of a competitive equilibrium will efficiency in production be achieved. *(LO4)*

17.4 On the new production possibilities frontier, the maximum quantity of food that can be produced is unchanged. At every level of food production, the corresponding amount of clothing that can be produced is exactly double the original amount. *(LO5)*

Government

Local telephone companies—however little we think about them today—are nonetheless regulated monopolies, so governmental regulators must rule on all their charges to the public. Historically, regulatory agencies prevented charges for directory assistance calls in the belief that such charges would "diminish the value of a vital public communications network." This conclusion, needless to say, seemed hopelessly vague to most economists. Directory assistance calls cost the phone company (and hence society) a lot of money to provide, and the economist's immediate fear is that people will be uneconomical in their use of this or any other resource for which they do not have to pay.

Some years ago, the New York State Public Service Commission (which regulates New York telephone companies) proposed that the companies begin charging 10 cents for every call made to directory assistance. This sensible proposal to give people an incentive to look numbers up for themselves in the phone book earned cheers from economists, but drew a much different response from consumer advocates. These groups hired sociologists and other expert witnesses, who testified that the social fabric would deteriorate sharply if people were penalized for attempting to get in touch with one another. Other witnesses complained that the charges would impose an unacceptable burden on the poor.

The proposal seemed doomed, when the commission proposed a brilliant amendment, one that would preserve its efficiency gains while at the same time eliminating any adverse effects on the poor. The amendment was that every telephone subscriber would be given a 30-cent credit on his or her monthly telephone bill in reflection of the costs saved on directory assistance calls. For example, someone who made one directory assistance call per month would be charged 10 cents, which, when combined with the credit, would make his monthly bill 20 cents less than before. Someone who made three directory assistance calls per month would break even, someone with four would pay 10 cents more than before, and so on. On the plausible assumption that a charge of 10 cents per call would be more likely to induce a low-income person than a high-income person to cut down on directory assistance calls, the net effect of the amended proposal was actually to increase the real purchasing power of the poor.

CHAPTER PREVIEW

The directory assistance episode illustrates two critically important points about government economic policy: (1) that distributional concerns permeate discussion of even the most seemingly trivial policies and (2) that the most efficient solution to a public policy problem is one that enables both rich and poor alike to do better than before. The sense in which "efficient" both does and doesn't mean "best"—an issue that confronted us in Chapter 16—will now get our complete attention.

In this chapter we explore two important functions of government: the provision of public goods and the direct redistribution of income. Concerns about both fairness and efficiency, we'll see, are inextricably linked in both areas.

It's not a necessary attribute of a public good that it be provided by government. We'll examine a variety of ingenious schemes, ranging from free commercial television—a media delivery system that transformed the United States in the years following World War II—to highly structured collective legal contracts, whereby public goods are provided with virtually no direct government involvement.

Next we'll take up the question of how societies make choices between competing public projects, with particular focus on cost-benefit analysis as an alternative to majority voting schemes.

We'll address a problem that plagues all mechanisms of public decision making—namely, that self-interested parties have an incentive to influence outcomes in their own favor. This problem goes by the name of rent-seeking, and it is often a serious threat to our social welfare.

From the problems of public choice, which themselves have important distributional implications, we'll turn to the topic of direct income transfer programs. Here our focus will be on how such transfers might be accomplished without undermining incentives to work and take risks. While this text has been concerned with these questions since its early editions in the 1990s, intense contemporary concerns with increasing inequality in the United States and other societies make questions around effective policy responses more relevant than ever. We will look at direct redistribution proposals and jobs guarantee proposals, and compare these proposals in terms of effectiveness in reducing inequality.

PUBLIC GOODS

Public goods are those goods or services that possess, in varying degrees, the properties of *nondiminishability* and *nonexcludability*. The nondiminishability property says that any one person's consumption of a public good has no effect on the amount of it available for others. Nonexcludability means that it is either impossible or prohibitively costly to exclude nonpayers from consuming the good.

pure public good a good that has a high degree of nondiminishability and nonexcludability.

collective good a good that is excludable and has a high degree only of nondiminishability.

Goods that have high degrees of both of these properties are often called **pure public goods,** the classic example of which is national defense. Goods that have only the nondiminishability property are sometimes referred to as collective goods. **Collective goods** are sometimes provided by government, sometimes by private companies. Most pure public goods are provided by government, but even here there are exceptional cases in which profit-seeking companies have devised schemes for providing them.

Let's begin our analysis with the case of an entity trying to decide what quantity to provide of some pure public good—an often-used example is that of security guards at a shopping mall. For simplicity, imagine that the mall has only two stores, A and B. Since A sells fancy electronic equipment and B sells frozen yogurt, A assigns a higher value to any given quantity of guards that the mall might hire. In Figure 18.1, the horizontal axis measures the number of security-guard-hours per week. The curve labeled AA' represents the amount A would be willing to pay for an additional guard-hour, and BB' represents the corresponding curve for B. Thus, at a level of 40 hours (one guard), A would be willing to pay $30/hr for an additional guard, while B would be willing to pay only $25/hr. The fact that the two willingness-to-pay curves are downward-sloping

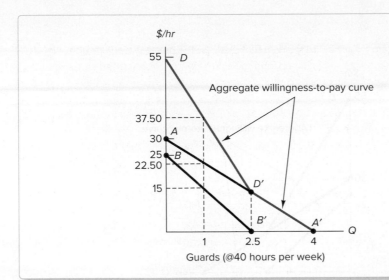

FIGURE 18.1

The Aggregate Willingness-to-Pay Curve for a Public Good

AA' and *BB'* represent the respective amounts that *A* and *B* are willing to pay for an additional unit of the public good. The aggregate willingness-to-pay curve is the vertical summation of the individual willingness-to-pay curves, the curve labeled *DD'A'*.

reflects the fact that the more hours guards are putting in, the less valuable an additional hour would be.

The central fact about providing any pure public good is that each stakeholder gets the same amount of it. If the mall hires one guard, each store gets the services of that one guard. In markets for private goods, by contrast, each stakeholder can consume whatever amount she or he chooses at the prevailing price. To obtain the market demand curve for a private good, we simply added the individual demand curves horizontally. In the case of public goods, the analog to the market demand curve is the aggregate willingness-to-pay curve. It is obtained by adding the individual willingness-to-pay curves not horizontally but vertically. At $Q = 1$ guard in Figure 18.1, for example, A and B together are willing to pay a total of $15 + 22.50 = \$37.50$/hr for an additional hour of guard service. The curve labeled *DD'A'* represents the vertical summation of the two individual's willingness-to-pay curves.

SELF-TEST 18.1

Ten homogeneous consumers all have individual willingness-to-pay curves $P = 12 - \frac{1}{5}Q$ for a public good—say, a concert in an open park (where P is measured in dollars and Q is measured in minutes). Construct and graph the aggregate willingness-to-pay curve. For a 30-minute concert, what is the maximum each individual would be willing to pay?

Optimal Quantity of Public Good

Given the aggregate willingness-to-pay curve we saw in Figure 18.1, what is the optimal number of guards? The answer depends, in this case, on the hourly cost for guards. In this simple example, there are no fixed costs, and the marginal cost is a constant hourly rate. In Figure 18.2, the curve labeled *DD'A'* again represents the aggregate willingness-to-pay curve for security guards. The curve labeled MC represents the constant marginal cost equivalent to the guards' hourly wage, here fixed at \$20/hr. The intersection of these two curves establishes $Q^* = 2$, the optimal number of guards. At $Q^* = 2$, the amounts that A and B would be willing to pay for another hour of guard service add to exactly the cost (\$20/hr) of producing another unit. If this equality did not hold, we could easily show that stores would be better off by either expanding or contracting the of hours.

FIGURE 18.2

The Aggregate Willingness-to-Pay Curve for Public Good without Fixed Costs

The aggregate willingness-to-pay curve is the vertical summation of the individual willingness-to-pay curves, the curve labeled *DD'A'*. The curve labeled MC represents the constant) marginal cost equivalent to the guards' hourly wage, here fixed at $20/hr. The intersection of these two curves establishes $Q^* = 2$, the optimal number of guards. At $Q^* = 2$, the amounts that A and B would be willing to pay for another hour of guard service add to exactly the cost ($20/hr) of producing another unit.

$/hr

Aggregate willingness-to-pay curve

Guards (@40 hours)

SELF-TEST 18.2

Consider the scenario described in Self-Test 18.1, and suppose that the marginal cost of providing the concert is MC = 2Q. Determine the optimal length of the concert.

Paying for Q*

Let's keep Figure 18.2 in mind, but instead of security guards, let's consider the case of police officers, who are provided by government and paid for by taxes. If the government is to produce Q^* numbers of police, it must somehow raise sufficient tax revenue to cover the total production costs of that amount.

Suppose, for the sake of discussion, that the government funds each of its programs with a separate tax and the government's tax structure requires the collection of equal tax payments from all citizens. In the example in Figure 18.2, *B*'s willingness to pay for the public good is smaller than *A*'s. It follows that *B* will vote for the provision of Q^* only if the total cost of Q^* is less than twice the area under *BB'* up to Q^*. For example, if the total cost of the good is 100, and each party must be taxed equally, *B* will vote for it only if his total willingness to pay exceeds 50. If the amount *B* is willing to pay for the public good is only, say, 40, this condition will not be satisfied, and so the project will not win approval. The same risk clearly applies to the situation in Figure 18.2.

And yet we know that this public good is one whose benefits to all citizens add up to more than its costs. Compared with the alternative in which the public good is not provided, both *A* and *B* can be made better off by providing Q^* of it and then taxing *A* more heavily than *B* in order to pay for it. It follows that a tax structure that levies the same tax on all citizens cannot in general be Pareto efficient.

The situation here is analogous to the case in which the incomes of two spouses differ substantially. Suppose Julie earns $200,000/yr while her husband, Bruce, earns only $30,000. Given her income, Julie as an individual would want to spend much more than Bruce would on housing, travel, entertainment, and the many other items they consume in common. But suppose the couple adopted a rule that each had to contribute an equal share toward the purchase of such items. The result would be to constrain the couple to live in a small house, to take only inexpensive vacations, to skimp on entertainment and dining out, and so on. And so, it is easy to imagine that Julie would find it attractive to pay considerably more than 50 percent for jointly consumed goods, thereby enabling both of them to consume in the manner their combined income affords.

As in the case of private goods, the willingness to pay for public goods is generally an increasing function of income. The rich, on the average, assign greater value to public goods than the poor do, not because they have different tastes but because they have more money. A tax system that taxed the poor just as heavily as the rich would result in the rich getting smaller amounts of public goods than they want. Rather than see that happen, the rich would gladly agree to a tax system that assigns them a larger share of the tax burden. It would be missing the point to criticize such a system by saying that the system is unfair because it enables the poor to enjoy the services of public goods for a smaller price. It does have this property, to be sure; but from the viewpoint of the rich, its terms are still attractive because the tax payments of the poor, though small, mean the rich end up paying less than if they had to finance public goods all by themselves.

PRIVATE PROVISION OF PUBLIC GOODS

Governments are not the exclusive providers of public goods in any society. Substantial quantities of such goods are routinely provided through a variety of private channels. If it is impractical to exclude people from consuming a public good, the pressing question is, How can the good be paid for, if not by mandatory taxes?

Funding by Donation

One method for funding public goods is through voluntary donations. As we have already seen, people make contributions to viewer-supported TV stations. They donate great artwork to museums. They also make contributions to food banks, animal shelters, and medical research. Motives for such donations are as varied as the projects they support. Some see charitable giving as a means to achieve respect and admiration in the community. Others may give because they are inspired by the example of other visible givers.[1] Still others may feel pressure to give in order to avoid social ostracism. These motives are really two sides of the same coin—social reward in the first case and social penalty in the second. Where such social forces are effective, they are a practical way of excluding nonpayers from full enjoyment of the public good.

Alternatively, people may donate because the increment to the public good that their contribution will finance is simply worth that much money to them. This motive is most likely to be important in situations in which one person's action can significantly affect the scale of the public good. Someone who lives at the end of a short dirt road in a rural area, for example, may find it worthwhile to pave the entire road at his own expense. He would naturally be happier if everyone who lived on the road chipped in. But rather than do without the road altogether, it may be worthwhile for him to pave it himself. Similarly, a person who plants a flower garden in front of her house provides a public good for neighbors to enjoy. If her own personal enjoyment from the garden exceeds its cost, pure self-interest is a sufficient motive for her to plant it.

But self-interested motives do not seem sufficient to explain why people make anonymous donations that will have no appreciable effect on the benefits they themselves receive. In the case of listener-supported radio stations, no single person's contribution

[1]For this beneficial social contagion to occur, donations must become public knowledge. Most charitable organizations publicize their lists of donors.

will make a perceptible difference in the nature or quality of programming. The station will either continue to operate in its current form, or else improve, or else get worse—irrespective of what any one person does.

free riding choosing not to donate to a cause but still benefiting from the donations of others.

In such situations, the logic of pure self-interest seems to dictate **free riding**—abstaining in the hope that others will contribute. And yet millions of people contribute to such enterprises each year. For many of these people, the satisfaction of giving—of having contributed to the common good—is an end in itself. And as we saw in Chapter 7, there may well be important material advantages in being such a person.

The fact that public goods are often supported through voluntary contributions does not necessarily mean, however, that they are supported at socially optimal levels. Residents might be perfectly willing to pay sufficient taxes to build the socially optimal road. And yet, in the absence of taxes, the road that actually gets built is likely to be considerably smaller. Similarly, many people might strongly want society to invest more in public television programming. But these same people might be reluctant to give voluntarily as much as they would be willing to pay in taxes.

Sale of By-Products

Free-rider problems are sometimes solved by devising novel means to finance the public good. One such way is the sale of an important by-product of the public good. In the case of commercial television, for example, financing comes from sponsors, generally private corporations, who pay for the right to beam advertising messages to the audience attracted by the broadcast. The captive viewing audience is a by-product of the broadcast, and sponsors are willing to pay a lot for access to it. As the following example makes clear, however, this system does not always assure an optimal allocation of broadcast resources.

EXAMPLE 18.1   **Free-Rider Problem**

In a given time slot, a television network faces the alternative of broadcasting either *Real Housewives of New Jersey* or *Masterpiece Theater*. If it chooses *Real Housewives*, it will win 20 percent of the viewing audience, but only 18 percent if it chooses *Masterpiece Theater*. Suppose those who would choose *Real Housewives* would collectively be willing to pay $10 million for the right to see that program, while those who choose *Masterpiece Theater* would be willing to pay $30 million. And suppose, finally, that the time slot is to be financed by a detergent company. Which program will the network choose? Which program would be socially optimal?

The sponsor cares primarily about the number of people who will see its advertisements, and will thus choose the program that will attract the largest audience—here, *Real Housewives*. The fact that those who prefer *Masterpiece Theater* would be willing to pay a lot more to see it is of little concern to the sponsor. But this difference in willingness to pay is critical when it comes to determining the optimal result from society's point of view. Because the people who prefer *Masterpiece Theater* could more than compensate the *Real Housewives* viewers for relinquishing the time slot, *Masterpiece Theater* is a Pareto-superior outcome. But unless its supporters happen to buy more soap in total than the *Real Housewives* viewers, *Real Housewives* will prevail. The difficulty with reliance on advertising and other indirect mechanisms for financing public goods is that there is no assurance that they will reflect the relevant benefits to society.

Development of New Means to Exclude Nonpayers

Another way to finance public goods privately is to devise cheap new ways of excluding people who do not pay for the good. In broadcast television, it was once impossible to prevent any household from tuning in to a program once it was sent out over the airwaves. Since the advent of cable TV, however, households are now simple to exclude. With the ability to charge for specific programs, it is no longer necessary to make programming decisions on the basis of which program will garner the largest audience. In our *Real Housewives* versus *Masterpiece Theater* example, a broadcasting company that can exclude nonpayers would have every incentive to show *Masterpiece Theater,* because its proponents now have a practical means of translating their greater willingness to pay into profits for the producer.

But note that whereas the outcome of pay-per-view TV is more efficient in the sense of selecting the programs the public most values, it is less efficient in one other important respect. By charging each household a fee for viewing, it discourages some households from tuning in. And since the marginal social cost of an additional household watching a program is exactly zero, it is inefficient to limit the audience in this way. Which of the two inefficiencies is more important—free TV's inefficiency in choosing between programs or pay TV's inefficiency in excluding potential beneficiaries—is an empirical question.

Private Contracts

Legal contracts among private individuals offer yet another means for overcoming some of the difficulties associated with the free-rider problem. Consider, for example, the public good consisting of residential maintenance and beautification. As neighborhoods are customarily organized, it is impractical to exclude your neighbors from the benefits they will reap if you keep your house well painted and your yard neatly trimmed. Nor would it be efficient to exclude them, because their consumption of these benefits does not diminish their value to you and others in any way. In this respect, home maintenance and beautification satisfy the definition of a pure public good and, for this reason, will generally be undersupplied by private individuals.

We saw in Chapter 16 that if transactions were costless, your neighbors could subsidize your investments in home maintenance and beautification, and you could do likewise for them. Set at the proper levels, subsidies of this sort would result in the optimal levels of investment by every homeowner. But in general it is costly to negotiate such subsidies on a case-by-case basis, and so the level of investment in home maintenance often ends up being well below optimal.

The organizers of condominiums, cooperatives, and other forms of legal residential associations have come up with an effective solution to this problem. The condominium contract requires each owner to contribute a specified sum each month toward maintenance and beautification. This payment functions much like a tax in the sense that it is mandatory for all parties to the contract. The advantage is that it is less coercive than a tax in one important respect: People who wish to spend less on home maintenance are free to live elsewhere.

Similar selection may occur between neighborhoods in different school districts. One district may choose higher spending levels on schools (and higher taxes to fund them) than another district nearby. Households then self-select: Families with children choose to live in the high-tax area, and singles and retirees choose to live in the other district.[2]

The Economics of Clubs

A pure public good has the property that an additional person's consumption of the good does not limit the amount of it available to others. Stated another way, the marginal cost of additional consumption of the public good is exactly zero. Many privately produced

---

[2]See also the subsequent discussion of local public goods.

goods have the property that marginal cost, although not zero, declines sharply with the number of users accommodated. The swimming pool is a case in point. The number of swimmers it can accommodate rises in proportion to its surface area, but its cost rises much more slowly. The difference between such goods and goods that satisfy the nondiminishability criterion perfectly is thus one of degree rather than of kind.

When the marginal cost of expanding the capacity of a private good is low relative to its average cost, consumers face an economic incentive to share the purchase and use of the good. In the swimming pool example, the cost to each of 20 families of a pool large enough for all to share will be much smaller than the cost of a pool large enough to serve the needs of only a single family. Indeed, the same statement is true of virtually any good that is not kept in continuous use by a single user. For example, most homeowners use extension ladders only once or twice a year, making it possible for several families to cut costs by sharing a single ladder.

The disadvantage of sharing, besides the fact that it requires someone to take the initiative to organize the arrangement, is that it limits both privacy and flexibility of access to the good. Thus, a homeowner might want to use the ladder on a particular Saturday afternoon, only to find it already in use by one of its other co-owners. Sometimes such inconveniences are trivial in relation to the cost savings; other times they will not be.

Opportunities for shared ownership thus confront the consumer with a variant of the standard consumer choice problem. To illustrate, consider again the choice between a privately owned pool and a shared pool. If we measure privacy and flexibility in the use of a pool on a scale from 0 to 1.0, a private pool would take the value 1.0, representing maximal privacy and flexibility. The limiting case at the other extreme is a large pool shared by infinitely many other people; the flexibility index for such a pool takes the value 0, representing virtually no privacy or flexibility.

The vertical axis in Figure 18.3 measures the amount the consumer spends on all other goods besides pools. If she buys her own private pool, at a cost of $Y' - Y_0$, she will achieve a privacy and flexibility index of 1.0. The other extreme represents a completely crowded pool, at a cost of 0 and a flexibility index of 0. Pools of intermediate size and crowdedness are represented by intermediate points on the budget constraint BB' in Figure 18.3. The consumer's best option is (F^*, Y^*), the point for which this budget constraint is tangent to an indifference curve (IC^*).

On the plausible assumption that the demand for privacy increases with income, we would predict that high-income consumers would be more likely to purchase their own pools than low-income consumers. But even consumers with very high incomes will find

FIGURE 18.3

The Trade-Off between Privacy and Cost

When the marginal cost of accommodating an extra user of a consumption good is less than the average cost, consumers can save money by forming clubs that share ownership of such goods. The optimal club for members with the same tastes is one for which the marginal rate of substitution between all other goods and privacy is exactly equal to the cost of additional privacy.

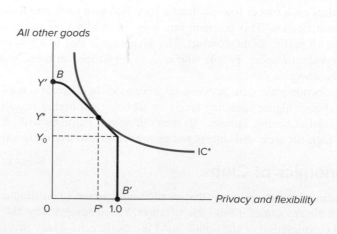

it attractive to participate in sharing arrangements for extremely costly consumption goods. Rather than maintain exclusive rights to operate an airplane that would sit idle on the tarmac most hours of the week, for example, even wealthy amateur pilots often choose to become members of flying clubs, the use of whose aircraft is shared with other members.

In the case of very inexpensive goods, by contrast, we would expect the demand for privacy to take precedence over the lure of cost savings even for consumers of relatively modest means. A privately owned toothbrush, like a privately owned airplane or swimming pool, is destined to remain idle for most hours of the day. Its cost per owner could be lowered substantially if it were shared by the members of a toothbrushing club. But the savings from such a transaction would be far too small to justify the sacrifice in privacy. Virtually everyone, even the poorest citizen, finds it worthwhile to maintain exclusive access to his personal toothbrush.

PUBLIC CHOICE

Whether public goods are provided by governments, charitable organizations, or private clubs, decisions must be made about the types and quantities to provide. The budget constraint confronting the group is often clear enough. The much more difficult aspect of the problem is to devise some means for translating the diverse preferences of the group's members into a single voice.

Majority Voting

One method of discerning group preferences is the majority vote.[3] By this standard, projects favored by a majority—in either a direct referendum or a vote taken by elected representatives—are adopted and all others abandoned. In recent years, much attention has been given to the fact that majority voting often leads to intransitivities in the ranking of alternatives. To illustrate, consider a legislative body with three members— Thune, Romney, and Murphy—each of whom has a well-ordered ranking of three alternative projects:

1. A new defensive system that will protect U.S. Navy ships from attack by ship-to-ship and shore-to-ship missiles. Navy ships on close-to-shore patrols are increasingly threatened by swarms of small fast motorboats that carry such missiles.

2. A large medical research project that shows promise in finding treatments to a wide range of serious auto-immune disorders, from diabetes to arthritis to multiple sclerosis.

3. An expansion of the Medicaid program that will substantially access to health care for low-income families.

Murphy likes the medical research project best, the Medicaid expansion next best, and the new missile system least. Thune likes the new missile best, the research program next best, and the Medicaid expansion least. Romney likes the Medicaid expansion best, the new missile program next best, and the research program last. These rankings are summarized in Table 18.1.

The budget has room for only one of these programs. This means that a decision among the projects can only be reached by successively voting on pairs of alternatives.

---

[3]We consider *majority* voting because our focus is on provision of public goods rather than election to office. The *plurality*—or first-past-the-post—voting system used for most state and federal election in the United States, UK, and Canada is often criticized for creating the intransitivities discussed below, especially in multi-candidate or multi-party elections. The *runoff* system used in some southern U.S. states as well as in French presidential elections achieves majorities and thereby reduces intransitivities but requires multiple elections. *Ranked-choice* voting, used (as of early 2020) in many U.S. communities but for state and federal races only in Maine, accomplishes the "runoff" in a single round of voting by allocating voter second and third choices if no candidate receives a first-choice majority. However, in the legislative example used in this section, ranked-choice voting would not produce a majority.

TABLE 18.1

Preferences That Produce Intransitive Rankings in Majority Voting

	Murphy	Thune	Romney
Best	Research program	New missile	Medicaid expansion
Second	Medicaid expansion	Research program	New missile
Third	New missile	Medicaid expansion	Research program

> In a majority vote, the missile defeats the research program, which in turn defeats the expansion of Medicaid. And yet the Medicaid expansion wins when paired against the missile. Majority voting schemes can lead to intransitivities even when individual preference orderings are transitive.

Why is this? It's clear that if we put all three programs "on the ballot" at the same time, none of them would pass, as each would get one vote. A ranked-choice vote that considered the senators' second and third choices would do no better. And if we gave each of the programs an up-or-down vote, none might pass—or all might pass, which would violate out budget constraint.[4]

So, pairwise voting it is. Given the rankings in Table 18.1, note what happens. In deciding which of any pair of alternatives to vote for, each voter—or, in this case, senator—will naturally choose the one he or she prefers to the other. Thus, in a vote between a new missile and medical research, the missile will get 2 votes (Thune and Romney); the research only 1 (Murphy). In a vote between research and Medicaid expansion, research gets 2 votes (Murphy and Thune); Medicaid only 1 (Romney). And finally, in a vote between Medicaid expansion and the missile, Medicaid gets 2 votes (Romney and Murphy); the missile only 1 (Thune). Thus, the missile defeats the research program and the research program defeats expanding Medicaid eligibility, and yet the Medicaid expansion defeats the missile program! Such intransitivities were assumed not to occur in individual preference orderings but can easily happen if social choice takes place by successive majority votes between pairs of alternatives.

Agenda Manipulation

No actual legislative process, obviously, is limited to sequential choice between pairs. And our three-programs/three-voters setup, just as obviously, was designed to emphasize what can go wrong. But the above illustration shows the importance of being able to set the rules and control the legislative agenda because the order in which alternatives are voted is critically important. Suppose, for example, that Romney is in charge. His first priority will be to avoid a direct confrontation between the missile, his most favored project, and the Medicaid expansion, which he knows will defeat the missile in a majority vote. He can ensure the missile's success by first conducting a vote between the Medicaid expansion and the research project, followed by a vote between the winner of that election and the missile. The research project will win the first vote and will then be defeated by the missile in the second. Given power to set the agenda, either Murphy or Thune could have taken similar steps to ensure victory for either the research project or expanded Medicaid. The takeaway is that the importance of controlling the rules and agenda is not limited to our example. Numerous important examples occur in practice in which majority voting leads to intransitive rankings, making the power to set the agenda tantamount to the power to choose the final outcome. Indeed, when a legislator is said to be "powerful," it is just this sort of beyond-his-or-her-own-vote control the term implies.

---

[4]Of course, if there is no budget constraint, then there is no problem with each program getting an up-or-down vote. There is also no need for a theory. Economic theory can illuminate choices only where those choices face some kind of constraint. The point of the somewhat artificial setup of our example is to put that constraint front and center.

Cost-Benefit Analysis

The difficulty of public choice by majority voting is not just that it sometimes leads to intransitivities. An even more serious problem is that it almost completely obscures important differences in the intensity with which different voters hold their preferences.

How is this a problem? Some people might hold that intensity of preferences should not matter. "This is a democracy," they might say. "Every person gets one vote." In practice, however, politicians have no choice but to be keenly aware of what issues are hot—and for whom. A system that did not give any recognition to voter intensity would become intensely frustrating to its most-motivated participants. But how can the system recognize intensity of preferences other than by reducing itself to a shouting match?

Cost-benefit analysis is an alternative to majority voting that attempts to take explicit account of how strongly people feel about each of the alternatives under consideration. Its method for measuring intensity of preference is to estimate how much people would be willing to pay in order to have the various alternatives. We encountered willingness-to-pay in the public TV example earlier in this chapter. In that example, community members' stated willingness to pay (or not) for a given level of public TV programming added up to a programming budget for the local public TV station and also provided an indication of the level of support the station would receive if it attempted to expand programming. With cost-benefit analysis, we go one step further; we calculate the "benefit" side of a proposed public good by netting out what a proposal's supporters would pay to have it go forward against what its opponents would pay to stop it.

To illustrate, let's consider how it would deal with the missile-research-health care decision we discussed earlier. Suppose Murphy, Thune, and Romney have to let program selection be determined by cost-benefit analysis. They have been in intense contact with the voters in their districts and have worked their staffs and with survey specialists to compile the valuations shown in Table 18.2. Positive entries in the table represent the amounts the legislator believes his or her district would pay for a desired program. Negative entries represent what the aggregated voters in the district would pay to prevent program from happening. The entries in the second column of the table, for instance, indicate that Thune's district would pay 100 to have the missile program go forward, 35 to have the medical research program, and 20 to avoid the expansion of Medicaid. Note that each district's ranking of the alternatives is the same in Table 18.2 as its legislator's was in Table 18.1. As before, we assume that because of budgetary shortages, only one of the three programs can be undertaken. To keep the discussion simple, we assume the cost of each program is 100 and also, crucially, that the amounts the voters in the three districts would pay for each program accurately capture all relevant benefits.

How will the decision be made? A glance at the Total Benefit column in Table 18.2 tells the story. Once the matter is referred to the "cost-benefit office," the recommendation

TABLE 18.2
Cost-Benefit Calculation, Based on Willingness to Pay, for Three Projects
(Each Project has Cost = 100)

	Murphy District	Thune District	Romney District	Total Benefit	Benefit over Cost
New missile	−25	100	45	120	20
Medical research	90	35	40	165	65
Medicaid expansion	60	−20	95	135	35

Cost-benefit analysis chooses the project with the largest surplus of benefits over costs. In this case, with benefit measured by willingness to pay, the medical research program wins.

will come back to the legislators to authorize the medical research program. Note that, unlike what we saw with the majority voting outcome, there is no intransitivity in preferences; the most-valued program gets the nod.

But what if, after all this commitment to the cost-benefit approach, Thune and Romney still hesitate? Might they not gang up and impose a different solution? It's possible, but the numbers make this unlikely. In fact, the Research program's large benefit over cost number makes it likely that if things have to be "worked out," they will get worked out in the Research program's favor. Since voters are willing to pay 65 units more than the research program will cost, this clearly creates the opportunity to fund 65 units of programs that will be more palatable to Thune's and Romney's constituencies. The very fact that the voters value the research program most is a powerful driver towards going forward with it; the most-valued program creates the most possibilities for everyone. This "room to cut a deal" is analogous to the Edgeworth box situation we saw in Chapter 17. Aaliyah and Bahjat, from their initial allocations between food and clothing, had the ability to trade less preferred items for more preferred (Figures 17.2 through 17.8); a similar opportunity for Pareto improvement exists here.

If cost-benefit analysis satisfies the Pareto criterion—that is, if it better reflects preferences—than majority voting, why do we so often use majority voting for making collective choices? One objection to cost-benefit analysis is that because it measures benefits by what people are willing to pay, it gives insufficient weight to the interests of people with little money. On this view, the poorer voters may feel very strongly about an issue, and yet their feelings will not count for much in cost-benefit analysis because they don't translate into large willingness-to-pay values. Even in cases with "room to cut a deal," like the research program above, there is no guarantee that compensation, if it were offered to low-income stakeholders, would be commensurate to the "true" intensity of their preferences.

But recall from Chapter 17 that the Pareto criteria *only* have force in relation to the initial allocation. If we look at Figure 18.4 (redrawn from Figure 17.4), we make no claim that that Aaliyah, starting with additional endowments *F*, is in a good position compared to Bahat, even if she can negotiate her way to point *V*. The only claim is that *V*, or any point between *U* and *V*, is better than *F*. The only way to make points between *W* and *Z* to available to Aaliyah is to change her initial endowments, and that change requires us to look at the redistributive potential of the tax system, employment laws, and other large-scale interventions. Pending these changes, it is counterproductive to interfere with Pareto-improving results that can reached through cost-benefit analysis and associated stakeholder negotiations. That such negotiations are needed for Aaliyah to "get to *V*" only underscores the micro-level importance of community organizers, stakeholder advocacy groups, and open and transparent processes.

FIGURE 18.4

Initial Endowments Constrain Final Outcomes (Revisited)

Starting from *F*, Aaliyah can do no better than negotiate her way to *V*. If she is to reach a point between *W* and *Z*, we must find a way to shift her initial endowment position to a point like *G*.

There is, however, a second objection to cost-benefit analysis, one that is sometimes raised in connection with the previous inequality objection and sometimes independently. Cass Sunstein has summarized the objection as the assertion that "people are citizens, not consumers."[5]

While the objection is phrased in positive terms, it is obviously normative. Its sense is that, in making decisions about public goods, we should have our citizen hat on, not our consumer hat, or at least not *only* our consumer hat. This is another way of saying that we should consider established legal and social norms in addition to transient measures like willingness to pay.

It is easy to come up with examples where the objection seems significant. Let's say initially that a wealthy group of people want to put up $1,000 each to put additional bathroom facilities in national parks. A poorer group, who would prefer that investments be made in their local communities, can only put up $100 each in response. If the added-up thousands outweigh the aggregated hundreds, cost-benefit analysis has no problem with telling the group on the short end to work out the best deal they can. For most questions, the Pareto improvements to be had from the process outweigh the likely benefits of political interference.

But now let's tweak the example. Suppose the proposed upgrade to national park facilities is not just to improve and increase the facilities, but create racially segregated bathrooms. What does economics say then? Should the most dollars win?

The example would seem to create difficulties for economists. To discount the objection would seem to admit society is just a market, that everything is always for sale, that there is no firewall anywhere between cheap and dear and right and wrong. One response of economists might be that, while there is no identity between economy and society, there is a strong analogy. Society, at least in one sense, *is* like a market, in that there is no assured steady state where previously established laws or previously won rights can simply be taken for granted or maintained without sacrifice. Proposals that violate basic norms *should* meet a groundswell of opposition—if they don't, what does that say?—and most economists would grant that when the goods at issue include basic rights, the concept of willingness to pay naturally extends to include nonfinancial participation in the debate. Cherished beliefs about freedom and justice have little meaning apart from the question of whether we will stand up for those beliefs—and how. At some point, willingness to pay must transform itself into personal involvement in the political process.

Rent Seeking

For cost-benefit outcomes to be trusted, the benefits of public choices must be broadly shared. And if cost-benefit analysis depends, at the limit, on broader citizen involvement, then questions of fair process become inescapable. As a practical matter, however, the gains from public choices or from changes in regulations are often large and concentrated in the hands of a few, whereas the costs, while also large, are spread among many. The upshot is that unlike those who stand to lose from a change, those who stand to benefit may find it practical to organize and lobby for it. The result of such "rent-seeking," all too frequently, is that projects are approved and rules are changed even when the benefits do not exceed the costs. While it is perhaps the "regulatory capture" side of the problem that receives the most current attention,[6] the impact of lobbying and political contributions on the awarding of government contracts is also legend.

A related difficulty arises in the case of similar projects whose benefits do exceed their costs. Because there are large gains to be had from the project, private parties are willing to spend large sums in order to enhance their odds of being chosen as its beneficiaries. One consequence of this form of rent-seeking is that the expected gains

[5]Sunstein, *The Cost-Benefit Revolution*, p. 57.
[6]Steven K. Vogel, "Rethinking Stigler's Theory of Regulation: Regulatory Capture or Deregulatory Capture?" Stigler Center, University of Chicago Booth School of Business, May 15, 2018, https://promarket.org/rethinking-stiglers-theory-regulation-regulatory-capture-deregulatory-capture/.

from government projects are often squandered by the competition among potential beneficiaries.

Consider, for example, a local government faced with the task of awarding the local cable TV franchise. Unless the government is prepared to engage in strict rate-of-return regulation, which most local governments are not, the franchisee can expect to earn substantial monopoly profits. The likelihood of any applicant being awarded the franchise is an increasing function of the amount of money it spends lobbying local legislators. The lure of the franchise's expected profits thus causes applicants to engage in a lobbying war to win the franchise. Such lobbying wars can dissipate much or all of the expected profits. If cable TV service is provided, unprofitably, by an exhausted vendor, the public ends up the just as much the loser had the service gone to vendor with a sweetheart contract.

INCOME DISTRIBUTION

In market economies, the main means of earning income is by selling factors of production. Some people, by far the minority, earn a significant portion of their income from their direct ownership of companies or by owning stocks, bonds, and other financial instruments. Most people depend primarily on the proceeds from the sale of their own labor. The great growth economists of the 1950s (Robert Solow, Nicholas Kaldor, and others) characterized these two income streams as the *capital share* and the *labor share*—and noted that in industrialized economies, the two shares' ratio seemed roughly constant, with the capital share averaging about 35 percent of the whole.

As a theory of income distribution, the growth models of the 1950s were far from perfect—imagine the level of abstraction required to sum up the production function we used to describe one product of one company into a production function for the entire economy—but these models possessed several attractive properties. First, they led to a determinate outcome: The theory of competitive factor markets tells us that each factor will be paid the value of its marginal product and that in long-run competitive equilibrium, these payments will add up to exactly the total product available for distribution.[7] Given the obvious potential for claims to exceed available output in any system, the fact that standard production theory clearly identifies a feasible payment for every party is no small advantage. A second attractive feature of the theory is that it rewards initiative, effort, and risk taking. Indeed, the successor growth models of the 1990s sought to capture just this feature of a dynamic economy. Work by Paul Romer and others modeled the role of innovation and the success and failure of firms under competition in an attempt to give mathematical precision to Joseph Schumpeter's famous summation of a capitalist economy as "creative destruction."

But what was being destroyed? During the three decades after World War II, which was precisely the time in which the 1950s growth models were developed, incomes of rich, middle-income, and poor families in the United States grew at about the same rate—almost 3 percent a year. But since then, almost all gains have gone to top earners. For one thing, the labor share has gotten smaller, falling by some calculations from more than 65 percent in 1950 to less than 57 percent in 2018.[8] But, within the labor share, the top 1 percent of earners, who received less than 9 percent of total income in 1973, saw their share rise to 22 percent by 2015. Gains grow ever larger as we move up the economic ladder. The top one-tenth of 1 percent of earners, for instance, saw their share of total income to rise more than sixfold during those same years. Members of

[7]Recall that long-run competitive equilibrium occurs at the minimum point of every firm's long-run average cost curve; at that point there are constant returns in production. It is a property of production functions with constant returns that $F(K, L) = K\partial F/\partial K + L\partial F/\partial L$, which says that paying each factor its marginal product will exactly exhaust the total product available. Of course, the rapidly changing income distribution of the last 30–40 years in the United States raises the question of whether such a simple production function can account for the distributional dynamics of the economy.

[8]See James Manyika et al., "A New Look at the Declining Labor Share of Income in the United States," McKinsey Global Institute Discussion paper, May 2019, www.mckinsey.com/featured-insights/employment-and-growth/a-new-look-at-the-declining-labor-share-of-income-in-the-united-states.

this group had an average income of $6.75 million in 2015. Earnings of the CEOs of the largest American companies have grown even more rapidly. In 2016 they earned 347 times as much as the average worker, up from 42 times as much in 1980.[9] But, looking away from the concentrated gains among the top few percent, we also see a great divergence among workers with high and low educational attainments. As MIT economist David Autor notes, the earnings gap between the college-educated and high school–educated U.S. males grew from $17,411 in 1979, measured in constant 2012 dollars, to $34,969 in 2012.[10]

The Rawlsian Critique

The figures in the previous section amply demonstrate that the current U.S. economy is generating inequality at an increasing rate, but they don't tell us how or why. Multiple theories have been proposed since Thomas Piketty addressed this question in his influential 2013 book.[11] Piketty's argument was that—absent institutional constraints such as a minimum wage, a progressive income tax, and significant taxes on wealth and large inheritances—inequality will tend to increase in market economies because during most periods, the rate of return to capital is greater than the overall growth rate of the economy.

Whatever the explanation for rising inequality, we can be sure that effort is not the biggest reason some people end up with vastly more than they can spend while others cannot meet their basic needs. We can acknowledge that talent plays an important role in most endeavors, and although it can be nurtured and developed if you have it, whether you have it in the first place is essentially a matter of luck.

Even having abundant talent is no guarantee of doing well. It is also necessary to have the right talent. Being able to hit a baseball 400 feet with consistency will earn you millions annually, while being the best fourth-grade teacher in the nation will earn you little; being the best handball player in the world will earn you virtually nothing. The baseball star earns so much more, not because he works harder or has more talent, but because he is lucky enough to be good at something people are willing to pay a lot for.

John Rawls, the late Harvard moral philosopher, constructed a cogent ethical critique of the type of economy described by marginal productivity theory, one based heavily on the microeconomic theory of choice itself.[12] The question he asked was "What constitutes a just distribution of income?" To answer it, he proposed the following thought experiment. Imagine that you and the other citizens of some country have been thrown together in a meeting to choose the rules for distributing income. This meeting takes place behind a "veil of ignorance," which conceals from each person any knowledge of what talents and abilities he and others have. No individual knows whether he is smart or dull, strong or weak, fast or slow, and so on—which means that no one knows which particular rules of distribution would work to his own advantage. Rawls argued that the rules people would choose in such a state of ignorance would necessarily be fair; and if the rules are fair, it follows that the distribution to which they give rise will also be fair.

What rules would people choose from behind a veil of ignorance? If the national income to be distributed were a fixed amount every year, it is likely that most would choose to give everyone an equal share. This is likely, Rawls argued, because most people

John Rawls argued that fair rules for distributing income would be chosen if people could be placed behind a "veil of ignorance" that prevented them from knowing their own talents and abilities.

[9]Inequality.org, "Income Inequality in the United States," https://inequality.org/facts/income-inequality/.
[10]David S. Autor, "Skills, Education, and the Rise of Earnings Inequality among the 'Other 99 Percent,'" *Science*, 344(6186): 843–851. These are median incomes for each group. The incomes gap among women of similar attainments, though lower in absolute terms, also approximately doubled. Because men and women of similar educational attainments tend to marry, the *household* gap grew from $30,298 to $58,249 over the same period. https://science.sciencemag.org/content/344/6186/843.full.
[11]Thomas Piketty, *Capital in the Twenty-First Century*, Cambridge, MA: Harvard University Press, 2014, Tr. by Arthur Goldhammer from *Le capital en XXI siècle*, Paris: Éditions du Seiul, 2013. The U.S. edition became a nonfiction bestseller.
[12]John A. Rawls, *A Theory of Justice*, Cambridge, MA: Harvard University Press, 2009 [1972].

are strongly risk-averse. Since an unequal distribution would involve not only a chance of doing well, but also a chance of doing poorly, most people would prefer to eliminate the risk by choosing an equal distribution.

The difficulty, however, is that the total amount of income available for distribution is not a fixed amount every year. The U.S. economy, for example, has been growing by an average of over 2 percent a year since the late nineteenth century. So, total income clearly depends on how hard people work, how much initiative and risk they take, technological innovation, and so on. If everyone were guaranteed an equal share of the national income at the outset, why would anyone work hard or take risks? Without rewards for hard work and risk taking, national income would be dramatically smaller than if such rewards existed. Of course, material rewards for effort and risk taking necessarily lead to inequality. But Rawls argues that people would be willing to accept a certain degree of inequality as long as these rewards produced a sufficiently large increase in the total amount of output available for distribution.

How much inequality? Much less than the amount produced by purely competitive factor markets, Rawls argued. The idea is that each person behind the veil of ignorance would rationally fear being in a disadvantaged position, and so each would choose distributional rules that would maximize the income of the poorest citizen. That is, additional inequality would be considered justified as long as it had the effect of raising the income of each and every citizen. Rawls's own critics responded that his proposal was unrealistically conservative—that most people would allow additional inequality if the effect were, say, to increase most incomes. But Rawls's basic point was that people behind a veil of ignorance would choose rules that would produce a more equal distribution of income than we get under the marginal productivity system. And since these choices define what constitutes a just distribution of income, he argued, fairness requires at least some attempt to reduce the inequality produced by competition-based market economies.

Reasons for Redistribution

The moral argument Rawls outlined has obvious force. But there are also compelling practical reasons, large and small, for limiting inequality. At the macro level, former World Bank research chief Branko Milanovic has written that:

> One of the most pernicious consequences of the rise in inequality in the rich countries has been the hollowing out of the middle class and the rising political importance of the rich. This danger, however, is coupled with its nemesis, a popular class rebellion, which tends to morph into populism or nativism. Neither populism nor plutocracy is compatible with the classical definition of democracy.[13]

Milanovic notes that between 1979 and 2010, the share of persons in the United States with disposable incomes between 25 percent above and below the median income fell from 33 to 27 percent. By this definition, he notes, the United States became one-fifth less composed of a "middle" class in only 30 years.[14]

In the "Public Goods" section earlier in this chapter, we already saw at a more micro level that in a society with unequal incomes, an equal tax levied on every citizen will generally result in under-provision of public goods. To the extent that willingness to pay for public goods increases with income, high-income citizens therefore have selfish reasons to support a progressive tax structure. The progressive tax, by this argument, enables the rich to pay for the public goods that everyone needs but that only the rich can afford. Because the public goods financed under such a tax system would be available to all, its result would be to reduce inequality by a "public goods effect" as well as by direct redistribution, yet the rich benefit along with everyone else.

---

[13]Branko Milanovic, *Global Inequality: A New Approach for the Age of Globalization*, Cambridge, MA: Harvard University Press, 2016: 191.
[14]Ibid., p. 195.

Recall also that we observed in Chapter 14 that within any single firm the tendency is for the most productive employees to be paid less than the values of their marginal products and for the least productive employees to be paid more. One reason for this pattern, we saw, is that heterogeneous collections of workers will not remain together in a firm unless those who hold positions of low rank are adequately compensated by those who hold high rank.

The same dynamic applies within society. It is obviously advantageous to occupy a position in the upper portion of society's income distribution. Such positions exist, however, only if there are others willing to occupy positions in the lower portion of the income distribution. Society has a clear interest in forging terms on which all members will view it as in their interests to remain part of society. Without such arrangements, lasting social cohesion may simply not be possible, and the stage is set for the "popular class rebellion" described above by Milanovic.

It is often said that the rich will not accept inequality-reducing measures. Perhaps the most important takeaway of this section is that inequality-reducing measures can be *practical* and, far from being brute confiscation, can meet Pareto-improvement criteria by benefitting everyone in society.

Fairness and Efficiency

We saw that efforts to reduce inequality may be justified on the basis of both moral and practical arguments. Some mix of such arguments has apparently been found compelling, for no modern economy leaves income distribution entirely to the marketplace. This underlying commitment to norms of equality is strong and plays a pivotal role in almost every debate on public policy.

The economist's natural advantage lies in answering questions related to efficiency. For this reason, many economists are reluctant even to discuss issues related to equity. Yet virtually every policy change will affect not only efficiency, but also the distribution of income. And we know that most societies seem prepared to reject efficient allocations if they do not pass muster on grounds of fairness. The result is that unless economists are prepared to work within social constraints on inequality, there will be little or no audience for their policy recommendations.

During a supply interruption of some important commodity, for example, economists are almost always quick to recommend letting the price rise to market-clearing levels. We know, after all, that this policy will lead to an efficient allocation of the scarce good. The social complaint, however, is that sharply rising prices will impose an unacceptable burden on the poor. And so, in the wake of shortages, governments often reject the free market path in favor of rationing, queues, and other, more cumbersome, methods of distribution.

The unfortunate irony in this response is that inefficient solutions make the economic pie smaller for everyone, rich and poor alike. If efficient solutions are adopted, it must be possible for everyone to receive a larger slice. But merely adopting an efficient policy does not guarantee that everyone will be made better off. Typically, it is also necessary to utilize some of the efficiency gains to compensate those who would be injured by the policy change. So when economists recommend a policy on grounds of efficiency, they must also be prepared to explain how its distributional consequences can be altered to meet social constraints. That economists have not always met this challenge has much to do with the battered reputation of economics, not only in the wake of the 2008 financial crises, but in the winners-versus-losers disputes created by accelerating globalization and the shift to a service economy.

A case in point is the episode with which we began this chapter. The issue, recall, was whether now-nearly-forgotten local telephone companies in New York should be permitted to charge for calls to directory assistance. The Public Service Commission's proposal that they should was greeted by complaints that this policy would impose unacceptable hardships on the poor. Commission officials salvaged the proposal by amending it to require that every telephone subscriber be given a 30-cent credit on his telephone bill in reflection of the costs saved from having fewer directory assistance calls.

FIGURE 18.5

Charging for Directory Assistance

When directory assistance calls are free, the consumer makes C_3 of them each month. Charging 10 cents each for them cuts down on the volume of these calls substantially, enough to finance a 30 cent per month credit for every customer. The new system is more efficient than the old and places more purchasing power in the hands of the typical customer.

Let's examine how this amended proposal works. In Figure 18.5, the horizontal axis measures directory assistance calls per month and the vertical axis measures expenditure on all other goods. The horizontal line labeled B_2 represents the budget constraint for a consumer with a monthly income of Y_0 in the event that there is no charge for directory assistance calls. B_1 represents the same person's budget when there is a 10-cent charge for such calls. And B_3 is the budget constraint when there is a 30-cent monthly credit in addition to the 10-cent charge per call. I_1, I_2, and I_3 are indifference curves. They have the conventional shape, except that beyond some number of calls each month they turn upward, reflecting the fact that most people would not choose to make an unlimited number of calls to directory assistance even if those calls were free. For the consumer shown, failure to charge for directory assistance calls results in C_3 calls/mo. A simple 10-cent charge results in C_1 calls/mo, a sharply lower number. The 10-cent charge with 30-cent credit results in C_2 calls/mo. On the plausible assumption that 30 cents/mo is a trivial amount of income even for a poor person, C_2 and C_1 should be almost the same. The 30-cent credit is financed by the cost savings that result when the number of calls falls from C_3 to C_2. This reduction in calls enables the telephone company to run its operations with fewer switchboards and operators—resources that are freed up to do something more useful.

A social scientist from another planet might find it hard to believe that the trivial hardship of paying for directory assistance calls would have dissuaded a regulatory commission from approving the charge. Yet such is the strength of distributional concerns in public policy debate. By taking care to share the cost savings with ratepayers in the form of a conspicuous 30-cent monthly credit, an otherwise doomed policy reform was salvaged.

In many other markets, such as those for food or energy, the distributional consequences of charging prices based on cost are much more pronounced than in the case of directory assistance calls. The problem is vastly amplified when we begin to look at the still-unpriced externalities that need to be recognized if we are to tame the process of climate change. In Chapter 5, we discussed ways to reduce carbon emissions without making inequality worse. We now consider the parallel issue of how to reduce inequality without incurring adverse social consequences.

Methods of Redistribution

The methods by which society redistributes income are subject to the same kinds of analysis that economists bring to bear on other programs and institutions. But these same methods—as promises, calls to action, or expressions of outrage—are the very stuff of politics.

Our discussion in this section takes as its starting point the persuasive normative case for redistribution presented in the previous section. Our focus is on the common objection that redistributive programs are misguided, even if well-intentioned. Standard economic theory does raise some concerns in this area, so we'll consider how to avoid poorly designed programs that could easily undo the very efficiency gains they were designed to create. In other words, we will ask what types of programs might work before we worry about how to pay for them.

Our Current Welfare Programs

Abba Lerner, one of my former professors in graduate school, once remarked that the main problem the poor confront is that they have too little income. The solution, in his view, was disarmingly simple. We should give them some money.

We shall take up Lerner's suggestion, including some recent variants, in the next section. Here we note that redistributive programs in the United States—often called "antipoverty" or "welfare" programs, since their original motivation was poverty reduction, not redistribution per se—have long presented a far more complicated picture. As of 2020, the six major federal antipoverty programs (or program clusters) in the United States (not counting pension or unemployment insurance programs) were as follows:

- *Temporary Assistance for Needy Families (TANF)*. TANF was created by reform legislation during the Clinton administration as a successor to the New Deal–era Aid to Families with Dependent Children (AFDC) program, which had long been the country's hallmark welfare program. As of March 2019, approximately 425,000 adults and 1.6 million children were receiving TANF assistance, with an average monthly benefit for a family of three of about $485. Less than 25 percent of families with children who would seem to be "living in poverty" under current federal guidelines[15] (e.g., families of three with less than $21,330 annual income) currently receive direct payments under TANF. Controversially, much of the TANF budget goes to state-chosen alternative programs—ranging from child care assistance to job search assistance to "programs to encourage two parent families"—instead of direct assistance. Cash payments to families have declined from nearly 60 percent of the TANF budget in 1998 to slightly over 25 percent in 2014.[16]

- *Supplemental Nutrition Assistance Program (SNAP)*, more commonly known as food stamps. Approximately 34 million people received an average of $130 per month in assistance in 2019.

- *Supplemental Security Income (SSI)*. Administered by the Social Security Administration, SSI is a supplemental, means-tested program for low-income seniors or people living with disabilities. Eight million people (6 million of them blind or disabled) received an average monthly benefit of $567 in 2019.

- *Housing and Energy Assistance Programs*. Federal housing assistance programs provide rent vouchers, subsidies to low-income housing providers, and direct funding for public housing. Additionally, about $3 billion ($9 per person per 2020 U.S. Census estimates) is budgeted for weatherization and energy bill assistance.

- *Earned Income Tax Credit (EITC)*. The closest of all the programs listed to pure redistribution, EITC provides tax credits to low-income wage earners, with the eligibility ceiling in tax year 2018 of about $56,000 for a family of four. Over 22 million

---

[15]As of 2019, families of three with less than $21,330 annual income were considered to be living in poverty. See "2019 Poverty Guidelines," Office of the Assistant Secretary for Planning and Evaluation, U.S. Department of Health and Human Services, https://aspe.hhs.gov/2019-poverty-guidelines.

[16]For a detailed breakdown of TANF expenditures as of 2014, see Andrew Flowers, "Most Welfare Dollars Don't Go Directly to Poor People Anymore," *FiveThirtyEight*, August 25, 2016, https://fivethirtyeight.com/features/most-welfare-dollars-dont-go-directly-to-poor-people-anymore/.

individuals and families received credits, which lifted 56.6 million people over the official poverty line, in 2018.

■ *Medicaid and the Child's Health Insurance Program (CHIP)*. The largest of these programs by far, Medicaid provided access to health services for over 71 million eligible participants in 2019.[17]

So, beyond the fact that anyone could raise concerns about the eligibility or benefit levels of any of the programs listed, what's the problem with the above approach? The three big issues raised by our welfare system are inefficiency, disincentives to work, and nagging political resentment.

Of these, *inefficiency* is the most obvious, though it might be the least serious. Daunting complexity and difficulty of obtaining information about multiple programs may cause many eligible individuals to be underserved. On the delivery side, the increased administrative costs incurred from the need to coordinate multiple programs, each with its own eligibility determination, are substantial—although wildly high and frequently reported multiples of administrative cost-to-benefit ratios are not be believed. However, the administrative "bite" of a program with highly detailed eligibility requirements, like TANF, is about 10 percent, which is significant. (The administrative costs of programs like SSI and EITC, which are run through the Social Security and Tax systems, are far lower.)

Multiple programs also create disincentives to work. The issue here is not the "work versus leisure" trade-off we discussed in Chapter 14—poor people are no more subject to this dynamic than anyone else—but a multiplicity of eligibility-related programs can magnify the disincentive to work.

To illustrate the difficulty, it is necessary first to describe some of the administrative details of the programs. Each program has a full benefit level that all persons who earn less than some threshold income level are eligible to receive. Once a beneficiary begins to earn more than that threshold, his or her benefits are reduced by some fraction of each additional dollar earned. This fraction is called the *marginal benefit reduction rate*. Figure 18.6 shows how benefits vary with income for a program with a full benefit level of $1,000 per year, a threshold income level of $4,000 per year, and a marginal benefit reduction rate of 50 percent.

The real problem comes when a person participates in several welfare programs at once, as is common under our current system. Consider, for example, a person enrolled in four programs like the one shown in Figure 18.6. Once that person's income reaches $4,000 a year, he will lose $2 in benefits (50 cents from each of the four programs) for every additional dollar he earns. So the downward-sloping portion of the benefits versus income line in Figure 18.6 will become *four times as steep*. Needless to say, these

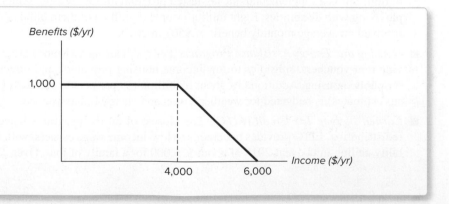

FIGURE 18.6

Benefits versus Income for a Typical Welfare Program

Persons who earn below $4,000/yr receive the full benefit level of $1,000/yr. For each dollar earned above $4,000, benefits go down by 50 cents. Once a person's income reaches $6,000/yr, all benefits cease.

[17]All the information about poverty programs, except when otherwise noted, is taken from Kimberly Amadeo, "US Welfare Programs, the Myths Versus the Facts: The 6 Major Welfare Programs," *The Balance*, 2019 (updated January 19, 2020), www.thebalance.com/welfare-programs-definition-and-list-3305759.

terms are hardly conducive to the expenditure of effort. The adverse effects on labor supply decisions are one of the most serious costs of our current welfare system. Obviously, many people are unable to work in their current circumstances. But probably just as many would benefit more, dollar for dollar, from working than from receiving public assistance. We should not design antipoverty programs to make work a losing proposition.

But perhaps the largest problem raised by the current welfare system comes from political discord and loss of social cohesion. It is seemingly a fixed star of American politics that welfare "handouts" are highly resented by persons who are a rung or two higher on the economic ladder than welfare recipients, but who still feel underserved.

That resentment against welfare recipients is often based on misperceptions is of little practical help. Misinformation about our various welfare program is simply another cost of complexity. A "working poor" family has no way of comparing the tax credit it may or may not get this *next* year with the benefits they imagine a non-working family to be receiving *this* year.[18] Our welfare system does not support the public conception of a "big tent" under which everyone (at least potentially) contributes and everyone benefits (or is at least insured). In this sense, it is a Pareto failure.

The Negative Income Tax

In 1969, at the urging of economist Milton Friedman, the Nixon administration proposed replacing existing U.S. welfare programs with a negative income tax under which a family of four with no other income would receive $1,600 in cash and $800 in food stamps per person annually—a combined $20,558 in early 2020 dollars. The proposal passed the U.S. House of Representative but failed on a 10–6 vote in Senate finance committee, where, according to Michael Tanner, the program was seen as too stingy by liberals and too expensive by conservatives.[19]

The term most-often used today for direct redistribution programs is *universal basic income* (sometimes "guaranteed income") or UBI. Recent strong-selling books[20] have touted the idea, and in late 2019 polling organizations reported that approximately half of Americans supported the UBI proposal floated by then-presidential candidate Andrew Yang.[21] If we use the term *negative income tax* (or NIT) here, it's because the idea has historically been studied under that name and because it is simplest to model and explain as an extension to the income tax system everyone already knows.

In Milton Friedman's version, the NIT starts out by giving every man, woman, and child—rich or poor—an income tax credit that is large enough to sustain a minimally adequate standard of living. Someone who earned no income would receive this credit in cash. People with earned or interest or pension income would then be taxed on their income at some rate less than 100 percent. The initial credit and the tax rate combine to determine a breakeven income level at which each person's tax liability exactly offsets his initial tax credit. People earning below that level would receive a net benefit payment from the government, while those earning more would make a net tax payment.

Figure 18.7 shows how the program would work with a tax credit of $4,000/yr and—for simplicity of illustration—a flat tax rate of 50 percent. The breakeven income level for these program values is $8,000/yr. Someone earning $4,000/yr would receive a net benefit payment of $2,000/yr, while someone earning $12,000/yr would make a tax payment of $2,000/yr.

---

[18]For a discussion of working-class resentment of benefits received by below-poverty-level citizens, see Joan C. Williams, *White Working Class: Overcoming Class Cluelessness in America*, Cambridge MA: Harvard Business School Press, 2017: 13–23.

[19]Michael Tanner, "The Pros and Cons of a Guaranteed National Income," Policy *Analysis* #773, Washington DC: Cato Institute, May 12, 2015. www.cato.org/sites/cato/files/pubs/pdf/pa773.pdf. In 2019, the U.S. government-defined poverty threshold for a family of four was $25,750. While under the threshold, the proposal was significantly more generous than any likely combination of 2020 programs.

[20]For example, Annie Lowrey, *Give People Money*, New York: Crown Publishing Group, 2018.

[21]Tess Bonn, "Voter Support for Universal Basic Income Grows: Poll," *The Hill*, September 19, 2019, https://thehill.com/hilltv/rising/463055-more-voters-support-universal-basic-income.

FIGURE 18.7

A Negative Income Tax Program

This NIT starts each person out with a tax credit of $4,000/yr. People who earn no income receive that amount in cash. All earned income is then taxed, here at the rate of 50 percent, resulting in a breakeven income level of $8,000/yr. People who earn less than that amount receive a net benefit payment from the government; people who earn more make a net tax payment.

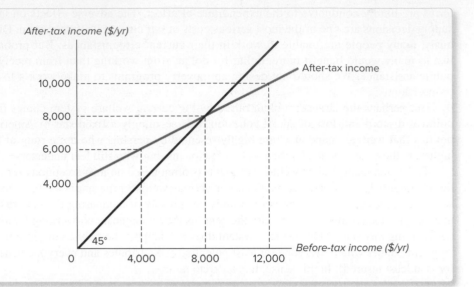

SELF-TEST 18.3

Find the breakeven income level for a program whose tax credit is $6,000 and whose tax rate is 40 percent. What is the net benefit received by a person who earns $4,000/yr from paid employment?

The NIT would be administered in much the same way as our current income tax—that is, like the admittedly-more-restrictive Earned Income Tax Credit, through the tax system itself. One strong advantage of the NIT is thus its promise to eliminate the over-lapping bureaucracies of our current programs. At the same time, going back to our Edgeworth box in Figure 18.4, it accomplishes the change in initial endowments that we pictured, and it does it automatically via the filing of a tax return. It also has the large attraction to economists of having a much less perverse effect on work incentives than current programs do. Because the marginal tax rate confronting poor people would never exceed 100 percent under the NIT, people would be assured of having more after-tax income if they worked longer hours.

This is not to say there are no incentive issues. If the NIT were to replace all our current welfare programs and become to be the sole means of insulating people against poverty, its payment to people with no earned income would have to be at least as large as the poverty threshold. And if the payment were large enough to live on, some fear that it would inevitably induce many people to stop working. This possibility was confirmed by federal experiments with the NIT during the 1970s.[22] Although the labor force withdrawals observed in these experiments were small—and not larger perhaps than could be explained by taking time to search between jobs or, in the case of women, using the benefit as a short period of paid family leave—they were nonetheless noticeable.[23]

This raises the concern that the NIT will be vulnerable to the same, politically potent, resentment-of-welfare-recipients dynamic noted in the last section. Even if the NIT induced only a handful of people to pursue lives of leisure at taxpayer expense, critics would find these people, and there would be an eager audience for reports of their doings

[22]Robert A Moffitt, "The Negative Income Tax: Would It Discourage Work?" *Monthly Labor Review*, Bureau of Labor Statistics, U.S. Department of Labor, April 1981, pp. 23–27.
[23]For a recent discussion of the experiments, with input from MIT econometrist Joshua Angrist, see Rebecca Linke, "Negative Income Tax, Explained," MIT Sloan *Ideas Made to Matter* blog, February 7, 2018, https://mitsloan.mit.edu/ideas-made-to-matter/negative-income-tax-explained.

on the nightly news. Viewers would be chagrined at the sight of NIT recipients practicing their guitars and playing volleyball on Monday mornings. In the face of such images, an NIT with a grant large enough to support able-bodied people who chose not to work would be under constant political attack.

But the preceding analysis considers the NIT purely as an antipoverty program. Would it suffer from the same political dynamics as an *inequality* program? If the benefits of the NIT tax credit were palpable to recipients who *above* the poverty line, there is a chance the program could be popular. If the illustrative the $4,000 credit we saw in Figure 18.7 is not taxed away too quickly when it is added to earned income, then we may have less reason to fear the images on the evening news.

So, the real challenge faced by the NIT is program design. Can an NIT be broad enough in its benefits to popular and still be acceptable to the wealthier echelons of voters who will be required to pay for it? We will return to this question after considering the main rival that has emerged to the guaranteed income idea: guaranteed jobs.

Guaranteed Jobs Proposals

On February 7, 2019, Senator Edward Markey and Representative Alexandria Ocasio-Cortez introduced into the 116th Congress a 14-page "Green New Deal" resolution.[24] Prominent in the resolution's many proposals was one that the U.S. government guarantee "a job with a family-sustaining wage, adequate family and medical leave, paid vacations, and retirement security to all people of the United States." While lacking specifics, the proposal was in many a reflection of more detailed proposals put forward by groups that prominently Feature Duke economist Sandy Darity and SUNY Stony Brook economist Stephanie Kelton.[25]

Of course, public jobs programs were a big part of the original New Deal in the 1930s. More recently, proposals for public jobs for the disadvantaged received much attention during the early days of President Lyndon Johnson's War on Poverty. These proposals had the obvious appeal of not providing handouts for people who could support themselves. In the language of program advocates, the government would serve as the "employer of last resort," the guarantor of "decent employment at a decent wage" to all who were unable to find such work in the private sector.

As the sole mechanism for lifting the poor from poverty, the public jobs idea fell victim to several criticisms. Perhaps the most important was that guaranteed public employment would cause people to desert the private sector in droves. The recent Green New Deal versions of these proposals have been greeted by the same criticism, not least because the proposed beginning full-time wage is the neighborhood of $12 an hour (plus benefits), more than low-skilled workers are paid by the private sector in many parts of the country. Advocates say this will induce the private sector to "step up its game." Opponents predict a very different kind of adjustment.

Guaranteed-jobs advocates have worked hard to deflect the second criticism of opponents of previous proposals, which was that public jobs for the disadvantaged would inevitably be make-work tasks, no more useful in themselves than the jobs

---

[24]For the House version, see: https://ocasio-cortez.house.gov/sites/ocasio-cortez.house.gov/files/Resolution%20on%20a%20Green%20New%20Deal.pdf.

[25]Mark Paul, William Darity Jr., Darrick Hamilton, and Khaing Zaw, "A Path to Ending Poverty by Way of Ending Unemployment: A Federal Job Guarantee," *RSF: The Russell Sage Foundation Journal of the Social Sciences* 4(3): 44–63, www.rsfjournal.org/content/rsfjss/4/3/44.full.pdf; Mark Paul, William Darity Jr., and Darrick Hamilton, "The Federal Job Guarantee—A Policy to Achieve Permanent Full Employment," Center on Budget and Policy Priorities, March 9, 2018, www.cbpp.org/sites/default/files/atoms/files/3-9-18fe.pdf; L. Randall Wray, Flavia Dantas, Scott Fullwiler, Pavlina R. Tcherneva, and Stephanie A. Kelton, "Public Service Employment: A Path to Full Employment," Levy Economics Institute of Bard College, April 1918, www.levyinstitute.org/pubs/rpr_4_18.pdf. Of the first two papers, the Russel Sage Foundation version considers objections while the CBPP version goes further into implementation details. Timothy Taylor, Managing Editor of *The Journal of Economic Perspectives*, provides a detailed discussion and critique—far more than can be attempted here—on his "Conversable Economist" blog: http://conversableeconomist.blogspot.com/2018/04/the-job-guarantee-controversy.html.

described in John Maynard Keynes's famous remark that, in a time of economic crisis, government should pay people to dig holes one day and fill them up the next. Darity and his co-writers, who call their proposal the National Investment Employment Corps (NIEC), assert:

> The NIEC can be deployed to cover a wide scope of activities including, but not limited to, the repair, maintenance, and expansion of the nation's infrastructure, housing stock, and public buildings; energy efficiency upgrades to public and private buildings; assistance with ecological restoration and services to reduce the country's carbon footprint; engagement in community development projects; provision of high-quality preschool and afterschool services; provision of teachers' aids; provision of high-quality elder care and companionship; rejuvenation of the nation's defunded postal service; support for the arts; and other activities that shall support the public good.[26]

The vision is impressive, but of course it raises more questions. One is how the workers who sign up for NIEC are going to be matched with available jobs by skill and location and, on the other side, how the program is going to provide the right types of jobs in the right places.

If coal mine shuts down, some of the displaced workers, joining for the NIEC, will no doubt be happy to use the same massive machines to "greenify" the site and plant wind turbines on top of it, but what will they do once this task is completed? And will the displaced miners who do not get the restoration jobs be content to provide "afterschool services" or "elder care and companionship"? We ask these questions not to suggest they couldn't find satisfactory answers in a particular case, but to point out that a program like the NIEC will face *thousands* of such questions in an unending stream, a massive challenge for coordination and administration. Not even the largest, most complex corporation on earth faces the task of finding suitable, productive, and lasting work for everyone who asks for it.

A second question concerns the target activities themselves. The NIEC's "investment" objectives sound worthwhile, but compared to what?" Do they really represent the kind of private-sector underinvestment (or "market failure"), such as we see in the case of provision of individual health insurance, that requires the government to step in? The pressure to keep millions of NIEC employees busy is likely to cause many "worthwhile" programs to be stood up at a far higher cost than the market, or the public through higher taxation, was willing to pay for them. In that case, the "make-work" objection returns through the back door.

Given the predisposition in the United States has often been to view all government jobs as make-work, it will be important for advocates for programs like the NIEC to link their proposal to the difficult but foreseeable adjustments faced by our economy. The NIEC looks like a hard-sell at a time of near-full employment figures, when the problems are the quiet ones of low job quality for unskilled workers and low labor market participation. The real test will come when the unemployment numbers go back up. This could be because of another sudden economic crisis, or it could come from structural trends we can glimpse today. The "green" part of the Green New Deal, or any response to climate change, is not going to come without job losses and economic dislocations, and the "Second Machine Age" prophesied by robotics and AI experts has led to even more dire predictions of a "post-work" economy.[27]

In that kind of environment, jobs themselves may become the most important measure of economic output. Comprehensive job guarantee programs may then be seen not as warmed-over make-work proposals but as broader how-we-will-work visions for a continuously changing economy. In other words, if massive economic change creates a need to "make work," we should do it without apology.

---

[26]Paul, Darity, and Hamilton, "The Federal Job Guarantee," p. 9.
[27]Erik Brynjolfsson and Andrew McAfee, *The Second Machine Age: Work, Progress, and Prosperity in a Time of Brilliant Technologies*, New York: W. W. Norton, 2014.

Taking Stock on Redistribution

As means of addressing inequality, how does a negative income tax or a jobs guarantee stack up against our current welfare system?

Neither program is without hazards. Left to decide on their own, economists would almost certainly prefer the NIT: its simplicity, adjustability, and directness—"directness" means address income inequality by moving around income, just as we showed in the Edgeworth box diagram in Figure 18.4—carries the day, assuming that design challenges can be met.

The biggest challenge is that a "big tent"—a program that addresses the bottom half of the income distribution and not just the bottom tenth or so—would cost a lot of money. That cost has led to the "tax the rich" proposals we have seen from social engineering economists[28] and political office seekers.

The point here is not to endorse any specific proposal. But recall from Chapter 7 that higher taxes would not threaten the interests of prosperous voters. That's because their ability to bid successfully for the special extras in life depends on their relative disposable income, which is unaffected by higher taxes. I labeled failure to appreciate that simple point "the mother of all cognitive illusions" because the tax resistance it has spawned has made it so difficult to finance much-needed public investment. The important practical question, then, is whether the sufficiently many prosperous voters can be persuaded to abandon this illusion.

The jobs guarantee, by contrast, presents a less attractive option to most economists. The administrative burdens, the matching and coordination problems, the potentially for "inefficiency"—to use that dreaded word—all give pause. And it's not clear that the government's provision of just-over-poverty-line jobs really addresses the economic inequality issue, which extends far up the income distribution.

One irreducible issue with *work* programs is that some people can't work or can only do so intermittently. Mental illness, addiction, and overwhelming personal circumstances all take a toll that is exacerbated by unemployment in some cases but is not a function of employment per se. A significant percentage of the population is going to need public assistance. We can build that assistance into the tax system, or we can provide it with "welfare" programs. The need is not going to go away.

All this said, programs to put people to work will have greater appeal in a time of acute economic crisis and may emerge in a whole different light if climate change, technological change, or some other development pushes us in the direction of a "post-work" economy. In an economy where actual production was performed by robots and drones, the benefits of a job will be measured in social terms and, in the increasing-scale world of robots, these benefits may far outweigh the costs.

As a last aside, a remaining issue with work programs is that some people can't work or can only do so intermittently. For many, the suffering associated with mental illness, addiction, and overwhelming personal circumstances cannot be alleviated by an offer of employment. A significant percentage of the population will continue to need public assistance. We can build that assistance into the tax system or we can provide it with "welfare" programs, but the need will not simply go away.

REPRISE: THINKING LIKE AN ECONOMIST

We began the book by using cost-benefit analysis to examine small-bore issues like phone calls to friends and shopping trips to Walmart. We end it by advocating the same need to weigh benefits and costs for decisions involving far greater stakes.

The Nobel laureate Robert Solow, in his 95th year and still professionally active as this edition goes to press, once wrote that "Economics is not the physics of society."[29]

---

[28]See, Piketty, *Capital in the Twenty-First Century*, and, more recently, Emmanuel Saez and Gabriel Zucman, *The Triumph of Injustice: How the Rich Dodge Taxes and How to Make Them Pay*, New York: WW Norton, 2019.

[29]Robert M. Solow and Jean-Philippe Touffut (Eds.), *What's Right With Macroeconomics?* Cheltenham UK: Edward Elgar, 2012: 2.

His point was that economic models cannot hope to offer complete explanations of forces that are only partly economic in nature. A similar recognition drove us to call this textbook *Microeconomics and Behavior*. However much the theory of rational choice can illuminate our options, it cannot make choices for us, much less anticipate their myriad side effects.

The world is complicated. We influence each other in ways that go beyond our purely economic impact, and those influences, in turn, have an impact on us. Few economists predicted, for example, the extent to which the adoption of photovoltaic panels proved to be socially contagious. The direct environmental impact of an early solar panel installation was negligible, just as portrayed in conventional models. But those models overlooked that each new adoption would inspire a host of neighbors and friends to follow suit. The total effect of an additional installation was thus anything but negligible.

Whether the YIMBY movement will succeed in reducing urban zoning restrictions is similarly difficult to predict. But economic models can help us anticipate the effects of liberalized zoning, which in turn can help us decide whether changes would be desirable.

Most of all, economic analysis encourages a deeper appreciation of the importance of efficiency. When both cost and benefits are inclusively measured, a change is efficient if its benefit exceeds its cost. Put differently, a change that that meets this test is said to make the economic pie larger. And just as is true of a pumpkin pie, any change that makes the economic pie larger necessarily creates at least the possibility of everyone having a larger slice than before.

No matter what role you play on any team in life, your knowledge of basic economic principles will help you identify opportunities to increase the efficiency of your team's efforts. You'll discover that paying close attention to how the relevant pies are divided will reliably boost your teammates' willingness to take advantage of those opportunities.

SUMMARY

- Public goods are like other goods in that their value can be measured by what people would be willing to pay to have more of them. But whereas the aggregate demand curve for a private good is formed by adding the individual demand curves horizontally, the aggregate willingness-to-pay curve for a public good is the vertical summation of the corresponding individual curves. This difference arose because the quantity of a public good must be the same for every consumer. In the private case, by contrast, the price is the same for different buyers, who then select different quantities. *(LO1, LO2)*

- As with private goods, the supply curve of a public good is simply the marginal cost of producing it. The optimal quantity of a public good is the level for which the aggregate willingness-to-pay curve intersects the supply curve. In order to pay for the optimal quantities of public goods, where the goods are supported by taxation, it will generally be necessary for individual tax payments to vary directly with the amounts that individuals are willing to pay for public goods. To the extent that people with higher incomes demand higher quantities of public goods, the result is that both rich and poor will favor a tax system that places a larger share of the total tax burden on the rich. *(LO2)*

- The mere fact that a good has the characteristics of a public good does not mean that it must necessarily be provided by government. There are many ingenious schemes, ranging from free commercial television to highly structured collective legal contracts, whereby public goods are provided with virtually no involvement by government. *(LO3)*

- Problems similar to those that arise in connection with public goods are encountered whenever there are significant indivisibilities or economies of scale in the production of private consumption goods. In such situations, we saw, it is common for clubs to form in which members share the costs of important consumption goods. The trade-off confronting a potential member of such a club is between cost savings and reduced privacy in the use of the good. *(LO3)*

- Majority voting sometimes produces intransitive rankings among projects. When it does, the power to choose the order in which different pairs of alternatives are considered is often tantamount to the power to determine the final outcome. There is a special class of issues in which majority voting is not vulnerable to agenda manipulation. With respect to single issues in which each voter ranks every alternative in terms of its distance from his ideal choice, the final outcome will be the one most preferred by the median voter, no matter what order the votes are taken in. This result is known as the median voter theorem. *(LO4)*

- Cost-benefit analysis is a simple but very powerful alternative to majority voting. Applied in the proper way to a sufficiently large number of small decisions, it almost always satisfies the Pareto criterion. *(LO4)*

- Even with a perfect mechanism for revealing public sentiments about the relative desirability of different public goods, there will still be difficult choices about which goods to produce. The problem is that the types of public goods strongly favored by some groups are often strongly opposed by others. If heterogeneous voters are forced to coexist in a single jurisdiction, the frequent result is a painful compromise that satisfies no one. But the need for such compromises is greatly reduced if voters are able to group themselves into communities with relatively homogeneous tastes. *(LO4)*

- A problem that plagues all mechanisms of public decision making is that self-interested parties have an incentive to influence outcomes in their own favor. This problem goes by the name of rent seeking and has become an increasingly serious threat to our social welfare. *(LO4)*

- The primary mechanism for distributing income in market economies is the factor market. People sell their labor in return for a payment equal to the value of its marginal product. And they invest their savings at interest rates that are similarly linked to the marginal productivity of capital. This method of income distribution has several desirable properties on efficiency grounds—in particular, it rewards effort and the willingness to incur risk—but in the last 40 years, it has lead to increasing inequality of wealth and income in the United States. But critics, notably John Rawls, have argued that people would never voluntarily choose to live under a process that yields such highly unequal outcomes as we see in untempered factor markets. *(LO5)*

- In addition to the moral argument Rawls has offered, there are at least two practical reasons for income redistribution. First, the rich would favor paying more than an equal share of the total tax burden because otherwise they would end up with an inefficiently small provision of public goods. And second, redistribution may be necessary to maintain a voluntary sense of social cohesion, something as much in the interests of the rich as of the poor. *(LO5)*

- Our current array of welfare programs is a costly and inadequate approach to reducing inequality. Alternative "guaranteed income" and "guaranteed jobs" proposals are prominent features of contemporary political campaigns and policy debates. *(LO5)*

KEY TERMS

collective good	free riding	pure public good

REVIEW QUESTIONS

1. Why are the individual willingness-to-pay curves added vertically, not horizontally, to get the aggregate willingness-to-pay curve for a public good? *(LO1)*

2. How are jointly produced private goods analogous to public goods? *(LO1)*

3. Why would even rich citizens be likely to oppose having equal tax payments by rich and poor alike? *(LO5)*

4. In what way does a private good produced under conditions of increasing returns to scale resemble a public good? Describe the trade-off between flexibility and cost that confronts users of such goods. *(LO4)*

5. How does majority voting lead to intransitive social rankings? *(LO4)*

6. Describe two forms of inefficiency associated with rent seeking. *(LO4)*

7. Why would many economists prefer a negative income tax to a guaranteed jobs program as a means of reducing inequality? *(LO5)*

PROBLEMS

McGraw Hill connect

1. A government is trying to decide how much of a public good to provide. The willingness-to-pay curves for each of its two citizens are as given in the diagram. The marginal cost curve for the public good is given by $MC = Q/2$, where Q is the quantity of the good. There is also a fixed cost of 10 associated with production of the good. *(LO2)*

a. What is the optimal quantity of the public good?

b. If both citizens must be taxed equally to provide the good, will it receive a majority vote?

2. On the assumption that the public good described in Problem 1 is provided at the optimal level, how much should the state charge each citizen each time he or she uses the public good? *(LO2)*

3. Ten identical consumers all have individual willingness-to-pay curves $P = 5 - \frac{1}{20}Q$ for a public good—say, local parks (where P is measured in hundreds of dollars and Q is measured in acres). Construct and graph the aggregate willingness-to-pay curve. For 50 acres of parks, what is the maximum each individual would be willing to pay? *(LO2)*

4. Consider the scenario described in Problem 3, but now consider that the marginal cost of providing parks measured in hundreds of dollars is $MC = \frac{1}{2}Q$. Determine the optimal size of local parks. *(LO2)*

5. Viewer-supported television stations often give contributors "free" gifts for making contributions at various levels. ("Two stainless steel *News Hour* coffee tumblers for a donation of $120.") Based on what you know about the psychology of framing decisions (see Chapter 8), explain why this practice might help stations raise more money. *(LO3)*

6. Colleges and universities commonly name buildings and business or medical schools after substantial donors (witness Ohio State's Max Fisher School of Business and Schottenstein Center/Value City Arena). Meanwhile, few donors care to earmark their gifts for routine maintenance of university buildings. How might the social benefits of charitable giving explain these observations? *(LO3)*

7. *True or false:* Because the issues at stake in national presidential elections are much more important than those at stake in a small village mayoral election, rational choice theory says a much larger proportion of voters will turn out in the former than in the latter. Explain. *(LO4)*

8. *True or false:* The fact that the voter turnout is significantly greater in close presidential elections than in one-sided ones provides clear support for the proposition that voters are rational. Explain. *(LO4)*

9. A sorority consisting of 20 sophomores, 20 juniors, and 20 seniors is about to elect its next president. Cressida, Destiny, and Kai are the three candidates. Members of each class have the ranking schemes given in the table:

Class	Best	Next best	Last
Seniors	Cressida	Destiny	Kai
Juniors	Destiny	Kai	Cressida
Sophs	Kai	Cressida	Destiny

The tradition in the sorority is to pit two candidates against each other and then pit the winner of that contest against the third candidate. If you were a sophomore, whom would you pair off in the preliminary round? If you were a senior? *(LO4)*

10. Shen, who is currently unemployed, is a participant in four welfare programs that offer daily benefits of $10 each to people with no earned income. Each program then curtails its benefits by 50 cents for every dollar of income a recipient earns. Shen's identical twin brother, Sean, is enrolled in an experimental negative income tax program that gives him $40/day in benefits and then taxes him at the rate of 50 percent on each dollar of earned income. Now suppose Shen is offered a job that pays $4/hr, the same wage his brother earns. *(LO6)*

a. Draw the budget constraint for each twin.

b. How many hours would they have to work before Shen ends up with more net cash and benefits than his brother?

11. Whether you smoke very largely depends on whether your parents or friends smoke. This is an example of negative social contagion. Propose some behaviors that might cause positive social contagion—actions that might do more good than their direct economic impact because they may inspire others to do the same. *(LO3)*

ANSWERS TO SELF-TESTS

18.1 The aggregate willingness-to-pay curve would be $P = 120 - 2Q$, the vertical summation of the individual willingness-to-pay curves (see graph). For $Q = 30$ minutes, each individual would be willing to pay up to $P = 12 - \frac{1}{5}Q = 12 - \frac{1}{5}(30) = \$6$, for a total of \$60 from 10 consumers. *(LO2)*

18.2 To find the optimal duration of the concert, equate the aggregate willingness-to-pay $P = 120 - 2Q$ and the marginal cost $MC = 2Q$ to find $Q = 30$ minutes. Refer to the figure as shown. *(LO2)*

18.3 Let Y^* denote the breakeven income level. To calculate Y^*, we solve $6{,}000 + (1 - 0.4)Y^* = Y^*$, which yields $Y^* = \$15{,}000/\text{yr}$. A person who earns \$4,000/yr would pay $0.4(\$4{,}000) = \$1{,}600/\text{yr}$ in taxes, and would thus receive a net annual benefit of $\$6{,}000 - \$1{,}600 = \$4{,}400$. *(LO5)*

Willingness to pay ($)

INDEX

Page numbers followed by n refer to notes.